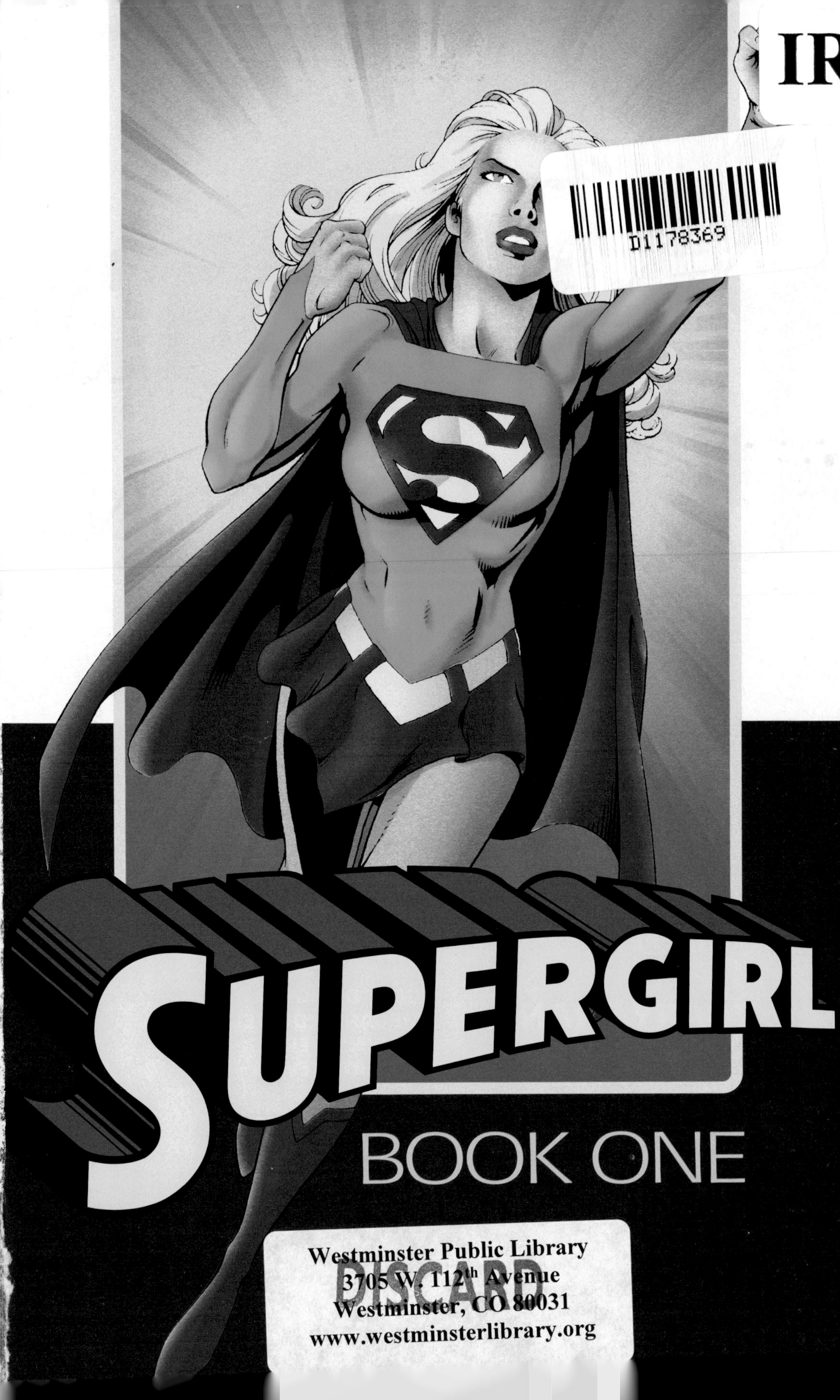

SUPERGIRL
BOOK ONE

SUPERGIRL

BOOK ONE

PETER DAVID
GARY FRANK
CHUCK DIXON
JOE LANSDALE
NEAL BARRETT JR.
BARBARA KESEL
KARL KESEL
writers

GARY FRANK
TERRY DODSON
MIKE MANLEY
BRET BLEVINS
JENNIFER GRAVES
RON WAGNER
ROBERT TERANISHI
DICK GIORDANO
pencillers

CAM SMITH
KARL STORY
JOHN NYBERG
CHUCK DROST
BILL REINHOLD
STAN WOCH
GEORGE PÉREZ
inkers

GENE D'ANGELO
MEGAN McDOWELL
MARIE SEVERIN
ROBERTA TEWES
colorists

PAT PRENTICE
ALBERT DE GUZMAN
GASPAR SALADINO
letterers

DIGITAL CHAMELEON
separations

Original series and collection cover art by **GARY FRANK** & **CAM SMITH**

SUPERGIRL ANNUAL #1 cover art by **RON WAGNER** & **BILL REINHOLD**

SUPERGIRL based on characters created by **JERRY SIEGEL** and **JOE SHUSTER**
SUPERMAN created by **JERRY SIEGEL** and **JOE SHUSTER**
By special arrangement with the JERRY SIEGEL family

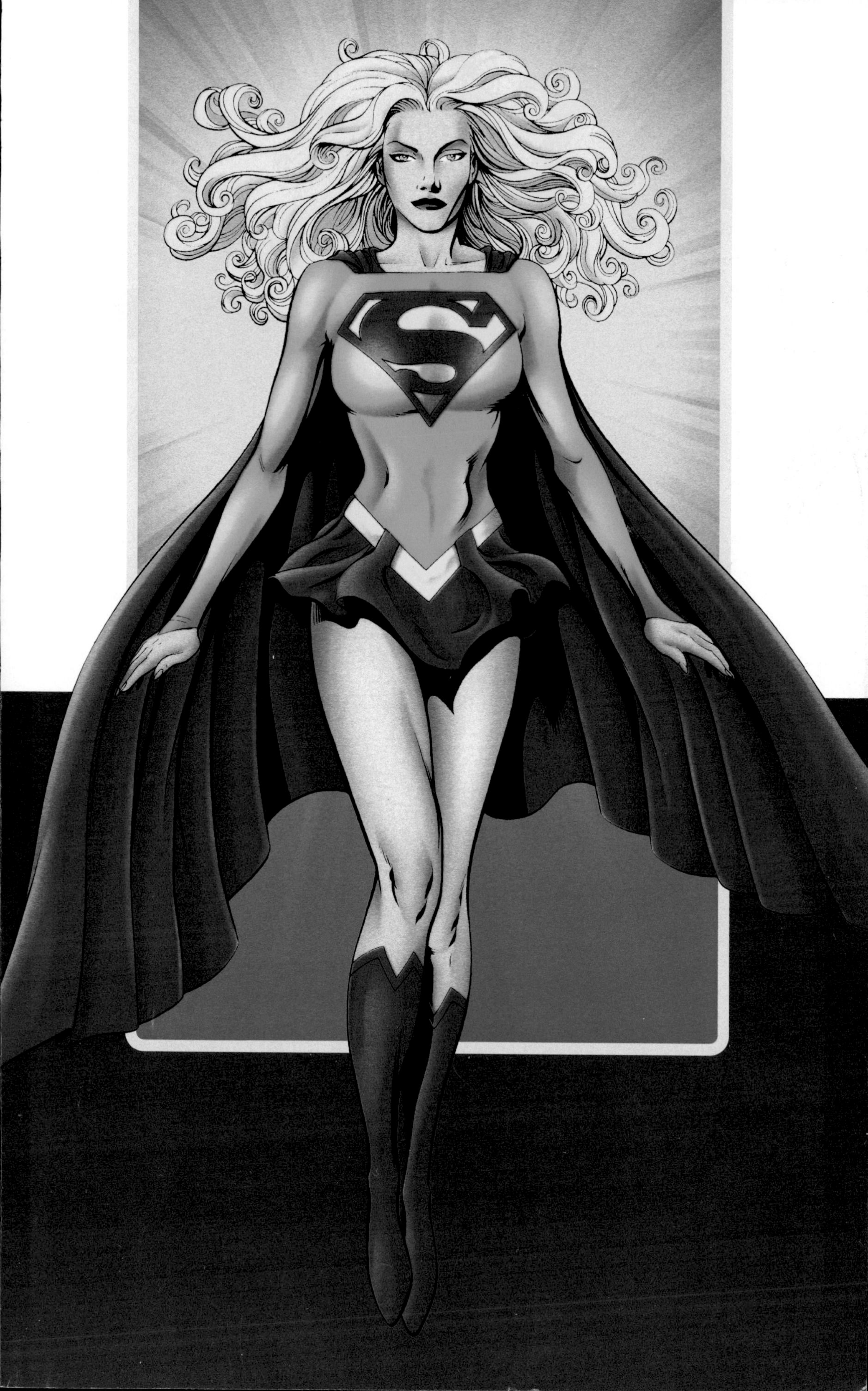

CHRIS DUFFY FRANK PITTARESE
Editors – Original Series
JEB WOODARD
Group Editor – Collected Editions
LIZ ERICKSON
Editor – Collected Edition
STEVE COOK
Design Director – Books
CURTIS KING JR.
Publication Design
BOB HARRAS
Senior VP – Editor-in-Chief, DC Comics

DIANE NELSON
President
DAN DIDIO and JIM LEE
Co-Publishers
GEOFF JOHNS
Chief Creative Officer
AMIT DESAI
Senior VP – Marketing & Global Franchise Management
NAIRI GARDINER
Senior VP – Finance
SAM ADES
VP – Digital Marketing
BOBBIE CHASE
VP – Talent Development
MARK CHIARELLO
Senior VP – Art, Design & Collected Editions
JOHN CUNNINGHAM
VP – Content Strategy

ANNE DEPIES
VP – Strategy Planning & Reporting
DON FALLETTI
VP – Manufacturing Operations
LAWRENCE GANEM
VP – Editorial Administration & Talent Relations
ALISON GILL
Senior VP – Manufacturing & Operations
HANK KANALZ
Senior VP – Editorial Strategy & Administration
JAY KOGAN
VP – Legal Affairs
DEREK MADDALENA
Senior VP – Sales & Business Development
JACK MAHAN
VP – Business Affairs
DAN MIRON
VP – Sales Planning & Trade Development
NICK NAPOLITANO
VP – Manufacturing Administration
CAROL ROEDER
VP – Marketing
EDDIE SCANNELL
VP – Mass Account & Digital Sales
COURTNEY SIMMONS
Senior VP – Publicity & Communications
JIM (SKI) SOKOLOWSKI
VP – Comic Book Specialty & Newsstand Sales
SANDY YI
Senior VP – Global Franchise Management

SUPERGIRL BOOK ONE
Published by DC Comics. Compilation and all new material Copyright © 2016 DC Comics.
All Rights Reserved. Originally published in single magazine form in SHOWCASE '96 8, SUPERGIRL
PLUS, SUPERGIRL 1-9, SUPERGIRL ANNUAL 1 © 1996, 1997 DC Comics. All Rights Reserved.
All characters, their distinctive likenesses and related elements featured in this publication are
trademarks of DC Comics. The stories, characters and incidents featured in this publication
are entirely fictional. DC Comics does not read or accept unsolicited ideas, stories or artwork.

DC Comics, 2900 West Alameda Ave., Burbank, CA 91505
Printed by RR Donnelley, Salem, VA, USA. 9/16/16. First Printing.
ISBN: 978-1-4012-6092-7

Library of Congress Cataloging-in-Publication Data is available.

PEFC Certified
Printed on paper from
sustainably managed
forests and controlled
sources

PEFC/29-31-75   www.pefc.org

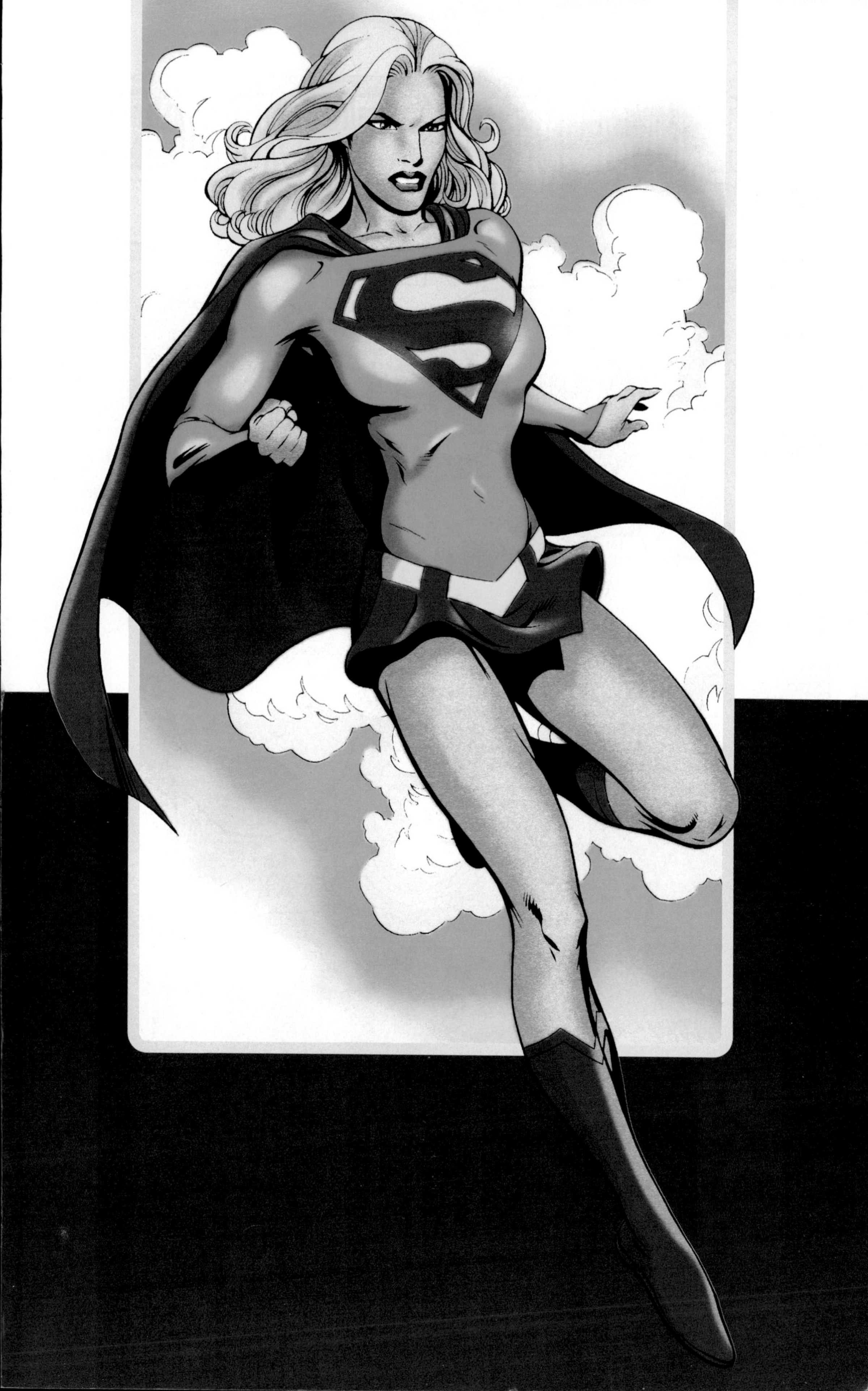

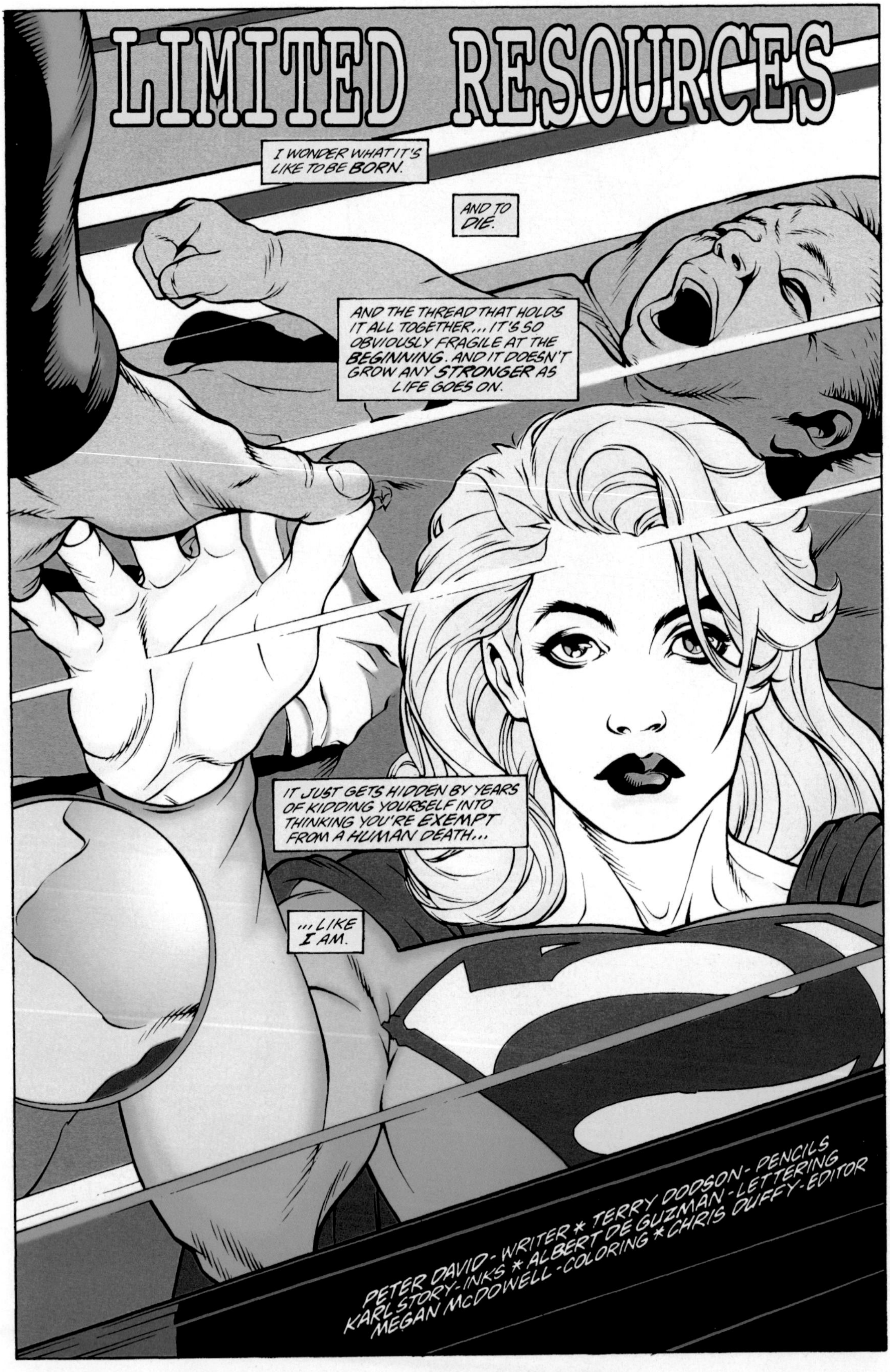
LIMITED RESOURCES
I WONDER WHAT IT'S LIKE TO BE BORN.
AND TO DIE.
AND THE THREAD THAT HOLDS IT ALL TOGETHER... IT'S SO OBVIOUSLY FRAGILE AT THE BEGINNING. AND IT DOESN'T GROW ANY STRONGER AS LIFE GOES ON.
IT JUST GETS HIDDEN BY YEARS OF KIDDING YOURSELF INTO THINKING YOU'RE EXEMPT FROM A HUMAN DEATH...
...LIKE I AM.
PETER DAVID-WRITER ✶ TERRY DODSON-PENCILS
KARL STORY-INKS ✶ ALBERT DE GUZMAN-LETTERING
MEGAN McDOWELL-COLORING ✶ CHRIS DUFFY-EDITOR

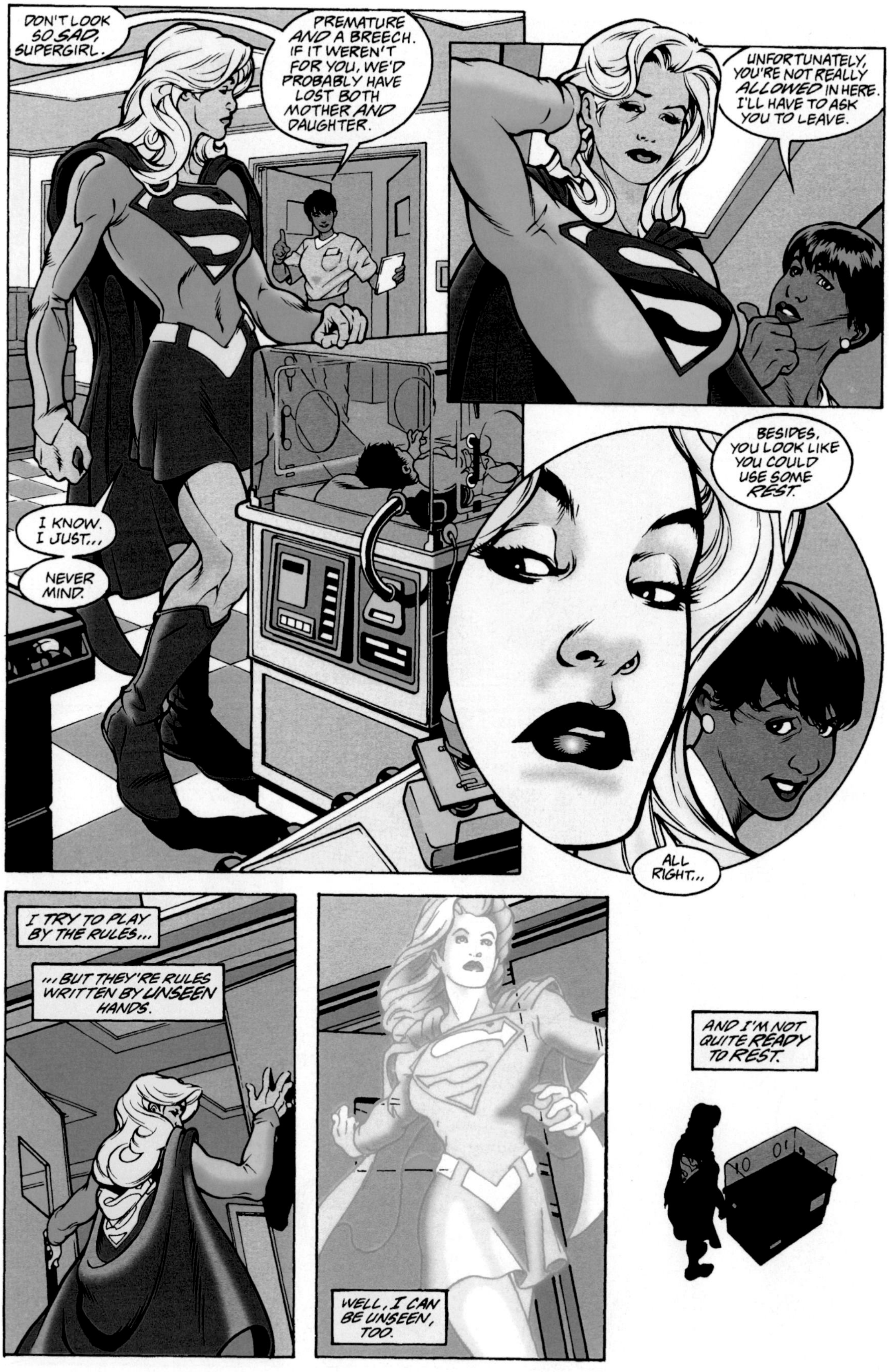

DON'T LOOK SO SAD, SUPERGIRL.
PREMATURE AND A BREECH. IF IT WEREN'T FOR YOU, WE'D PROBABLY HAVE LOST BOTH MOTHER AND DAUGHTER.
I KNOW. I JUST...
NEVER MIND.
UNFORTUNATELY, YOU'RE NOT REALLY ALLOWED IN HERE. I'LL HAVE TO ASK YOU TO LEAVE.
BESIDES, YOU LOOK LIKE YOU COULD USE SOME REST.
ALL RIGHT...
I TRY TO PLAY BY THE RULES...
...BUT THEY'RE RULES WRITTEN BY UNSEEN HANDS.
WELL, I CAN BE UNSEEN, TOO.
AND I'M NOT QUITE READY TO REST.

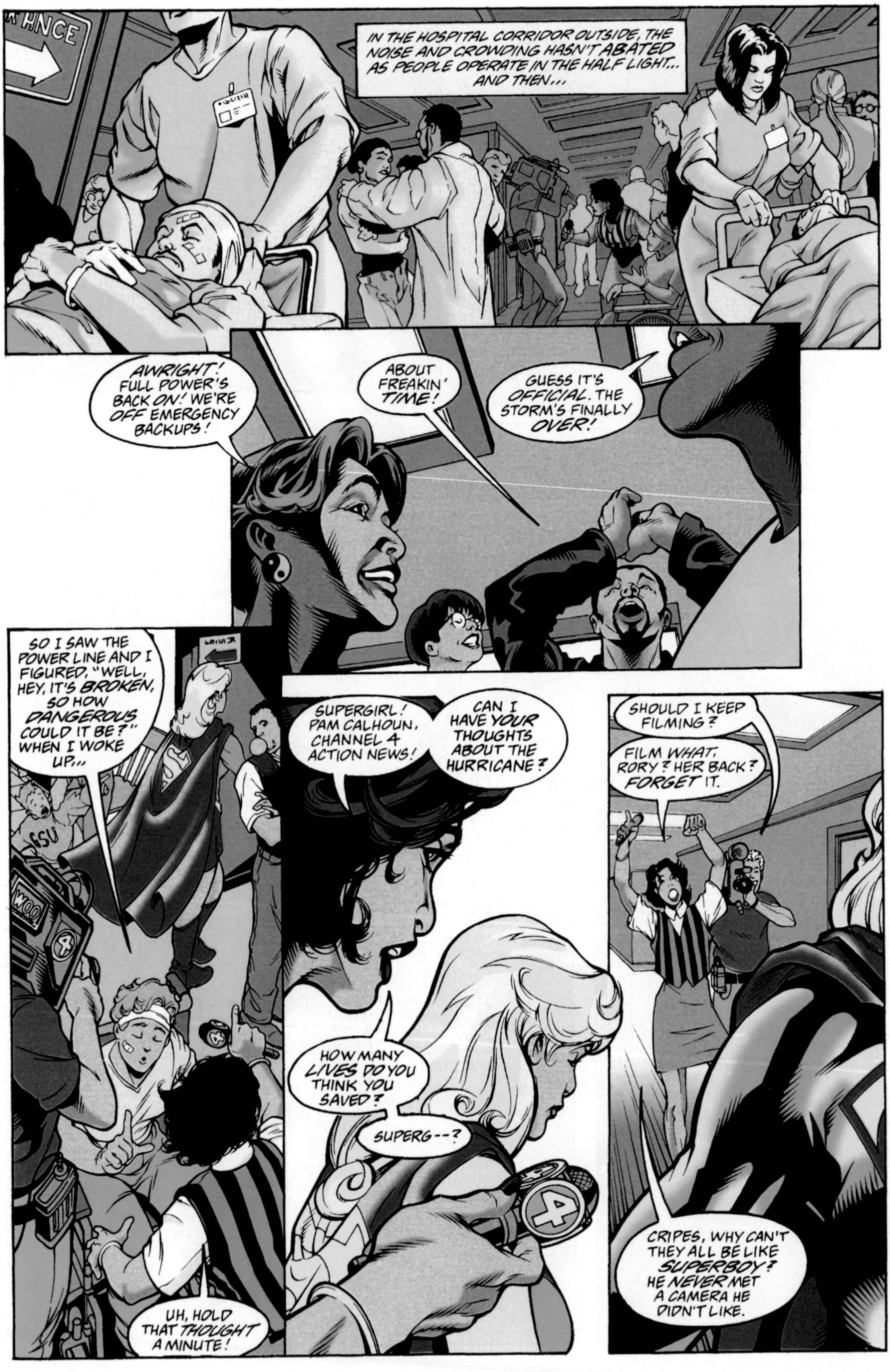
IN THE HOSPITAL CORRIDOR OUTSIDE, THE NOISE AND CROWDING HASN'T ABATED AS PEOPLE OPERATE IN THE HALF LIGHT... AND THEN...
AWRIGHT! FULL POWER'S BACK ON! WE'RE OFF EMERGENCY BACKUPS!
ABOUT FREAKIN' TIME!
GUESS IT'S OFFICIAL. THE STORM'S FINALLY OVER!
SO I SAW THE POWER LINE AND I FIGURED, "WELL, HEY, IT'S BROKEN, SO HOW DANGEROUS COULD IT BE?" WHEN I WOKE UP...
UH, HOLD THAT THOUGHT A MINUTE!
SUPERGIRL! PAM CALHOUN, CHANNEL 4 ACTION NEWS!
CAN I HAVE YOUR THOUGHTS ABOUT THE HURRICANE?
HOW MANY LIVES DO YOU THINK YOU SAVED?
SUPERG--?
SHOULD I KEEP FILMING?
FILM WHAT, RORY? HER BACK? FORGET IT.
CRIPES, WHY CAN'T THEY ALL BE LIKE SUPERBOY? HE NEVER MET A CAMERA HE DIDN'T LIKE.

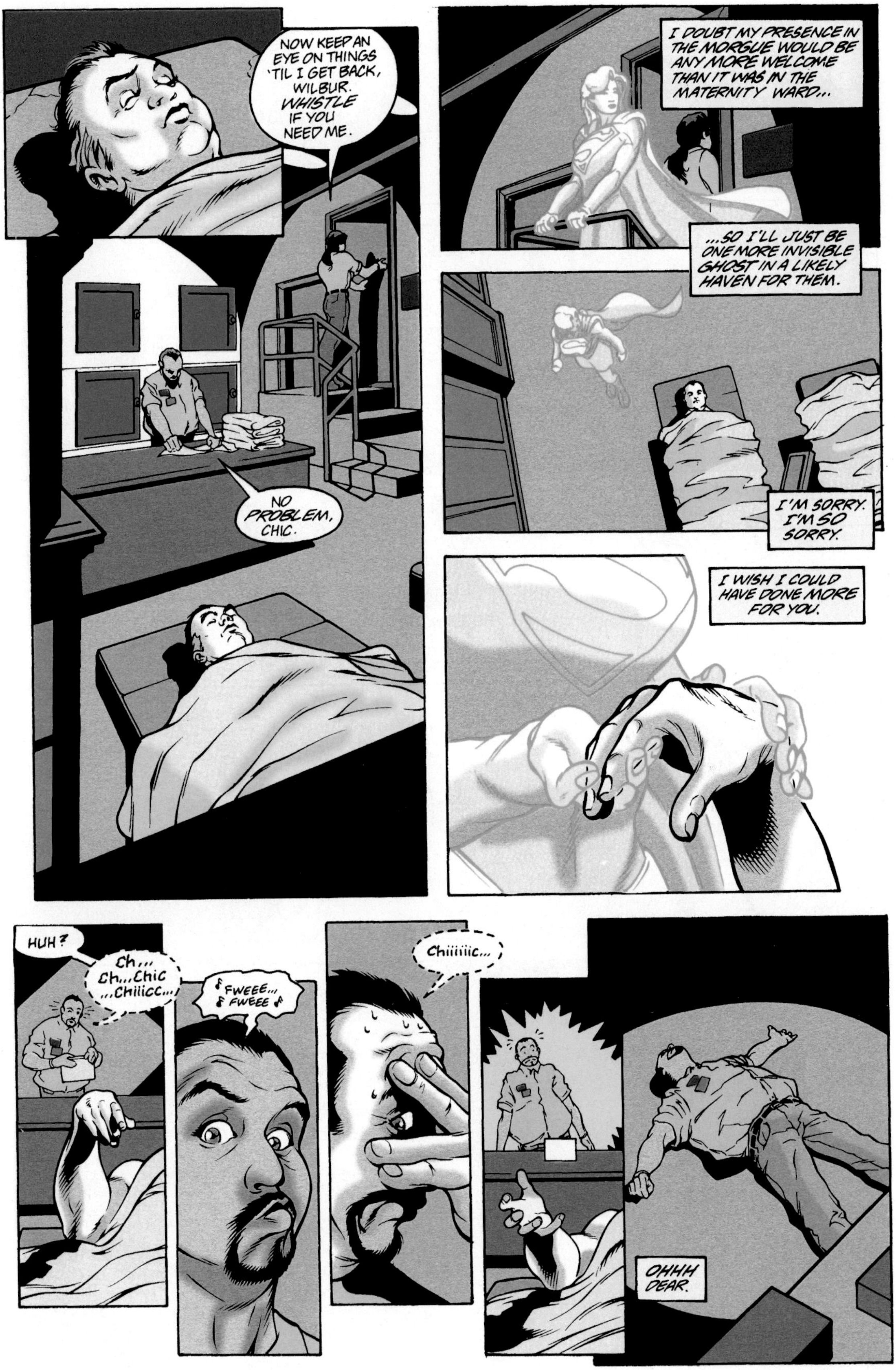
NOW KEEP AN EYE ON THINGS 'TIL I GET BACK, WILBUR. WHISTLE IF YOU NEED ME.
NO PROBLEM, CHIC.
I DOUBT MY PRESENCE IN THE MORGUE WOULD BE ANY MORE WELCOME THAN IT WAS IN THE MATERNITY WARD...
...SO I'LL JUST BE ONE MORE INVISIBLE GHOST IN A LIKELY HAVEN FOR THEM.
I'M SORRY. I'M SO SORRY.
I WISH I COULD HAVE DONE MORE FOR YOU.
HUH?
Ch... Ch...Chic ...Chiiicc...
FWEEE... FWEEE
Chiiiiiic...
OHHH DEAR.

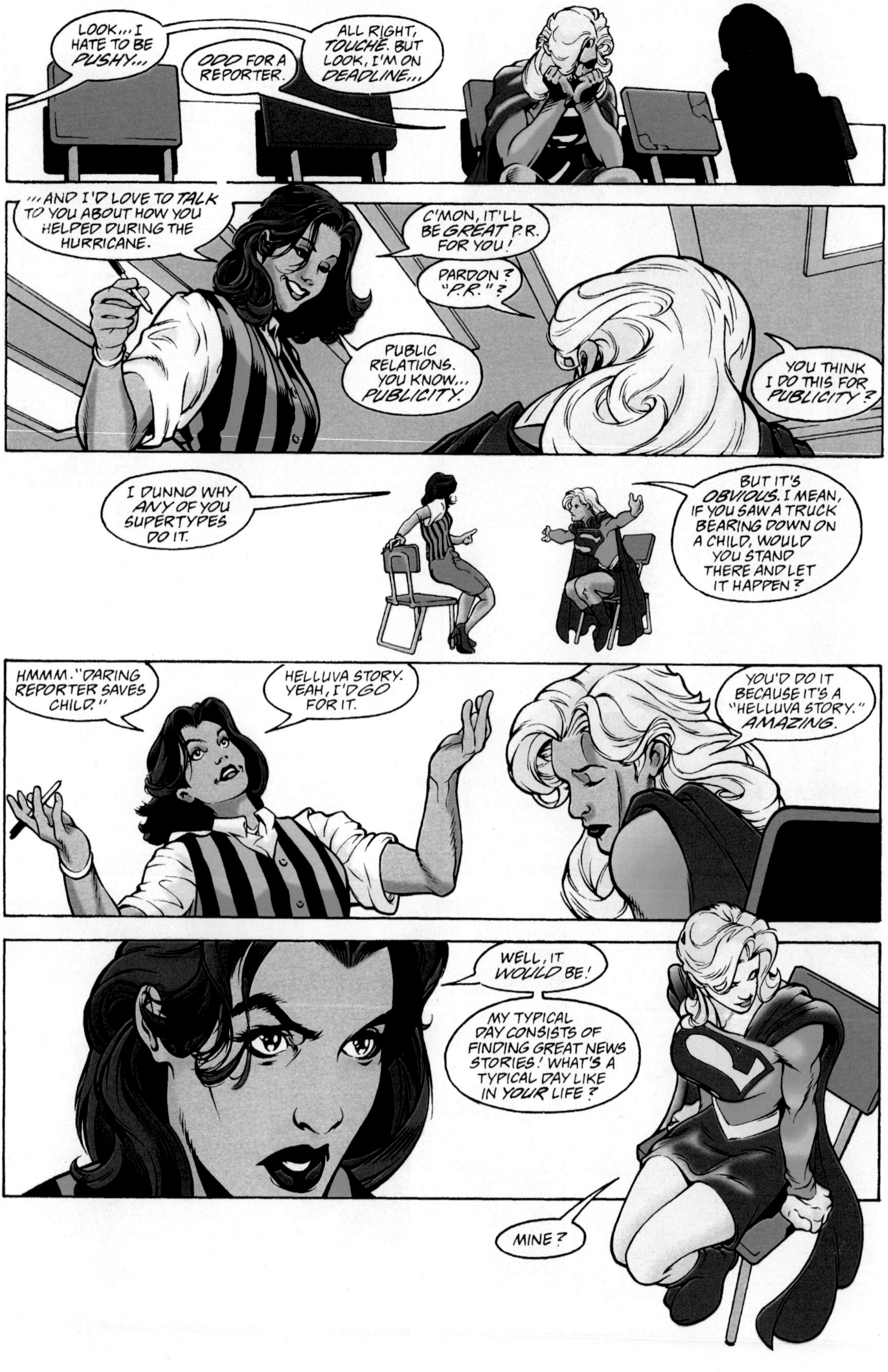
LOOK... I HATE TO BE PUSHY...
ODD FOR A REPORTER.
ALL RIGHT, TOUCHÉ. BUT LOOK, I'M ON DEADLINE...
...AND I'D LOVE TO TALK TO YOU ABOUT HOW YOU HELPED DURING THE HURRICANE.
C'MON, IT'LL BE GREAT P.R. FOR YOU!
PARDON? "P.R."?
PUBLIC RELATIONS. YOU KNOW... PUBLICITY.
YOU THINK I DO THIS FOR PUBLICITY?
I DUNNO WHY ANY OF YOU SUPERTYPES DO IT.
BUT IT'S OBVIOUS. I MEAN, IF YOU SAW A TRUCK BEARING DOWN ON A CHILD, WOULD YOU STAND THERE AND LET IT HAPPEN?
HMMM. "DARING REPORTER SAVES CHILD."
HELLUVA STORY. YEAH, I'D GO FOR IT.
YOU'D DO IT BECAUSE IT'S A "HELLUVA STORY." AMAZING.
WELL, IT WOULD BE!
MY TYPICAL DAY CONSISTS OF FINDING GREAT NEWS STORIES! WHAT'S A TYPICAL DAY LIKE IN YOUR LIFE?
MINE?

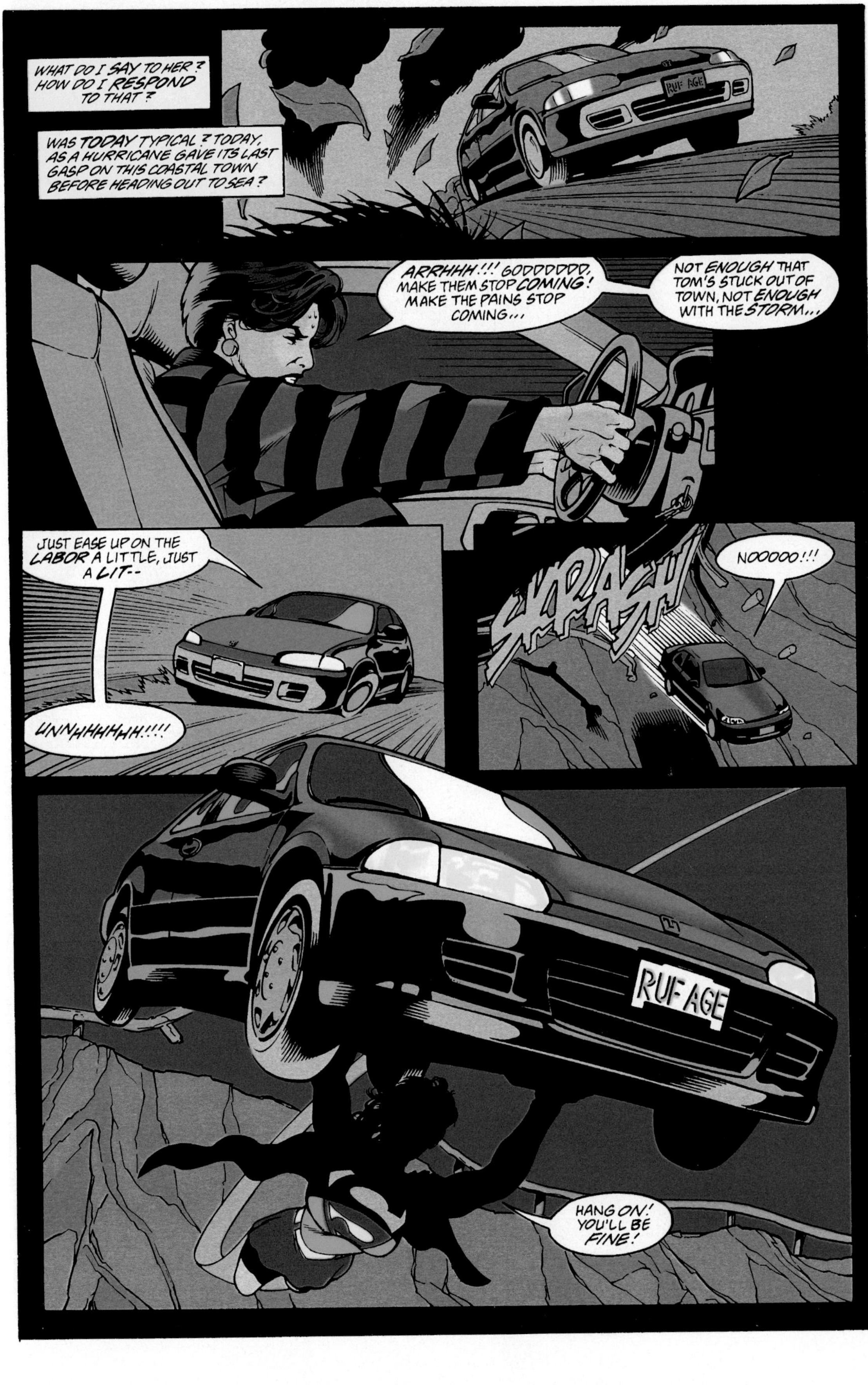
WHAT DO I SAY TO HER? HOW DO I RESPOND TO THAT?
WAS TODAY TYPICAL? TODAY, AS A HURRICANE GAVE ITS LAST GASP ON THIS COASTAL TOWN BEFORE HEADING OUT TO SEA?
RUF AGE
ARRHHH!!! GODDDDDDD, MAKE THEM STOP COMING! MAKE THE PAINS STOP COMING...
NOT ENOUGH THAT TOM'S STUCK OUT OF TOWN, NOT ENOUGH WITH THE STORM...
JUST EASE UP ON THE LABOR A LITTLE, JUST A LIT--
UNNHHHHHH!!!!
SKRASH
NOOOOO!!!
RUF AGE
HANG ON! YOU'LL BE FINE!

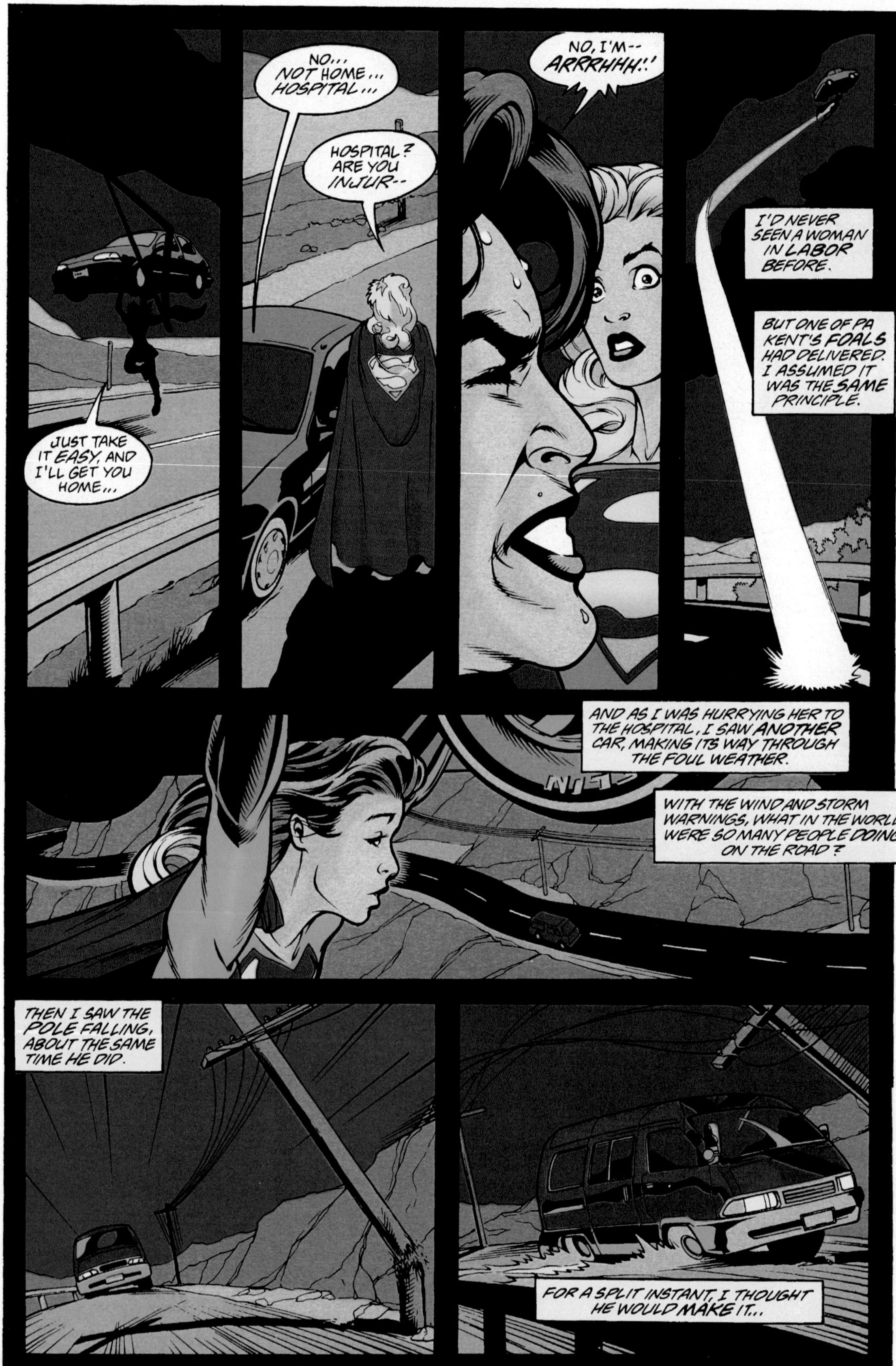
JUST TAKE IT EASY, AND I'LL GET YOU HOME...
NO... NOT HOME... HOSPITAL...
HOSPITAL? ARE YOU INJUR--
NO, I'M-- ARRRHHH!!
I'D NEVER SEEN A WOMAN IN LABOR BEFORE.
BUT ONE OF PA KENT'S FOALS HAD DELIVERED. I ASSUMED IT WAS THE SAME PRINCIPLE.
AND AS I WAS HURRYING HER TO THE HOSPITAL, I SAW ANOTHER CAR, MAKING ITS WAY THROUGH THE FOUL WEATHER.
WITH THE WIND AND STORM WARNINGS, WHAT IN THE WORLD WERE SO MANY PEOPLE DOING ON THE ROAD?
THEN I SAW THE POLE FALLING, ABOUT THE SAME TIME HE DID.
FOR A SPLIT INSTANT, I THOUGHT HE WOULD MAKE IT...

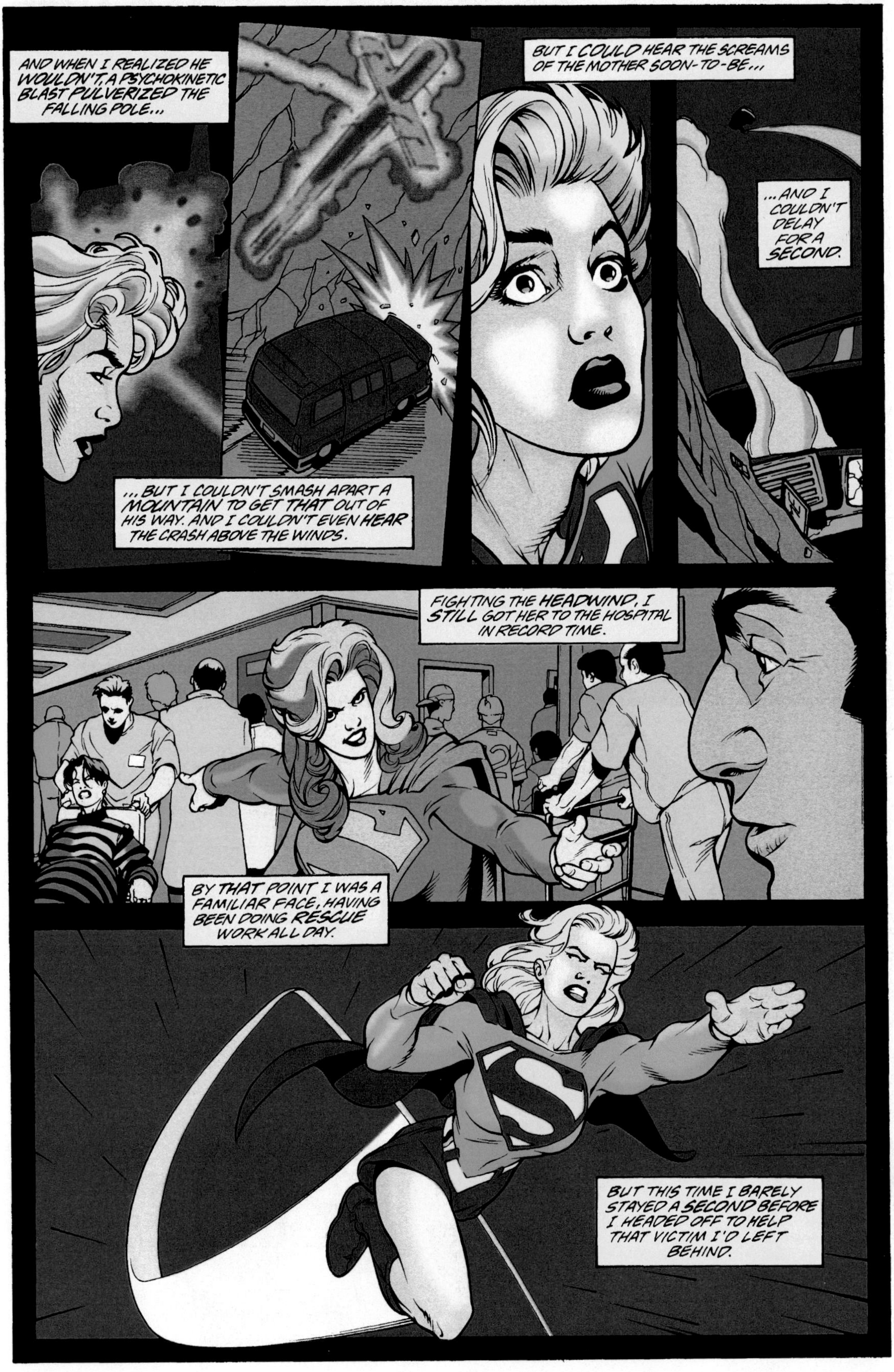
AND WHEN I REALIZED HE WOULDN'T, A PSYCHOKINETIC BLAST PULVERIZED THE FALLING POLE...
...BUT I COULDN'T SMASH APART A MOUNTAIN TO GET THAT OUT OF HIS WAY. AND I COULDN'T EVEN HEAR THE CRASH ABOVE THE WINDS.
BUT I COULD HEAR THE SCREAMS OF THE MOTHER SOON-TO-BE...
...AND I COULDN'T DELAY FOR A SECOND.
FIGHTING THE HEADWIND, I STILL GOT HER TO THE HOSPITAL IN RECORD TIME.
BY THAT POINT I WAS A FAMILIAR FACE, HAVING BEEN DOING RESCUE WORK ALL DAY.
BUT THIS TIME I BARELY STAYED A SECOND BEFORE I HEADED OFF TO HELP THAT VICTIM I'D LEFT BEHIND.

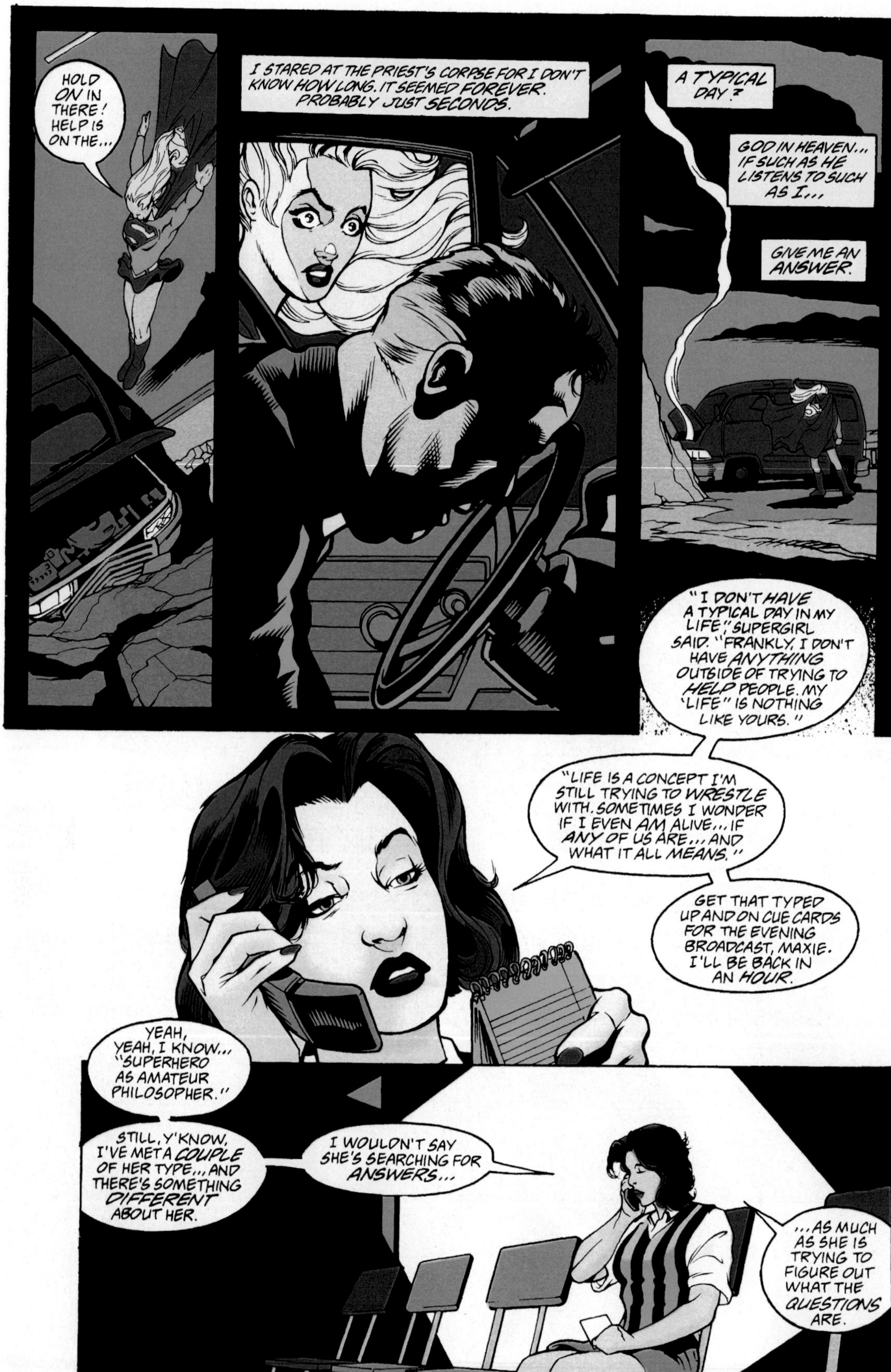
HOLD ON IN THERE! HELP IS ON THE...
I STARED AT THE PRIEST'S CORPSE FOR I DON'T KNOW HOW LONG. IT SEEMED FOREVER. PROBABLY JUST SECONDS.
A TYPICAL DAY?
GOD IN HEAVEN... IF SUCH AS HE LISTENS TO SUCH AS I...
GIVE ME AN ANSWER.
"I DON'T HAVE A TYPICAL DAY IN MY LIFE," SUPERGIRL SAID. "FRANKLY, I DON'T HAVE ANYTHING OUTSIDE OF TRYING TO HELP PEOPLE. MY 'LIFE' IS NOTHING LIKE YOURS."
"LIFE IS A CONCEPT I'M STILL TRYING TO WRESTLE WITH. SOMETIMES I WONDER IF I EVEN AM ALIVE... IF ANY OF US ARE... AND WHAT IT ALL MEANS."
GET THAT TYPED UP AND ON CUE CARDS FOR THE EVENING BROADCAST, MAXIE. I'LL BE BACK IN AN HOUR.
YEAH, YEAH, I KNOW... "SUPERHERO AS AMATEUR PHILOSOPHER."
STILL, Y'KNOW, I'VE MET A COUPLE OF HER TYPE... AND THERE'S SOMETHING DIFFERENT ABOUT HER.
I WOULDN'T SAY SHE'S SEARCHING FOR ANSWERS...
...AS MUCH AS SHE IS TRYING TO FIGURE OUT WHAT THE QUESTIONS ARE.

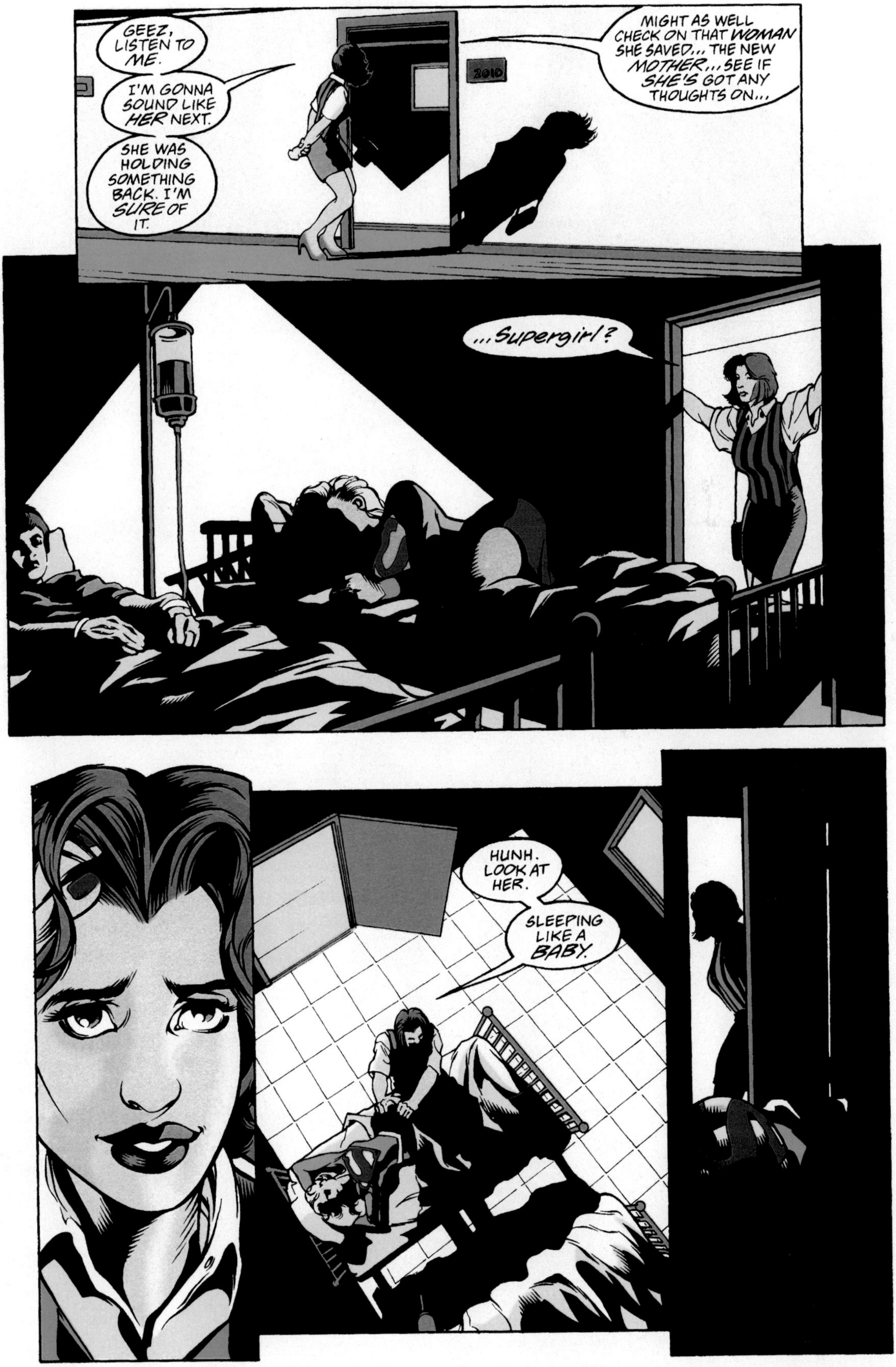
GEEZ, LISTEN TO ME.
I'M GONNA SOUND LIKE HER NEXT.
SHE WAS HOLDING SOMETHING BACK. I'M SURE OF IT.
2010
MIGHT AS WELL CHECK ON THAT WOMAN SHE SAVED... THE NEW MOTHER... SEE IF SHE'S GOT ANY THOUGHTS ON...
...Supergirl?
HUNH. LOOK AT HER.
SLEEPING LIKE A BABY.

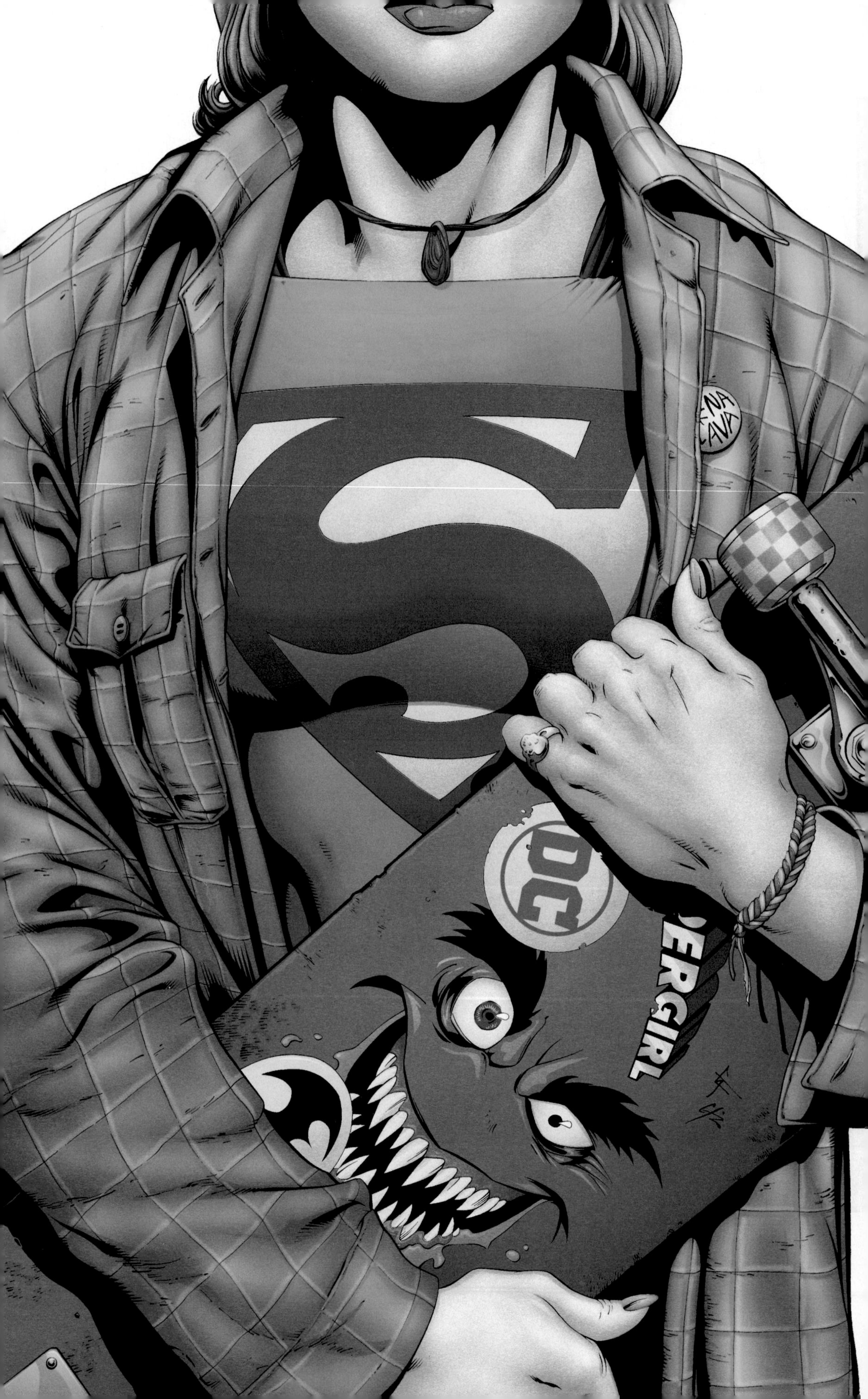
ERGIRL

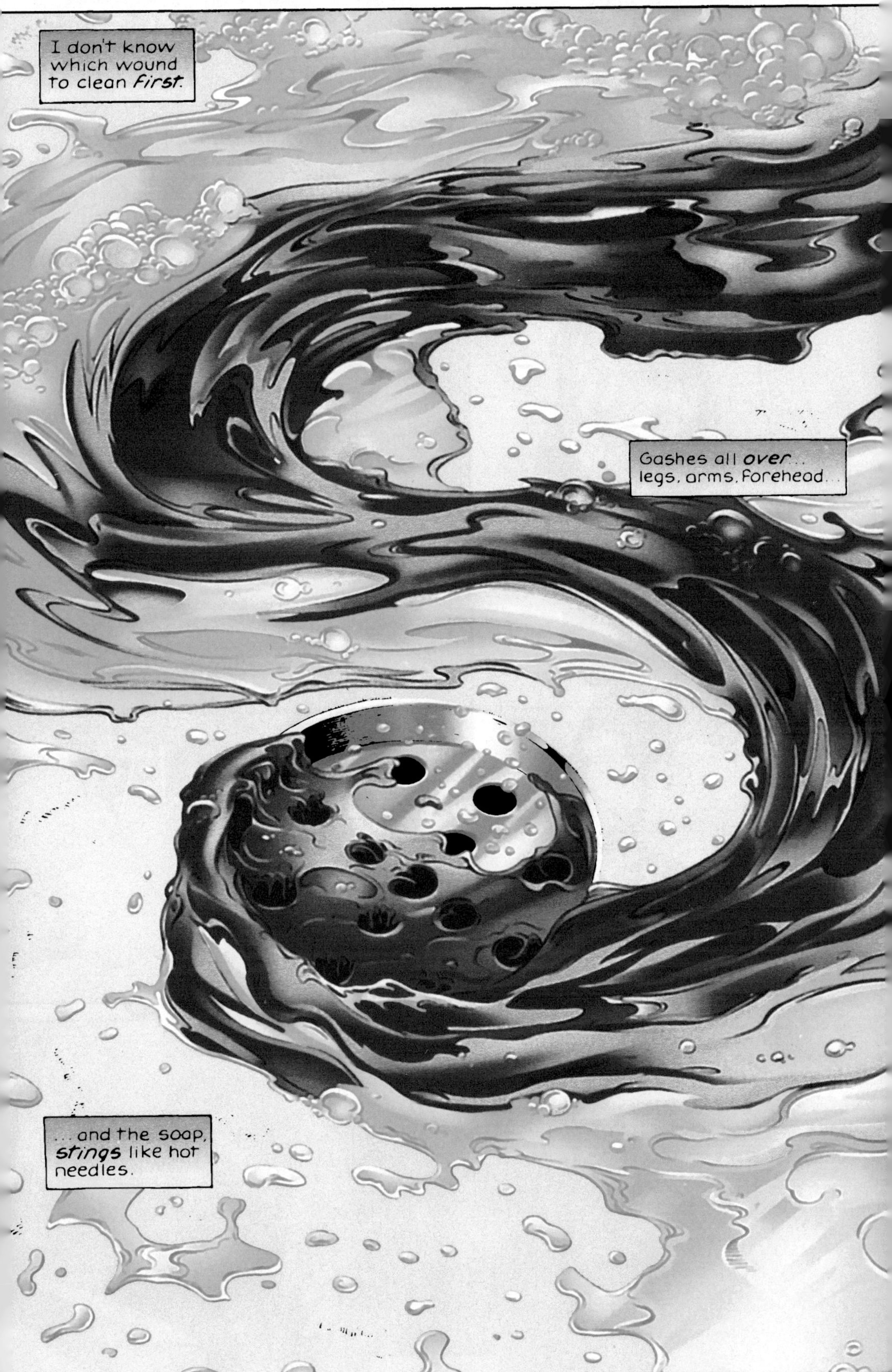
I don't know which wound to clean *first*.
Gashes all *over*... legs, arms, forehead...
...and the soap, *stings* like hot needles.

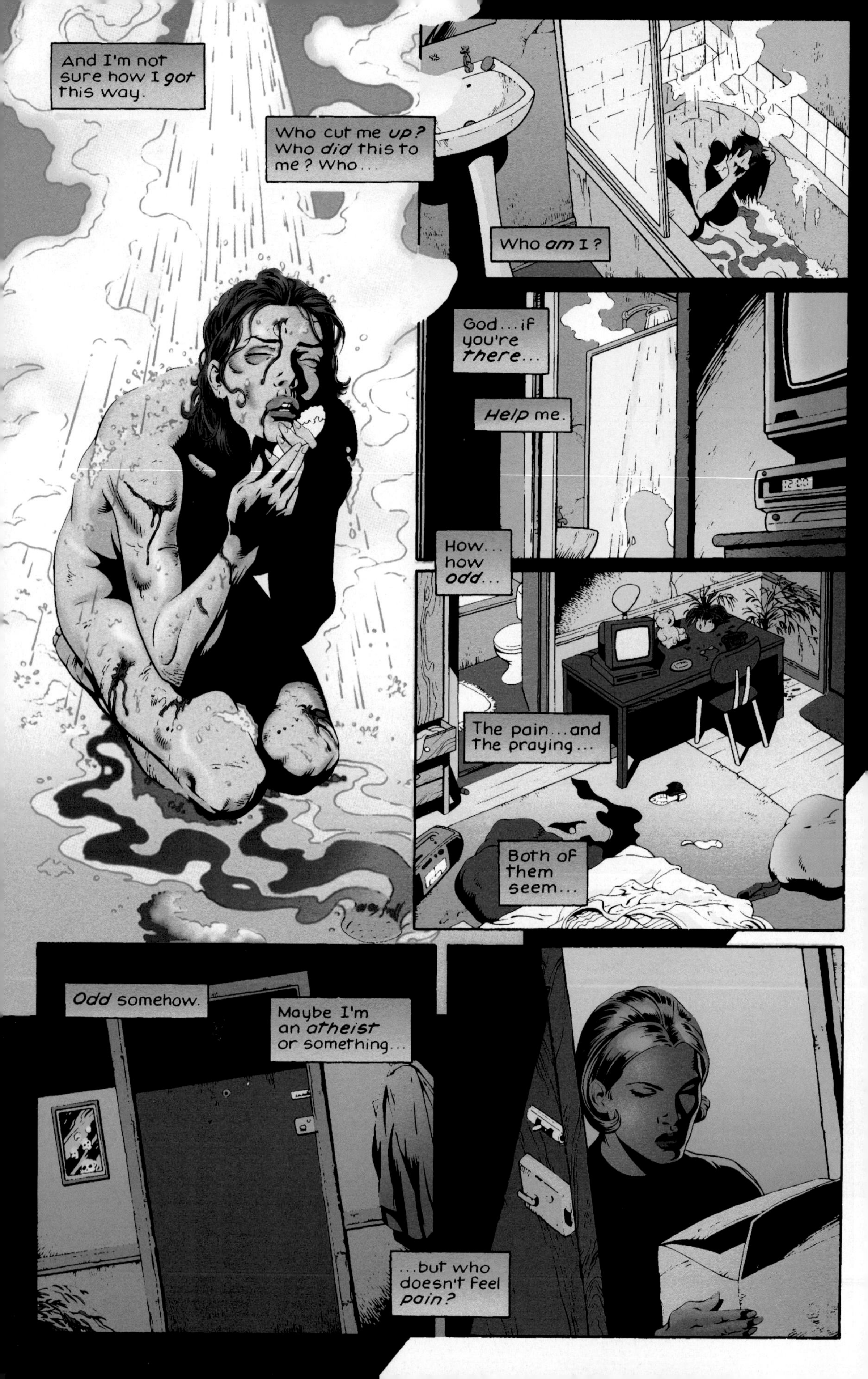
And I'm not sure how I got this way.
Who cut me up? Who did this to me? Who...
Who am I?
God...if you're there...
Help me.
How... how odd...
The pain...and the praying...
Both of them seem...
Odd somehow.
Maybe I'm an atheist or something...
...but who doesn't feel pain?

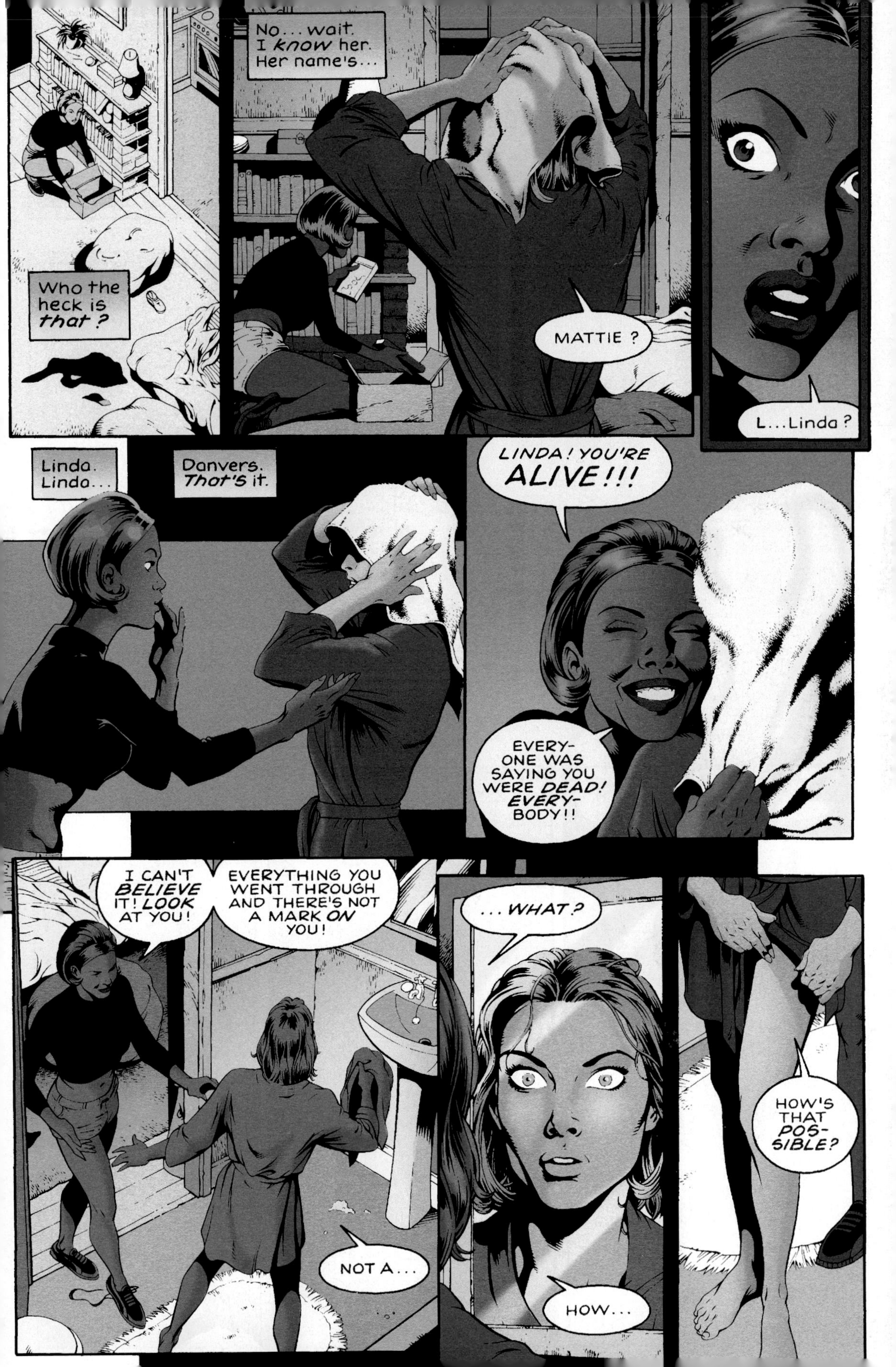
Who the heck is *that*?
No... wait. I *know* her. Her name's...
MATTIE?
L...Linda?
Linda. Linda...
Danvers. *That's* it.
LINDA! YOU'RE **ALIVE!!!**
EVERY-ONE WAS SAYING YOU WERE *DEAD! EVERY*-BODY!!
I CAN'T *BELIEVE* IT! *LOOK* AT YOU!
EVERYTHING YOU WENT THROUGH AND THERE'S NOT A MARK *ON* YOU!
NOT A...
...*WHAT?*
HOW...
HOW'S THAT *POS-SIBLE?*

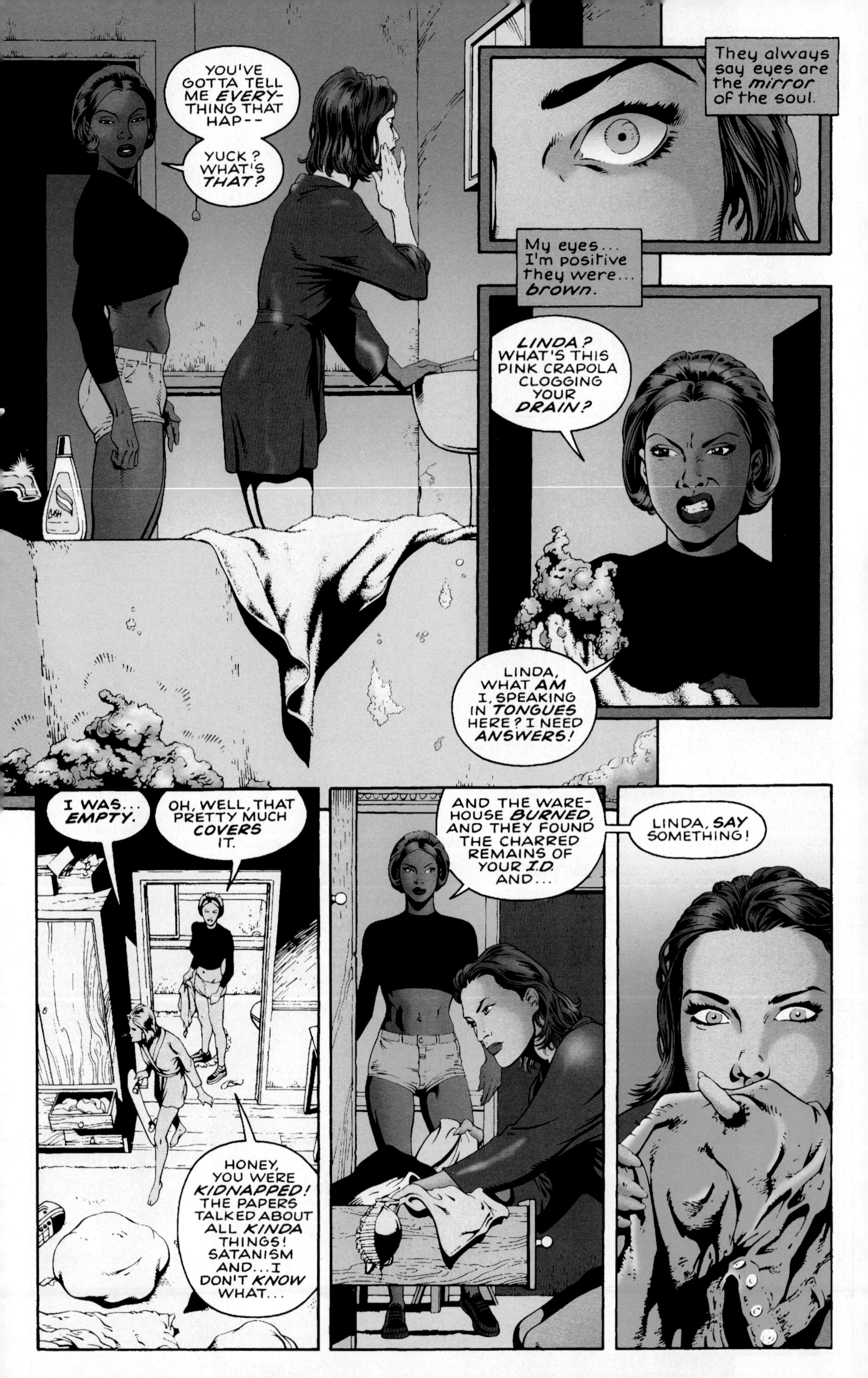

YOU'VE GOTTA TELL ME *EVERY*-THING THAT HAP--
YUCK? WHAT'S *THAT*?
They always say eyes are the *mirror* of the soul.
My eyes... I'm positive they were... *brown*.
LINDA? WHAT'S THIS PINK CRAPOLA CLOGGING YOUR *DRAIN?*
LINDA, WHAT *AM* I, SPEAKING IN *TONGUES* HERE? I NEED *ANSWERS!*
I WAS... *EMPTY*.
OH, WELL, THAT PRETTY MUCH *COVERS* IT.
HONEY, YOU WERE *KIDNAPPED!* THE PAPERS TALKED ABOUT ALL *KINDA* THINGS! SATANISM AND... I DON'T *KNOW* WHAT...
AND THE WARE-HOUSE *BURNED*, AND THEY FOUND THE CHARRED REMAINS OF YOUR *I.D.* AND...
LINDA, *SAY* SOMETHING!

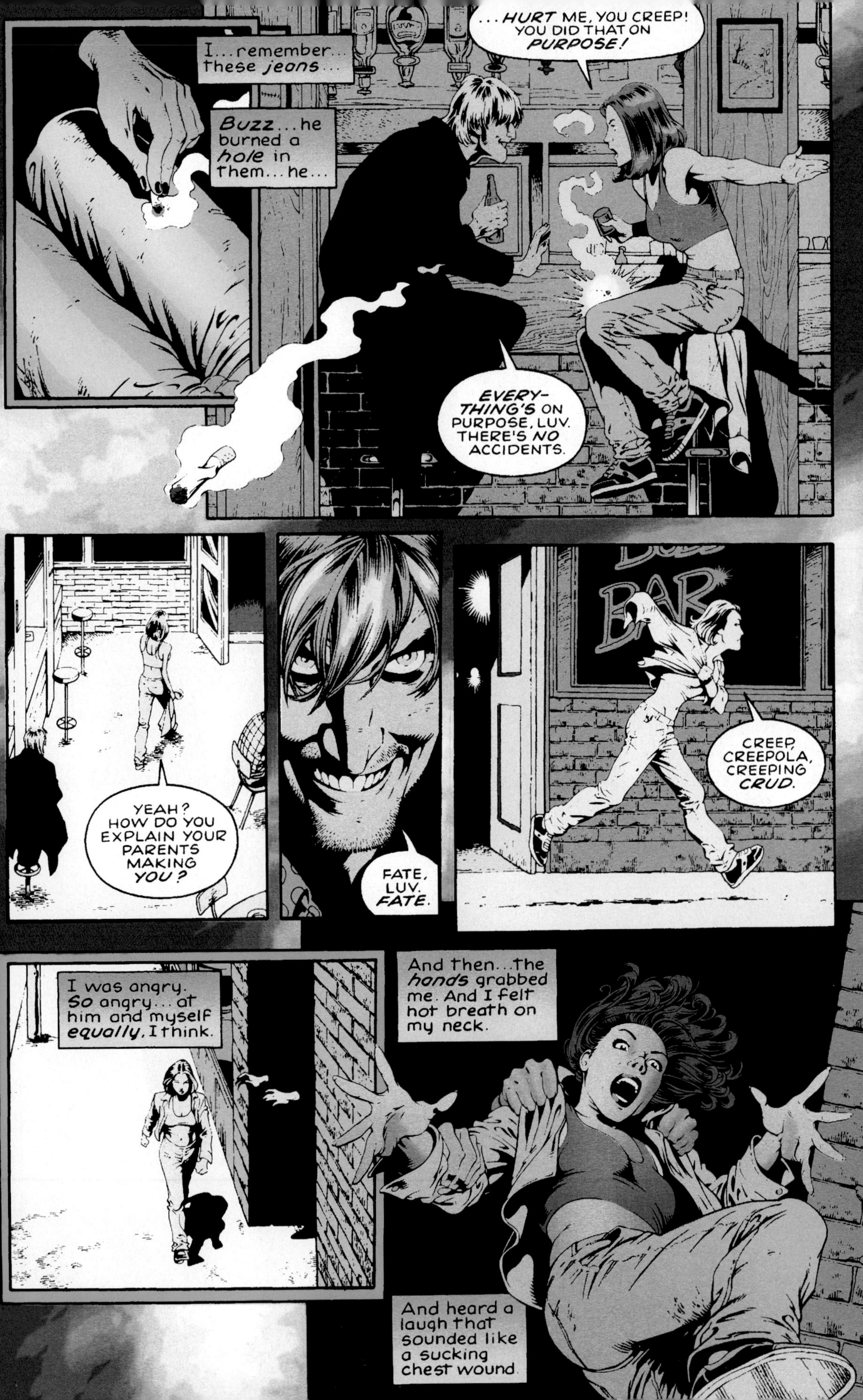
I... remember... these jeans...
Buzz... he burned a hole in them... he...
...HURT ME, YOU CREEP! YOU DID THAT ON PURPOSE!
EVERYTHING'S ON PURPOSE, LUV. THERE'S NO ACCIDENTS.
YEAH? HOW DO YOU EXPLAIN YOUR PARENTS MAKING YOU?
FATE, LUV. FATE.
CREEP, CREEPOLA, CREEPING CRUD.
I was angry. So angry... at him and myself equally, I think.
And then...the hands grabbed me. And I felt hot breath on my neck.
And heard a laugh that sounded like a sucking chest wound.

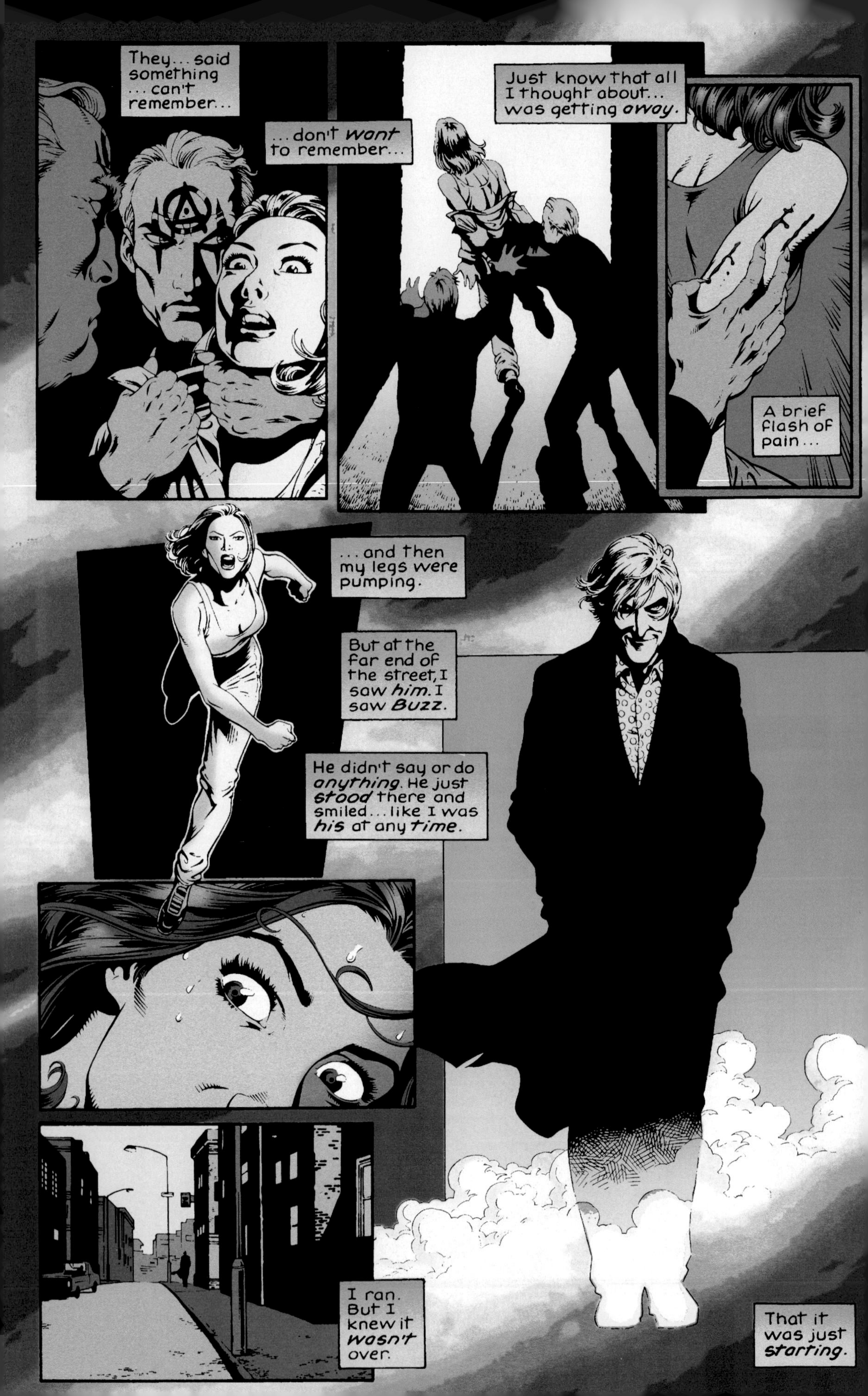
They... said something ...can't remember...
...don't want to remember...
Just know that all I thought about... was getting away.
A brief flash of pain...
...and then my legs were pumping.
But at the far end of the street, I saw him. I saw Buzz.
He didn't say or do anything. He just stood there and smiled... like I was his at any time.
I ran. But I knew it wasn't over.
That it was just starting.

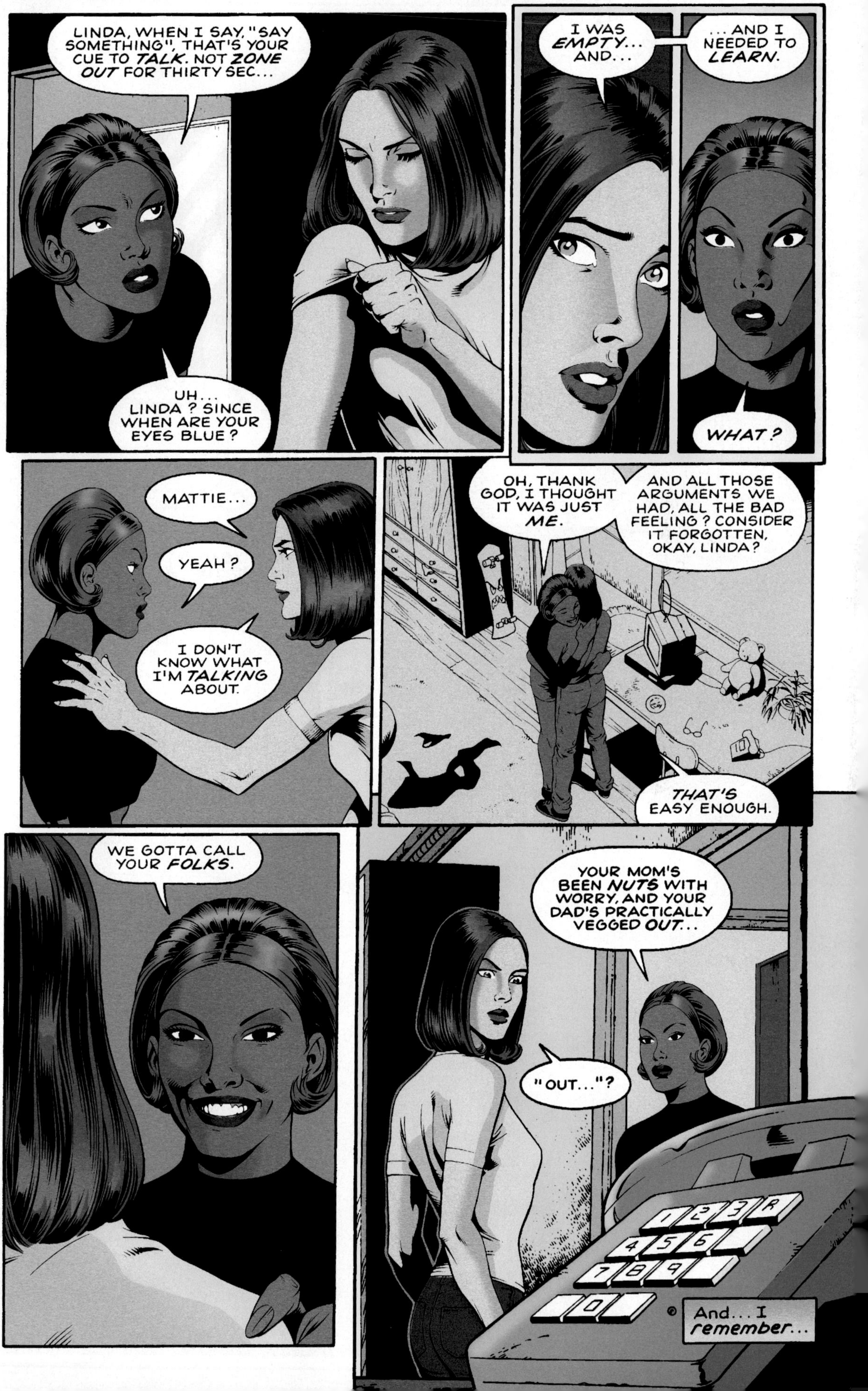
LINDA, WHEN I SAY, "SAY SOMETHING", THAT'S YOUR CUE TO TALK. NOT ZONE OUT FOR THIRTY SEC...
UH... LINDA? SINCE WHEN ARE YOUR EYES BLUE?
I WAS EMPTY... AND...
...AND I NEEDED TO LEARN.
WHAT?
MATTIE...
YEAH?
I DON'T KNOW WHAT I'M TALKING ABOUT.
OH, THANK GOD, I THOUGHT IT WAS JUST ME.
AND ALL THOSE ARGUMENTS WE HAD, ALL THE BAD FEELING? CONSIDER IT FORGOTTEN, OKAY, LINDA?
THAT'S EASY ENOUGH.
WE GOTTA CALL YOUR FOLKS.
YOUR MOM'S BEEN NUTS WITH WORRY, AND YOUR DAD'S PRACTICALLY VEGGED OUT...
"OUT..."?
And... I remember...

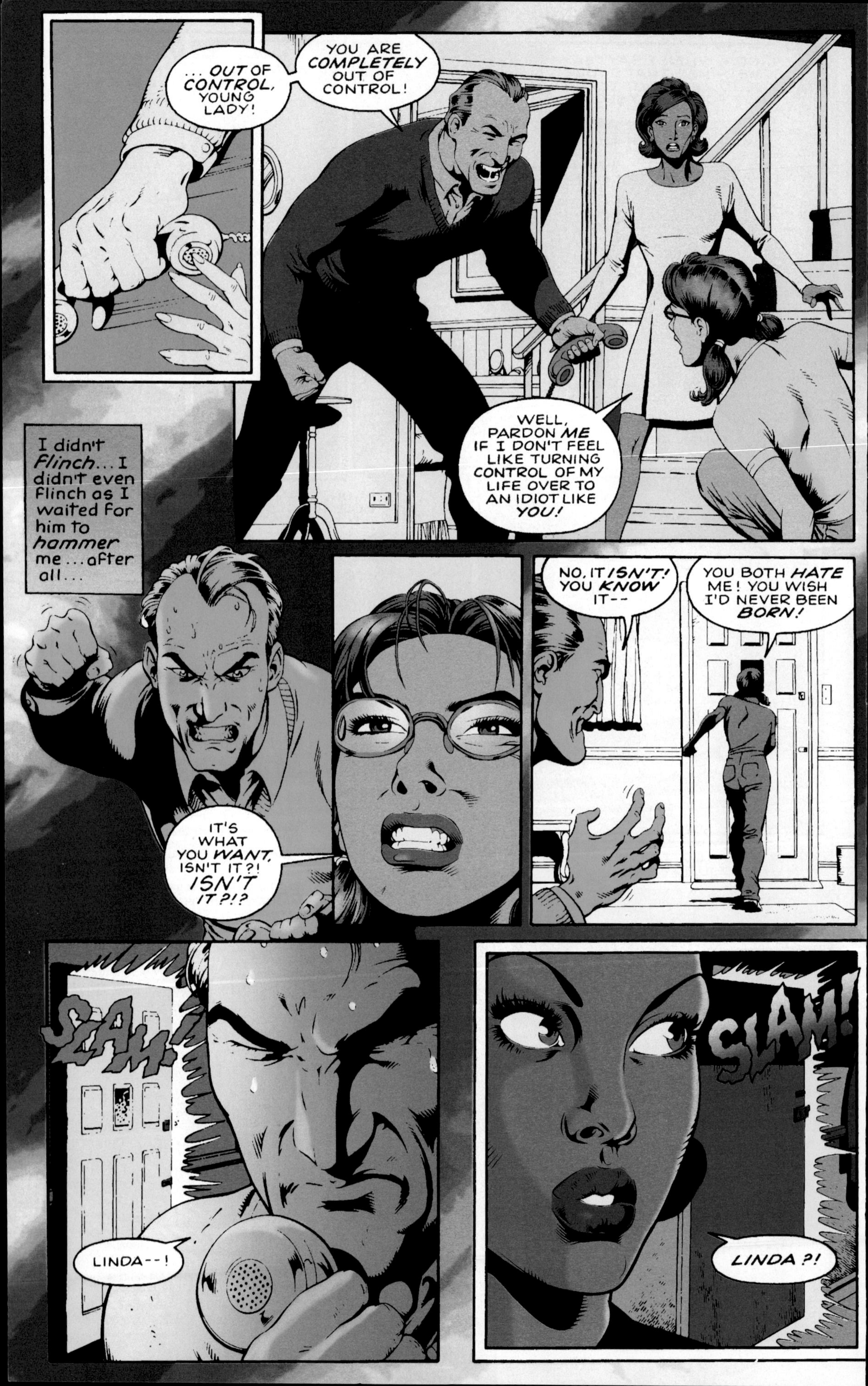
...OUT OF CONTROL, YOUNG LADY!
YOU ARE COMPLETELY OUT OF CONTROL!
WELL, PARDON ME IF I DON'T FEEL LIKE TURNING CONTROL OF MY LIFE OVER TO AN IDIOT LIKE YOU!
I didn't flinch... I didn't even flinch as I waited for him to hammer me... after all...
IT'S WHAT YOU WANT, ISN'T IT?! ISN'T IT?!?
NO, IT ISN'T! YOU KNOW IT--
YOU BOTH HATE ME! YOU WISH I'D NEVER BEEN BORN!
SLAM!
LINDA--!
SLAM!
LINDA?!

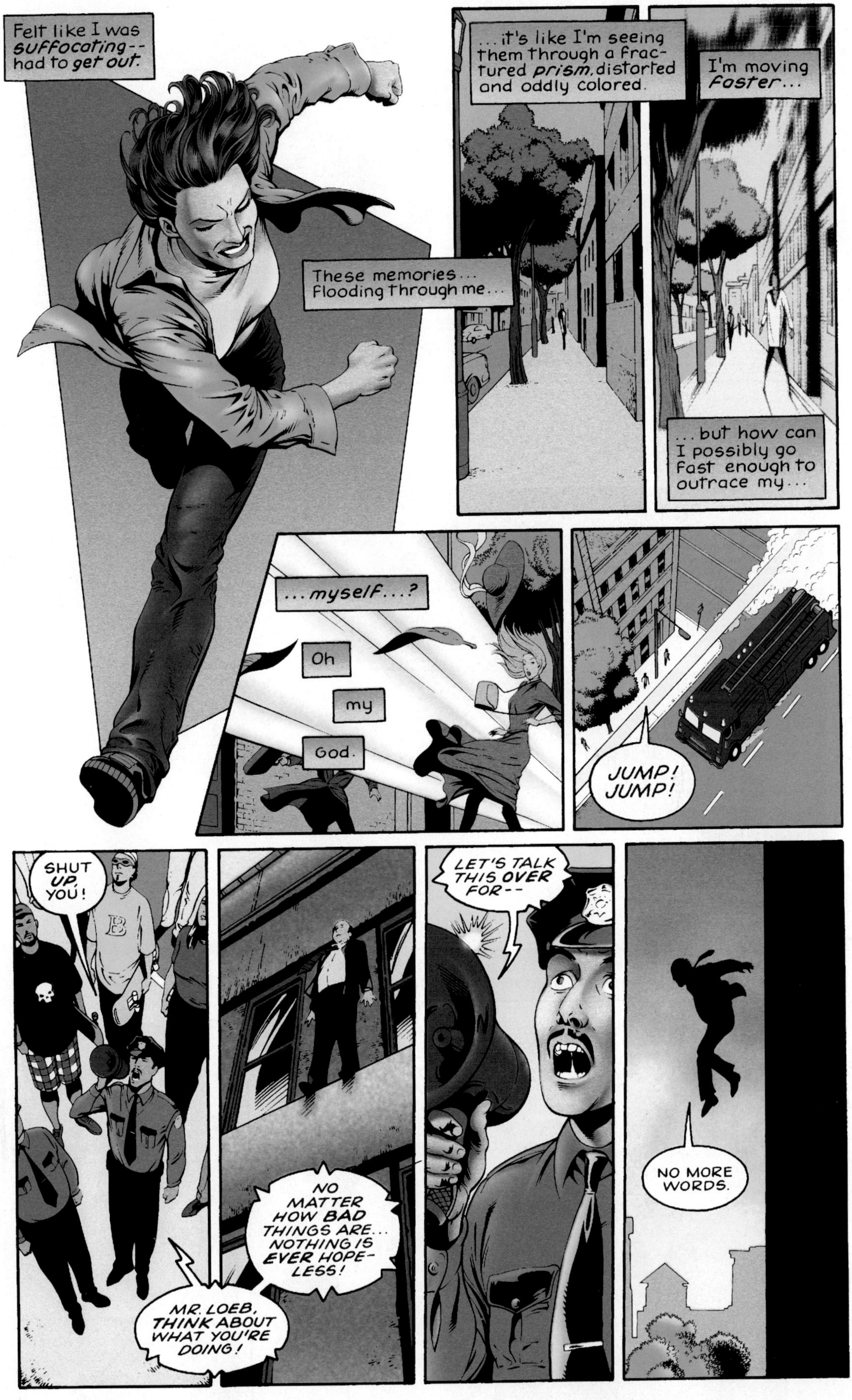
Felt like I was suffocating--had to get out.
These memories... flooding through me...
...it's like I'm seeing them through a fractured prism, distorted and oddly colored.
I'm moving faster...
...but how can I possibly go fast enough to outrace my...
...myself...?
Oh
my
God.
JUMP! JUMP!
SHUT UP, YOU!
MR. LOEB, THINK ABOUT WHAT YOU'RE DOING!
NO MATTER HOW BAD THINGS ARE... NOTHING IS EVER HOPELESS!
LET'S TALK THIS OVER FOR--
NO MORE WORDS.

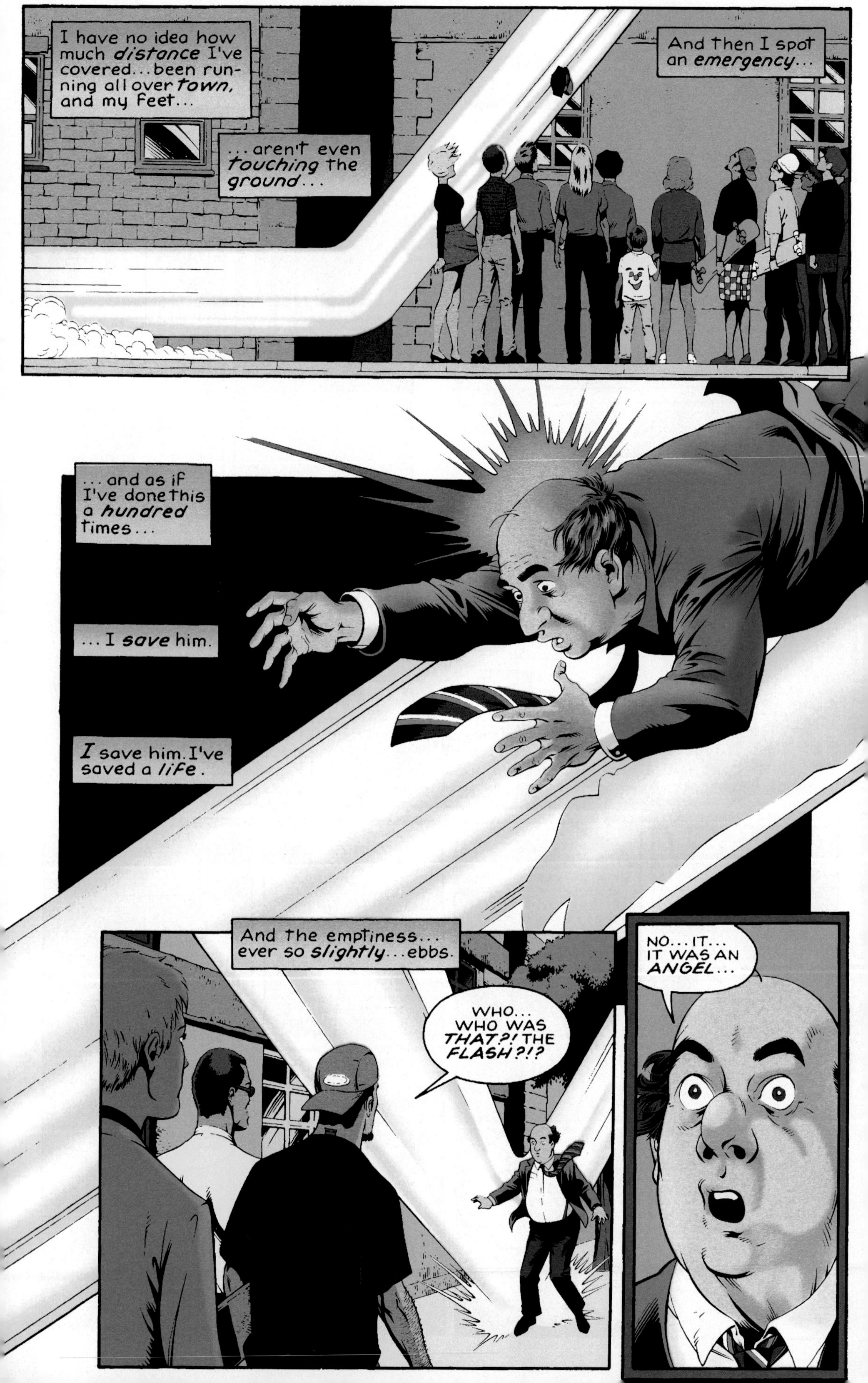
I have no idea how much distance I've covered... been running all over town, and my feet...
...aren't even touching the ground...
And then I spot an emergency...
...and as if I've done this a hundred times...
...I save him.
I save him. I've saved a life.
And the emptiness... ever so slightly...ebbs.
WHO... WHO WAS THAT?! THE FLASH?!?
NO... IT... IT WAS AN ANGEL...

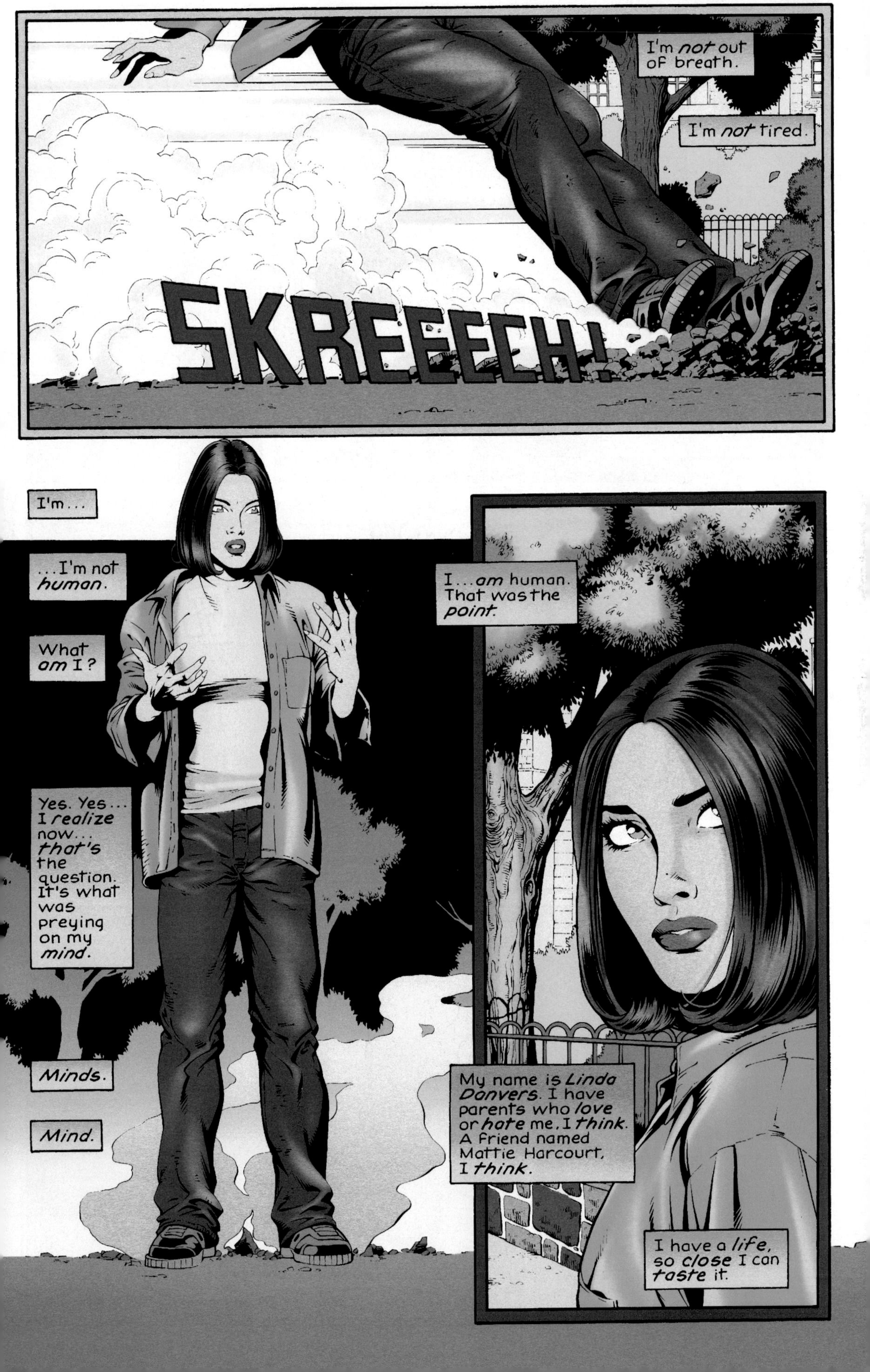

I'm not out of breath.
I'm not tired.
SKREEECH!
I'm...
...I'm not human.
What am I?
Yes. Yes... I realize now... that's the question. It's what was preying on my mind.
Minds.
Mind.
I...am human. That was the point.
My name is Linda Danvers. I have parents who love or hate me, I think. A friend named Mattie Harcourt, I think.
I have a life, so close I can taste it.

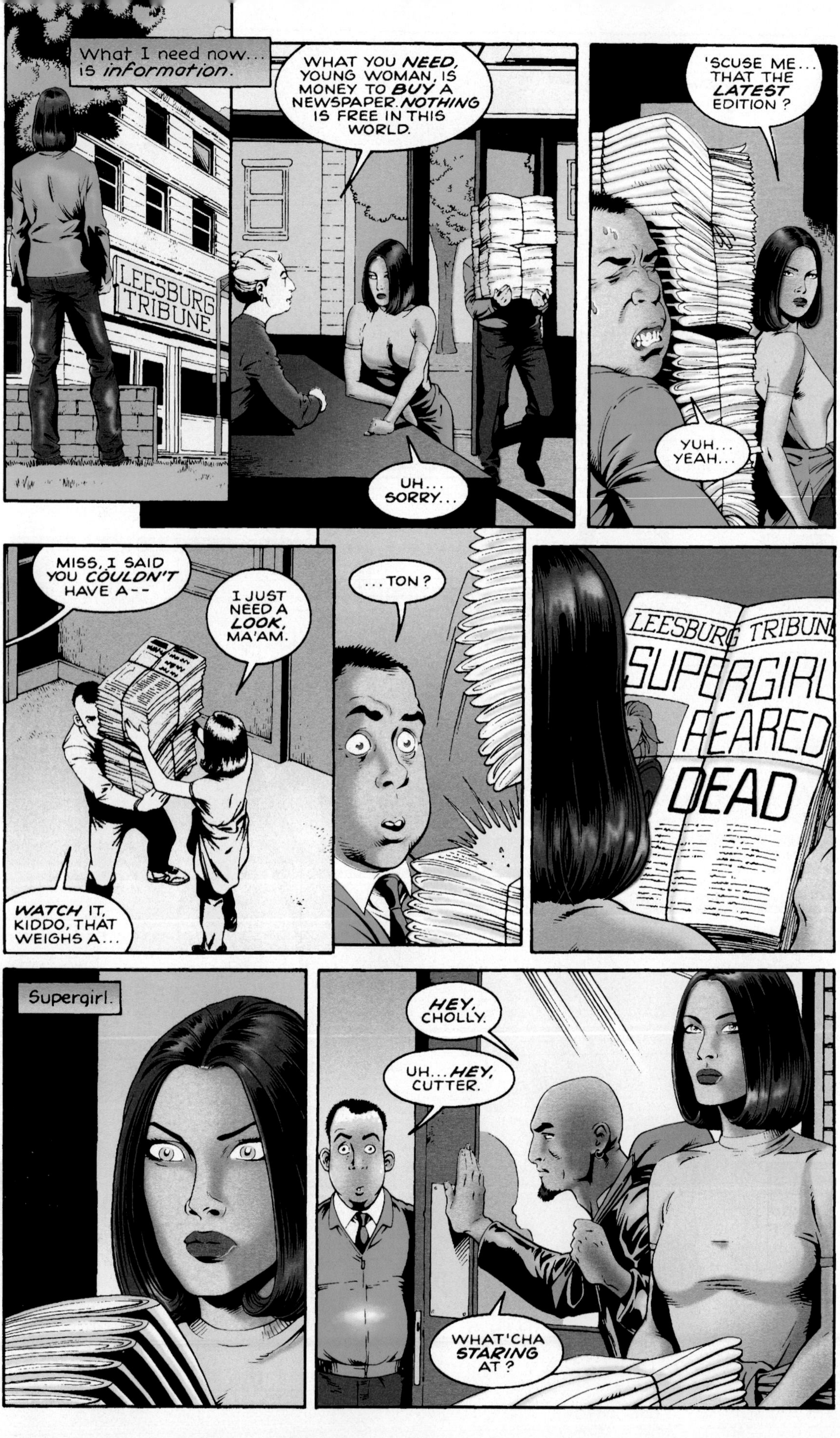
What I need now... is *information*.
LEESBURG TRIBUNE
WHAT YOU ***NEED,*** YOUNG WOMAN, IS MONEY TO ***BUY*** A NEWSPAPER. ***NOTHING*** IS FREE IN THIS WORLD.
UH... SORRY...
'SCUSE ME... THAT THE ***LATEST*** EDITION?
YUH... YEAH...
MISS, I SAID YOU ***COULDN'T*** HAVE A--
I JUST NEED A ***LOOK,*** MA'AM.
WATCH IT, KIDDO, THAT WEIGHS A...
...TON?
LEESBURG TRIBUNE
SUPERGIRL FEARED DEAD
Supergirl.
HEY, CHOLLY.
UH... ***HEY,*** CUTTER.
WHAT'CHA ***STARING*** AT?

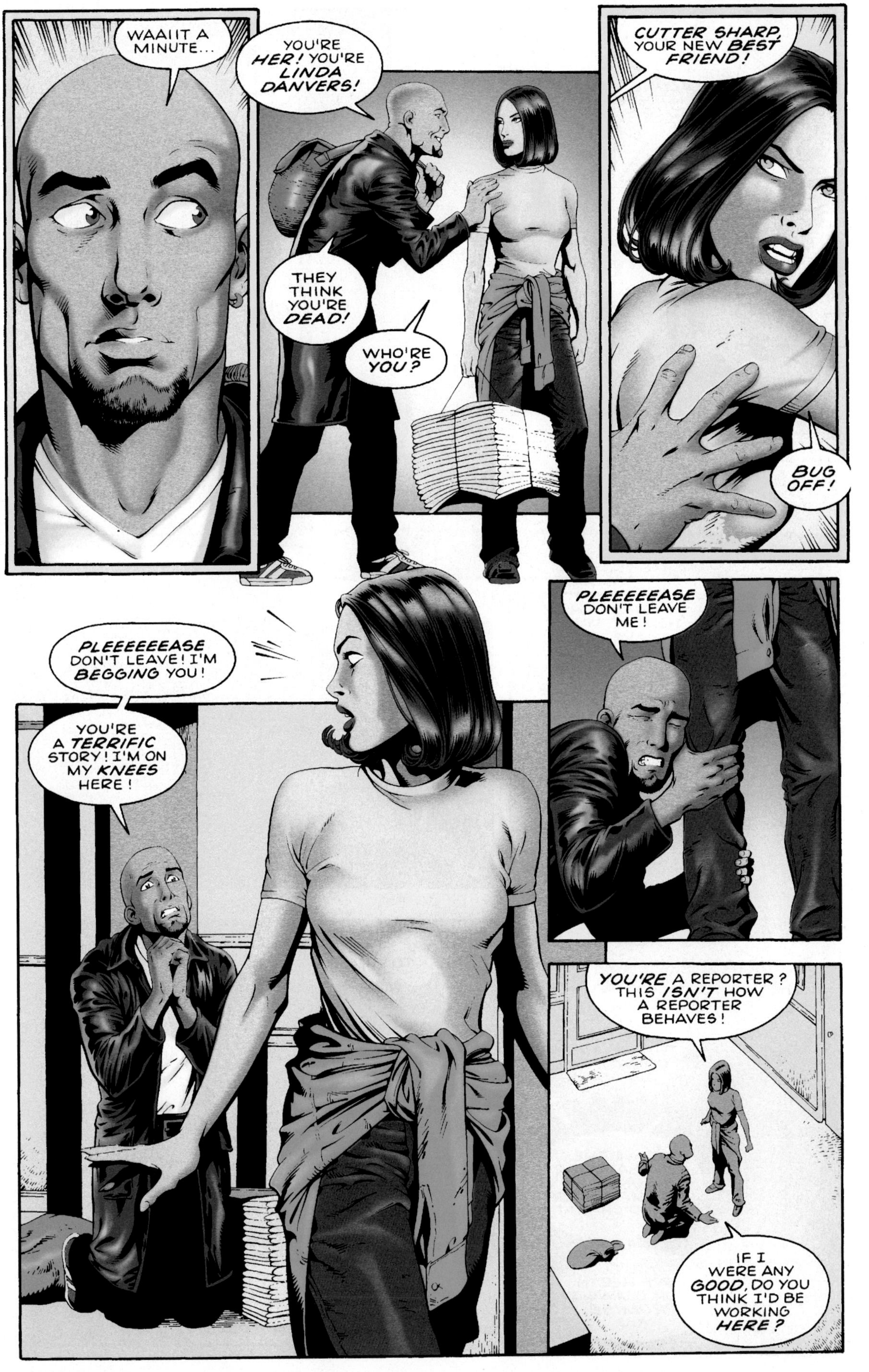
WAAIIT A MINUTE...
YOU'RE HER! YOU'RE LINDA DANVERS!
THEY THINK YOU'RE DEAD!
WHO'RE YOU?
CUTTER SHARP, YOUR NEW BEST FRIEND!
BUG OFF!
PLEEEEEEASE DON'T LEAVE! I'M BEGGING YOU!
YOU'RE A TERRIFIC STORY! I'M ON MY KNEES HERE!
PLEEEEEASE DON'T LEAVE ME!
YOU'RE A REPORTER? THIS ISN'T HOW A REPORTER BEHAVES!
IF I WERE ANY GOOD, DO YOU THINK I'D BE WORKING HERE?

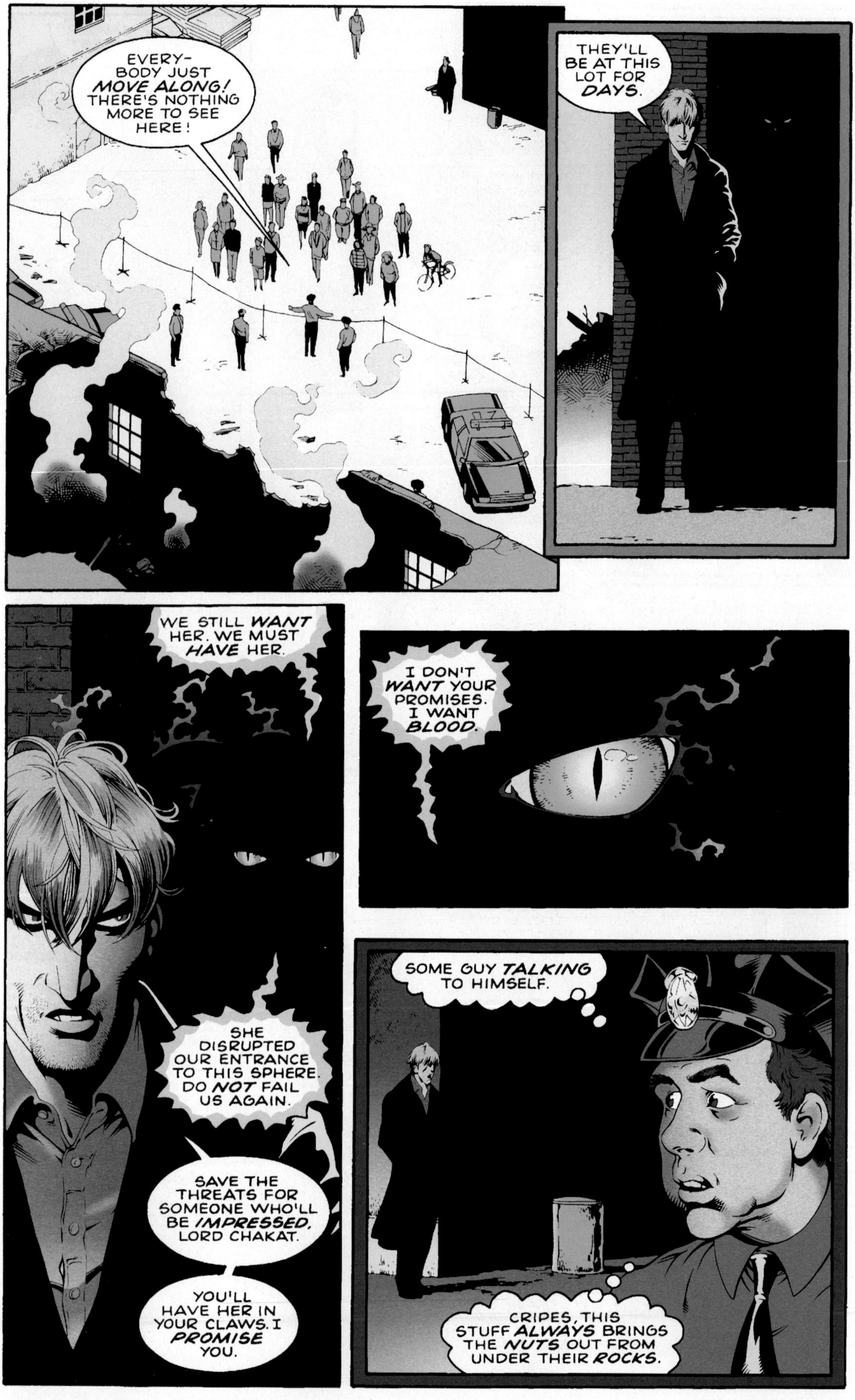
EVERY-BODY JUST MOVE ALONG! THERE'S NOTHING MORE TO SEE HERE!
THEY'LL BE AT THIS LOT FOR DAYS.
WE STILL WANT HER. WE MUST HAVE HER.
I DON'T WANT YOUR PROMISES. I WANT BLOOD.
SHE DISRUPTED OUR ENTRANCE TO THIS SPHERE. DO NOT FAIL US AGAIN.
SAVE THE THREATS FOR SOMEONE WHO'LL BE IMPRESSED, LORD CHAKAT.
YOU'LL HAVE HER IN YOUR CLAWS. I PROMISE YOU.
SOME GUY TALKING TO HIMSELF.
CRIPES, THIS STUFF ALWAYS BRINGS THE NUTS OUT FROM UNDER THEIR ROCKS.

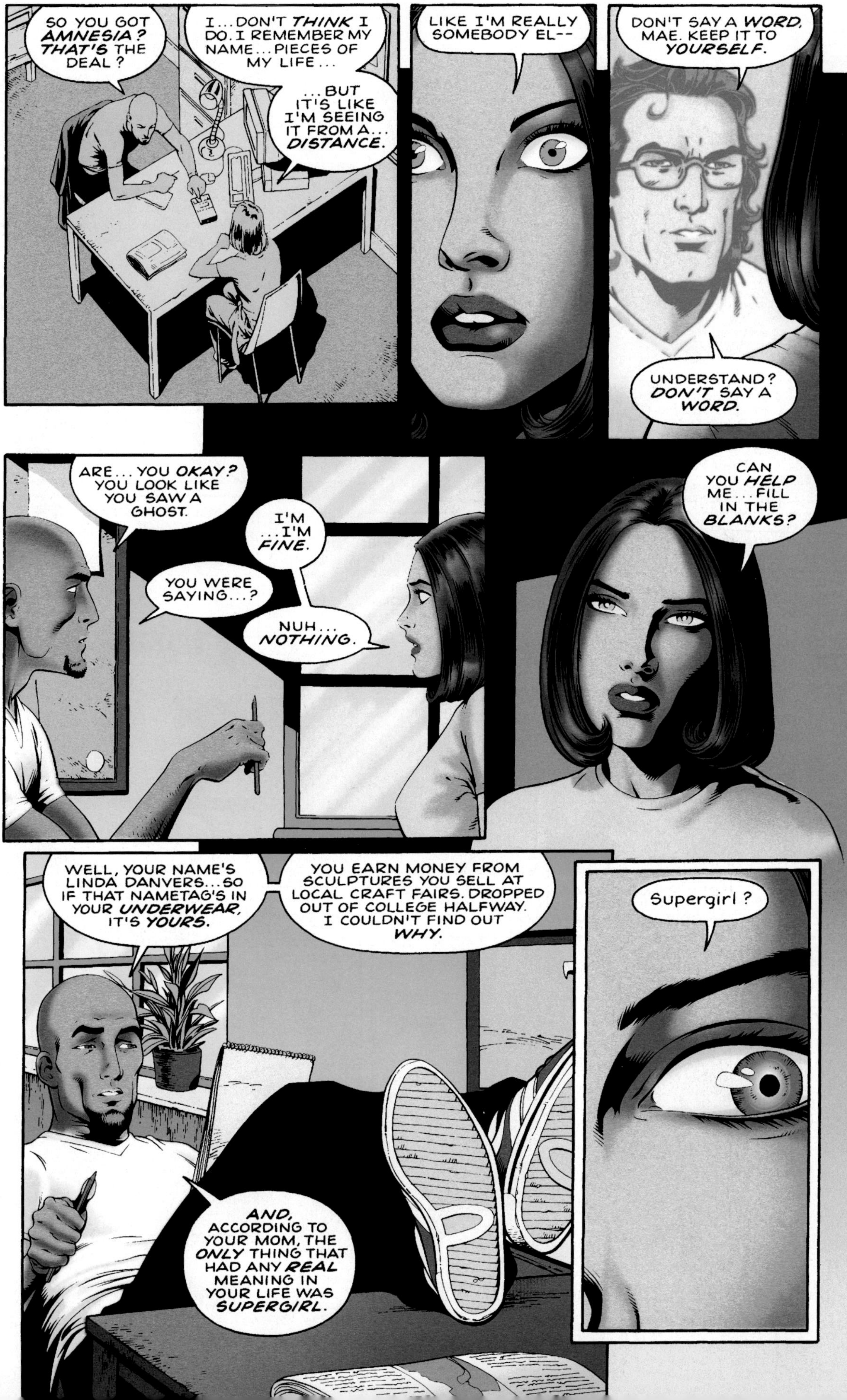

SO YOU GOT AMNESIA? THAT'S THE DEAL?
I... DON'T THINK I DO. I REMEMBER MY NAME... PIECES OF MY LIFE...
...BUT IT'S LIKE I'M SEEING IT FROM A... DISTANCE.
LIKE I'M REALLY SOMEBODY EL--
DON'T SAY A WORD, MAE. KEEP IT TO YOURSELF.
UNDERSTAND? DON'T SAY A WORD.
ARE... YOU OKAY? YOU LOOK LIKE YOU SAW A GHOST.
I'M ...I'M FINE.
YOU WERE SAYING...?
NUH... NOTHING.
CAN YOU HELP ME... FILL IN THE BLANKS?
WELL, YOUR NAME'S LINDA DANVERS... SO IF THAT NAMETAG'S IN YOUR UNDERWEAR, IT'S YOURS.
YOU EARN MONEY FROM SCULPTURES YOU SELL AT LOCAL CRAFT FAIRS. DROPPED OUT OF COLLEGE HALFWAY. I COULDN'T FIND OUT WHY.
AND, ACCORDING TO YOUR MOM, THE ONLY THING THAT HAD ANY REAL MEANING IN YOUR LIFE WAS SUPERGIRL.
Supergirl?

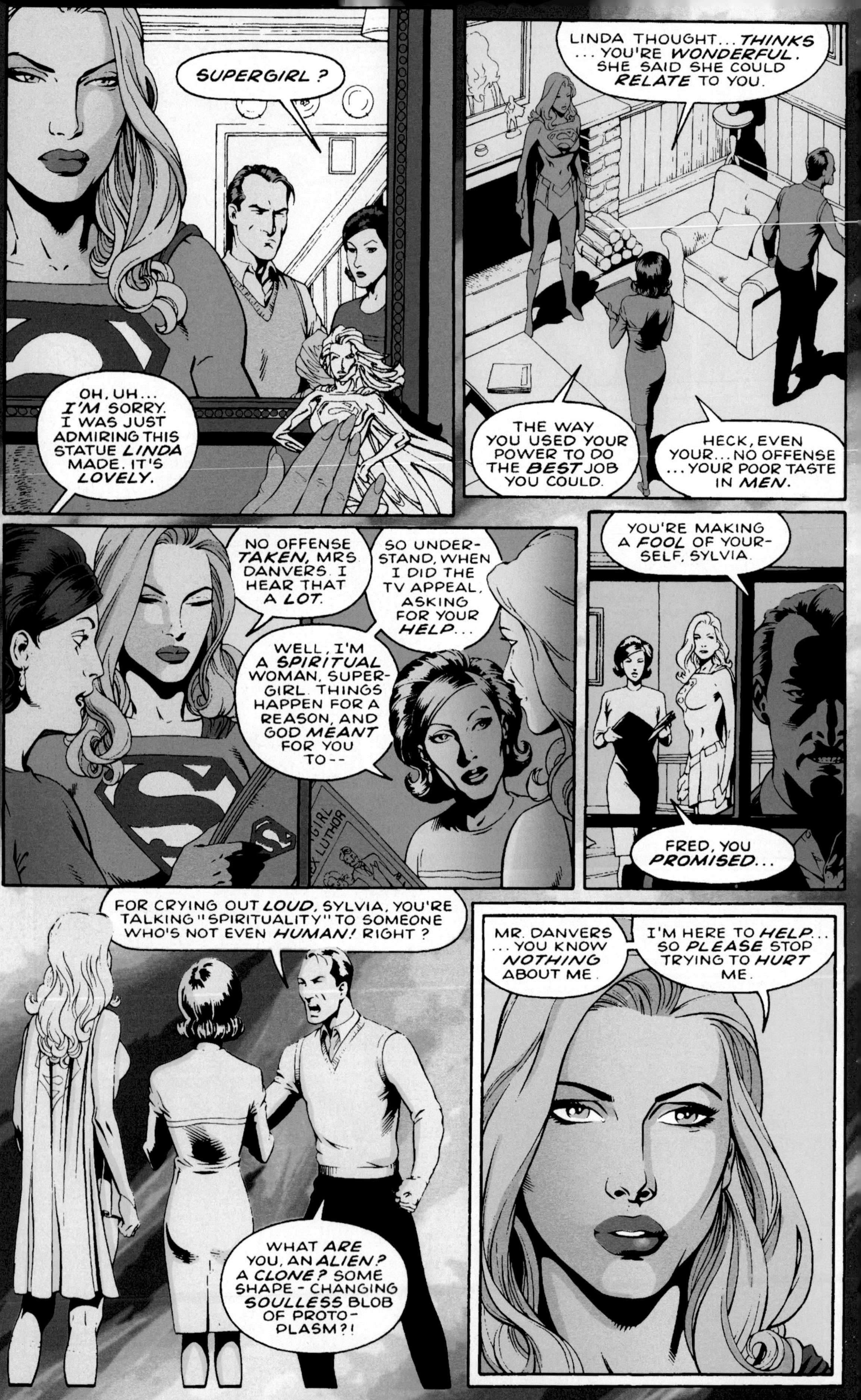
SUPERGIRL ?
OH, UH... I'M SORRY. I WAS JUST ADMIRING THIS STATUE LINDA MADE. IT'S LOVELY.
LINDA THOUGHT... THINKS ... YOU'RE WONDERFUL. SHE SAID SHE COULD RELATE TO YOU.
THE WAY YOU USED YOUR POWER TO DO THE BEST JOB YOU COULD.
HECK, EVEN YOUR... NO OFFENSE ... YOUR POOR TASTE IN MEN.
NO OFFENSE TAKEN, MRS DANVERS. I HEAR THAT A LOT.
SO UNDER-STAND, WHEN I DID THE TV APPEAL, ASKING FOR YOUR HELP...
WELL, I'M A SPIRITUAL WOMAN, SUPER-GIRL. THINGS HAPPEN FOR A REASON, AND GOD MEANT FOR YOU TO--
YOU'RE MAKING A FOOL OF YOUR-SELF, SYLVIA.
FRED, YOU PROMISED...
FOR CRYING OUT LOUD, SYLVIA, YOU'RE TALKING "SPIRITUALITY" TO SOMEONE WHO'S NOT EVEN HUMAN! RIGHT ?
WHAT ARE YOU, AN ALIEN? A CLONE? SOME SHAPE-CHANGING SOULLESS BLOB OF PROTO-PLASM?!
MR. DANVERS ... YOU KNOW NOTHING ABOUT ME.
I'M HERE TO HELP... SO PLEASE STOP TRYING TO HURT ME.

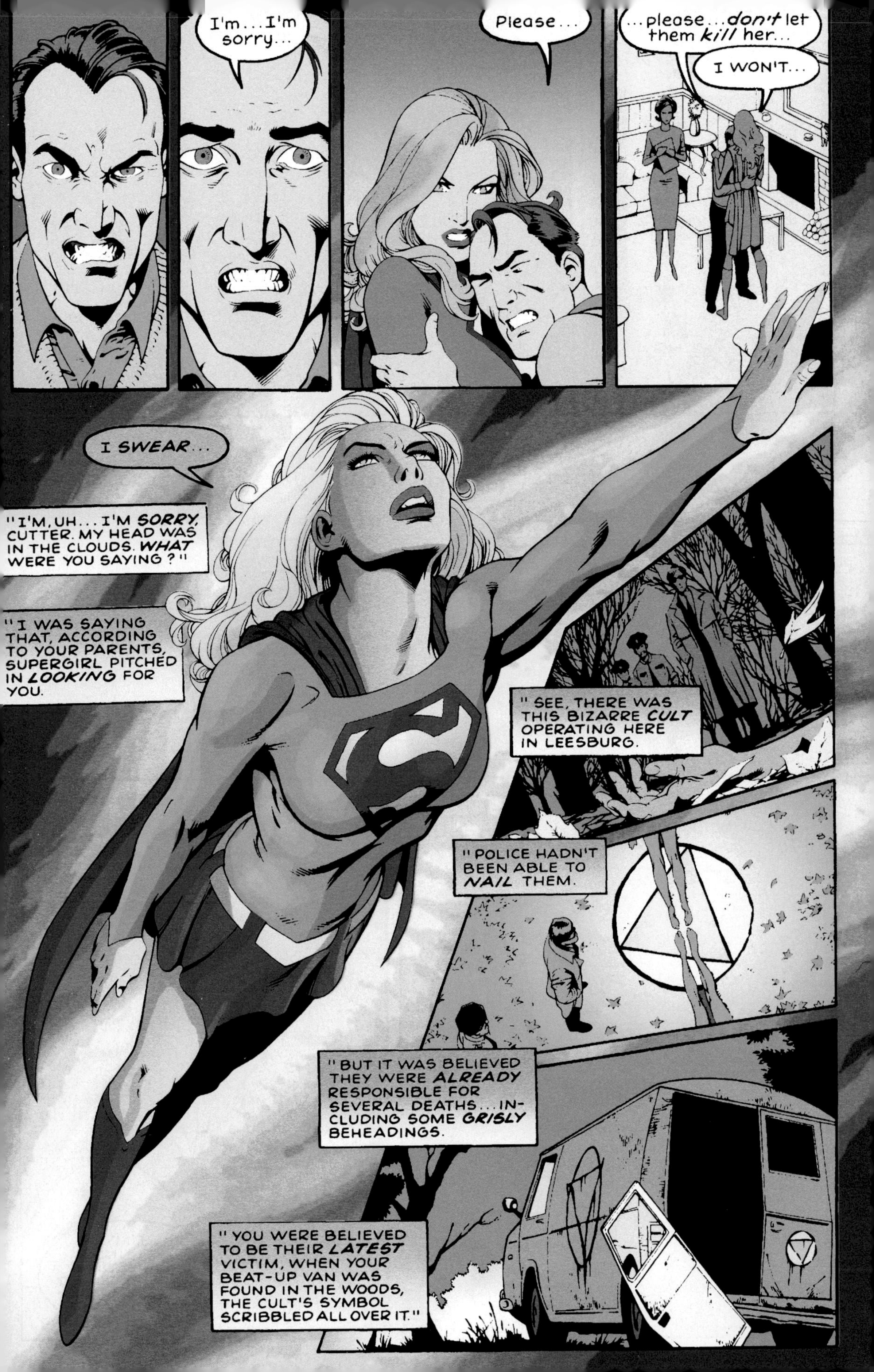

I'm...I'm sorry...
Please...
...please...don't let them kill her...
I WON'T...
I SWEAR...
"I'M, UH...I'M SORRY, CUTTER. MY HEAD WAS IN THE CLOUDS. WHAT WERE YOU SAYING?"
"I WAS SAYING THAT, ACCORDING TO YOUR PARENTS, SUPERGIRL PITCHED IN LOOKING FOR YOU.
"SEE, THERE WAS THIS BIZARRE CULT OPERATING HERE IN LEESBURG.
"POLICE HADN'T BEEN ABLE TO NAIL THEM.
"BUT IT WAS BELIEVED THEY WERE ALREADY RESPONSIBLE FOR SEVERAL DEATHS...INCLUDING SOME GRISLY BEHEADINGS.
"YOU WERE BELIEVED TO BE THEIR LATEST VICTIM, WHEN YOUR BEAT-UP VAN WAS FOUND IN THE WOODS, THE CULT'S SYMBOL SCRIBBLED ALL OVER IT."

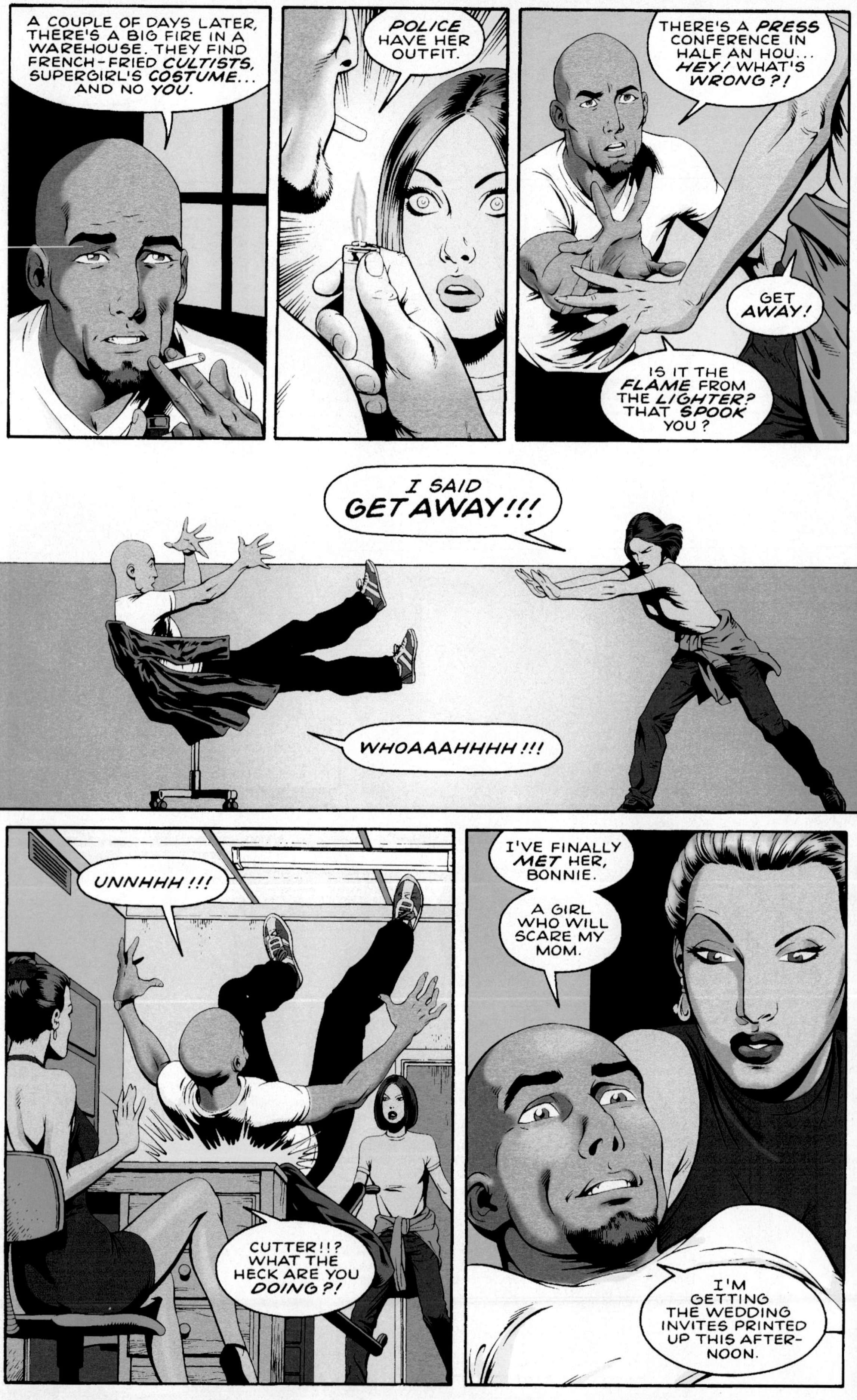
A COUPLE OF DAYS LATER, THERE'S A BIG FIRE IN A WAREHOUSE. THEY FIND FRENCH-FRIED *CULTISTS*, SUPERGIRL'S *COSTUME*... AND NO *YOU*.
POLICE HAVE HER OUTFIT.
THERE'S A *PRESS* CONFERENCE IN HALF AN HOU... *HEY!* WHAT'S *WRONG?!*
GET *AWAY!*
IS IT THE *FLAME* FROM THE *LIGHTER?* THAT *SPOOK* YOU?
I SAID **GET AWAY!!!**
WHOAAAHHHH!!!
UNNHHH!!!
CUTTER!!? WHAT THE HECK ARE YOU *DOING?!*
I'VE FINALLY *MET* HER, BONNIE.
A GIRL WHO WILL SCARE MY MOM.
I'M GETTING THE WEDDING INVITES PRINTED UP THIS AFTER-NOON.

He runs out onto the street, calling my name.

He looks around.

Doesn't look *up*.

But I... I look *inward*...

I see *her* ...I see *Supergirl* in pitched battle...

More than see... I can *feel* the heat, intense and rippling...

Somewhere there's the stench of burning human flesh, threatening to turn my *stomach*...

And there's something *else*... something *feral*, just beyond my consciousness...

A spell... they're trying to release some *thing*.

There's *flame* ...*every*where, there's flame...

And I'm *screaming*... screaming at *myself*...

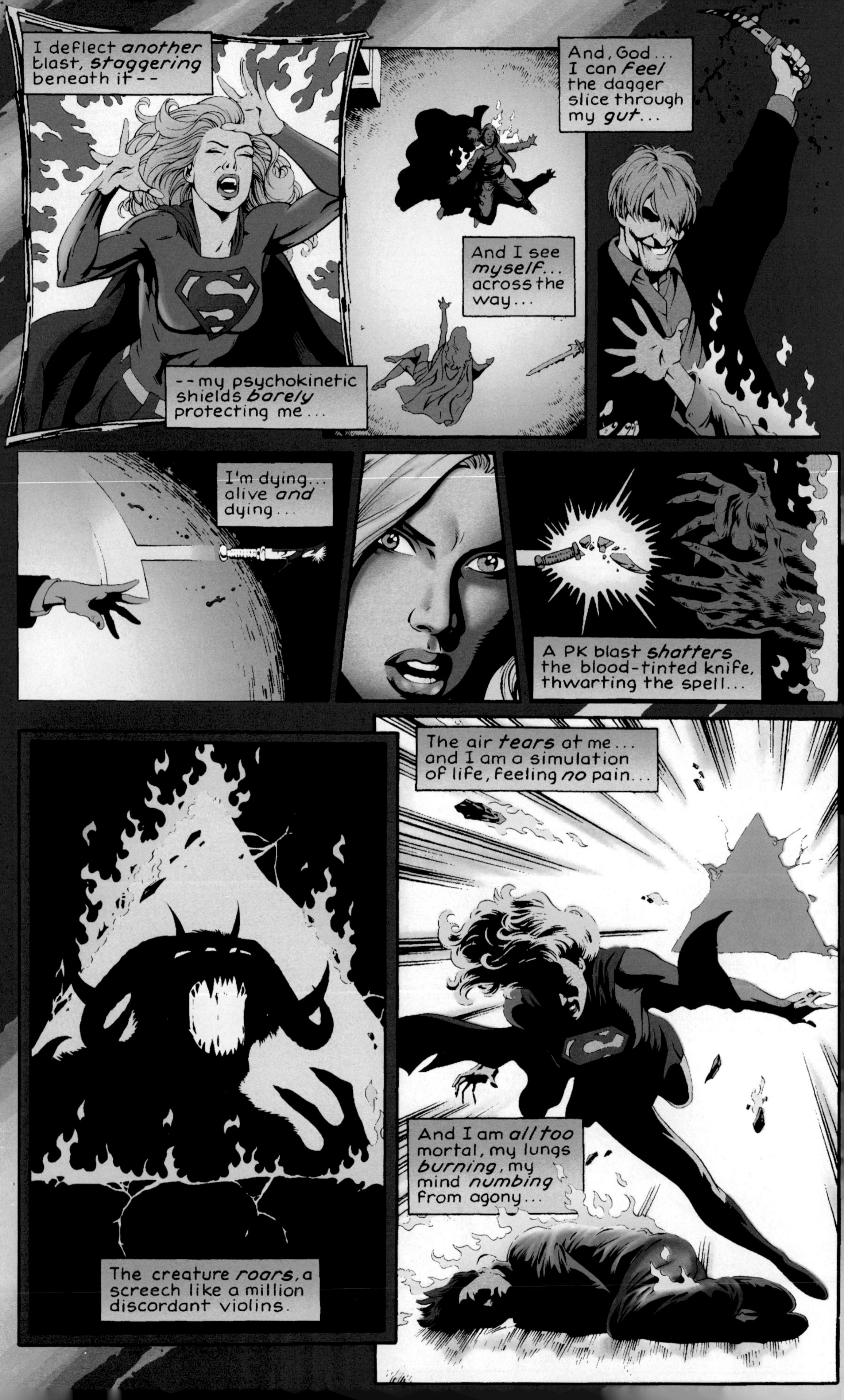
I deflect *another* blast, *staggering* beneath it --
--my psychokinetic shields *barely* protecting me...
And I see *myself*... across the way...
And, God... I can *feel* the dagger slice through my *gut*...
I'm dying... alive *and* dying...
A PK blast *shatters* the blood-tinted knife, thwarting the spell...
The creature *roars*, a screech like a million discordant violins.
The air *tears* at me... and I am a simulation of life, feeling *no* pain...
And I am *all too* mortal, my lungs *burning*, my mind *numbing* from agony...

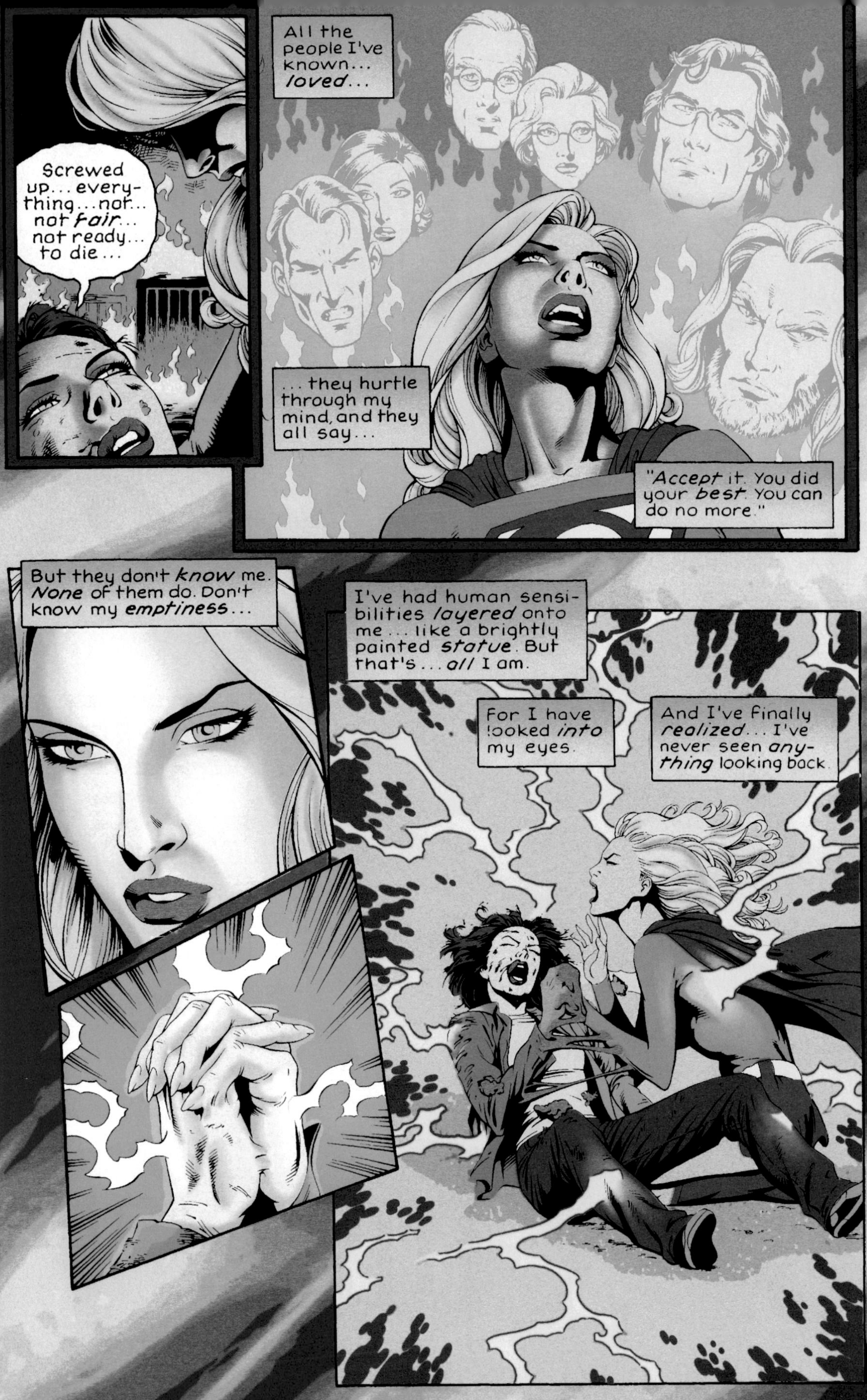
Screwed up... every-thing... not... not fair... not ready... to die...
All the people I've known... loved...
...they hurtle through my mind, and they all say...
"Accept it. You did your best. You can do no more."
But they don't know me. None of them do. Don't know my emptiness...
I've had human sensi-bilities layered onto me... like a brightly painted statue. But that's... all I am.
For I have looked into my eyes.
And I've finally realized... I've never seen any-thing looking back.

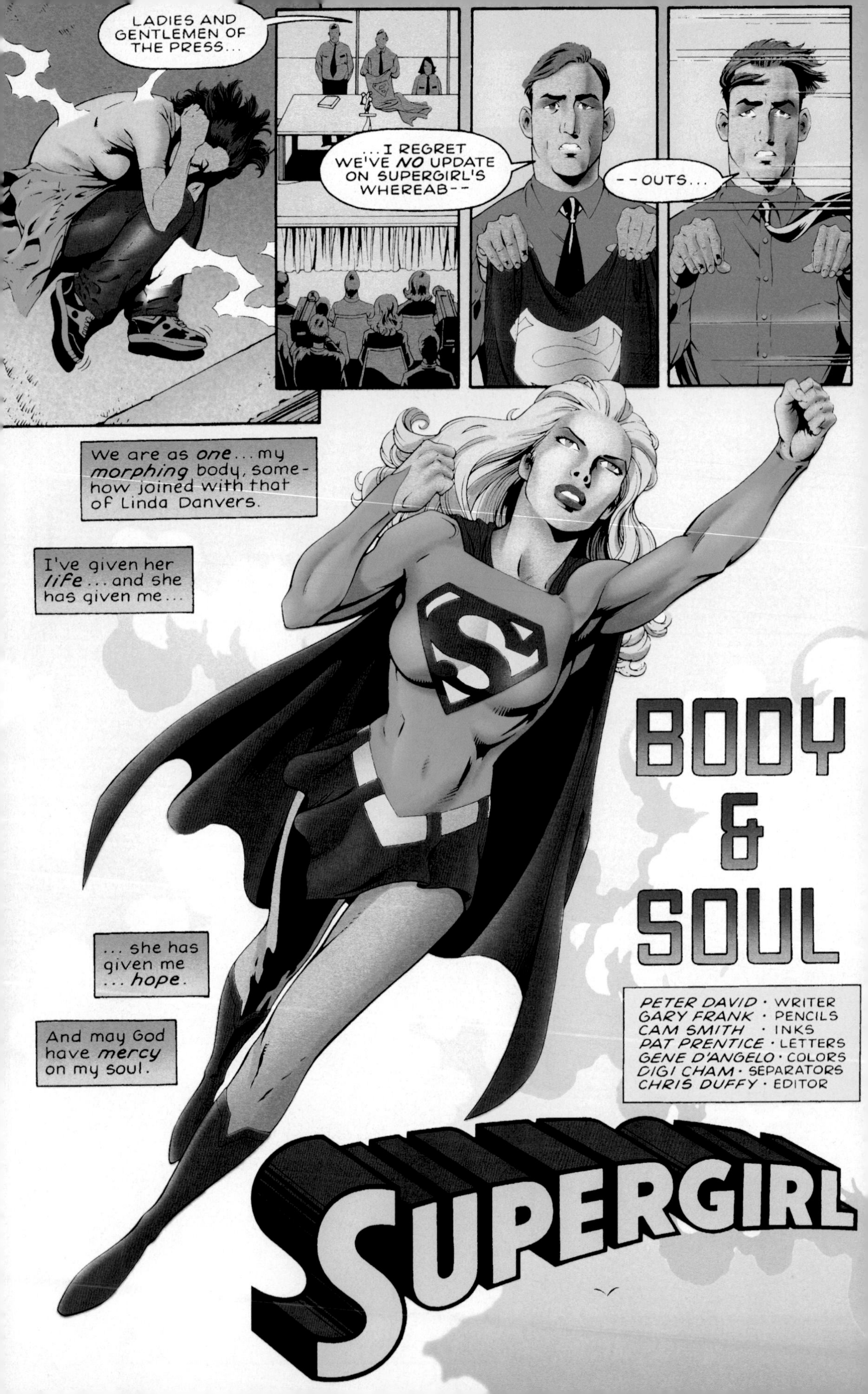
LADIES AND GENTLEMEN OF THE PRESS...
...I REGRET WE'VE NO UPDATE ON SUPERGIRL'S WHEREAB--
--OUTS...
We are as one... my morphing body, somehow joined with that of Linda Danvers.
I've given her life... and she has given me...
...she has given me ...hope.
And may God have mercy on my soul.
BODY & SOUL
PETER DAVID · WRITER
GARY FRANK · PENCILS
CAM SMITH · INKS
PAT PRENTICE · LETTERS
GENE D'ANGELO · COLORS
DIGI CHAM · SEPARATORS
CHRIS DUFFY · EDITOR
SUPERGIRL

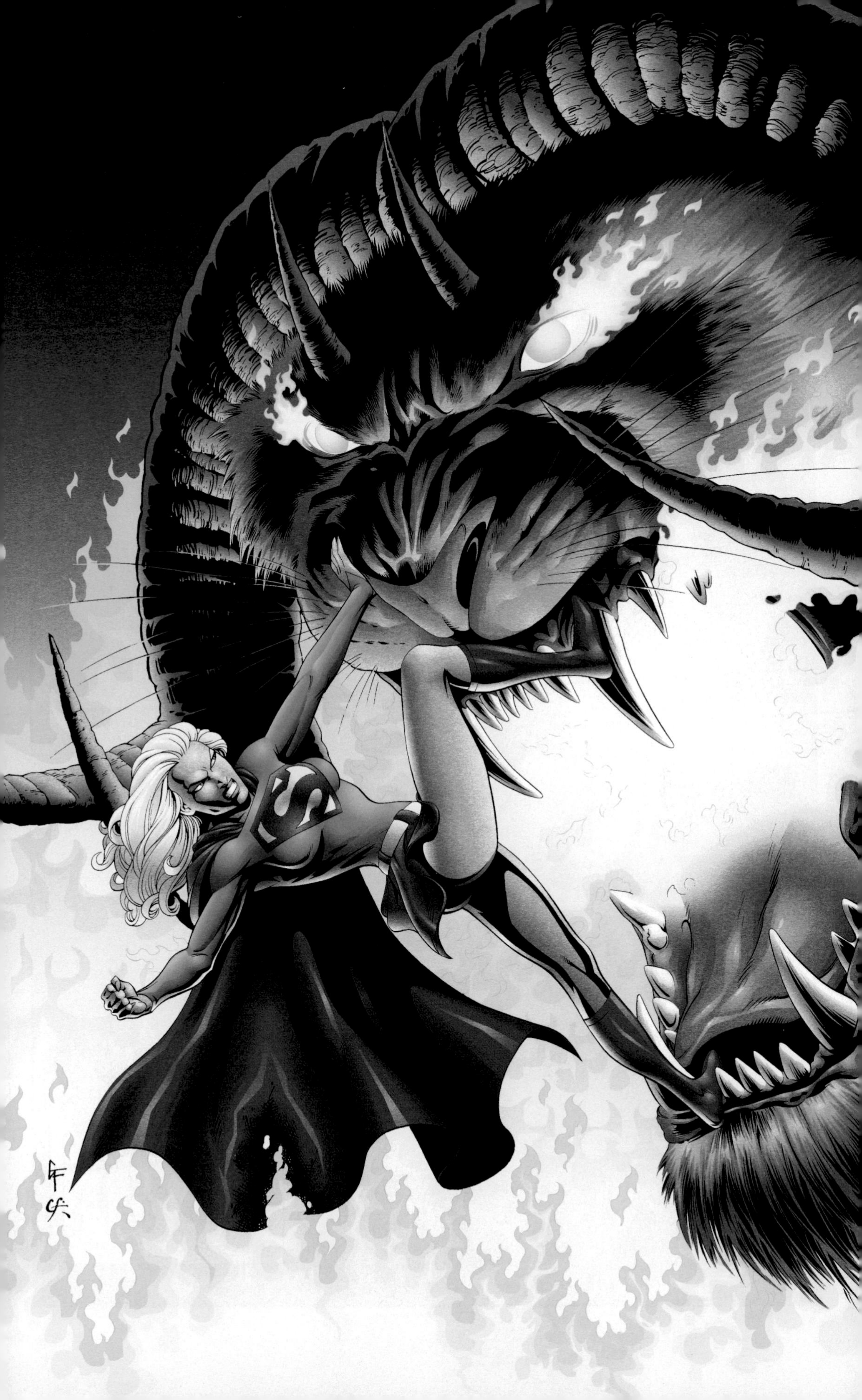

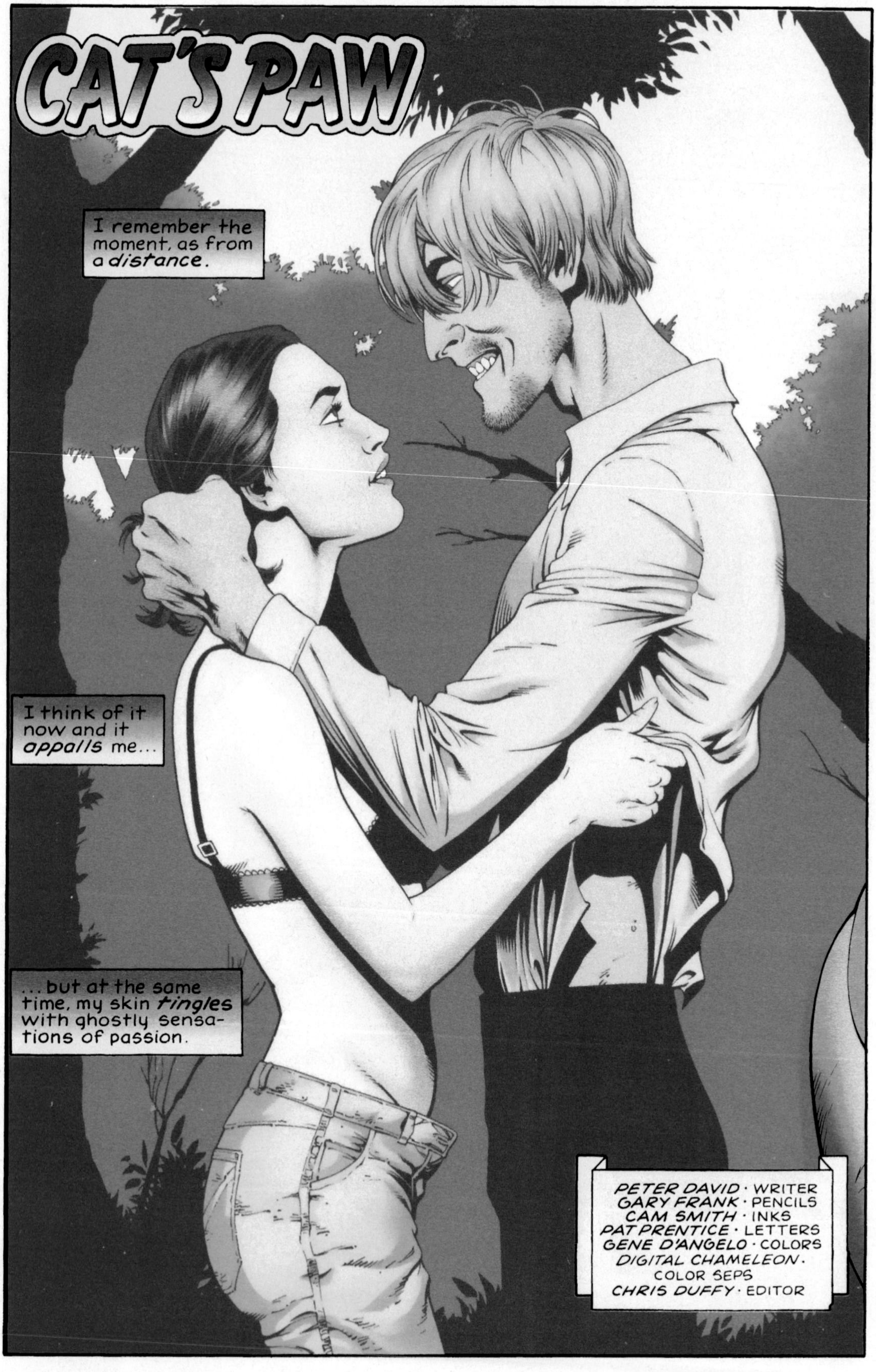
CAT'S PAW
I remember the moment, as from a distance.
I think of it now and it appalls me...
...but at the same time, my skin tingles with ghostly sensations of passion.
PETER DAVID · WRITER
GARY FRANK · PENCILS
CAM SMITH · INKS
PAT PRENTICE · LETTERS
GENE D'ANGELO · COLORS
DIGITAL CHAMELEON · COLOR SEPS
CHRIS DUFFY · EDITOR

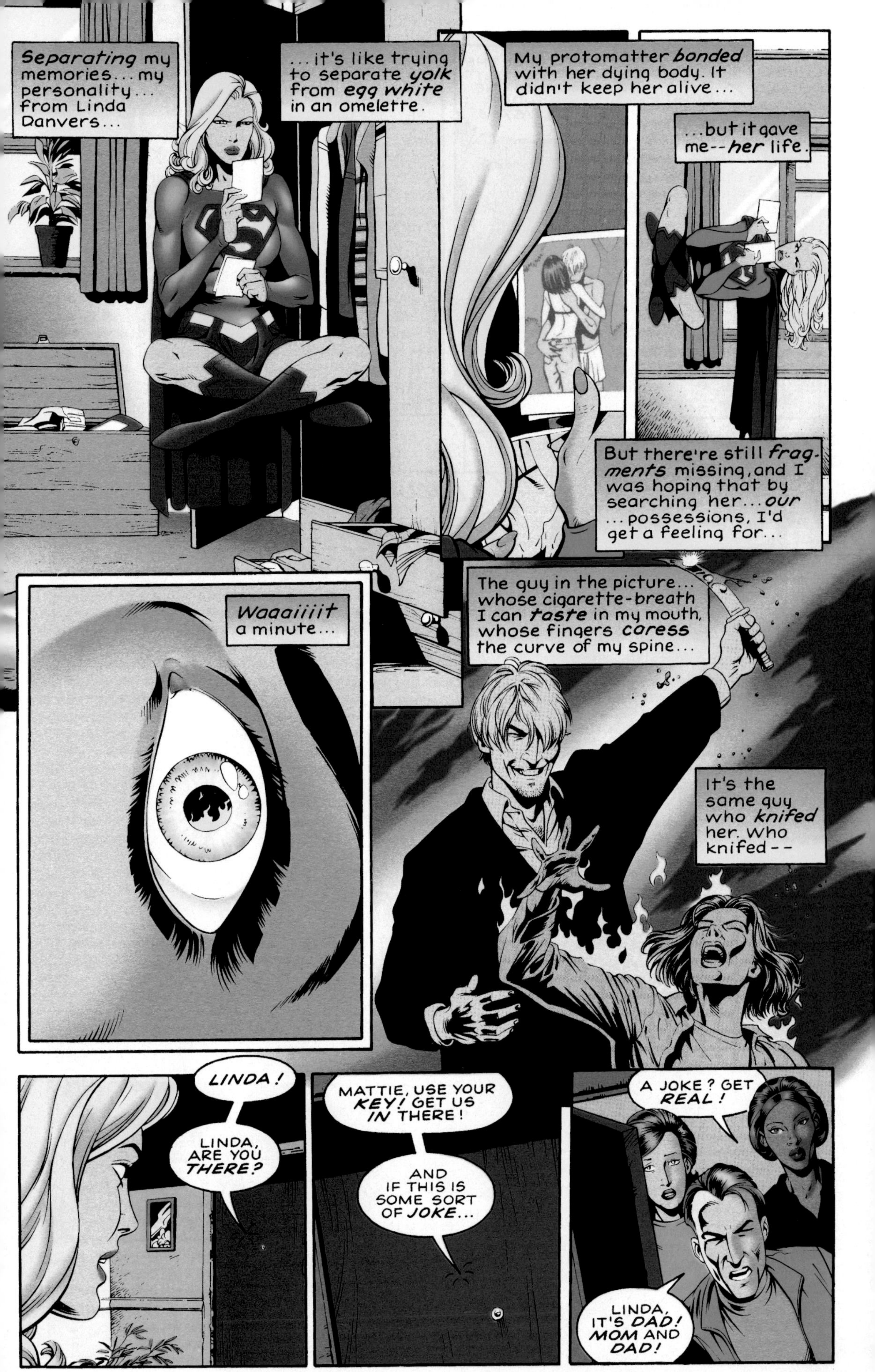
Separating my memories... my personality... from Linda Danvers...
...it's like trying to separate yolk from egg white in an omelette.
My protomatter bonded with her dying body. It didn't keep her alive...
...but it gave me--her life.
But there're still fragments missing, and I was hoping that by searching her...our...possessions, I'd get a feeling for...
Waaaiiiit a minute...
The guy in the picture... whose cigarette-breath I can taste in my mouth, whose fingers caress the curve of my spine...
It's the same guy who knifed her. Who knifed--
LINDA!
LINDA, ARE YOU THERE?
MATTIE, USE YOUR KEY! GET US IN THERE!
AND IF THIS IS SOME SORT OF JOKE...
A JOKE? GET REAL!
LINDA, IT'S DAD! MOM AND DAD!

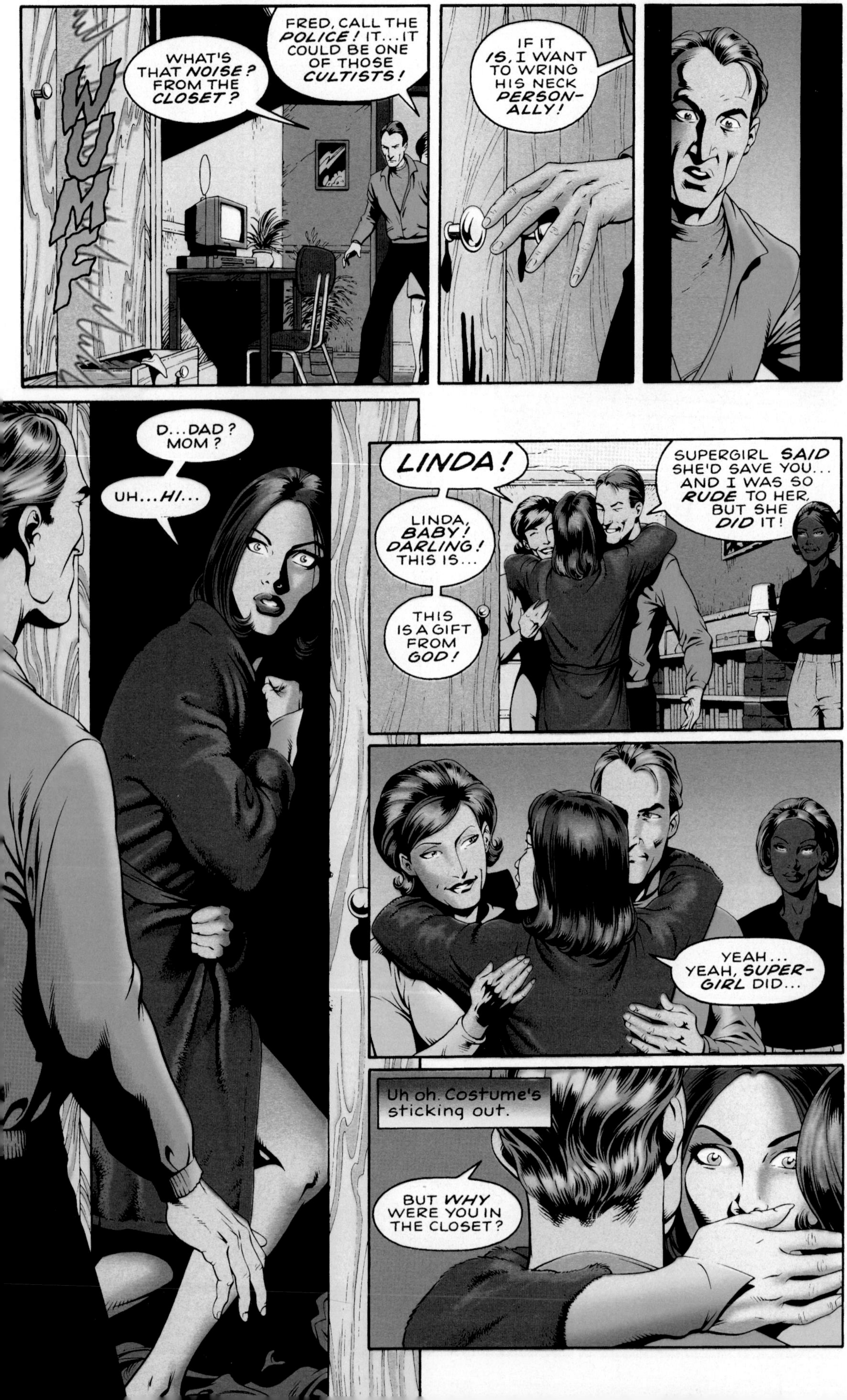
WUMF
WHAT'S THAT NOISE? FROM THE CLOSET?
FRED, CALL THE POLICE! IT...IT COULD BE ONE OF THOSE CULTISTS!
IF IT IS, I WANT TO WRING HIS NECK PERSON-ALLY!
D...DAD? MOM?
UH...HI...
LINDA!
LINDA, BABY! DARLING! THIS IS...
THIS IS A GIFT FROM GOD!
SUPERGIRL SAID SHE'D SAVE YOU... AND I WAS SO RUDE TO HER, BUT SHE DID IT!
YEAH... YEAH, SUPER-GIRL DID...
Uh oh. Costume's sticking out.
BUT WHY WERE YOU IN THE CLOSET?

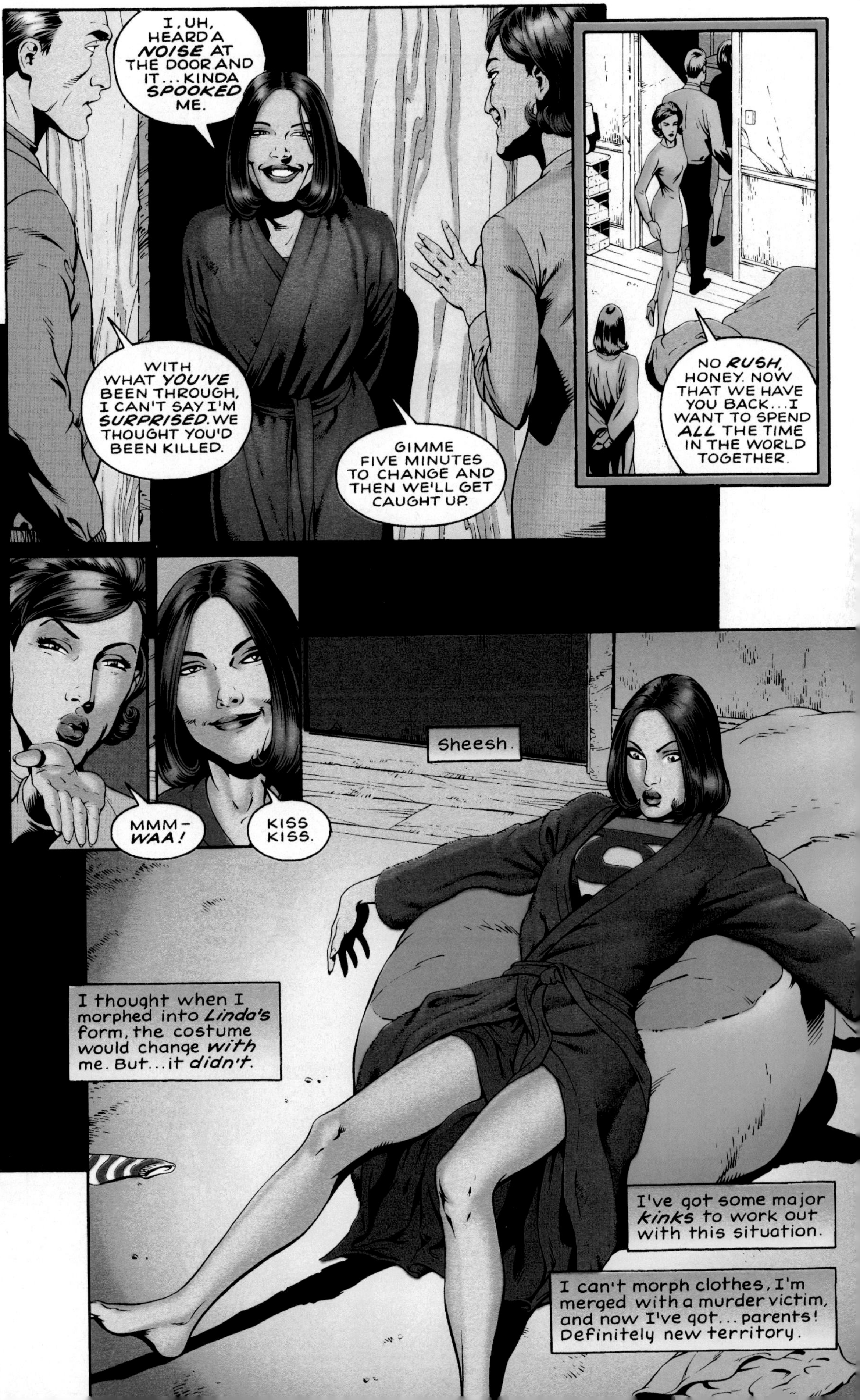
I, UH, HEARD A NOISE AT THE DOOR AND IT... KINDA SPOOKED ME.
WITH WHAT YOU'VE BEEN THROUGH, I CAN'T SAY I'M SURPRISED. WE THOUGHT YOU'D BEEN KILLED.
GIMME FIVE MINUTES TO CHANGE AND THEN WE'LL GET CAUGHT UP.
NO RUSH, HONEY. NOW THAT WE HAVE YOU BACK... I WANT TO SPEND ALL THE TIME IN THE WORLD TOGETHER.
MMM-WAA!
KISS KISS.
Sheesh.
I thought when I morphed into Linda's form, the costume would change with me. But...it didn't.
I've got some major kinks to work out with this situation.
I can't morph clothes, I'm merged with a murder victim, and now I've got... parents! Definitely new territory.

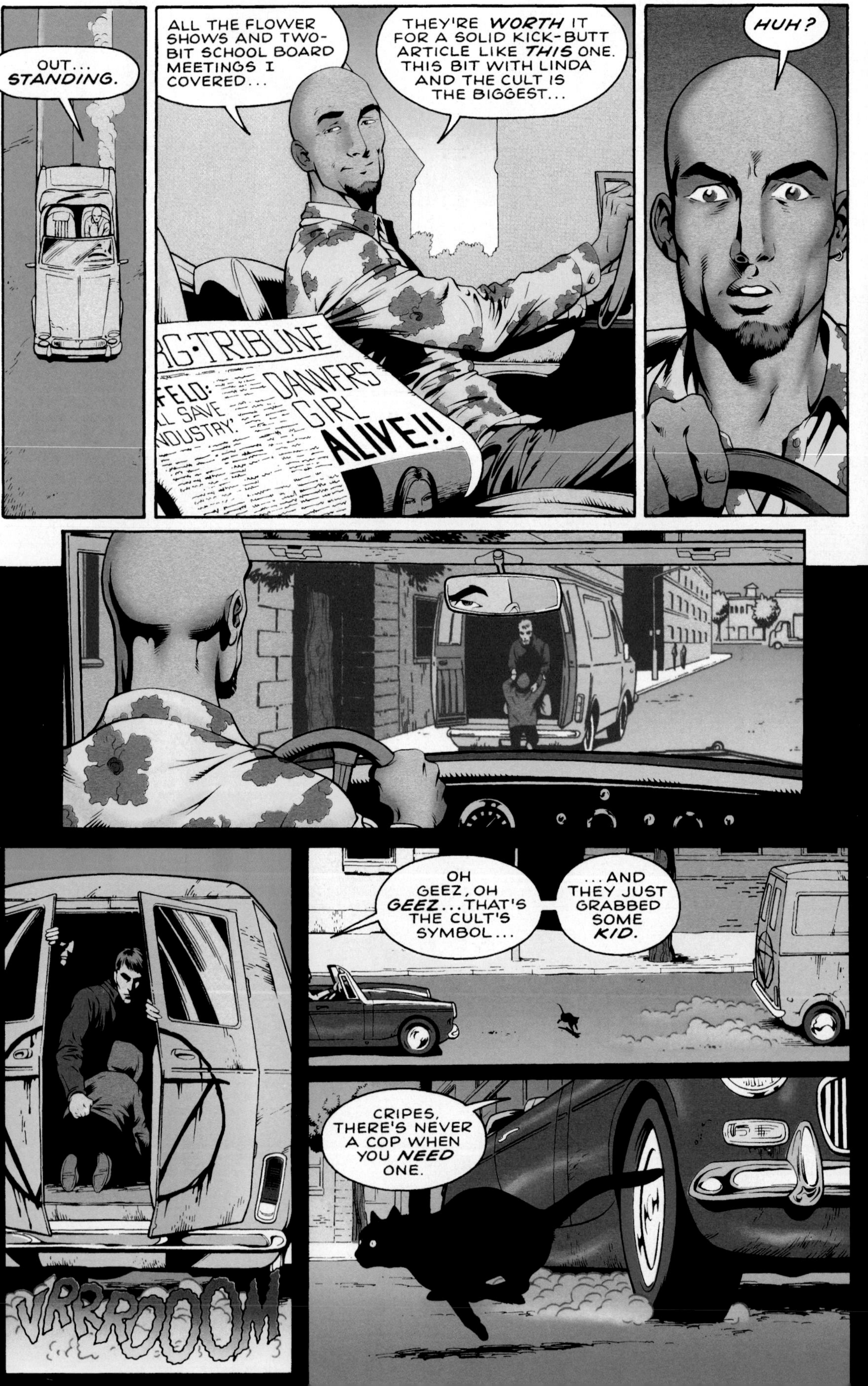
OUT... STANDING.
ALL THE FLOWER SHOWS AND TWO-BIT SCHOOL BOARD MEETINGS I COVERED...
THEY'RE WORTH IT FOR A SOLID KICK-BUTT ARTICLE LIKE THIS ONE. THIS BIT WITH LINDA AND THE CULT IS THE BIGGEST...
RG·TRIBUNE
FELD:
LL SAVE
NDUSTRY,'
DANVERS GIRL ALIVE!!
HUH?
VRRROOOM
OH GEEZ, OH GEEZ... THAT'S THE CULT'S SYMBOL...
...AND THEY JUST GRABBED SOME KID.
CRIPES, THERE'S NEVER A COP WHEN YOU NEED ONE.

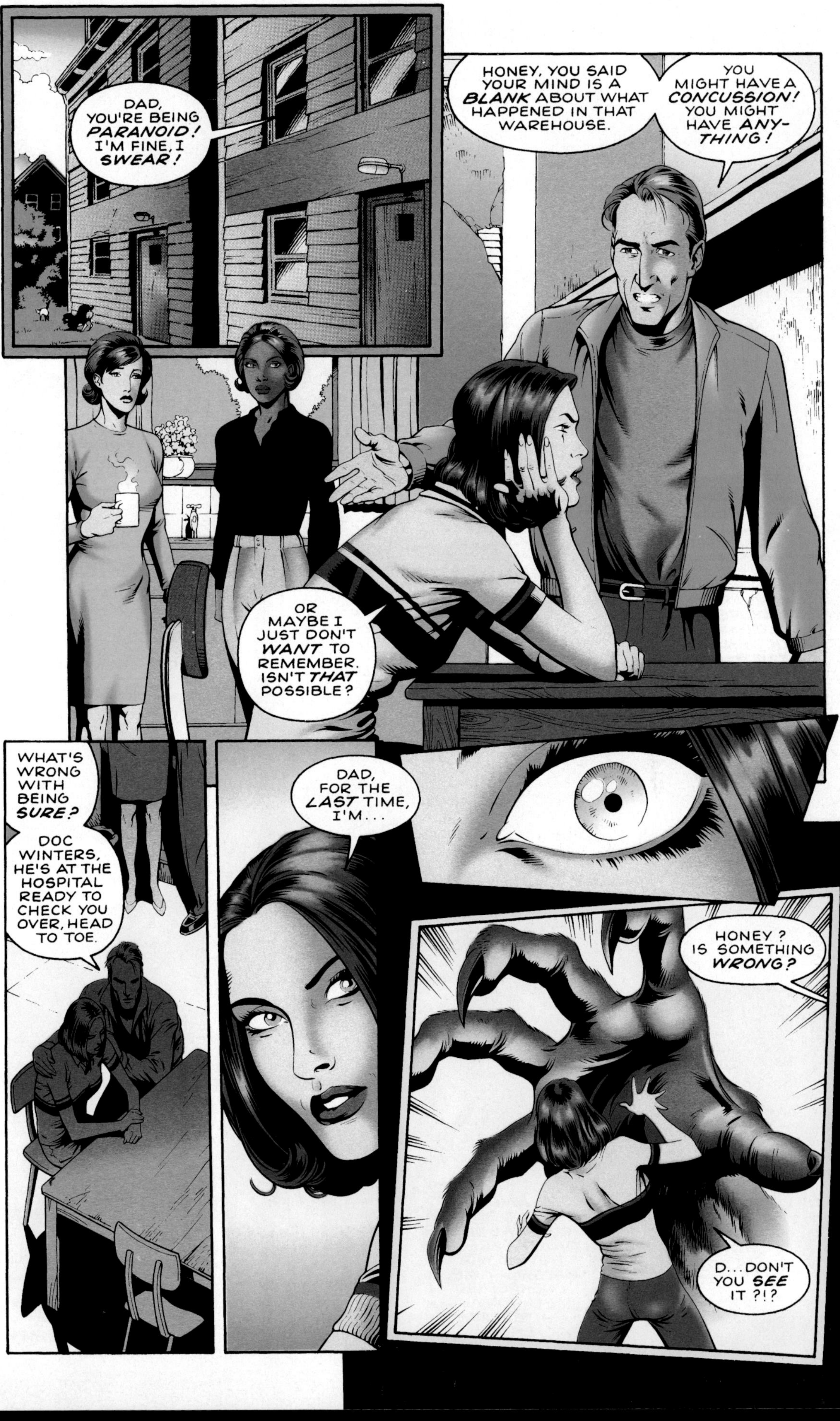
DAD, YOU'RE BEING PARANOID! I'M FINE, I SWEAR!
HONEY, YOU SAID YOUR MIND IS A BLANK ABOUT WHAT HAPPENED IN THAT WAREHOUSE.
YOU MIGHT HAVE A CONCUSSION! YOU MIGHT HAVE ANY-THING!
OR MAYBE I JUST DON'T WANT TO REMEMBER. ISN'T THAT POSSIBLE?
WHAT'S WRONG WITH BEING SURE?
DOC WINTERS, HE'S AT THE HOSPITAL READY TO CHECK YOU OVER, HEAD TO TOE.
DAD, FOR THE LAST TIME, I'M...
HONEY? IS SOMETHING WRONG?
D...DON'T YOU SEE IT?!?

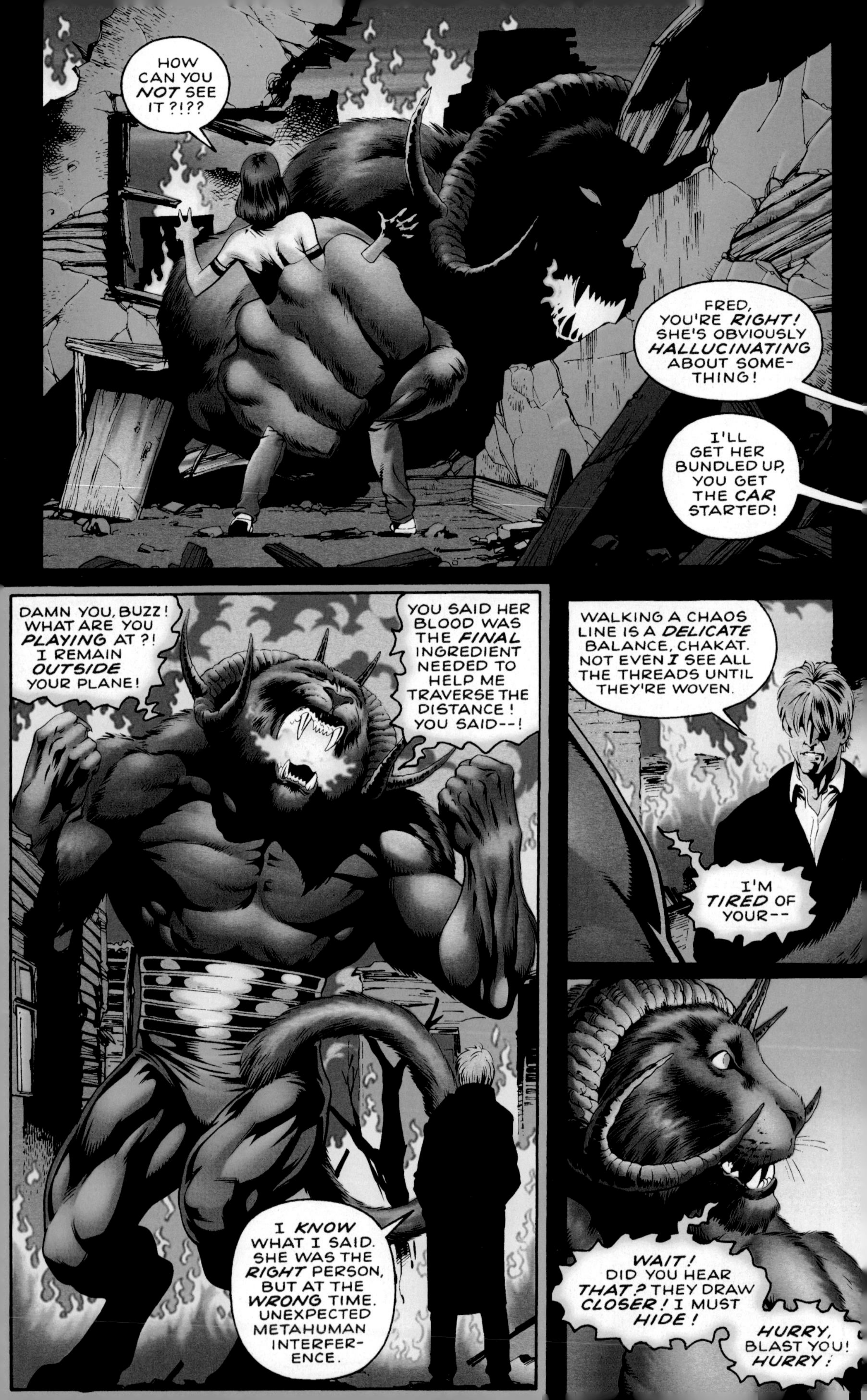
HOW CAN YOU NOT SEE IT ?!??
FRED, YOU'RE RIGHT! SHE'S OBVIOUSLY HALLUCINATING ABOUT SOME-THING!
I'LL GET HER BUNDLED UP, YOU GET THE CAR STARTED!
DAMN YOU, BUZZ! WHAT ARE YOU PLAYING AT ?! I REMAIN OUTSIDE YOUR PLANE!
YOU SAID HER BLOOD WAS THE FINAL INGREDIENT NEEDED TO HELP ME TRAVERSE THE DISTANCE ! YOU SAID--!
I KNOW WHAT I SAID. SHE WAS THE RIGHT PERSON, BUT AT THE WRONG TIME. UNEXPECTED METAHUMAN INTERFER-ENCE.
WALKING A CHAOS LINE IS A DELICATE BALANCE, CHAKAT. NOT EVEN I SEE ALL THE THREADS UNTIL THEY'RE WOVEN.
I'M TIRED OF YOUR--
WAIT! DID YOU HEAR THAT? THEY DRAW CLOSER! I MUST HIDE!
HURRY, BLAST YOU! HURRY!

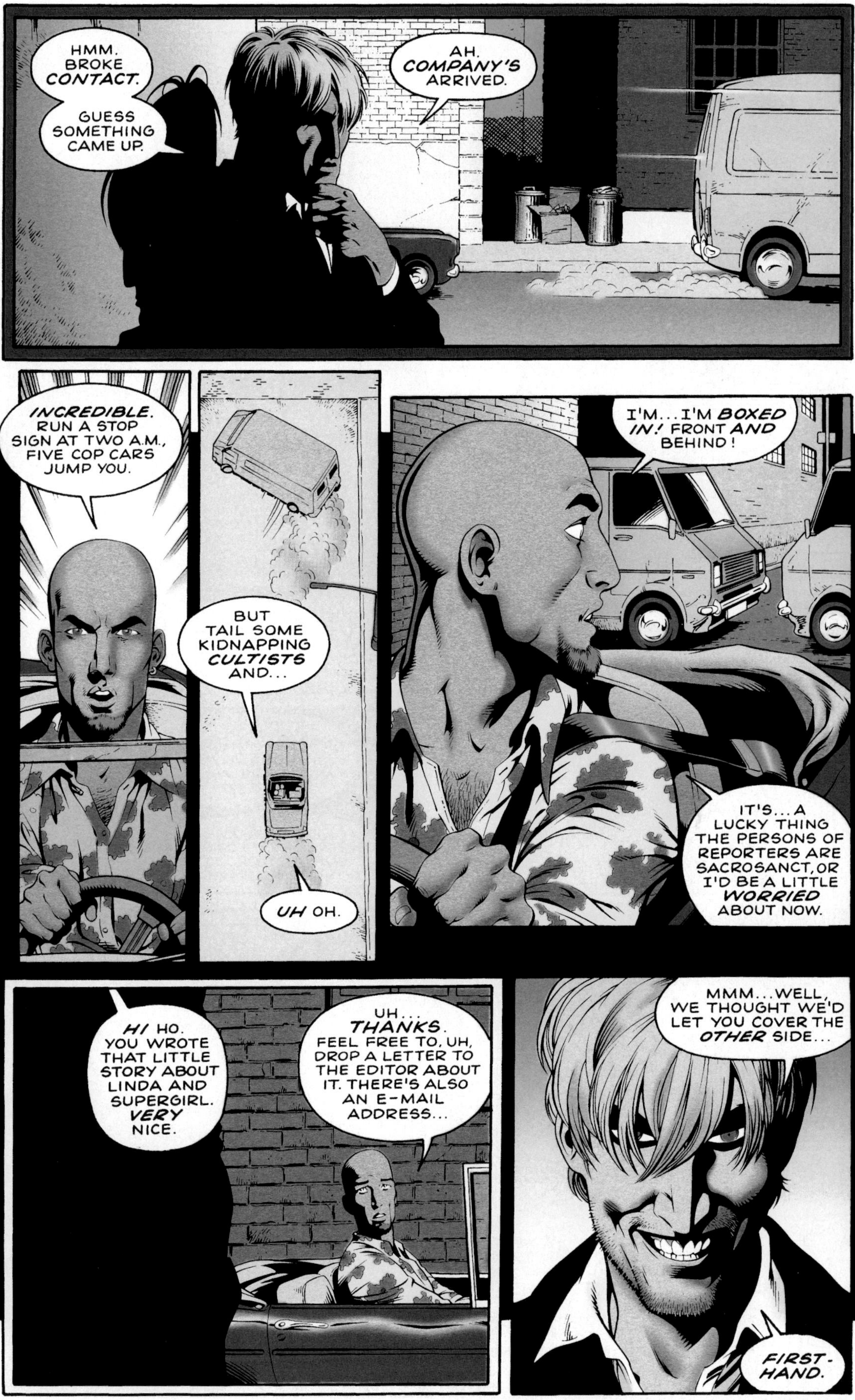
HMM. BROKE CONTACT.
GUESS SOMETHING CAME UP.
AH. COMPANY'S ARRIVED.
INCREDIBLE. RUN A STOP SIGN AT TWO A.M., FIVE COP CARS JUMP YOU.
BUT TAIL SOME KIDNAPPING CULTISTS AND...
UH OH.
I'M...I'M BOXED IN! FRONT AND BEHIND!
IT'S...A LUCKY THING THE PERSONS OF REPORTERS ARE SACROSANCT, OR I'D BE A LITTLE WORRIED ABOUT NOW.
HI HO. YOU WROTE THAT LITTLE STORY ABOUT LINDA AND SUPERGIRL. VERY NICE.
UH... THANKS. FEEL FREE TO, UH, DROP A LETTER TO THE EDITOR ABOUT IT. THERE'S ALSO AN E-MAIL ADDRESS...
MMM...WELL, WE THOUGHT WE'D LET YOU COVER THE OTHER SIDE...
FIRST-HAND.

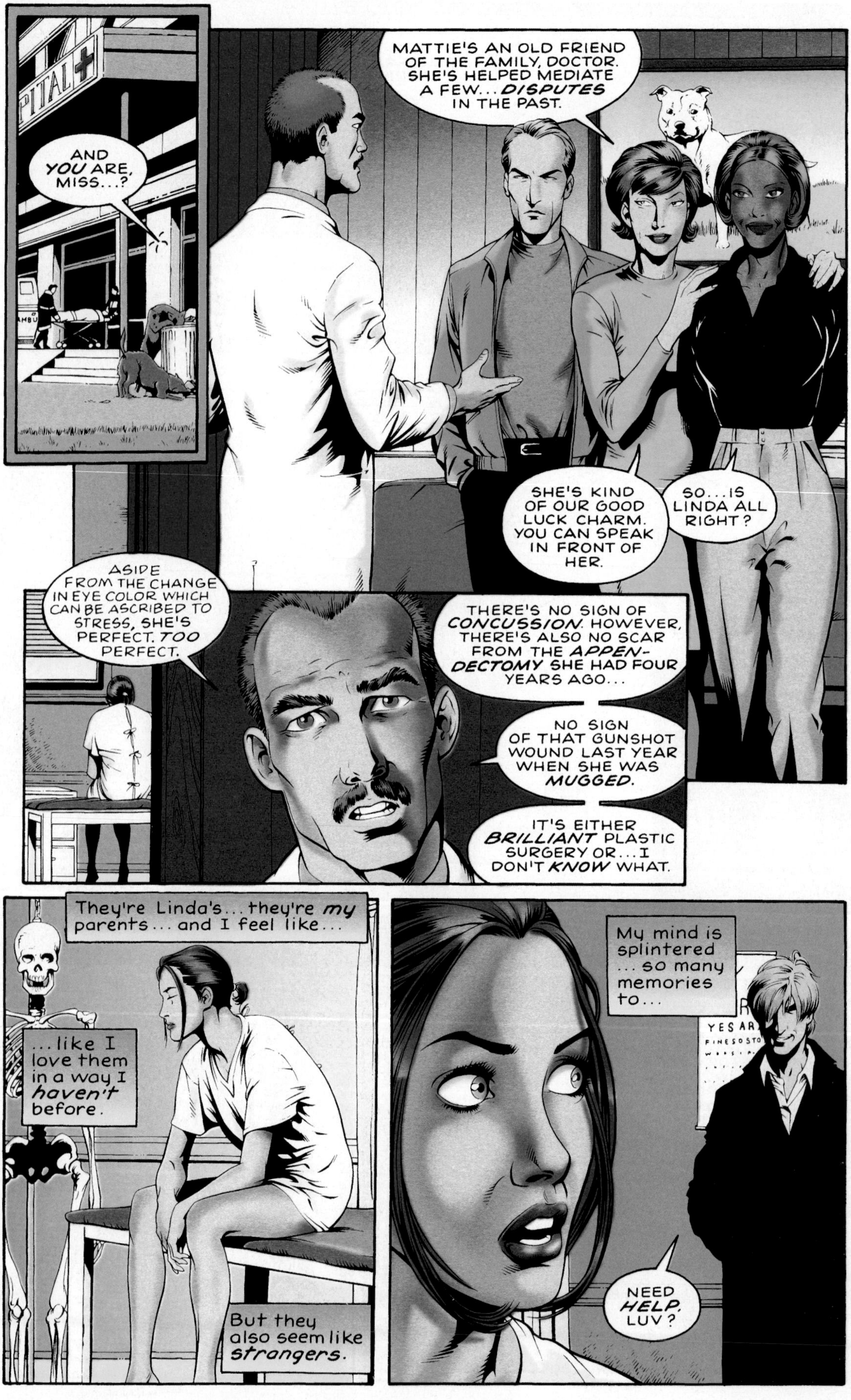
AND YOU ARE, MISS...?
MATTIE'S AN OLD FRIEND OF THE FAMILY, DOCTOR. SHE'S HELPED MEDIATE A FEW... DISPUTES IN THE PAST.
SHE'S KIND OF OUR GOOD LUCK CHARM. YOU CAN SPEAK IN FRONT OF HER.
SO... IS LINDA ALL RIGHT?
ASIDE FROM THE CHANGE IN EYE COLOR WHICH CAN BE ASCRIBED TO STRESS, SHE'S PERFECT. TOO PERFECT.
THERE'S NO SIGN OF CONCUSSION. HOWEVER, THERE'S ALSO NO SCAR FROM THE APPENDECTOMY SHE HAD FOUR YEARS AGO...
NO SIGN OF THAT GUNSHOT WOUND LAST YEAR WHEN SHE WAS MUGGED.
IT'S EITHER BRILLIANT PLASTIC SURGERY OR... I DON'T KNOW WHAT.
They're Linda's... they're my parents... and I feel like...
...like I love them in a way I haven't before.
But they also seem like strangers.
My mind is splintered ... so many memories to...
NEED HELP, LUV?

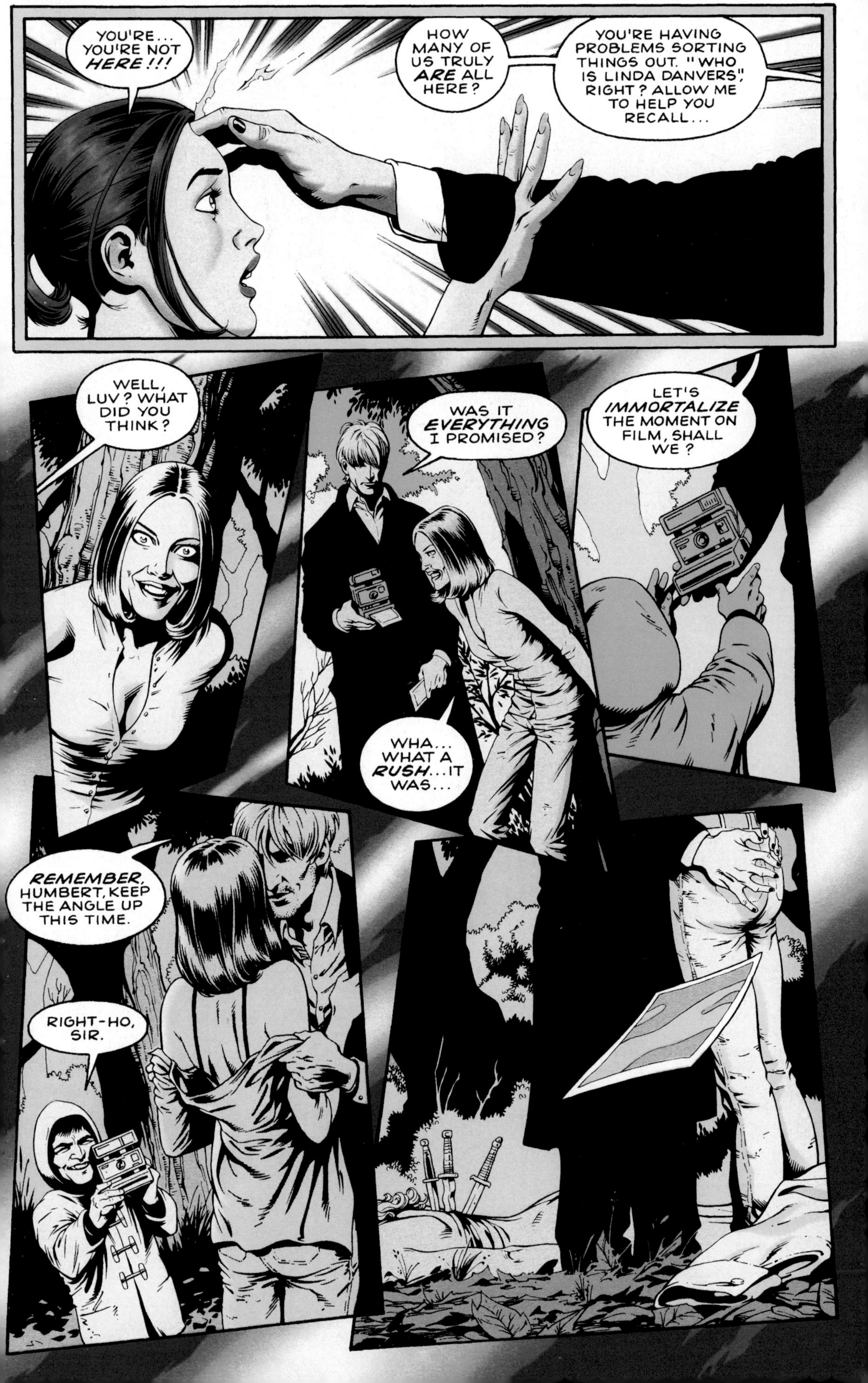
YOU'RE... YOU'RE NOT HERE!!!
HOW MANY OF US TRULY ARE ALL HERE?
YOU'RE HAVING PROBLEMS SORTING THINGS OUT. "WHO IS LINDA DANVERS", RIGHT? ALLOW ME TO HELP YOU RECALL...
WELL, LUV? WHAT DID YOU THINK?
WAS IT EVERYTHING I PROMISED?
WHA... WHAT A RUSH...IT WAS...
LET'S IMMORTALIZE THE MOMENT ON FILM, SHALL WE?
REMEMBER, HUMBERT, KEEP THE ANGLE UP THIS TIME.
RIGHT-HO, SIR.

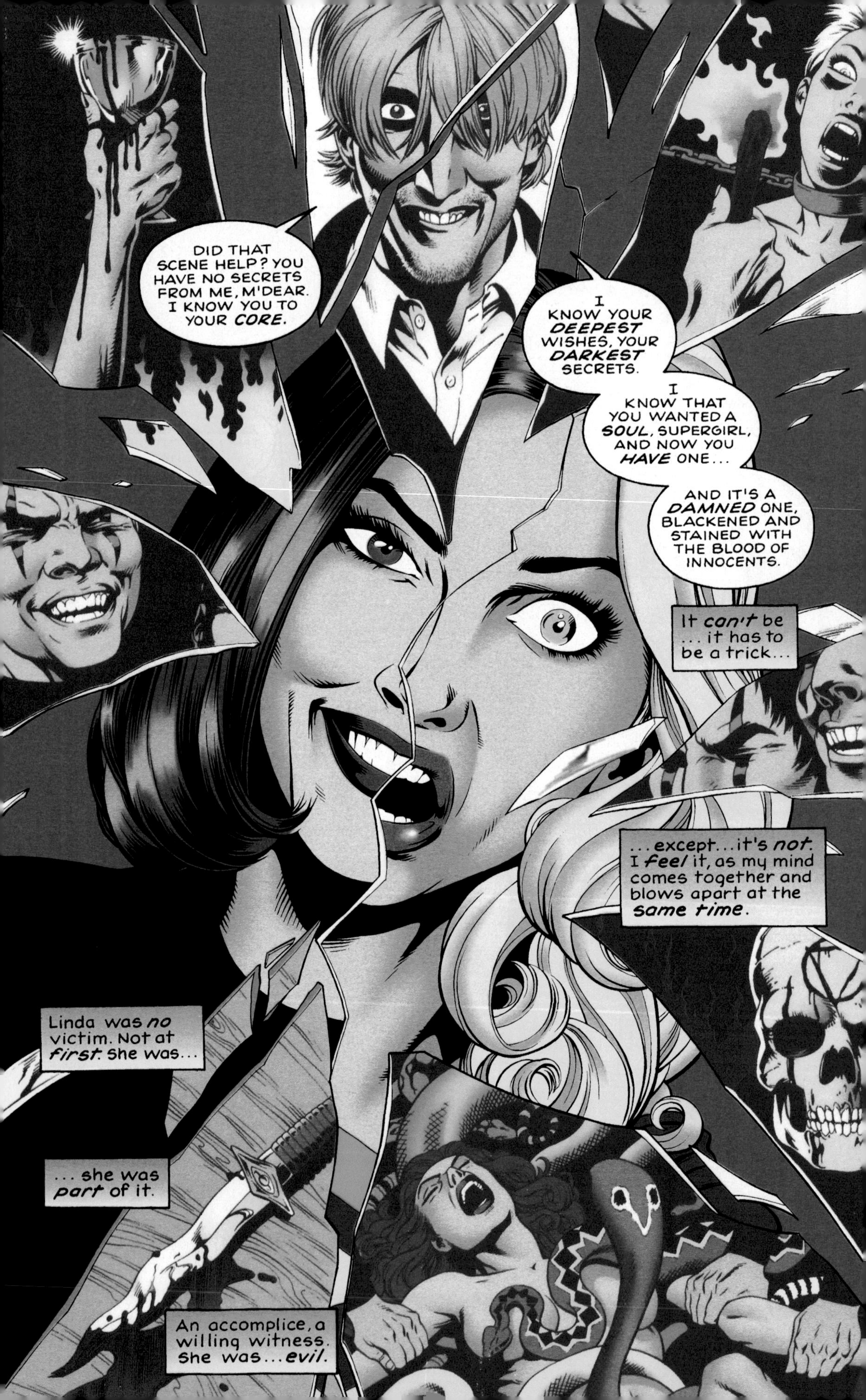
DID THAT SCENE HELP? YOU HAVE NO SECRETS FROM ME, M'DEAR. I KNOW YOU TO YOUR CORE.
I KNOW YOUR DEEPEST WISHES, YOUR DARKEST SECRETS.
I KNOW THAT YOU WANTED A SOUL, SUPERGIRL, AND NOW YOU HAVE ONE...
AND IT'S A DAMNED ONE, BLACKENED AND STAINED WITH THE BLOOD OF INNOCENTS.
It can't be ... it has to be a trick...
... except... it's not. I feel it, as my mind comes together and blows apart at the same time.
Linda was no victim. Not at first. She was...
... she was part of it.
An accomplice, a willing witness. She was... evil.

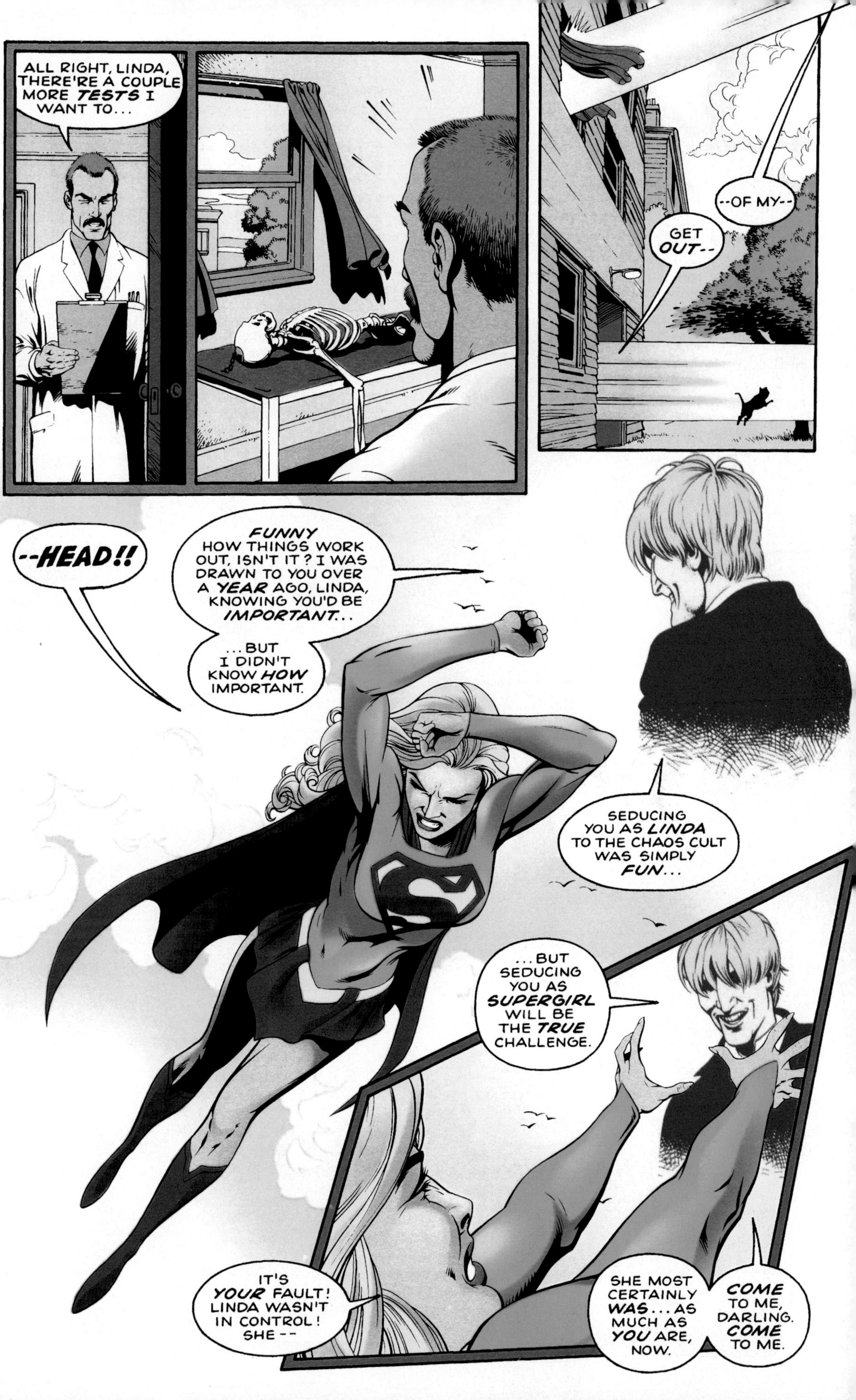

ALL RIGHT, LINDA, THERE'RE A COUPLE MORE TESTS I WANT TO...
GET OUT--
--OF MY--
--HEAD!!
FUNNY HOW THINGS WORK OUT, ISN'T IT? I WAS DRAWN TO YOU OVER A YEAR AGO, LINDA, KNOWING YOU'D BE IMPORTANT...
...BUT I DIDN'T KNOW HOW IMPORTANT.
SEDUCING YOU AS LINDA TO THE CHAOS CULT WAS SIMPLY FUN...
...BUT SEDUCING YOU AS SUPERGIRL WILL BE THE TRUE CHALLENGE.
IT'S YOUR FAULT! LINDA WASN'T IN CONTROL! SHE--
SHE MOST CERTAINLY WAS... AS MUCH AS YOU ARE, NOW.
COME TO ME, DARLING. COME TO ME.

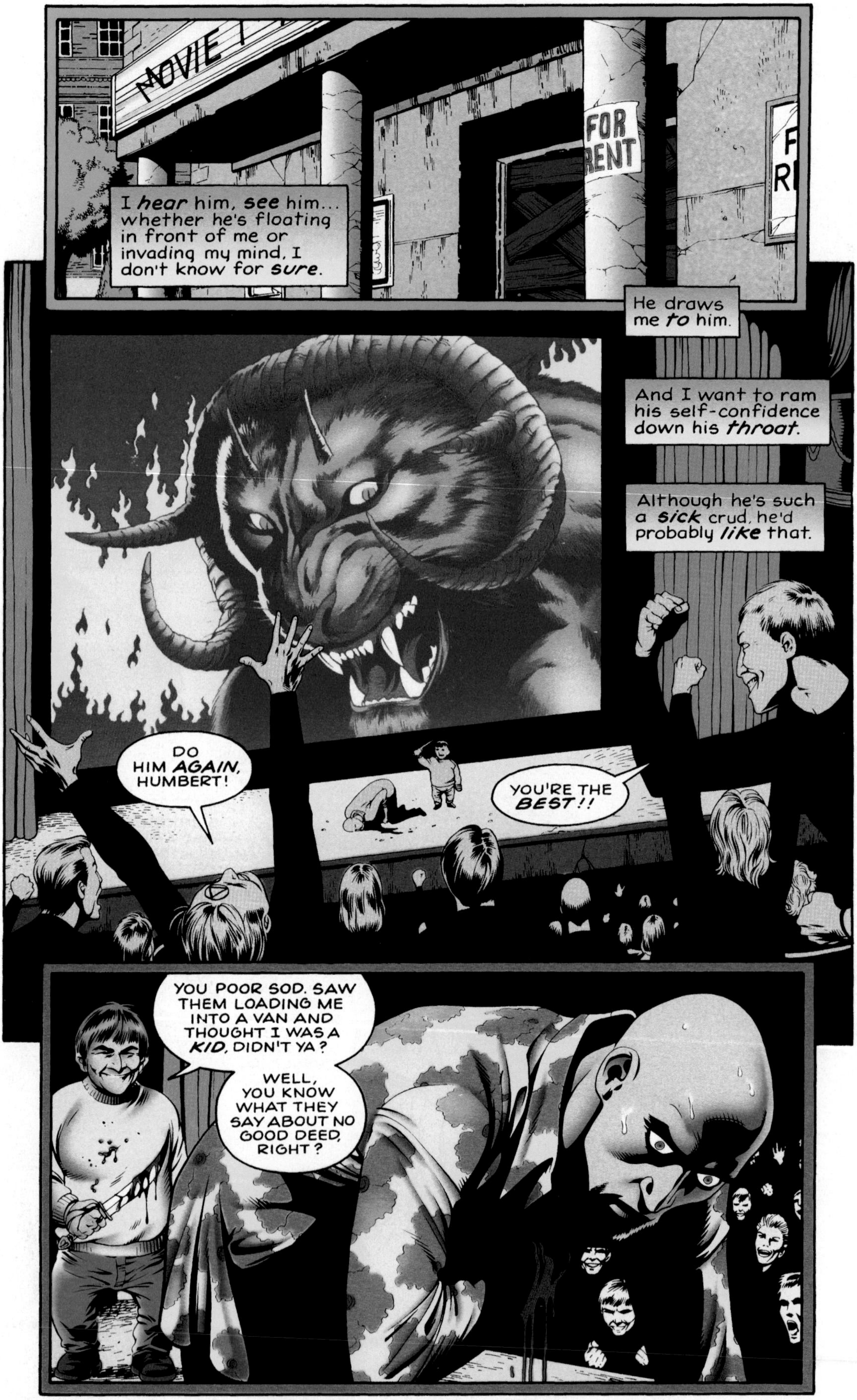
MOVIE
FOR RENT
I *hear* him, *see* him... whether he's floating in front of me or invading my mind, I don't know for *sure*.
He draws me *to* him.
And I want to ram his self-confidence down his *throat*.
Although he's such a *sick* crud, he'd probably *like* that.
DO HIM *AGAIN*, HUMBERT!
YOU'RE THE *BEST*!!
YOU POOR SOD. SAW THEM LOADING ME INTO A VAN AND THOUGHT I WAS A *KID*, DIDN'T YA?
WELL, YOU KNOW WHAT THEY SAY ABOUT NO GOOD DEED, RIGHT?

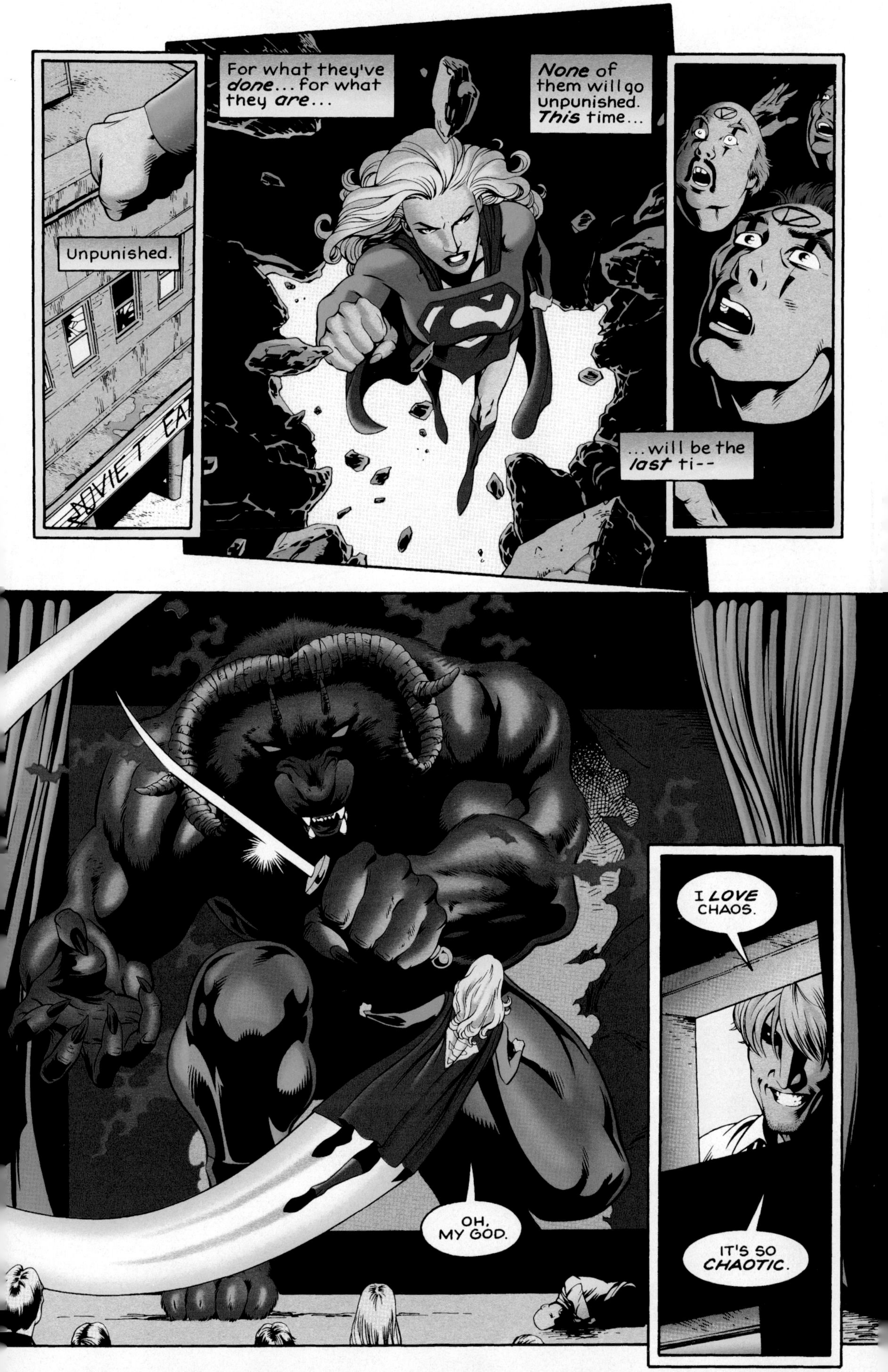
Unpunished.
For what they've done... for what they are...
None of them will go unpunished. This time...
...will be the last ti--
MOVIE T EA
I LOVE CHAOS.
OH, MY GOD.
IT'S SO CHAOTIC.

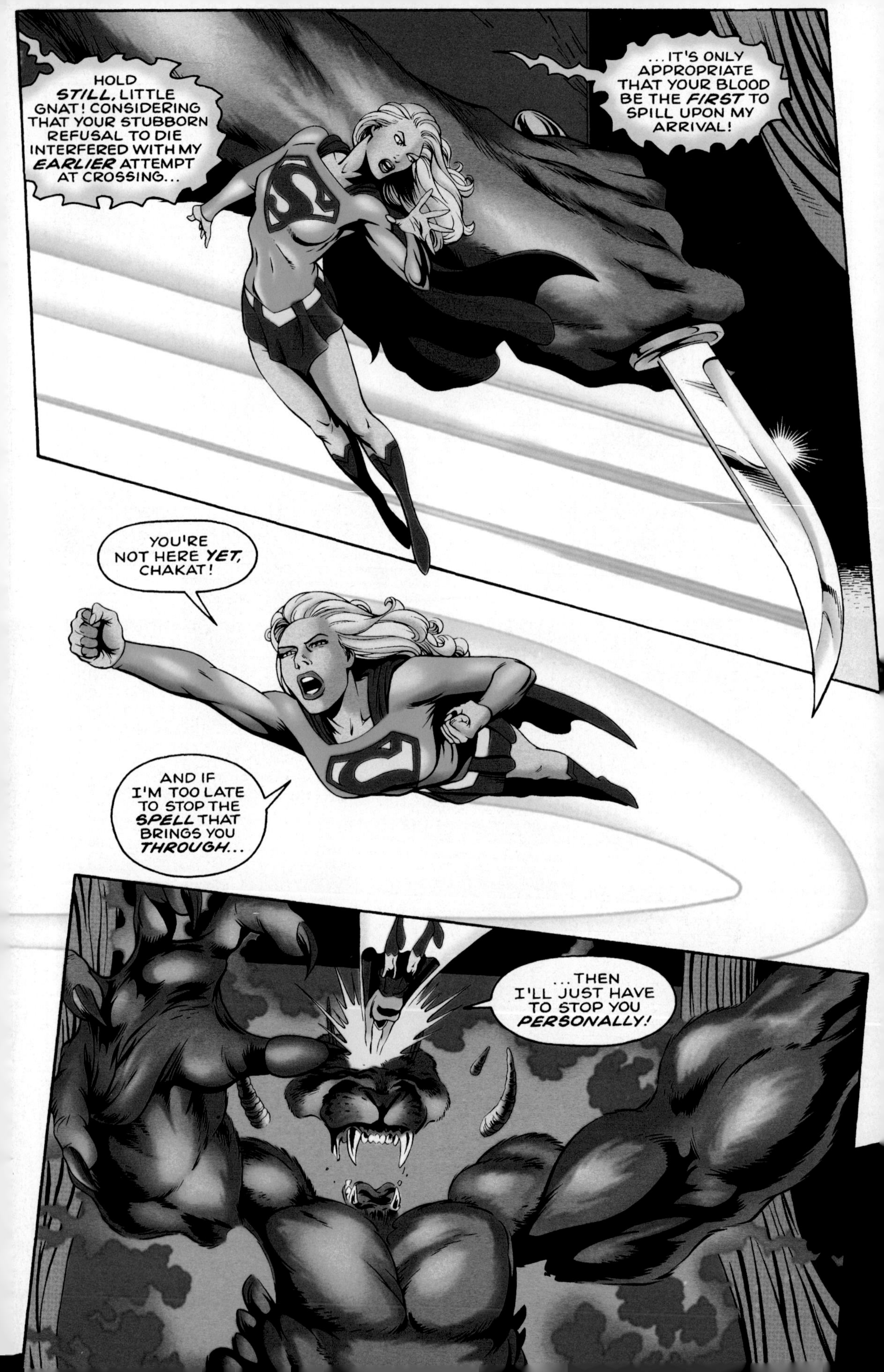
HOLD STILL, LITTLE GNAT! CONSIDERING THAT YOUR STUBBORN REFUSAL TO DIE INTERFERED WITH MY EARLIER ATTEMPT AT CROSSING...
...IT'S ONLY APPROPRIATE THAT YOUR BLOOD BE THE FIRST TO SPILL UPON MY ARRIVAL!
YOU'RE NOT HERE YET, CHAKAT!
AND IF I'M TOO LATE TO STOP THE SPELL THAT BRINGS YOU THROUGH...
...THEN I'LL JUST HAVE TO STOP YOU PERSONALLY!

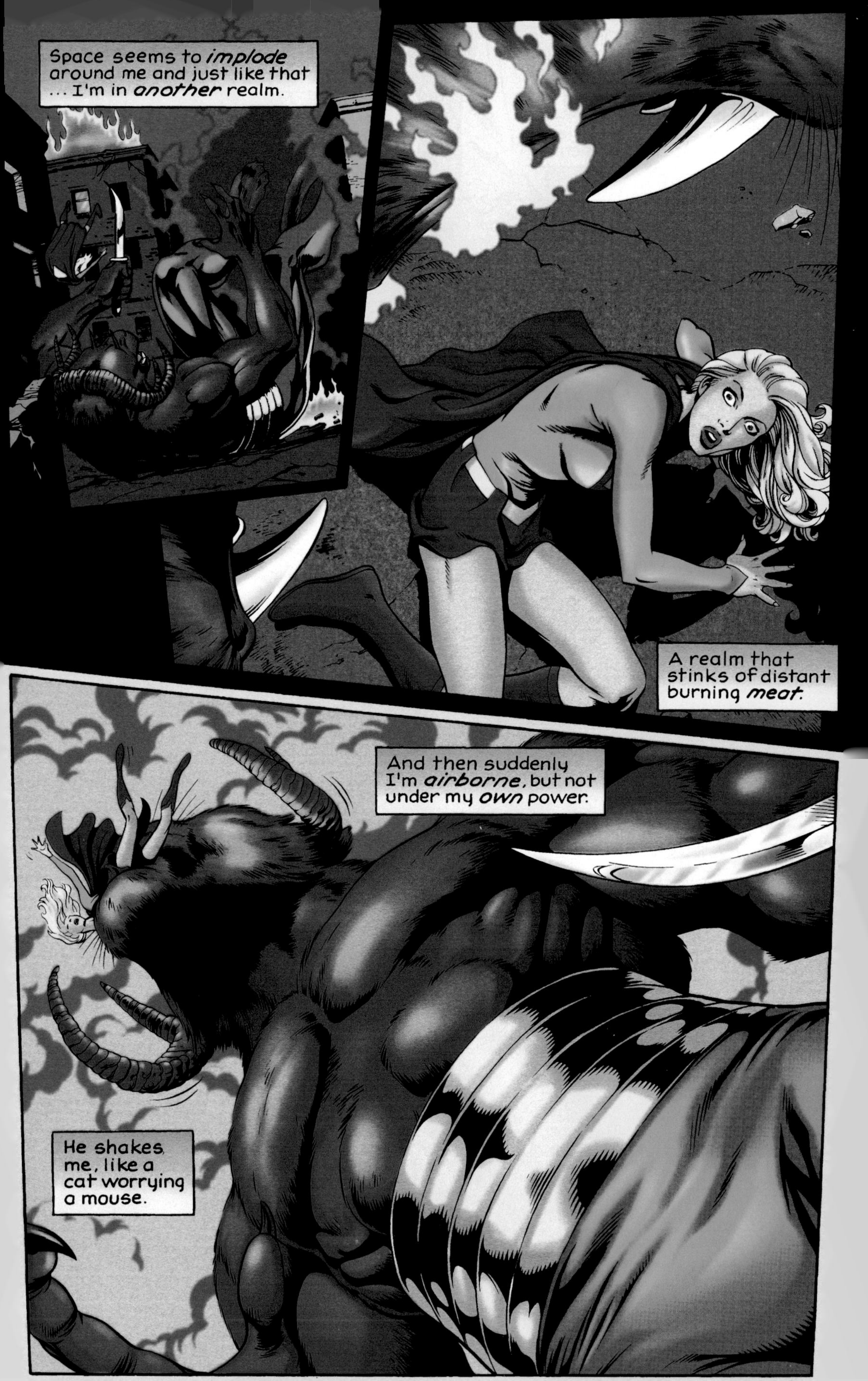
Space seems to implode around me and just like that ... I'm in another realm.
A realm that stinks of distant burning meat.
And then suddenly I'm airborne, but not under my own power.
He shakes me, like a cat worrying a mouse.

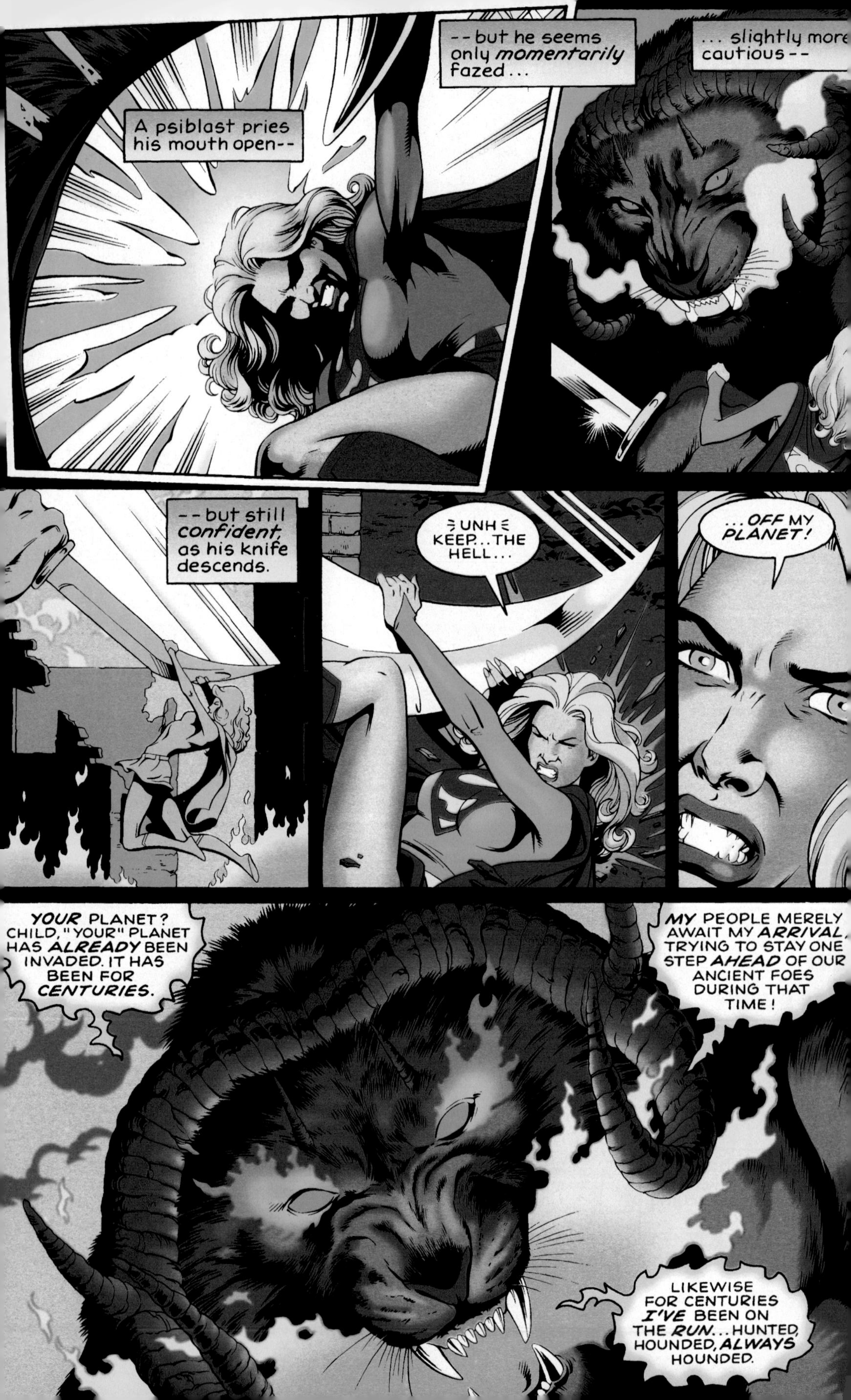
A psiblast pries his mouth open--
--but he seems only momentarily fazed...
...slightly more cautious--
--but still confident, as his knife descends.
UNH KEEP...THE HELL...
...OFF MY PLANET!
YOUR PLANET? CHILD, "YOUR" PLANET HAS ALREADY BEEN INVADED. IT HAS BEEN FOR CENTURIES.
MY PEOPLE MERELY AWAIT MY ARRIVAL, TRYING TO STAY ONE STEP AHEAD OF OUR ANCIENT FOES DURING THAT TIME!
LIKEWISE FOR CENTURIES I'VE BEEN ON THE RUN...HUNTED, HOUNDED, ALWAYS HOUNDED.

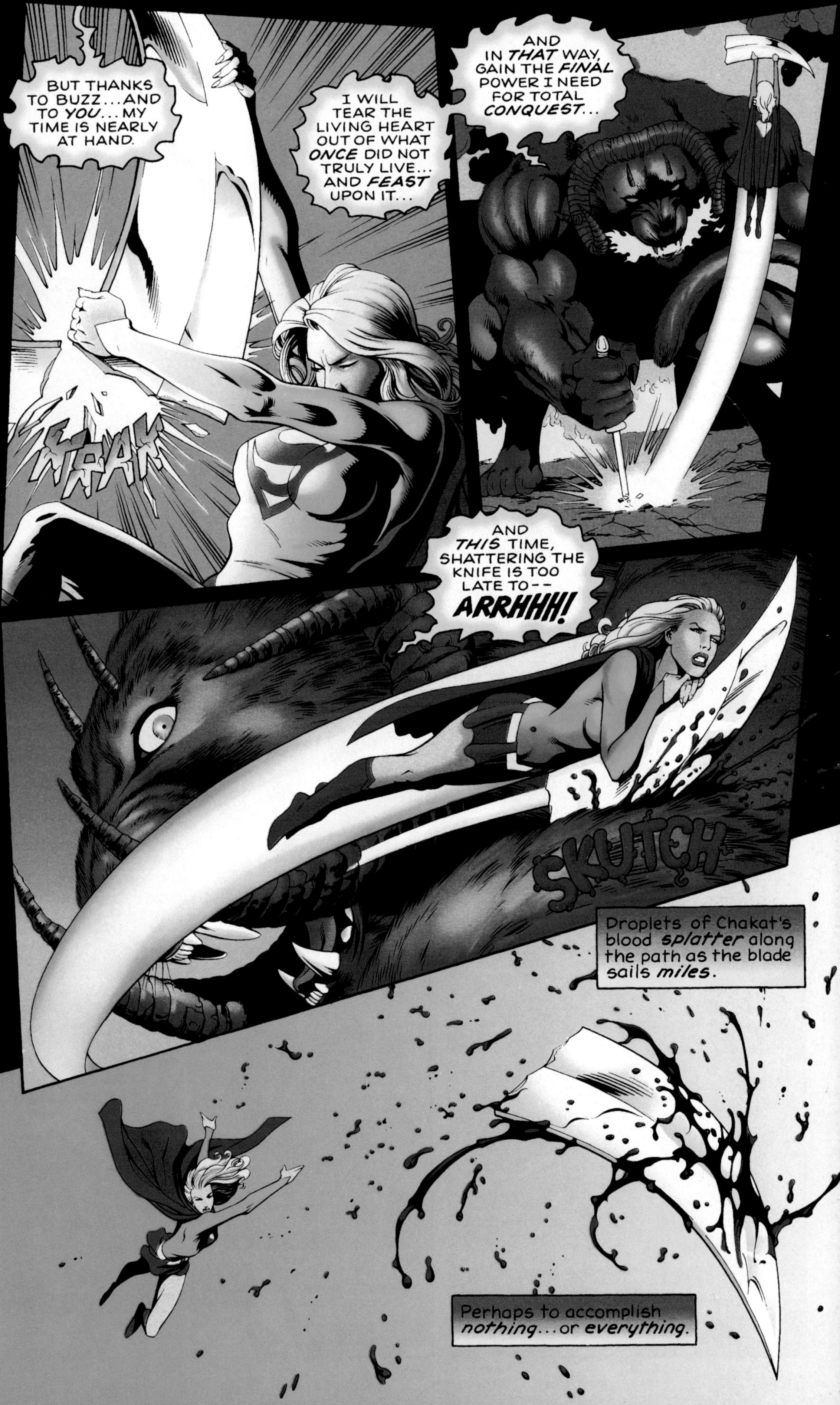
BUT THANKS TO BUZZ...AND TO YOU... MY TIME IS NEARLY AT HAND.
I WILL TEAR THE LIVING HEART OUT OF WHAT ONCE DID NOT TRULY LIVE... AND FEAST UPON IT...
WRAK
AND IN THAT WAY, GAIN THE FINAL POWER I NEED FOR TOTAL CONQUEST...
AND THIS TIME, SHATTERING THE KNIFE IS TOO LATE TO-- ARRHHH!
SKUTCH
Droplets of Chakat's blood splatter along the path as the blade sails miles.
Perhaps to accomplish nothing...or everything.

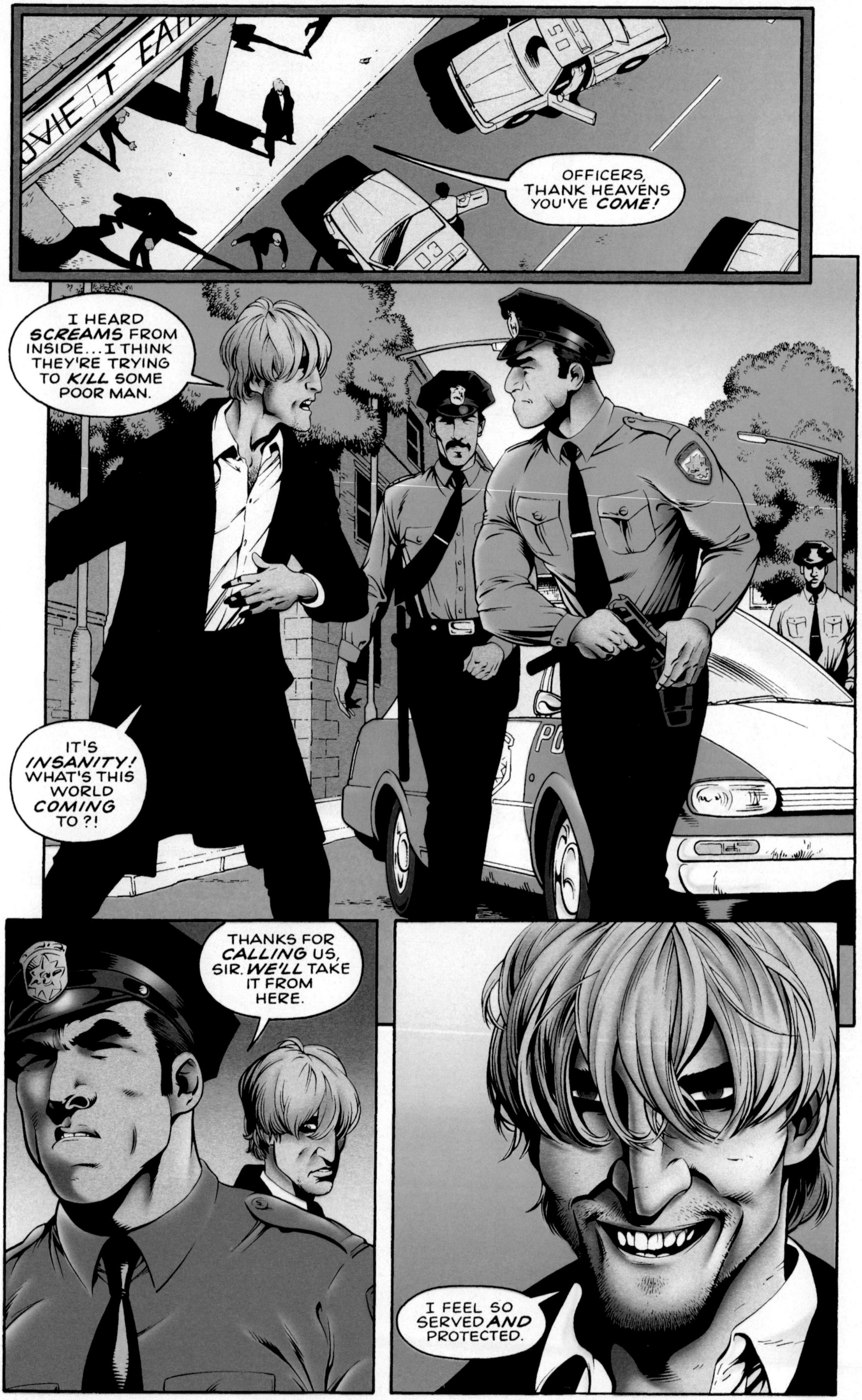
OFFICERS, THANK HEAVENS YOU'VE COME!
I HEARD SCREAMS FROM INSIDE... I THINK THEY'RE TRYING TO KILL SOME POOR MAN.
IT'S INSANITY! WHAT'S THIS WORLD COMING TO?!
THANKS FOR CALLING US, SIR. WE'LL TAKE IT FROM HERE.
I FEEL SO SERVED AND PROTECTED.

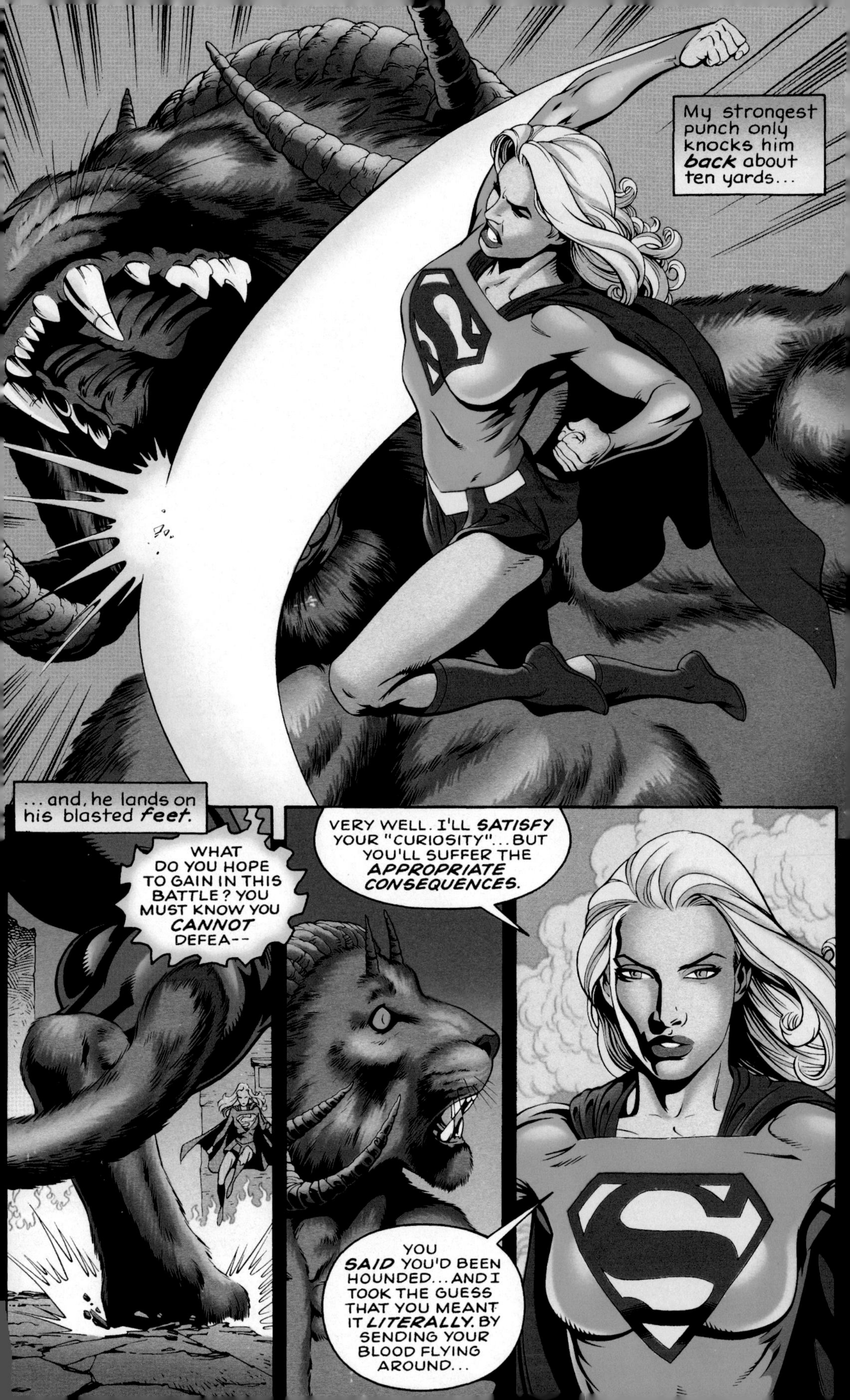
My strongest punch only knocks him *back* about ten yards...
...and, he lands on his blasted *feet*.
WHAT DO YOU HOPE TO GAIN IN THIS BATTLE? YOU MUST KNOW YOU *CANNOT* DEFEA--
VERY WELL. I'LL *SATISFY* YOUR "CURIOSITY"... BUT YOU'LL SUFFER THE *APPROPRIATE CONSEQUENCES*.
YOU *SAID* YOU'D BEEN HOUNDED... AND I TOOK THE GUESS THAT YOU MEANT IT *LITERALLY*. BY SENDING YOUR BLOOD FLYING AROUND...

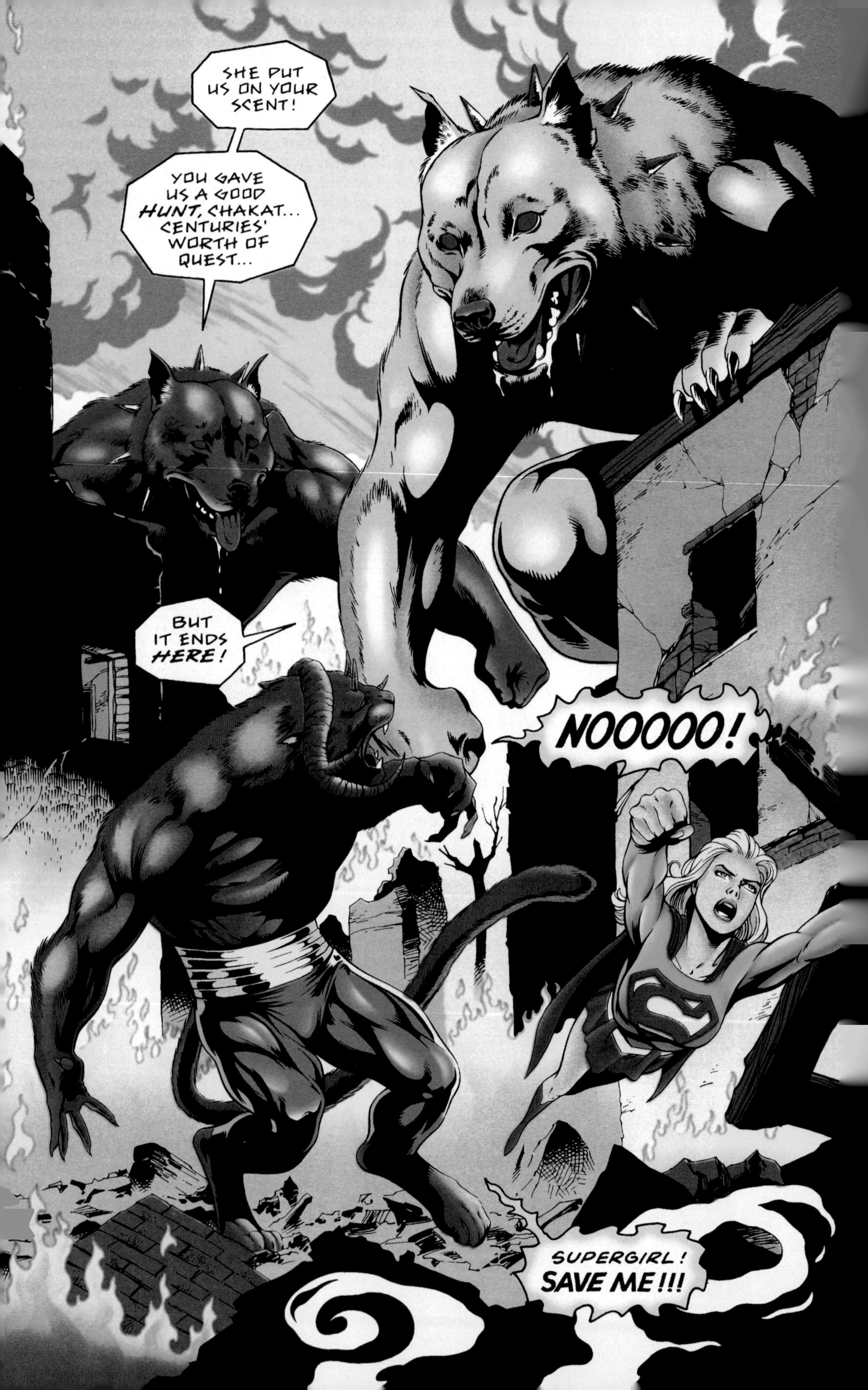
SHE PUT US ON YOUR SCENT!
YOU GAVE US A GOOD *HUNT*, CHAKAT... CENTURIES' WORTH OF QUEST...
BUT IT ENDS *HERE*!
NOOOOO!
SUPERGIRL! SAVE ME!!!

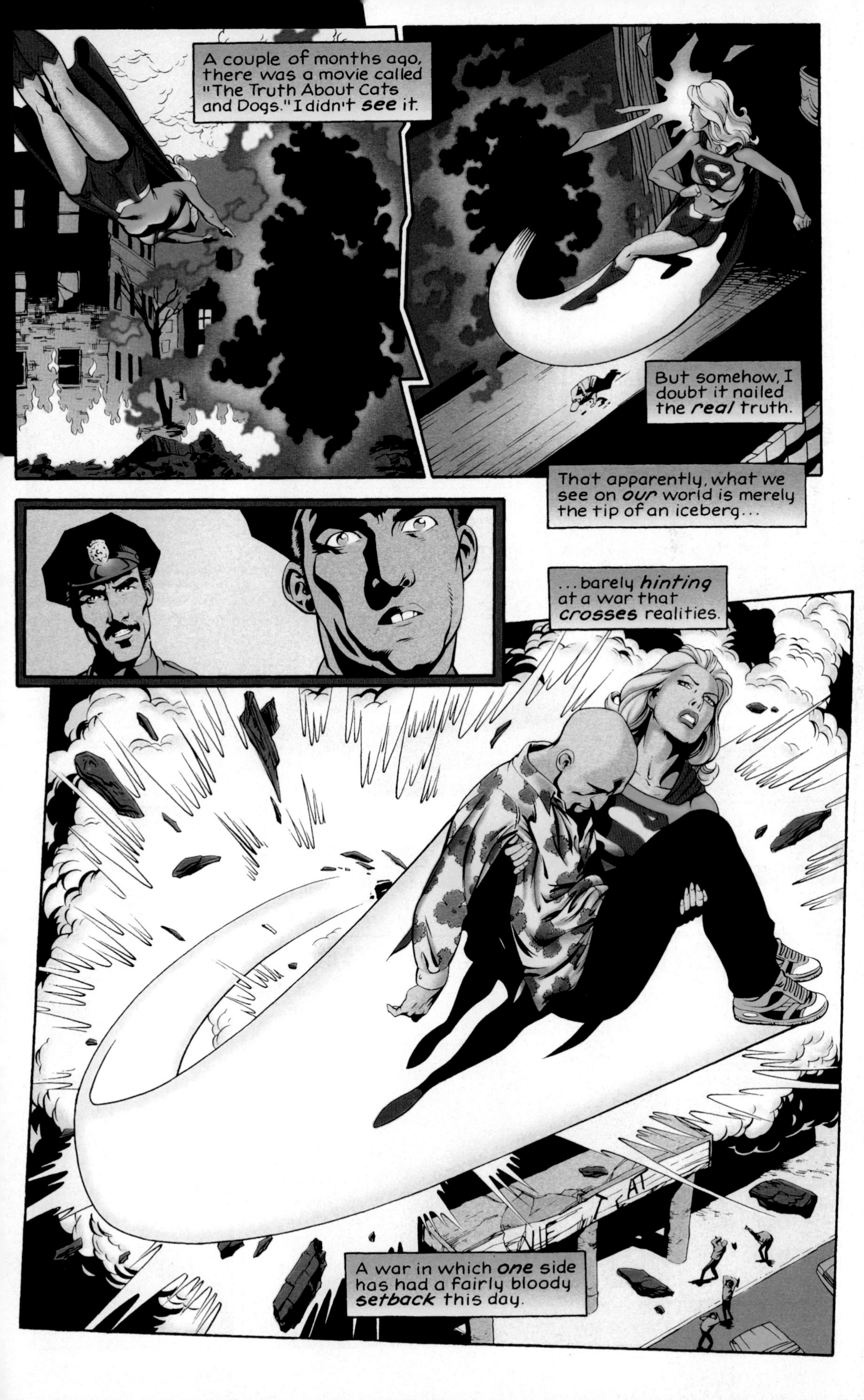
A couple of months ago, there was a movie called "The Truth About Cats and Dogs." I didn't see it.
But somehow, I doubt it nailed the real truth.
That apparently, what we see on our world is merely the tip of an iceberg...
...barely hinting at a war that crosses realities.
A war in which one side has had a fairly bloody setback this day.

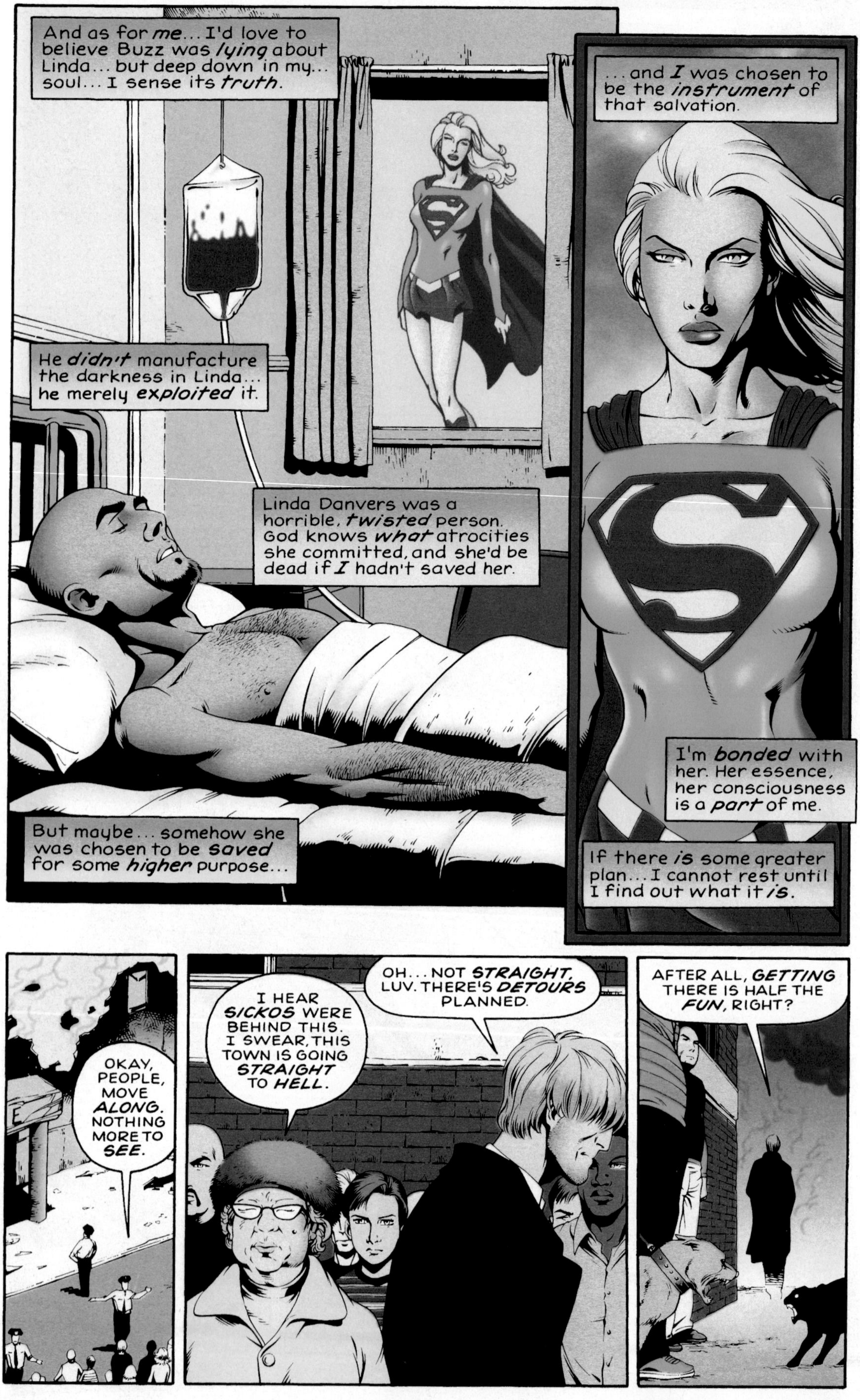
And as for me... I'd love to believe Buzz was lying about Linda... but deep down in my... soul... I sense its truth.
He didn't manufacture the darkness in Linda... he merely exploited it.
Linda Danvers was a horrible, twisted person. God knows what atrocities she committed, and she'd be dead if I hadn't saved her.
But maybe... somehow she was chosen to be saved for some higher purpose...
...and I was chosen to be the instrument of that salvation.
I'm bonded with her. Her essence, her consciousness is a part of me.
If there is some greater plan... I cannot rest until I find out what it is.
OKAY, PEOPLE, MOVE ALONG. NOTHING MORE TO SEE.
I HEAR SICKOS WERE BEHIND THIS. I SWEAR, THIS TOWN IS GOING STRAIGHT TO HELL.
OH... NOT STRAIGHT, LUV. THERE'S DETOURS PLANNED.
AFTER ALL, GETTING THERE IS HALF THE FUN, RIGHT?

WELCOME TO LEESBURG...

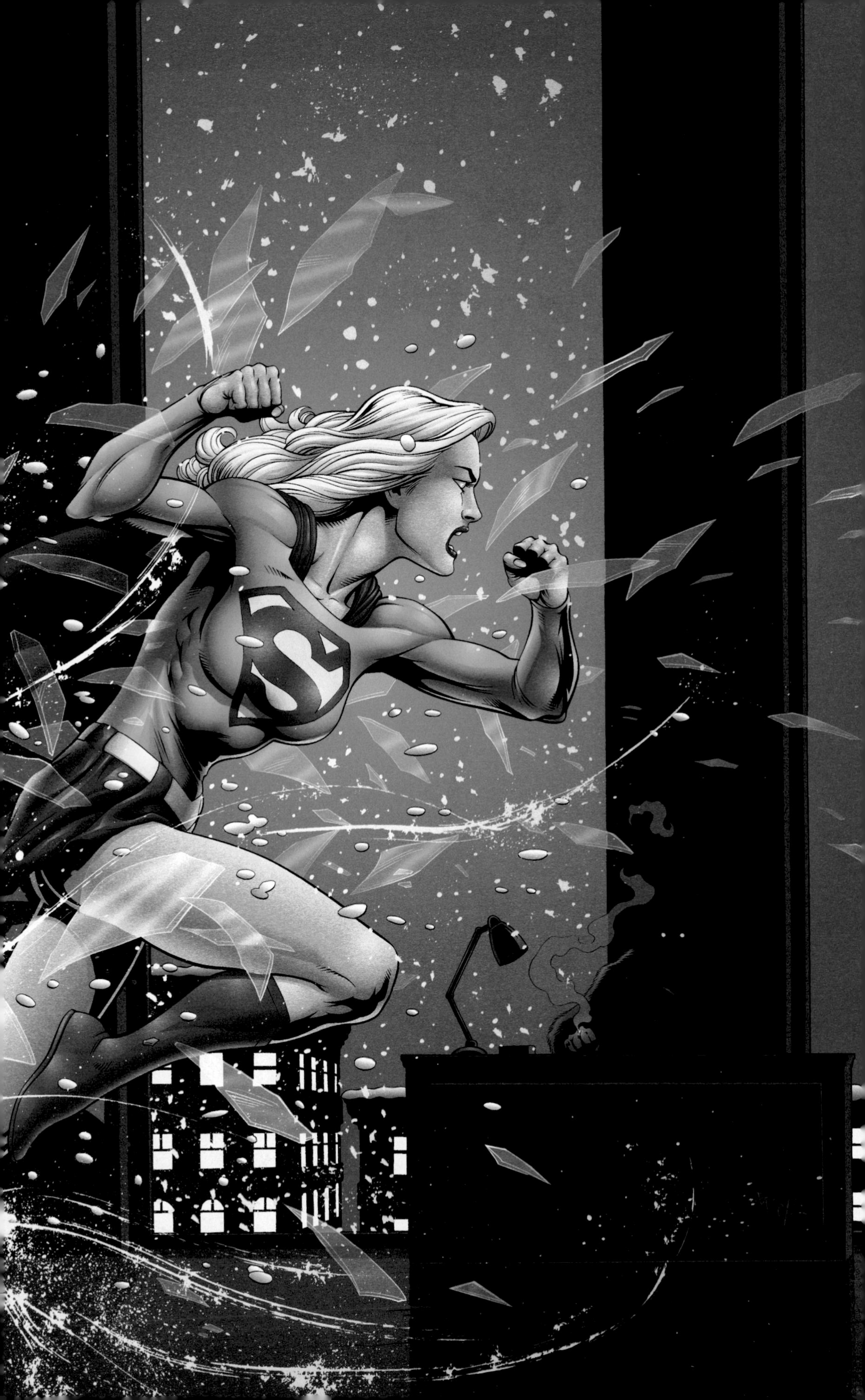

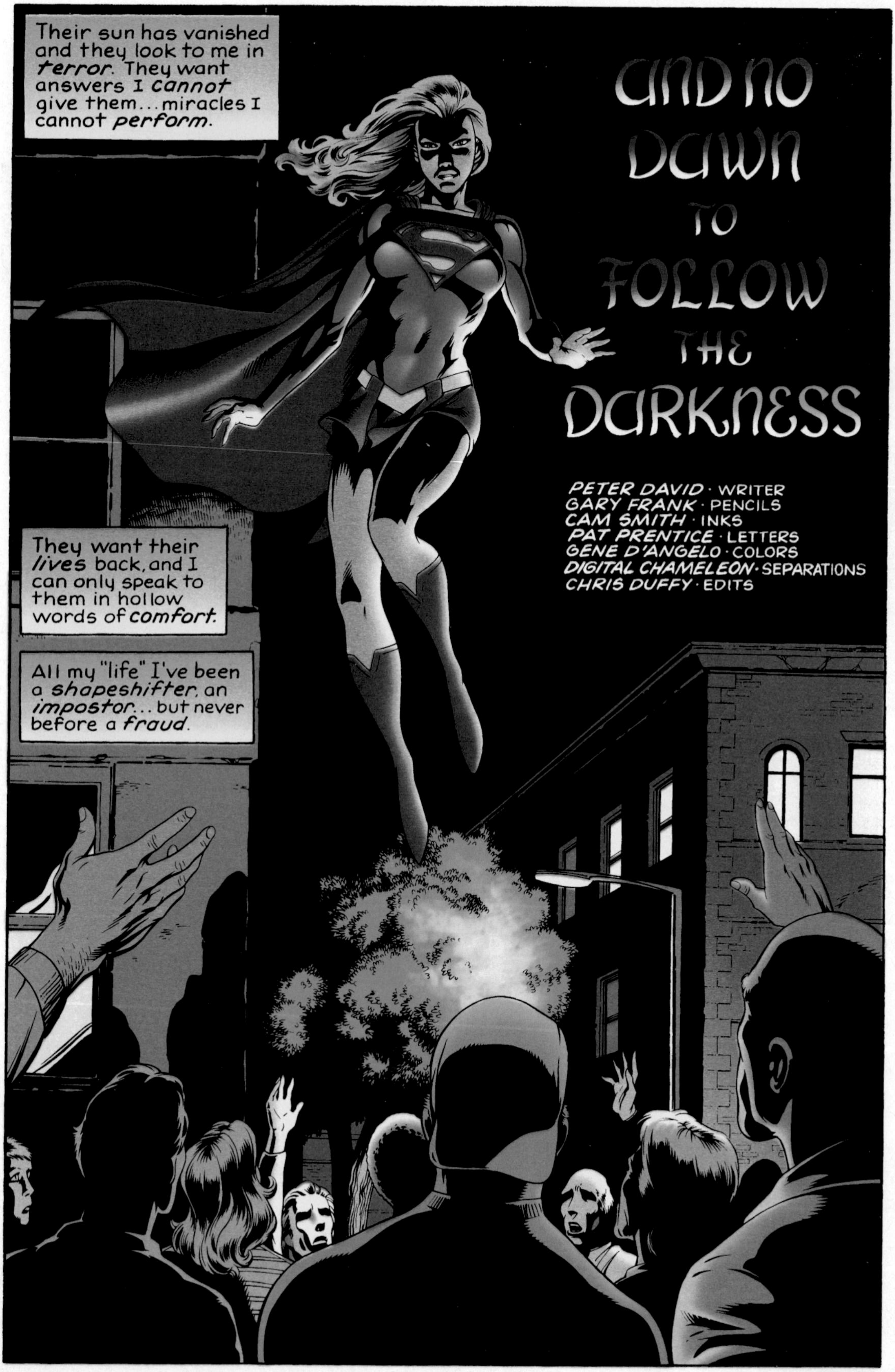

Their sun has vanished and they look to me in terror. They want answers I cannot give them... miracles I cannot perform.
AND NO DAWN TO FOLLOW THE DARKNESS
PETER DAVID · WRITER
GARY FRANK · PENCILS
CAM SMITH · INKS
PAT PRENTICE · LETTERS
GENE D'ANGELO · COLORS
DIGITAL CHAMELEON · SEPARATIONS
CHRIS DUFFY · EDITS
They want their lives back, and I can only speak to them in hollow words of comfort.
All my "life" I've been a shapeshifter, an impostor... but never before a fraud.

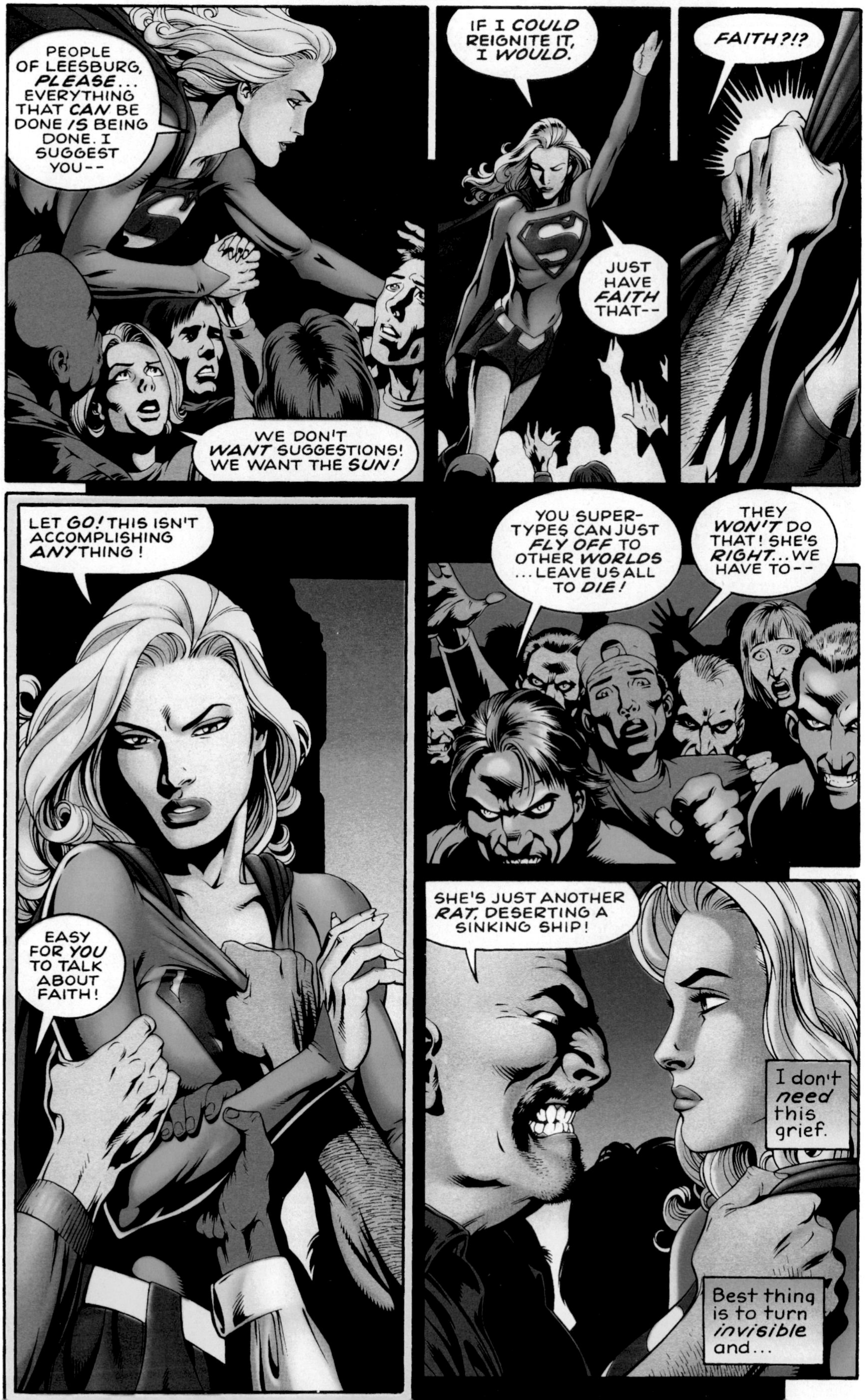
PEOPLE OF LEESBURG, PLEASE... EVERYTHING THAT CAN BE DONE IS BEING DONE. I SUGGEST YOU--
WE DON'T WANT SUGGESTIONS! WE WANT THE SUN!
IF I COULD REIGNITE IT, I WOULD.
JUST HAVE FAITH THAT--
FAITH?!?
LET GO! THIS ISN'T ACCOMPLISHING ANYTHING!
EASY FOR YOU TO TALK ABOUT FAITH!
YOU SUPER-TYPES CAN JUST FLY OFF TO OTHER WORLDS ...LEAVE US ALL TO DIE!
THEY WON'T DO THAT! SHE'S RIGHT...WE HAVE TO--
SHE'S JUST ANOTHER RAT, DESERTING A SINKING SHIP!
I don't need this grief.
Best thing is to turn invisible and...

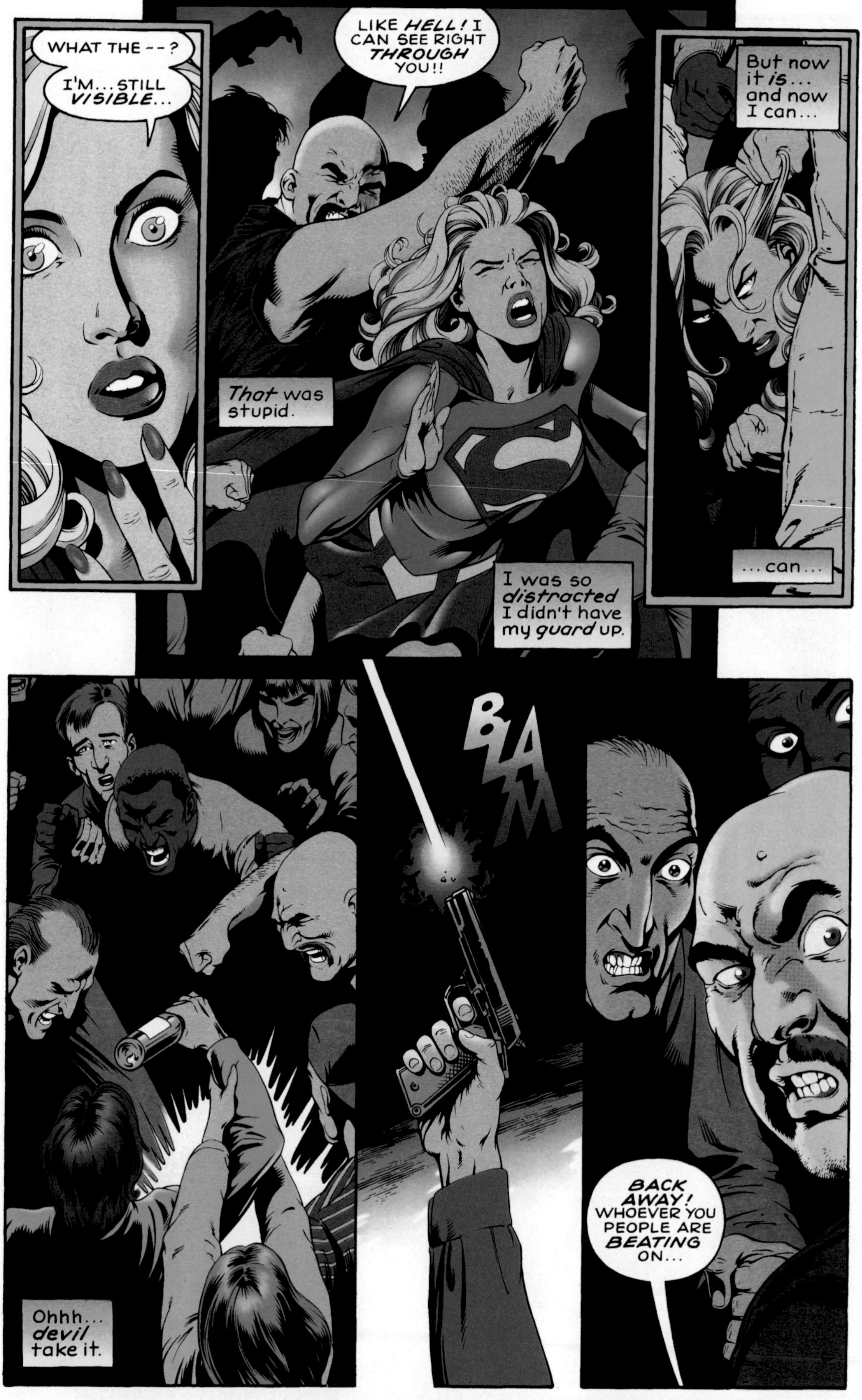

WHAT THE --?
I'M... STILL *VISIBLE*...
LIKE *HELL!* I CAN SEE RIGHT *THROUGH* YOU!!
That was stupid.
I was so *distracted* I didn't have my *guard* up.
But now it *is*... and now I can...
...can...
Ohhh... *devil* take it.
BLAM
BACK AWAY! WHOEVER YOU PEOPLE ARE *BEATING* ON...

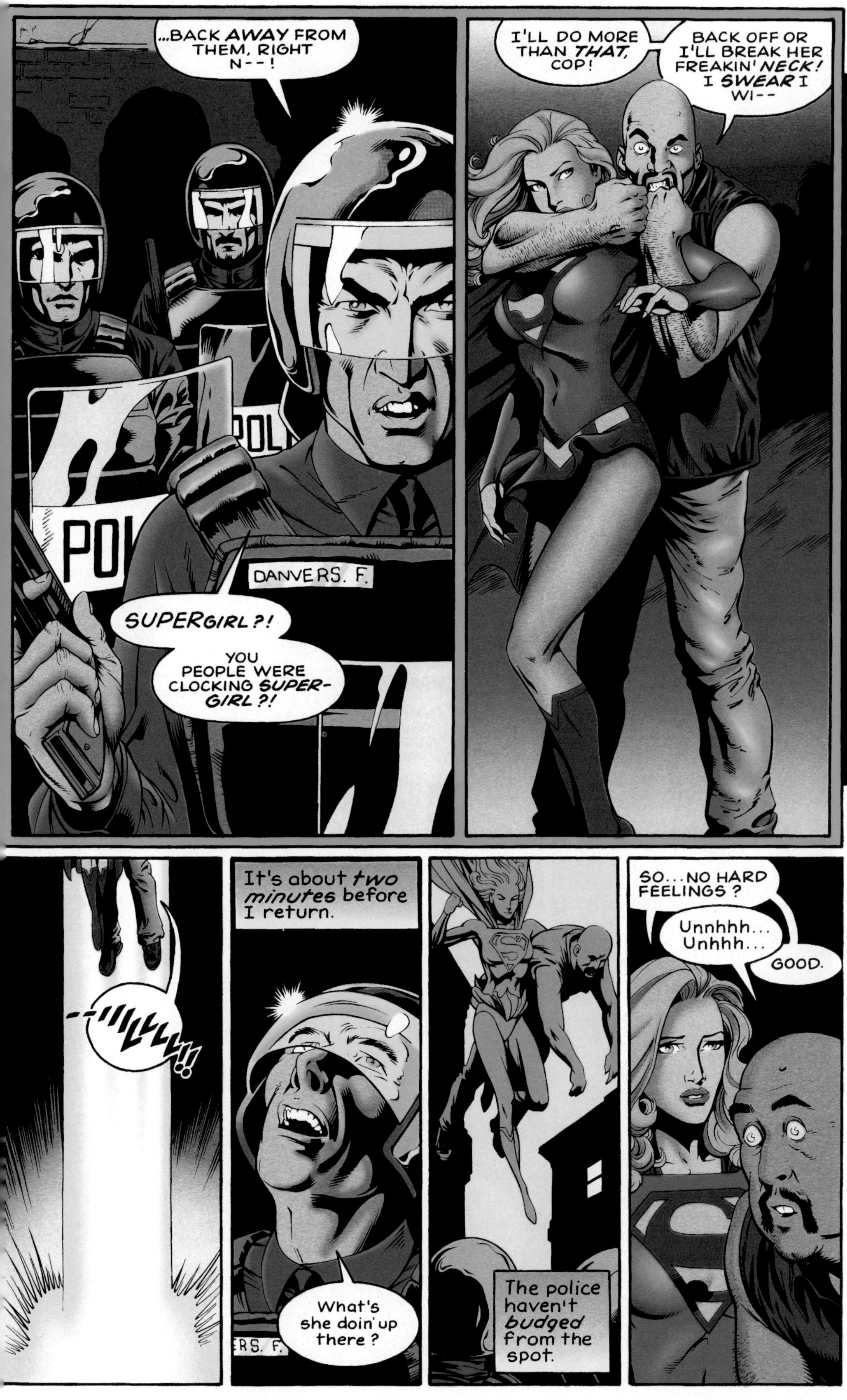
...BACK AWAY FROM THEM, RIGHT N--!
POL
POL
DANVERS. F.
SUPERGIRL?!
YOU PEOPLE WERE CLOCKING SUPER-GIRL?!
I'LL DO MORE THAN THAT, COP!
BACK OFF OR I'LL BREAK HER FREAKIN' NECK! I SWEAR I WI--
--ZZZZZZ!!
It's about two minutes before I return.
What's she doin' up there?
ERS. F.
The police haven't budged from the spot.
SO...NO HARD FEELINGS?
Unnhhh... Unhhh...
GOOD.

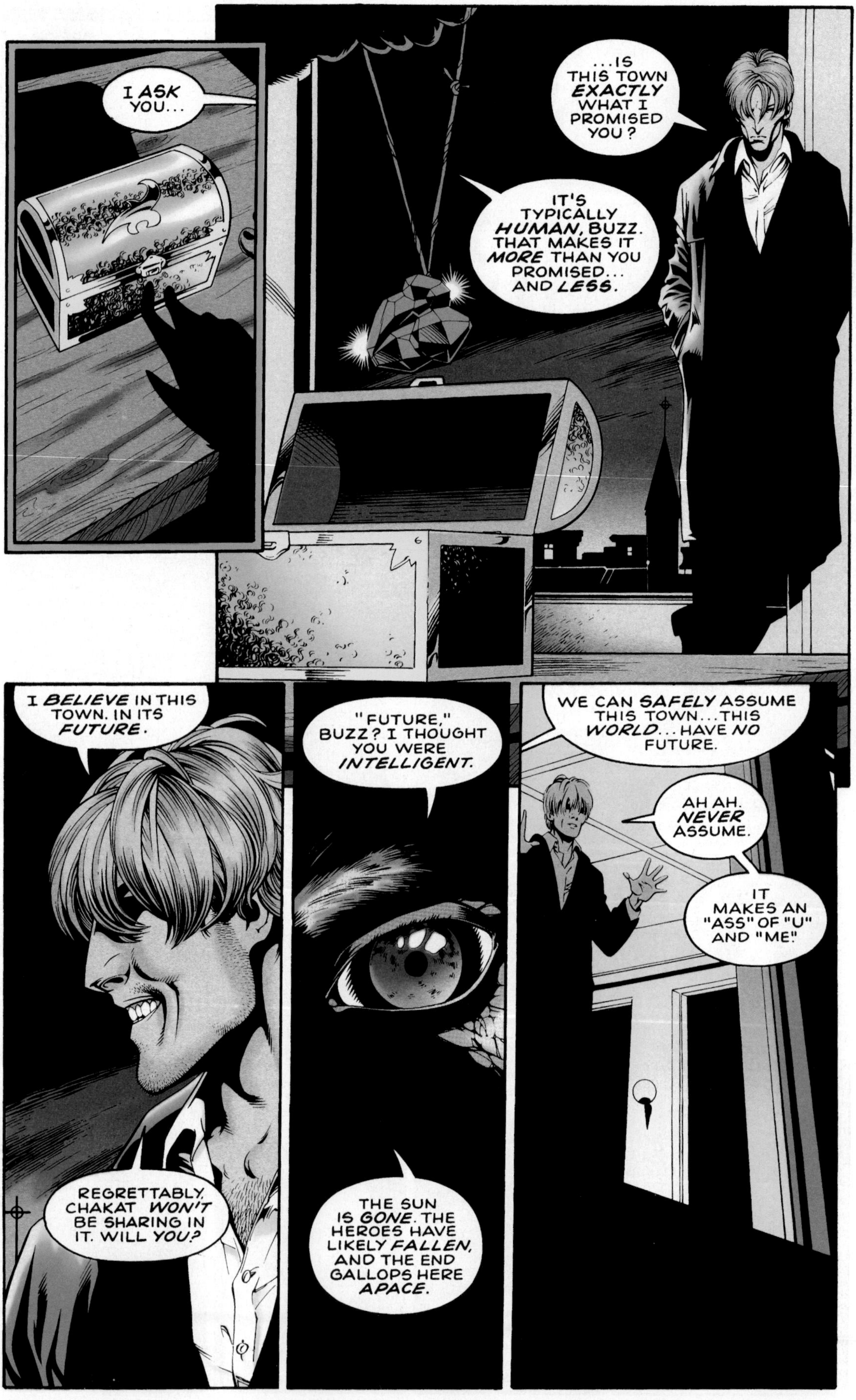
I ASK YOU...
...IS THIS TOWN EXACTLY WHAT I PROMISED YOU?
IT'S TYPICALLY HUMAN, BUZZ. THAT MAKES IT MORE THAN YOU PROMISED... AND LESS.
I BELIEVE IN THIS TOWN. IN ITS FUTURE.
REGRETTABLY, CHAKAT WON'T BE SHARING IN IT. WILL YOU?
"FUTURE," BUZZ? I THOUGHT YOU WERE INTELLIGENT.
THE SUN IS GONE. THE HEROES HAVE LIKELY FALLEN, AND THE END GALLOPS HERE APACE.
WE CAN SAFELY ASSUME THIS TOWN...THIS WORLD...HAVE NO FUTURE.
AH AH. NEVER ASSUME.
IT MAKES AN "ASS" OF "U" AND "ME."

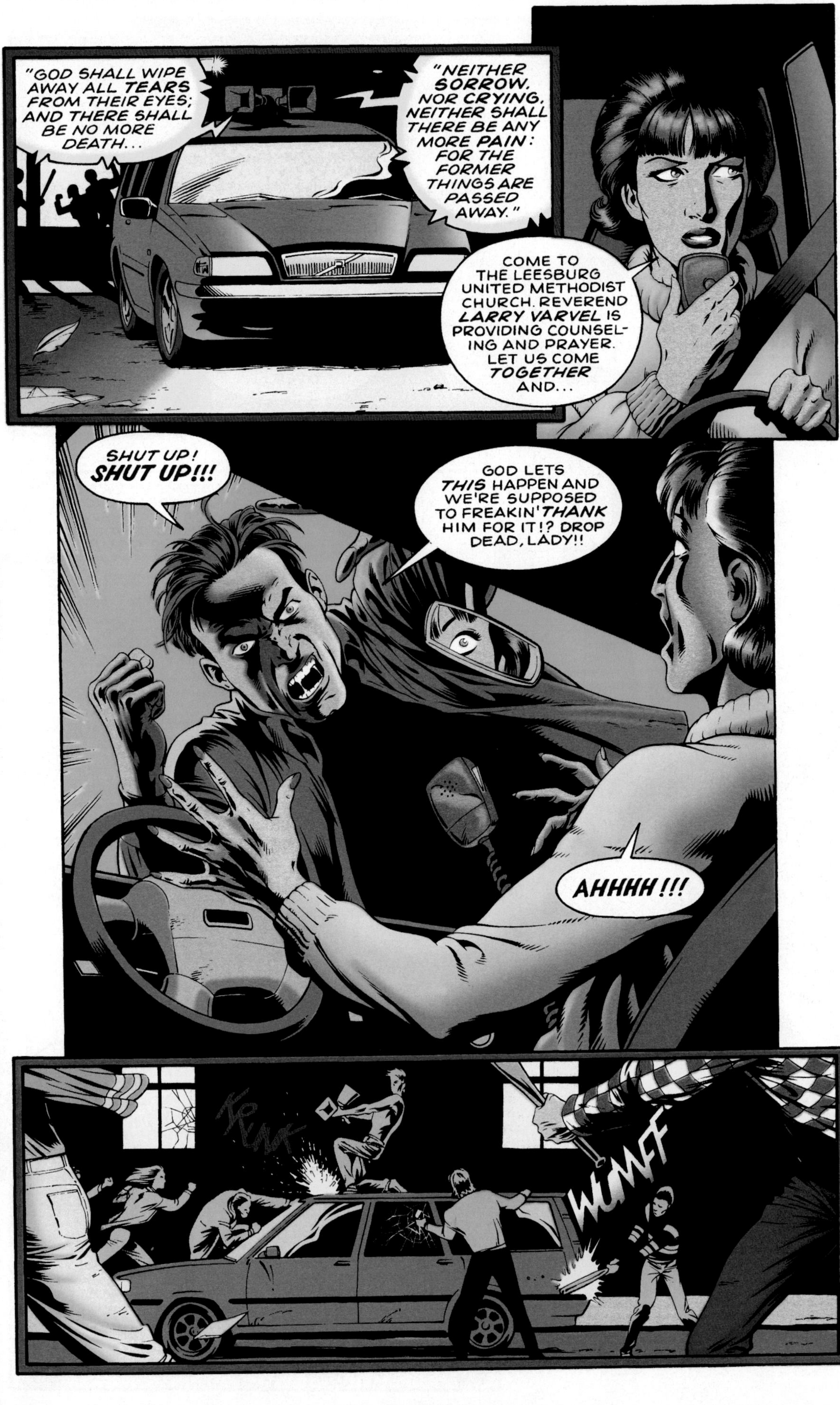
"GOD SHALL WIPE AWAY ALL TEARS FROM THEIR EYES; AND THERE SHALL BE NO MORE DEATH...
"NEITHER SORROW, NOR CRYING, NEITHER SHALL THERE BE ANY MORE PAIN: FOR THE FORMER THINGS ARE PASSED AWAY."
COME TO THE LEESBURG UNITED METHODIST CHURCH. REVEREND LARRY VARVEL IS PROVIDING COUNSELING AND PRAYER. LET US COME TOGETHER AND...
SHUT UP! SHUT UP!!!
GOD LETS THIS HAPPEN AND WE'RE SUPPOSED TO FREAKIN' THANK HIM FOR IT!? DROP DEAD, LADY!!
AHHHH!!!
WUMFF

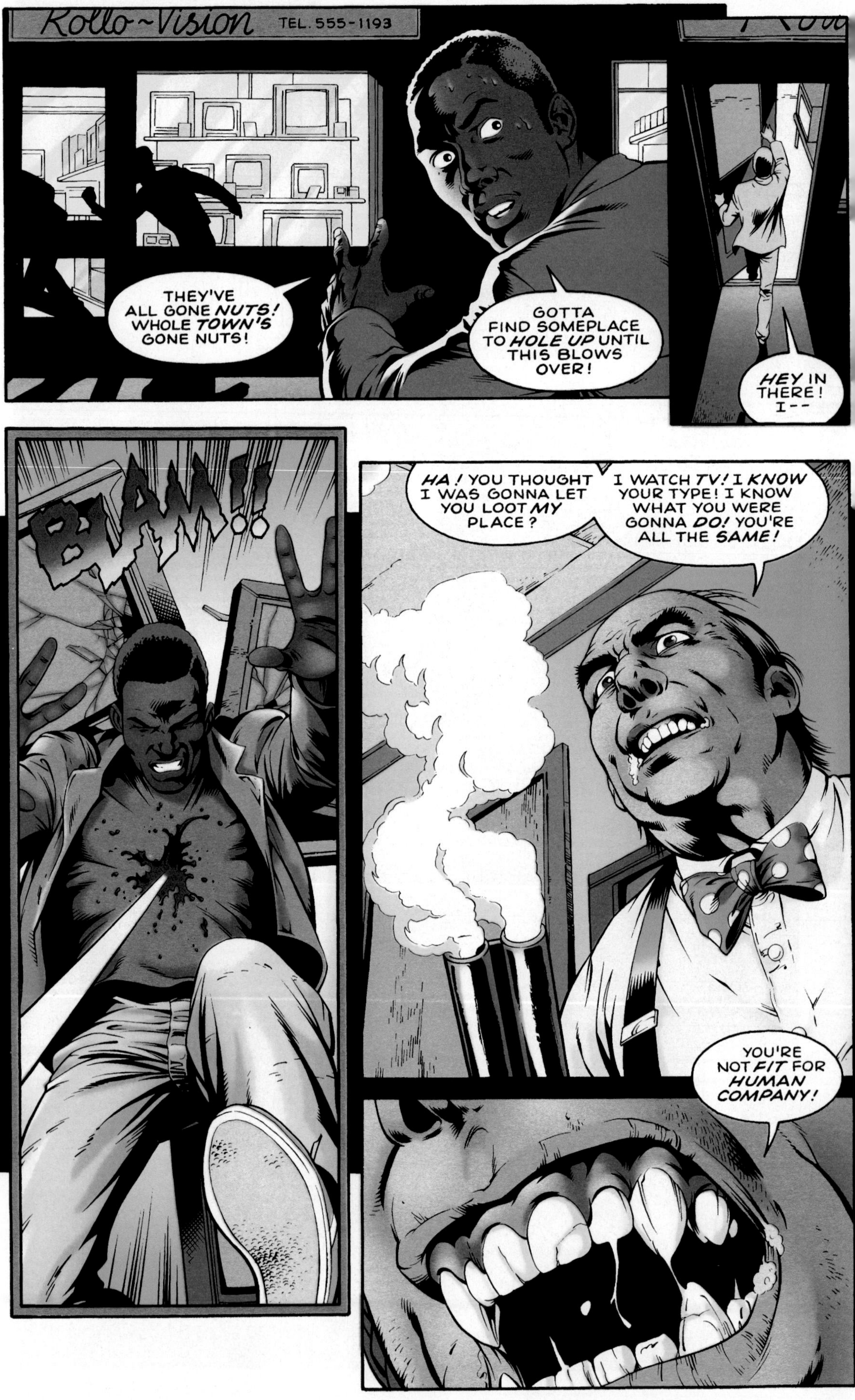
Rollo~Vision TEL. 555-1193
THEY'VE ALL GONE NUTS! WHOLE TOWN'S GONE NUTS!
GOTTA FIND SOMEPLACE TO HOLE UP UNTIL THIS BLOWS OVER!
HEY IN THERE! I--
BLAM!!
HA! YOU THOUGHT I WAS GONNA LET YOU LOOT MY PLACE?
I WATCH TV! I KNOW YOUR TYPE! I KNOW WHAT YOU WERE GONNA DO! YOU'RE ALL THE SAME!
YOU'RE NOT FIT FOR HUMAN COMPANY!

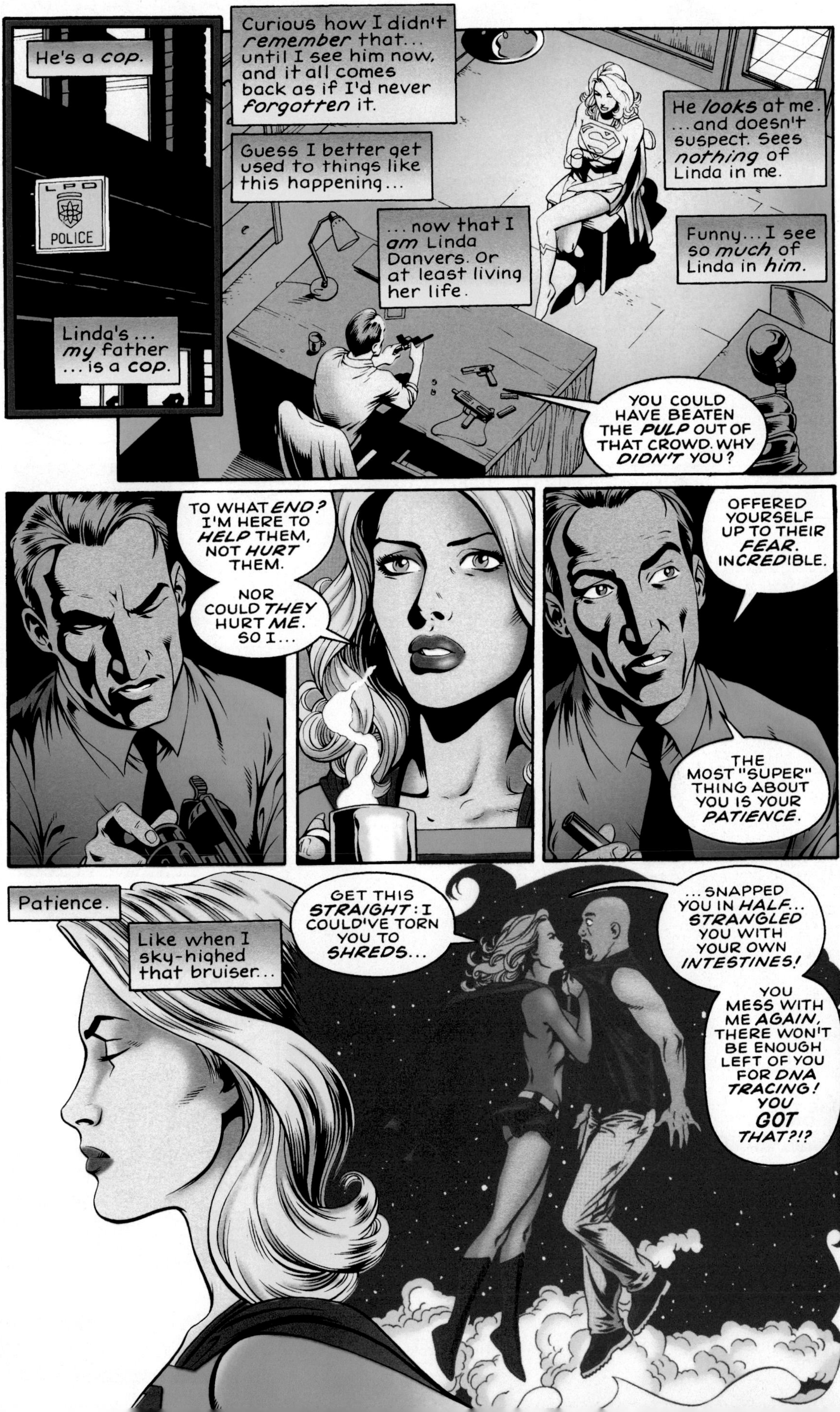
He's a cop.
Linda's... my father ...is a cop.
Curious how I didn't remember that... until I see him now, and it all comes back as if I'd never forgotten it.
Guess I better get used to things like this happening...
...now that I am Linda Danvers. Or at least living her life.
He looks at me. ...and doesn't suspect. Sees nothing of Linda in me.
Funny... I see so much of Linda in him.
LPD
POLICE
YOU COULD HAVE BEATEN THE PULP OUT OF THAT CROWD. WHY DIDN'T YOU?
TO WHAT END? I'M HERE TO HELP THEM, NOT HURT THEM.
NOR COULD THEY HURT ME. SO I...
OFFERED YOURSELF UP TO THEIR FEAR. INCREDIBLE.
THE MOST "SUPER" THING ABOUT YOU IS YOUR PATIENCE.
Patience.
Like when I sky-highed that bruiser...
GET THIS STRAIGHT: I COULD'VE TORN YOU TO SHREDS...
...SNAPPED YOU IN HALF... STRANGLED YOU WITH YOUR OWN INTESTINES!
YOU MESS WITH ME AGAIN, THERE WON'T BE ENOUGH LEFT OF YOU FOR DNA TRACING! YOU GOT THAT?!?

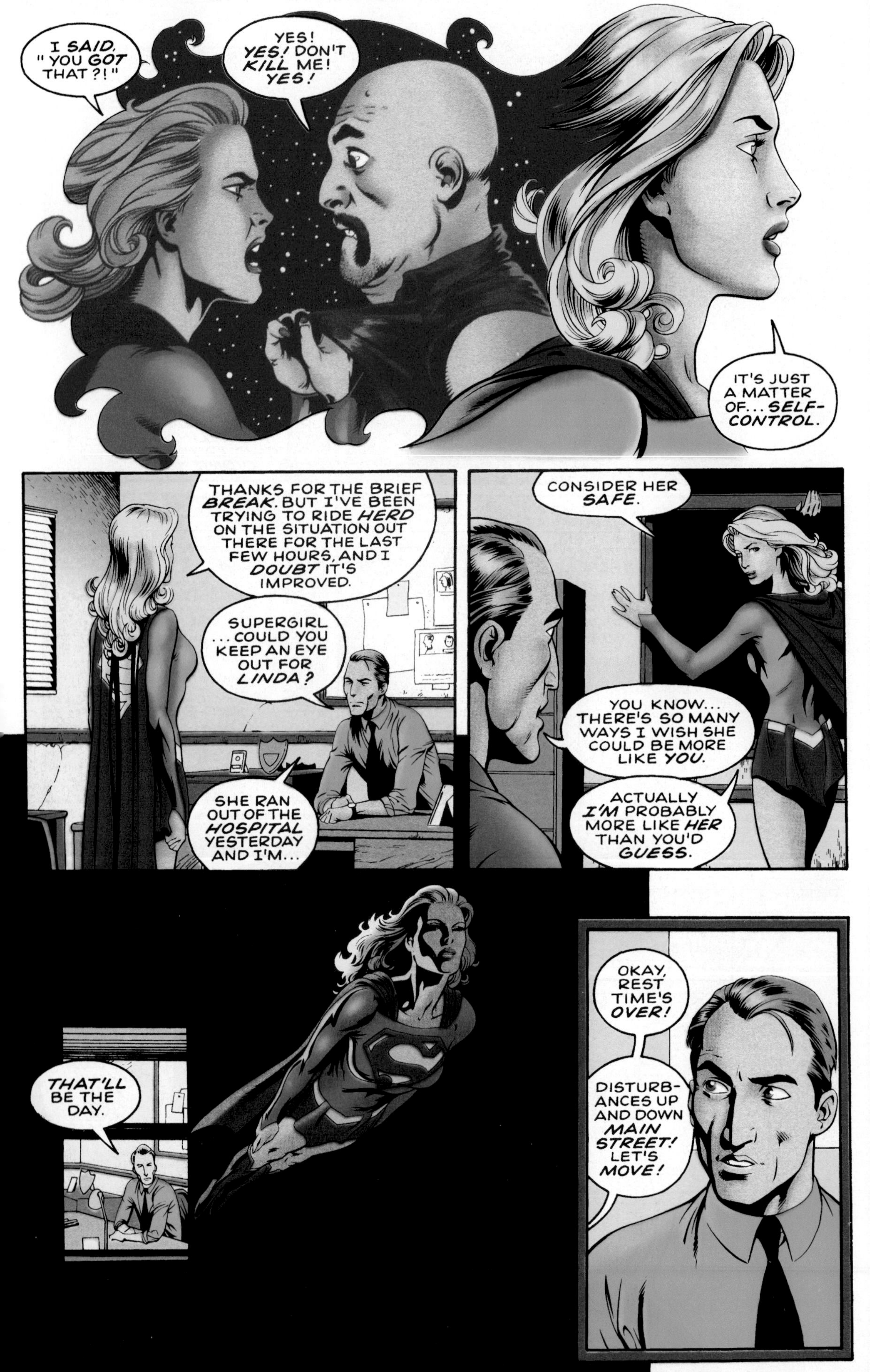

I SAID, "YOU GOT THAT?!"
YES! YES! DON'T KILL ME! YES!
IT'S JUST A MATTER OF... SELF-CONTROL.
THANKS FOR THE BRIEF BREAK. BUT I'VE BEEN TRYING TO RIDE HERD ON THE SITUATION OUT THERE FOR THE LAST FEW HOURS, AND I DOUBT IT'S IMPROVED.
SUPERGIRL ...COULD YOU KEEP AN EYE OUT FOR LINDA?
SHE RAN OUT OF THE HOSPITAL YESTERDAY AND I'M...
CONSIDER HER SAFE.
YOU KNOW... THERE'S SO MANY WAYS I WISH SHE COULD BE MORE LIKE YOU.
ACTUALLY I'M PROBABLY MORE LIKE HER THAN YOU'D GUESS.
THAT'LL BE THE DAY.
OKAY, REST TIME'S OVER!
DISTURB-ANCES UP AND DOWN MAIN STREET! LET'S MOVE!

MAN, *LOOK AT THAT!*

RIOTING IN THE STREETS... BEST STUFF TO HIT THIS BACKWATER TOWN SINCE SUPERGIRL SHOWED UP... AND *I'M* STUCK IN THE *HOSPITAL?*

NO WAY. I'M *BLOWING* THIS POPSICLE STAND.

AND WHAT DO YOU MEAN BY *THAT*, MR. SHARPE?

I MEAN I'M CHECKING MYSELF *OUT.*

MR. SHARPE, EVEN A RESIDENT LIKE *ME* KNOWS YOUR WOUNDS COULD OPEN *UP* AGAIN...

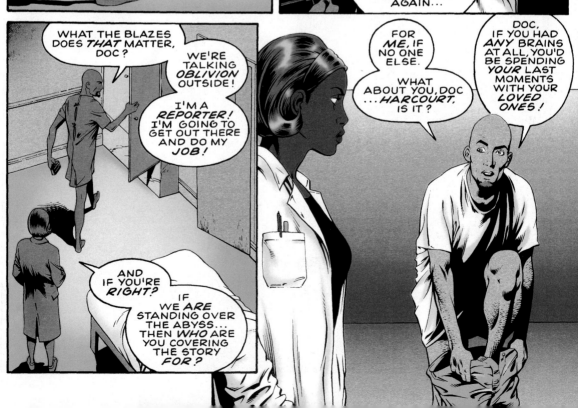

WHAT THE BLAZES DOES *THAT* MATTER, DOC?

WE'RE TALKING *OBLIVION* OUTSIDE!

I'M A *REPORTER!* I'M GOING TO GET OUT THERE AND DO MY *JOB!*

AND IF YOU'RE *RIGHT?*

IF WE *ARE* STANDING OVER THE ABYSS... THEN *WHO* ARE YOU COVERING THE STORY *FOR?*

FOR *ME*, IF NO ONE ELSE.

WHAT ABOUT YOU, DOC ...*HARCOURT*, IS IT?

DOC, IF YOU HAD *ANY* BRAINS AT ALL, YOU'D BE SPENDING *YOUR* LAST MOMENTS WITH YOUR *LOVED ONES!*

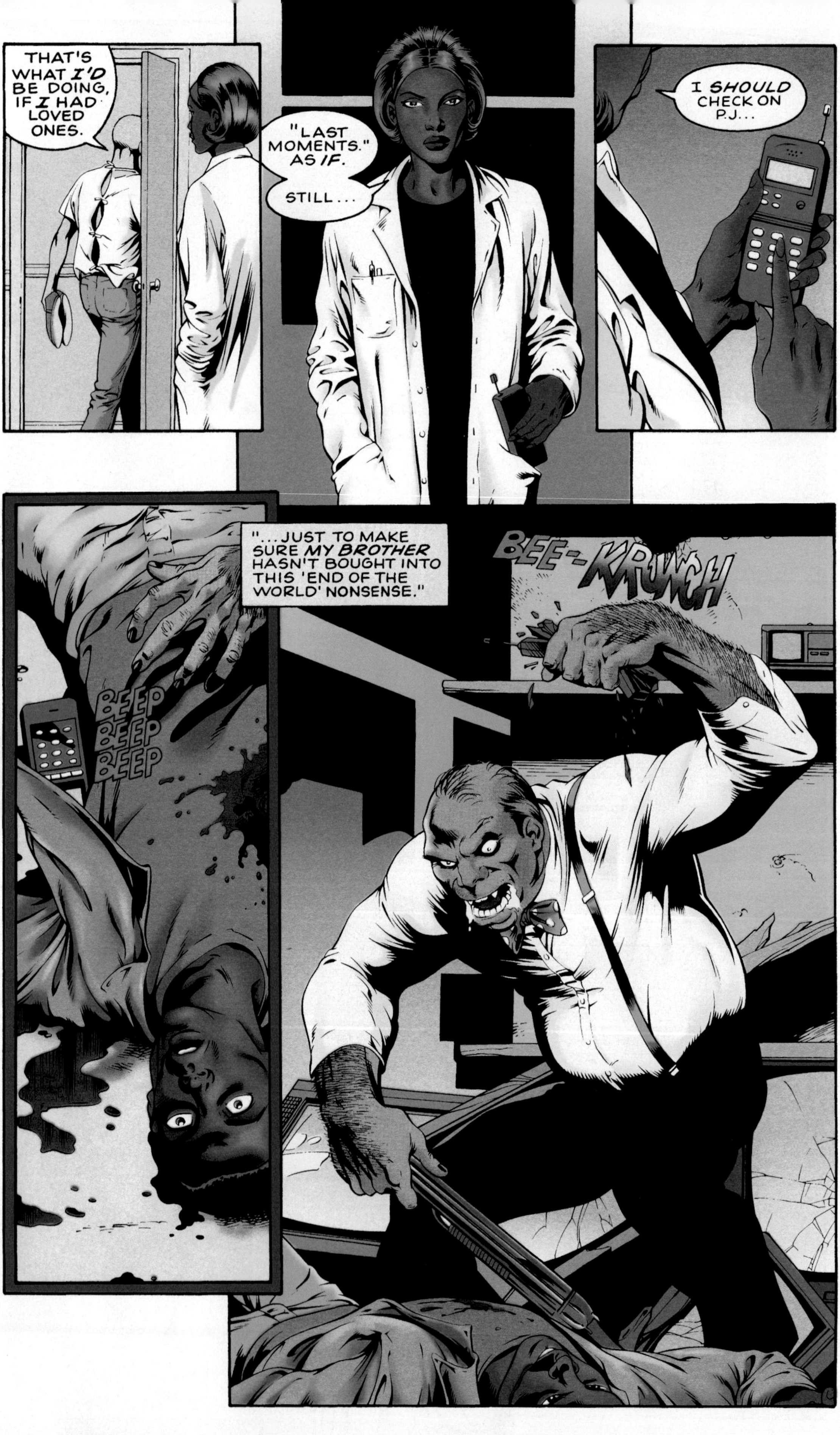
THAT'S WHAT *I'D* BE DOING, IF *I* HAD LOVED ONES.
"LAST MOMENTS." AS *IF*.
STILL...
I *SHOULD* CHECK ON P.J...
"...JUST TO MAKE SURE *MY BROTHER* HASN'T BOUGHT INTO THIS 'END OF THE WORLD' NONSENSE."
BEEP BEEP BEEP
BEE-KRUNCH

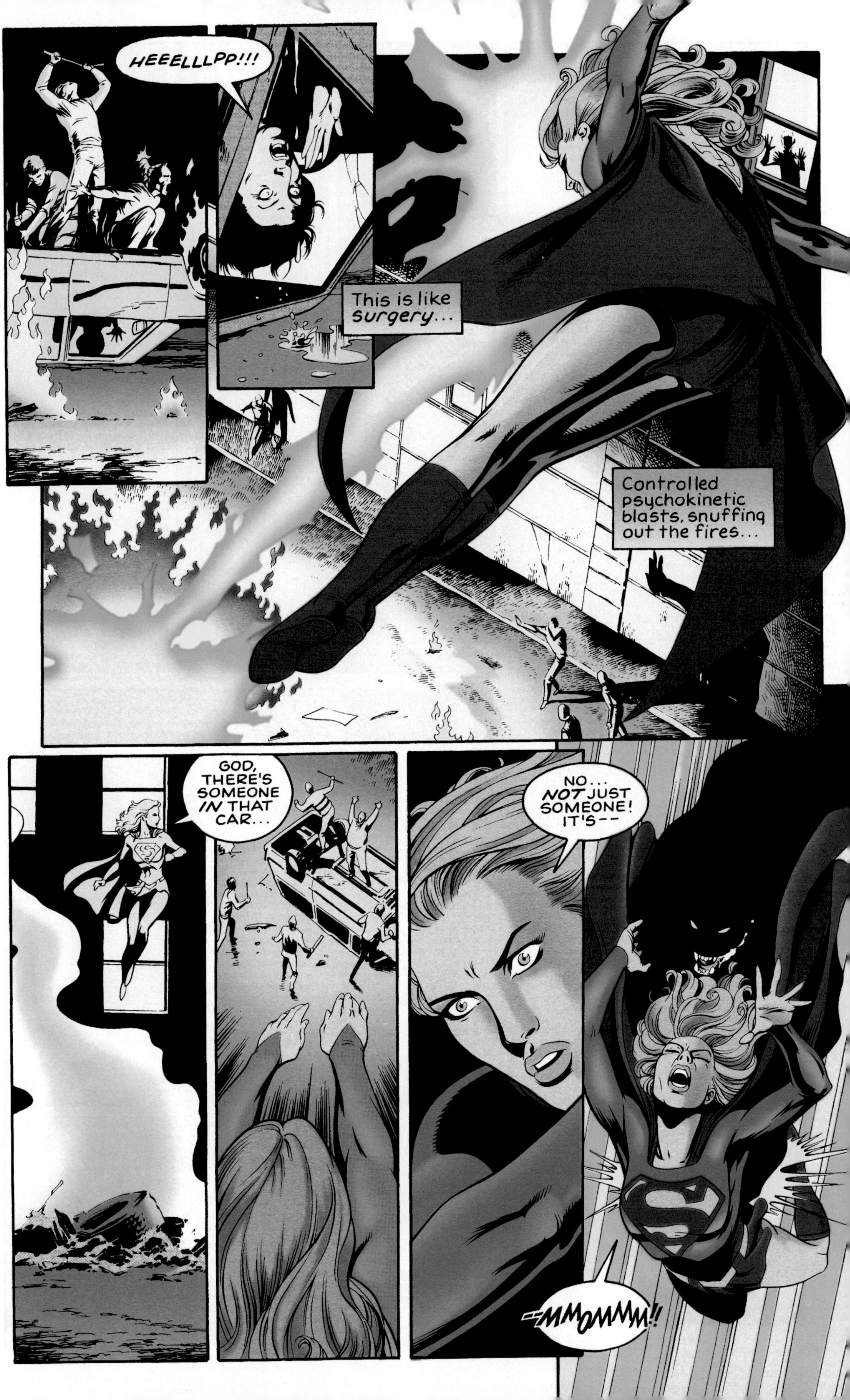
HEEELLLPP!!!
This is like surgery...
Controlled psychokinetic blasts, snuffing out the fires...
GOD, THERE'S SOMEONE IN THAT CAR...
NO... NOT JUST SOMEONE! IT'S--
--MMOMMM!!

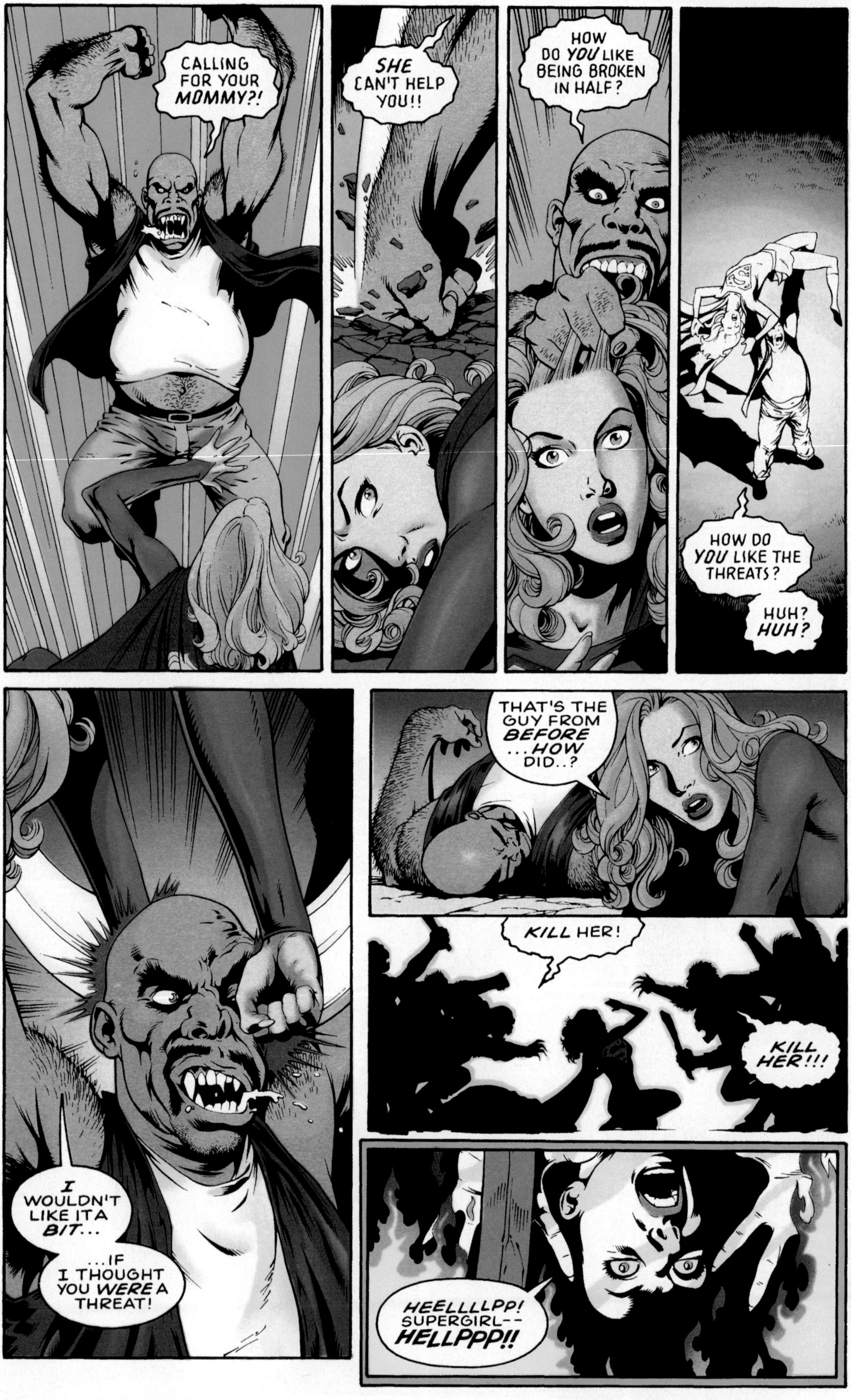
CALLING FOR YOUR MOMMY?!
SHE CAN'T HELP YOU!!
HOW DO YOU LIKE BEING BROKEN IN HALF?
HOW DO YOU LIKE THE THREATS?
HUH? HUH?
I WOULDN'T LIKE IT A BIT...
...IF I THOUGHT YOU WERE A THREAT!
THAT'S THE GUY FROM BEFORE ...HOW DID..?
KILL HER!
KILL HER!!!
HEELLLLPP! SUPERGIRL-- HELLPPP!!

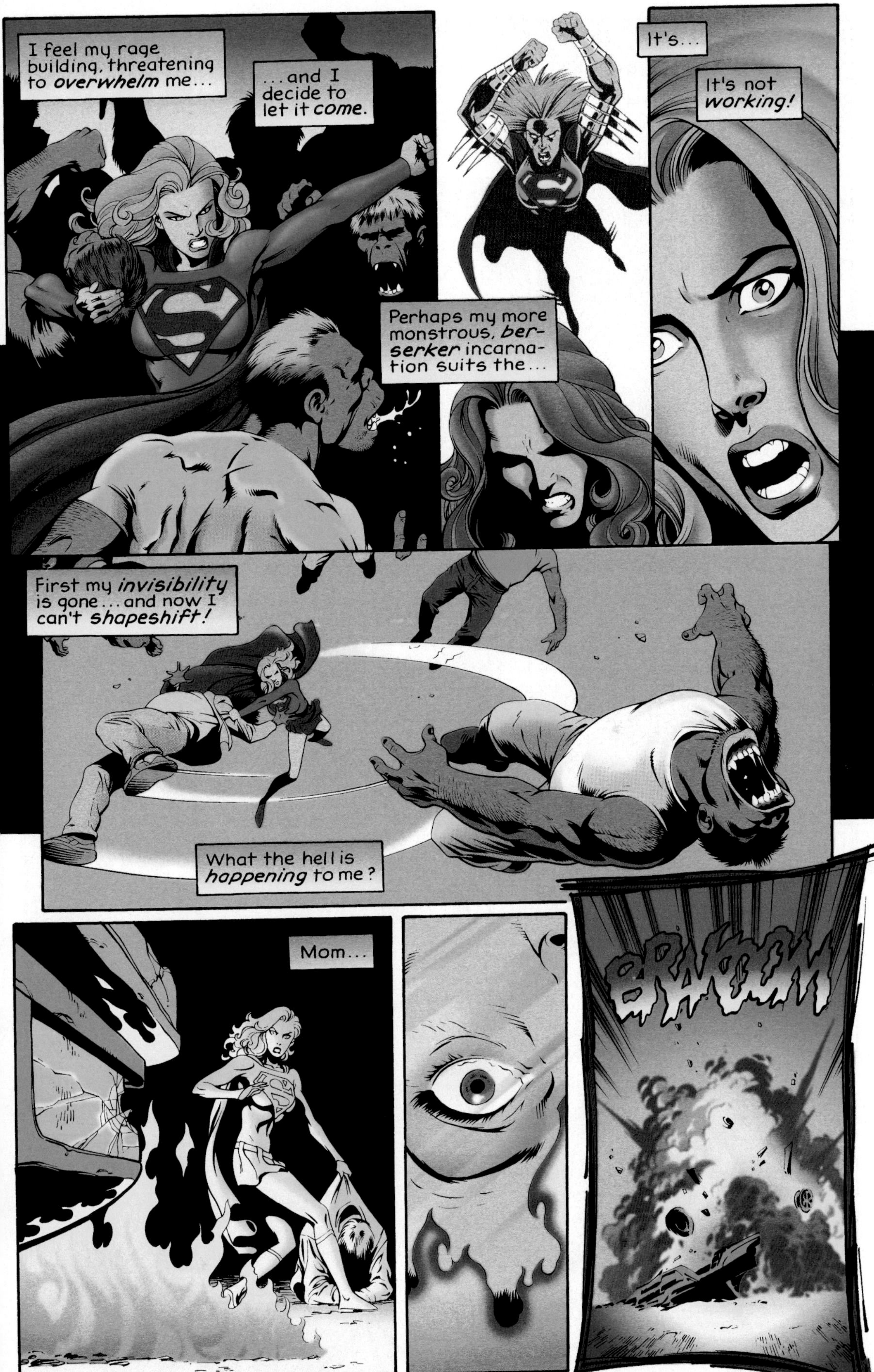
I feel my rage building, threatening to *overwhelm* me...
...and I decide to let it *come*.
It's...
It's not *working!*
Perhaps my more monstrous, *ber-serker* incarna-tion suits the...
First my *invisibility* is gone...and now I can't *shapeshift!*
What the hell is *happening* to me?
Mom...
BRAKOOM

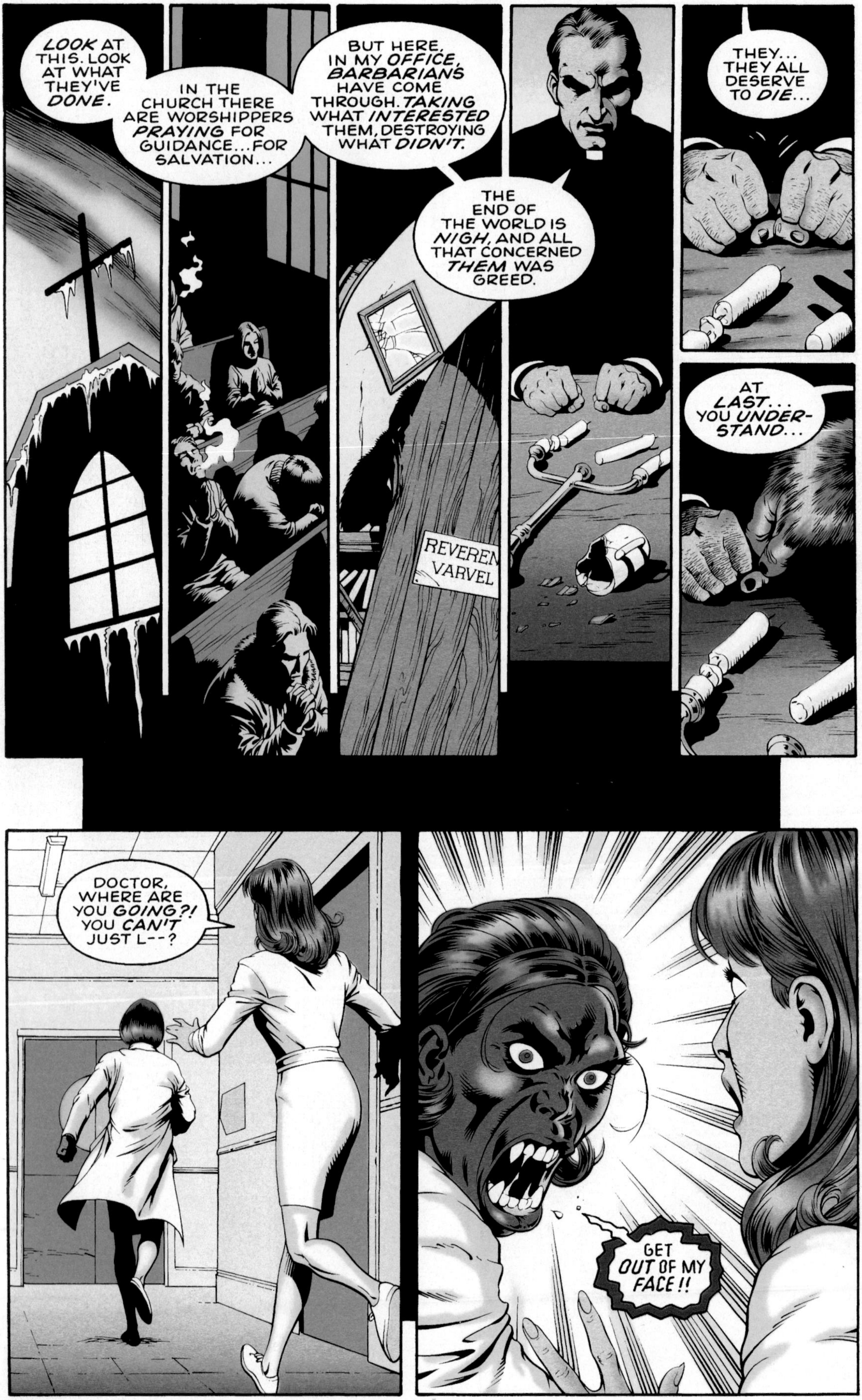
LOOK AT THIS. LOOK AT WHAT THEY'VE DONE.
IN THE CHURCH THERE ARE WORSHIPPERS PRAYING FOR GUIDANCE...FOR SALVATION...
BUT HERE, IN MY OFFICE, BARBARIANS HAVE COME THROUGH. TAKING WHAT INTERESTED THEM, DESTROYING WHAT DIDN'T.
REVEREN VARVEL
THE END OF THE WORLD IS NIGH, AND ALL THAT CONCERNED THEM WAS GREED.
THEY... THEY ALL DESERVE TO DIE...
AT LAST... YOU UNDERSTAND...
DOCTOR, WHERE ARE YOU GOING?! YOU CAN'T JUST L--?
GET OUT OF MY FACE!!

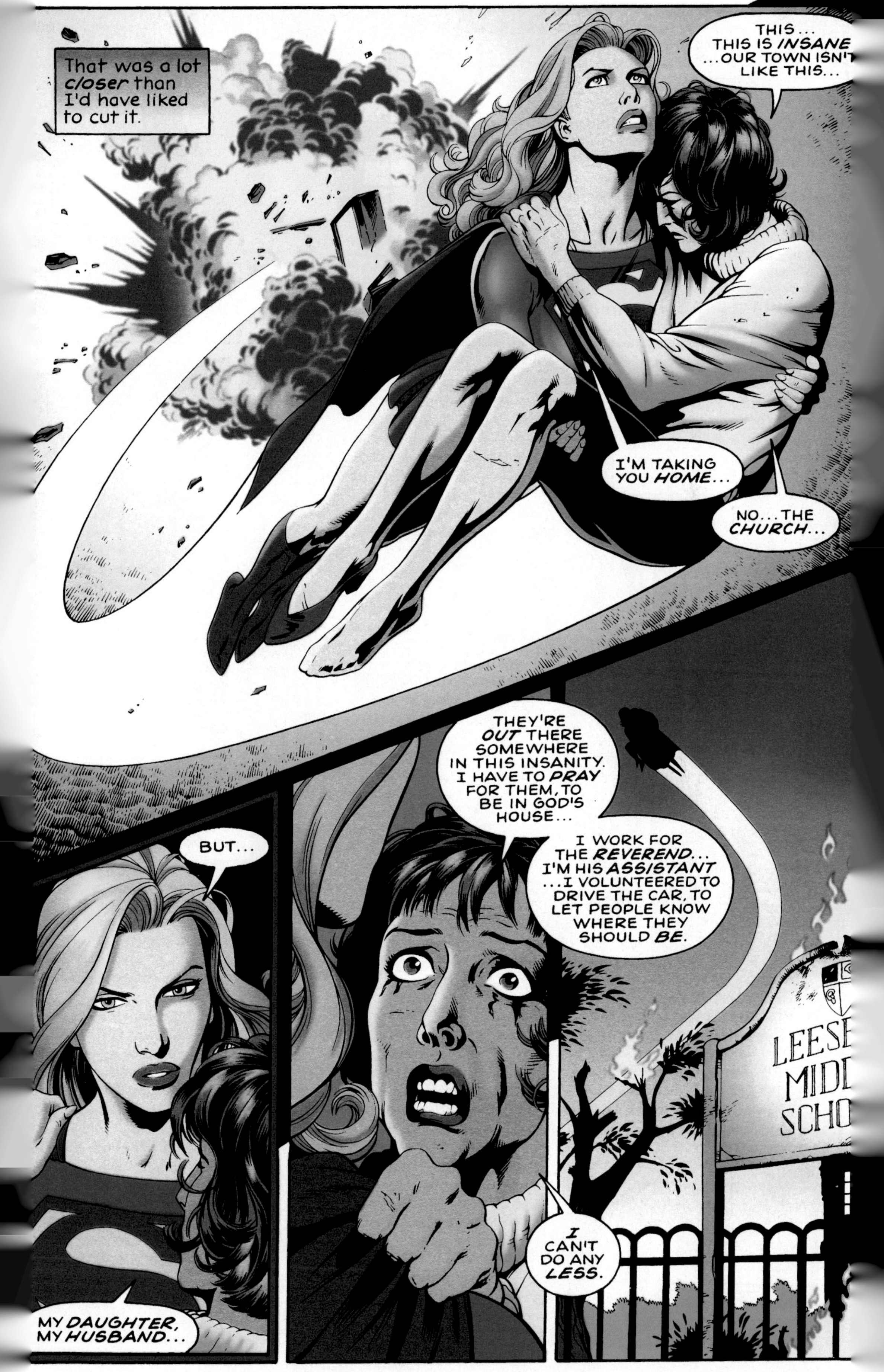
That was a lot closer than I'd have liked to cut it.
THIS... THIS IS INSANE ...OUR TOWN ISN'T LIKE THIS...
I'M TAKING YOU HOME...
NO... THE CHURCH...
BUT...
MY DAUGHTER, MY HUSBAND...
THEY'RE OUT THERE SOMEWHERE IN THIS INSANITY. I HAVE TO PRAY FOR THEM, TO BE IN GOD'S HOUSE...
I WORK FOR THE REVEREND... I'M HIS ASSISTANT ...I VOLUNTEERED TO DRIVE THE CAR, TO LET PEOPLE KNOW WHERE THEY SHOULD BE.
I CAN'T DO ANY LESS.

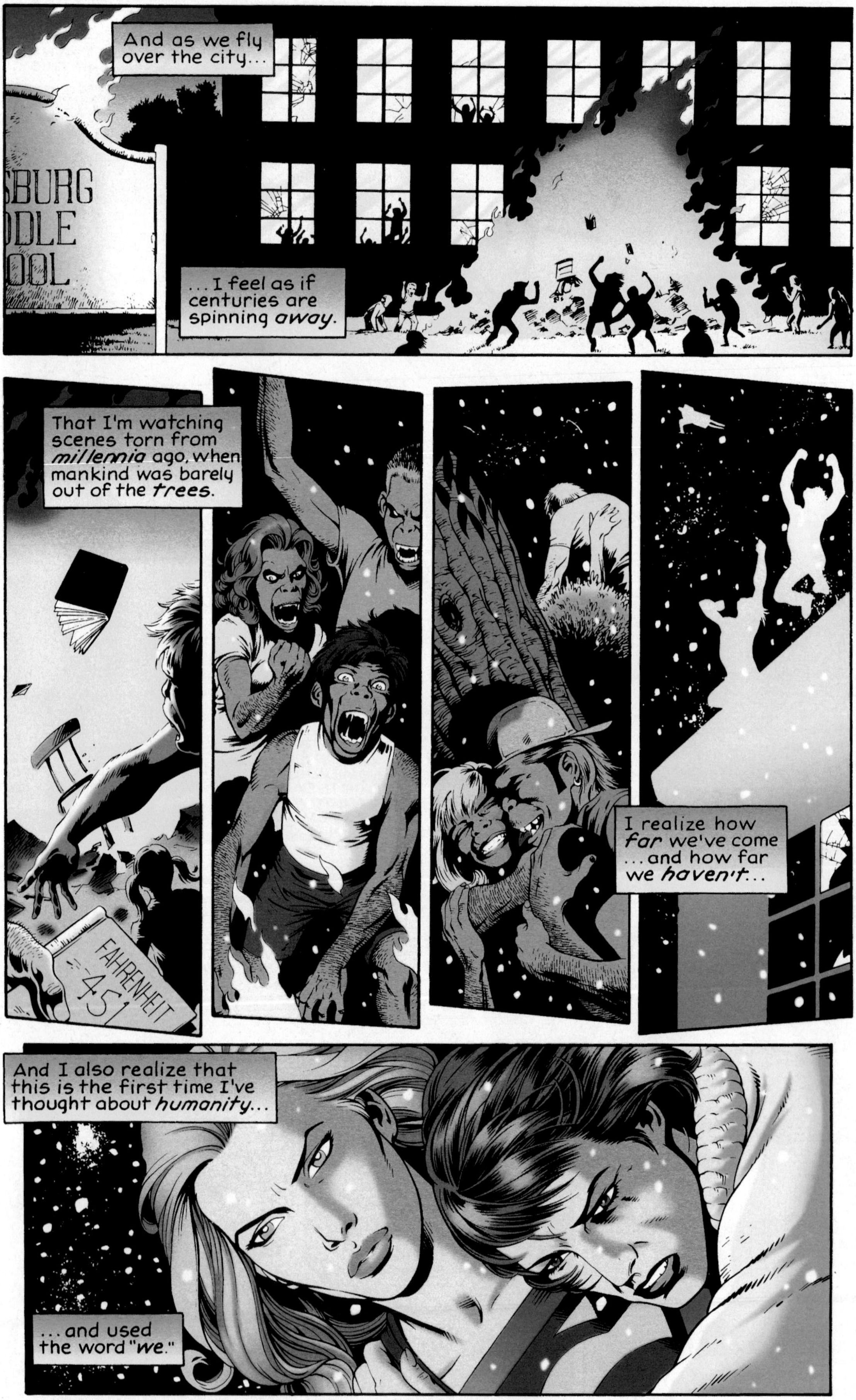

And as we fly over the city...
SBURG
DDLE
OOL
...I feel as if centuries are spinning *away*.
That I'm watching scenes torn from *millennia* ago, when mankind was barely out of the *trees*.
FAHRENHEIT 451
I realize how *far* we've come ...and how far we *haven't*...
And I also realize that this is the first time I've thought about *humanity*...
...and used the word "*we*."

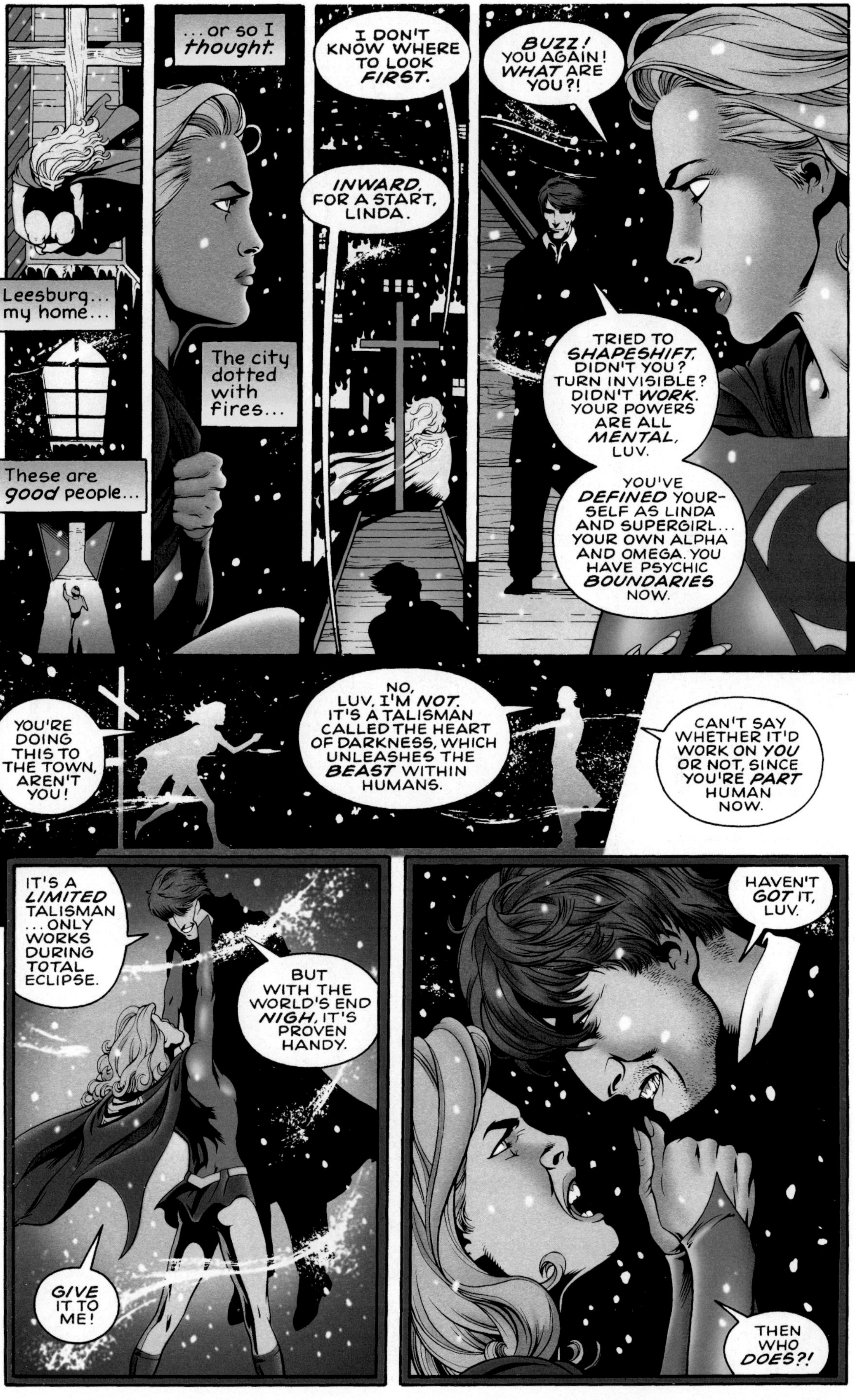

Leesburg... my home...
These are good people...
...or so I thought.
The city dotted with fires...
I DON'T KNOW WHERE TO LOOK FIRST.
INWARD, FOR A START, LINDA.
BUZZ! YOU AGAIN! WHAT ARE YOU?!
TRIED TO SHAPESHIFT, DIDN'T YOU? TURN INVISIBLE? DIDN'T WORK. YOUR POWERS ARE ALL MENTAL, LUV.
YOU'VE DEFINED YOURSELF AS LINDA AND SUPERGIRL... YOUR OWN ALPHA AND OMEGA. YOU HAVE PSYCHIC BOUNDARIES NOW.
YOU'RE DOING THIS TO THE TOWN, AREN'T YOU!
NO, LUV, I'M NOT. IT'S A TALISMAN CALLED THE HEART OF DARKNESS, WHICH UNLEASHES THE BEAST WITHIN HUMANS.
CAN'T SAY WHETHER IT'D WORK ON YOU OR NOT, SINCE YOU'RE PART HUMAN NOW.
IT'S A LIMITED TALISMAN ...ONLY WORKS DURING TOTAL ECLIPSE.
BUT WITH THE WORLD'S END NIGH, IT'S PROVEN HANDY.
GIVE IT TO ME!
HAVEN'T GOT IT, LUV.
THEN WHO DOES?!

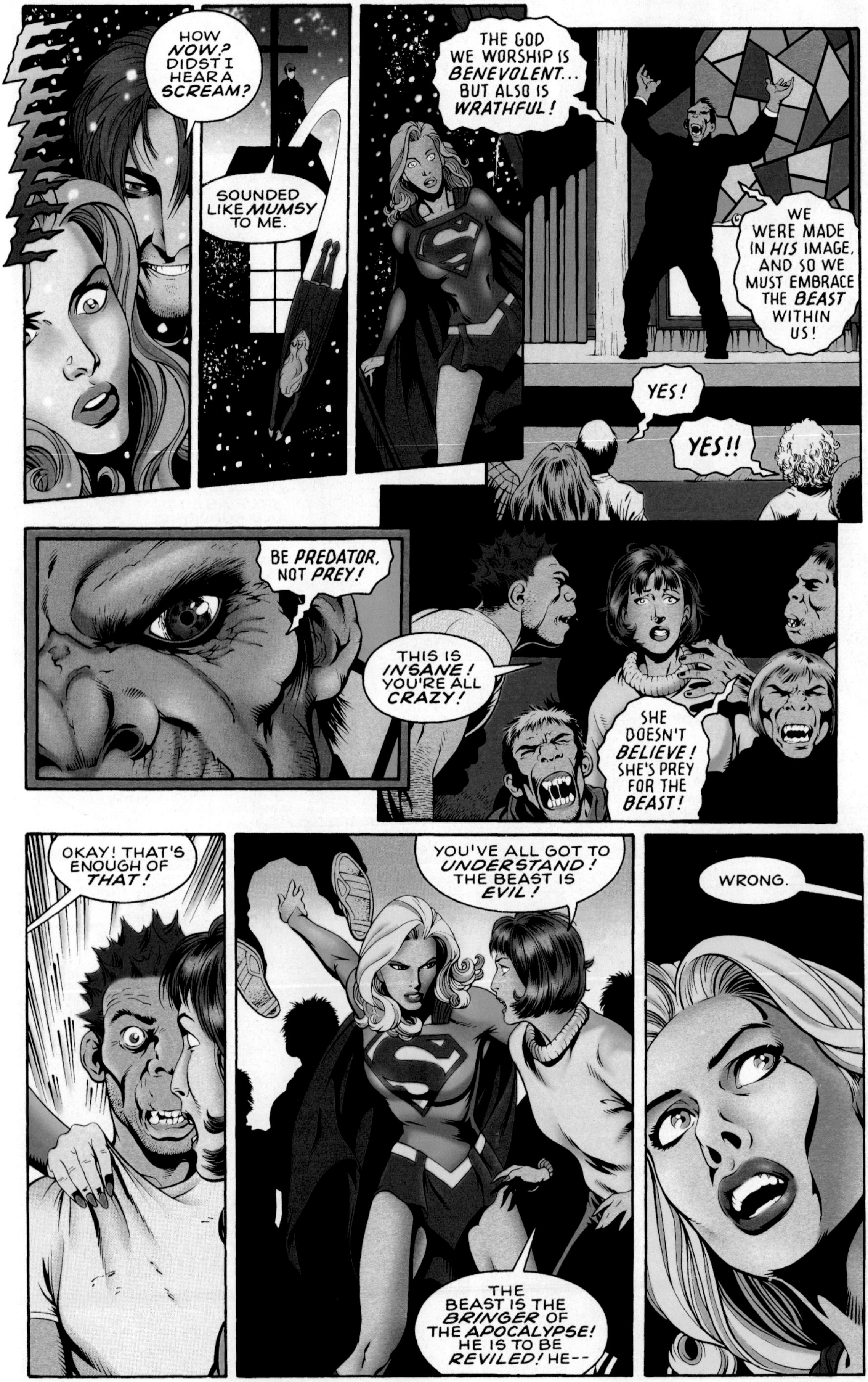
EEEEEEE
HOW NOW? DIDST I HEAR A SCREAM?
SOUNDED LIKE MUMSY TO ME.
THE GOD WE WORSHIP IS BENEVOLENT... BUT ALSO IS WRATHFUL!
WE WERE MADE IN HIS IMAGE, AND SO WE MUST EMBRACE THE BEAST WITHIN US!
YES!
YES!!
BE PREDATOR, NOT PREY!
THIS IS INSANE! YOU'RE ALL CRAZY!
SHE DOESN'T BELIEVE! SHE'S PREY FOR THE BEAST!
OKAY! THAT'S ENOUGH OF THAT!
YOU'VE ALL GOT TO UNDERSTAND! THE BEAST IS EVIL!
THE BEAST IS THE BRINGER OF THE APOCALYPSE! HE IS TO BE REVILED! HE--
WRONG.

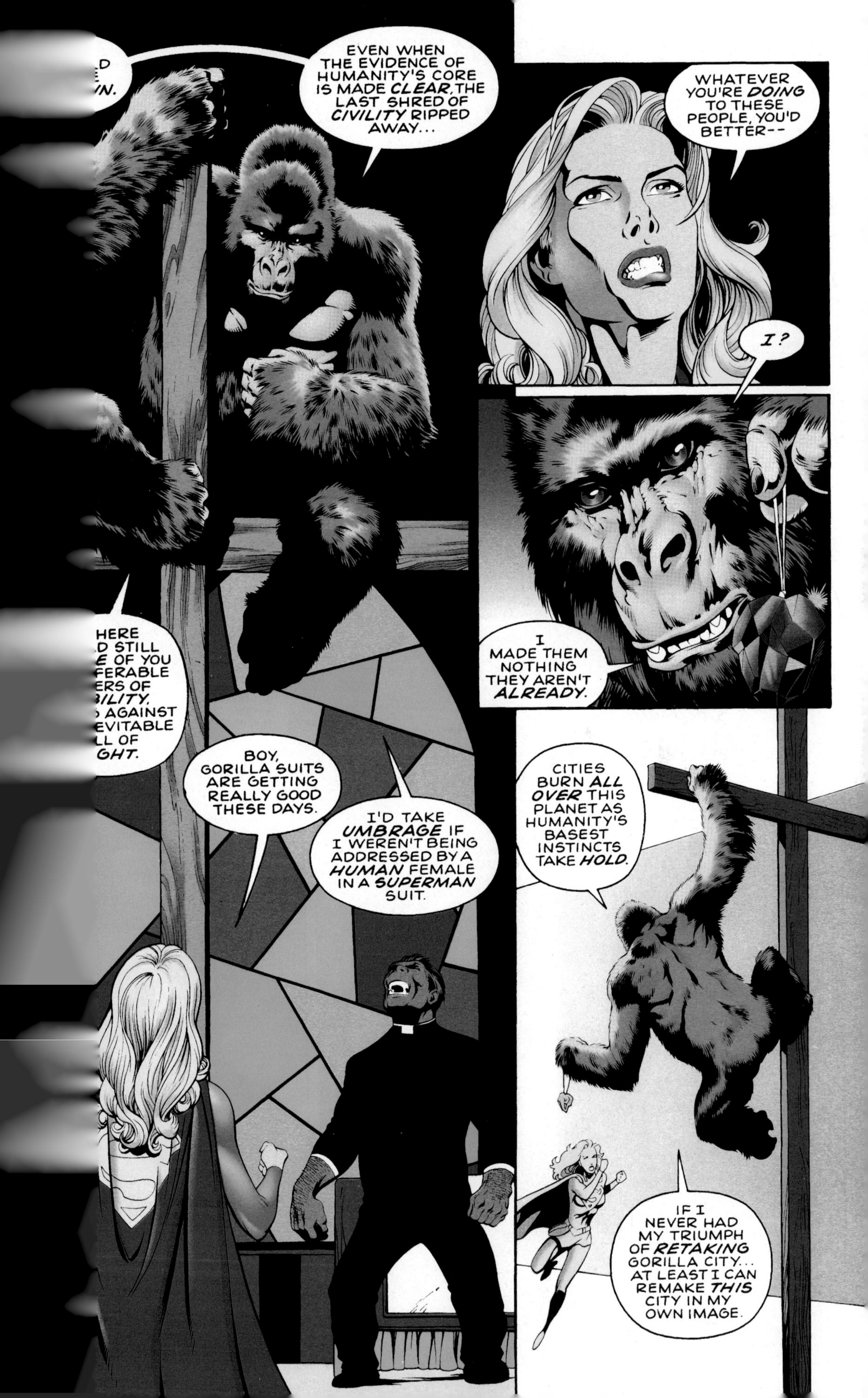
EVEN WHEN THE EVIDENCE OF HUMANITY'S CORE IS MADE *CLEAR*, THE LAST SHRED OF *CIVILITY* RIPPED AWAY...
WHATEVER YOU'RE *DOING* TO THESE PEOPLE, YOU'D BETTER--
I?
I MADE THEM NOTHING THEY AREN'T *ALREADY*.
BOY, GORILLA SUITS ARE GETTING REALLY GOOD THESE DAYS.
I'D TAKE *UMBRAGE* IF I WEREN'T BEING ADDRESSED BY A *HUMAN* FEMALE IN A *SUPERMAN* SUIT.
CITIES BURN *ALL OVER* THIS PLANET AS HUMANITY'S BASEST INSTINCTS TAKE *HOLD*.
IF I NEVER HAD MY TRIUMPH OF *RETAKING* GORILLA CITY... AT LEAST I CAN REMAKE *THIS* CITY IN MY OWN IMAGE.

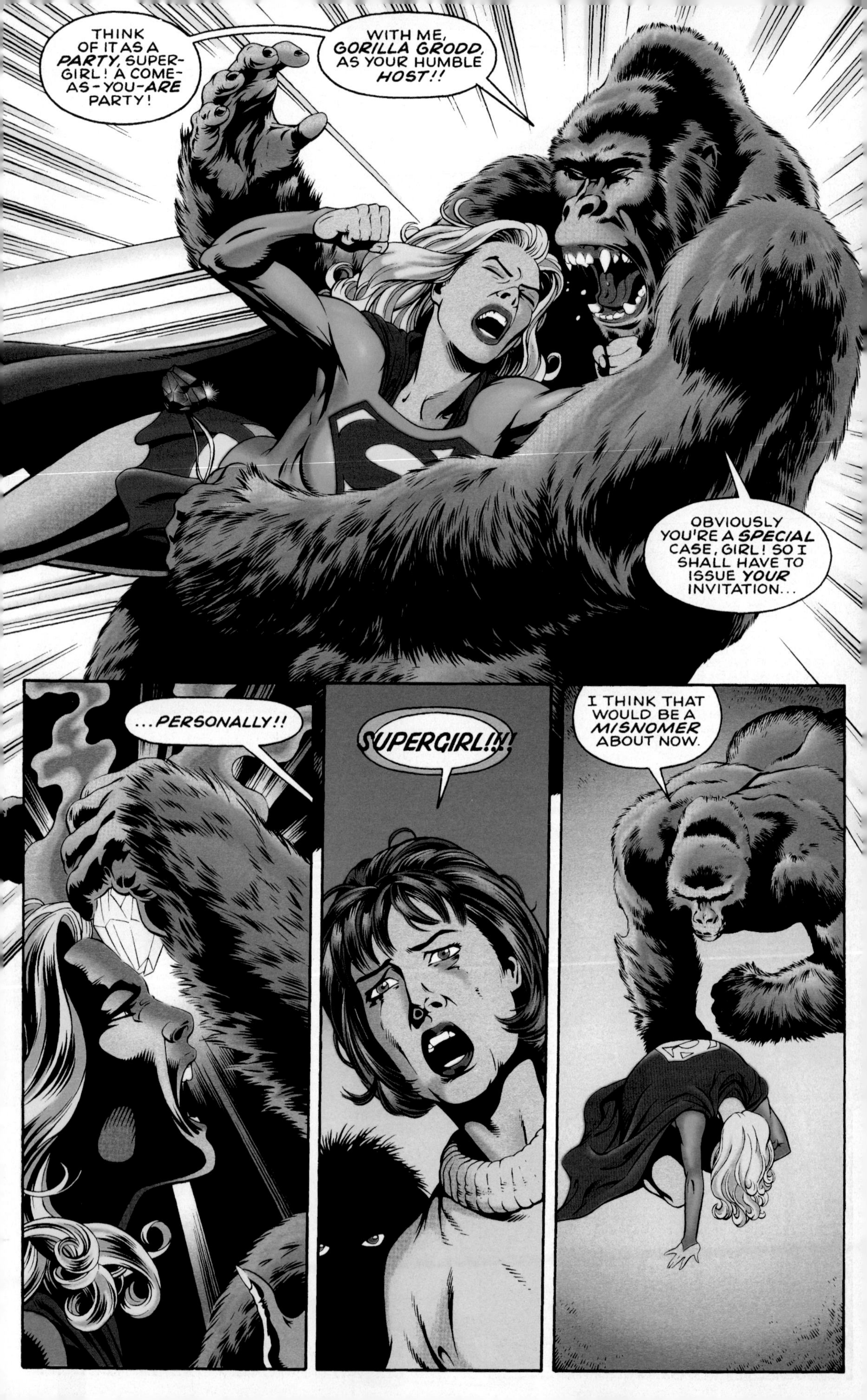
THINK OF IT AS A PARTY, SUPER-GIRL! A COME-AS-YOU-ARE PARTY!
WITH ME, GORILLA GRODD, AS YOUR HUMBLE HOST!!
OBVIOUSLY YOU'RE A SPECIAL CASE, GIRL! SO I SHALL HAVE TO ISSUE YOUR INVITATION...
...PERSONALLY!!
SUPERGIRL!!!
I THINK THAT WOULD BE A MISNOMER ABOUT NOW.

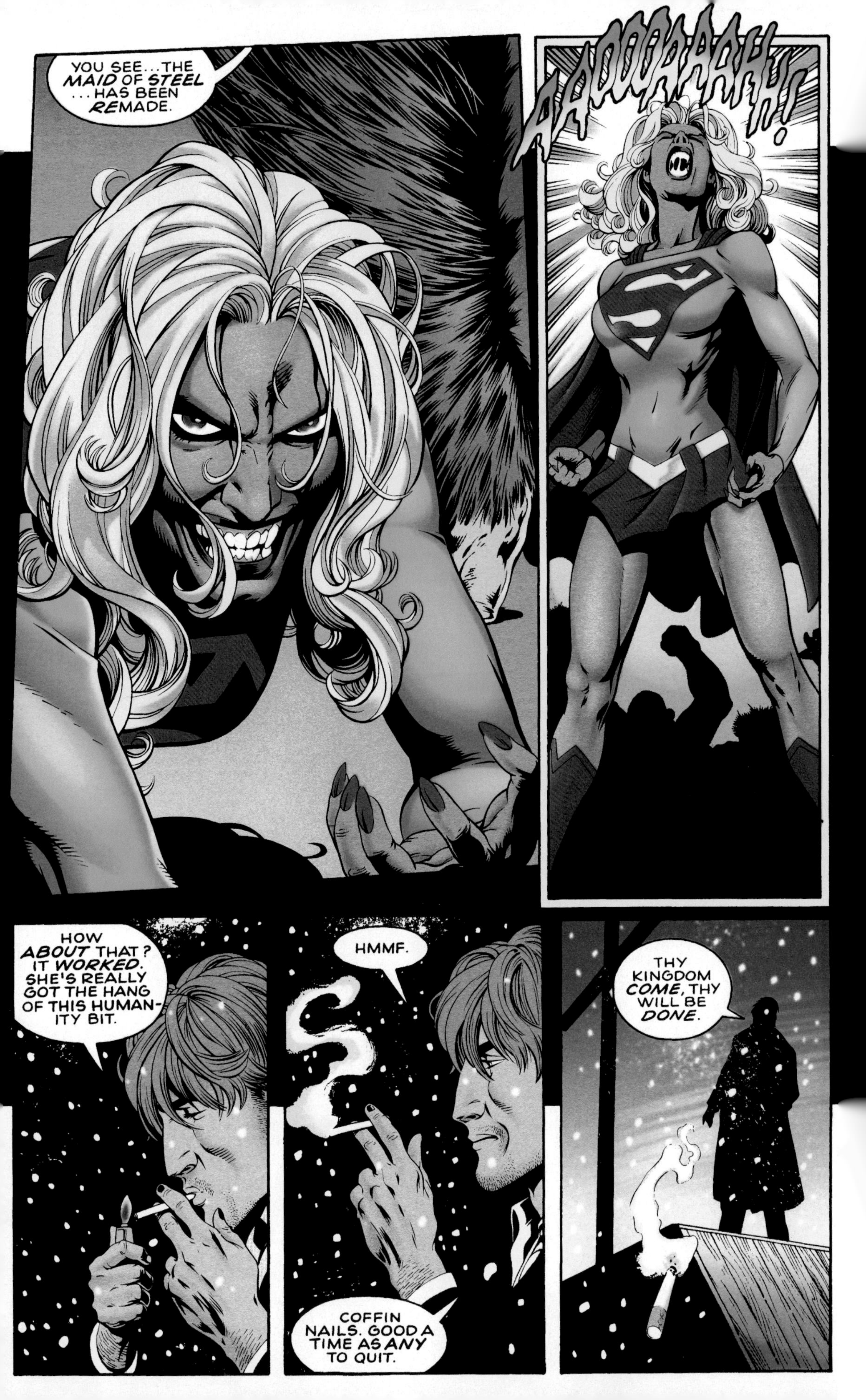
YOU SEE... THE MAID OF STEEL ...HAS BEEN REMADE.
AAOOORAARHH!
HOW ABOUT THAT? IT WORKED. SHE'S REALLY GOT THE HANG OF THIS HUMAN-ITY BIT.
HMMF.
COFFIN NAILS. GOOD A TIME AS ANY TO QUIT.
THY KINGDOM COME, THY WILL BE DONE.

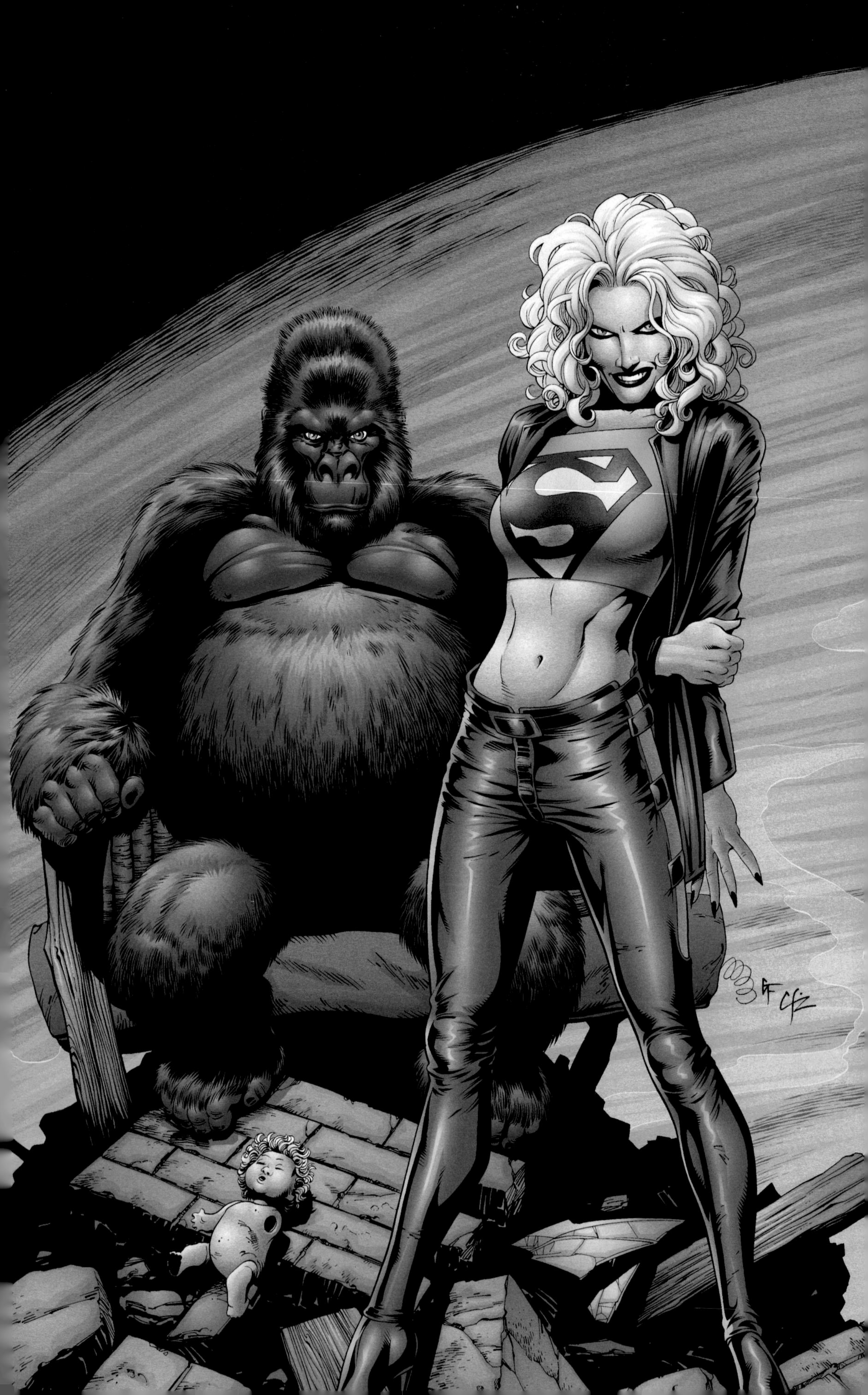

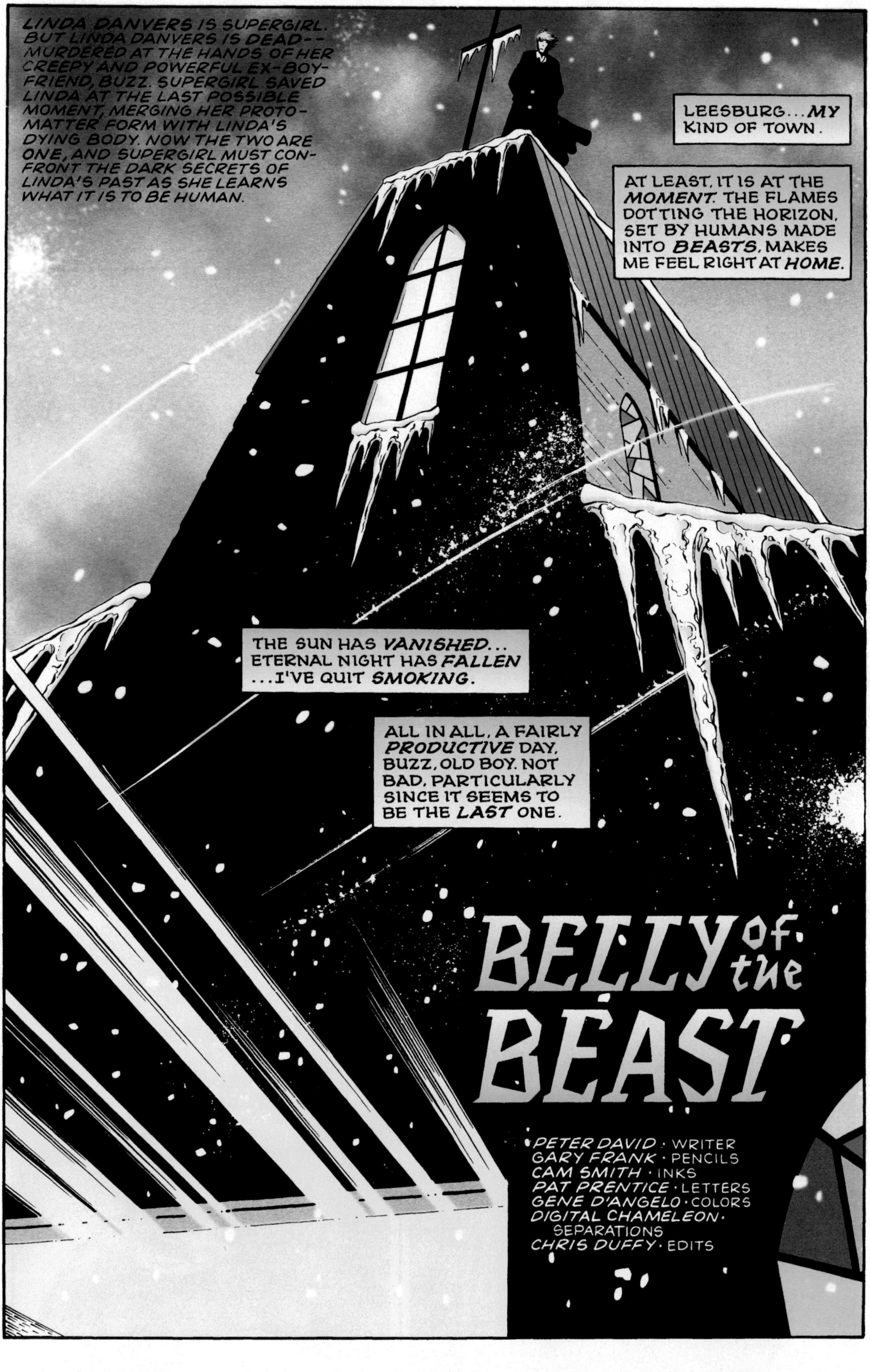
LINDA DANVERS IS SUPERGIRL. BUT LINDA DANVERS IS DEAD-- MURDERED AT THE HANDS OF HER CREEPY AND POWERFUL EX-BOY-FRIEND, BUZZ. SUPERGIRL SAVED LINDA AT THE LAST POSSIBLE MOMENT, MERGING HER PROTO-MATTER FORM WITH LINDA'S DYING BODY. NOW THE TWO ARE ONE, AND SUPERGIRL MUST CONFRONT THE DARK SECRETS OF LINDA'S PAST AS SHE LEARNS WHAT IT IS TO BE HUMAN.
LEESBURG... MY KIND OF TOWN.
AT LEAST, IT IS AT THE MOMENT. THE FLAMES DOTTING THE HORIZON, SET BY HUMANS MADE INTO BEASTS, MAKES ME FEEL RIGHT AT HOME.
THE SUN HAS VANISHED... ETERNAL NIGHT HAS FALLEN ...I'VE QUIT SMOKING.
ALL IN ALL, A FAIRLY PRODUCTIVE DAY, BUZZ, OLD BOY. NOT BAD, PARTICULARLY SINCE IT SEEMS TO BE THE LAST ONE.
BELLY of the BEAST
PETER DAVID · WRITER
GARY FRANK · PENCILS
CAM SMITH · INKS
PAT PRENTICE · LETTERS
GENE D'ANGELO · COLORS
DIGITAL CHAMELEON · SEPARATIONS
CHRIS DUFFY · EDITS

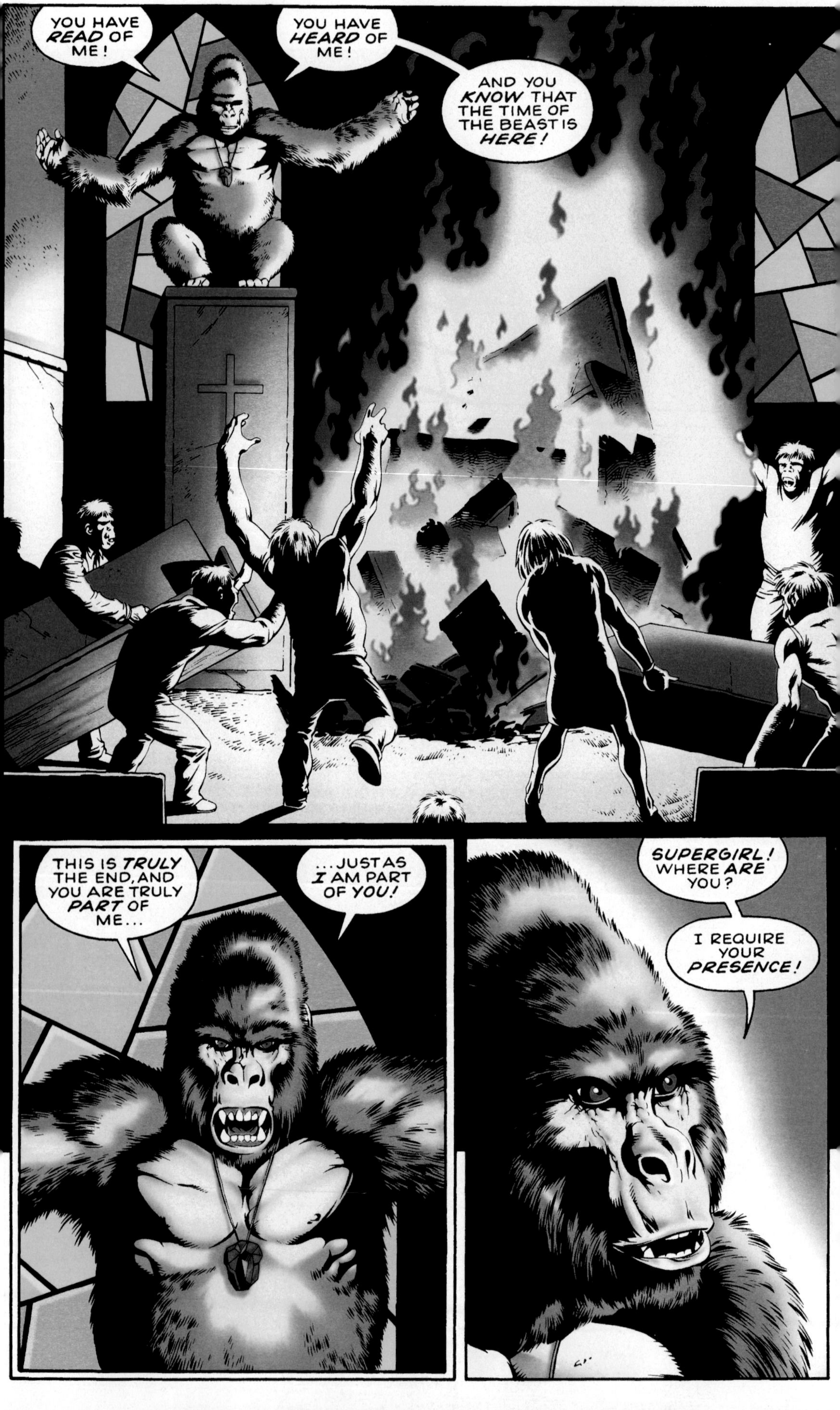
YOU HAVE READ OF ME!
YOU HAVE HEARD OF ME!
AND YOU KNOW THAT THE TIME OF THE BEAST IS HERE!
THIS IS TRULY THE END, AND YOU ARE TRULY PART OF ME...
...JUST AS I AM PART OF YOU!
SUPERGIRL! WHERE ARE YOU?
I REQUIRE YOUR PRESENCE!

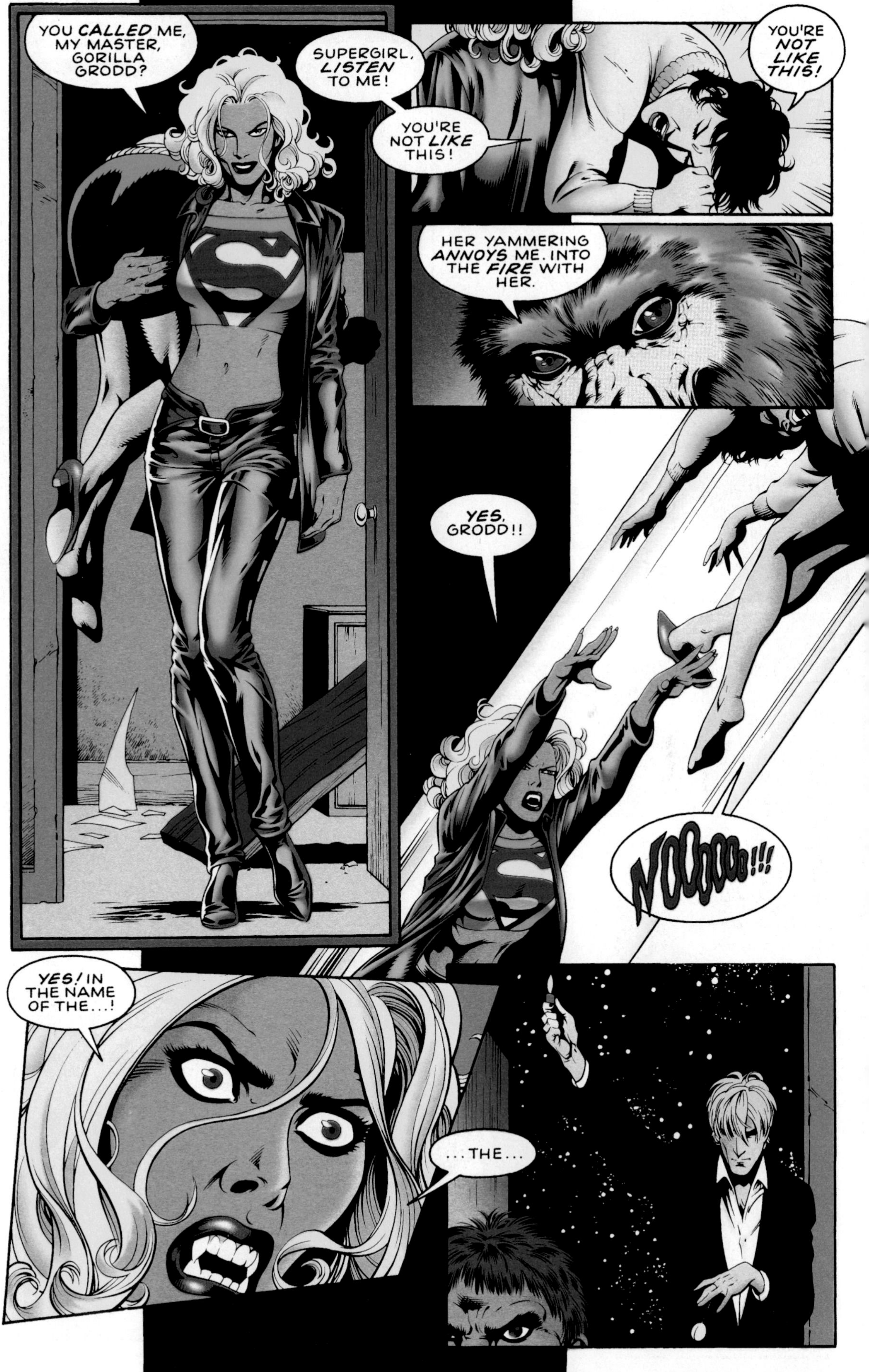

YOU CALLED ME, MY MASTER, GORILLA GRODD?
SUPERGIRL, LISTEN TO ME!
YOU'RE NOT LIKE THIS!
YOU'RE NOT LIKE THIS!
HER YAMMERING ANNOYS ME. INTO THE FIRE WITH HER.
YES, GRODD!!
NOOOOO!!!
YES! IN THE NAME OF THE...!
...THE...

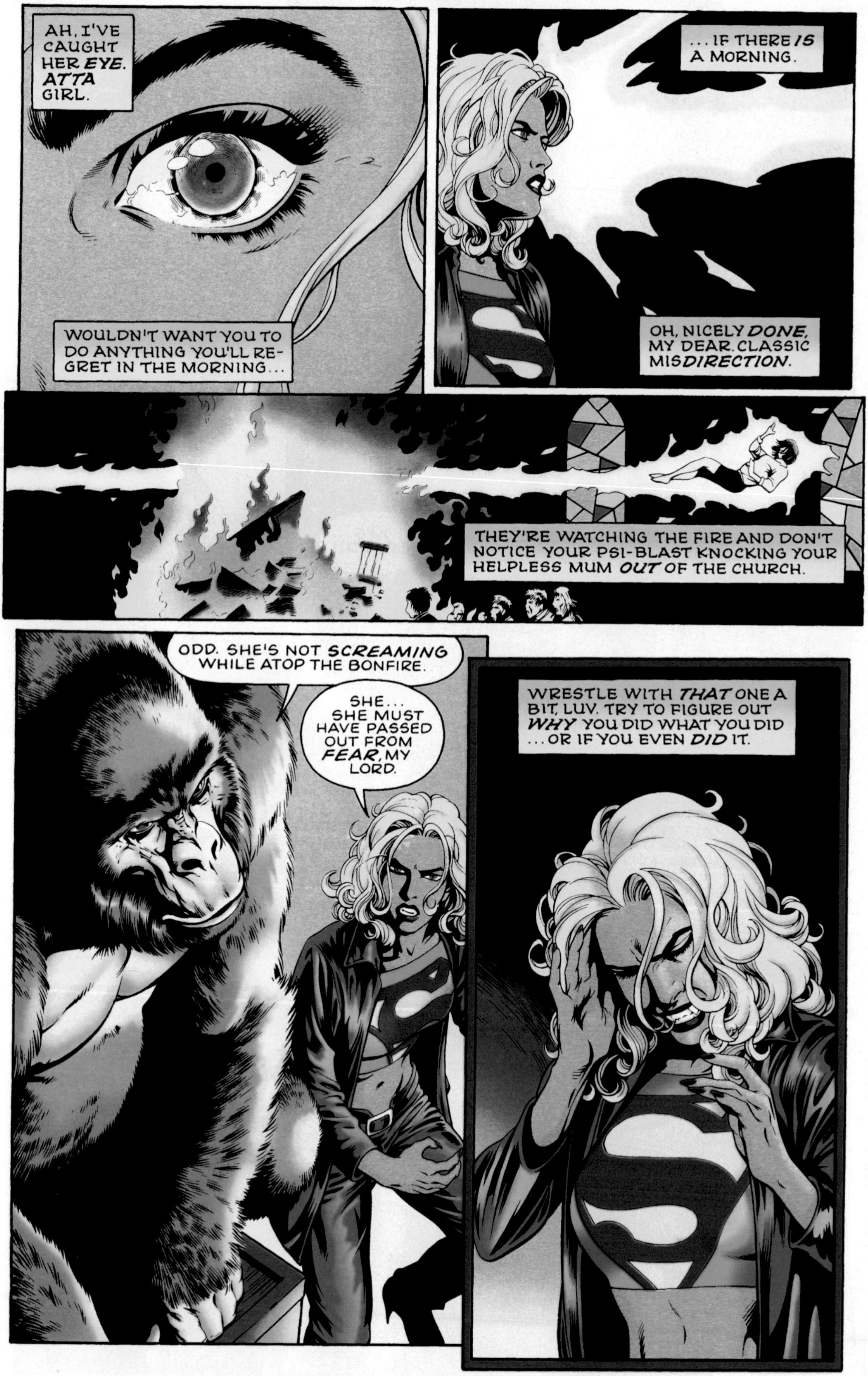
AH, I'VE CAUGHT HER EYE. ATTA GIRL.
WOULDN'T WANT YOU TO DO ANYTHING YOU'LL RE-GRET IN THE MORNING...
...IF THERE IS A MORNING.
OH, NICELY DONE, MY DEAR. CLASSIC MISDIRECTION.
THEY'RE WATCHING THE FIRE AND DON'T NOTICE YOUR PSI-BLAST KNOCKING YOUR HELPLESS MUM OUT OF THE CHURCH.
ODD. SHE'S NOT SCREAMING WHILE ATOP THE BONFIRE.
SHE... SHE MUST HAVE PASSED OUT FROM FEAR, MY LORD.
WRESTLE WITH THAT ONE A BIT, LUV. TRY TO FIGURE OUT WHY YOU DID WHAT YOU DID ...OR IF YOU EVEN DID IT.

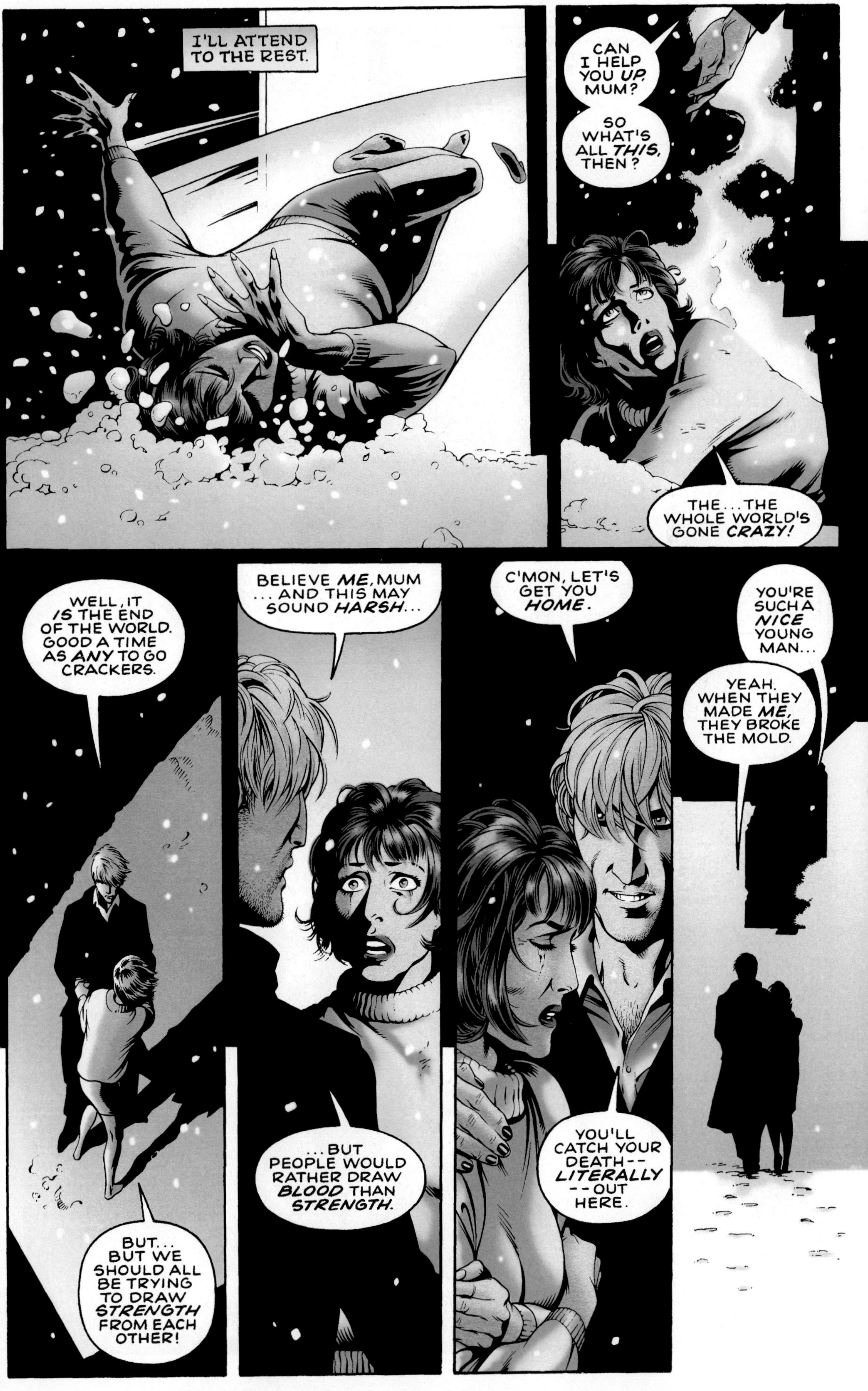
I'LL ATTEND TO THE REST.
CAN I HELP YOU UP, MUM?
SO WHAT'S ALL THIS, THEN?
THE... THE WHOLE WORLD'S GONE CRAZY!
WELL, IT IS THE END OF THE WORLD. GOOD A TIME AS ANY TO GO CRACKERS.
BUT... BUT WE SHOULD ALL BE TRYING TO DRAW STRENGTH FROM EACH OTHER!
BELIEVE ME, MUM ...AND THIS MAY SOUND HARSH...
...BUT PEOPLE WOULD RATHER DRAW BLOOD THAN STRENGTH.
C'MON, LET'S GET YOU HOME.
YOU'LL CATCH YOUR DEATH-- LITERALLY --OUT HERE.
YOU'RE SUCH A NICE YOUNG MAN...
YEAH. WHEN THEY MADE ME, THEY BROKE THE MOLD.

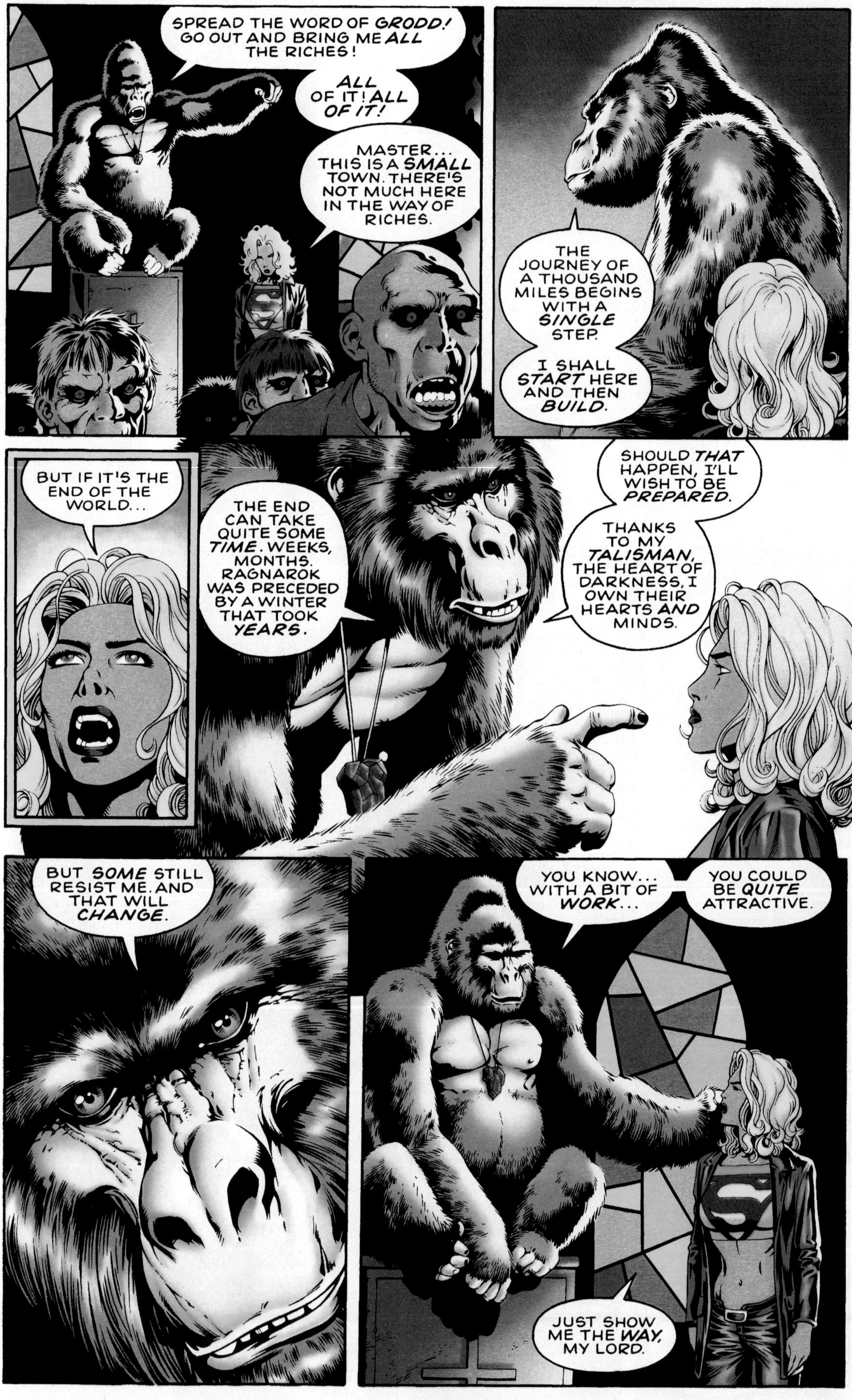
SPREAD THE WORD OF GRODD! GO OUT AND BRING ME ALL THE RICHES!
ALL OF IT! ALL OF IT!
MASTER... THIS IS A SMALL TOWN. THERE'S NOT MUCH HERE IN THE WAY OF RICHES.
THE JOURNEY OF A THOUSAND MILES BEGINS WITH A SINGLE STEP.
I SHALL START HERE AND THEN BUILD.
BUT IF IT'S THE END OF THE WORLD...
THE END CAN TAKE QUITE SOME TIME. WEEKS, MONTHS. RAGNAROK WAS PRECEDED BY A WINTER THAT TOOK YEARS.
SHOULD THAT HAPPEN, I'LL WISH TO BE PREPARED.
THANKS TO MY TALISMAN, THE HEART OF DARKNESS, I OWN THEIR HEARTS AND MINDS.
BUT SOME STILL RESIST ME. AND THAT WILL CHANGE.
YOU KNOW... WITH A BIT OF WORK...
YOU COULD BE QUITE ATTRACTIVE.
JUST SHOW ME THE WAY, MY LORD.

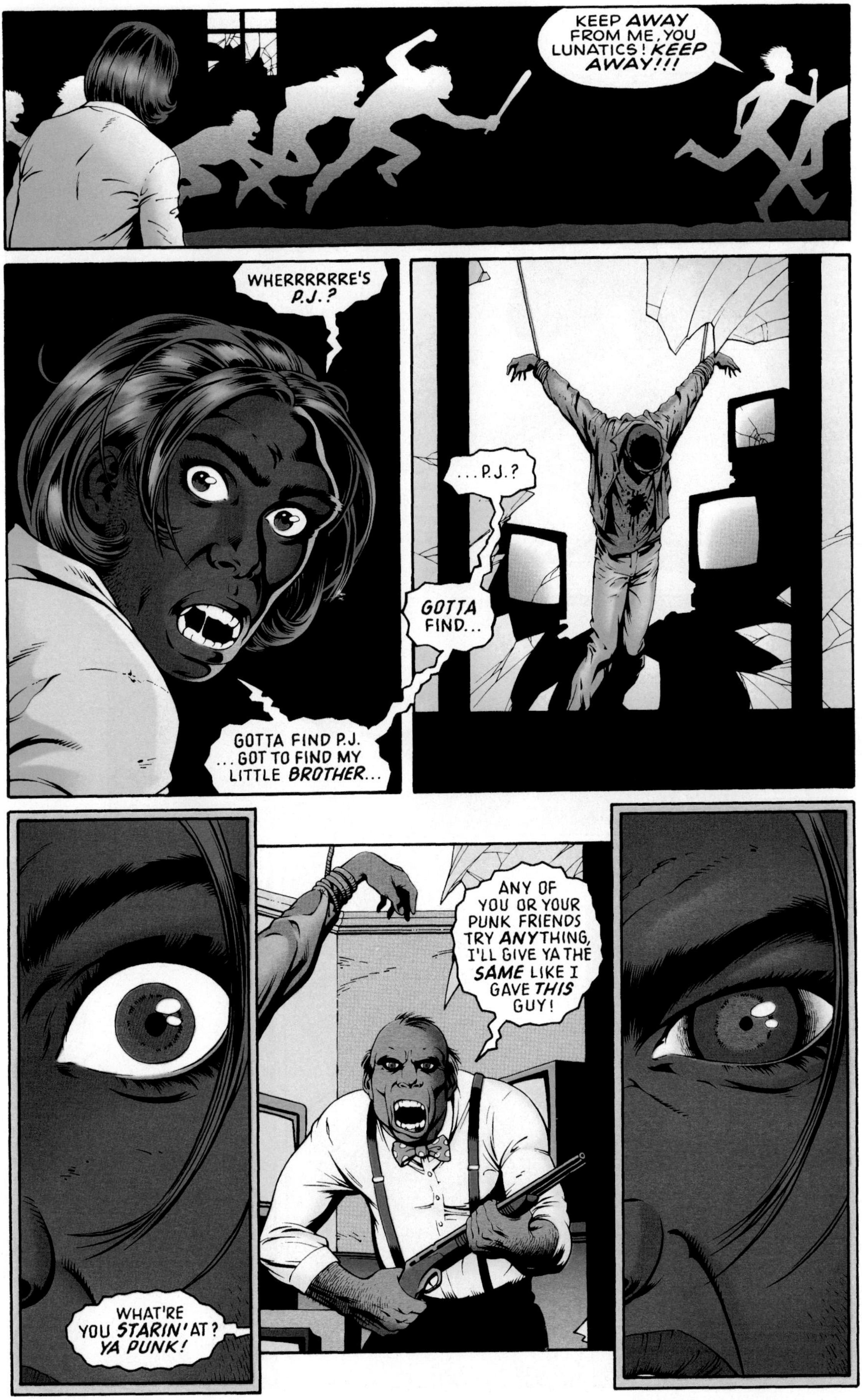
KEEP AWAY FROM ME, YOU LUNATICS! KEEP AWAY!!!
WHERRRRRRE'S P.J.?
GOTTA FIND P.J. ...GOT TO FIND MY LITTLE BROTHER...
...P.J.?
GOTTA FIND...
ANY OF YOU OR YOUR PUNK FRIENDS TRY ANYTHING, I'LL GIVE YA THE SAME LIKE I GAVE THIS GUY!
WHAT'RE YOU STARIN' AT? YA PUNK!

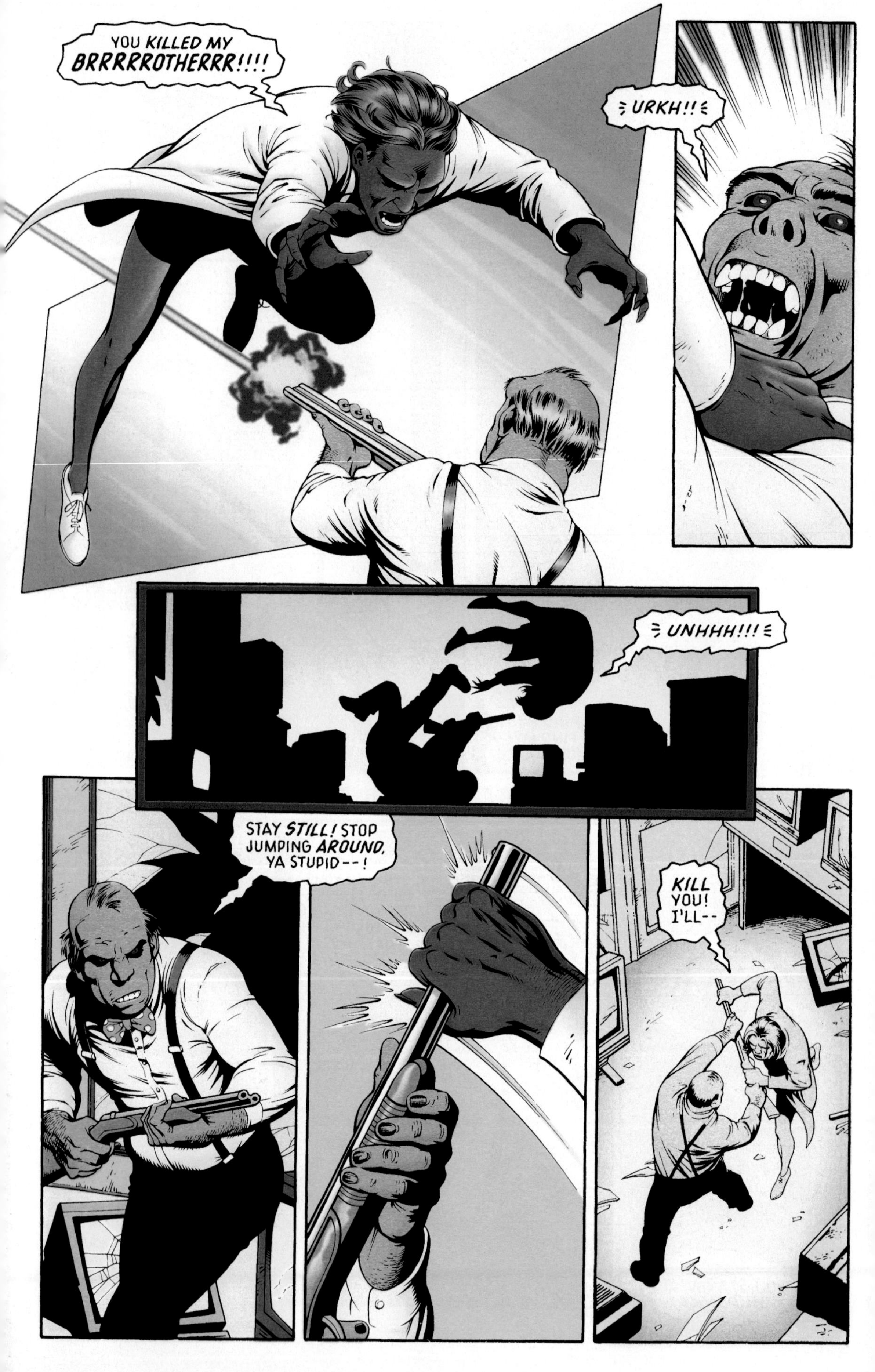
YOU KILLED MY BRRRRROTHERRR!!!!
URKH!!
UNHHH!!!
STAY STILL! STOP JUMPING AROUND, YA STUPID--!
KILL YOU! I'LL--

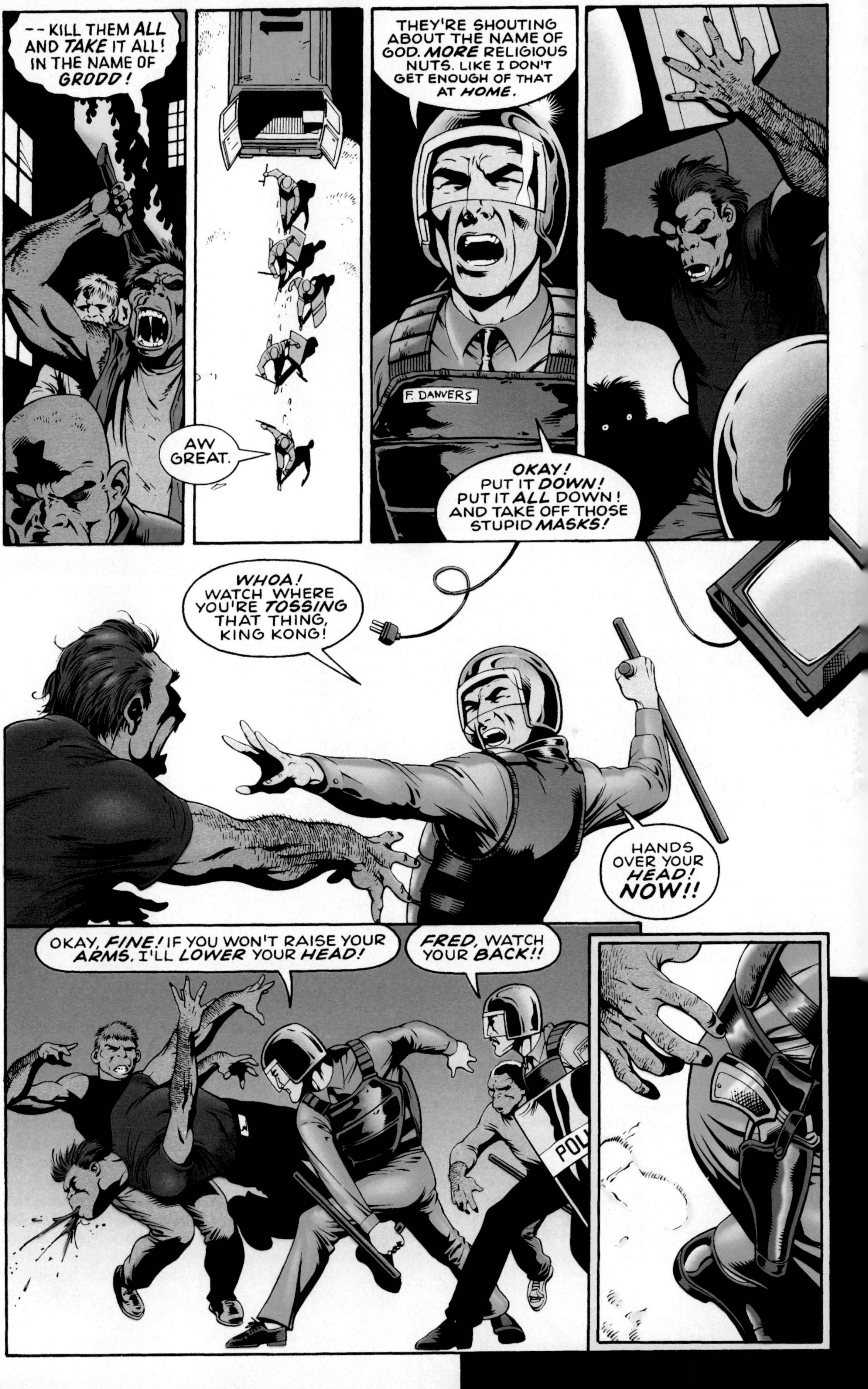

--KILL THEM ALL AND TAKE IT ALL! IN THE NAME OF GRODD!
AW GREAT.
THEY'RE SHOUTING ABOUT THE NAME OF GOD. MORE RELIGIOUS NUTS. LIKE I DON'T GET ENOUGH OF THAT AT HOME.
F. DANVERS
OKAY! PUT IT DOWN! PUT IT ALL DOWN! AND TAKE OFF THOSE STUPID MASKS!
WHOA! WATCH WHERE YOU'RE TOSSING THAT THING, KING KONG!
HANDS OVER YOUR HEAD! NOW!!
OKAY, FINE! IF YOU WON'T RAISE YOUR ARMS, I'LL LOWER YOUR HEAD!
FRED, WATCH YOUR BACK!!
POL

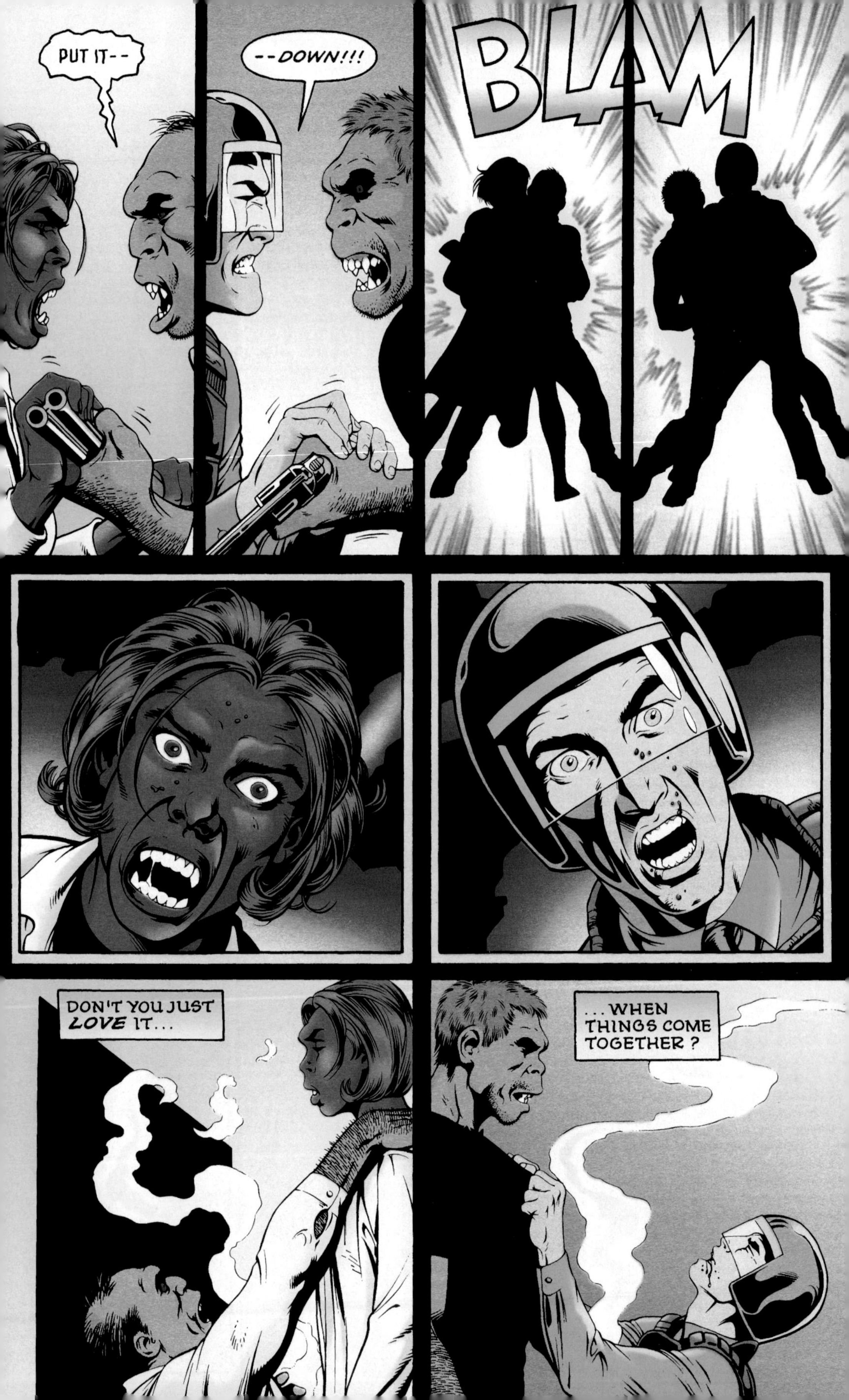
PUT IT--
--DOWN!!!
BLAM
DON'T YOU JUST LOVE IT...
...WHEN THINGS COME TOGETHER?

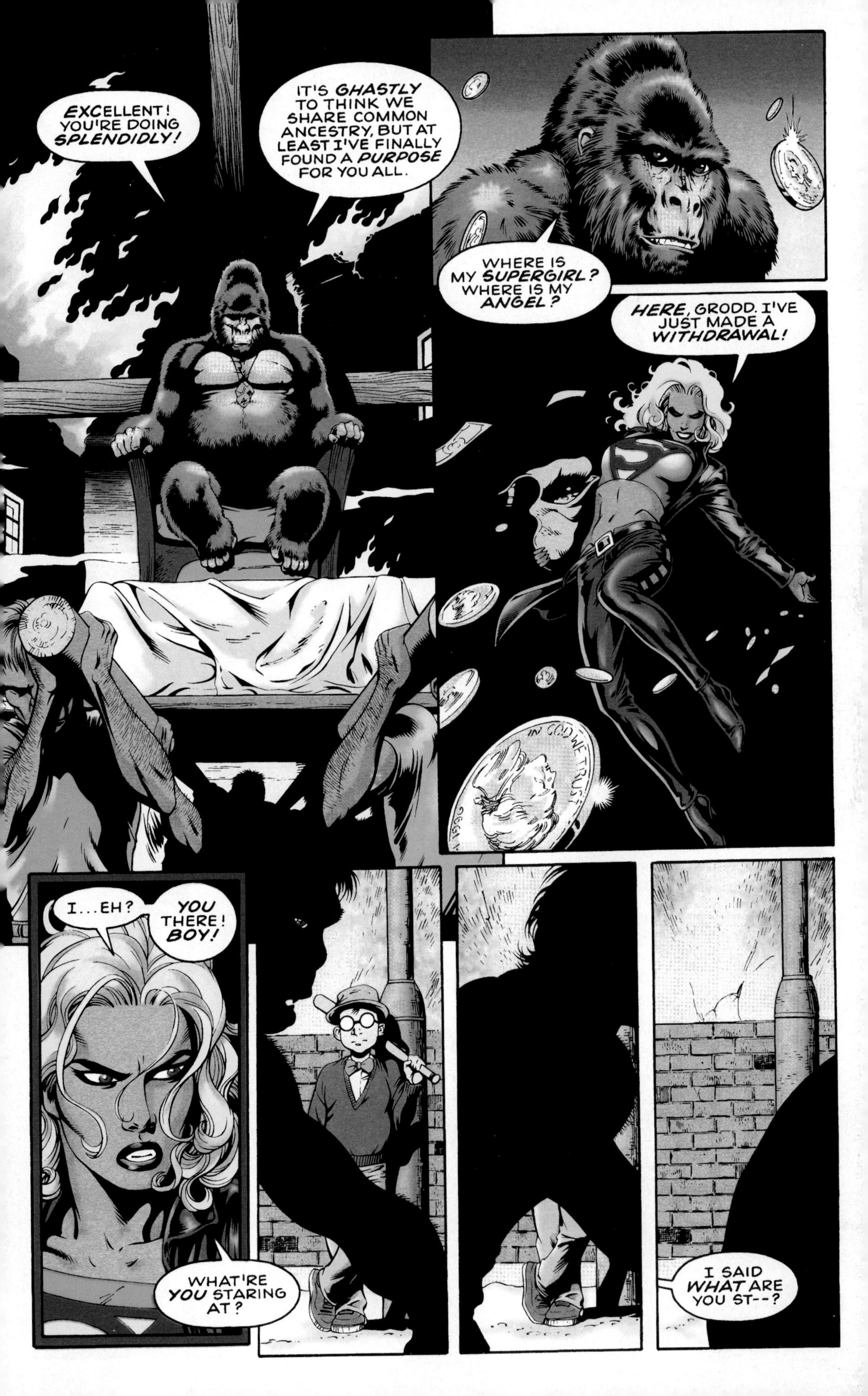
EXCELLENT! YOU'RE DOING SPLENDIDLY!
IT'S GHASTLY TO THINK WE SHARE COMMON ANCESTRY, BUT AT LEAST I'VE FINALLY FOUND A PURPOSE FOR YOU ALL.
WHERE IS MY SUPERGIRL? WHERE IS MY ANGEL?
HERE, GRODD. I'VE JUST MADE A WITHDRAWAL!
IN GOD WE TRUST
I...EH?
YOU THERE! BOY!
WHAT'RE YOU STARING AT?
I SAID WHAT ARE YOU ST--?

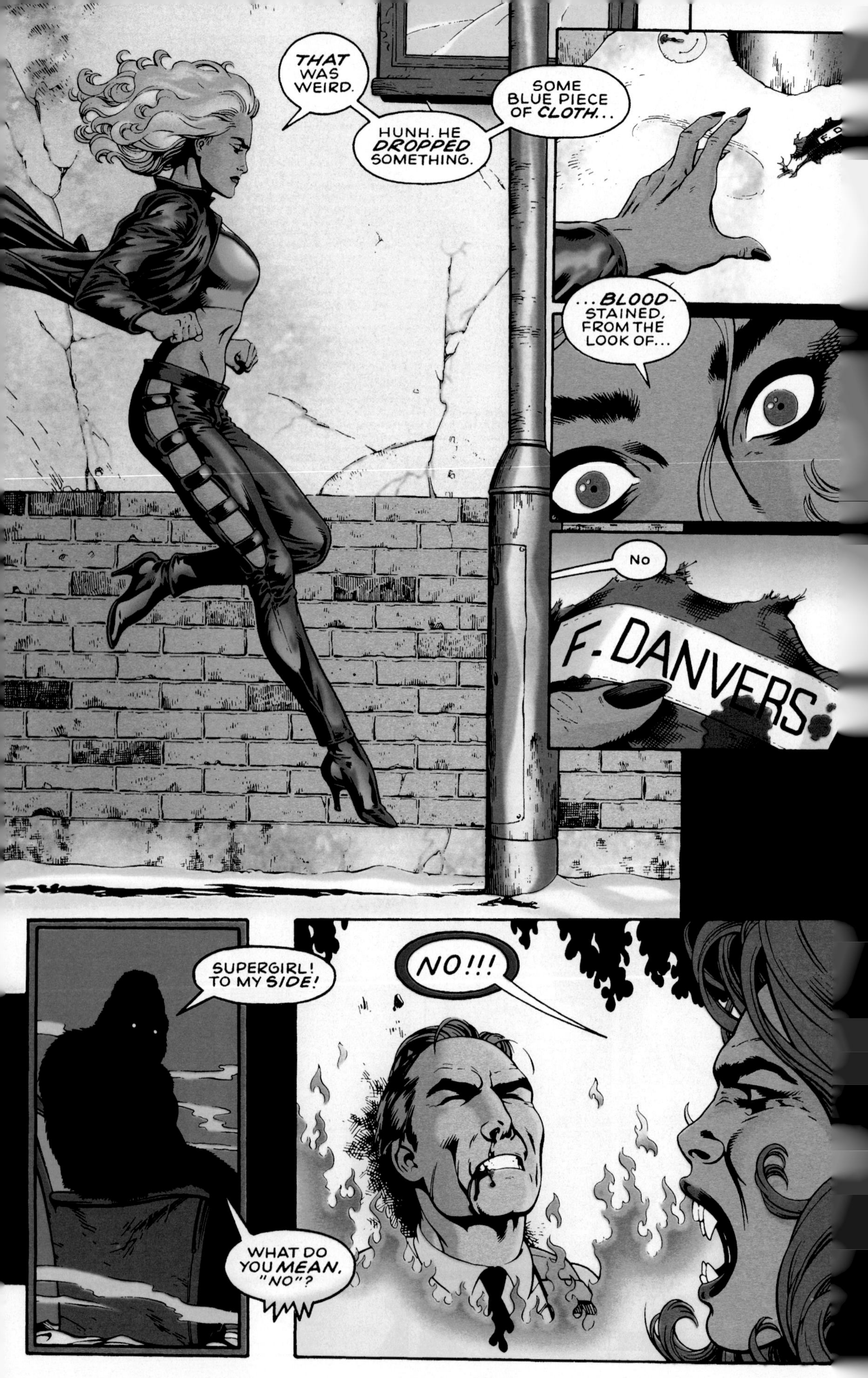
THAT WAS WEIRD.
HUNH. HE DROPPED SOMETHING.
SOME BLUE PIECE OF CLOTH...
...BLOOD-STAINED, FROM THE LOOK OF...
No
F. DANVERS
SUPERGIRL! TO MY SIDE!
NO!!!
WHAT DO YOU MEAN, "NO"?

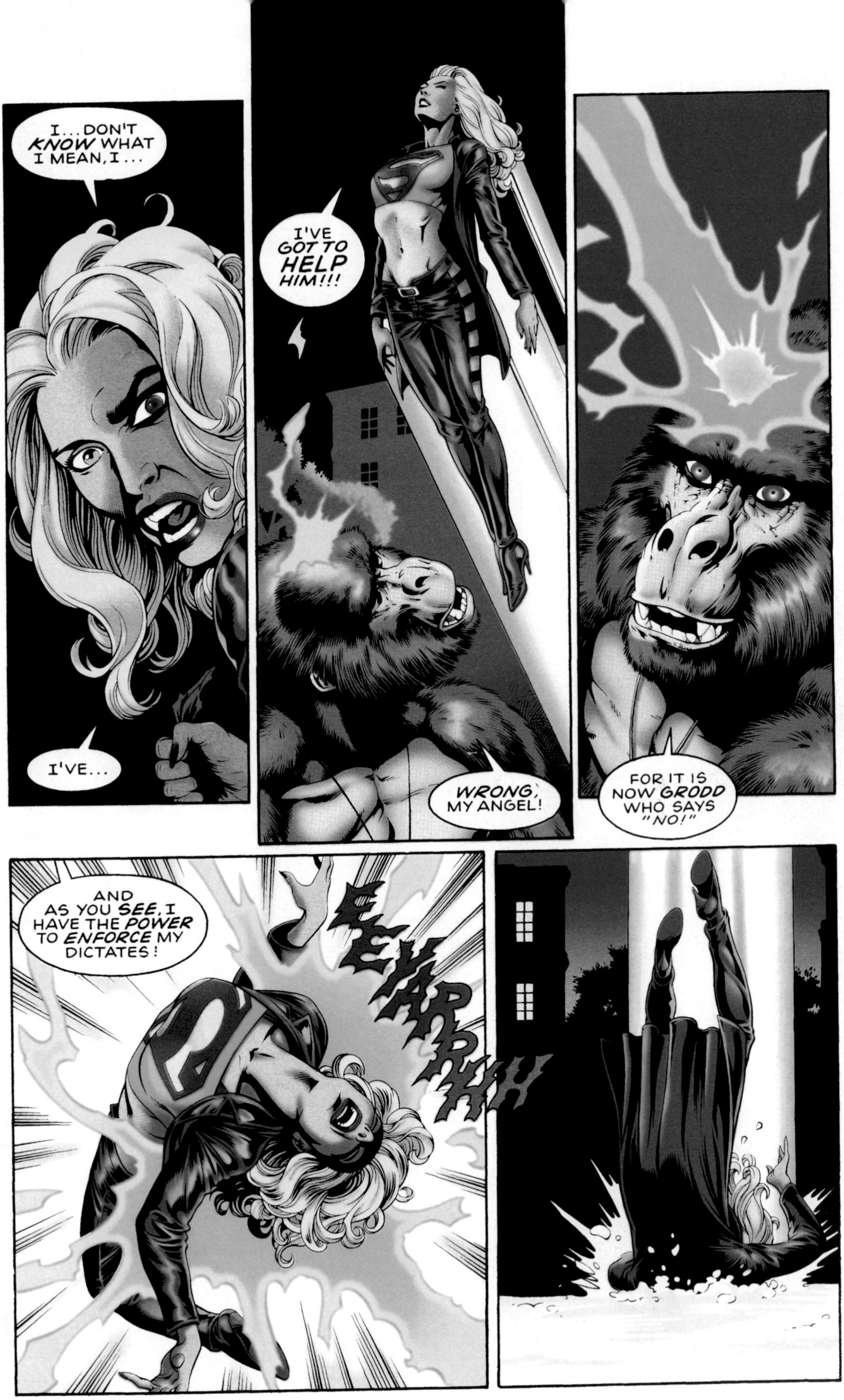
I...DON'T KNOW WHAT I MEAN, I...
I'VE...
I'VE GOT TO HELP HIM!!!
WRONG, MY ANGEL!
FOR IT IS NOW GRODD WHO SAYS "NO!"
AND AS YOU SEE, I HAVE THE POWER TO ENFORCE MY DICTATES!
EEEYARRHH

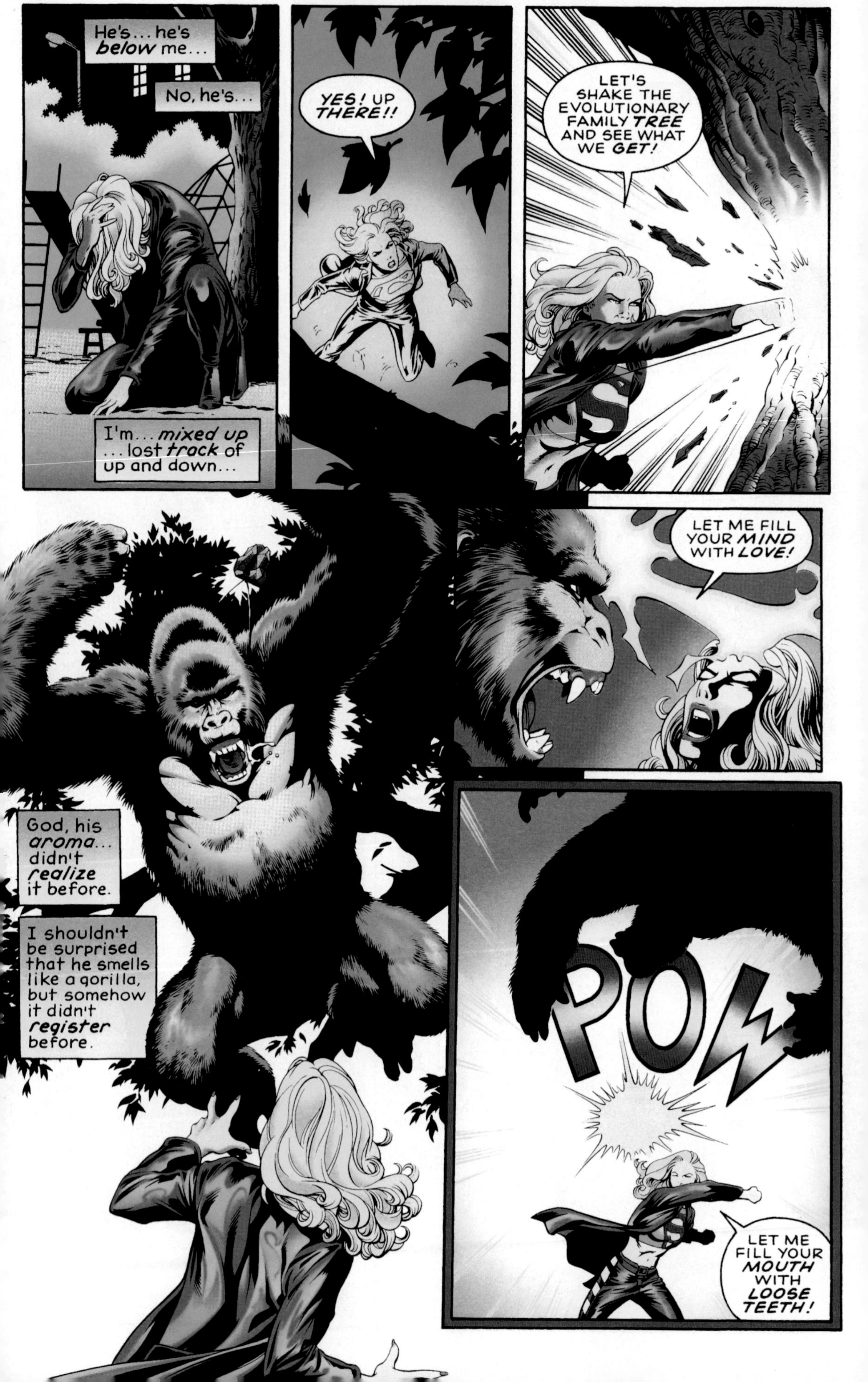
He's... he's below me...
No, he's...
I'm... mixed up ...lost track of up and down...
YES! UP THERE!!
LET'S SHAKE THE EVOLUTIONARY FAMILY TREE AND SEE WHAT WE GET!
God, his aroma... didn't realize it before.
I shouldn't be surprised that he smells like a gorilla, but somehow it didn't register before.
LET ME FILL YOUR MIND WITH LOVE!
POW
LET ME FILL YOUR MOUTH WITH LOOSE TEETH!

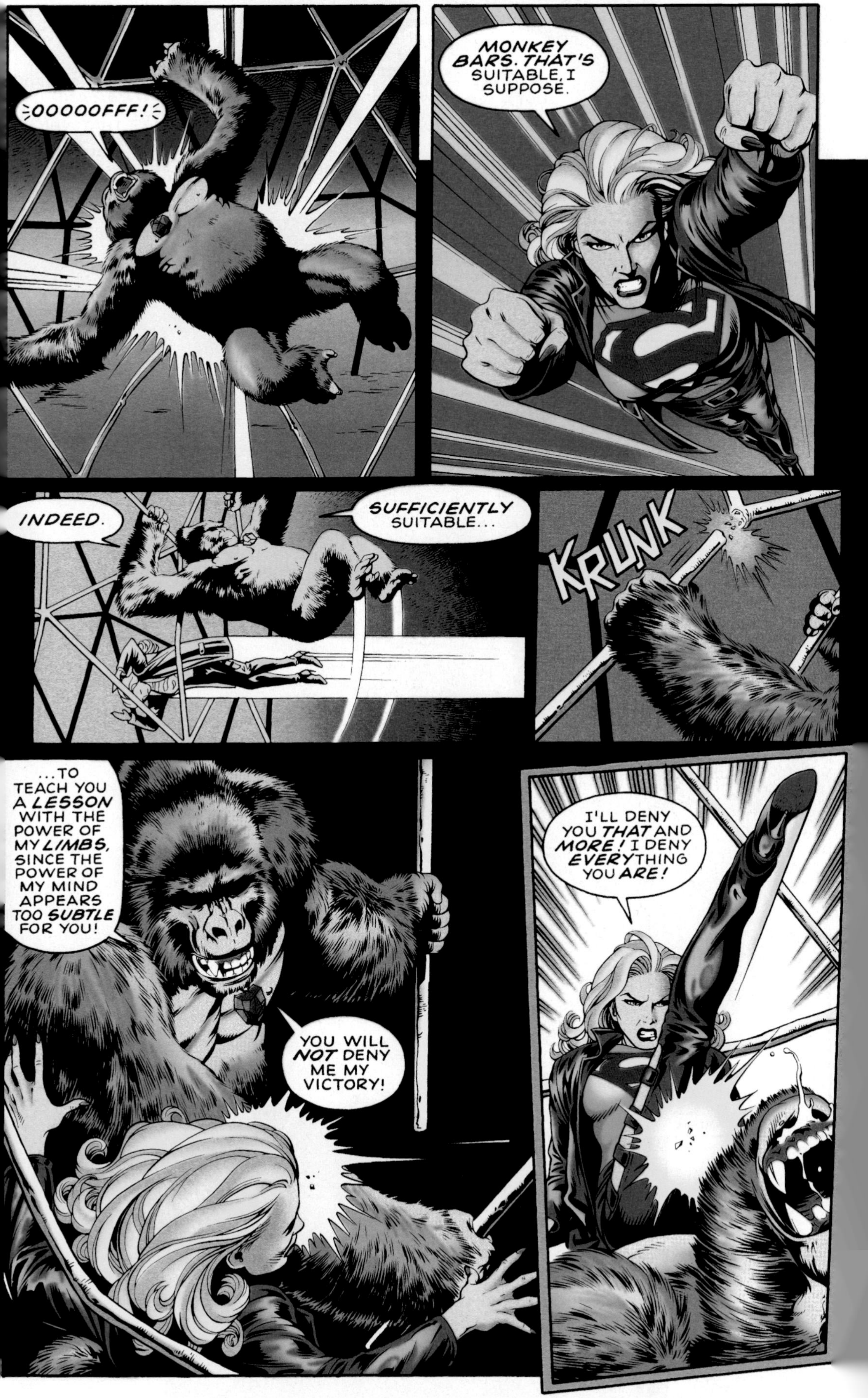
OOOOOFFF!
MONKEY BARS. THAT'S SUITABLE, I SUPPOSE.
INDEED.
SUFFICIENTLY SUITABLE...
KRUNK
...TO TEACH YOU A LESSON WITH THE POWER OF MY LIMBS, SINCE THE POWER OF MY MIND APPEARS TOO SUBTLE FOR YOU!
YOU WILL NOT DENY ME MY VICTORY!
I'LL DENY YOU THAT AND MORE! I DENY EVERYTHING YOU ARE!

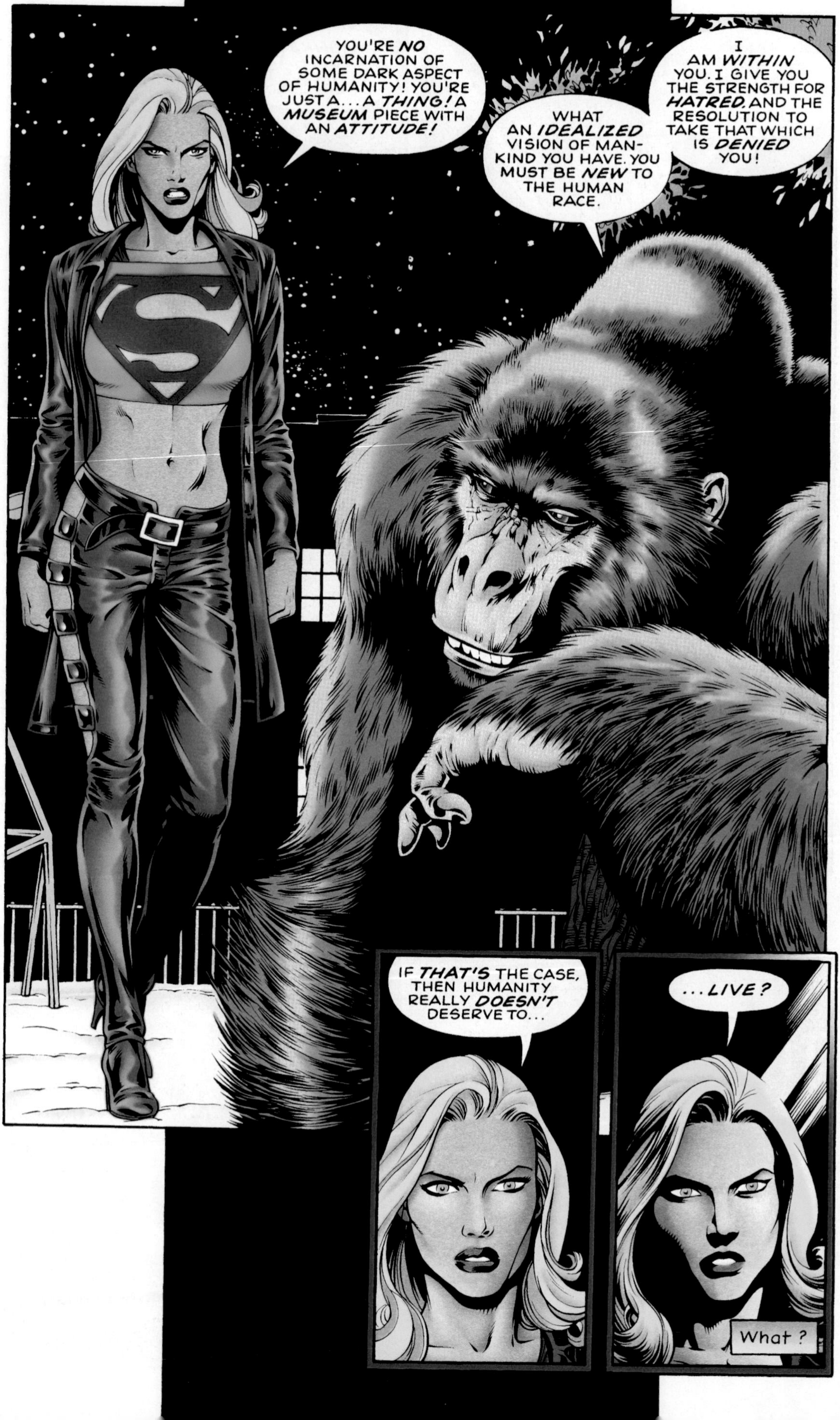
YOU'RE NO INCARNATION OF SOME DARK ASPECT OF HUMANITY! YOU'RE JUST A... A THING! A MUSEUM PIECE WITH AN ATTITUDE!
WHAT AN IDEALIZED VISION OF MANKIND YOU HAVE. YOU MUST BE NEW TO THE HUMAN RACE.
I AM WITHIN YOU. I GIVE YOU THE STRENGTH FOR HATRED, AND THE RESOLUTION TO TAKE THAT WHICH IS DENIED YOU!
IF THAT'S THE CASE, THEN HUMANITY REALLY DOESN'T DESERVE TO...
...LIVE?
What?

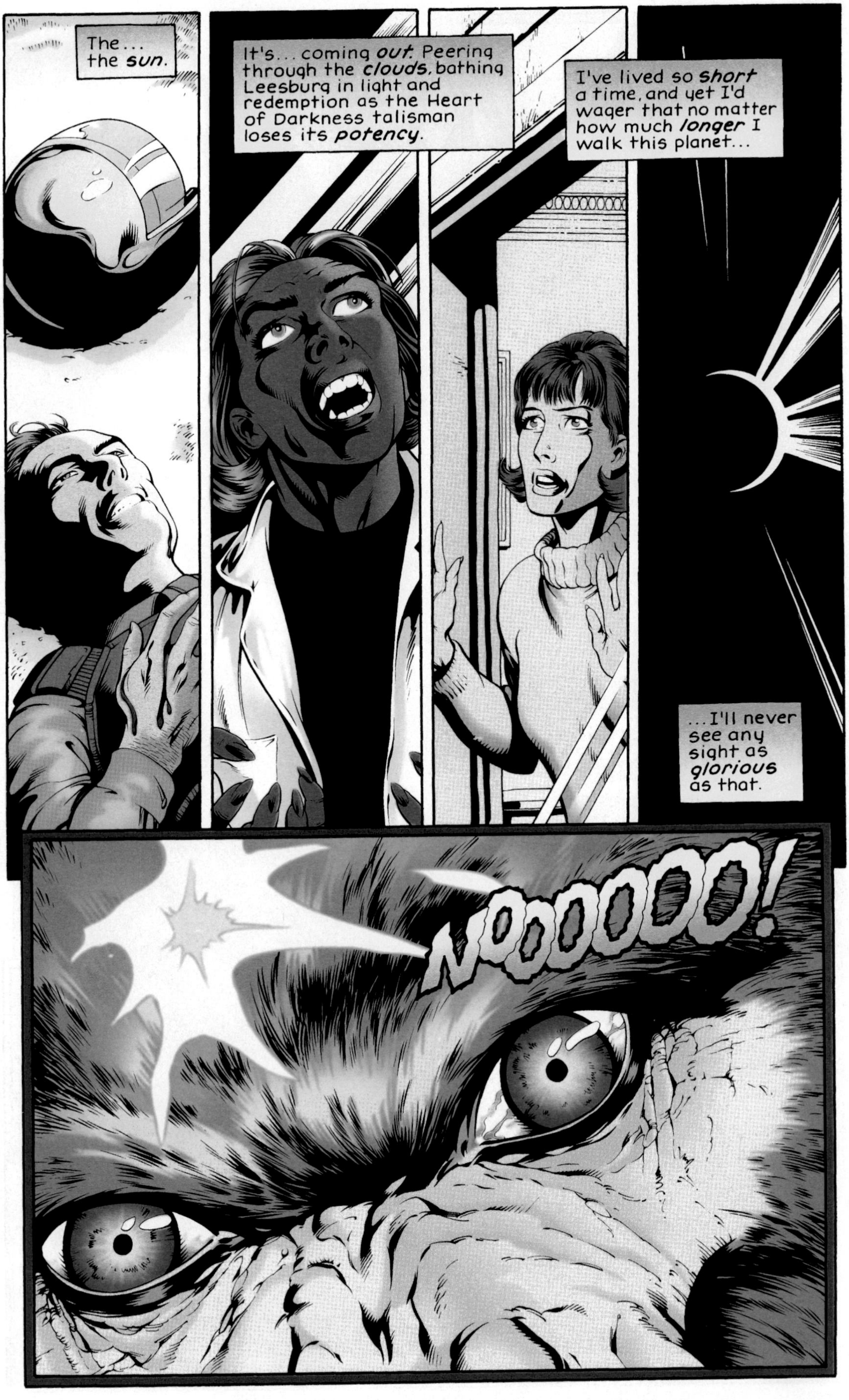
The... the sun.
It's... coming out. Peering through the clouds, bathing Leesburg in light and redemption as the Heart of Darkness talisman loses its potency.
I've lived so short a time, and yet I'd wager that no matter how much longer I walk this planet...
...I'll never see any sight as glorious as that.
NOOOOOO!

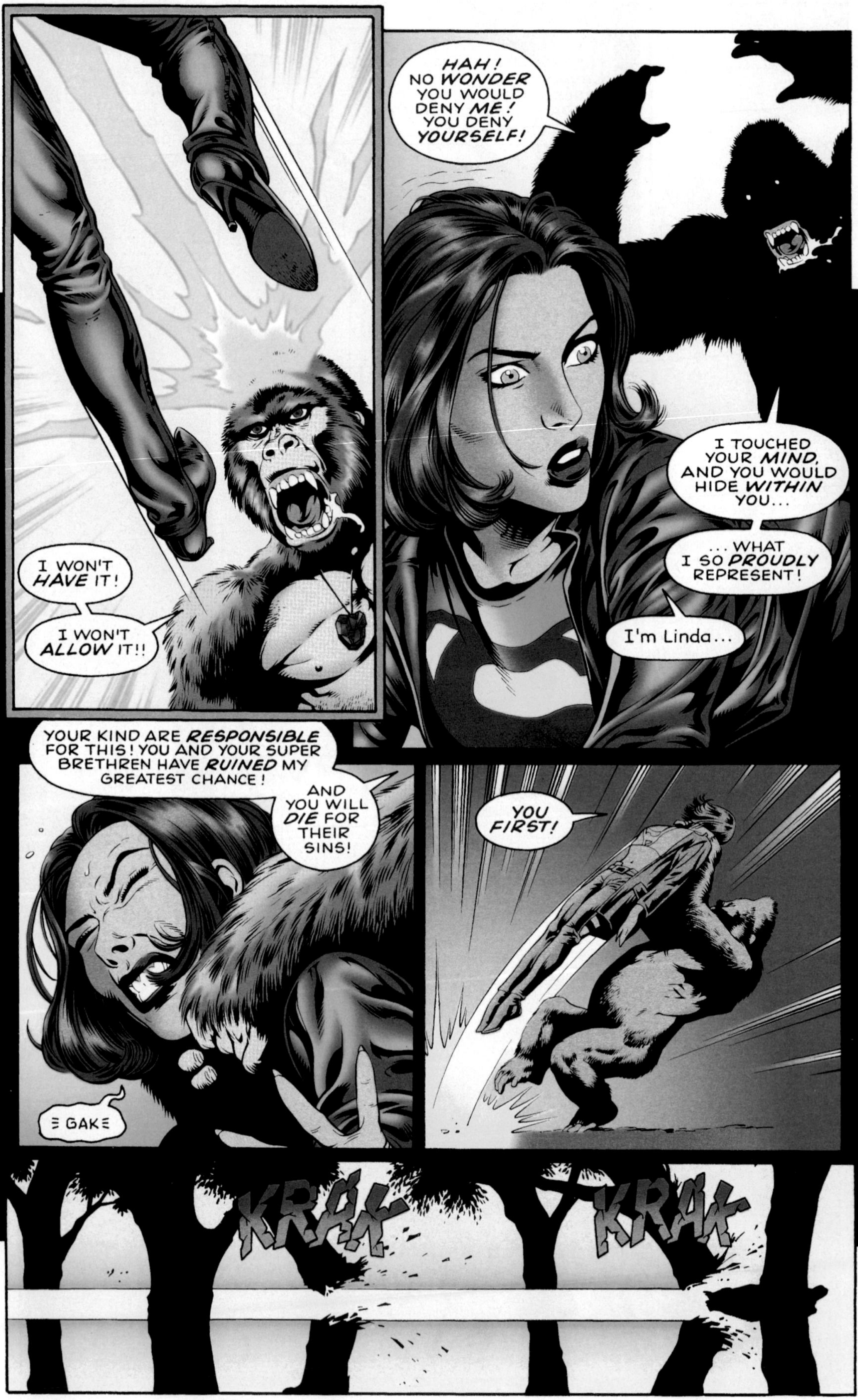
HAH! NO WONDER YOU WOULD DENY ME! YOU DENY YOURSELF!
I TOUCHED YOUR MIND, AND YOU WOULD HIDE WITHIN YOU...
... WHAT I SO PROUDLY REPRESENT!
I'm Linda...
I WON'T HAVE IT!
I WON'T ALLOW IT!!
YOUR KIND ARE RESPONSIBLE FOR THIS! YOU AND YOUR SUPER BRETHREN HAVE RUINED MY GREATEST CHANCE!
AND YOU WILL DIE FOR THEIR SINS!
GAK
YOU FIRST!
KRAK
KRAK

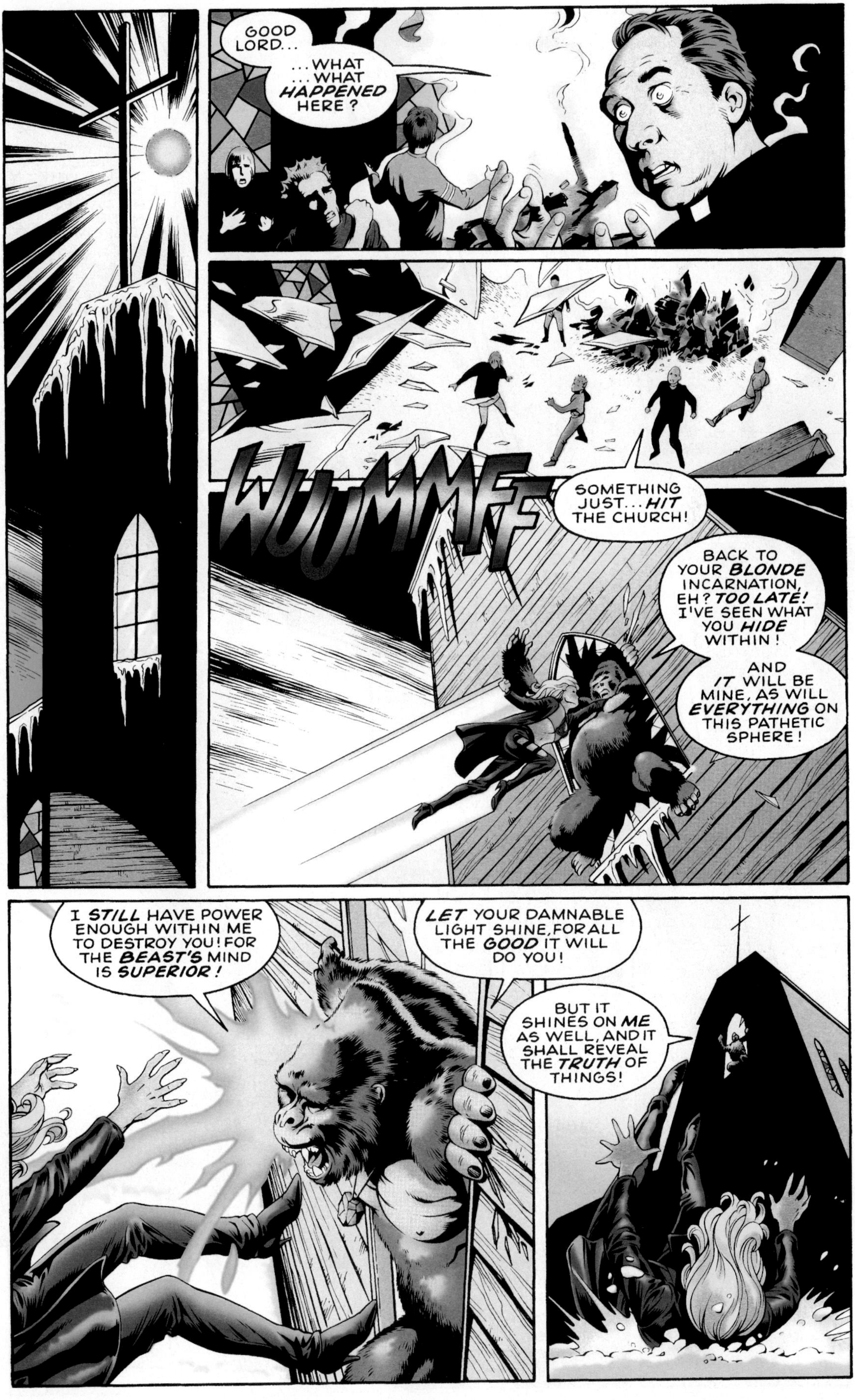
GOOD LORD...
...WHAT ...WHAT HAPPENED HERE?
WUUMMFF
SOMETHING JUST... HIT THE CHURCH!
BACK TO YOUR BLONDE INCARNATION, EH? TOO LATE! I'VE SEEN WHAT YOU HIDE WITHIN!
AND IT WILL BE MINE, AS WILL EVERYTHING ON THIS PATHETIC SPHERE!
I STILL HAVE POWER ENOUGH WITHIN ME TO DESTROY YOU! FOR THE BEAST'S MIND IS SUPERIOR!
LET YOUR DAMNABLE LIGHT SHINE, FOR ALL THE GOOD IT WILL DO YOU!
BUT IT SHINES ON ME AS WELL, AND IT SHALL REVEAL THE TRUTH OF THINGS!

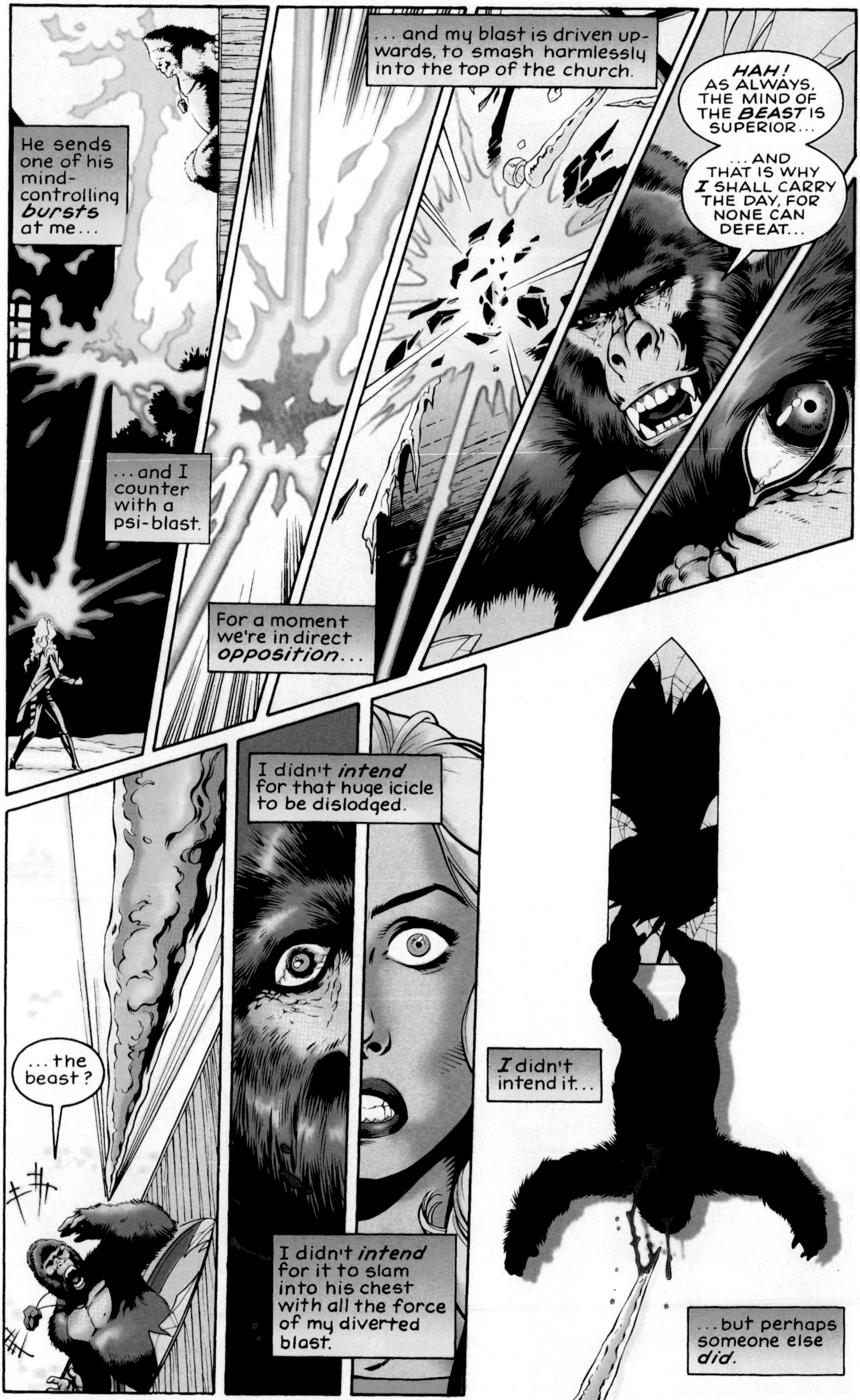
He sends one of his mind-controlling *bursts* at me...
...and I counter with a psi-blast.
For a moment we're in direct *opposition*...
...and my blast is driven upwards, to smash harmlessly into the top of the church.
HAH! AS ALWAYS, THE MIND OF THE *BEAST* IS SUPERIOR...
...AND THAT IS WHY *I* SHALL CARRY THE DAY, FOR NONE CAN DEFEAT...
...the beast?
I didn't *intend* for that huge icicle to be dislodged.
I didn't *intend* for it to slam into his chest with all the force of my diverted blast.
I didn't intend it...
...but perhaps someone else *did*.

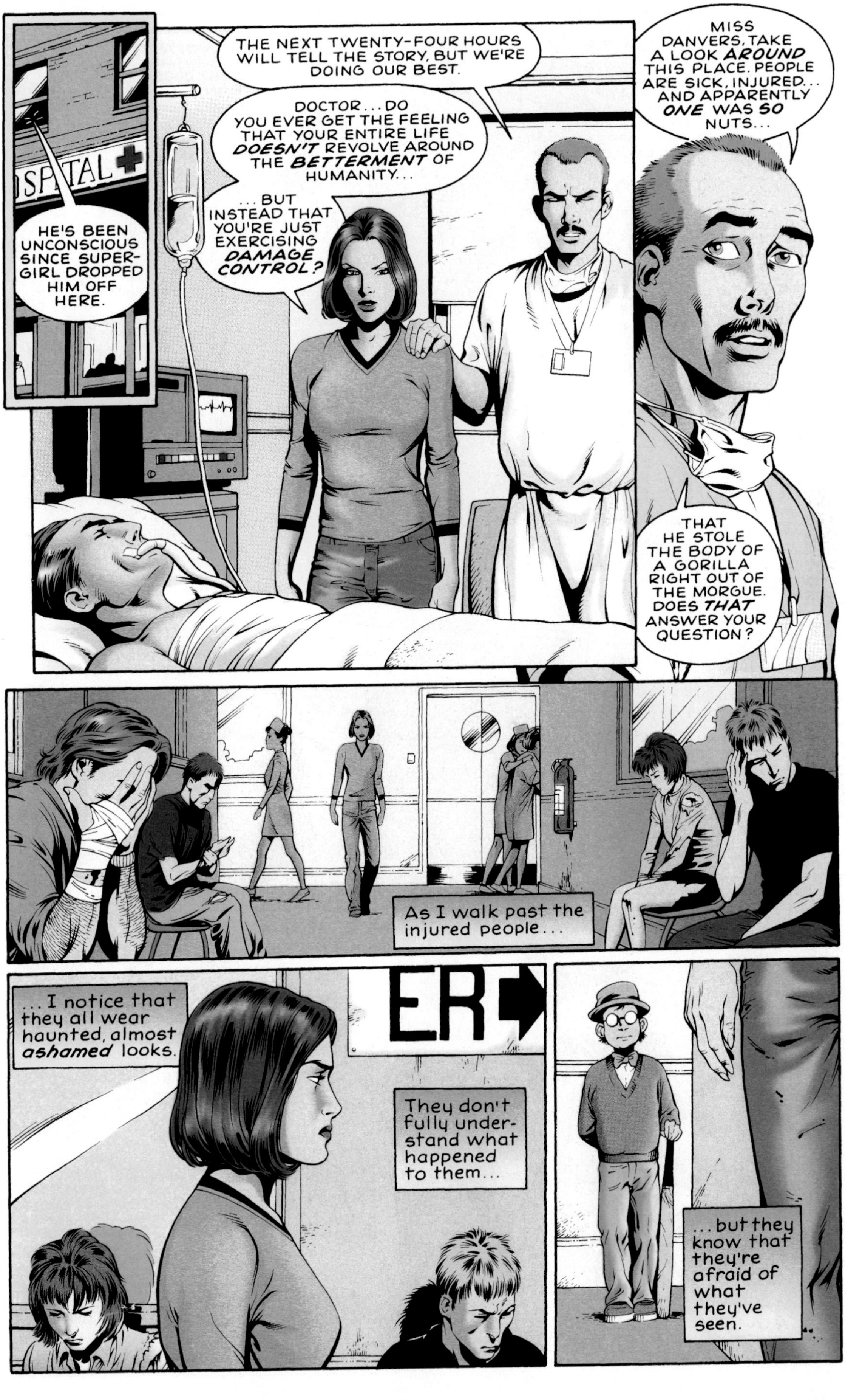

OSPITAL
HE'S BEEN UNCONSCIOUS SINCE SUPER-GIRL DROPPED HIM OFF HERE.
THE NEXT TWENTY-FOUR HOURS WILL TELL THE STORY, BUT WE'RE DOING OUR BEST.
DOCTOR... DO YOU EVER GET THE FEELING THAT YOUR ENTIRE LIFE DOESN'T REVOLVE AROUND THE BETTERMENT OF HUMANITY...
...BUT INSTEAD THAT YOU'RE JUST EXERCISING DAMAGE CONTROL?
MISS DANVERS, TAKE A LOOK AROUND THIS PLACE. PEOPLE ARE SICK, INJURED... AND APPARENTLY ONE WAS SO NUTS...
THAT HE STOLE THE BODY OF A GORILLA RIGHT OUT OF THE MORGUE. DOES THAT ANSWER YOUR QUESTION?
As I walk past the injured people...
...I notice that they all wear haunted, almost ashamed looks.
ER
They don't fully under-stand what happened to them...
...but they know that they're afraid of what they've seen.

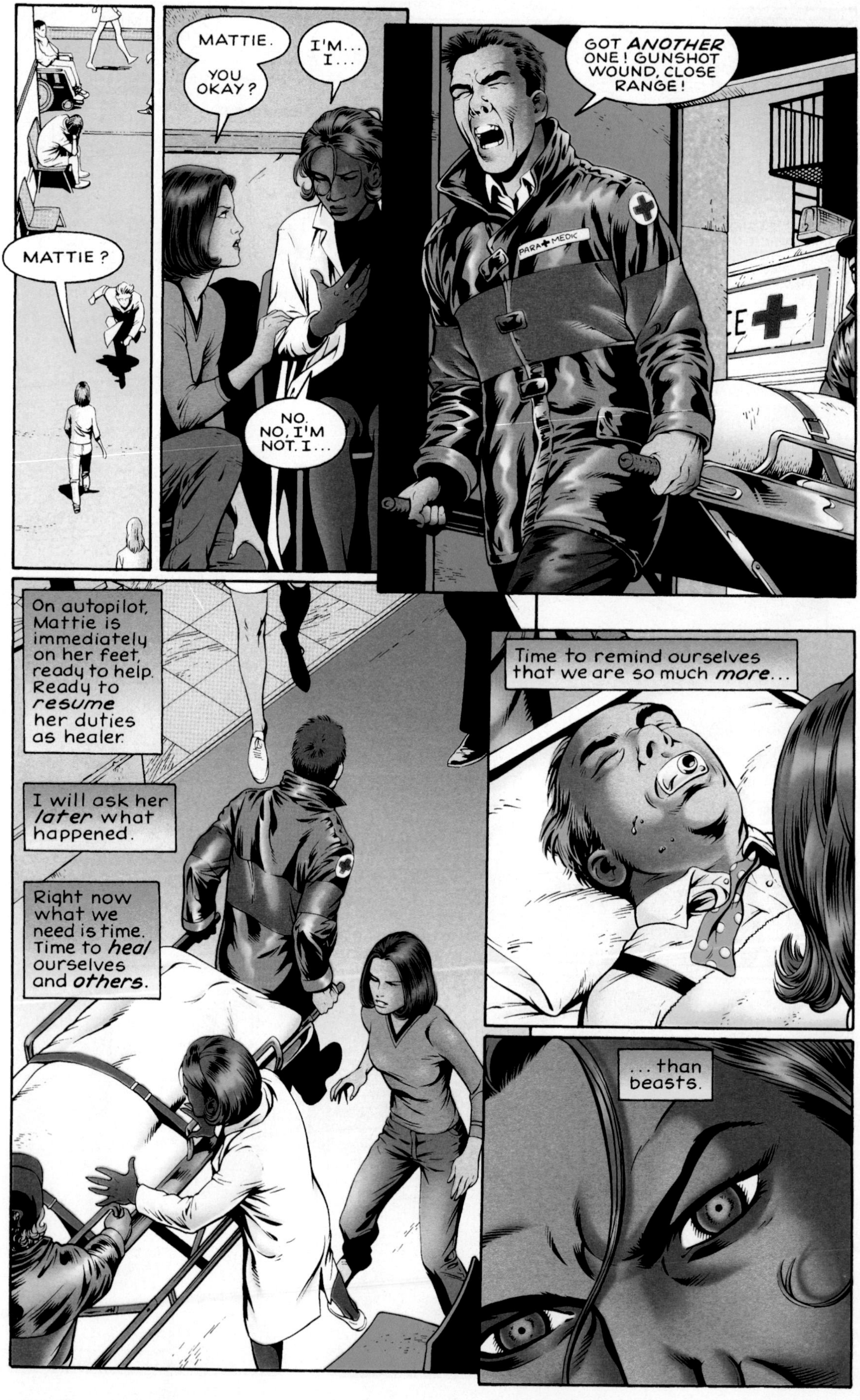
MATTIE?
MATTIE.
YOU OKAY?
I'M... I...
NO. NO, I'M NOT. I...
GOT ANOTHER ONE! GUNSHOT WOUND, CLOSE RANGE!
PARA MEDIC
On autopilot, Mattie is immediately on her feet, ready to help. Ready to resume her duties as healer.
I will ask her later what happened.
Right now what we need is time. Time to heal ourselves and others.
Time to remind ourselves that we are so much more...
...than beasts.

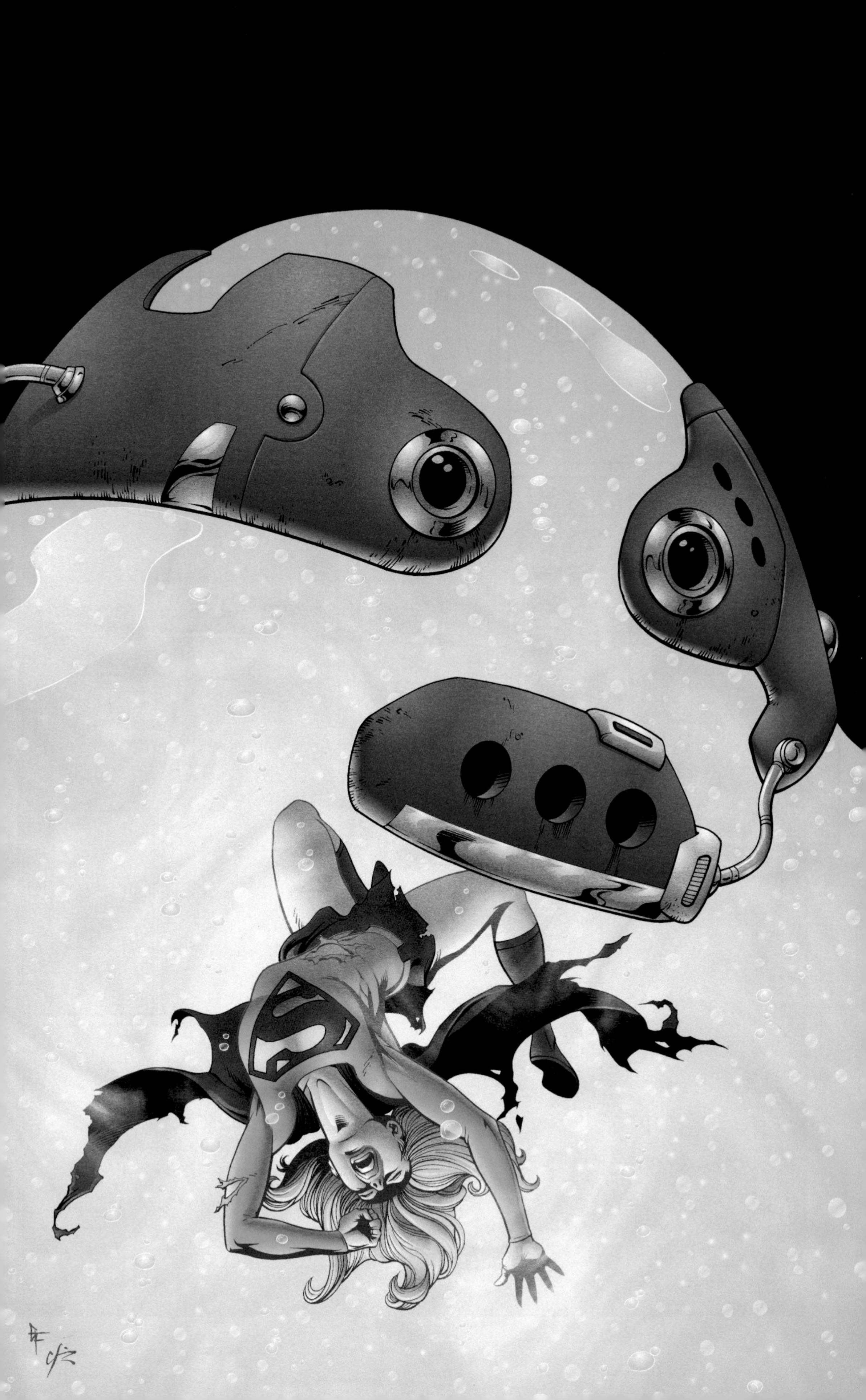

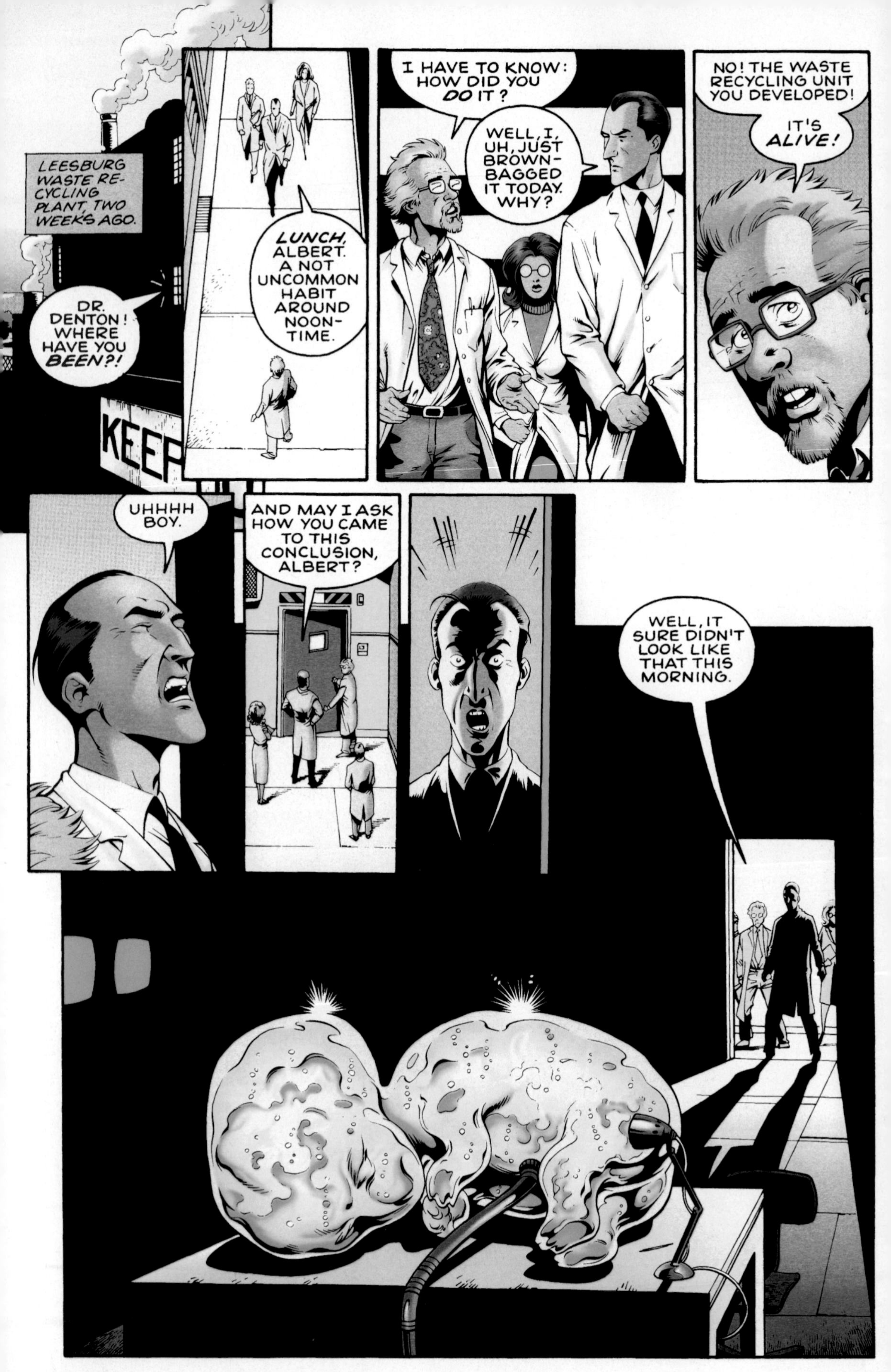
LEESBURG WASTE RE-CYCLING PLANT, TWO WEEKS AGO.
DR. DENTON! WHERE HAVE YOU BEEN?!
LUNCH, ALBERT. A NOT UNCOMMON HABIT AROUND NOON-TIME.
KEEP
I HAVE TO KNOW: HOW DID YOU DO IT?
WELL, I, UH, JUST BROWN-BAGGED IT TODAY. WHY?
NO! THE WASTE RECYCLING UNIT YOU DEVELOPED!
IT'S ALIVE!
UHHHH BOY.
AND MAY I ASK HOW YOU CAME TO THIS CONCLUSION, ALBERT?
WELL, IT SURE DIDN'T LOOK LIKE THAT THIS MORNING.

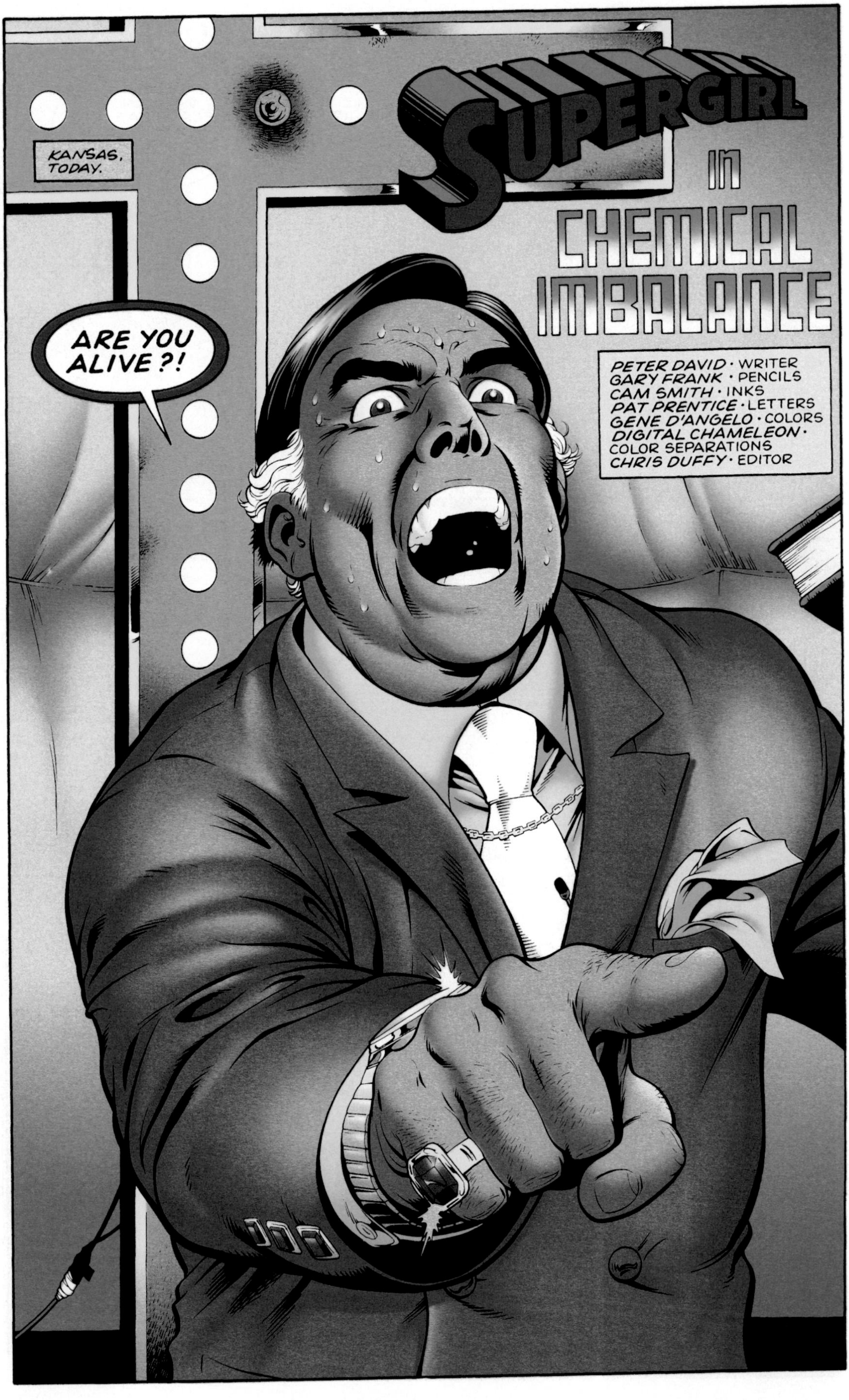
SUPERGIRL
in
CHEMICAL IMBALANCE
PETER DAVID · WRITER
GARY FRANK · PENCILS
CAM SMITH · INKS
PAT PRENTICE · LETTERS
GENE D'ANGELO · COLORS
DIGITAL CHAMELEON · COLOR SEPARATIONS
CHRIS DUFFY · EDITOR
KANSAS, TODAY.
ARE YOU ALIVE?!

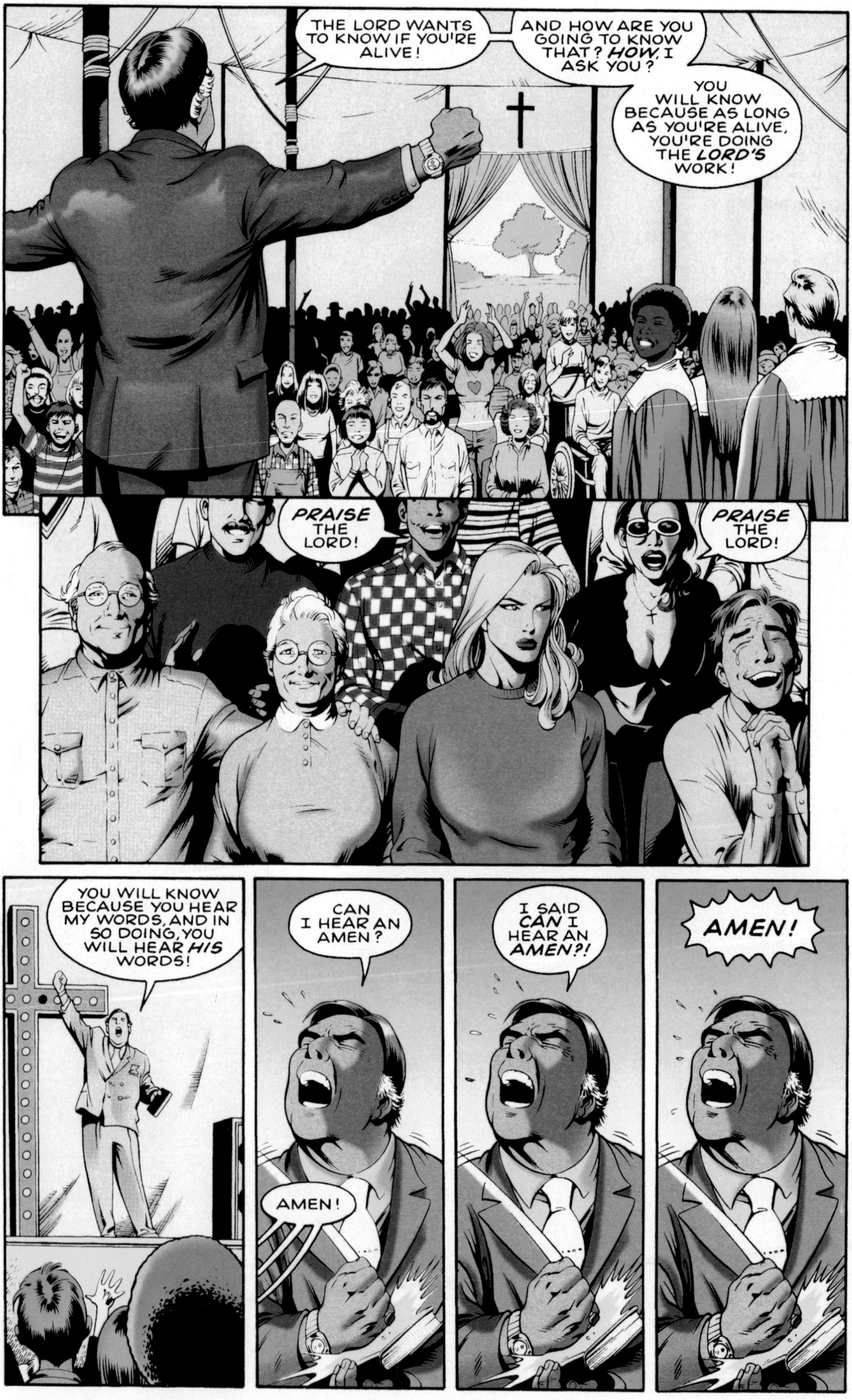
THE LORD WANTS TO KNOW IF YOU'RE ALIVE!
AND HOW ARE YOU GOING TO KNOW THAT? HOW, I ASK YOU?
YOU WILL KNOW BECAUSE AS LONG AS YOU'RE ALIVE, YOU'RE DOING THE LORD'S WORK!
PRAISE THE LORD!
PRAISE THE LORD!
YOU WILL KNOW BECAUSE YOU HEAR MY WORDS, AND IN SO DOING, YOU WILL HEAR HIS WORDS!
CAN I HEAR AN AMEN?
AMEN!
I SAID CAN I HEAR AN AMEN?!
AMEN!

AND YOU WILL KNOW, MY FRIENDS... YOU WILL KNOW YOU'RE ALIVE...

...BECAUSE YOU'RE WILLING TO GIVE. *GIVE*, MY FRIENDS. GIVE UNTIL IT HURTS, BECAUSE THE LORD *WANTS* YOU TO.

HE WANTS YOU TO HELP ME CONTINUE HIS GOOD WORKS.

WHEN YOU HELP ME, THEN YOU HELP ALL OF US GET CLOSER TO GOD!

These people ...scraping a few dollars together...

...to buy into his barnstorming rhetoric.

While he sports expensive jewelry.

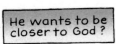

He wants to be closer to God?

Let's see if a half-strength psi-blast can bring him closer than he *anticipated*.

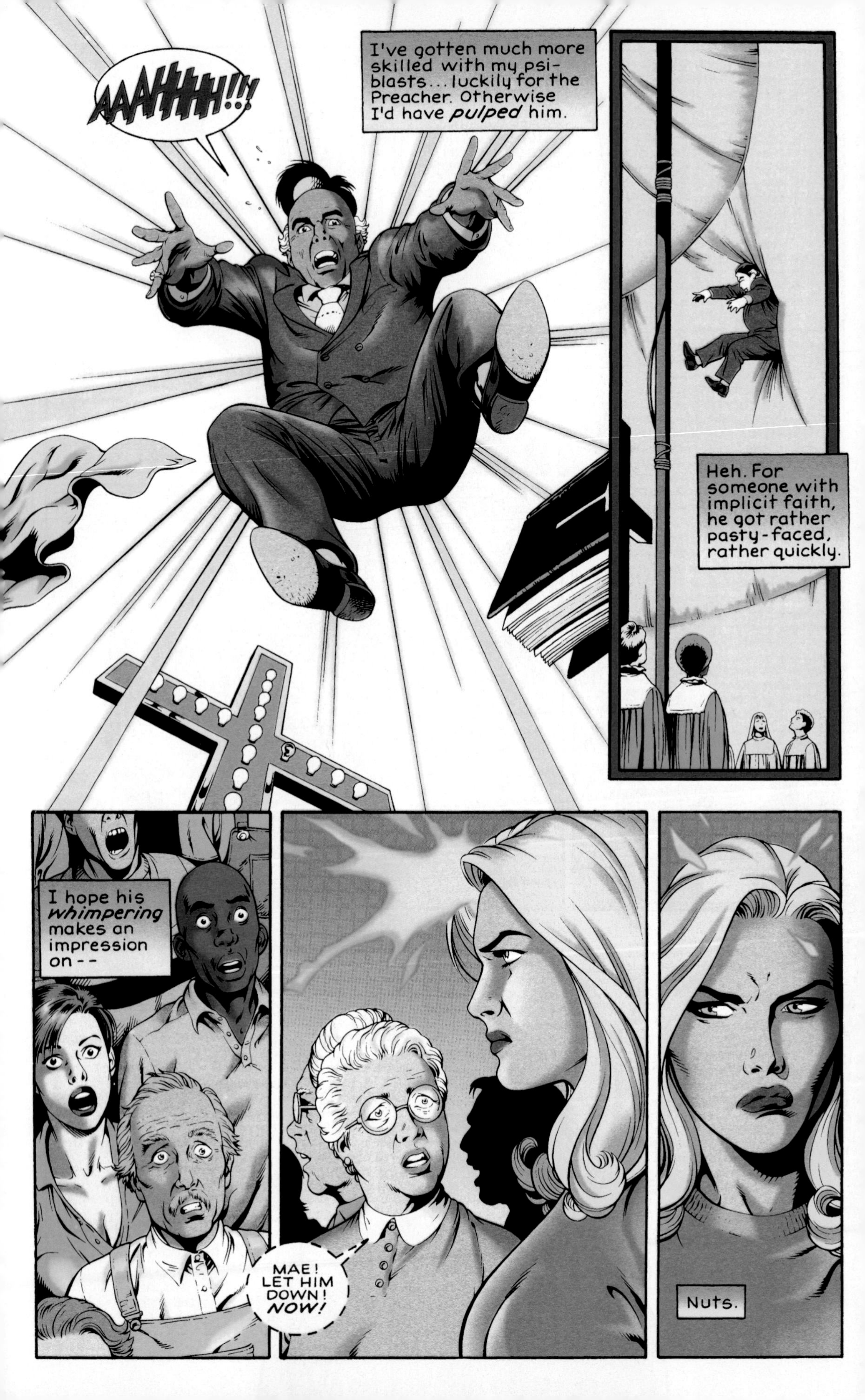
AAAHHHH!!!
I've gotten much more skilled with my psi-blasts... luckily for the Preacher. Otherwise I'd have *pulped* him.
Heh. For someone with implicit faith, he got rather pasty-faced, rather quickly.
I hope his *whimpering* makes an impression on --
MAE! LET HIM DOWN! *NOW!*
Nuts.

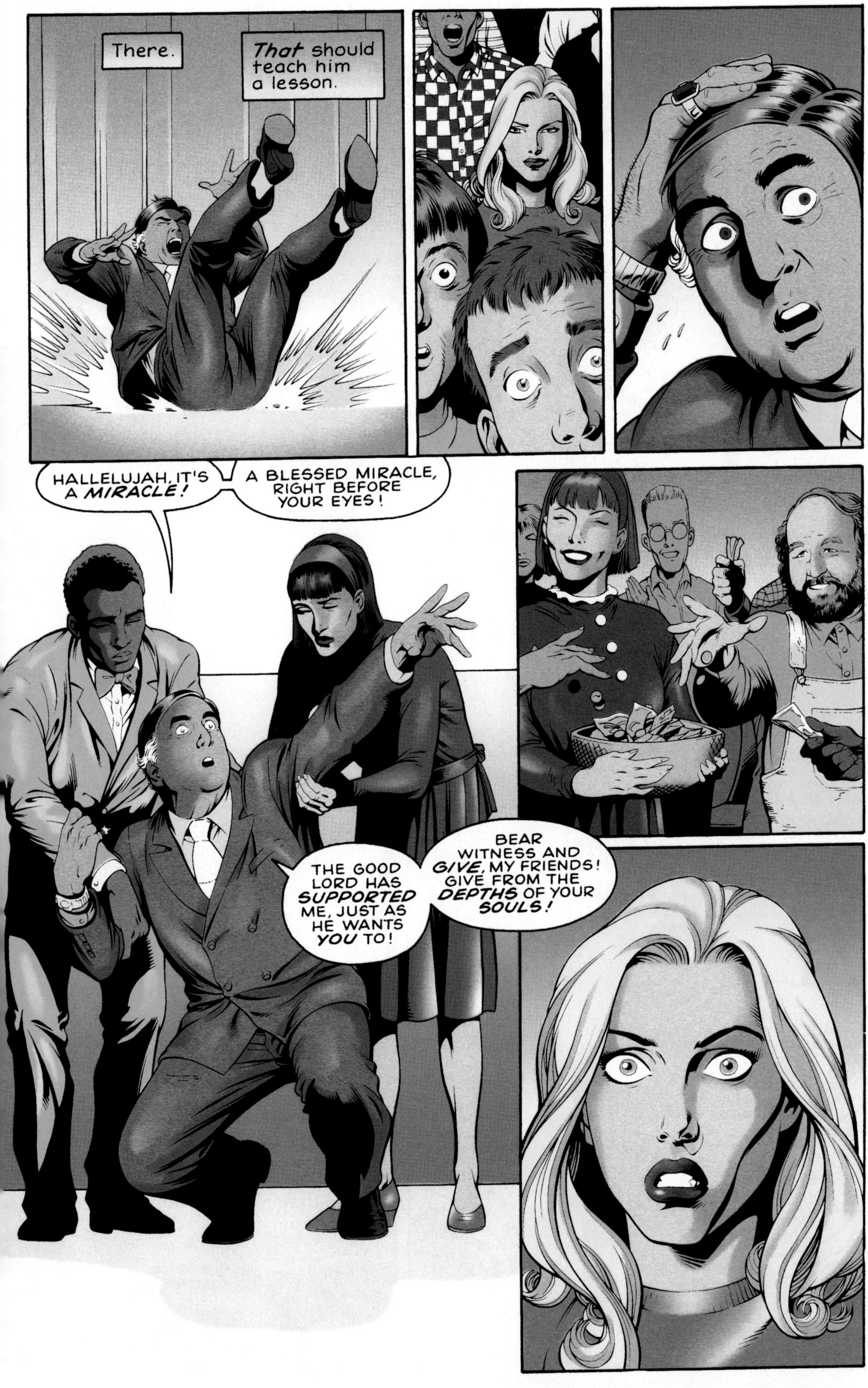

There.
That should teach him a lesson.
HALLELUJAH, IT'S A *MIRACLE*!
A BLESSED MIRACLE, RIGHT BEFORE YOUR EYES!
THE GOOD LORD HAS *SUPPORTED* ME, JUST AS HE WANTS *YOU* TO!
BEAR WITNESS AND *GIVE*, MY FRIENDS! GIVE FROM THE *DEPTHS* OF YOUR *SOULS*!

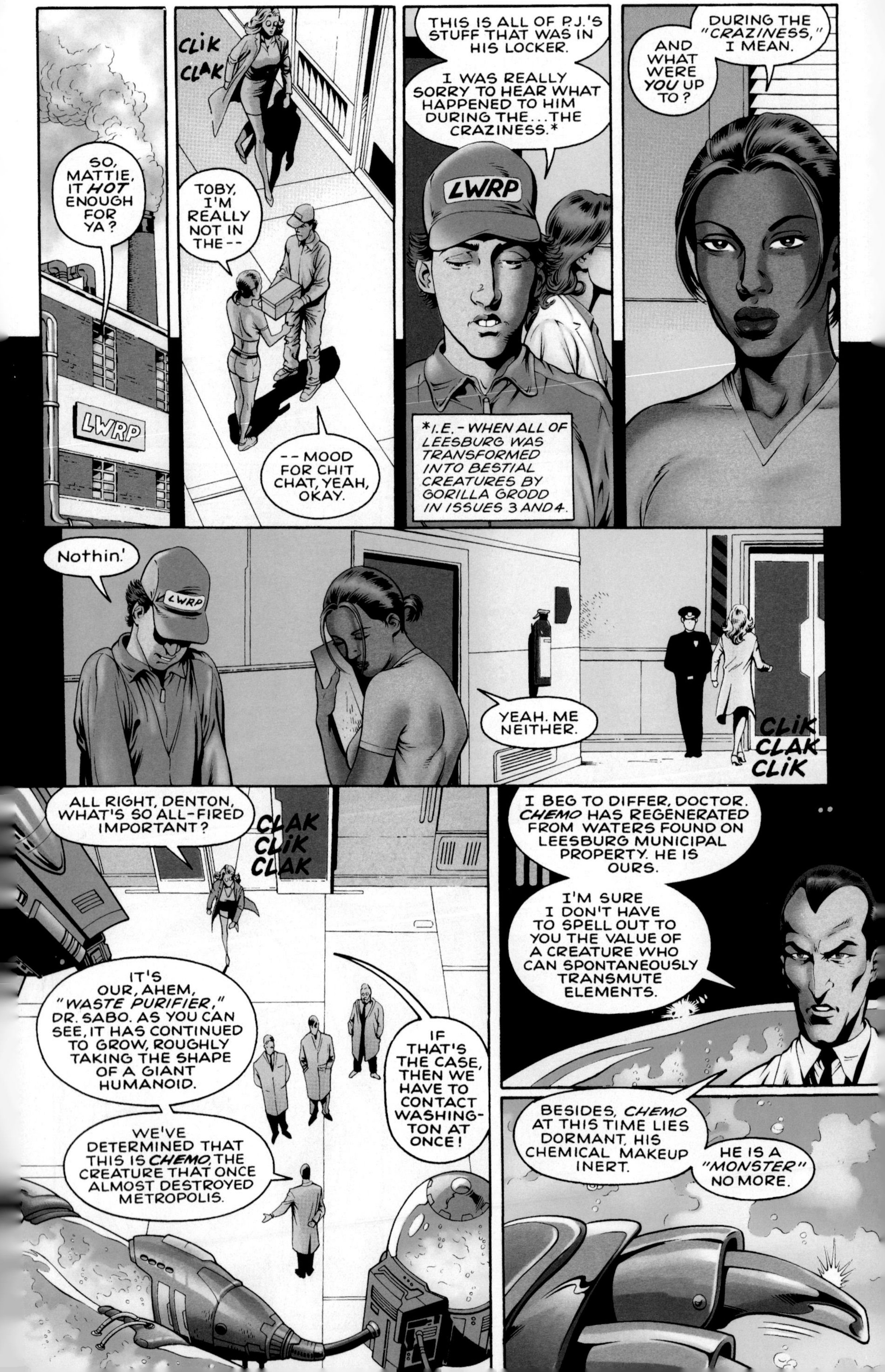
SO, MATTIE, IT HOT ENOUGH FOR YA?
CLIK
CLAK
TOBY, I'M REALLY NOT IN THE--
--MOOD FOR CHIT CHAT, YEAH, OKAY.
THIS IS ALL OF P.J.'S STUFF THAT WAS IN HIS LOCKER.
I WAS REALLY SORRY TO HEAR WHAT HAPPENED TO HIM DURING THE...THE CRAZINESS.*
LWRP
*I.E.-WHEN ALL OF LEESBURG WAS TRANSFORMED INTO BESTIAL CREATURES BY GORILLA GRODD IN ISSUES 3 AND 4.
DURING THE "CRAZINESS," I MEAN.
AND WHAT WERE YOU UP TO?
Nothin.'
YEAH. ME NEITHER.
CLIK
CLAK
CLIK
ALL RIGHT, DENTON, WHAT'S SO ALL-FIRED IMPORTANT?
CLAK
CLIK
CLAK
IT'S OUR, AHEM, "WASTE PURIFIER," DR. SABO. AS YOU CAN SEE, IT HAS CONTINUED TO GROW, ROUGHLY TAKING THE SHAPE OF A GIANT HUMANOID.
WE'VE DETERMINED THAT THIS IS CHEMO, THE CREATURE THAT ONCE ALMOST DESTROYED METROPOLIS.
IF THAT'S THE CASE, THEN WE HAVE TO CONTACT WASHINGTON AT ONCE!
I BEG TO DIFFER, DOCTOR. CHEMO HAS REGENERATED FROM WATERS FOUND ON LEESBURG MUNICIPAL PROPERTY. HE IS OURS.
I'M SURE I DON'T HAVE TO SPELL OUT TO YOU THE VALUE OF A CREATURE WHO CAN SPONTANEOUSLY TRANSMUTE ELEMENTS.
BESIDES, CHEMO AT THIS TIME LIES DORMANT, HIS CHEMICAL MAKEUP INERT.
HE IS A "MONSTER" NO MORE.

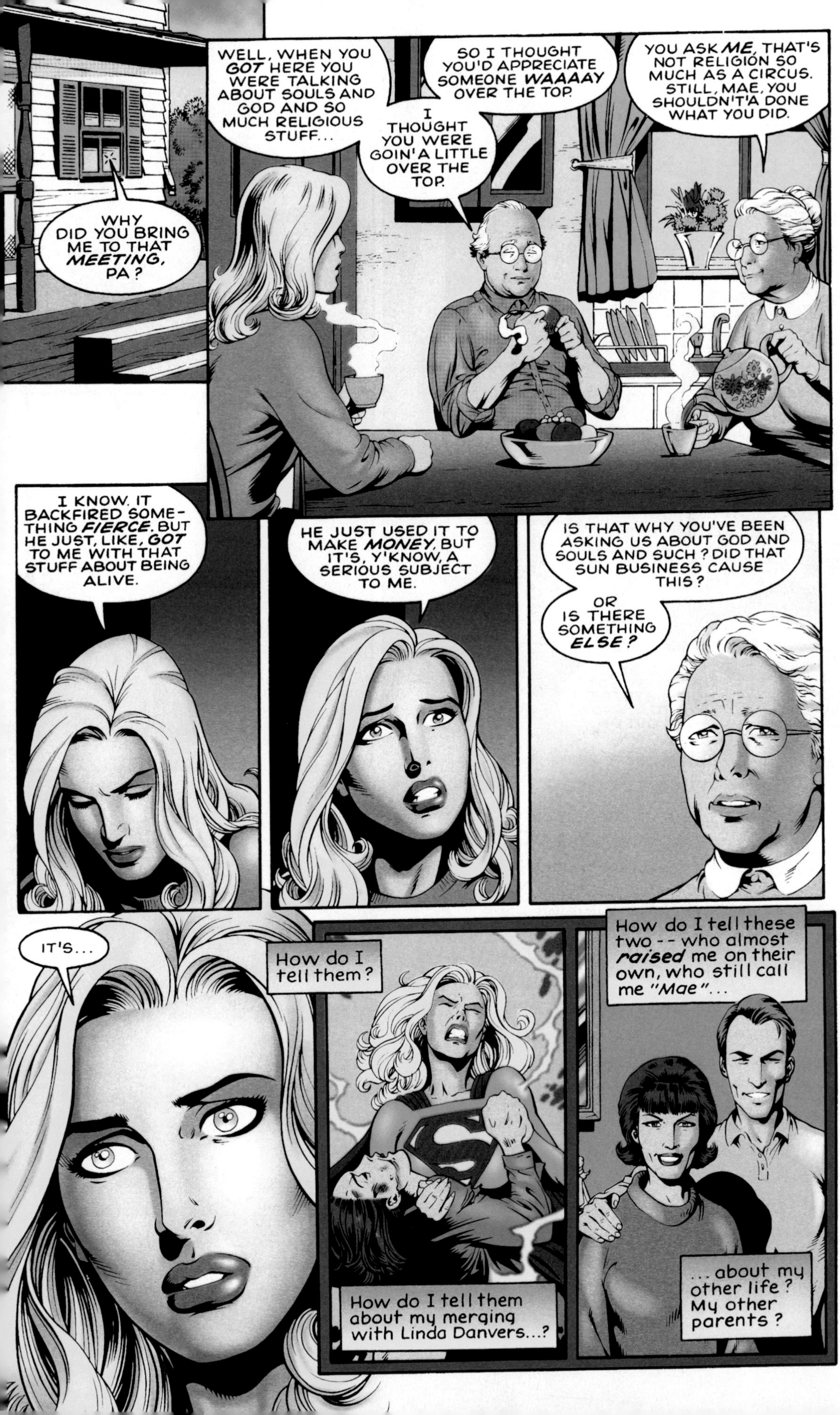
WHY DID YOU BRING ME TO THAT MEETING, PA?
WELL, WHEN YOU GOT HERE YOU WERE TALKING ABOUT SOULS AND GOD AND SO MUCH RELIGIOUS STUFF...
I THOUGHT YOU WERE GOIN' A LITTLE OVER THE TOP.
SO I THOUGHT YOU'D APPRECIATE SOMEONE WAAAAY OVER THE TOP.
YOU ASK ME, THAT'S NOT RELIGION SO MUCH AS A CIRCUS. STILL, MAE, YOU SHOULDN'T'A DONE WHAT YOU DID.
I KNOW. IT BACKFIRED SOME-THING FIERCE. BUT HE JUST, LIKE, GOT TO ME WITH THAT STUFF ABOUT BEING ALIVE.
HE JUST USED IT TO MAKE MONEY, BUT IT'S, Y'KNOW, A SERIOUS SUBJECT TO ME.
IS THAT WHY YOU'VE BEEN ASKING US ABOUT GOD AND SOULS AND SUCH? DID THAT SUN BUSINESS CAUSE THIS?
OR IS THERE SOMETHING ELSE?
IT'S...
How do I tell them?
How do I tell them about my merging with Linda Danvers...?
How do I tell these two -- who almost raised me on their own, who still call me "Mae"...
...about my other life? My other parents?

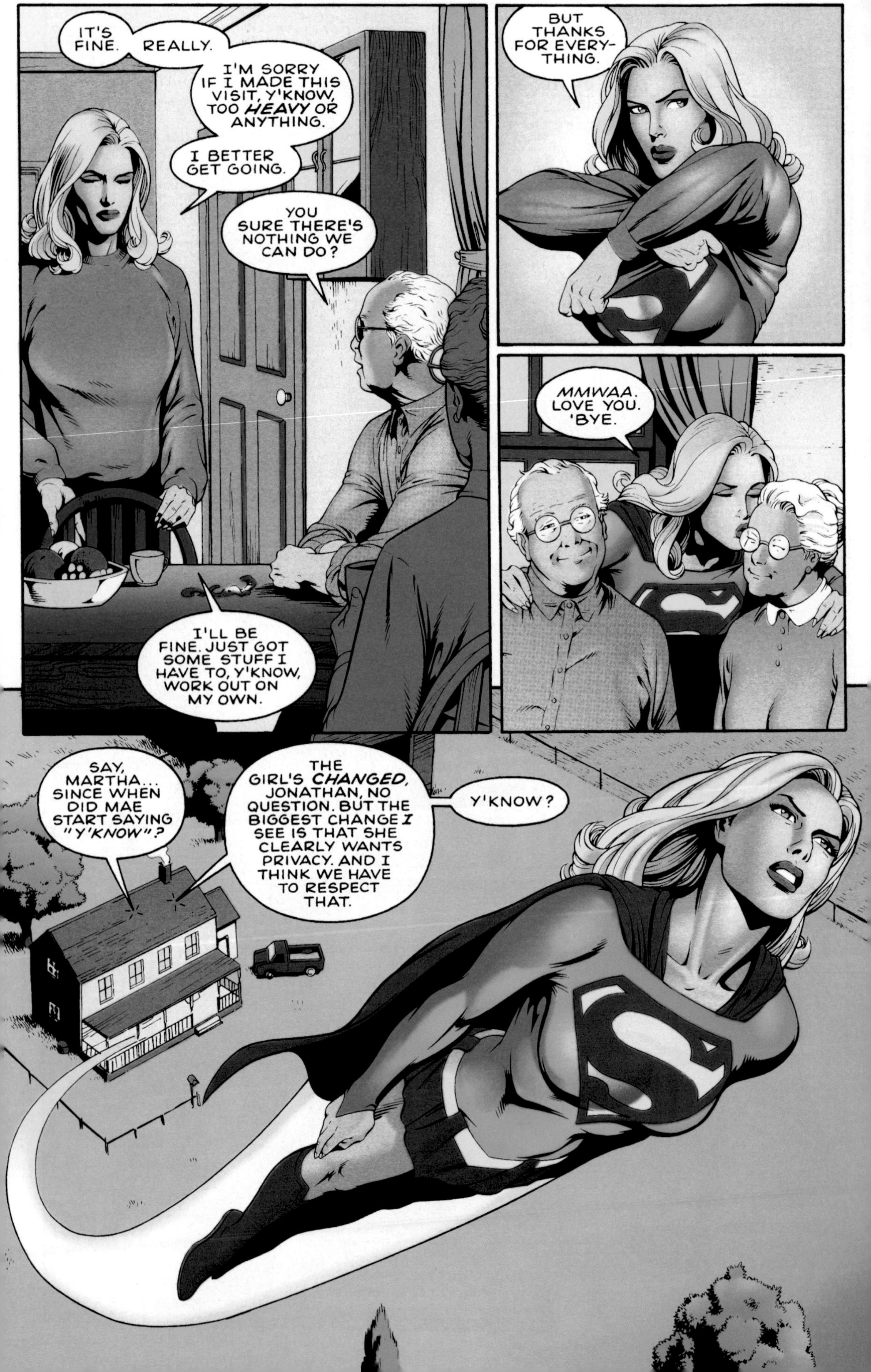
IT'S FINE.
REALLY.
I'M SORRY IF I MADE THIS VISIT, Y'KNOW, TOO *HEAVY* OR ANYTHING.
I BETTER GET GOING.
YOU SURE THERE'S NOTHING WE CAN DO?
I'LL BE FINE. JUST GOT SOME STUFF I HAVE TO, Y'KNOW, WORK OUT ON MY OWN.
BUT THANKS FOR EVERY-THING.
MMWAA. LOVE YOU. 'BYE.
SAY, MARTHA... SINCE WHEN DID MAE START SAYING *"Y'KNOW"*?
THE GIRL'S *CHANGED,* JONATHAN, NO QUESTION. BUT THE BIGGEST CHANGE *I* SEE IS THAT SHE CLEARLY WANTS PRIVACY. AND I THINK WE HAVE TO RESPECT THAT.
Y'KNOW?

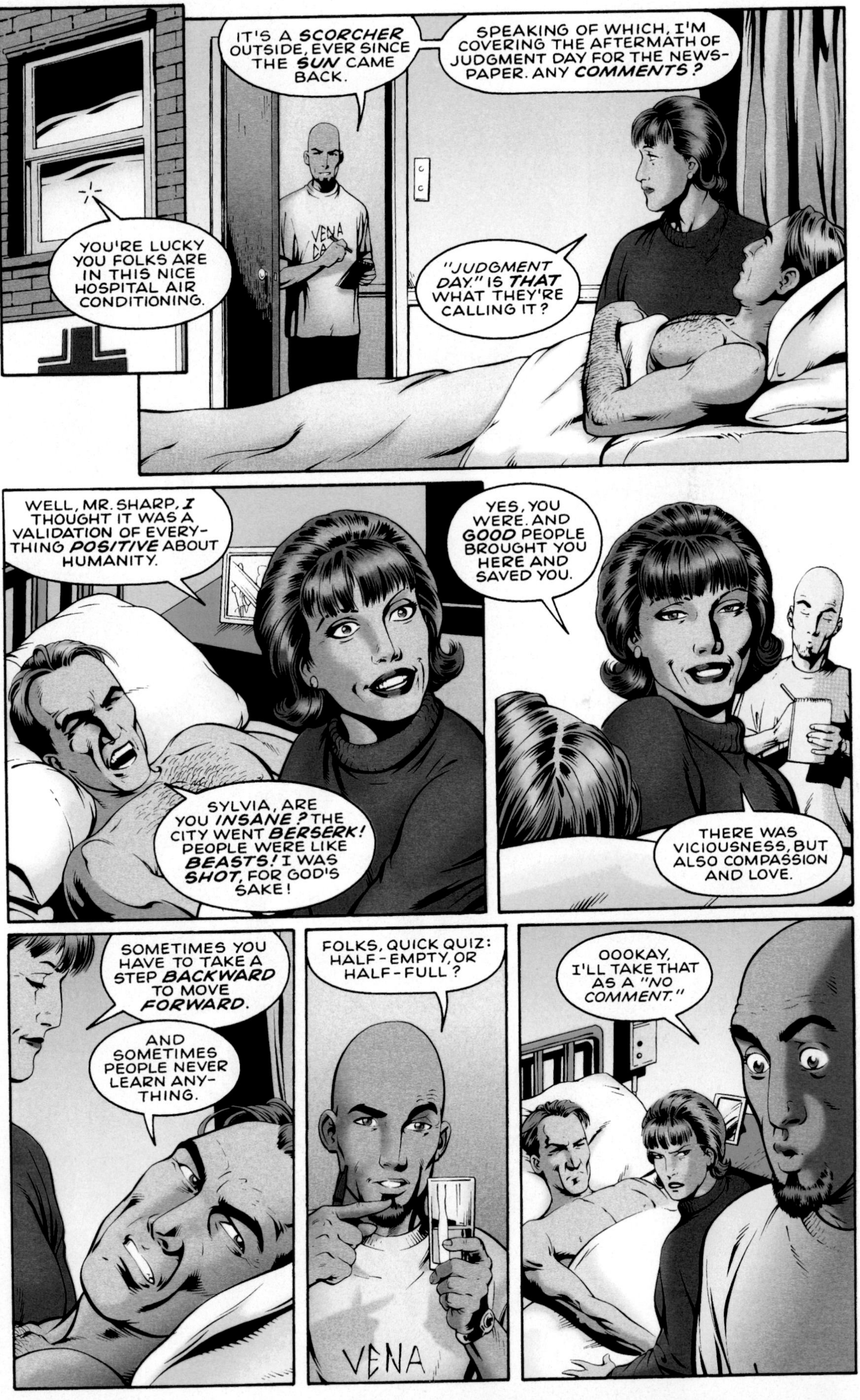
IT'S A SCORCHER OUTSIDE, EVER SINCE THE SUN CAME BACK.
YOU'RE LUCKY YOU FOLKS ARE IN THIS NICE HOSPITAL AIR CONDITIONING.
SPEAKING OF WHICH, I'M COVERING THE AFTERMATH OF JUDGMENT DAY FOR THE NEWSPAPER. ANY COMMENTS?
"JUDGMENT DAY." IS THAT WHAT THEY'RE CALLING IT?
WELL, MR. SHARP, I THOUGHT IT WAS A VALIDATION OF EVERYTHING POSITIVE ABOUT HUMANITY.
SYLVIA, ARE YOU INSANE? THE CITY WENT BERSERK! PEOPLE WERE LIKE BEASTS! I WAS SHOT, FOR GOD'S SAKE!
YES, YOU WERE. AND GOOD PEOPLE BROUGHT YOU HERE AND SAVED YOU.
THERE WAS VICIOUSNESS, BUT ALSO COMPASSION AND LOVE.
SOMETIMES YOU HAVE TO TAKE A STEP BACKWARD TO MOVE FORWARD.
AND SOMETIMES PEOPLE NEVER LEARN ANYTHING.
FOLKS, QUICK QUIZ: HALF-EMPTY, OR HALF-FULL?
VENA
OOOKAY, I'LL TAKE THAT AS A "NO COMMENT."

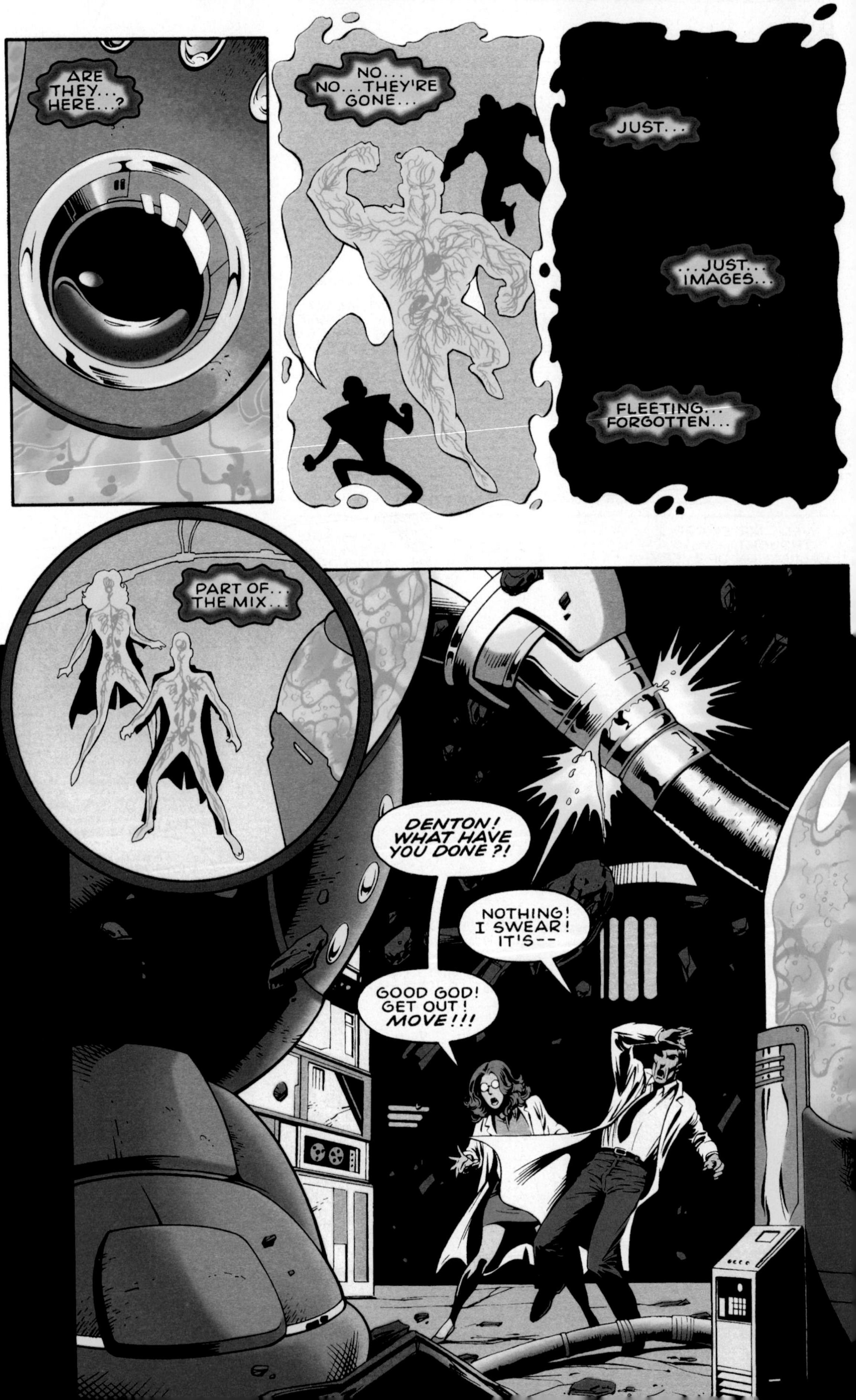
ARE THEY...HERE...?
NO... NO...THEY'RE GONE...
JUST...
...JUST... IMAGES...
FLEETING... FORGOTTEN...
PART OF... THE MIX...
DENTON! WHAT HAVE YOU DONE?!
NOTHING! I SWEAR! IT'S--
GOOD GOD! GET OUT! MOVE!!!

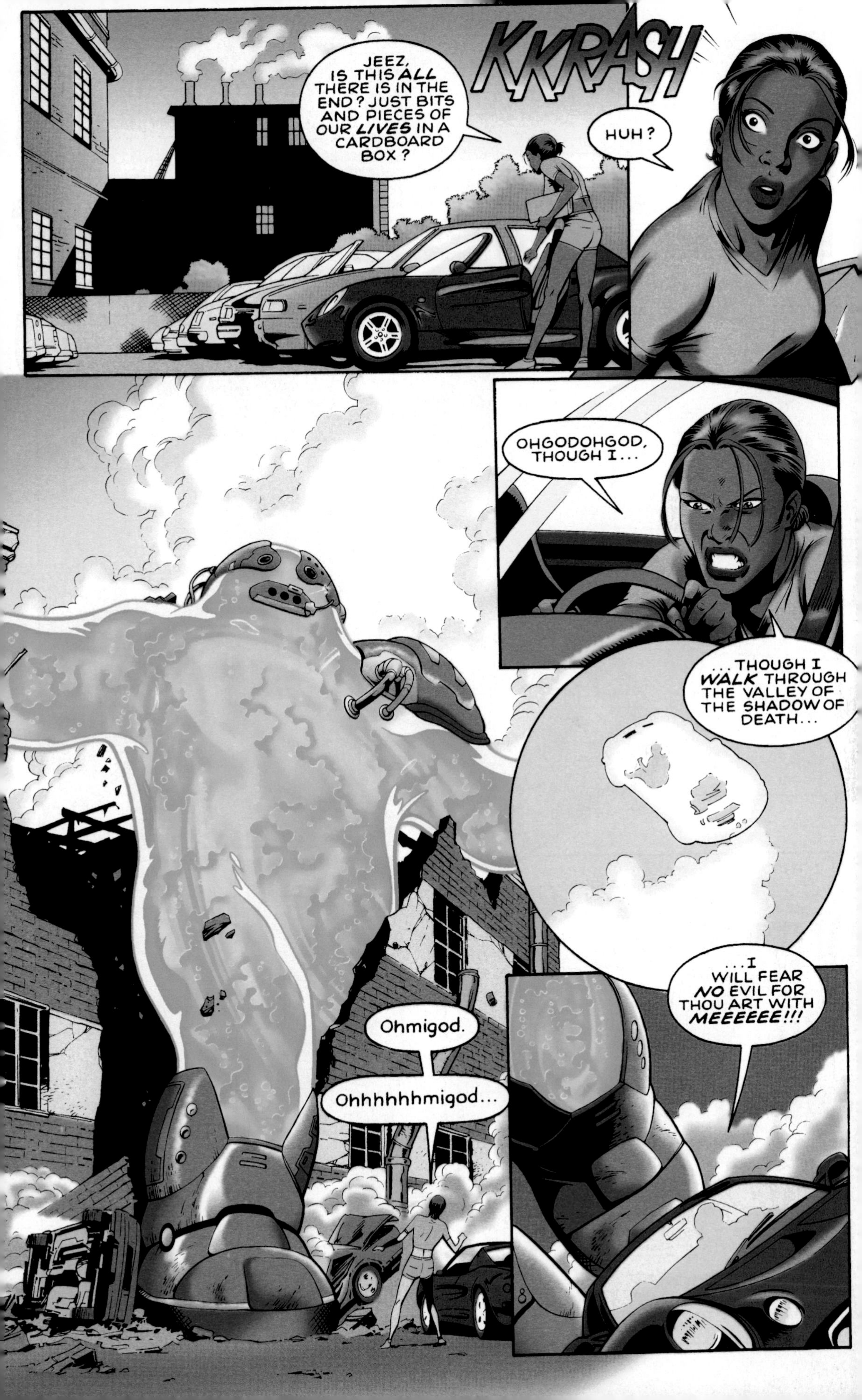
JEEZ, IS THIS ALL THERE IS IN THE END? JUST BITS AND PIECES OF OUR LIVES IN A CARDBOARD BOX?
KKRASH
HUH?
OHGODOHGOD, THOUGH I...
...THOUGH I WALK THROUGH THE VALLEY OF THE SHADOW OF DEATH...
Ohmigod.
Ohhhhhhmigod...
...I WILL FEAR NO EVIL FOR THOU ART WITH MEEEEEE!!!

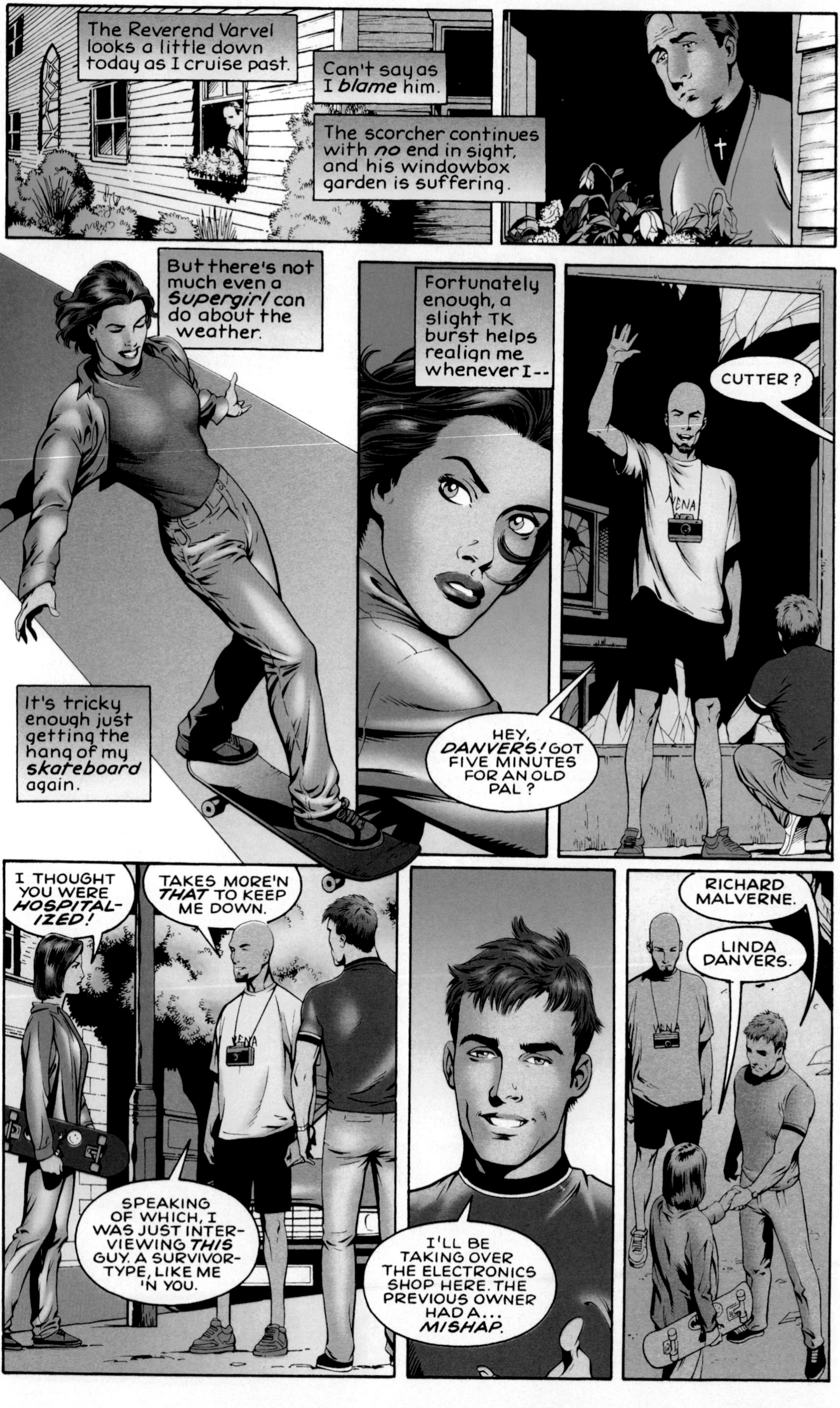
The Reverend Varvel looks a little down today as I cruise past.
Can't say as I *blame* him.
The scorcher continues with *no* end in sight, and his windowbox garden is suffering.
But there's not much even a *Supergirl* can do about the weather.
It's tricky enough just getting the hang of my *skateboard* again.
Fortunately enough, a slight TK burst helps realign me whenever I--
CUTTER?
HEY, *DANVERS!* GOT FIVE MINUTES FOR AN OLD PAL?
VENA
I THOUGHT YOU WERE *HOSPITALIZED!*
TAKES MORE'N *THAT* TO KEEP ME DOWN.
SPEAKING OF WHICH, I WAS JUST INTERVIEWING *THIS* GUY. A SURVIVOR-TYPE, LIKE ME 'N YOU.
I'LL BE TAKING OVER THE ELECTRONICS SHOP HERE. THE PREVIOUS OWNER HAD A... *MISHAP*.
RICHARD MALVERNE.
LINDA DANVERS.

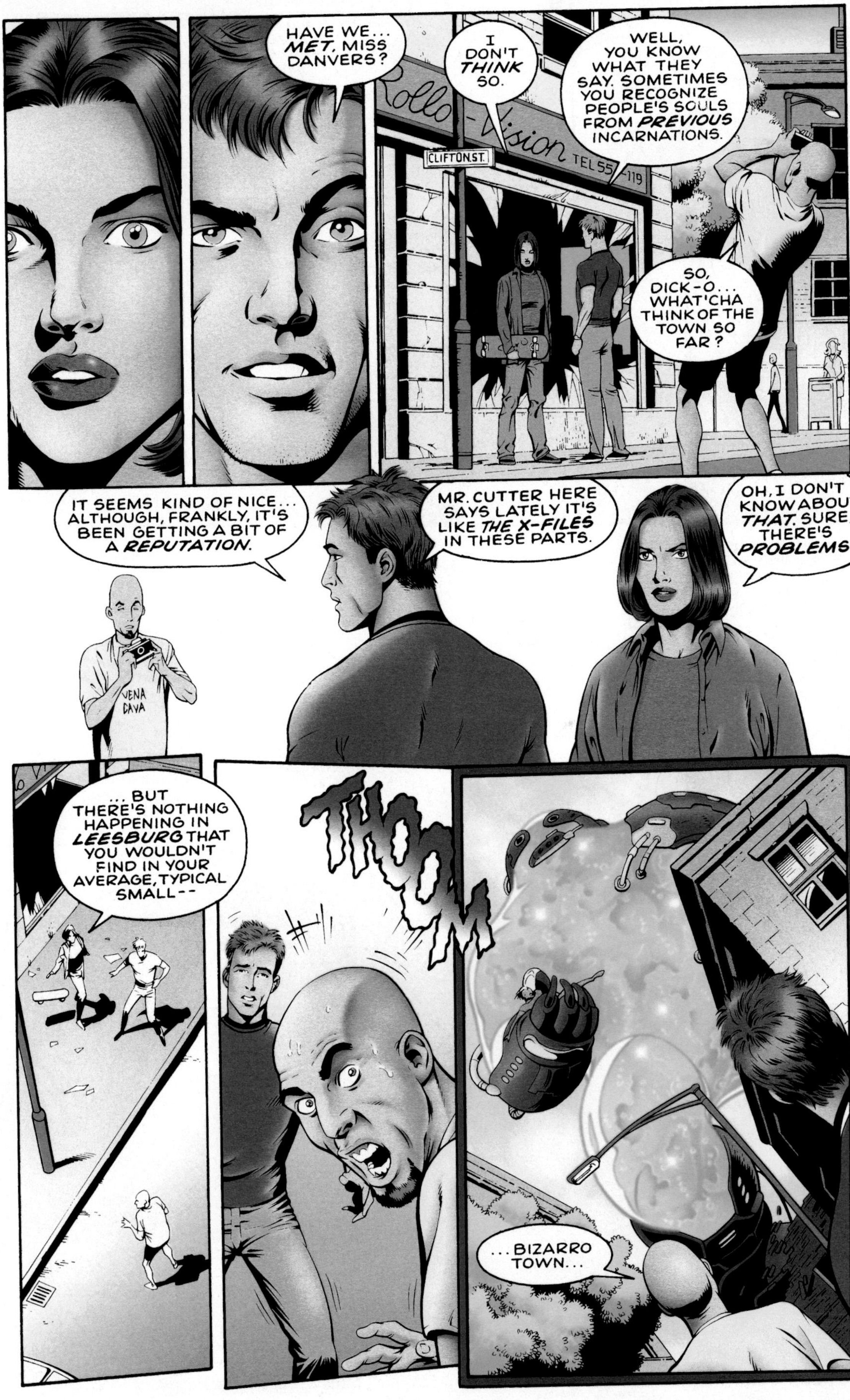
HAVE WE... MET, MISS DANVERS?
I DON'T THINK SO.
WELL, YOU KNOW WHAT THEY SAY. SOMETIMES YOU RECOGNIZE PEOPLE'S SOULS FROM PREVIOUS INCARNATIONS.
Rollo-Vision TEL 55 -119
CLIFTON ST.
SO, DICK-O... WHAT'CHA THINK OF THE TOWN SO FAR?
IT SEEMS KIND OF NICE... ALTHOUGH, FRANKLY, IT'S BEEN GETTING A BIT OF A REPUTATION.
MR. CUTTER HERE SAYS LATELY IT'S LIKE THE X-FILES IN THESE PARTS.
OH, I DON'T KNOW ABOUT THAT. SURE, THERE'S PROBLEMS...
VENA CAVA
... BUT THERE'S NOTHING HAPPENING IN LEESBURG THAT YOU WOULDN'T FIND IN YOUR AVERAGE, TYPICAL SMALL--
THOOM
... BIZARRO TOWN...

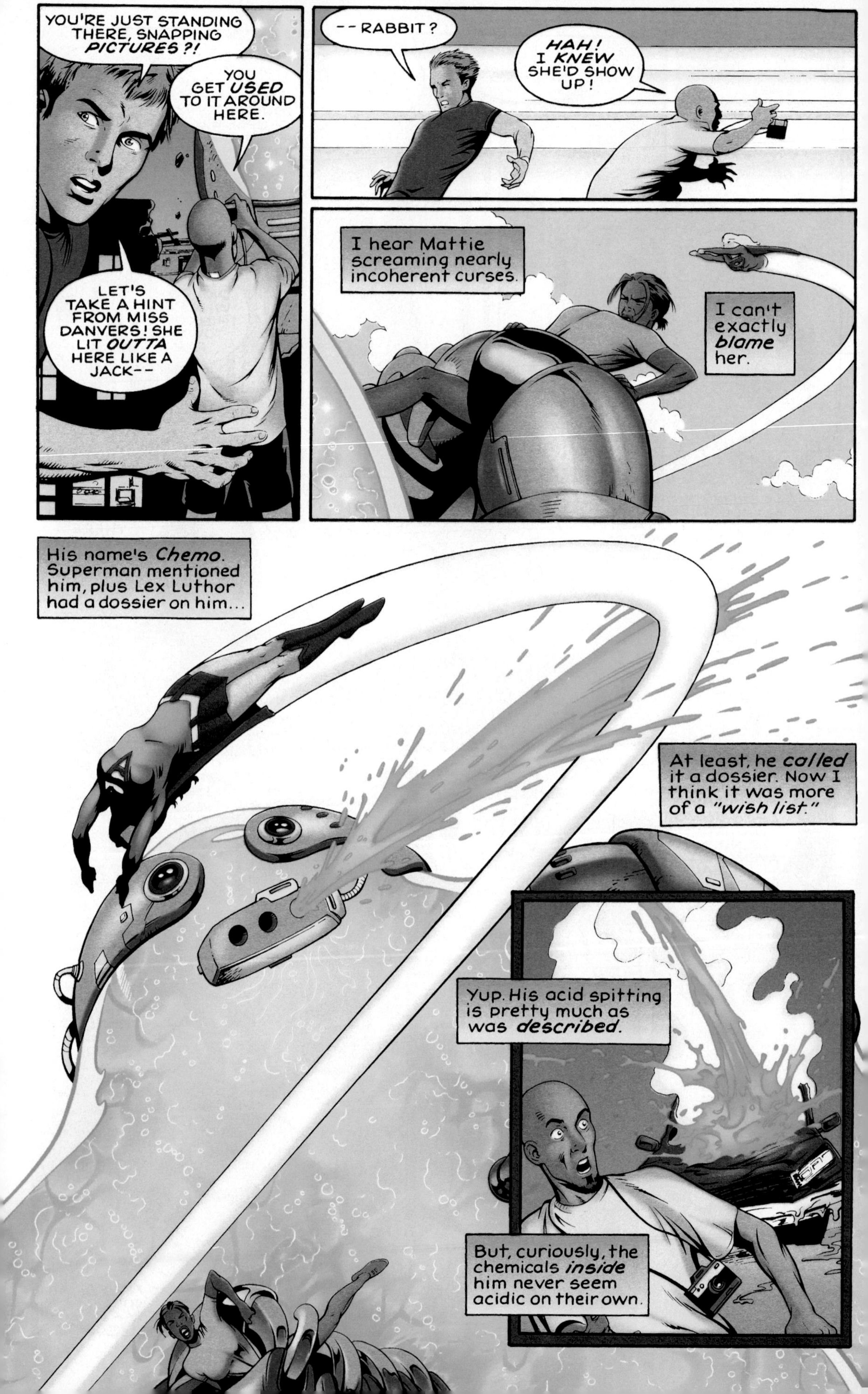
YOU'RE JUST STANDING THERE, SNAPPING PICTURES?!
YOU GET USED TO IT AROUND HERE.
LET'S TAKE A HINT FROM MISS DANVERS! SHE LIT OUTTA HERE LIKE A JACK--
--RABBIT?
HAH! I KNEW SHE'D SHOW UP!
I hear Mattie screaming nearly incoherent curses.
I can't exactly blame her.
His name's Chemo. Superman mentioned him, plus Lex Luthor had a dossier on him...
At least, he called it a dossier. Now I think it was more of a "wish list."
Yup. His acid spitting is pretty much as was described.
But, curiously, the chemicals inside him never seem acidic on their own.

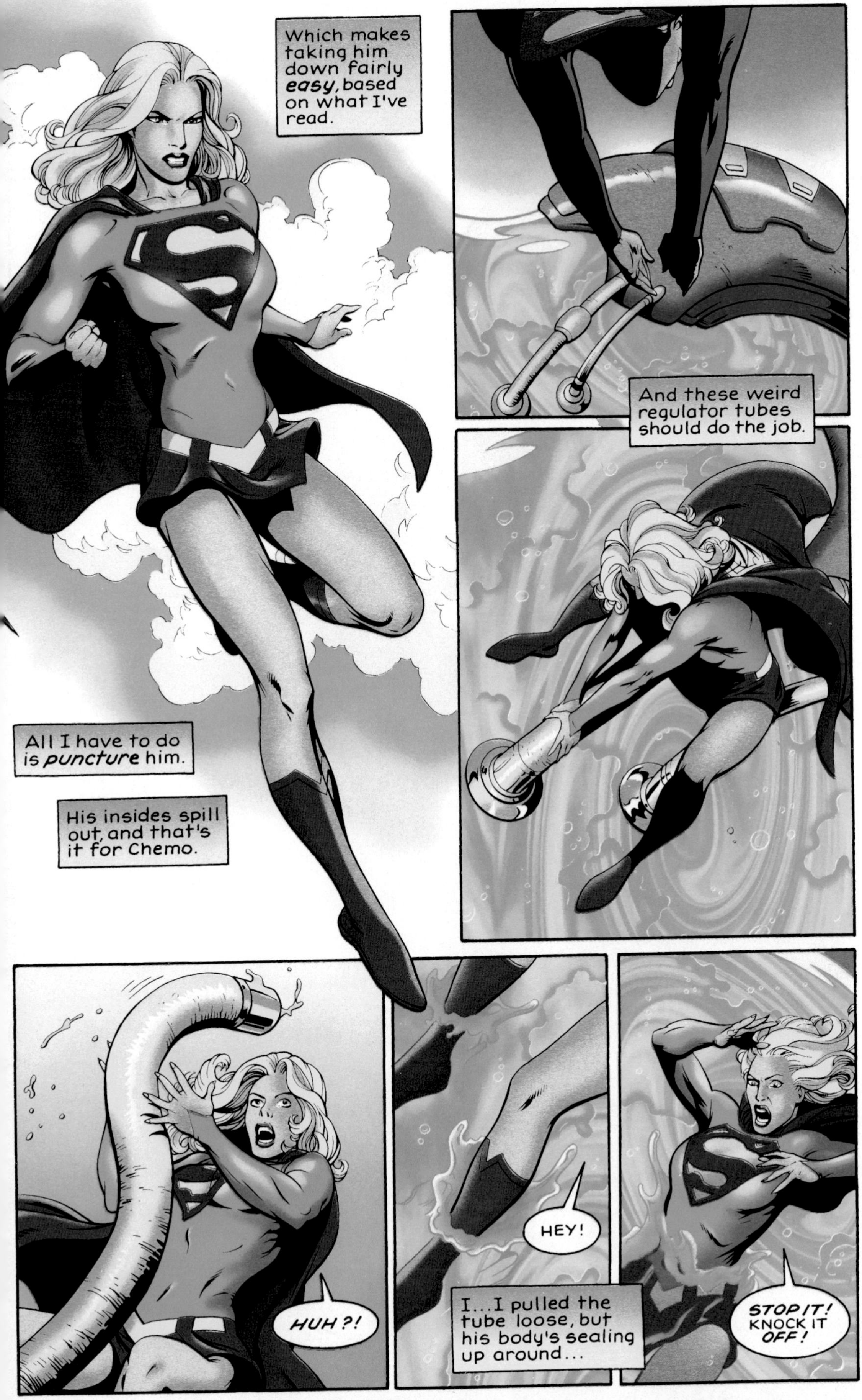
Which makes taking him down fairly *easy*, based on what I've read.
All I have to do is *puncture* him.
His insides spill out, and that's it for Chemo.
And these weird regulator tubes should do the job.
HUH?!
HEY!
I...I pulled the tube loose, but his body's sealing up around...
STOP IT! KNOCK IT *OFF!*

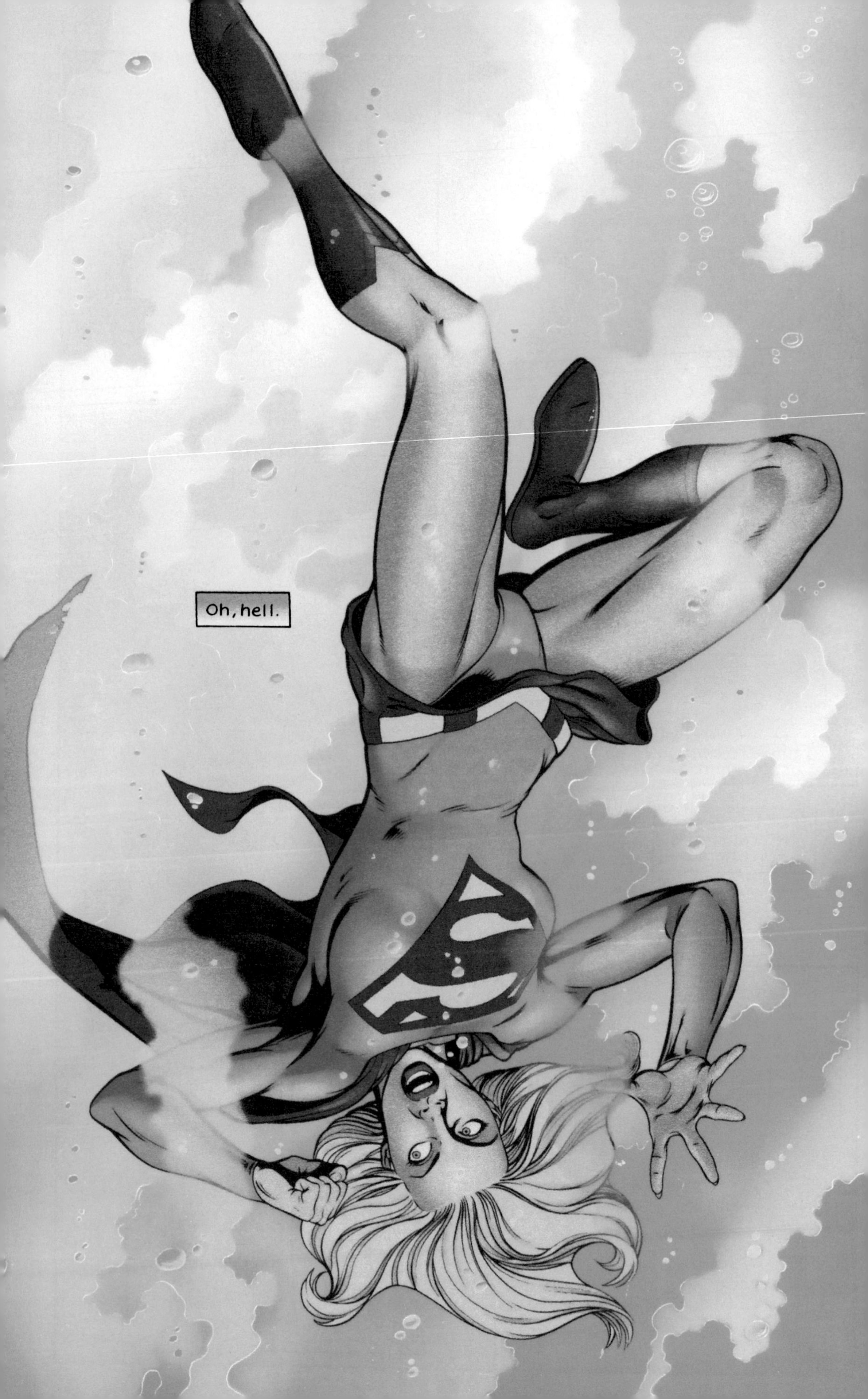
Oh, hell.

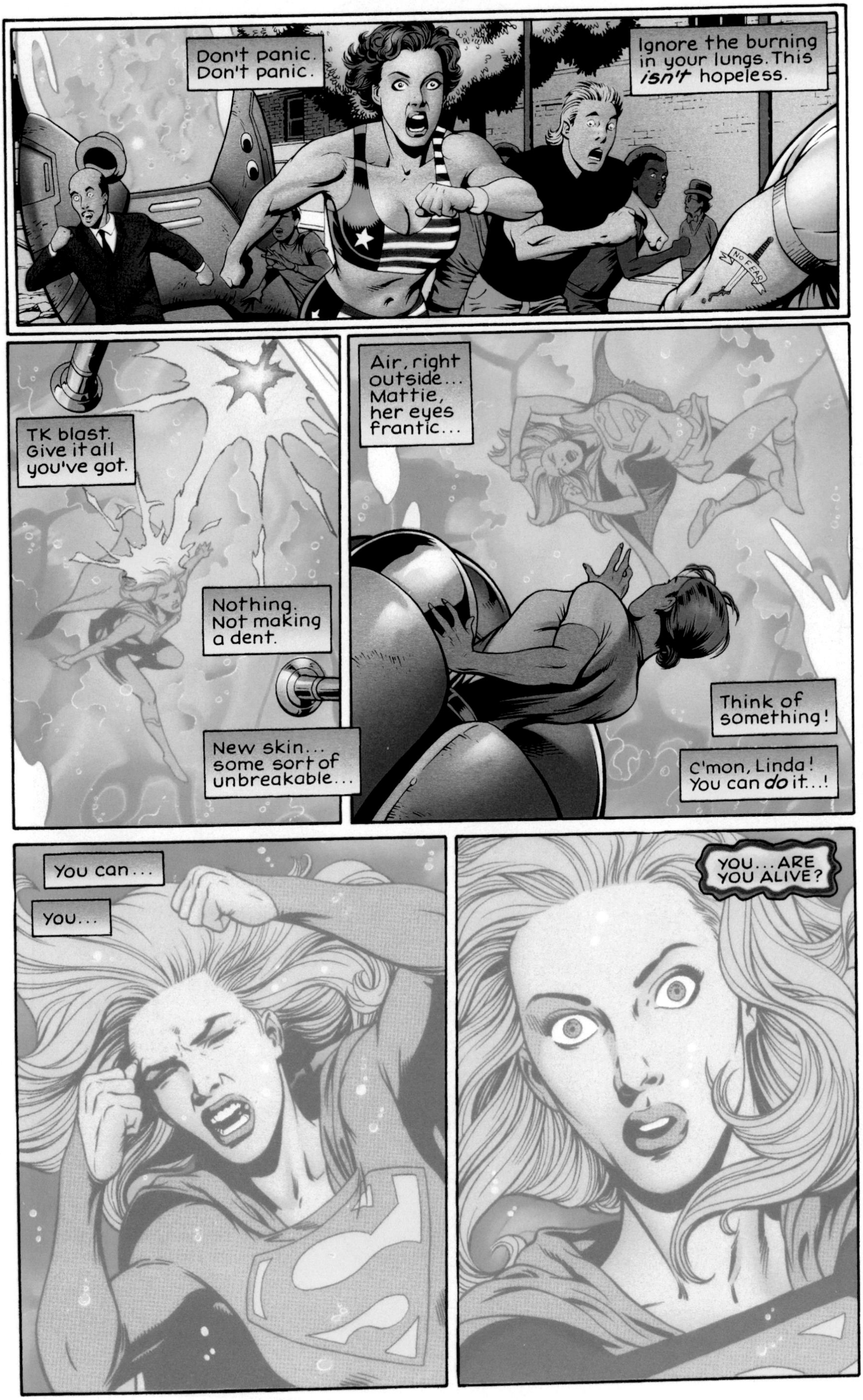
Don't panic.
Don't panic.
Ignore the burning in your lungs. This *isn't* hopeless.
NO FEAR
TK blast. Give it all you've got.
Nothing. Not making a dent.
New skin... some sort of unbreakable...
Air, right outside... Mattie, her eyes frantic...
Think of something!
C'mon, Linda! You can *do* it...!
You can...
You...
YOU... ARE YOU ALIVE?

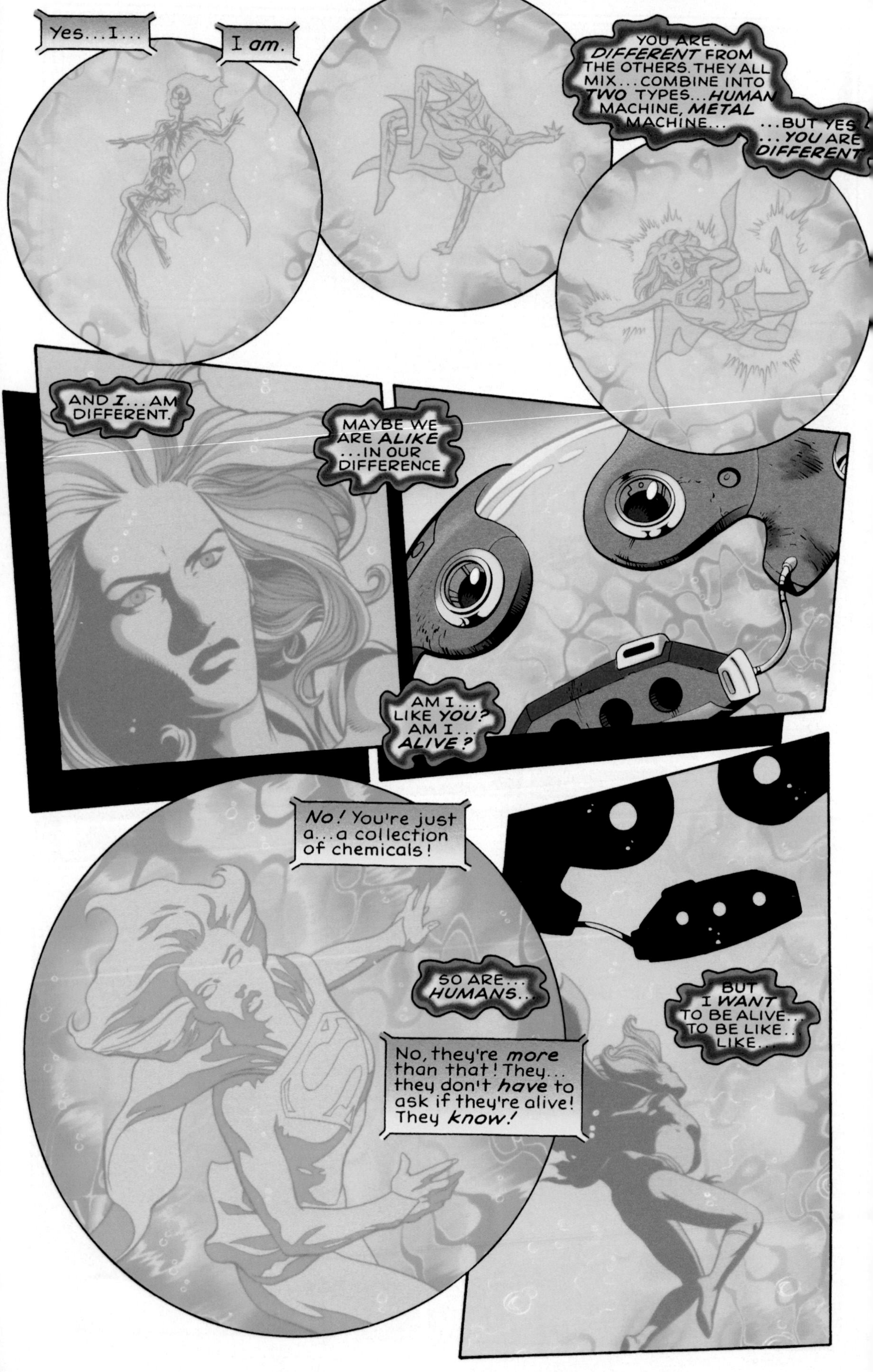
Yes... I...
I am.
YOU ARE... DIFFERENT FROM THE OTHERS. THEY ALL MIX... COMBINE INTO TWO TYPES... HUMAN MACHINE, METAL MACHINE...
...BUT YES ...YOU ARE DIFFERENT
AND I... AM DIFFERENT.
MAYBE WE ARE ALIKE ...IN OUR DIFFERENCE.
AM I... LIKE YOU? AM I... ALIVE?
No! You're just a... a collection of chemicals!
SO ARE... HUMANS...
No, they're more than that! They... they don't have to ask if they're alive! They know!
BUT I WANT TO BE ALIVE... TO BE LIKE... LIKE...

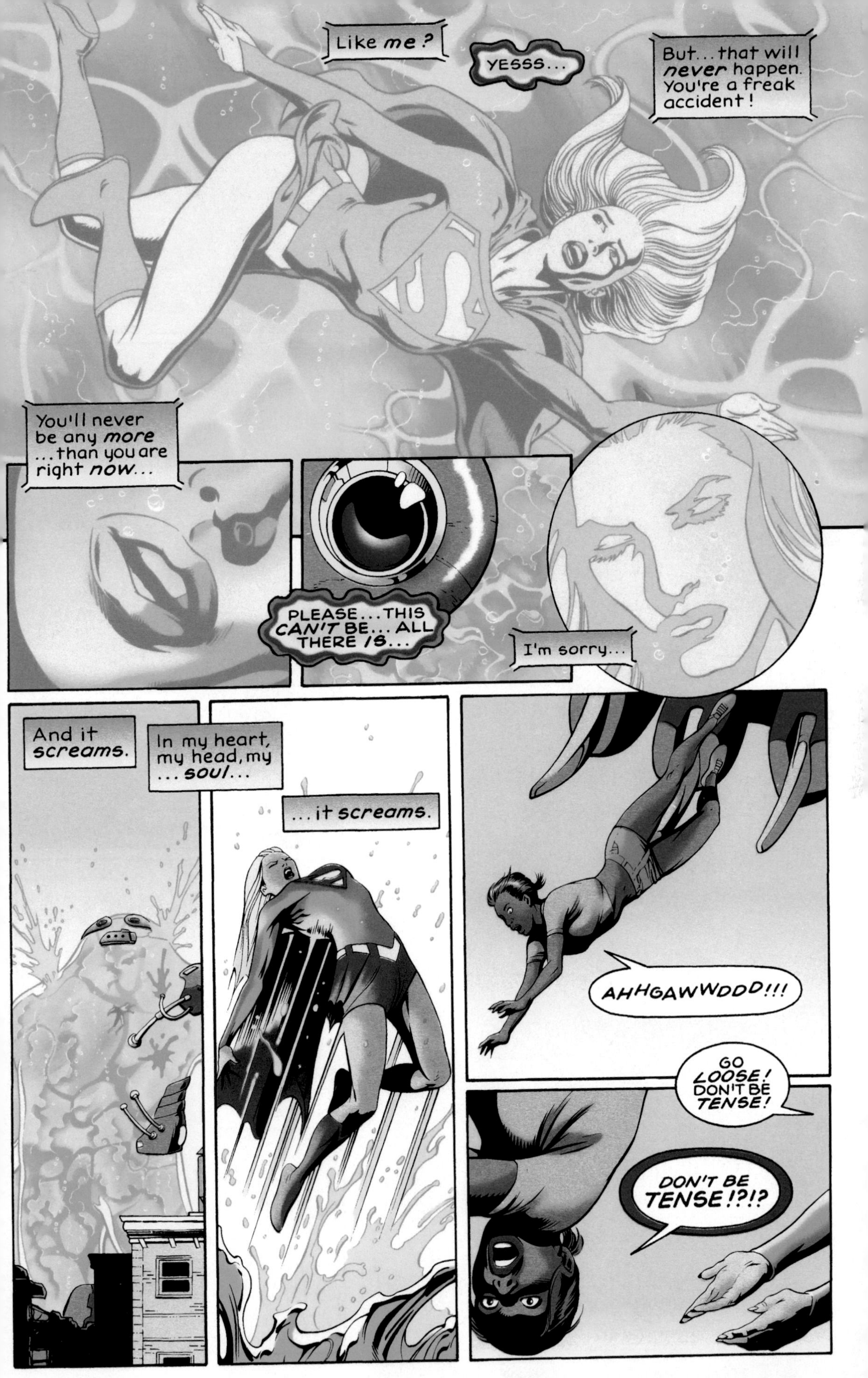

Like *me*?
YESSS...
But... that will *never* happen. You're a freak accident!
You'll never be any *more* ...than you are right *now*...
PLEASE... THIS *CAN'T* BE... ALL THERE *IS*...
I'm sorry...
And it *screams*.
In my heart, my head, my ... *soul*...
...it *screams*.
AHHGAWWDDD!!!
GO *LOOSE*! DON'T BE *TENSE*!
DON'T BE *TENSE*!?!?

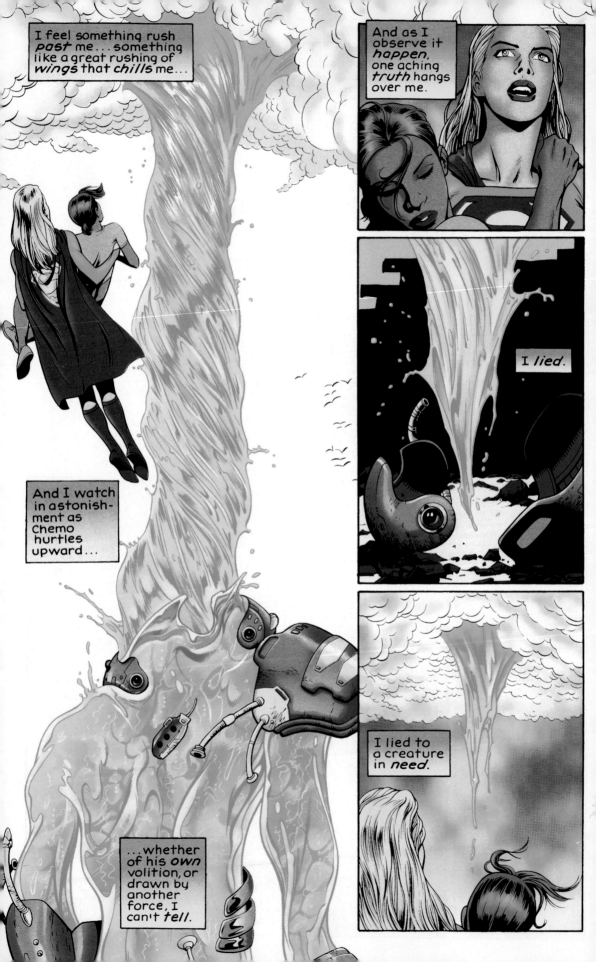

I feel something rush *past* me...something like a great rushing of *wings* that *chills* me...

And I watch in astonishment as Chemo hurtles upward...

...whether of his *own* volition, or drawn by another force, I can't *tell*.

And as I observe it *happen*, one aching *truth* hangs over me.

I *lied*.

I lied to a creature in *need*.

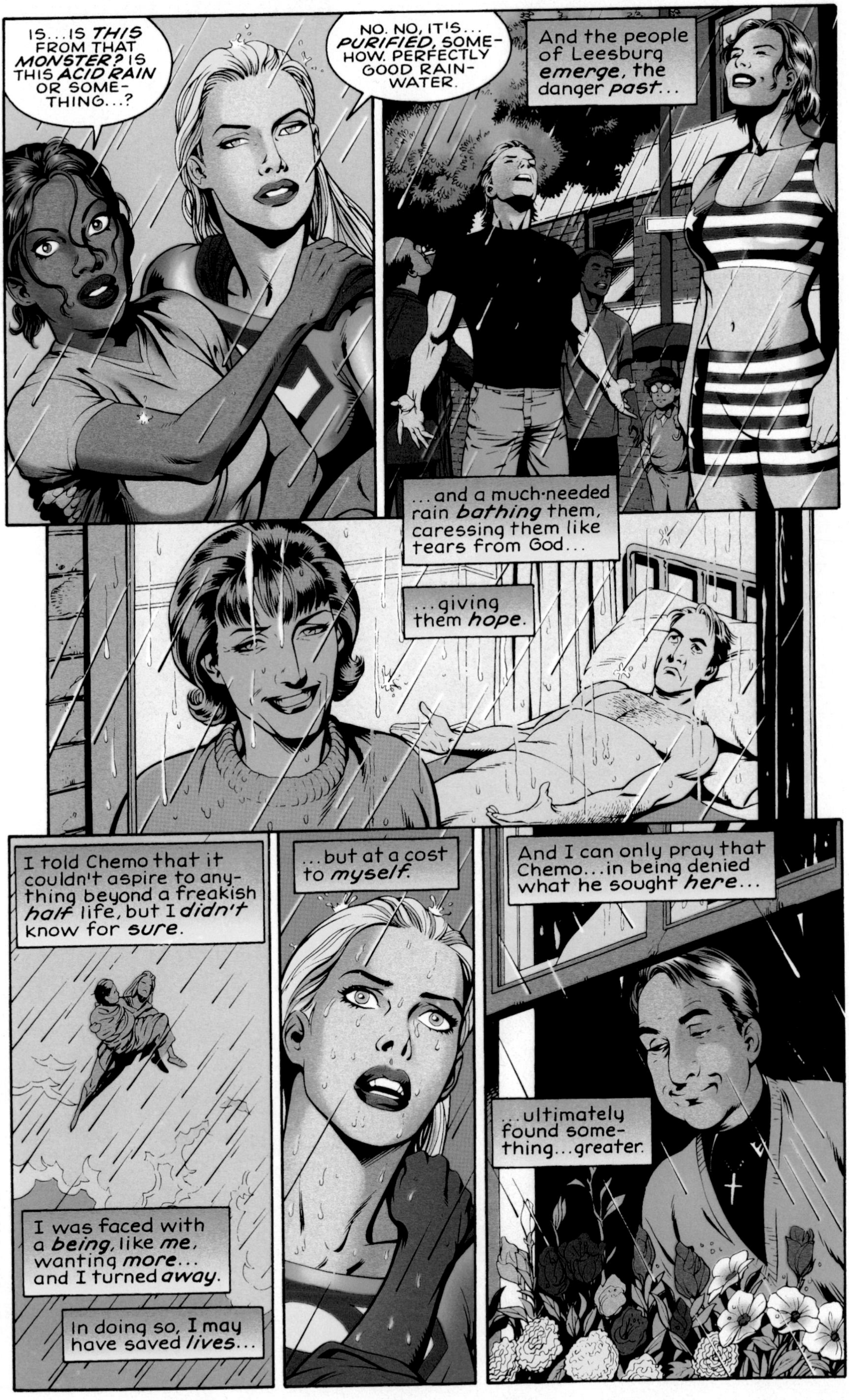
IS... IS THIS FROM THAT MONSTER? IS THIS ACID RAIN OR SOMETHING...?
NO. NO, IT'S... PURIFIED, SOMEHOW. PERFECTLY GOOD RAINWATER.
And the people of Leesburg emerge, the danger past...
...and a much-needed rain bathing them, caressing them like tears from God...
...giving them hope.
I told Chemo that it couldn't aspire to anything beyond a freakish half life, but I didn't know for sure.
I was faced with a being, like me, wanting more... and I turned away.
In doing so, I may have saved lives...
...but at a cost to myself.
And I can only pray that Chemo... in being denied what he sought here...
...ultimately found something... greater.

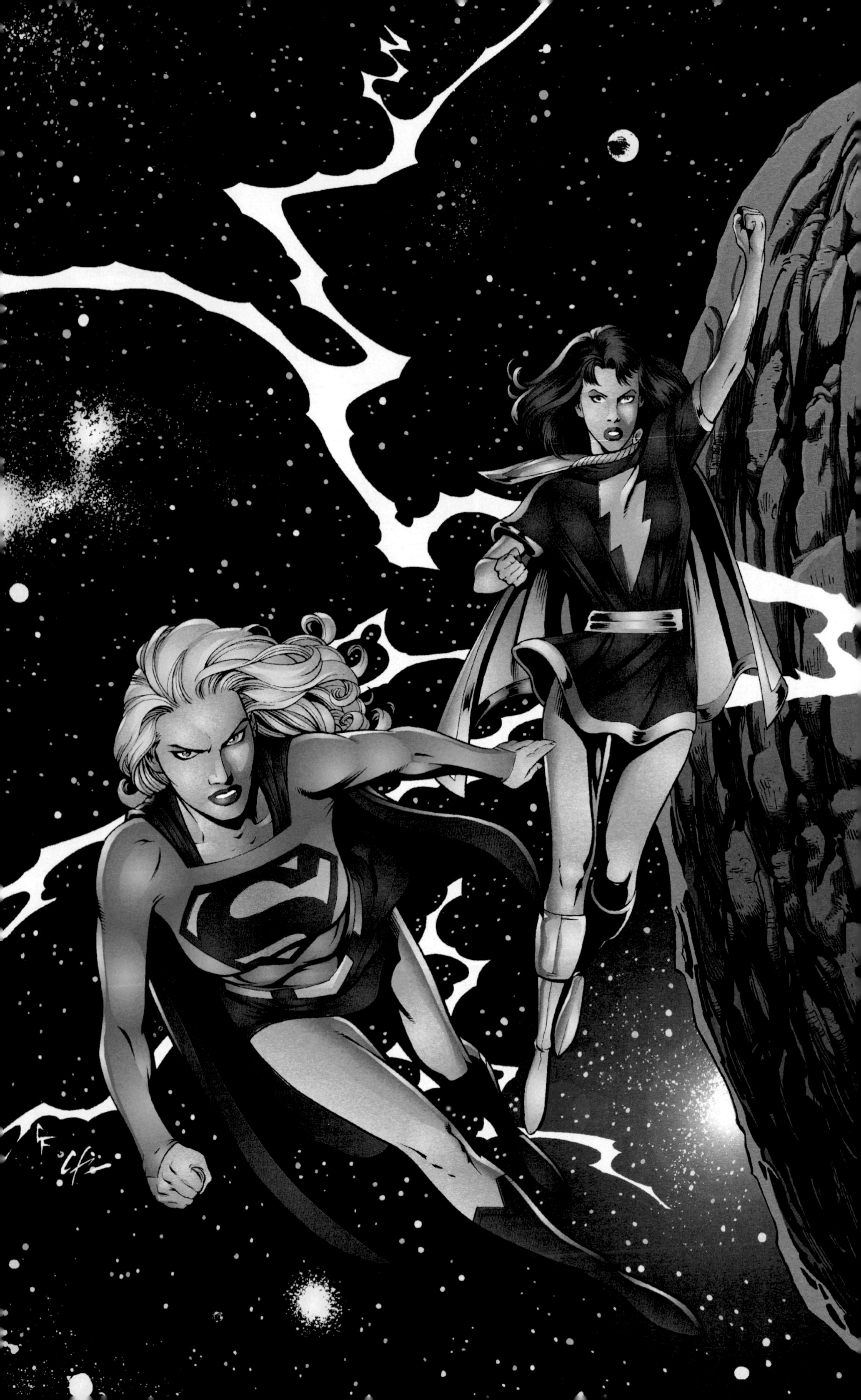

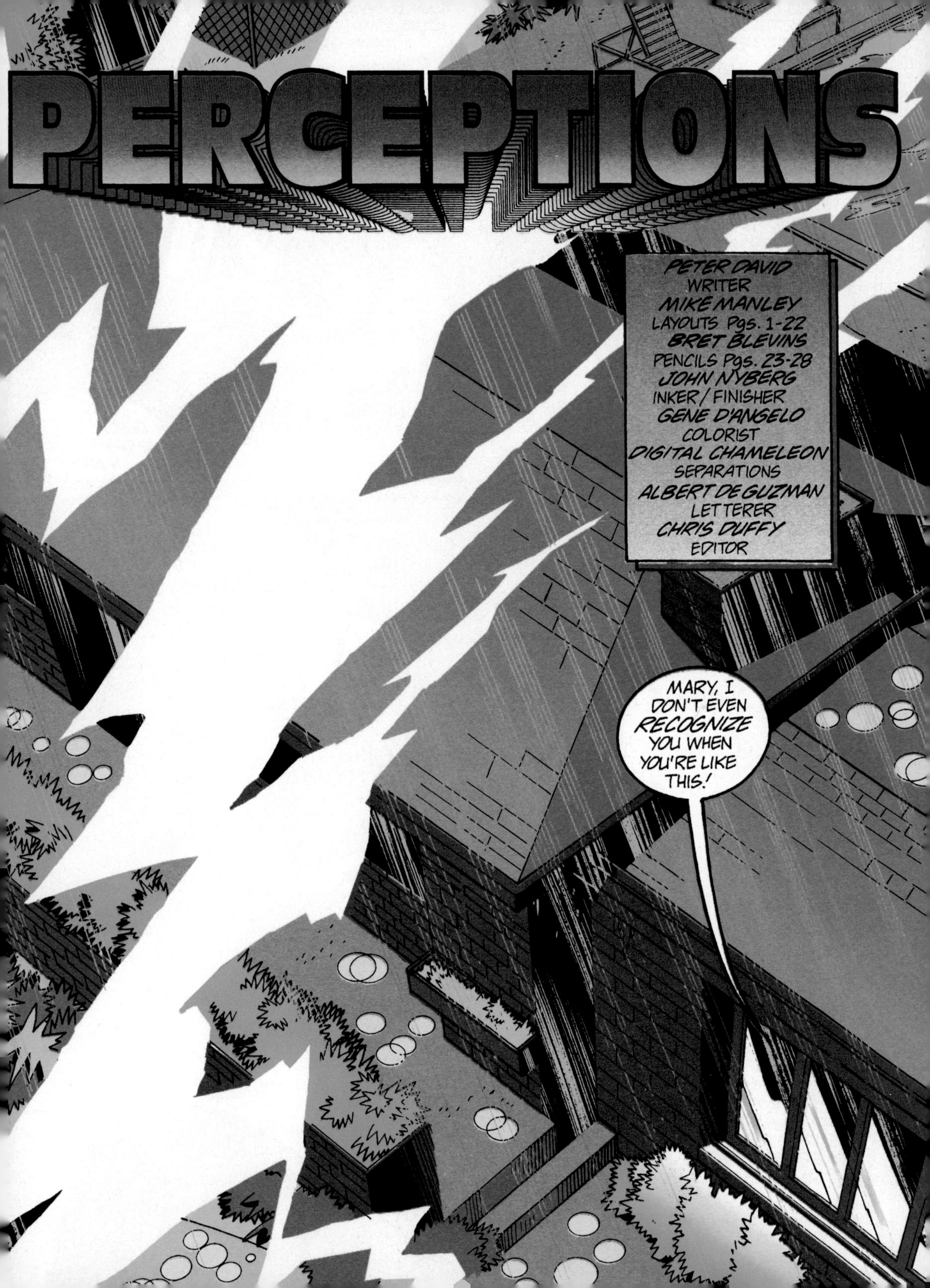
PERCEPTIONS
PETER DAVID
WRITER
MIKE MANLEY
LAYOUTS Pgs. 1-22
BRET BLEVINS
PENCILS Pgs. 23-28
JOHN NYBERG
INKER/FINISHER
GENE D'ANGELO
COLORIST
DIGITAL CHAMELEON
SEPARATIONS
ALBERT DE GUZMAN
LETTERER
CHRIS DUFFY
EDITOR
MARY, I DON'T EVEN RECOGNIZE YOU WHEN YOU'RE LIKE THIS!

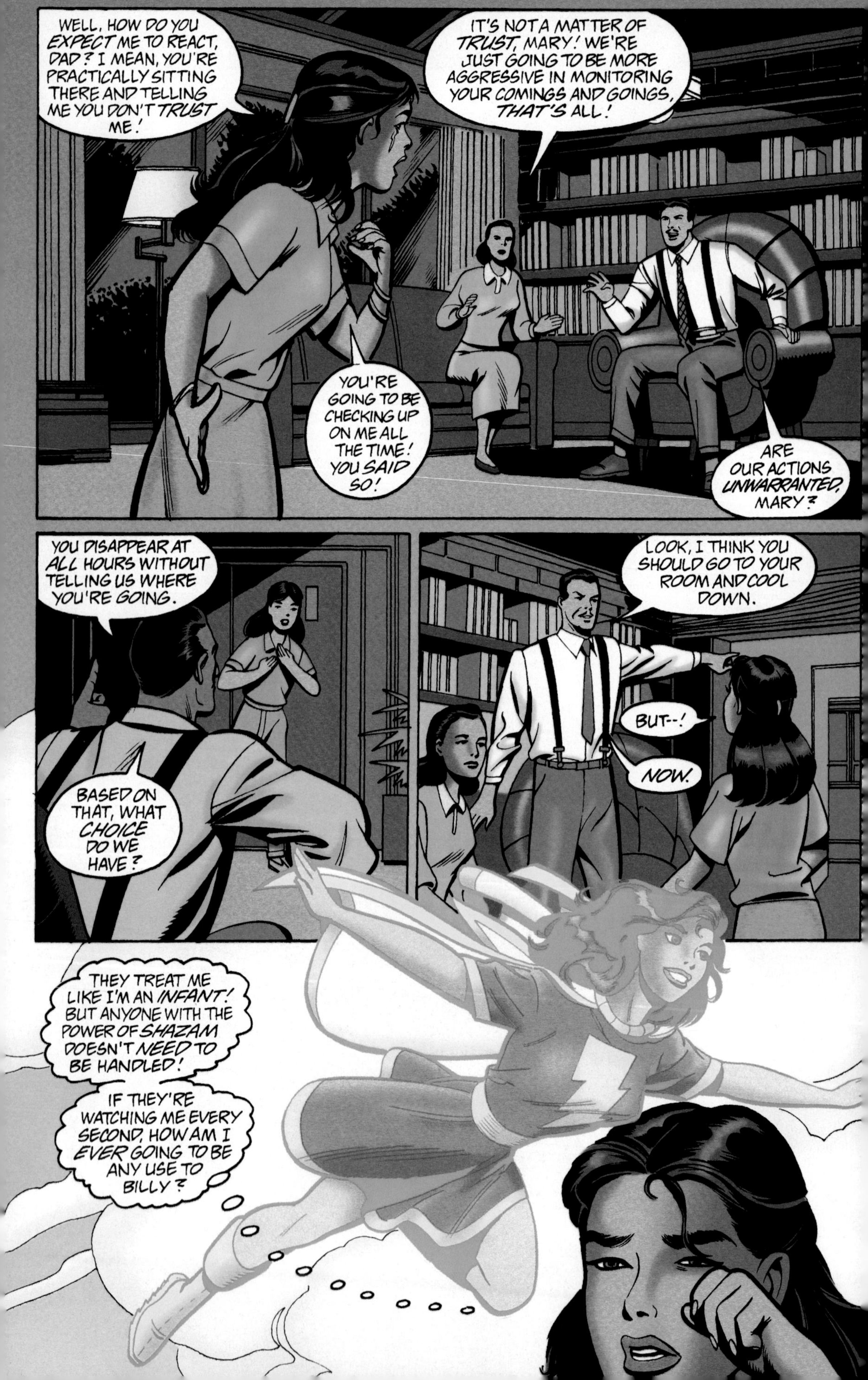
WELL, HOW DO YOU EXPECT ME TO REACT, DAD? I MEAN, YOU'RE PRACTICALLY SITTING THERE AND TELLING ME YOU DON'T TRUST ME!
IT'S NOT A MATTER OF TRUST, MARY! WE'RE JUST GOING TO BE MORE AGGRESSIVE IN MONITORING YOUR COMINGS AND GOINGS, THAT'S ALL!
YOU'RE GOING TO BE CHECKING UP ON ME ALL THE TIME! YOU SAID SO!
ARE OUR ACTIONS UNWARRANTED, MARY?
YOU DISAPPEAR AT ALL HOURS WITHOUT TELLING US WHERE YOU'RE GOING.
BASED ON THAT, WHAT CHOICE DO WE HAVE?
LOOK, I THINK YOU SHOULD GO TO YOUR ROOM AND COOL DOWN.
BUT--!
NOW.
THEY TREAT ME LIKE I'M AN INFANT! BUT ANYONE WITH THE POWER OF SHAZAM DOESN'T NEED TO BE HANDLED!
IF THEY'RE WATCHING ME EVERY SECOND, HOW AM I EVER GOING TO BE ANY USE TO BILLY?

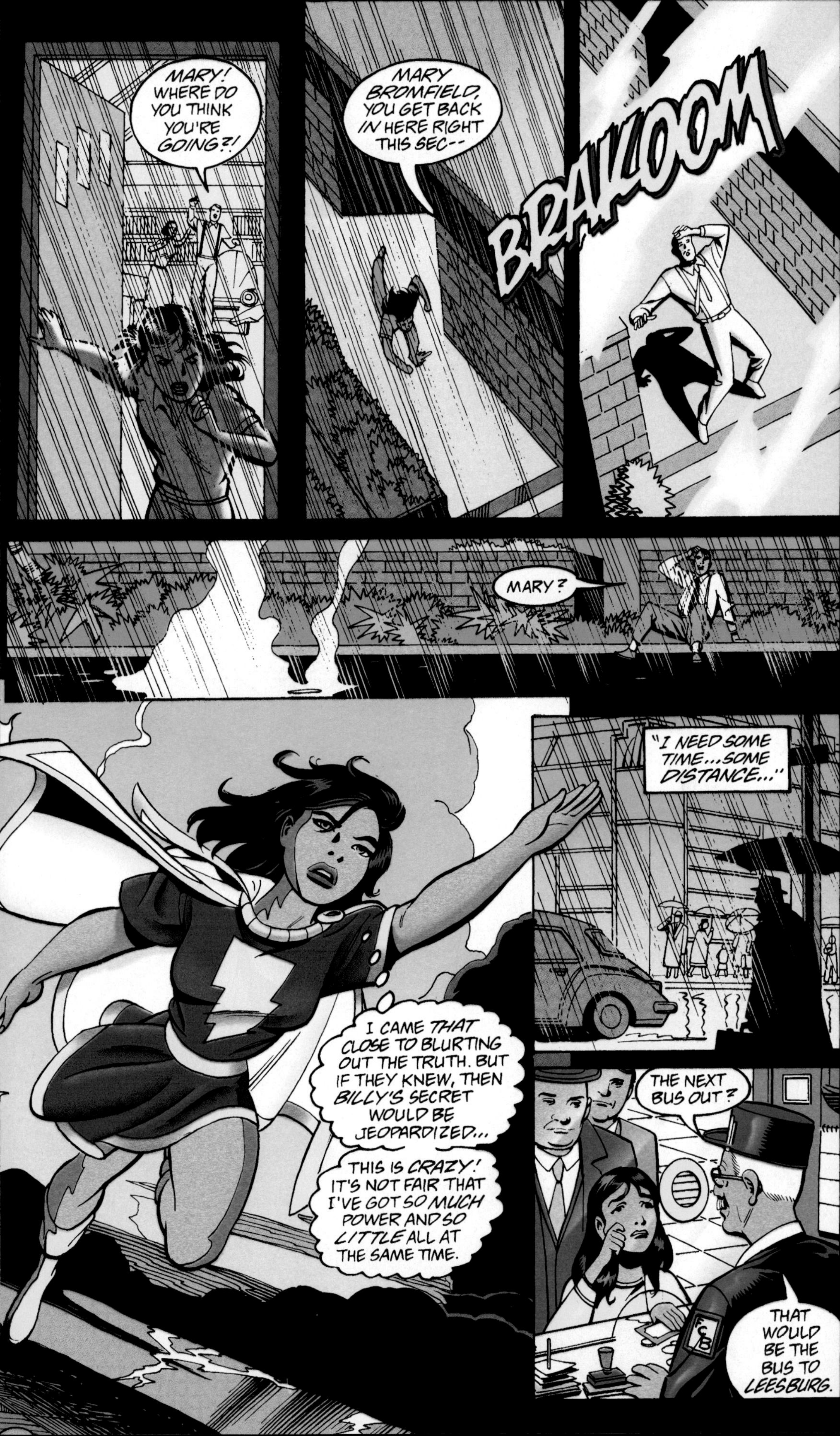
MARY! WHERE DO YOU THINK YOU'RE GOING?!
MARY BROMFIELD, YOU GET BACK IN HERE RIGHT THIS SEC--
BRAKOOOM
MARY?
"I NEED SOME TIME... SOME DISTANCE..."
I CAME THAT CLOSE TO BLURTING OUT THE TRUTH. BUT IF THEY KNEW, THEN BILLY'S SECRET WOULD BE JEOPARDIZED...
THIS IS CRAZY! IT'S NOT FAIR THAT I'VE GOT SO MUCH POWER AND SO LITTLE ALL AT THE SAME TIME.
THE NEXT BUS OUT?
THAT WOULD BE THE BUS TO LEESBURG.

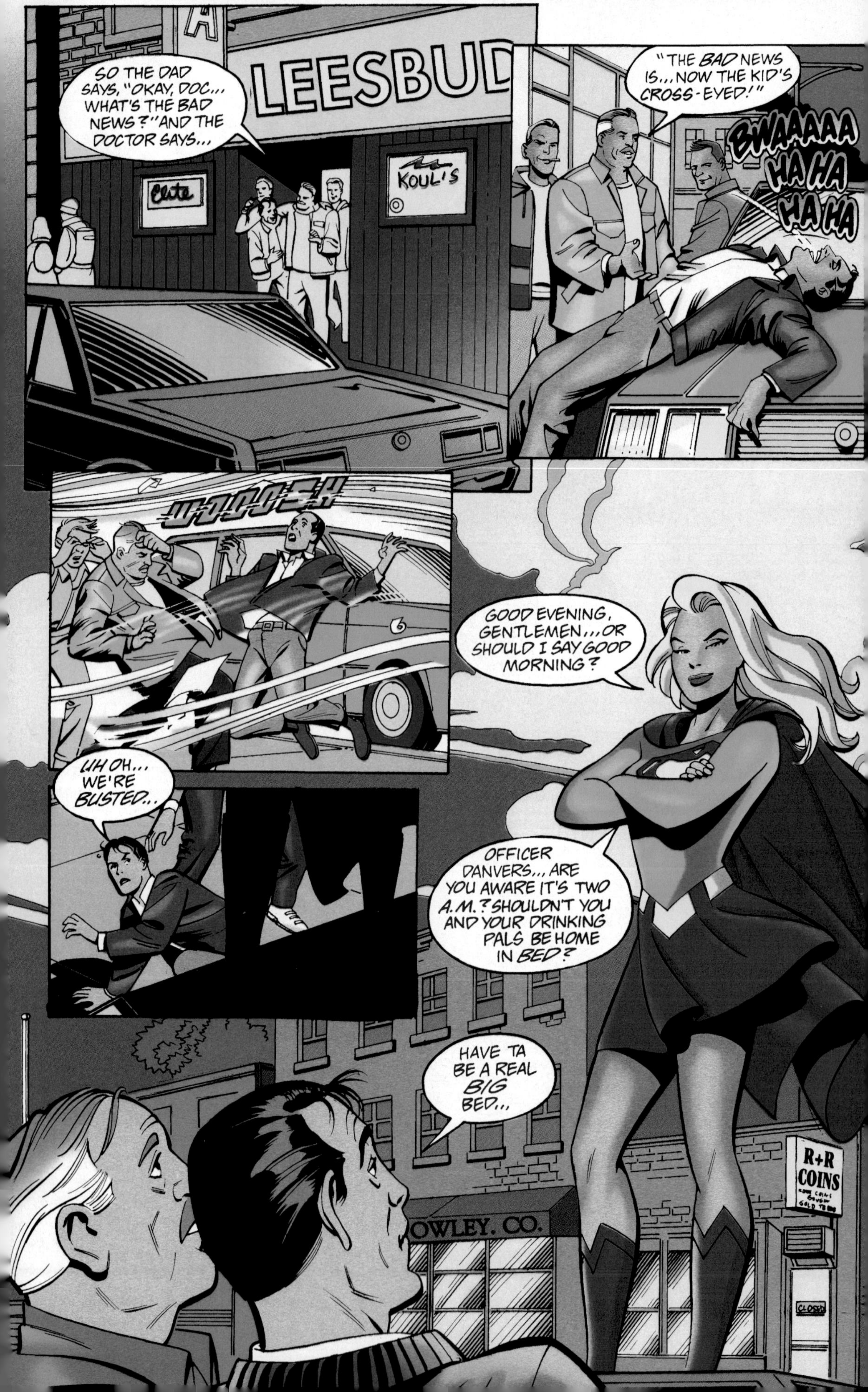
LEESBUD
SO THE DAD SAYS, "OKAY, DOC... WHAT'S THE BAD NEWS?" AND THE DOCTOR SAYS...
Elite
KOULI'S
"THE BAD NEWS IS... NOW THE KID'S CROSS-EYED!"
BWAAAAA HA HA HA HA
GOOD EVENING, GENTLEMEN... OR SHOULD I SAY GOOD MORNING?
UH OH... WE'RE BUSTED...
OFFICER DANVERS... ARE YOU AWARE IT'S TWO A.M.? SHOULDN'T YOU AND YOUR DRINKING PALS BE HOME IN BED?
HAVE TA BE A REAL BIG BED...
R+R COINS
OWLEY. CO.
CLOSED

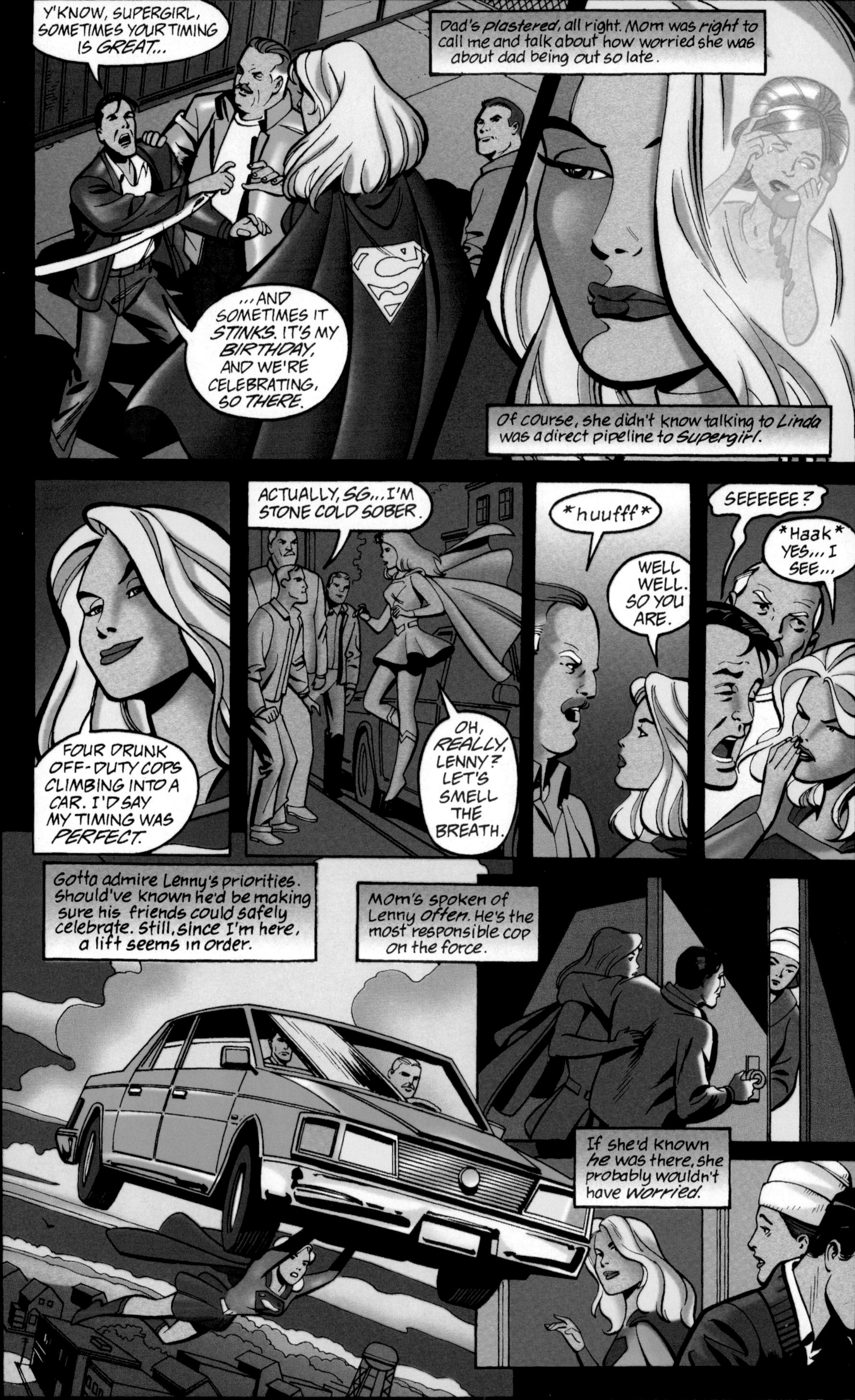
Y'KNOW, SUPERGIRL, SOMETIMES YOUR TIMING IS GREAT...
Dad's plastered, all right. Mom was right to call me and talk about how worried she was about dad being out so late.
...AND SOMETIMES IT STINKS. IT'S MY BIRTHDAY, AND WE'RE CELEBRATING, SO THERE.
Of course, she didn't know talking to Linda was a direct pipeline to Supergirl.
FOUR DRUNK OFF-DUTY COPS CLIMBING INTO A CAR. I'D SAY MY TIMING WAS PERFECT.
ACTUALLY, SG... I'M STONE COLD SOBER.
OH, REALLY, LENNY? LET'S SMELL THE BREATH.
huufff
WELL WELL. SO YOU ARE.
SEEEEEE?
Haak YES... I SEE...
Gotta admire Lenny's priorities. Should've known he'd be making sure his friends could safely celebrate. Still, since I'm here, a lift seems in order.
Mom's spoken of Lenny often. He's the most responsible cop on the force.
If she'd known he was there, she probably wouldn't have worried.

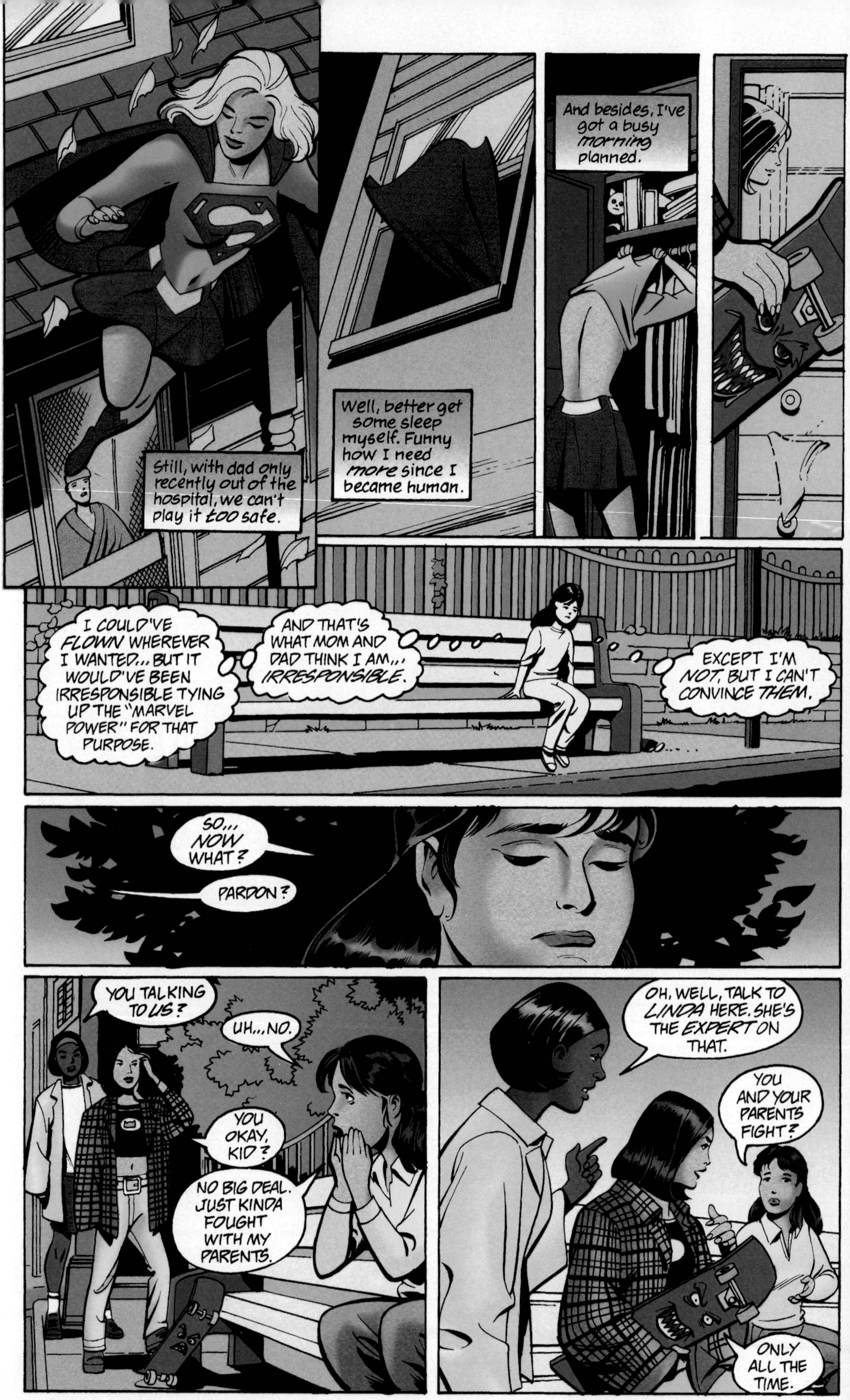
Still, with dad only recently out of the hospital, we can't play it too safe.
Well, better get some sleep myself. Funny how I need more since I became human.
And besides, I've got a busy morning planned.
I COULD'VE FLOWN WHEREVER I WANTED... BUT IT WOULD'VE BEEN IRRESPONSIBLE TYING UP THE "MARVEL POWER" FOR THAT PURPOSE.
AND THAT'S WHAT MOM AND DAD THINK I AM... IRRESPONSIBLE.
EXCEPT I'M NOT, BUT I CAN'T CONVINCE THEM.
SO... NOW WHAT?
PARDON?
YOU TALKING TO US?
UH... NO.
YOU OKAY, KID?
NO BIG DEAL. JUST KINDA FOUGHT WITH MY PARENTS.
OH, WELL, TALK TO LINDA HERE. SHE'S THE EXPERT ON THAT.
YOU AND YOUR PARENTS FIGHT?
ONLY ALL THE TIME.

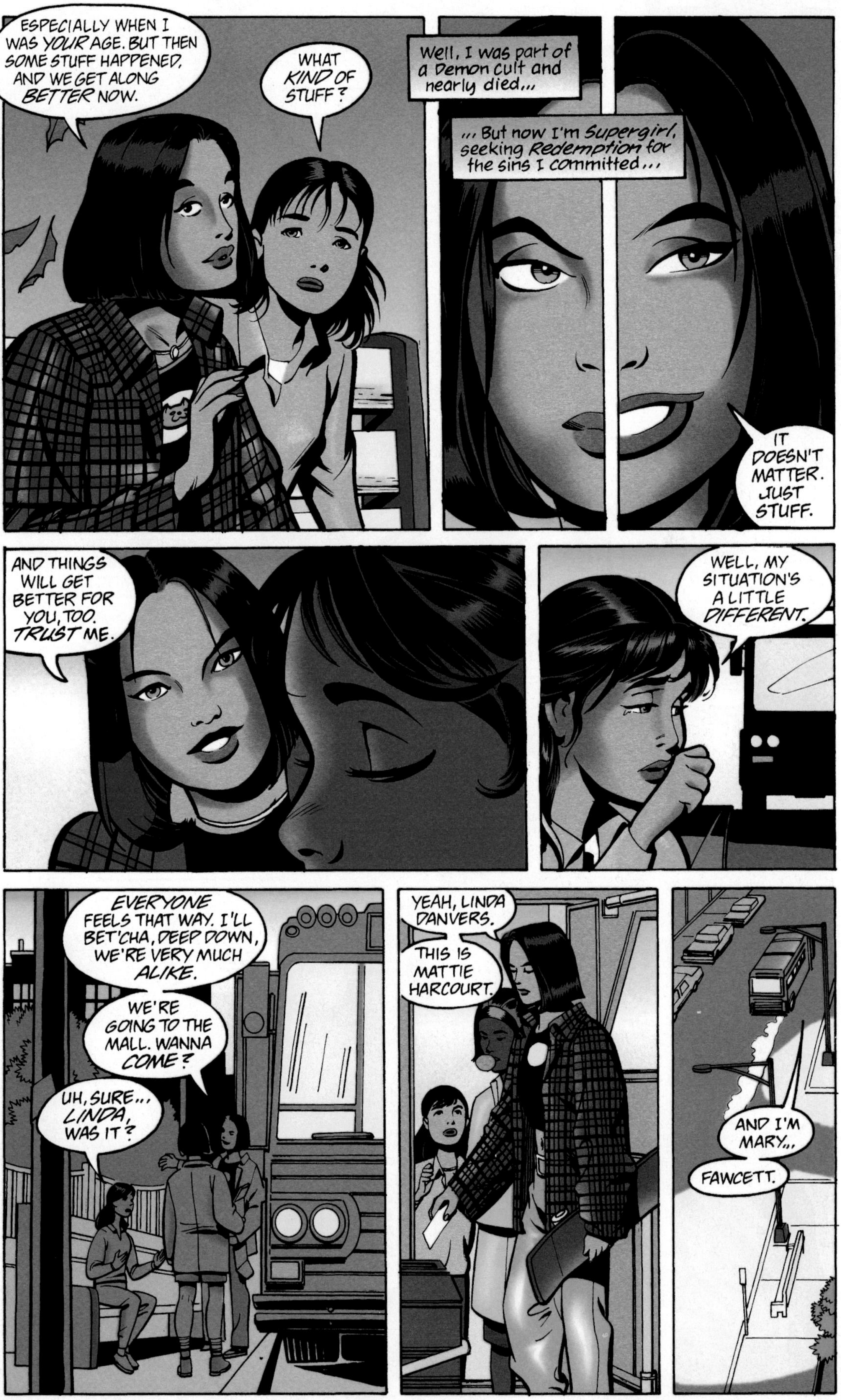
ESPECIALLY WHEN I WAS YOUR AGE. BUT THEN SOME STUFF HAPPENED, AND WE GET ALONG BETTER NOW.
WHAT KIND OF STUFF?
Well, I was part of a Demon cult and nearly died...
...But now I'm Supergirl, seeking Redemption for the sins I committed...
IT DOESN'T MATTER. JUST STUFF.
AND THINGS WILL GET BETTER FOR YOU, TOO. TRUST ME.
WELL, MY SITUATION'S A LITTLE DIFFERENT.
EVERYONE FEELS THAT WAY. I'LL BET'CHA, DEEP DOWN, WE'RE VERY MUCH ALIKE.
WE'RE GOING TO THE MALL. WANNA COME?
UH, SURE... LINDA, WAS IT?
YEAH, LINDA DANVERS.
THIS IS MATTIE HARCOURT.
AND I'M MARY...
FAWCETT.

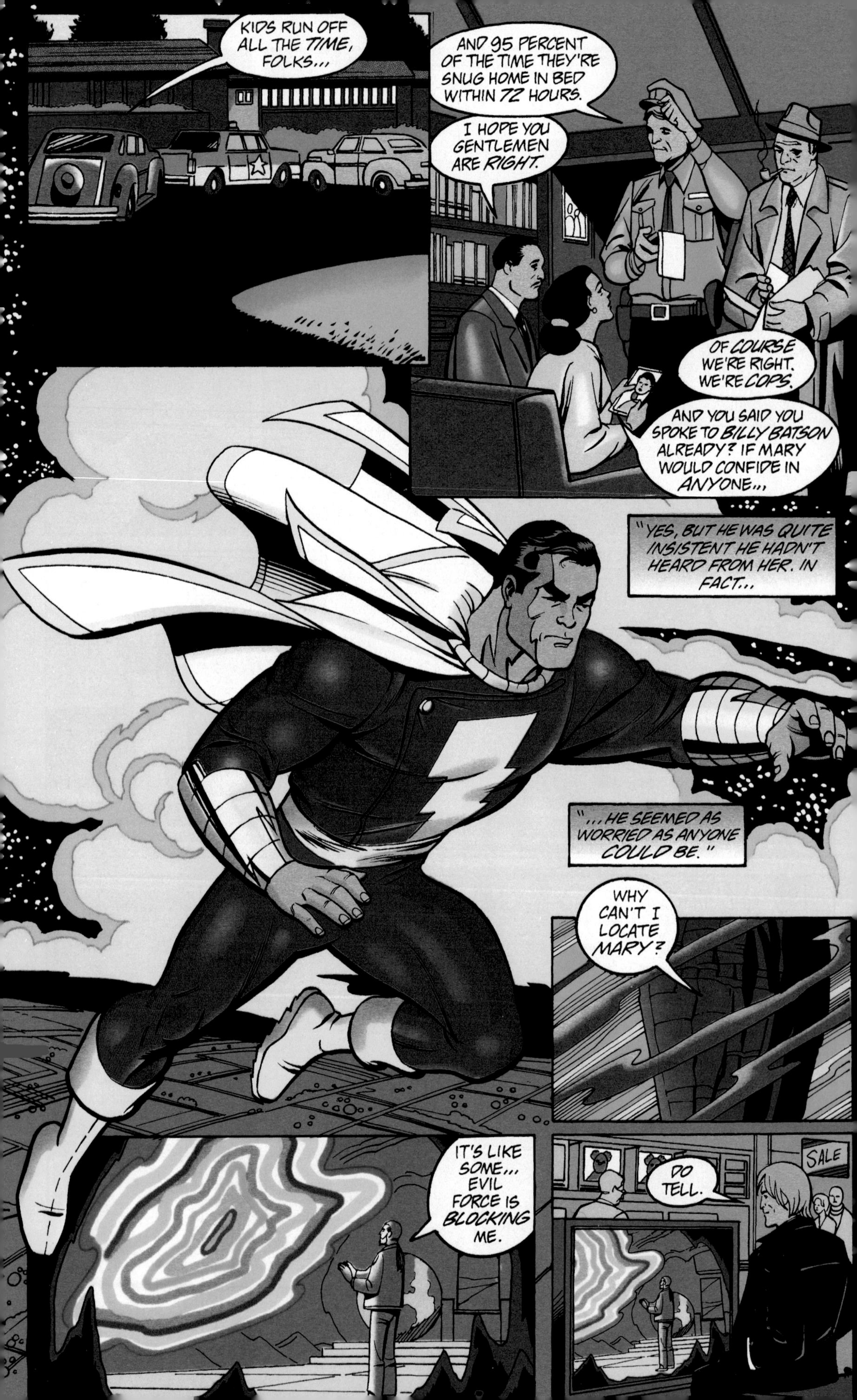
KIDS RUN OFF ALL THE TIME, FOLKS...
AND 95 PERCENT OF THE TIME THEY'RE SNUG HOME IN BED WITHIN 72 HOURS.
I HOPE YOU GENTLEMEN ARE RIGHT.
OF COURSE WE'RE RIGHT. WE'RE COPS.
AND YOU SAID YOU SPOKE TO BILLY BATSON ALREADY? IF MARY WOULD CONFIDE IN ANYONE...
"YES, BUT HE WAS QUITE INSISTENT HE HADN'T HEARD FROM HER. IN FACT...
"...HE SEEMED AS WORRIED AS ANYONE COULD BE."
WHY CAN'T I LOCATE MARY?
IT'S LIKE SOME... EVIL FORCE IS BLOCKING ME.
SALE
DO TELL.

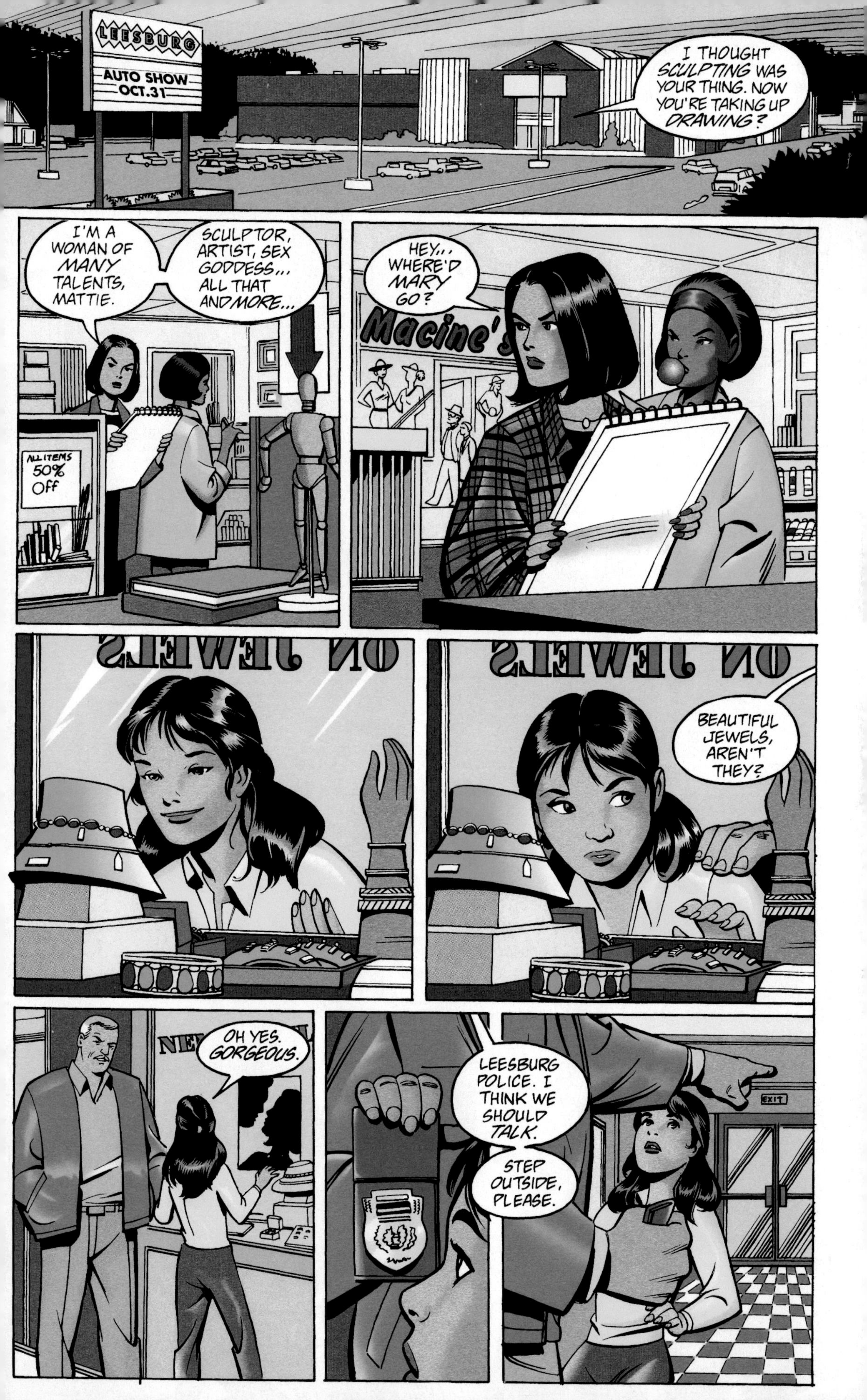
LEESBURG
AUTO SHOW OCT.31
I THOUGHT SCULPTING WAS YOUR THING. NOW YOU'RE TAKING UP DRAWING?
I'M A WOMAN OF MANY TALENTS, MATTIE.
SCULPTOR, ARTIST, SEX GODDESS... ALL THAT AND MORE...
ALL ITEMS 50% OFF
HEY... WHERE'D MARY GO?
Macine's
BEAUTIFUL JEWELS, AREN'T THEY?
OH YES. GORGEOUS.
LEESBURG POLICE. I THINK WE SHOULD TALK.
STEP OUTSIDE, PLEASE.
EXIT

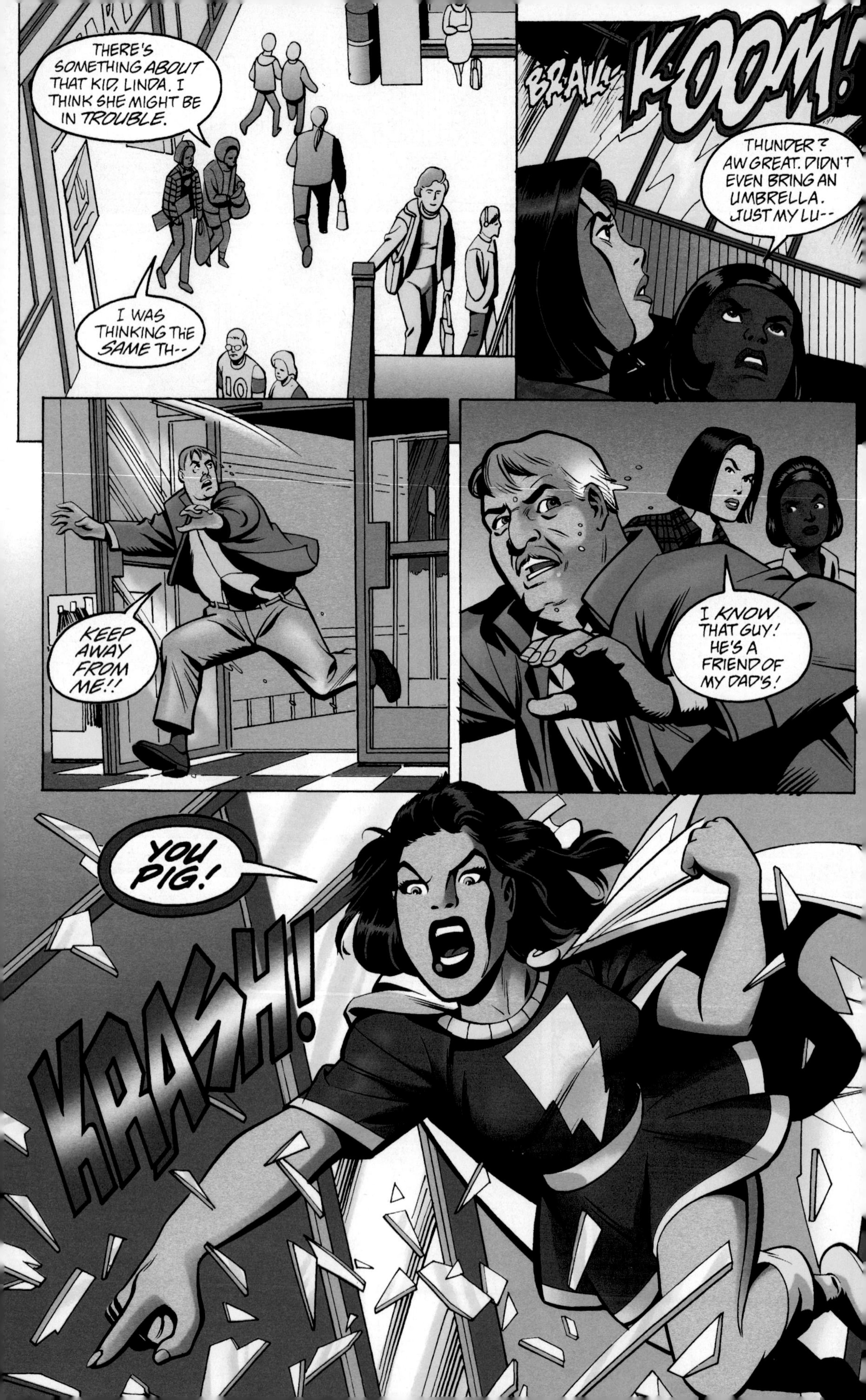
THERE'S SOMETHING ABOUT THAT KID, LINDA. I THINK SHE MIGHT BE IN TROUBLE.
I WAS THINKING THE SAME TH--
BRAKA-KOOM!
THUNDER? AW GREAT. DIDN'T EVEN BRING AN UMBRELLA. JUST MY LU--
KEEP AWAY FROM ME!!
I KNOW THAT GUY! HE'S A FRIEND OF MY DAD'S!
YOU PIG!
KRASH!

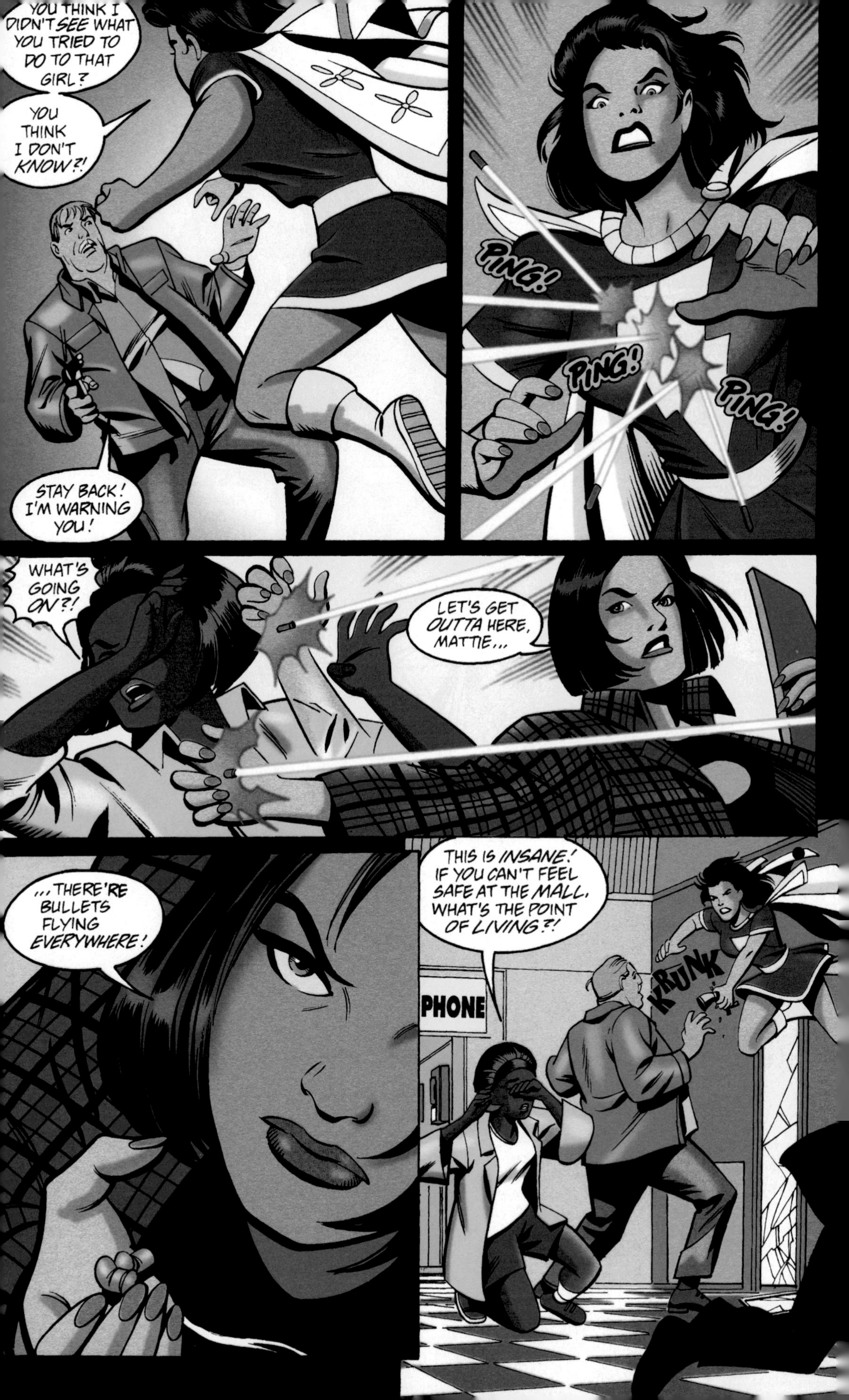
YOU THINK I DIDN'T SEE WHAT YOU TRIED TO DO TO THAT GIRL?
YOU THINK I DON'T KNOW?!
STAY BACK! I'M WARNING YOU!
PING!
PING!
PING!
WHAT'S GOING ON?!
LET'S GET OUTTA HERE, MATTIE...
...THERE'RE BULLETS FLYING EVERYWHERE!
THIS IS INSANE! IF YOU CAN'T FEEL SAFE AT THE MALL, WHAT'S THE POINT OF LIVING?!
PHONE
KRUNK

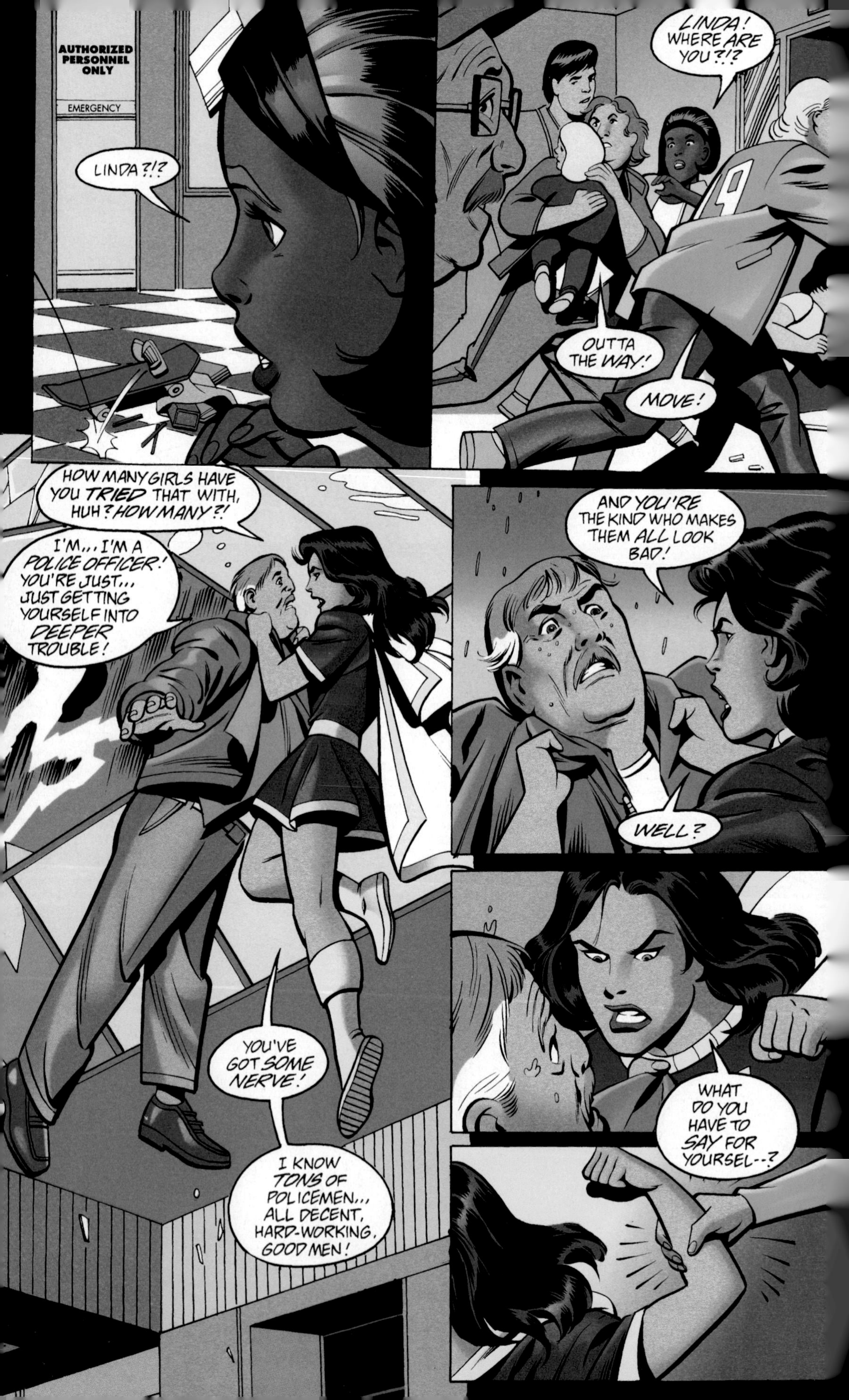
AUTHORIZED PERSONNEL ONLY
EMERGENCY
LINDA?!?
LINDA! WHERE ARE YOU?!?
OUTTA THE WAY!
MOVE!
HOW MANY GIRLS HAVE YOU TRIED THAT WITH, HUH? HOW MANY?!
I'M... I'M A POLICE OFFICER! YOU'RE JUST... JUST GETTING YOURSELF INTO DEEPER TROUBLE!
YOU'VE GOT SOME NERVE!
I KNOW TONS OF POLICEMEN... ALL DECENT, HARD-WORKING, GOOD MEN!
AND YOU'RE THE KIND WHO MAKES THEM ALL LOOK BAD!
WELL?
WHAT DO YOU HAVE TO SAY FOR YOURSEL--?

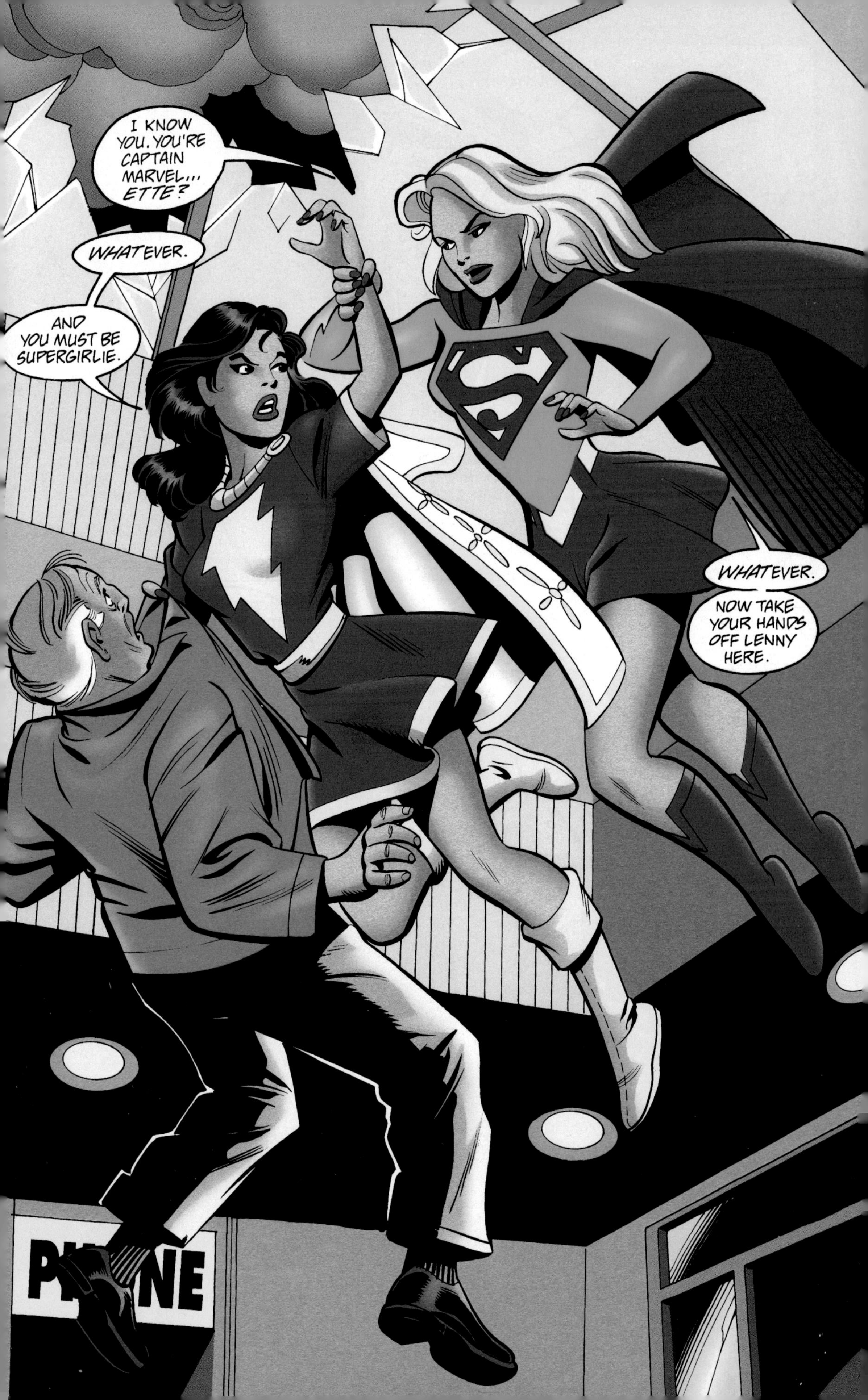
I KNOW YOU. YOU'RE CAPTAIN MARVEL,.. ETTE?
WHATEVER.
AND YOU MUST BE SUPERGIRLIE.
WHATEVER.
NOW TAKE YOUR HANDS OFF LENNY HERE.
PHONE

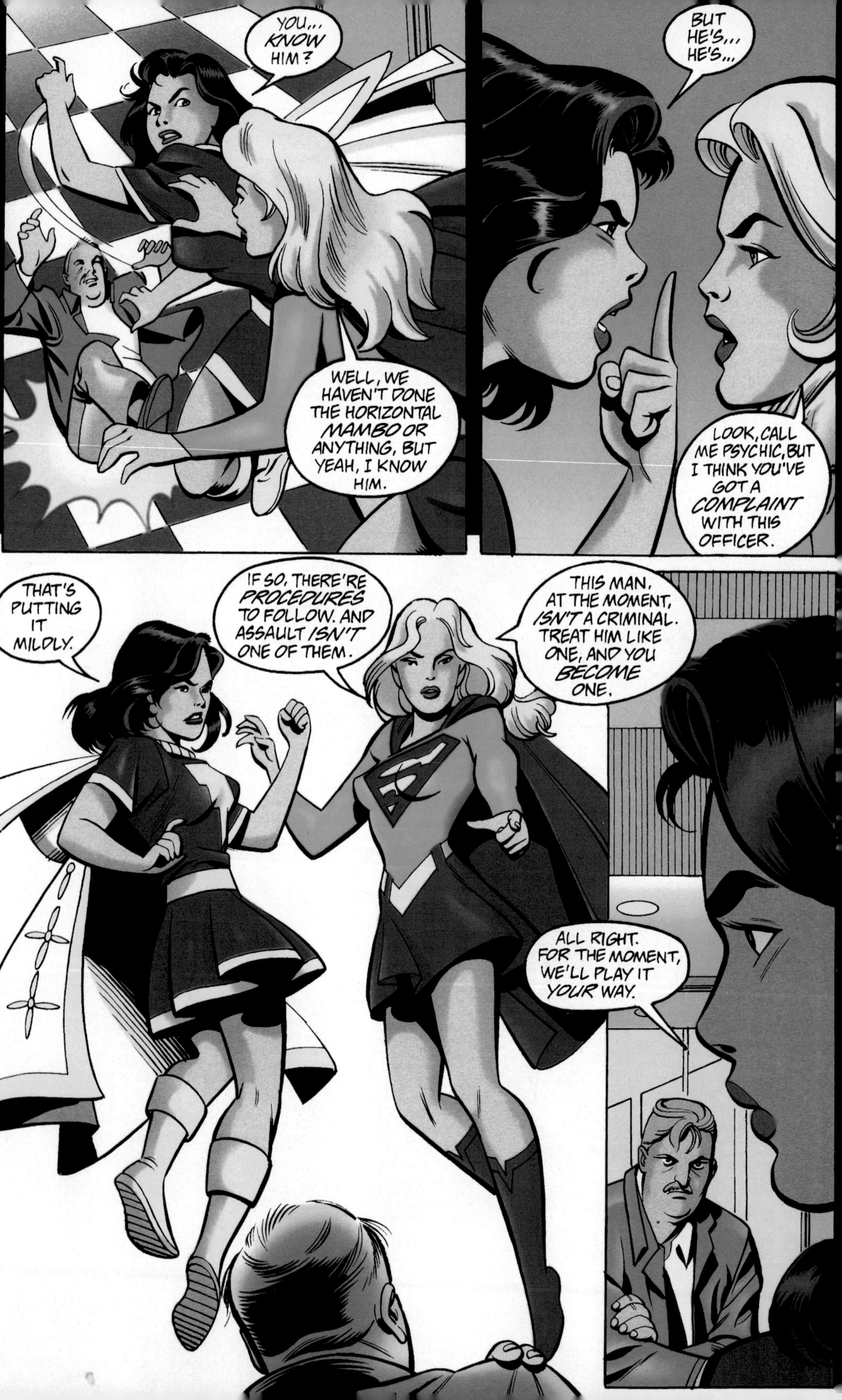
YOU... KNOW HIM?
WELL, WE HAVEN'T DONE THE HORIZONTAL MAMBO OR ANYTHING, BUT YEAH, I KNOW HIM.
BUT HE'S... HE'S...
LOOK, CALL ME PSYCHIC, BUT I THINK YOU'VE GOT A COMPLAINT WITH THIS OFFICER.
THAT'S PUTTING IT MILDLY.
IF SO, THERE'RE PROCEDURES TO FOLLOW. AND ASSAULT ISN'T ONE OF THEM.
THIS MAN, AT THE MOMENT, ISN'T A CRIMINAL. TREAT HIM LIKE ONE, AND YOU BECOME ONE.
ALL RIGHT. FOR THE MOMENT, WE'LL PLAY IT YOUR WAY.

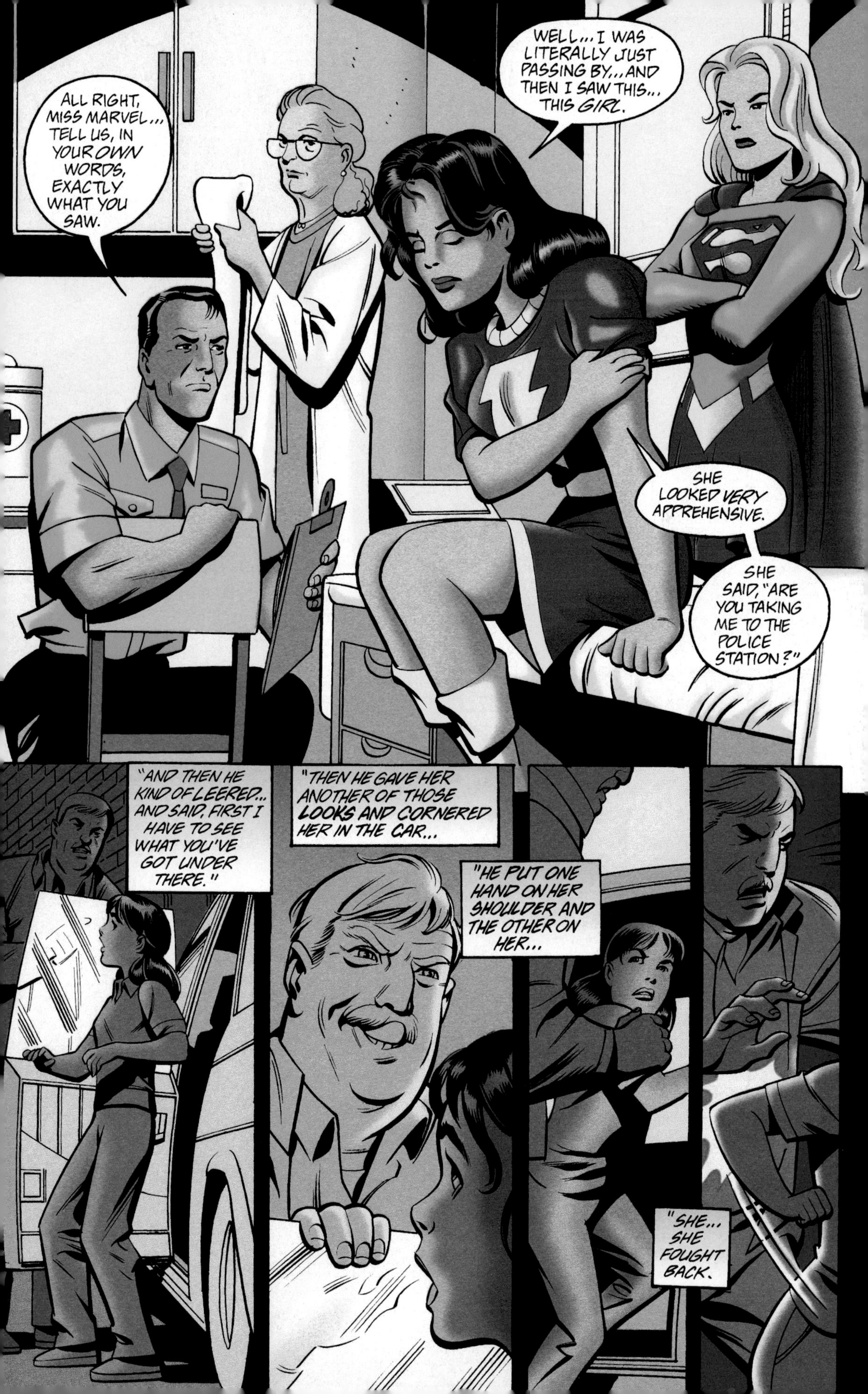
ALL RIGHT, MISS MARVEL... TELL US, IN YOUR OWN WORDS, EXACTLY WHAT YOU SAW.
WELL... I WAS LITERALLY JUST PASSING BY... AND THEN I SAW THIS... THIS GIRL.
SHE LOOKED VERY APPREHENSIVE.
SHE SAID, "ARE YOU TAKING ME TO THE POLICE STATION?"
"AND THEN HE KIND OF LEERED... AND SAID, FIRST I HAVE TO SEE WHAT YOU'VE GOT UNDER THERE."
"THEN HE GAVE HER ANOTHER OF THOSE LOOKS AND CORNERED HER IN THE CAR...
"HE PUT ONE HAND ON HER SHOULDER AND THE OTHER ON HER...
"SHE... SHE FOUGHT BACK.

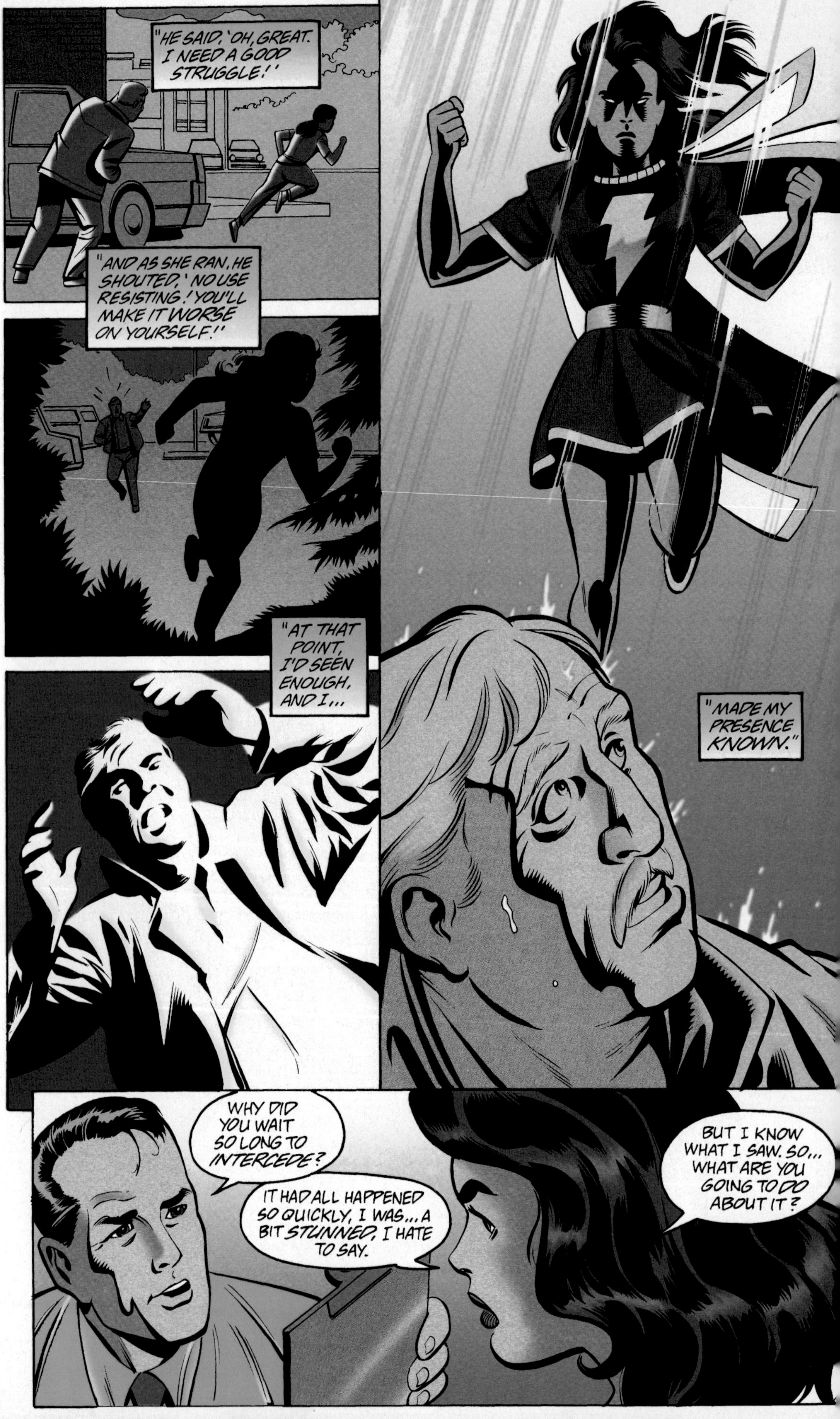
"HE SAID, 'OH, GREAT. I NEED A GOOD STRUGGLE!'
"AND AS SHE RAN, HE SHOUTED, 'NO USE RESISTING! YOU'LL MAKE IT WORSE ON YOURSELF!'
"AT THAT POINT, I'D SEEN ENOUGH, AND I...
"MADE MY PRESENCE KNOWN."
WHY DID YOU WAIT SO LONG TO INTERCEDE?
IT HAD ALL HAPPENED SO QUICKLY, I WAS... A BIT STUNNED, I HATE TO SAY.
BUT I KNOW WHAT I SAW. SO... WHAT ARE YOU GOING TO DO ABOUT IT?

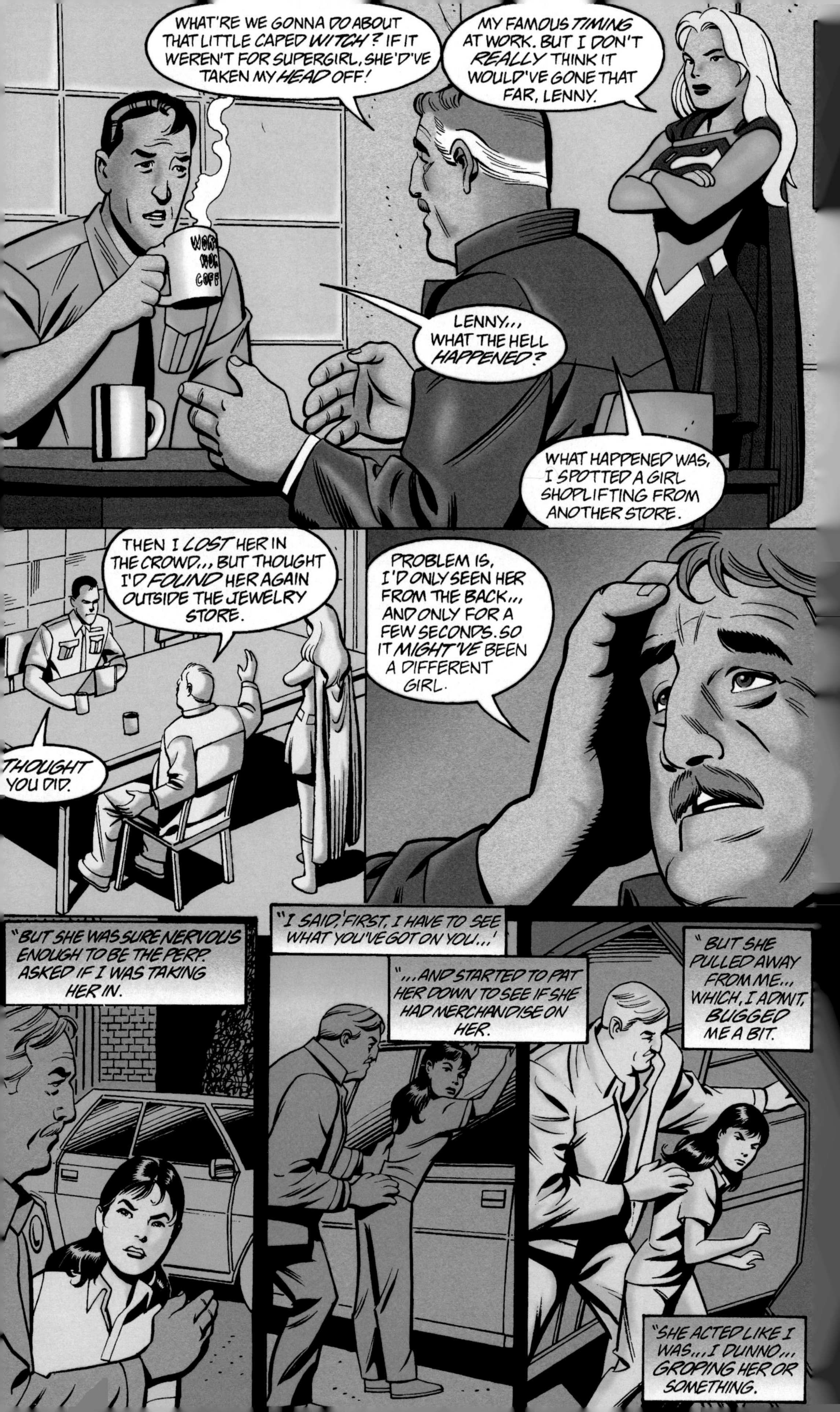
WHAT'RE WE GONNA DO ABOUT THAT LITTLE CAPED WITCH? IF IT WEREN'T FOR SUPERGIRL, SHE'D'VE TAKEN MY HEAD OFF!
MY FAMOUS TIMING AT WORK. BUT I DON'T REALLY THINK IT WOULD'VE GONE THAT FAR, LENNY.
LENNY... WHAT THE HELL HAPPENED?
WHAT HAPPENED WAS, I SPOTTED A GIRL SHOPLIFTING FROM ANOTHER STORE.
THEN I LOST HER IN THE CROWD... BUT THOUGHT I'D FOUND HER AGAIN OUTSIDE THE JEWELRY STORE.
THOUGHT YOU DID.
PROBLEM IS, I'D ONLY SEEN HER FROM THE BACK... AND ONLY FOR A FEW SECONDS. SO IT MIGHT'VE BEEN A DIFFERENT GIRL.
"BUT SHE WAS SURE NERVOUS ENOUGH TO BE THE PERP. ASKED IF I WAS TAKING HER IN.
"I SAID, 'FIRST, I HAVE TO SEE WHAT YOU'VE GOT ON YOU...'
"...AND STARTED TO PAT HER DOWN TO SEE IF SHE HAD MERCHANDISE ON HER.
"BUT SHE PULLED AWAY FROM ME... WHICH, I ADMIT, BUGGED ME A BIT.
"SHE ACTED LIKE I WAS... I DUNNO... GROPING HER OR SOMETHING.

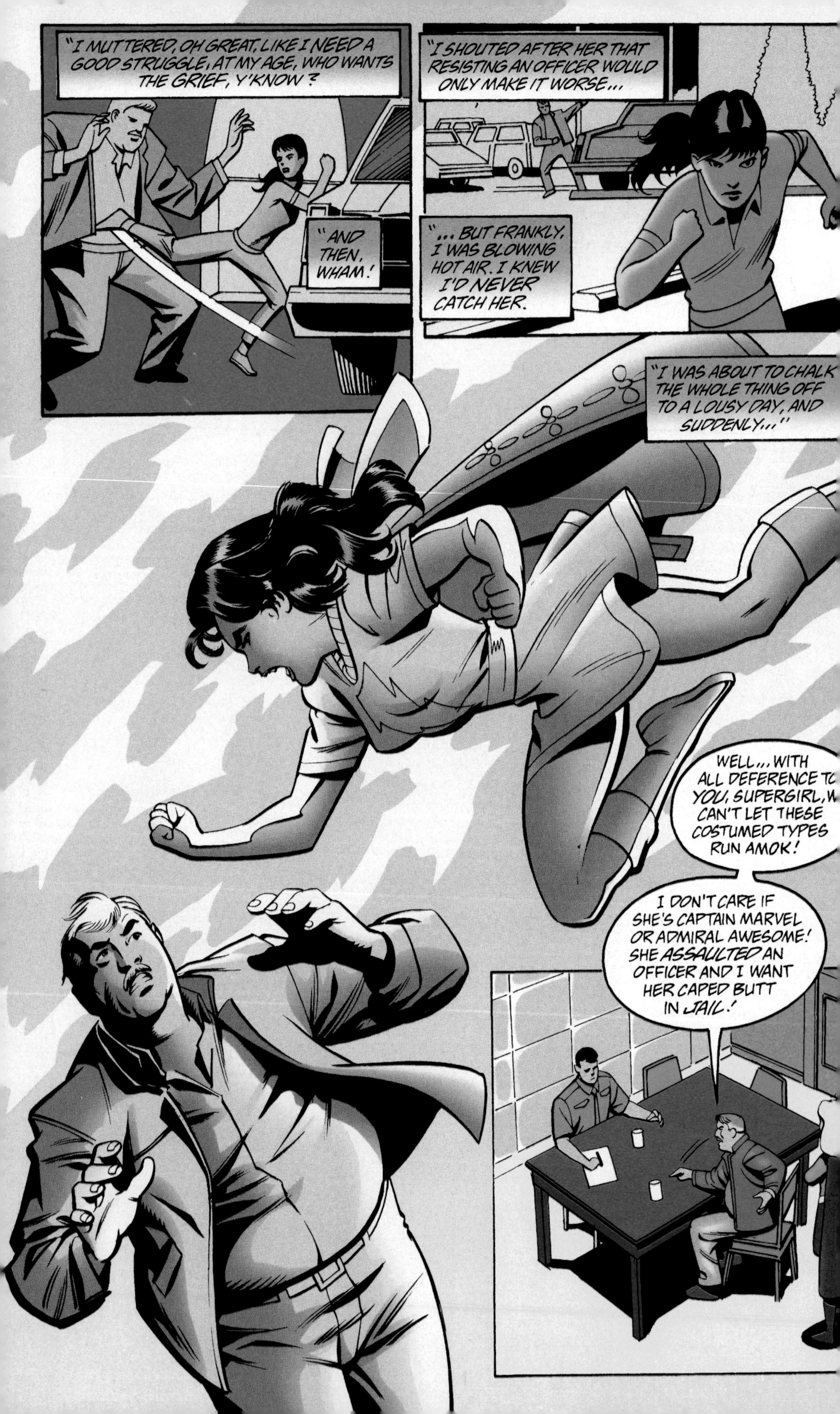
"I MUTTERED, OH GREAT, LIKE I NEED A GOOD STRUGGLE, AT MY AGE, WHO WANTS THE GRIEF, Y'KNOW?
"AND THEN, WHAM!
"I SHOUTED AFTER HER THAT RESISTING AN OFFICER WOULD ONLY MAKE IT WORSE...
"...BUT FRANKLY, I WAS BLOWING HOT AIR. I KNEW I'D NEVER CATCH HER.
"I WAS ABOUT TO CHALK THE WHOLE THING OFF TO A LOUSY DAY, AND SUDDENLY..."
WELL... WITH ALL DEFERENCE TO YOU, SUPERGIRL, W CAN'T LET THESE COSTUMED TYPES RUN AMOK!
I DON'T CARE IF SHE'S CAPTAIN MARVEL OR ADMIRAL AWESOME! SHE ASSAULTED AN OFFICER AND I WANT HER CAPED BUTT IN JAIL!

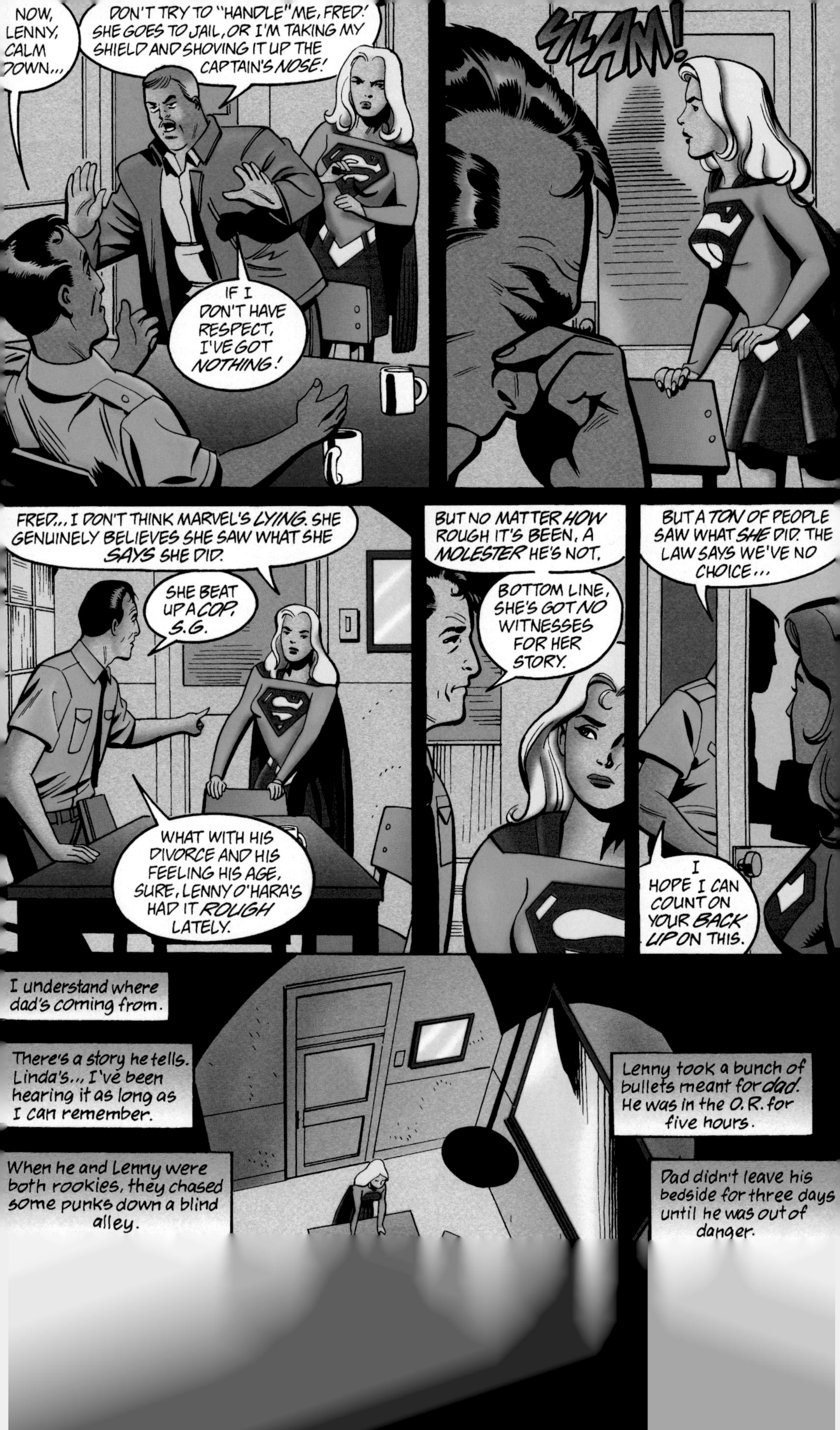
NOW, LENNY, CALM DOWN...
DON'T TRY TO "HANDLE" ME, FRED! SHE GOES TO JAIL, OR I'M TAKING MY SHIELD AND SHOVING IT UP THE CAPTAIN'S NOSE!
IF I DON'T HAVE RESPECT, I'VE GOT NOTHING!
SLAM!
FRED... I DON'T THINK MARVEL'S LYING. SHE GENUINELY BELIEVES SHE SAW WHAT SHE SAYS SHE DID.
SHE BEAT UP A COP, S.G.
WHAT WITH HIS DIVORCE AND HIS FEELING HIS AGE, SURE, LENNY O'HARA'S HAD IT ROUGH LATELY.
BUT NO MATTER HOW ROUGH IT'S BEEN, A MOLESTER HE'S NOT.
BOTTOM LINE, SHE'S GOT NO WITNESSES FOR HER STORY.
BUT A TON OF PEOPLE SAW WHAT SHE DID. THE LAW SAYS WE'VE NO CHOICE...
I HOPE I CAN COUNT ON YOUR BACK UP ON THIS.
I understand where dad's coming from.
There's a story he tells. Linda's... I've been hearing it as long as I can remember.
When he and Lenny were both rookies, they chased some punks down a blind alley.
Lenny took a bunch of bullets meant for dad. He was in the O.R. for five hours.
Dad didn't leave his bedside for three days until he was out of danger.

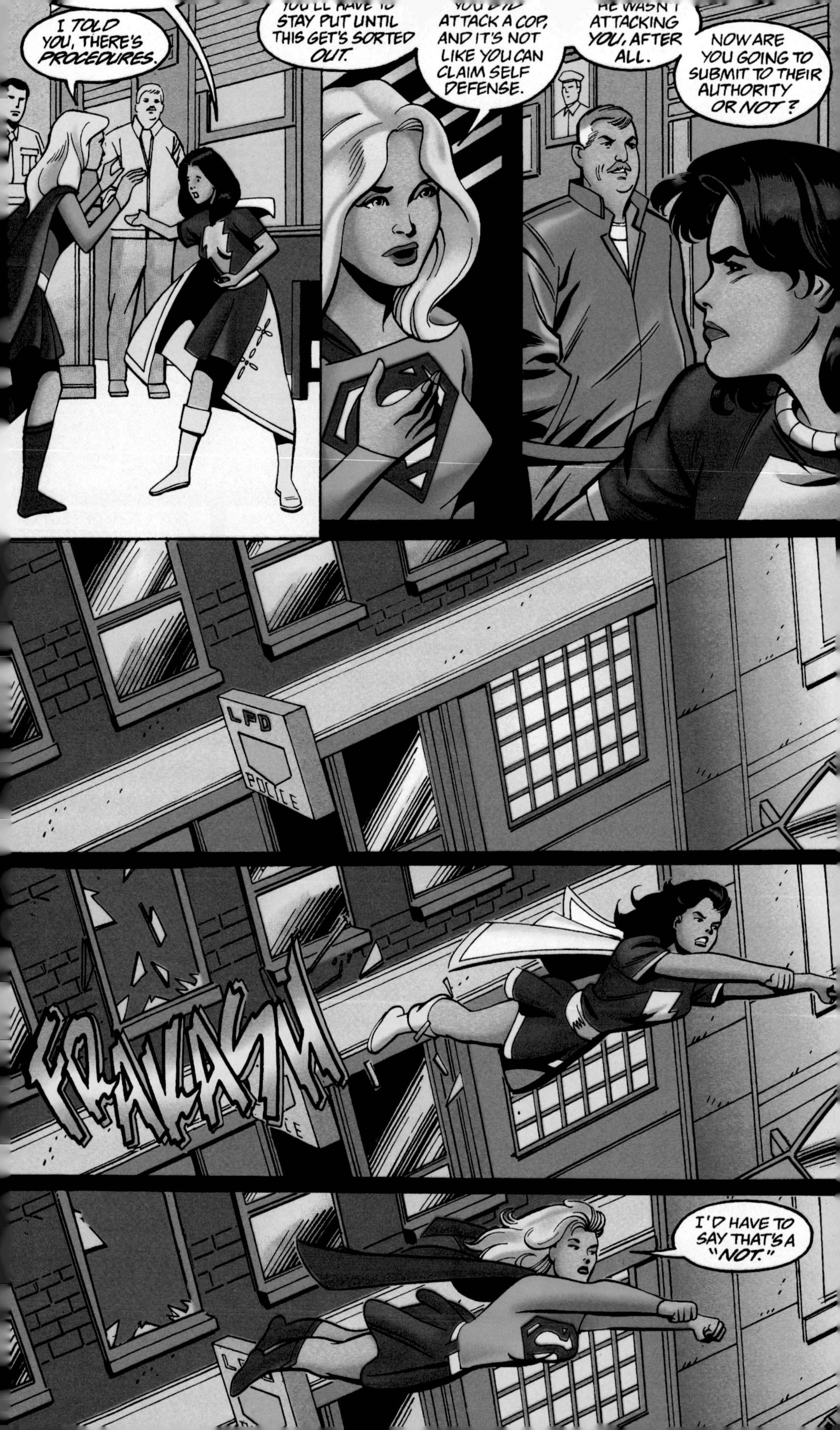
I TOLD YOU, THERE'S PROCEDURES.
YOU'LL HAVE TO STAY PUT UNTIL THIS GET'S SORTED OUT.
YOU DID ATTACK A COP, AND IT'S NOT LIKE YOU CAN CLAIM SELF DEFENSE.
HE WASN'T ATTACKING YOU, AFTER ALL.
NOW ARE YOU GOING TO SUBMIT TO THEIR AUTHORITY OR NOT?
LPD
POLICE
I'D HAVE TO SAY THAT'S A "NOT."

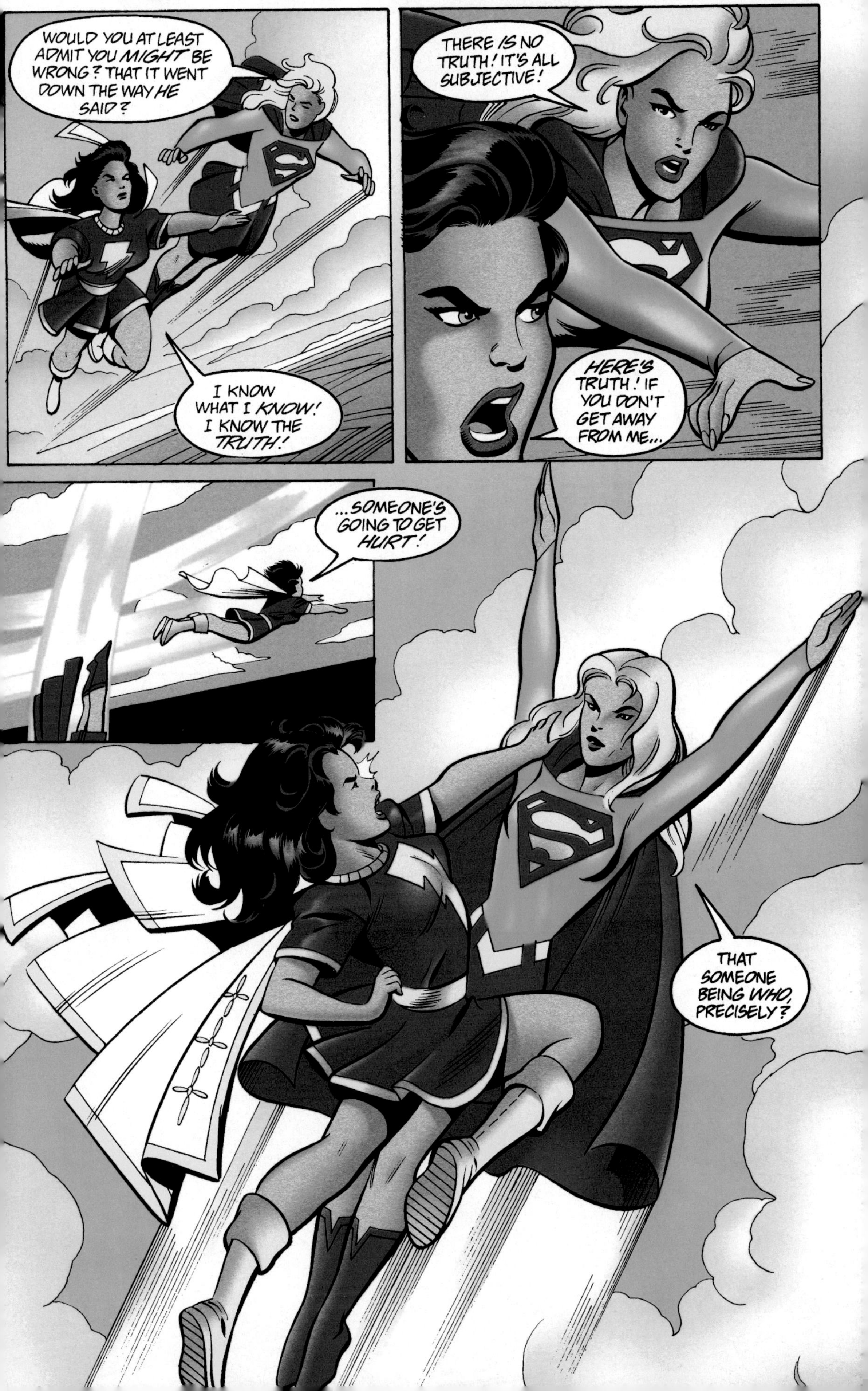
WOULD YOU AT LEAST ADMIT YOU *MIGHT* BE WRONG? THAT IT WENT DOWN THE WAY *HE* SAID?
I KNOW WHAT I *KNOW*! I KNOW THE *TRUTH*!
THERE *IS* NO TRUTH! IT'S ALL SUBJECTIVE!
HERE'S TRUTH! IF YOU DON'T GET AWAY FROM ME...
...SOMEONE'S GOING TO GET *HURT*!
THAT SOMEONE BEING *WHO*, PRECISELY?

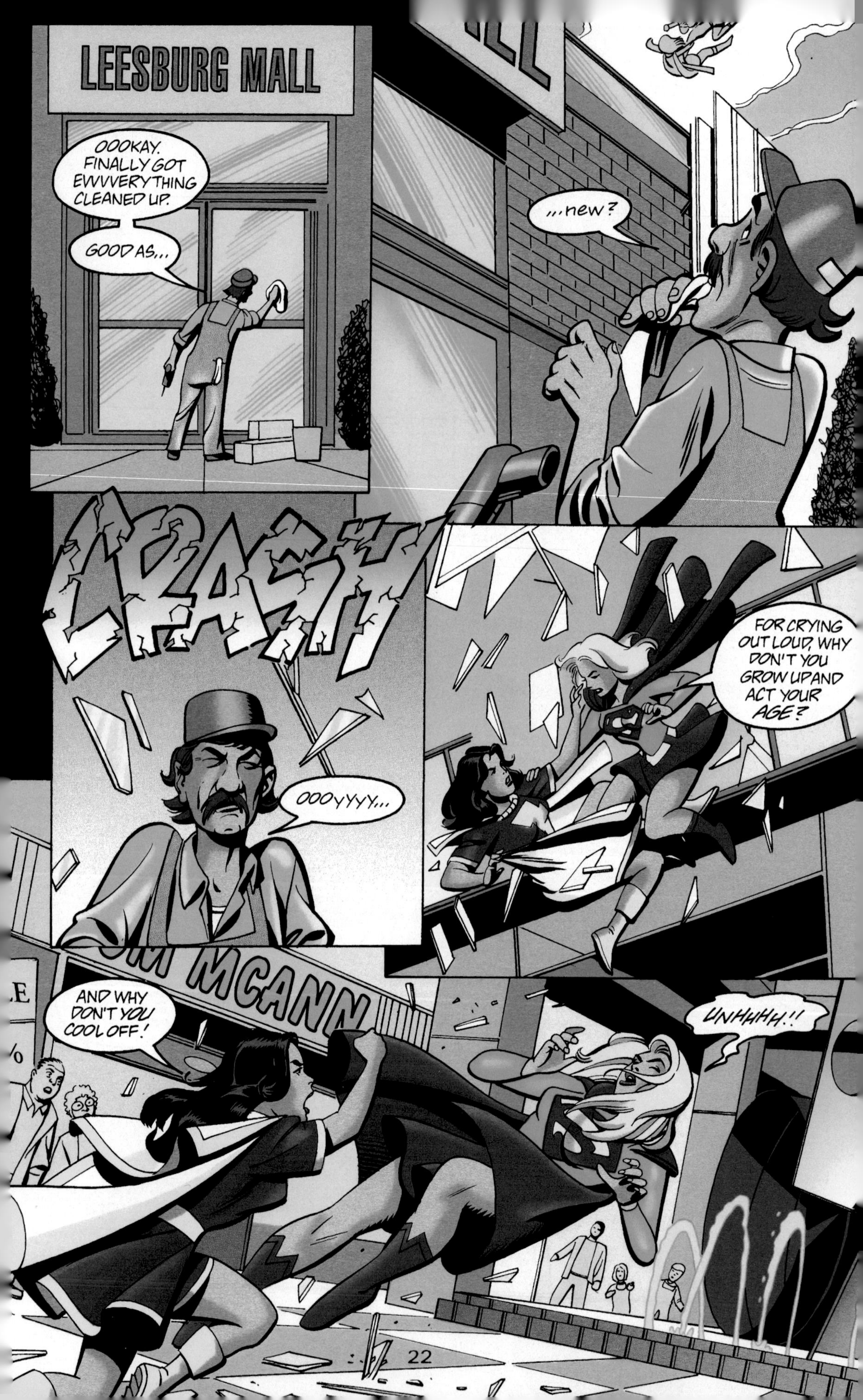
LEESBURG MALL
OOOKAY. FINALLY GOT EVVVERYTHING CLEANED UP.
GOOD AS,..
,,,new?
CRASH
OOOYYYY,,,
FOR CRYING OUT LOUD, WHY DON'T YOU GROW UP AND ACT YOUR AGE?
AND WHY DON'T YOU COOL OFF!
UNHHHH!!

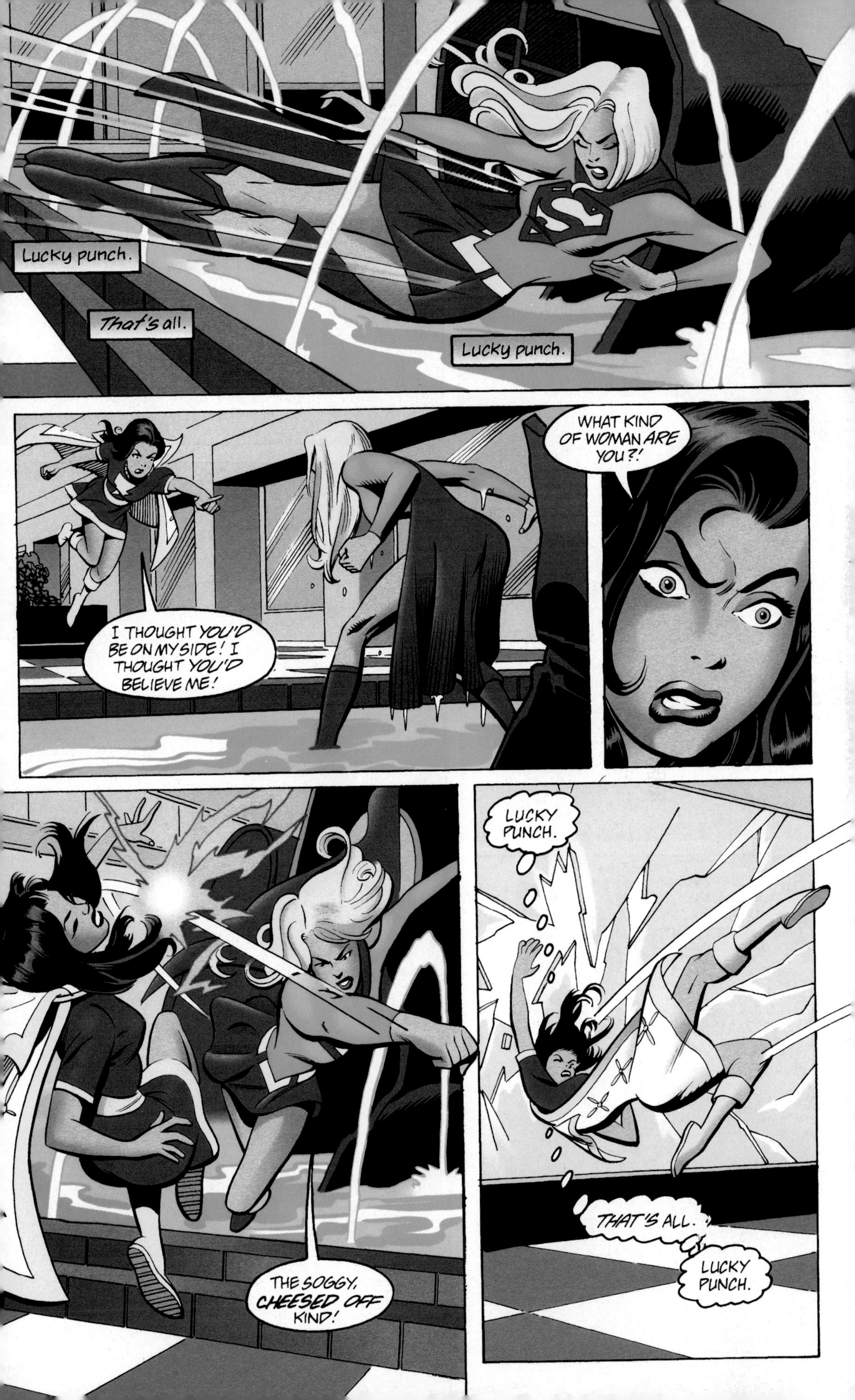
Lucky punch.
That's all.
Lucky punch.
WHAT KIND OF WOMAN ARE YOU?!
I THOUGHT YOU'D BE ON MY SIDE! I THOUGHT YOU'D BELIEVE ME!
THE SOGGY, CHEESED OFF KIND!
LUCKY PUNCH.
THAT'S ALL.
LUCKY PUNCH.

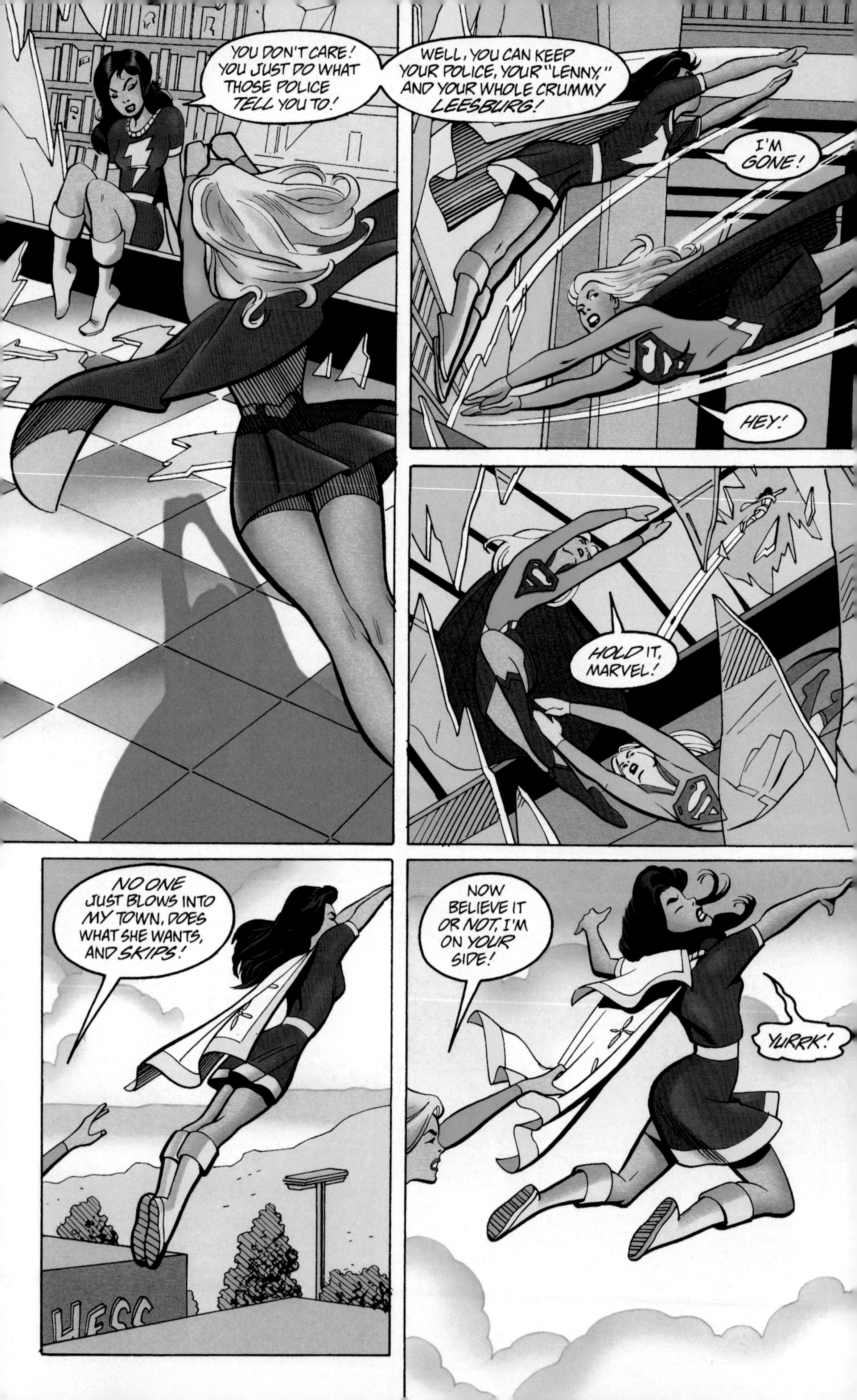
YOU DON'T CARE! YOU JUST DO WHAT THOSE POLICE TELL YOU TO!
WELL, YOU CAN KEEP YOUR POLICE, YOUR "LENNY," AND YOUR WHOLE CRUMMY LEESBURG!
I'M GONE!
HEY!
HOLD IT, MARVEL!
NO ONE JUST BLOWS INTO MY TOWN, DOES WHAT SHE WANTS, AND SKIPS!
NOW BELIEVE IT OR NOT, I'M ON YOUR SIDE!
YURRK!

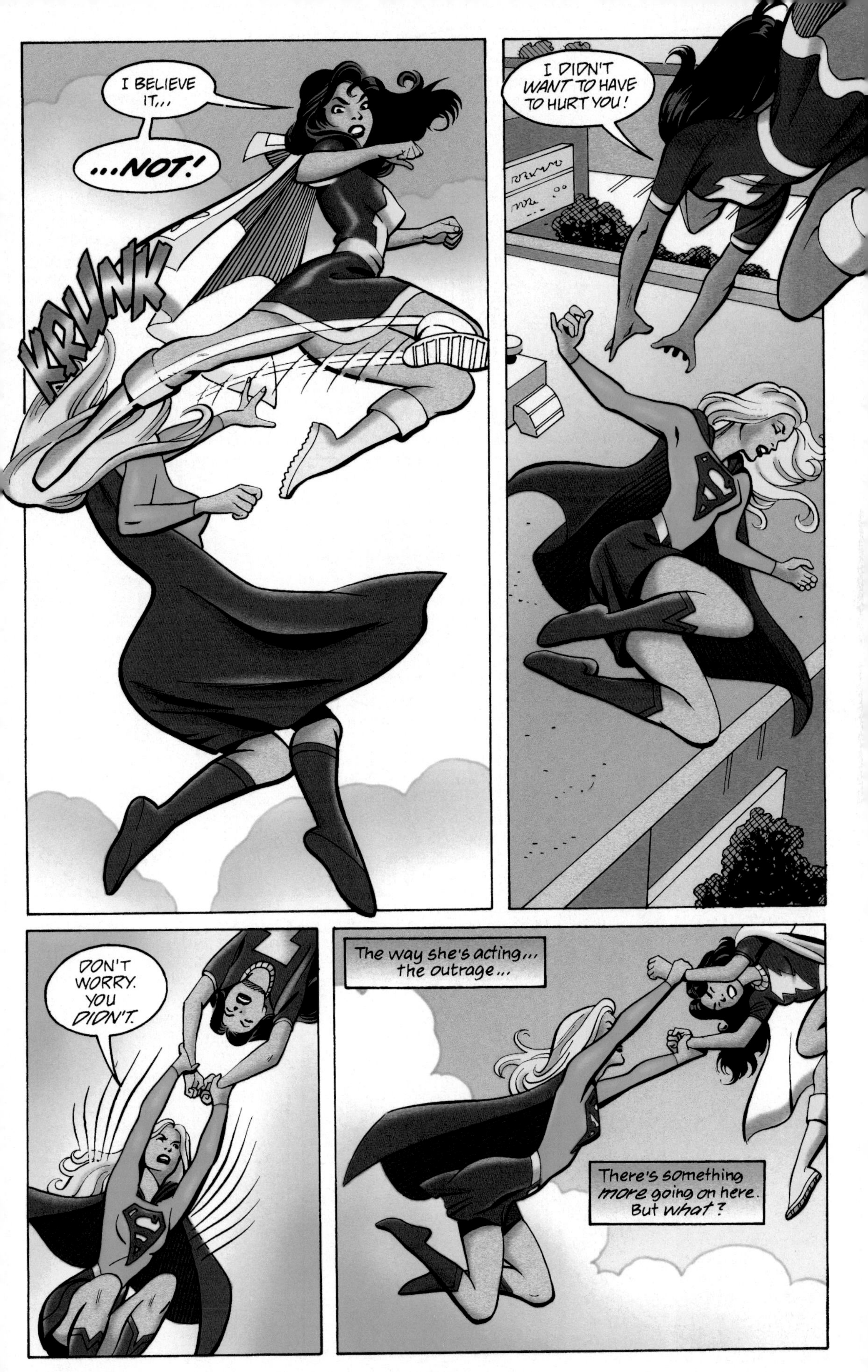
I BELIEVE IT,,,
...NOT!
KRUNK
I DIDN'T WANT TO HAVE TO HURT YOU!
DON'T WORRY. YOU DIDN'T.
The way she's acting,,, the outrage...
There's something more going on here. But what?

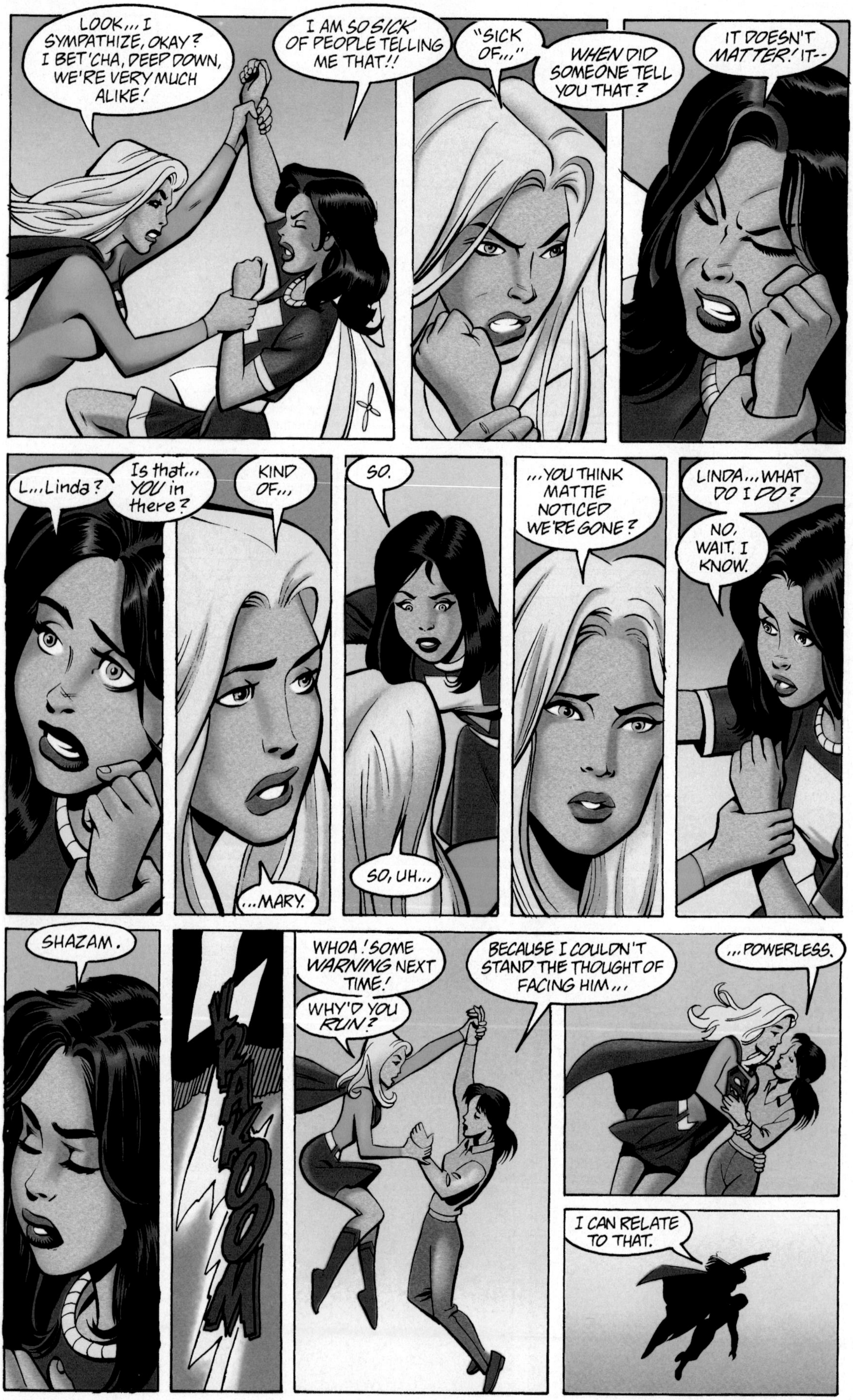

LOOK,... I SYMPATHIZE, OKAY? I BET'CHA, DEEP DOWN, WE'RE VERY MUCH ALIKE!
I AM SO SICK OF PEOPLE TELLING ME THAT!!
"SICK OF..."
WHEN DID SOMEONE TELL YOU THAT?
IT DOESN'T MATTER! IT--
L...Linda?
Is that... YOU in there?
KIND OF...
...MARY.
SO.
SO, UH...
...YOU THINK MATTIE NOTICED WE'RE GONE?
LINDA... WHAT DO I DO?
NO, WAIT. I KNOW.
SHAZAM.
WHOA! SOME WARNING NEXT TIME!
WHY'D YOU RUN?
BECAUSE I COULDN'T STAND THE THOUGHT OF FACING HIM...
...POWERLESS.
I CAN RELATE TO THAT.

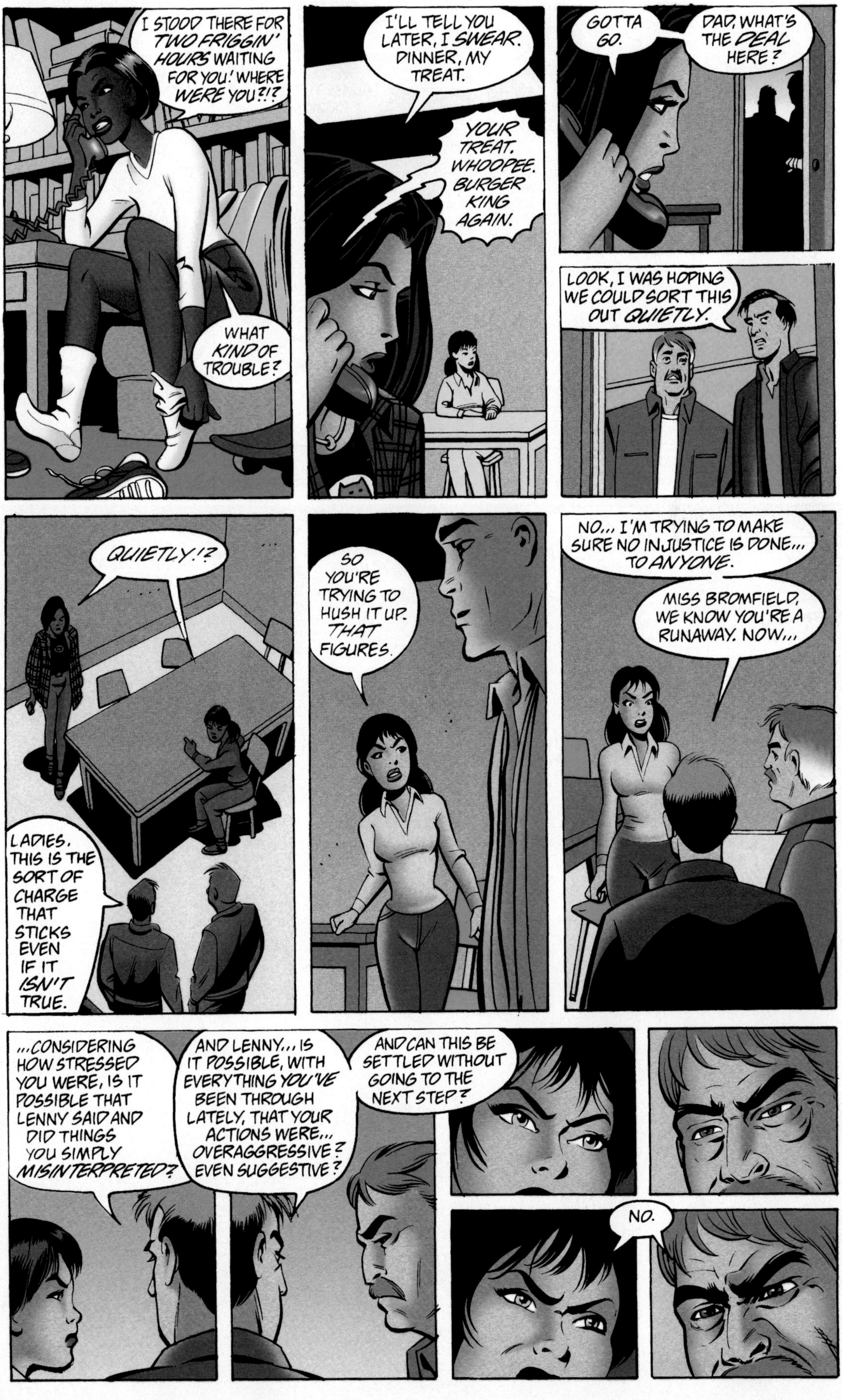
I STOOD THERE FOR TWO FRIGGIN' HOURS WAITING FOR YOU! WHERE WERE YOU?!?
WHAT KIND OF TROUBLE?
I'LL TELL YOU LATER, I SWEAR. DINNER, MY TREAT.
YOUR TREAT. WHOOPEE. BURGER KING AGAIN.
GOTTA GO.
DAD, WHAT'S THE DEAL HERE?
LOOK, I WAS HOPING WE COULD SORT THIS OUT QUIETLY.
QUIETLY!?
...
...
LADIES. THIS IS THE SORT OF CHARGE THAT STICKS EVEN IF IT ISN'T TRUE.
SO YOU'RE TRYING TO HUSH IT UP. THAT FIGURES.
NO... I'M TRYING TO MAKE SURE NO INJUSTICE IS DONE... TO ANYONE.
MISS BROMFIELD, WE KNOW YOU'RE A RUNAWAY. NOW...
...CONSIDERING HOW STRESSED YOU WERE, IS IT POSSIBLE THAT LENNY SAID AND DID THINGS YOU SIMPLY MISINTERPRETED?
AND LENNY... IS IT POSSIBLE, WITH EVERYTHING YOU'VE BEEN THROUGH LATELY, THAT YOUR ACTIONS WERE... OVERAGGRESSIVE? EVEN SUGGESTIVE?
AND CAN THIS BE SETTLED WITHOUT GOING TO THE NEXT STEP?
NO.

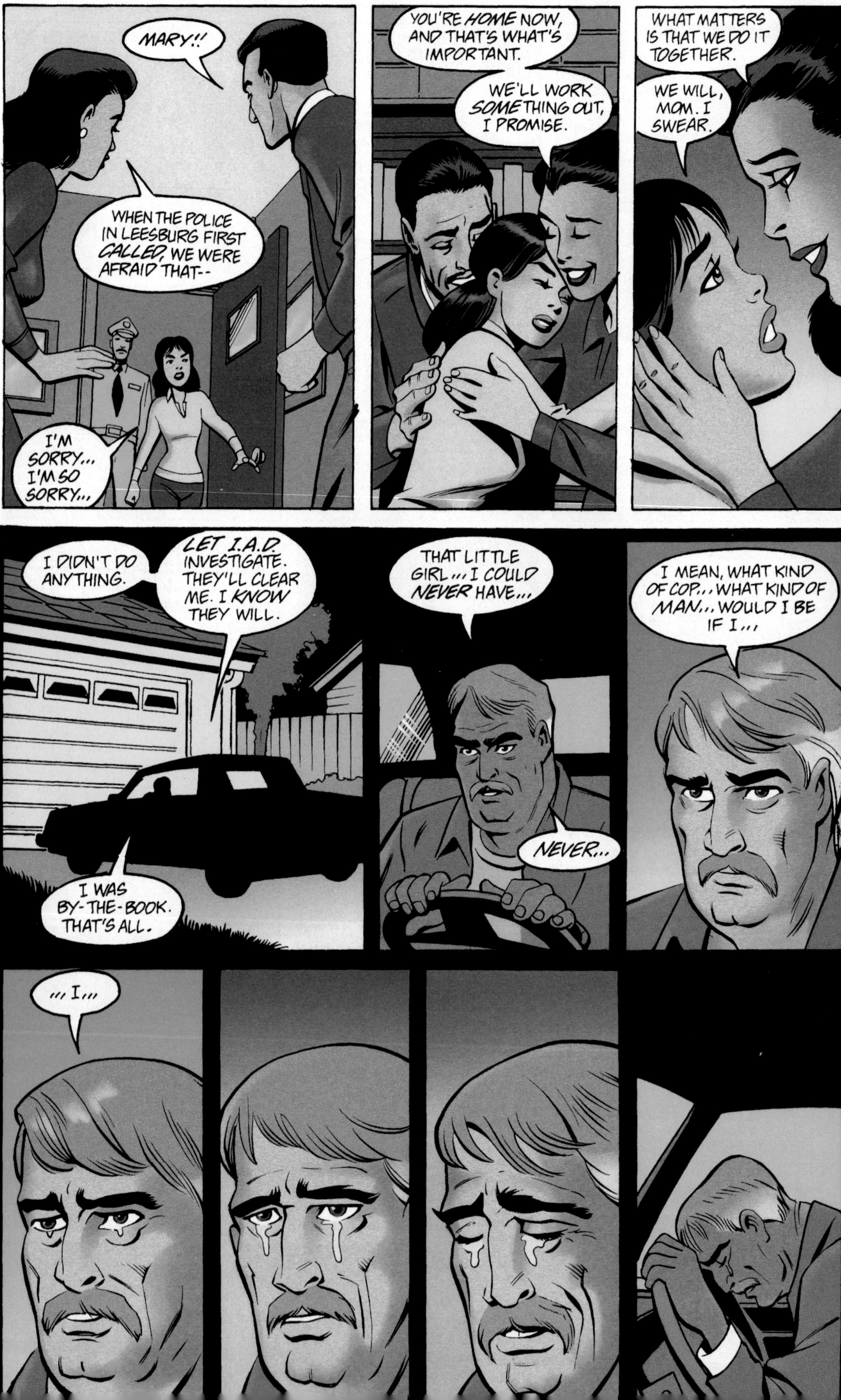
MARY!!
WHEN THE POLICE IN LEESBURG FIRST CALLED, WE WERE AFRAID THAT--
I'M SORRY... I'M SO SORRY...
YOU'RE HOME NOW, AND THAT'S WHAT'S IMPORTANT.
WE'LL WORK SOMETHING OUT, I PROMISE.
WHAT MATTERS IS THAT WE DO IT TOGETHER.
WE WILL, MOM. I SWEAR.
I DIDN'T DO ANYTHING.
LET I.A.D. INVESTIGATE. THEY'LL CLEAR ME. I KNOW THEY WILL.
I WAS BY-THE-BOOK. THAT'S ALL.
THAT LITTLE GIRL... I COULD NEVER HAVE...
NEVER...
I MEAN, WHAT KIND OF COP... WHAT KIND OF MAN... WOULD I BE IF I...
...I...

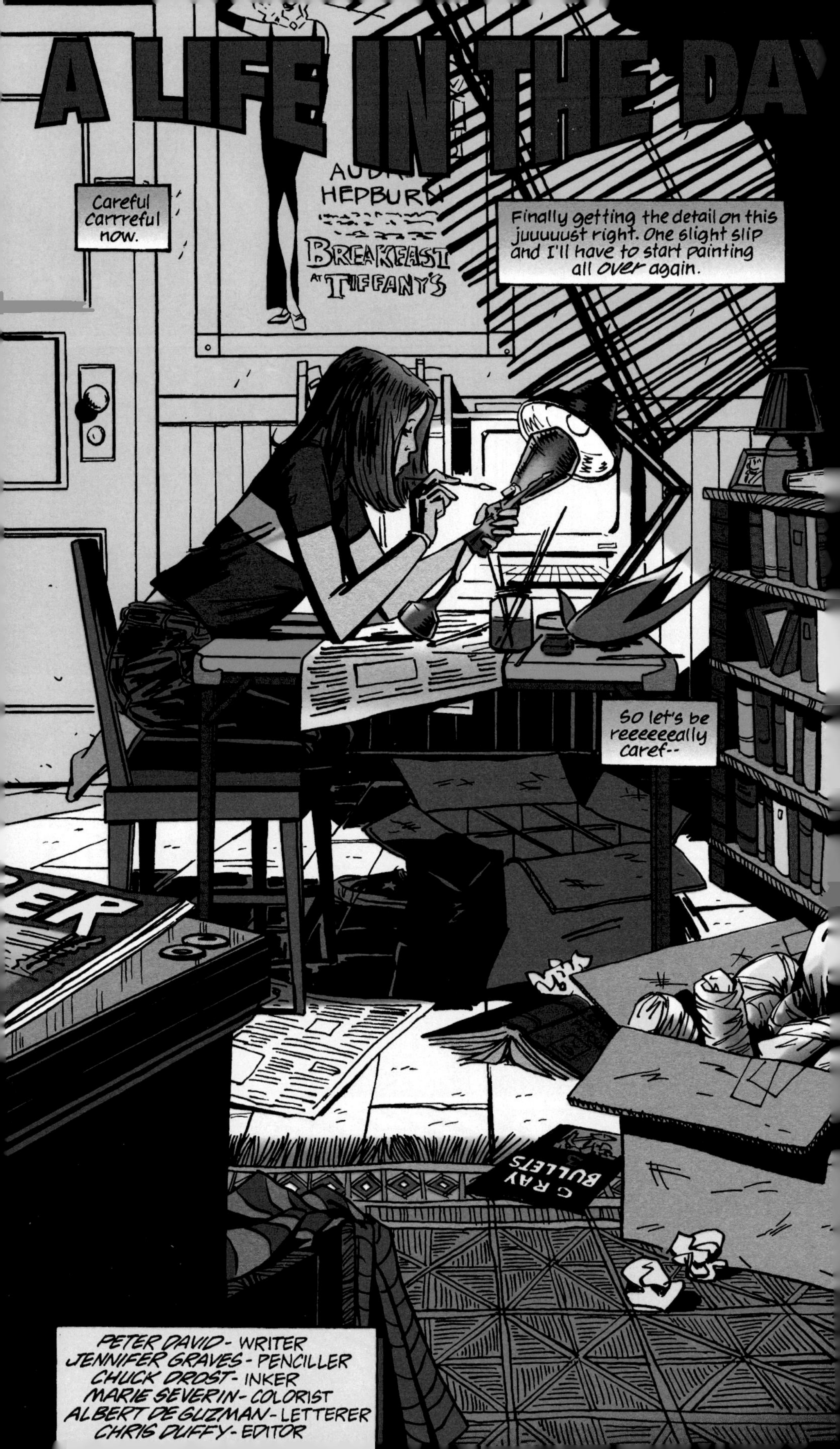
A LIFE IN THE DA
Careful carrreful now.
Finally getting the detail on this juuuuust right. One slight slip and I'll have to start painting all *over* again.
BREAKFAST AT TIFFANY'S
So let's be reeeeeeally caref--
PETER DAVID - WRITER
JENNIFER GRAVES - PENCILLER
CHUCK DROST - INKER
MARIE SEVERIN - COLORIST
ALBERT DE GUZMAN - LETTERER
CHRIS DUFFY - EDITOR

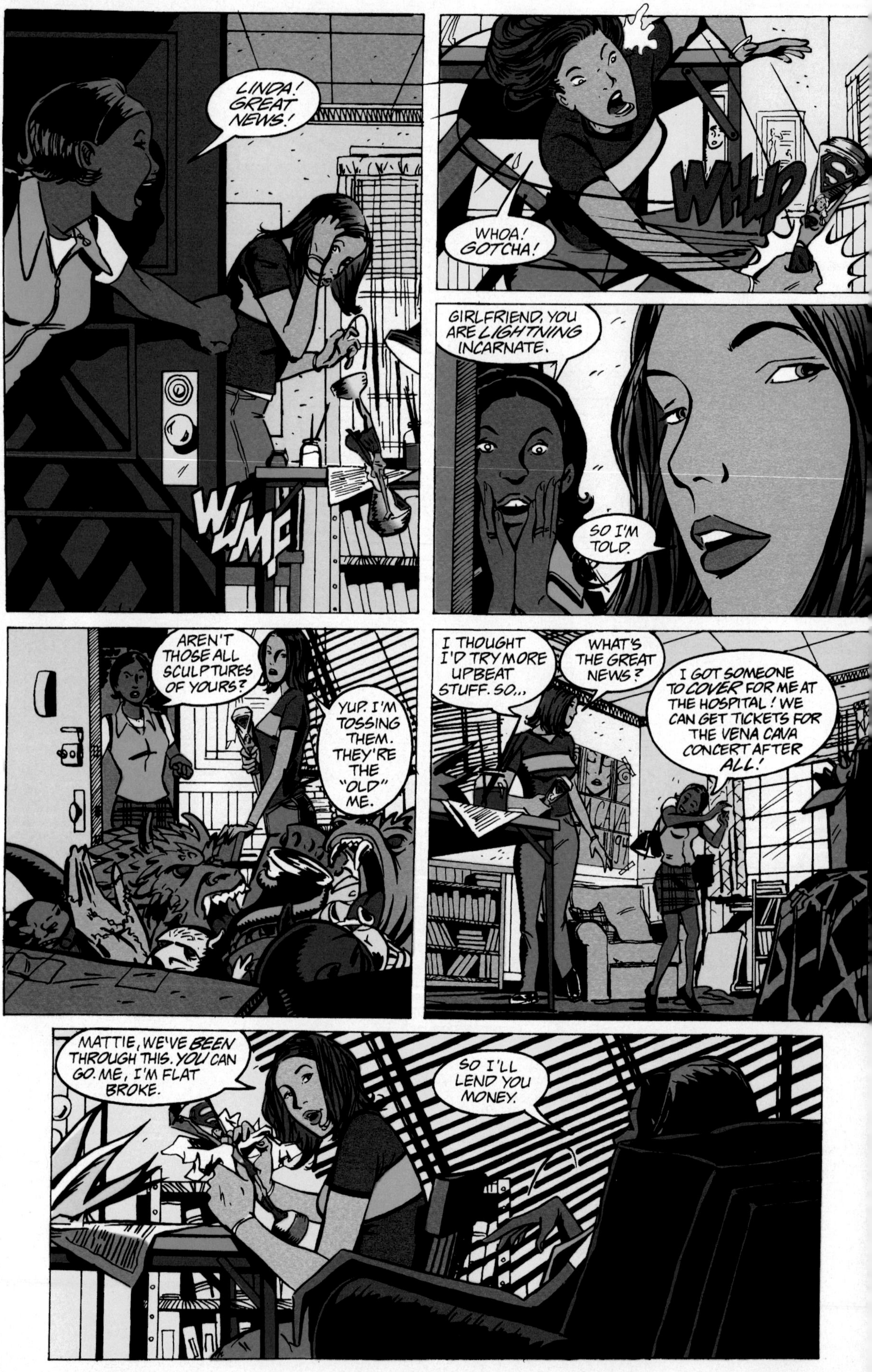
LINDA! GREAT NEWS!
WUMP
WHOA! GOTCHA!
WHUD
GIRLFRIEND, YOU ARE LIGHTNING INCARNATE.
SO I'M TOLD.
AREN'T THOSE ALL SCULPTURES OF YOURS?
YUP. I'M TOSSING THEM. THEY'RE THE "OLD" ME.
I THOUGHT I'D TRY MORE UPBEAT STUFF. SO...
WHAT'S THE GREAT NEWS?
I GOT SOMEONE TO COVER FOR ME AT THE HOSPITAL! WE CAN GET TICKETS FOR THE VENA CAVA CONCERT AFTER ALL!
MATTIE, WE'VE BEEN THROUGH THIS. YOU CAN GO. ME, I'M FLAT BROKE.
SO I'LL LEND YOU MONEY.

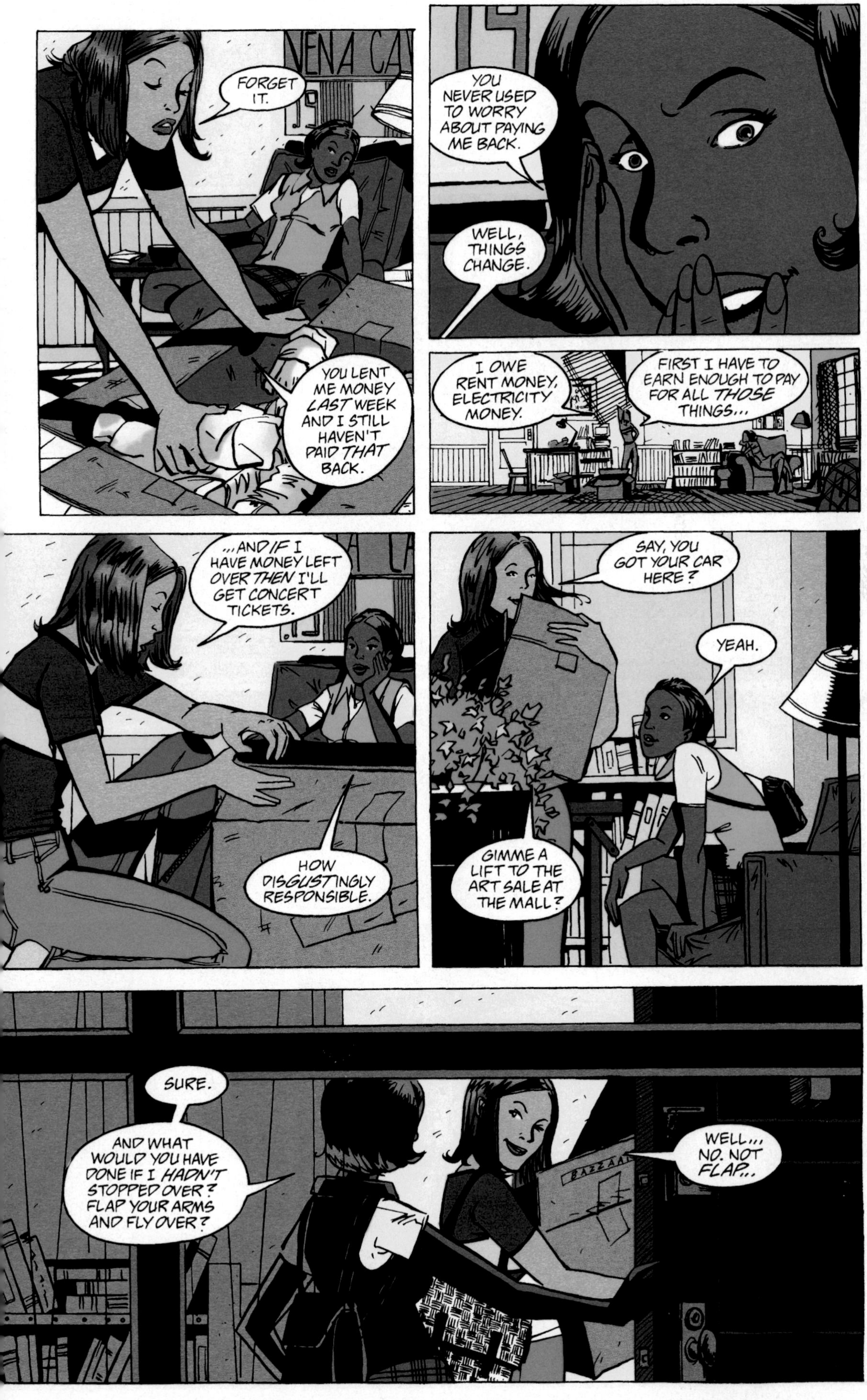
FORGET IT.
YOU LENT ME MONEY LAST WEEK AND I STILL HAVEN'T PAID THAT BACK.
YOU NEVER USED TO WORRY ABOUT PAYING ME BACK.
WELL, THINGS CHANGE.
I OWE RENT MONEY, ELECTRICITY MONEY.
FIRST I HAVE TO EARN ENOUGH TO PAY FOR ALL THOSE THINGS...
...AND IF I HAVE MONEY LEFT OVER THEN I'LL GET CONCERT TICKETS.
HOW DISGUSTINGLY RESPONSIBLE.
SAY, YOU GOT YOUR CAR HERE?
YEAH.
GIMME A LIFT TO THE ART SALE AT THE MALL?
SURE.
AND WHAT WOULD YOU HAVE DONE IF I HADN'T STOPPED OVER? FLAP YOUR ARMS AND FLY OVER?
WELL... NO. NOT FLAP...

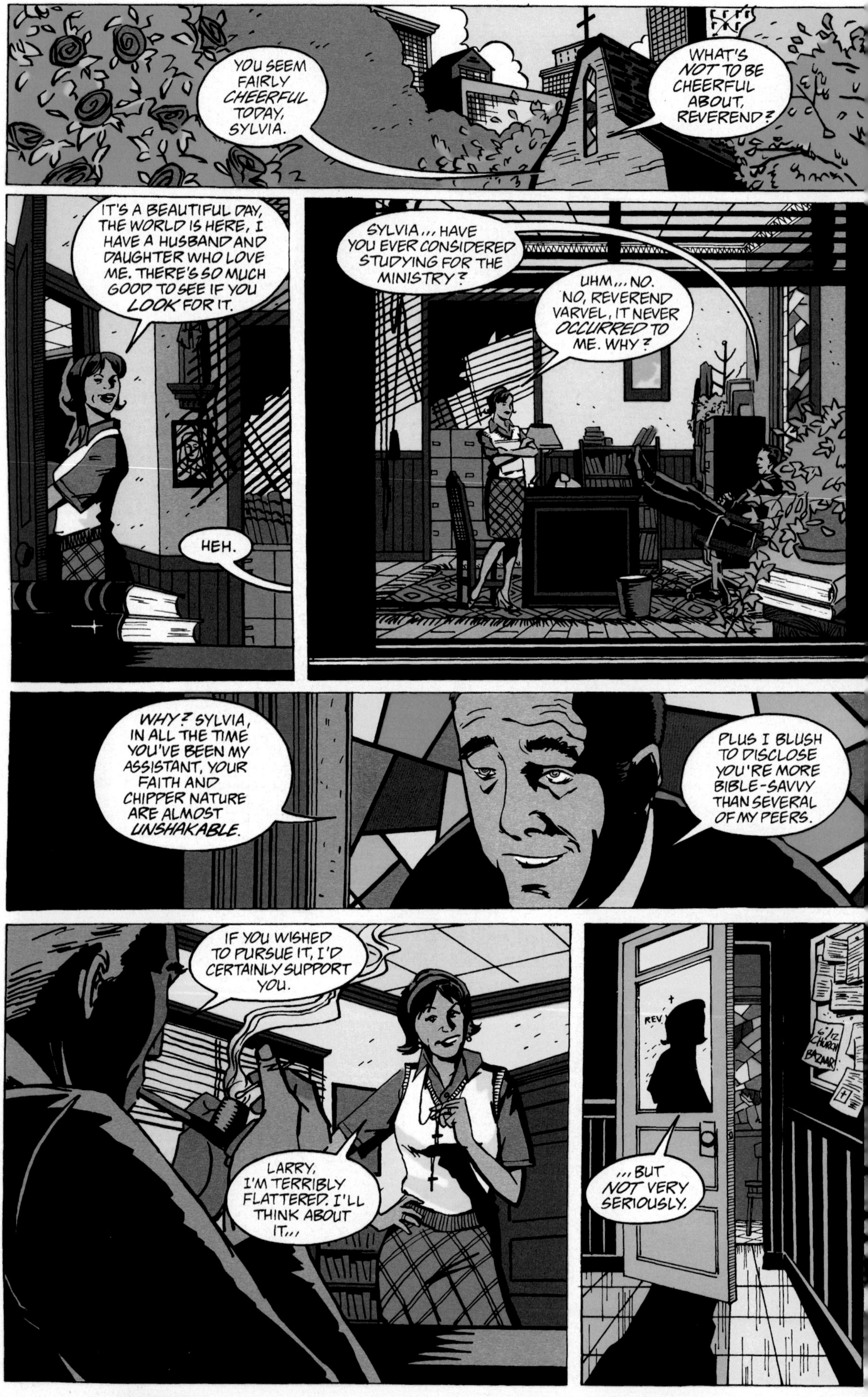
YOU SEEM FAIRLY CHEERFUL TODAY, SYLVIA.
WHAT'S NOT TO BE CHEERFUL ABOUT, REVEREND?
IT'S A BEAUTIFUL DAY, THE WORLD IS HERE, I HAVE A HUSBAND AND DAUGHTER WHO LOVE ME. THERE'S SO MUCH GOOD TO SEE IF YOU LOOK FOR IT.
HEH.
SYLVIA... HAVE YOU EVER CONSIDERED STUDYING FOR THE MINISTRY?
UHM... NO. NO, REVEREND VARVEL, IT NEVER OCCURRED TO ME. WHY?
WHY? SYLVIA, IN ALL THE TIME YOU'VE BEEN MY ASSISTANT, YOUR FAITH AND CHIPPER NATURE ARE ALMOST UNSHAKABLE.
PLUS I BLUSH TO DISCLOSE YOU'RE MORE BIBLE-SAVVY THAN SEVERAL OF MY PEERS.
IF YOU WISHED TO PURSUE IT, I'D CERTAINLY SUPPORT YOU.
LARRY, I'M TERRIBLY FLATTERED. I'LL THINK ABOUT IT...
REV.
6/12 CHURCH BAZAAR
...BUT NOT VERY SERIOUSLY.

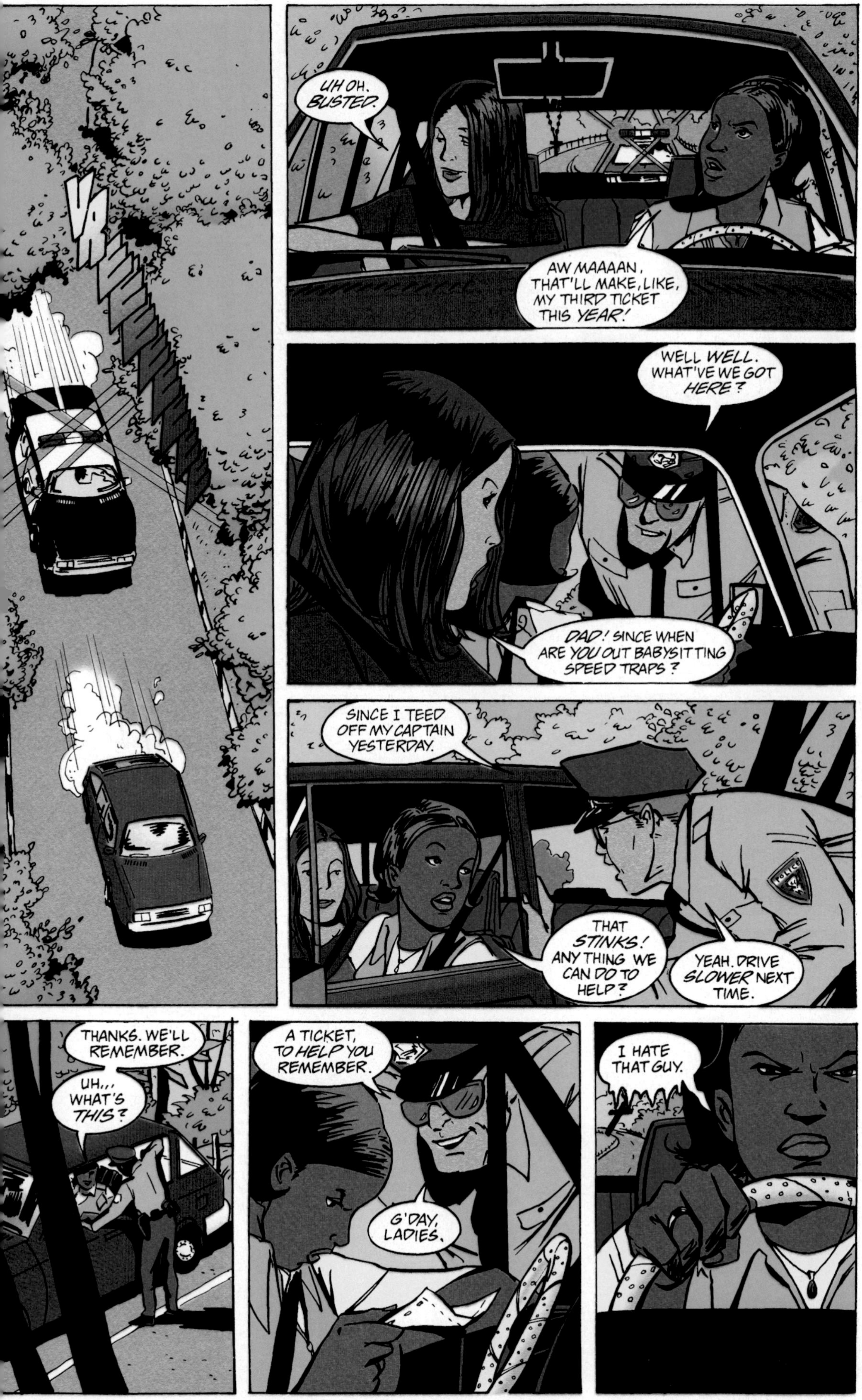
UH OH. BUSTED.
AW MAAAAN, THAT'LL MAKE, LIKE, MY THIRD TICKET THIS YEAR!
WELL WELL. WHAT'VE WE GOT HERE?
DAD! SINCE WHEN ARE YOU OUT BABYSITTING SPEED TRAPS?
SINCE I TEED OFF MY CAPTAIN YESTERDAY.
THAT STINKS! ANY THING WE CAN DO TO HELP?
YEAH. DRIVE SLOWER NEXT TIME.
THANKS. WE'LL REMEMBER.
UH... WHAT'S THIS?
A TICKET, TO HELP YOU REMEMBER.
G'DAY, LADIES.
I HATE THAT GUY.

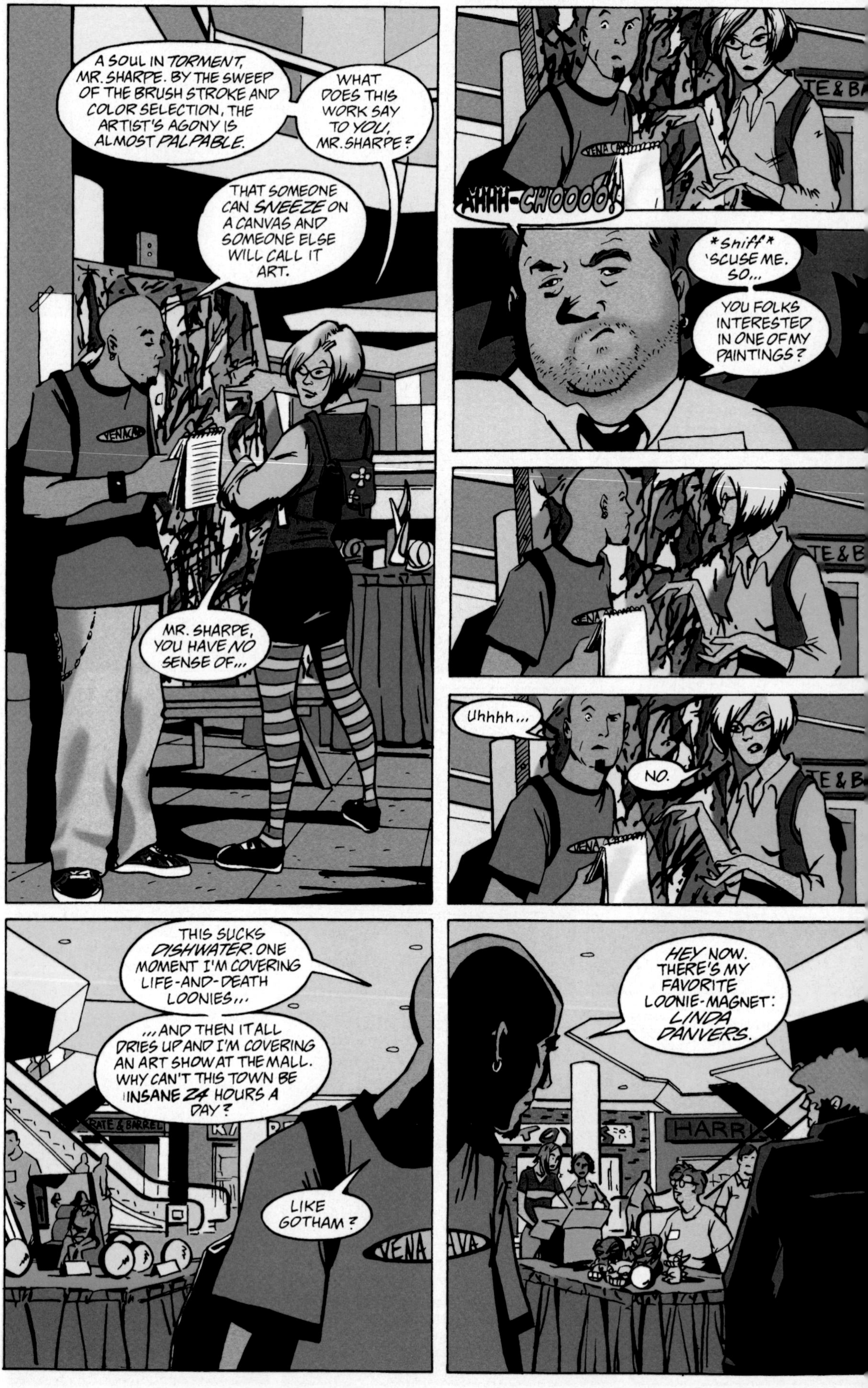
A SOUL IN TORMENT, MR. SHARPE. BY THE SWEEP OF THE BRUSH STROKE AND COLOR SELECTION, THE ARTIST'S AGONY IS ALMOST PALPABLE.
WHAT DOES THIS WORK SAY TO YOU, MR. SHARPE?
THAT SOMEONE CAN SNEEZE ON A CANVAS AND SOMEONE ELSE WILL CALL IT ART.
MR. SHARPE, YOU HAVE NO SENSE OF...
AHHH-CHOOOO!
Sniff 'SCUSE ME. SO...
YOU FOLKS INTERESTED IN ONE OF MY PAINTINGS?
Uhhhh...
NO.
THIS SUCKS DISHWATER. ONE MOMENT I'M COVERING LIFE-AND-DEATH LOONIES...
...AND THEN IT ALL DRIES UP AND I'M COVERING AN ART SHOW AT THE MALL. WHY CAN'T THIS TOWN BE INSANE 24 HOURS A DAY?
LIKE GOTHAM?
HEY NOW. THERE'S MY FAVORITE LOONIE-MAGNET: LINDA DANVERS.

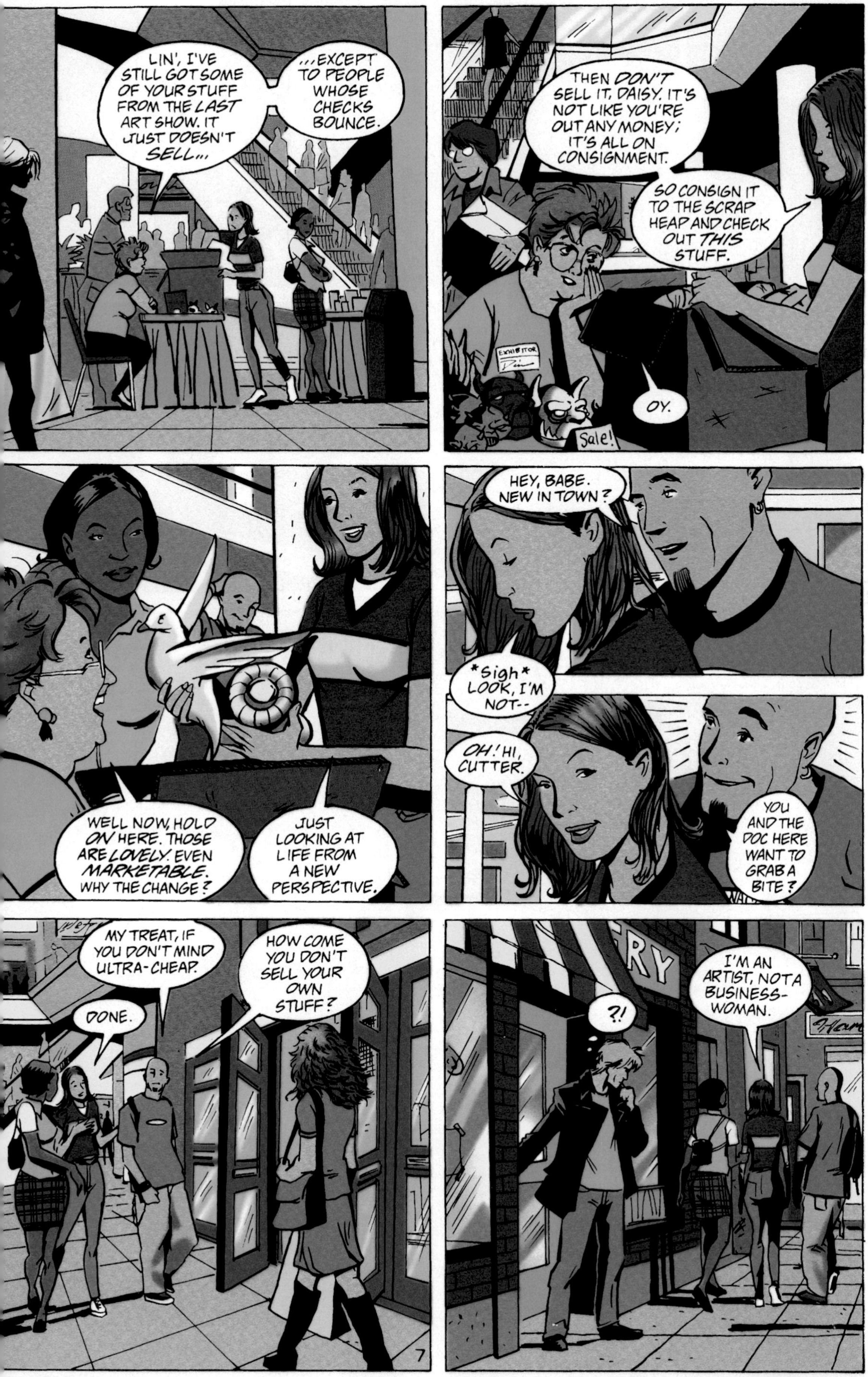

LIN', I'VE STILL GOT SOME OF YOUR STUFF FROM THE LAST ART SHOW. IT JUST DOESN'T SELL...
...EXCEPT TO PEOPLE WHOSE CHECKS BOUNCE.
THEN DON'T SELL IT, DAISY. IT'S NOT LIKE YOU'RE OUT ANY MONEY; IT'S ALL ON CONSIGNMENT.
SO CONSIGN IT TO THE SCRAP HEAP AND CHECK OUT THIS STUFF.
OY.
Sale!
WELL NOW, HOLD ON HERE. THOSE ARE LOVELY. EVEN MARKETABLE. WHY THE CHANGE?
JUST LOOKING AT LIFE FROM A NEW PERSPECTIVE.
HEY, BABE. NEW IN TOWN?
Sigh LOOK, I'M NOT--
OH! HI, CUTTER.
YOU AND THE DOC HERE WANT TO GRAB A BITE?
MY TREAT, IF YOU DON'T MIND ULTRA-CHEAP.
DONE.
HOW COME YOU DON'T SELL YOUR OWN STUFF?
?!
I'M AN ARTIST, NOT A BUSINESS-WOMAN.

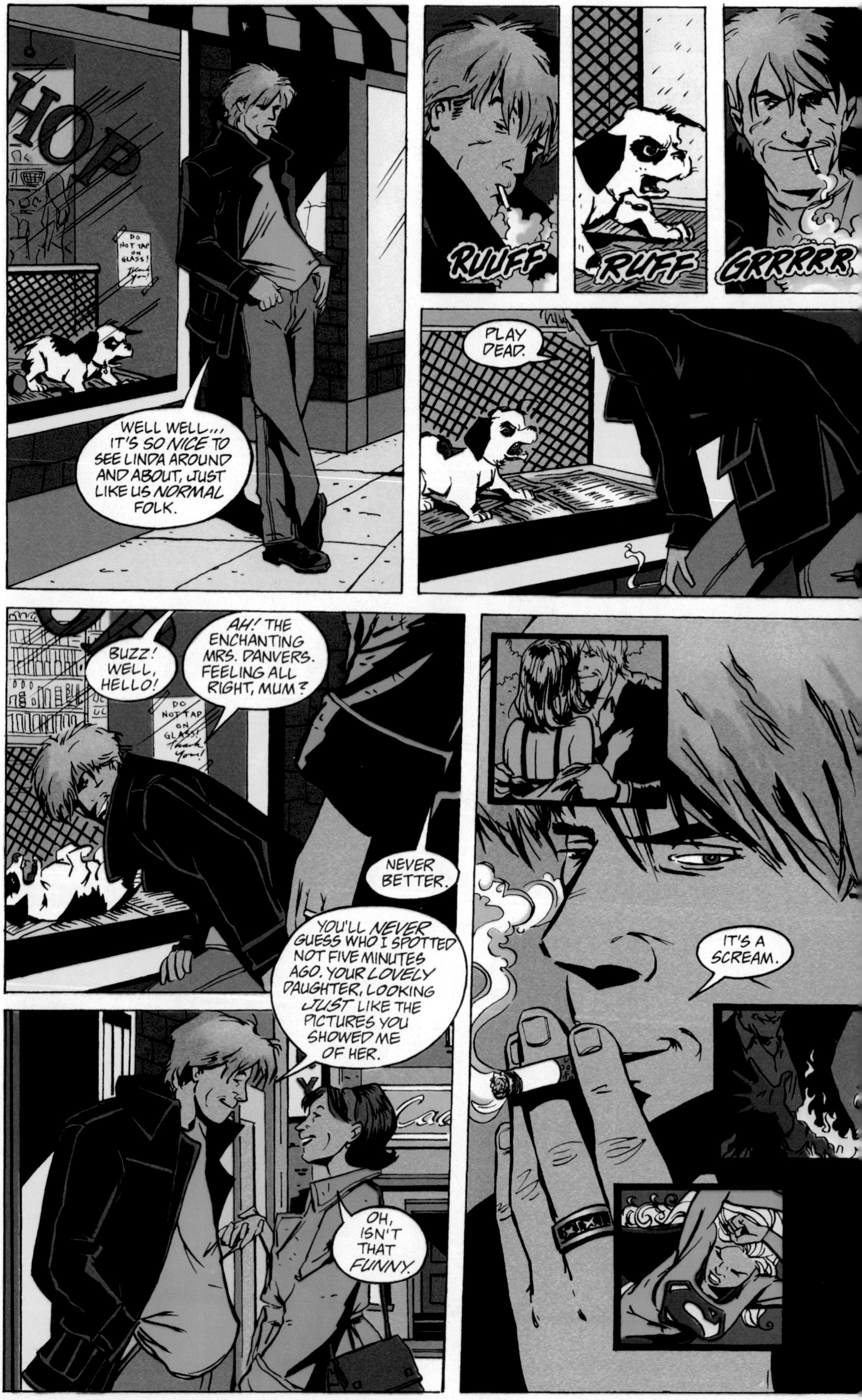

HOP
DO NOT TAP ON GLASS! Thank You!
WELL WELL... IT'S SO NICE TO SEE LINDA AROUND AND ABOUT, JUST LIKE US NORMAL FOLK.
RUUFF
RUFF
GRRRRR
PLAY DEAD.
BUZZ! WELL, HELLO!
AH! THE ENCHANTING MRS. DANVERS. FEELING ALL RIGHT, MUM?
DO NOT TAP ON GLASS! Thank You!
NEVER BETTER.
YOU'LL NEVER GUESS WHO I SPOTTED NOT FIVE MINUTES AGO. YOUR LOVELY DAUGHTER, LOOKING JUST LIKE THE PICTURES YOU SHOWED ME OF HER.
OH, ISN'T THAT FUNNY.
IT'S A SCREAM.

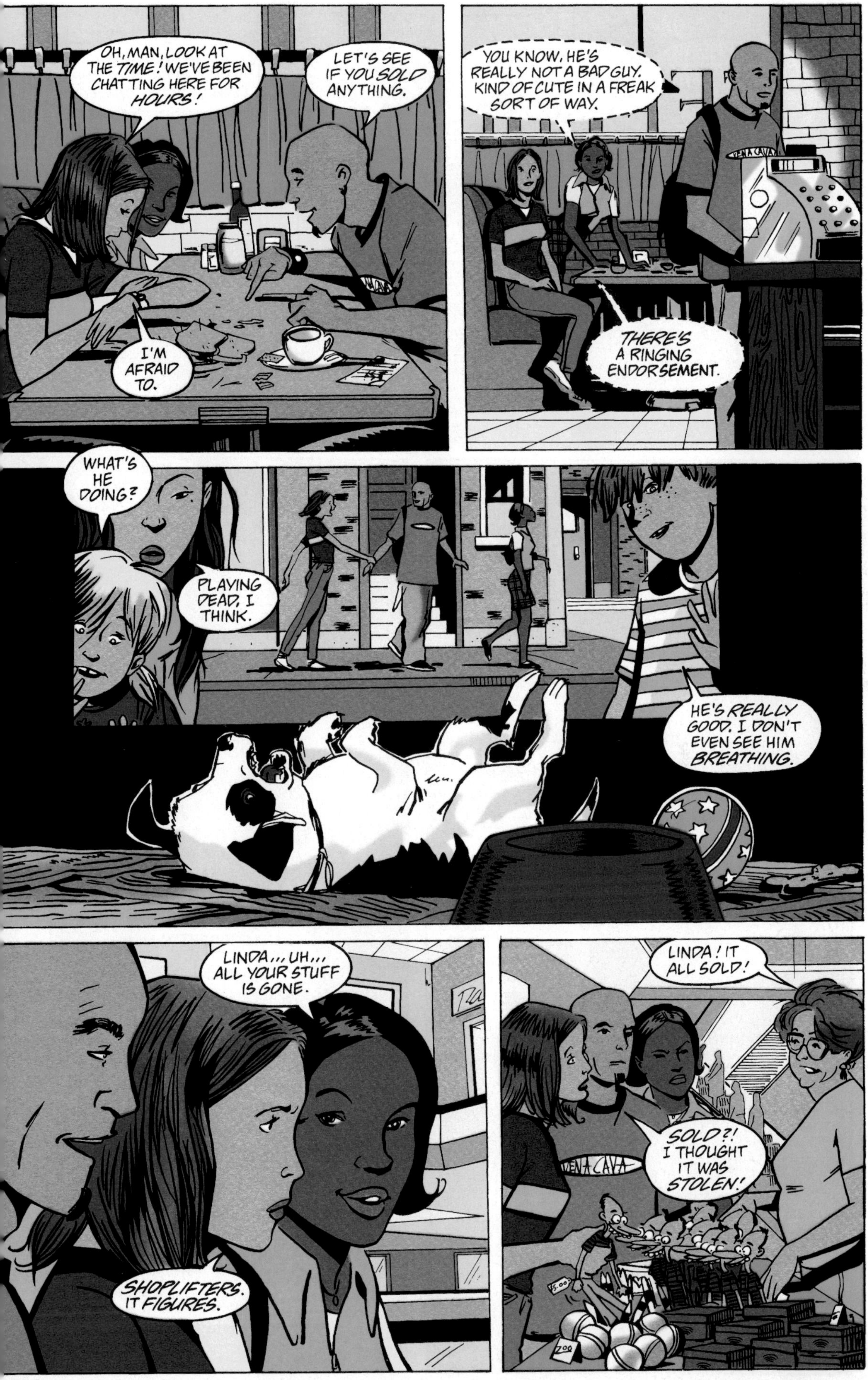
OH, MAN, LOOK AT THE TIME! WE'VE BEEN CHATTING HERE FOR HOURS!
LET'S SEE IF YOU SOLD ANYTHING.
I'M AFRAID TO.
YOU KNOW, HE'S REALLY NOT A BAD GUY. KIND OF CUTE IN A FREAK SORT OF WAY.
THERE'S A RINGING ENDORSEMENT.
WHAT'S HE DOING?
PLAYING DEAD, I THINK.
HE'S REALLY GOOD. I DON'T EVEN SEE HIM BREATHING.
LINDA... UH... ALL YOUR STUFF IS GONE.
SHOPLIFTERS. IT FIGURES.
LINDA! IT ALL SOLD!
SOLD?! I THOUGHT IT WAS STOLEN!

ONE WOMAN JUST FELL IN LOVE WITH *ALL* OF IT. BOUGHT EVERY PIECE OF YOURS I *HAD.* THE VASE, THE ANGELS,... EVERYTHING.

YOU'RE ROLLING IN DOUGH, YOUNG LADY.

VENA CAVA!

OUTSTANDING! OBVIOUSLY YOU WERE ON THE SAME WAVE LENGTH WITH *SOMEBODY.*

WISH I'D BEEN HERE TO MEET HER AND SAY THANKS!

WHAT THE HELL IS *THIS?*

YOUR WIFE DROPPED IT OFF, FRED. SAID SHE'D THOUGHT IT'D BRIGHTEN YOUR DAY.

AW, GREAT. *THANKS LOADS,* SYLVIA.

LEWIS
DROST
JORDAN
MILLER
SPALETA
DOHERTY
SMITH
WARNER
YARICH
PUPPY

021 GLEA
342 SPAD
681 SOTO
421 MAT

THAT SYLVIA...SO *THOUGHTFUL.*

THERE! IT LOOKS AS LOVELY THERE AS I *THOUGHT* IT WOULD.

THERE. THAT SHOULD BRIGHTEN UP MY LITTLE HELL HOLE.

ALL IN ALL... NOT A BAD DAY.

CONTINUED...IN **SUPERGIRL!**

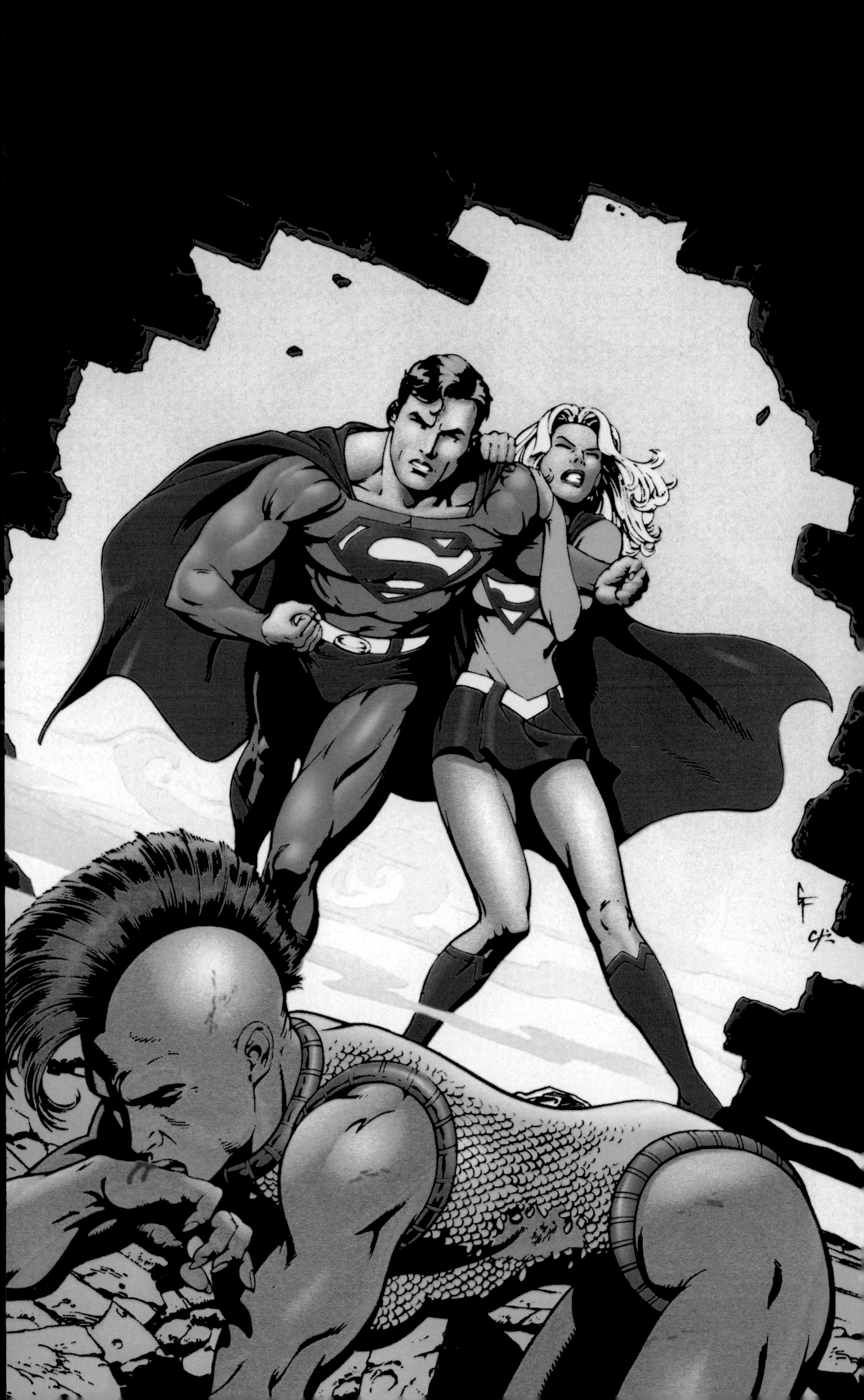

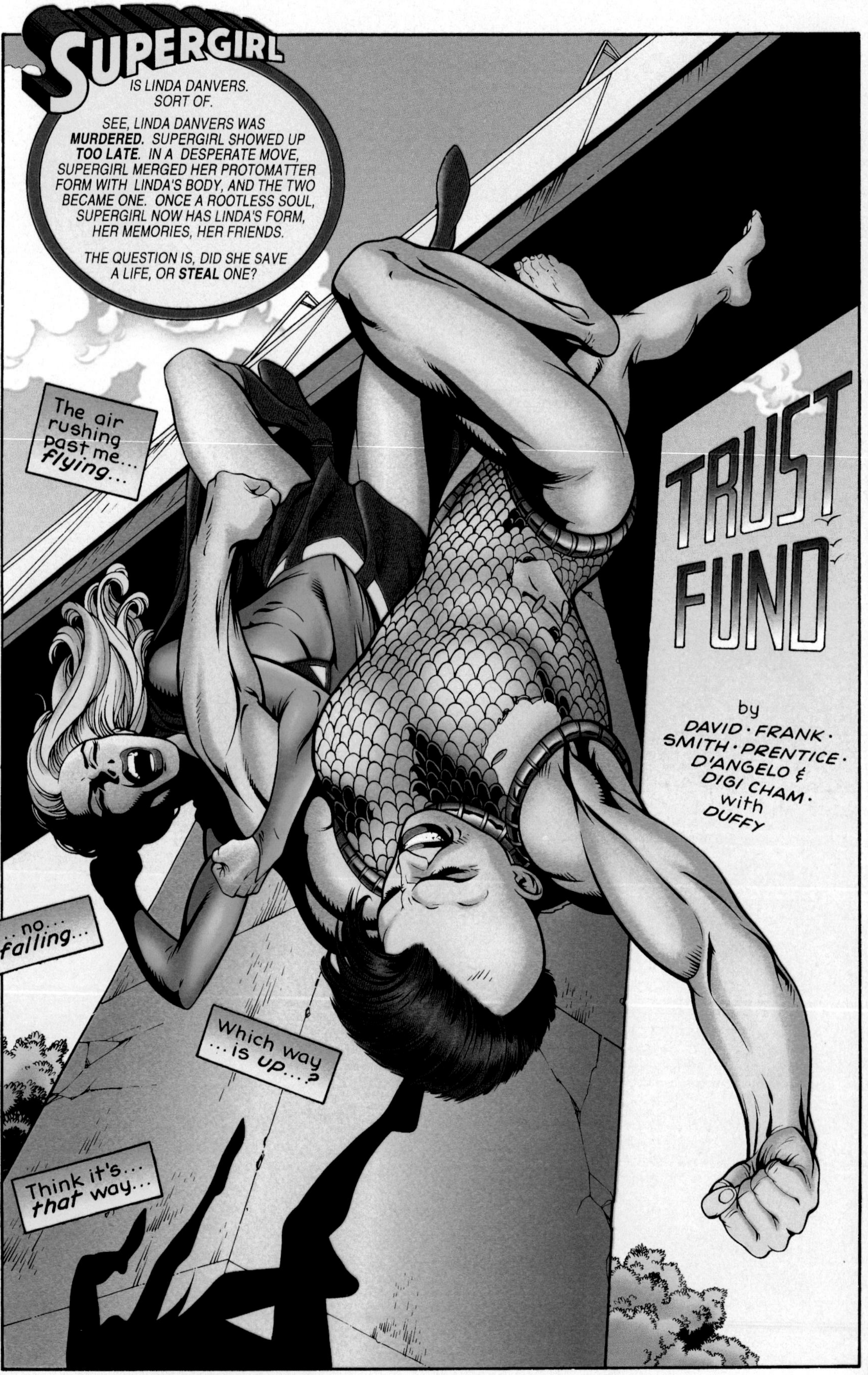
SUPERGIRL
IS LINDA DANVERS. SORT OF.
SEE, LINDA DANVERS WAS MURDERED. SUPERGIRL SHOWED UP TOO LATE. IN A DESPERATE MOVE, SUPERGIRL MERGED HER PROTOMATTER FORM WITH LINDA'S BODY, AND THE TWO BECAME ONE. ONCE A ROOTLESS SOUL, SUPERGIRL NOW HAS LINDA'S FORM, HER MEMORIES, HER FRIENDS.
THE QUESTION IS, DID SHE SAVE A LIFE, OR STEAL ONE?
The air rushing past me... flying...
...no... falling...
Which way ...is up...?
Think it's... that way...
TRUST FUND
by DAVID · FRANK · SMITH · PRENTICE · D'ANGELO & DIGI CHAM · with DUFFY

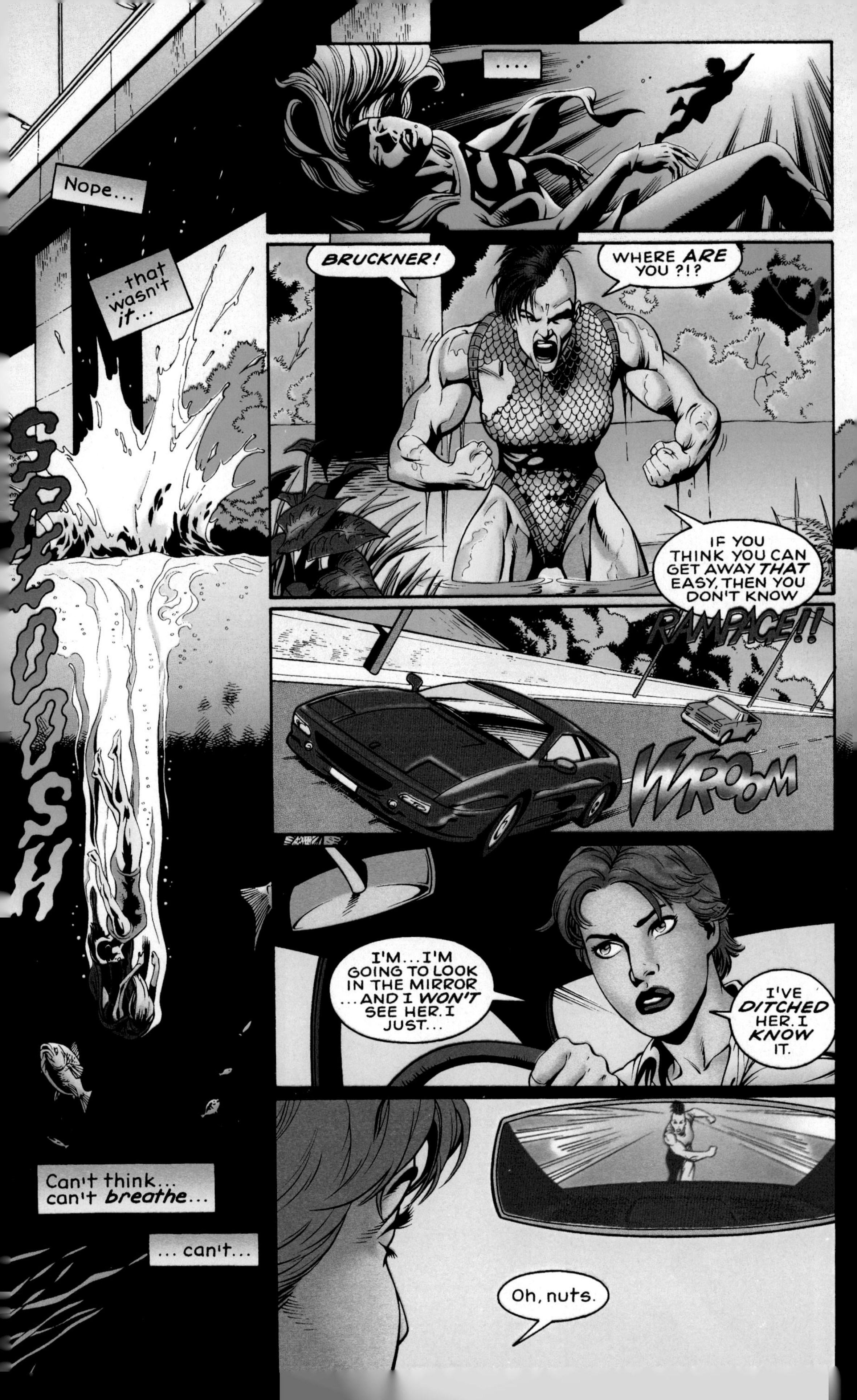

Nope...
. . . .
...that wasn't *it*...
SPLOOSH
BRUCKNER!
WHERE *ARE* YOU ?!?
IF YOU THINK YOU CAN GET AWAY *THAT* EASY, THEN YOU DON'T KNOW
RAMPAGE!!
WROOM
I'M...I'M GOING TO LOOK IN THE MIRROR ...AND I *WON'T* SEE HER. I JUST...
I'VE *DITCHED* HER. I *KNOW* IT.
Can't think... can't *breathe*...
... can't...
Oh, nuts.

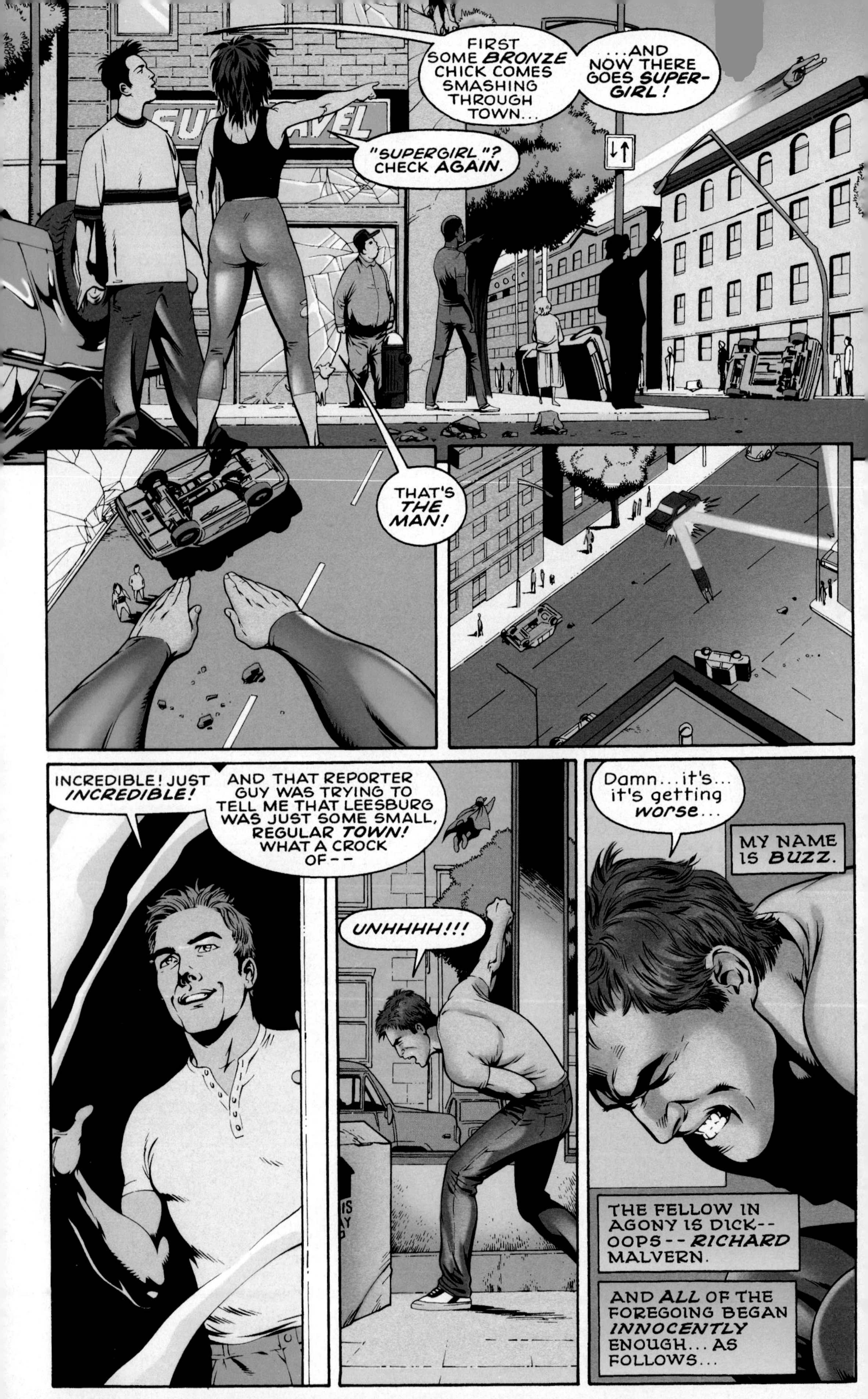
FIRST SOME BRONZE CHICK COMES SMASHING THROUGH TOWN...
...AND NOW THERE GOES SUPER-GIRL!
"SUPERGIRL"? CHECK AGAIN.
THAT'S THE MAN!
INCREDIBLE! JUST INCREDIBLE!
AND THAT REPORTER GUY WAS TRYING TO TELL ME THAT LEESBURG WAS JUST SOME SMALL, REGULAR TOWN! WHAT A CROCK OF--
UNHHHH!!!
Damn... it's... it's getting worse...
MY NAME IS BUZZ.
THE FELLOW IN AGONY IS DICK--OOPS--RICHARD MALVERN.
AND ALL OF THE FOREGOING BEGAN INNOCENTLY ENOUGH... AS FOLLOWS...

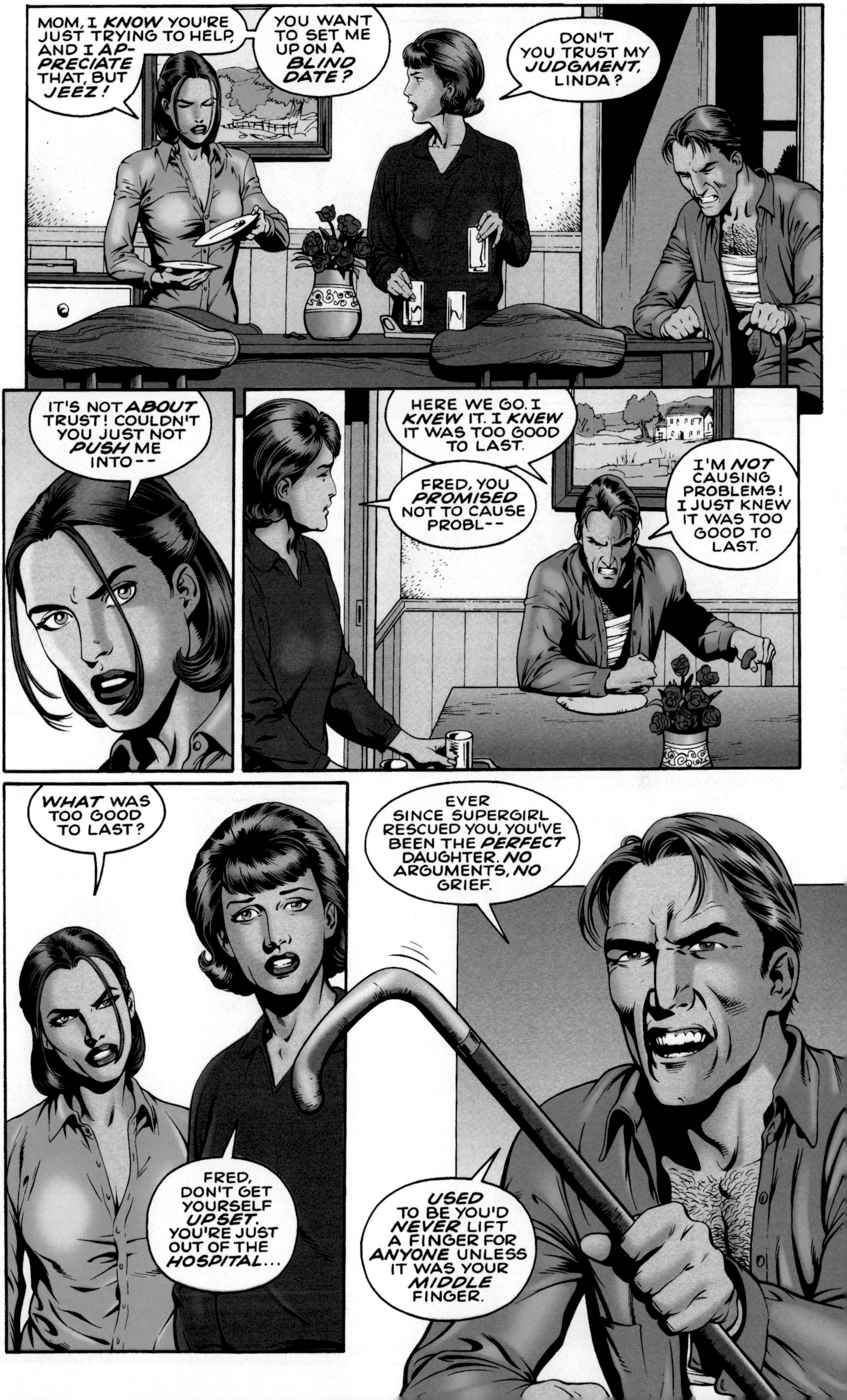
MOM, I KNOW YOU'RE JUST TRYING TO HELP, AND I AP-PRECIATE THAT, BUT JEEZ!
YOU WANT TO SET ME UP ON A BLIND DATE?
DON'T YOU TRUST MY JUDGMENT, LINDA?
IT'S NOT ABOUT TRUST! COULDN'T YOU JUST NOT PUSH ME INTO--
HERE WE GO. I KNEW IT. I KNEW IT WAS TOO GOOD TO LAST.
FRED, YOU PROMISED NOT TO CAUSE PROBL--
I'M NOT CAUSING PROBLEMS! I JUST KNEW IT WAS TOO GOOD TO LAST.
WHAT WAS TOO GOOD TO LAST?
EVER SINCE SUPERGIRL RESCUED YOU, YOU'VE BEEN THE PERFECT DAUGHTER. NO ARGUMENTS, NO GRIEF.
FRED, DON'T GET YOURSELF UPSET. YOU'RE JUST OUT OF THE HOSPITAL...
USED TO BE YOU'D NEVER LIFT A FINGER FOR ANYONE UNLESS IT WAS YOUR MIDDLE FINGER.

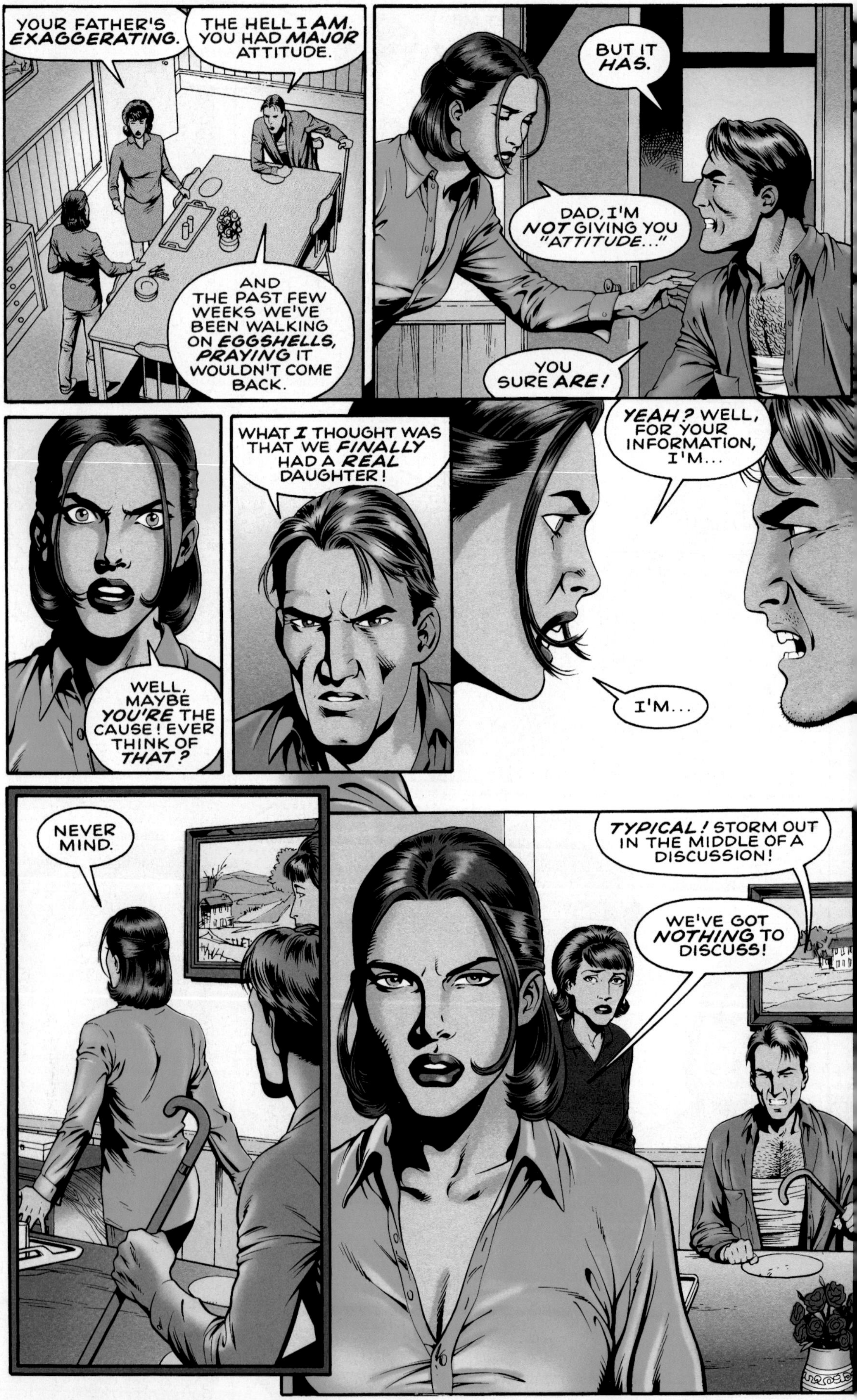
YOUR FATHER'S EXAGGERATING.
THE HELL I AM. YOU HAD MAJOR ATTITUDE.
AND THE PAST FEW WEEKS WE'VE BEEN WALKING ON EGGSHELLS, PRAYING IT WOULDN'T COME BACK.
BUT IT HAS.
DAD, I'M NOT GIVING YOU "ATTITUDE..."
YOU SURE ARE!
WELL, MAYBE YOU'RE THE CAUSE! EVER THINK OF THAT?
WHAT I THOUGHT WAS THAT WE FINALLY HAD A REAL DAUGHTER!
YEAH? WELL, FOR YOUR INFORMATION, I'M...
I'M...
NEVER MIND.
TYPICAL! STORM OUT IN THE MIDDLE OF A DISCUSSION!
WE'VE GOT NOTHING TO DISCUSS!

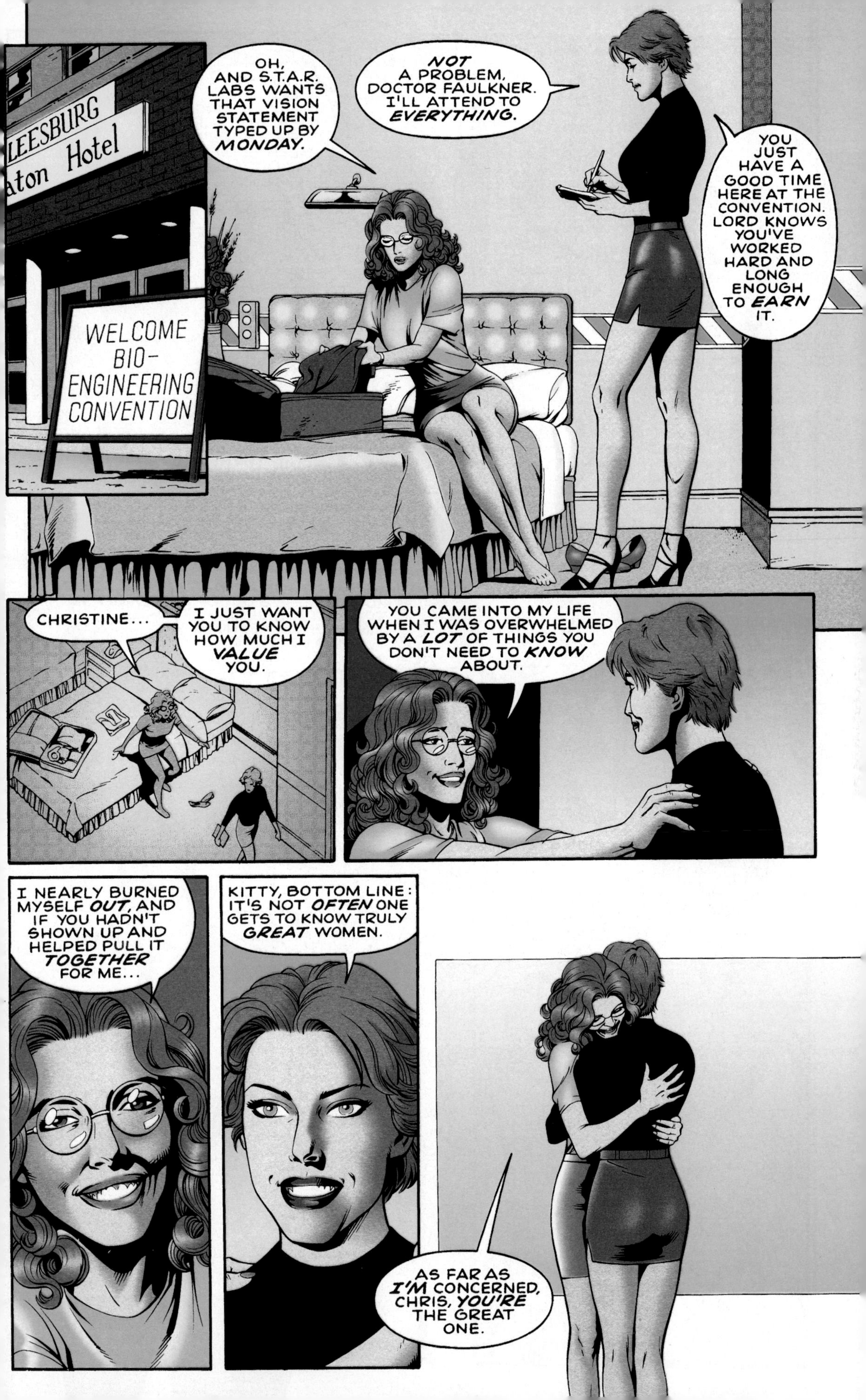
LEESBURG
aton Hotel
WELCOME BIO-ENGINEERING CONVENTION
OH, AND S.T.A.R. LABS WANTS THAT VISION STATEMENT TYPED UP BY MONDAY.
NOT A PROBLEM, DOCTOR FAULKNER. I'LL ATTEND TO EVERYTHING.
YOU JUST HAVE A GOOD TIME HERE AT THE CONVENTION. LORD KNOWS YOU'VE WORKED HARD AND LONG ENOUGH TO EARN IT.
CHRISTINE...
I JUST WANT YOU TO KNOW HOW MUCH I VALUE YOU.
YOU CAME INTO MY LIFE WHEN I WAS OVERWHELMED BY A LOT OF THINGS YOU DON'T NEED TO KNOW ABOUT.
I NEARLY BURNED MYSELF OUT, AND IF YOU HADN'T SHOWN UP AND HELPED PULL IT TOGETHER FOR ME...
KITTY, BOTTOM LINE: IT'S NOT OFTEN ONE GETS TO KNOW TRULY GREAT WOMEN.
AS FAR AS I'M CONCERNED, CHRIS, YOU'RE THE GREAT ONE.

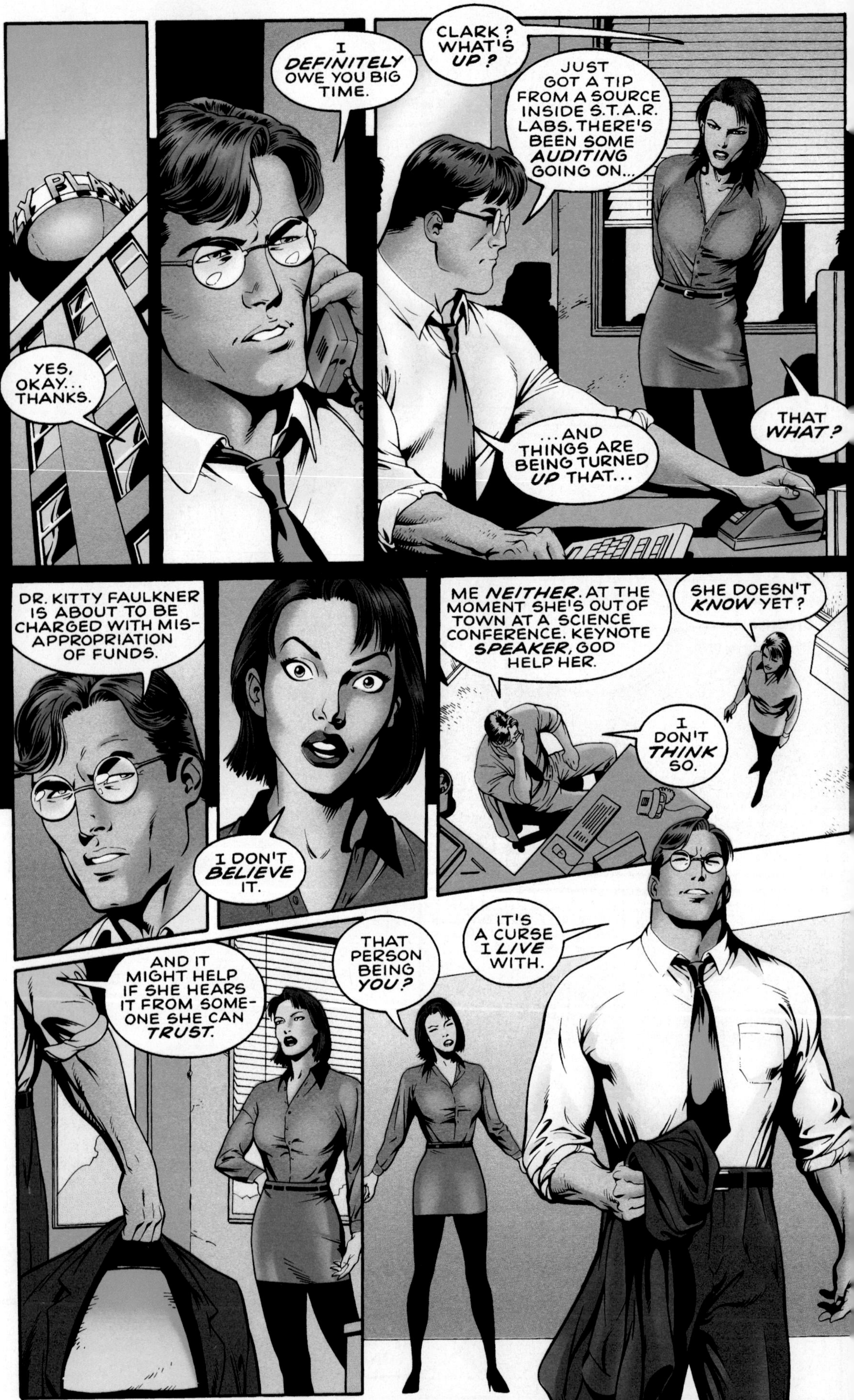
YES, OKAY... THANKS.
I DEFINITELY OWE YOU BIG TIME.
CLARK? WHAT'S UP?
JUST GOT A TIP FROM A SOURCE INSIDE S.T.A.R. LABS. THERE'S BEEN SOME AUDITING GOING ON...
...AND THINGS ARE BEING TURNED UP THAT...
THAT WHAT?
DR. KITTY FAULKNER IS ABOUT TO BE CHARGED WITH MIS-APPROPRIATION OF FUNDS.
I DON'T BELIEVE IT.
ME NEITHER. AT THE MOMENT SHE'S OUT OF TOWN AT A SCIENCE CONFERENCE. KEYNOTE SPEAKER, GOD HELP HER.
SHE DOESN'T KNOW YET?
I DON'T THINK SO.
AND IT MIGHT HELP IF SHE HEARS IT FROM SOME-ONE SHE CAN TRUST.
THAT PERSON BEING YOU?
IT'S A CURSE I LIVE WITH.

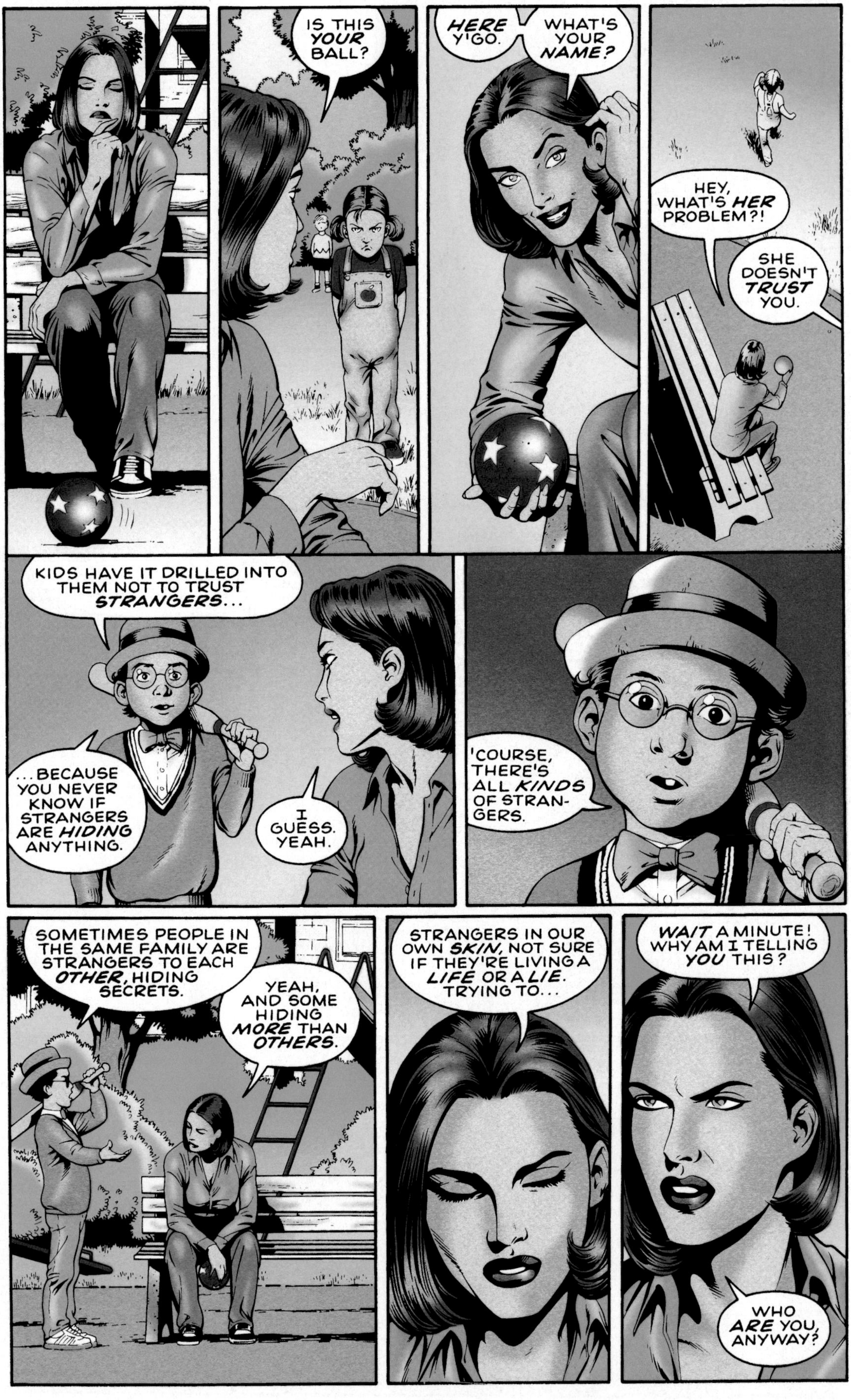
IS THIS YOUR BALL?
HERE Y'GO.
WHAT'S YOUR NAME?
HEY, WHAT'S HER PROBLEM?!
SHE DOESN'T TRUST YOU.
KIDS HAVE IT DRILLED INTO THEM NOT TO TRUST STRANGERS...
...BECAUSE YOU NEVER KNOW IF STRANGERS ARE HIDING ANYTHING.
I GUESS. YEAH.
'COURSE, THERE'S ALL KINDS OF STRAN- GERS.
SOMETIMES PEOPLE IN THE SAME FAMILY ARE STRANGERS TO EACH OTHER, HIDING SECRETS.
YEAH, AND SOME HIDING MORE THAN OTHERS.
STRANGERS IN OUR OWN SKIN, NOT SURE IF THEY'RE LIVING A LIFE OR A LIE. TRYING TO...
WAIT A MINUTE! WHY AM I TELLING YOU THIS?
WHO ARE YOU, ANYWAY?

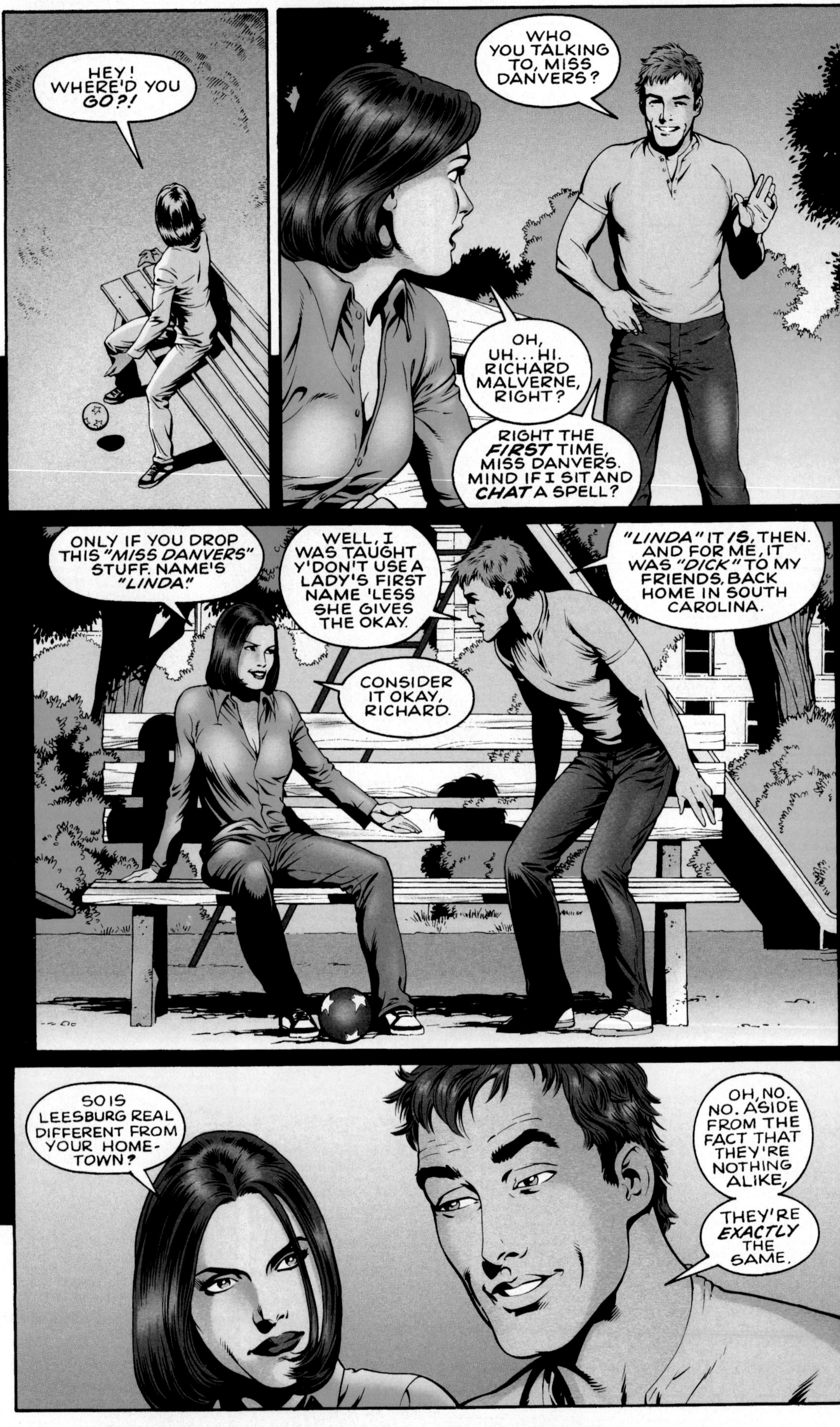
HEY! WHERE'D YOU GO?!
WHO YOU TALKING TO, MISS DANVERS?
OH, UH... HI. RICHARD MALVERNE, RIGHT?
RIGHT THE FIRST TIME, MISS DANVERS. MIND IF I SIT AND CHAT A SPELL?
ONLY IF YOU DROP THIS "MISS DANVERS" STUFF. NAME'S "LINDA."
WELL, I WAS TAUGHT Y'DON'T USE A LADY'S FIRST NAME 'LESS SHE GIVES THE OKAY.
"LINDA" IT IS, THEN. AND FOR ME, IT WAS "DICK" TO MY FRIENDS, BACK HOME IN SOUTH CAROLINA.
CONSIDER IT OKAY, RICHARD.
SO IS LEESBURG REAL DIFFERENT FROM YOUR HOME-TOWN?
OH, NO. NO. ASIDE FROM THE FACT THAT THEY'RE NOTHING ALIKE,
THEY'RE EXACTLY THE SAME.

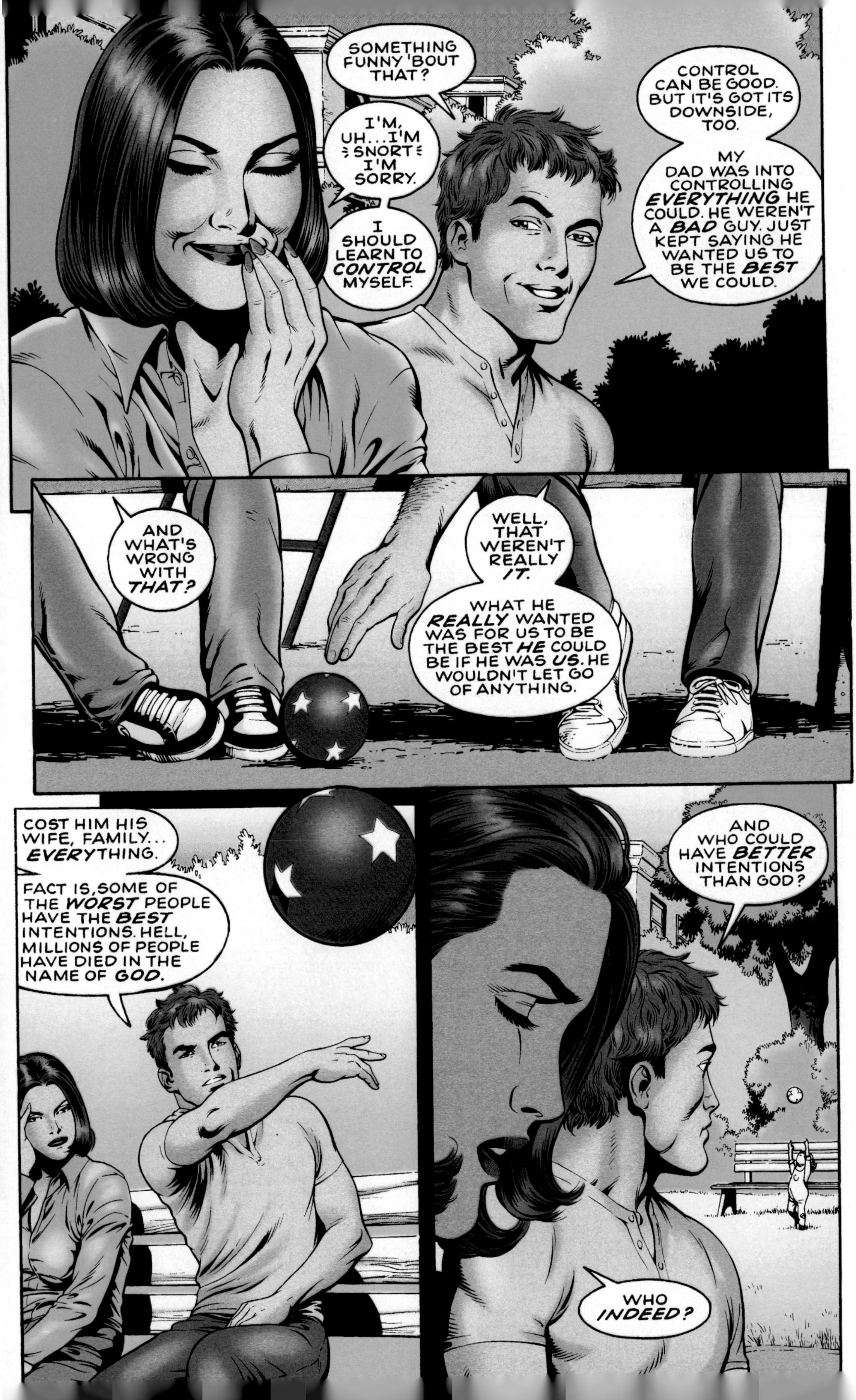
SOMETHING FUNNY 'BOUT THAT?
I'M, UH...I'M SNORT I'M SORRY.
I SHOULD LEARN TO CONTROL MYSELF.
CONTROL CAN BE GOOD. BUT IT'S GOT ITS DOWNSIDE, TOO.
MY DAD WAS INTO CONTROLLING EVERYTHING HE COULD. HE WEREN'T A BAD GUY. JUST KEPT SAYING HE WANTED US TO BE THE BEST WE COULD.
AND WHAT'S WRONG WITH THAT?
WELL, THAT WEREN'T REALLY IT.
WHAT HE REALLY WANTED WAS FOR US TO BE THE BEST HE COULD BE IF HE WAS US. HE WOULDN'T LET GO OF ANYTHING.
COST HIM HIS WIFE, FAMILY... EVERYTHING.
FACT IS, SOME OF THE WORST PEOPLE HAVE THE BEST INTENTIONS. HELL, MILLIONS OF PEOPLE HAVE DIED IN THE NAME OF GOD.
AND WHO COULD HAVE BETTER INTENTIONS THAN GOD?
WHO INDEED?

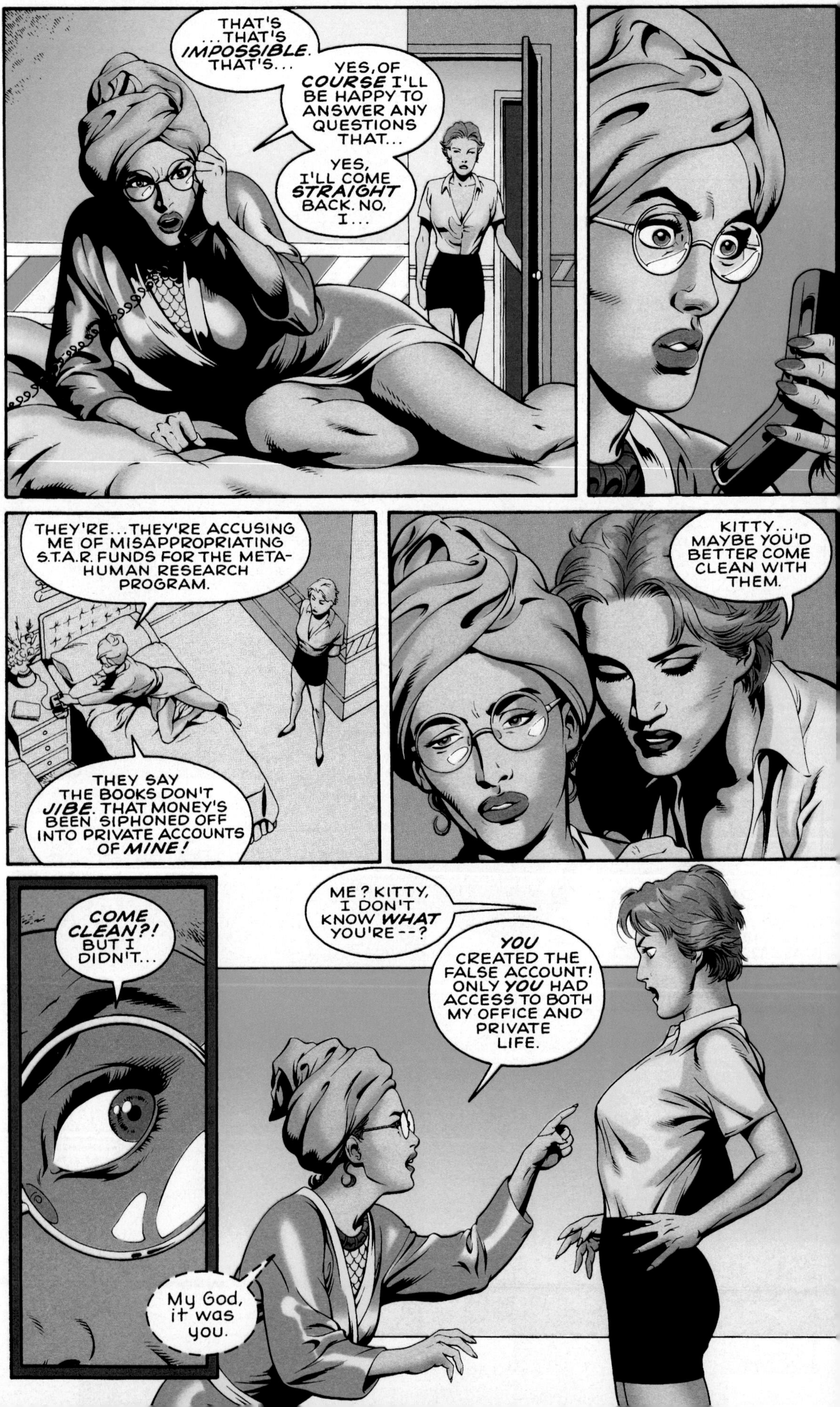
THAT'S ...THAT'S IMPOSSIBLE. THAT'S...
YES, OF COURSE I'LL BE HAPPY TO ANSWER ANY QUESTIONS THAT...
YES, I'LL COME STRAIGHT BACK. NO, I...
THEY'RE...THEY'RE ACCUSING ME OF MISAPPROPRIATING S.T.A.R. FUNDS FOR THE META-HUMAN RESEARCH PROGRAM.
THEY SAY THE BOOKS DON'T JIBE. THAT MONEY'S BEEN SIPHONED OFF INTO PRIVATE ACCOUNTS OF MINE!
KITTY... MAYBE YOU'D BETTER COME CLEAN WITH THEM.
COME CLEAN?! BUT I DIDN'T...
My God, it was you.
ME? KITTY, I DON'T KNOW WHAT YOU'RE--?
YOU CREATED THE FALSE ACCOUNT! ONLY YOU HAD ACCESS TO BOTH MY OFFICE AND PRIVATE LIFE.

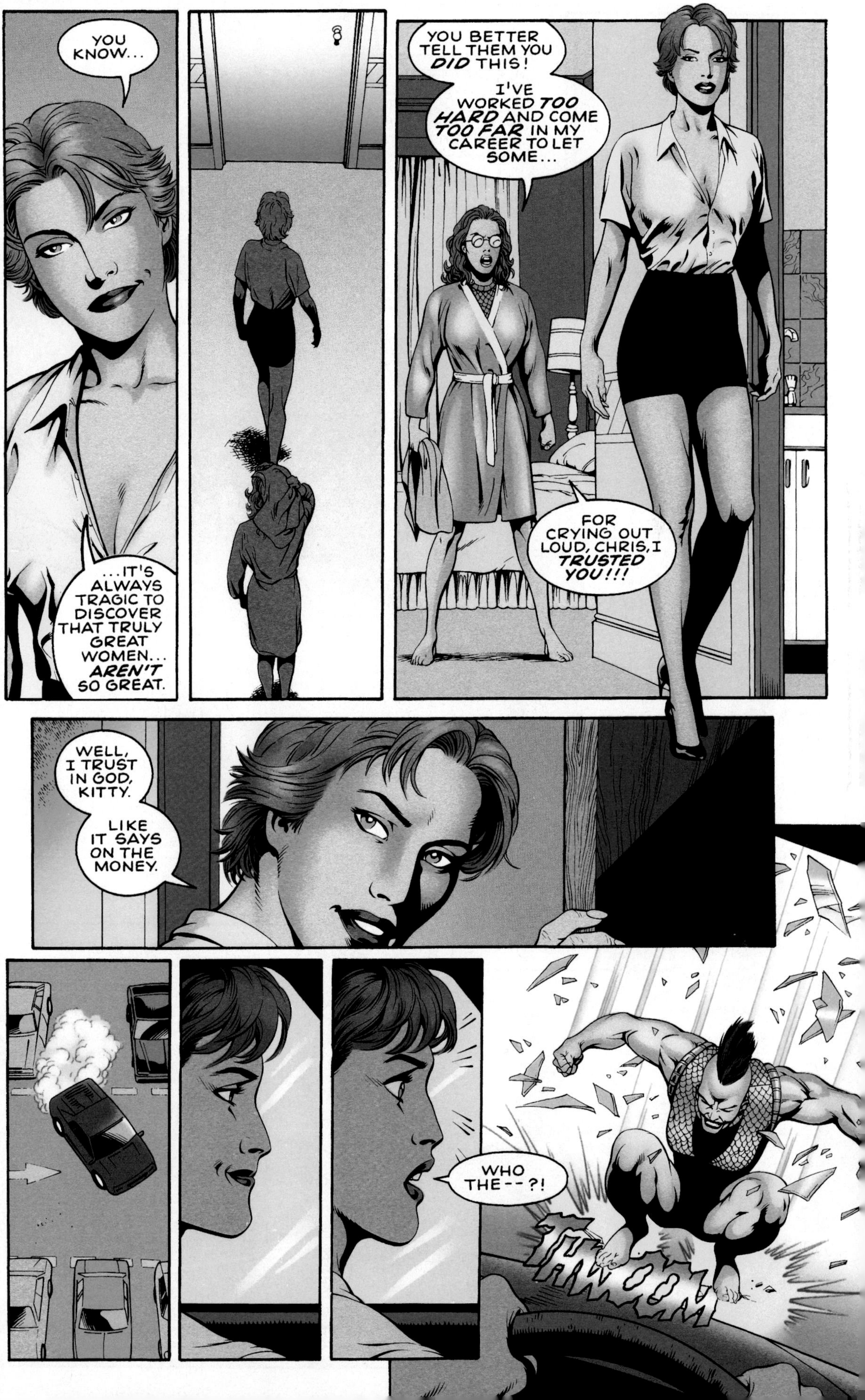
YOU KNOW...
...IT'S ALWAYS TRAGIC TO DISCOVER THAT TRULY GREAT WOMEN... AREN'T SO GREAT.
YOU BETTER TELL THEM YOU DID THIS!
I'VE WORKED TOO HARD AND COME TOO FAR IN MY CAREER TO LET SOME...
FOR CRYING OUT LOUD, CHRIS, I TRUSTED YOU!!!
WELL, I TRUST IN GOD, KITTY.
LIKE IT SAYS ON THE MONEY.
WHO THE--?!
THOOM

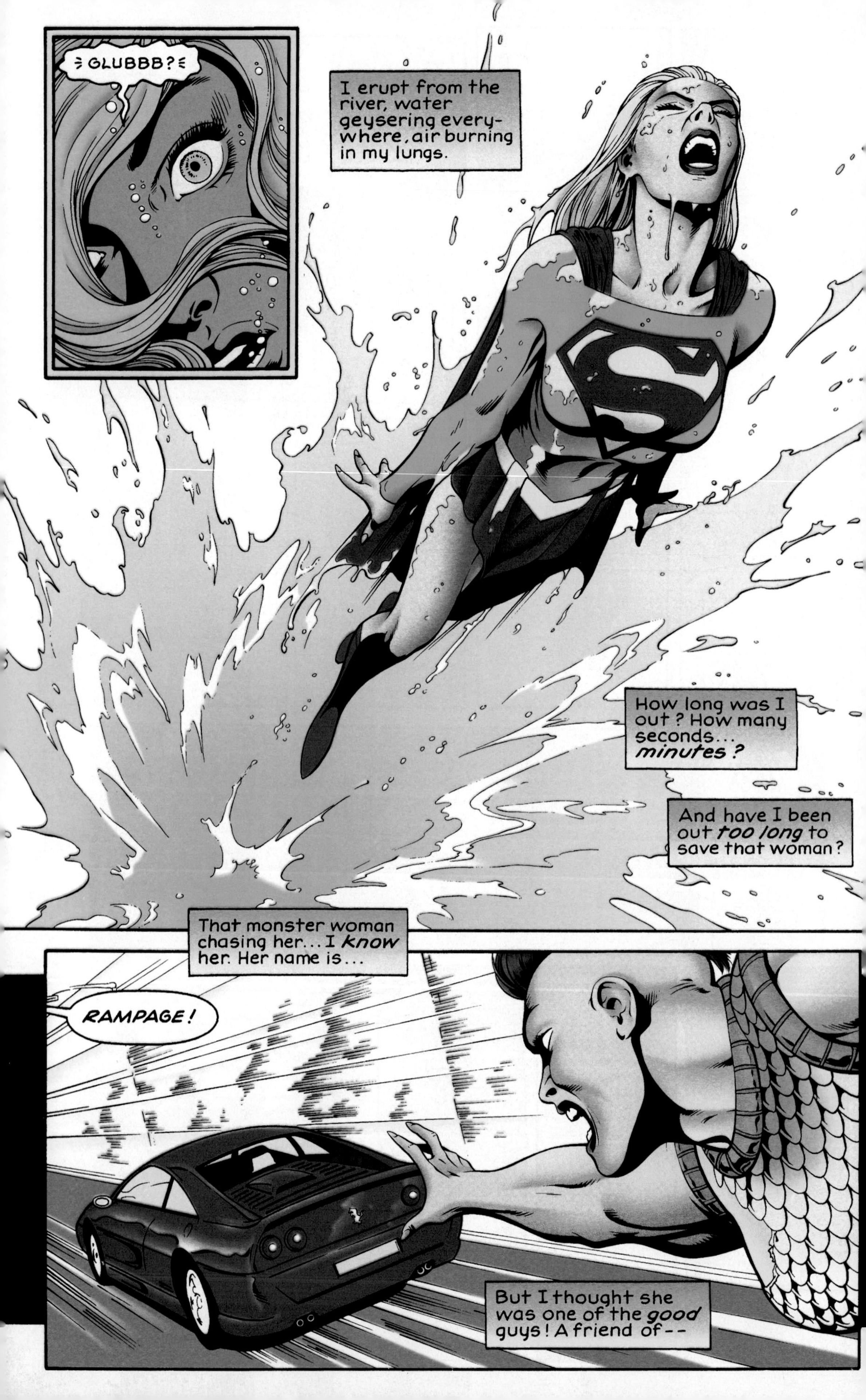
GLUBBB?
I erupt from the river, water geysering every-where, air burning in my lungs.
How long was I out? How many seconds... minutes?
And have I been out too long to save that woman?
That monster woman chasing her... I know her. Her name is...
RAMPAGE!
But I thought she was one of the good guys! A friend of--

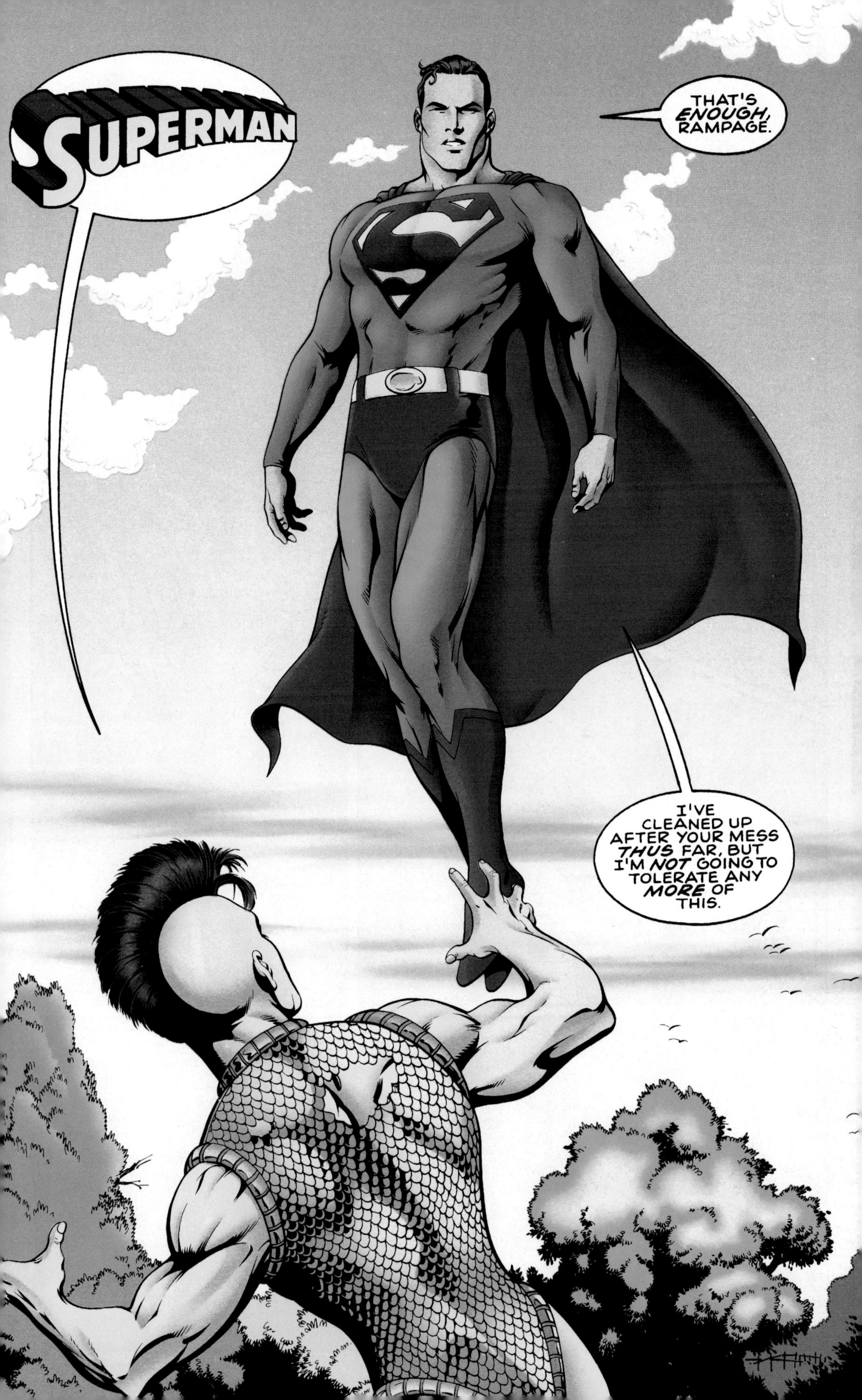
SUPERMAN
THAT'S ENOUGH, RAMPAGE.
I'VE CLEANED UP AFTER YOUR MESS THUS FAR, BUT I'M NOT GOING TO TOLERATE ANY MORE OF THIS.

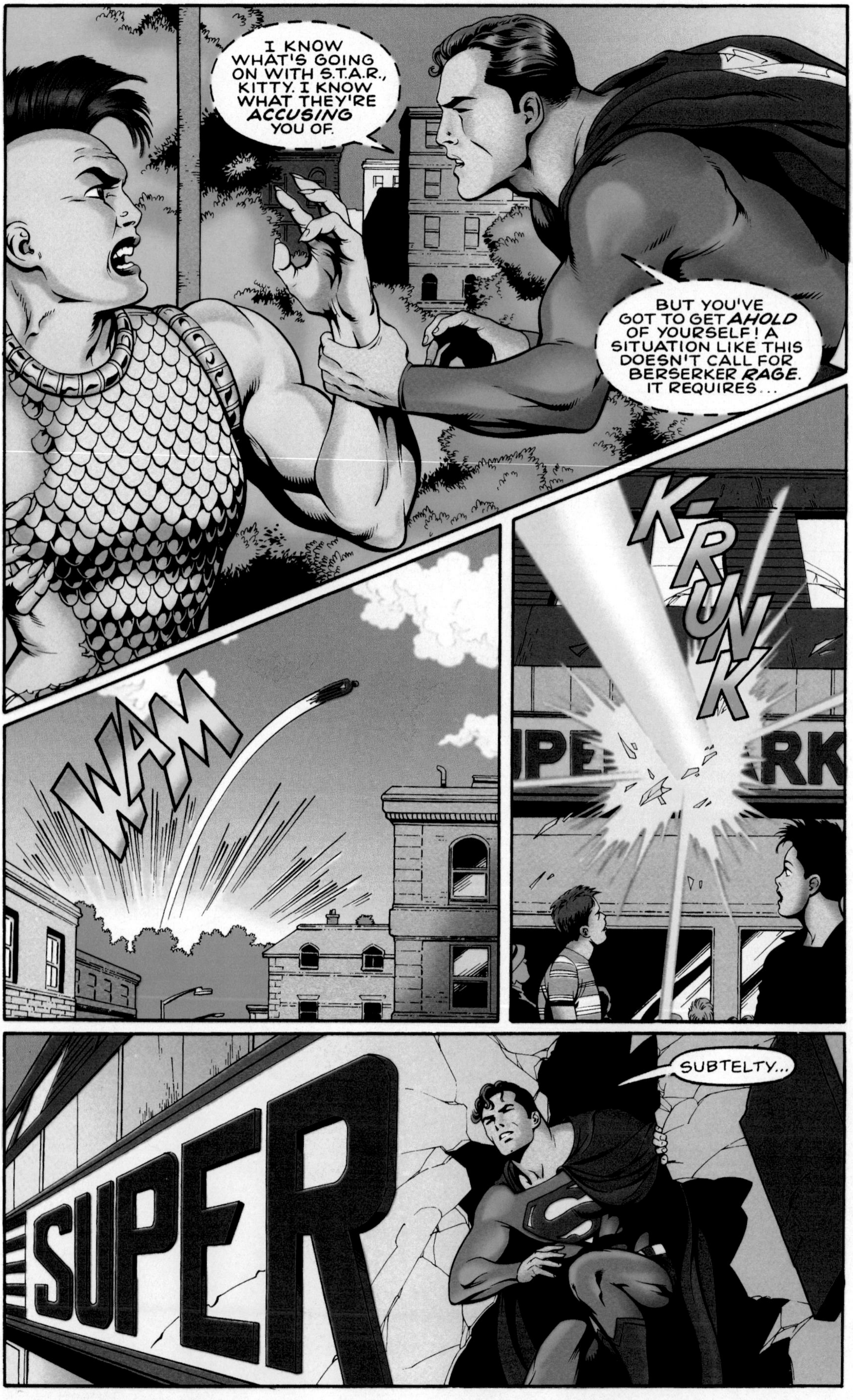
I KNOW WHAT'S GOING ON WITH S.T.A.R., KITTY. I KNOW WHAT THEY'RE ACCUSING YOU OF.
BUT YOU'VE GOT TO GET AHOLD OF YOURSELF! A SITUATION LIKE THIS DOESN'T CALL FOR BERSERKER RAGE. IT REQUIRES...
WAM
K-RUNK
SUBTELTY...
SUPER

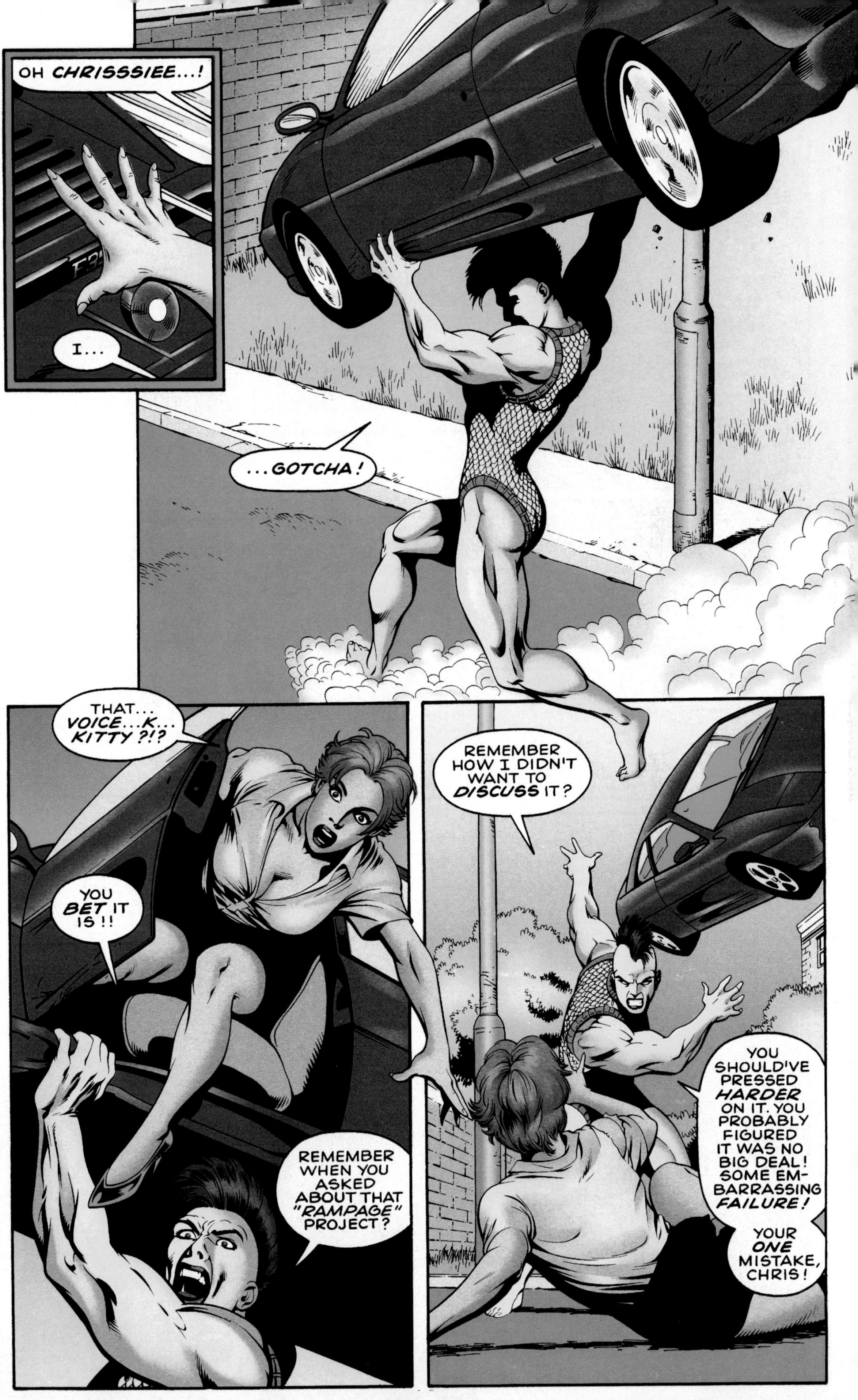

OH CHRISSSIEE...!
I...
...GOTCHA!
THAT... VOICE...K... KITTY ?!?
YOU BET IT IS!!
REMEMBER WHEN YOU ASKED ABOUT THAT "RAMPAGE" PROJECT?
REMEMBER HOW I DIDN'T WANT TO DISCUSS IT?
YOU SHOULD'VE PRESSED HARDER ON IT. YOU PROBABLY FIGURED IT WAS NO BIG DEAL! SOME EMBARRASSING FAILURE!
YOUR ONE MISTAKE, CHRIS!

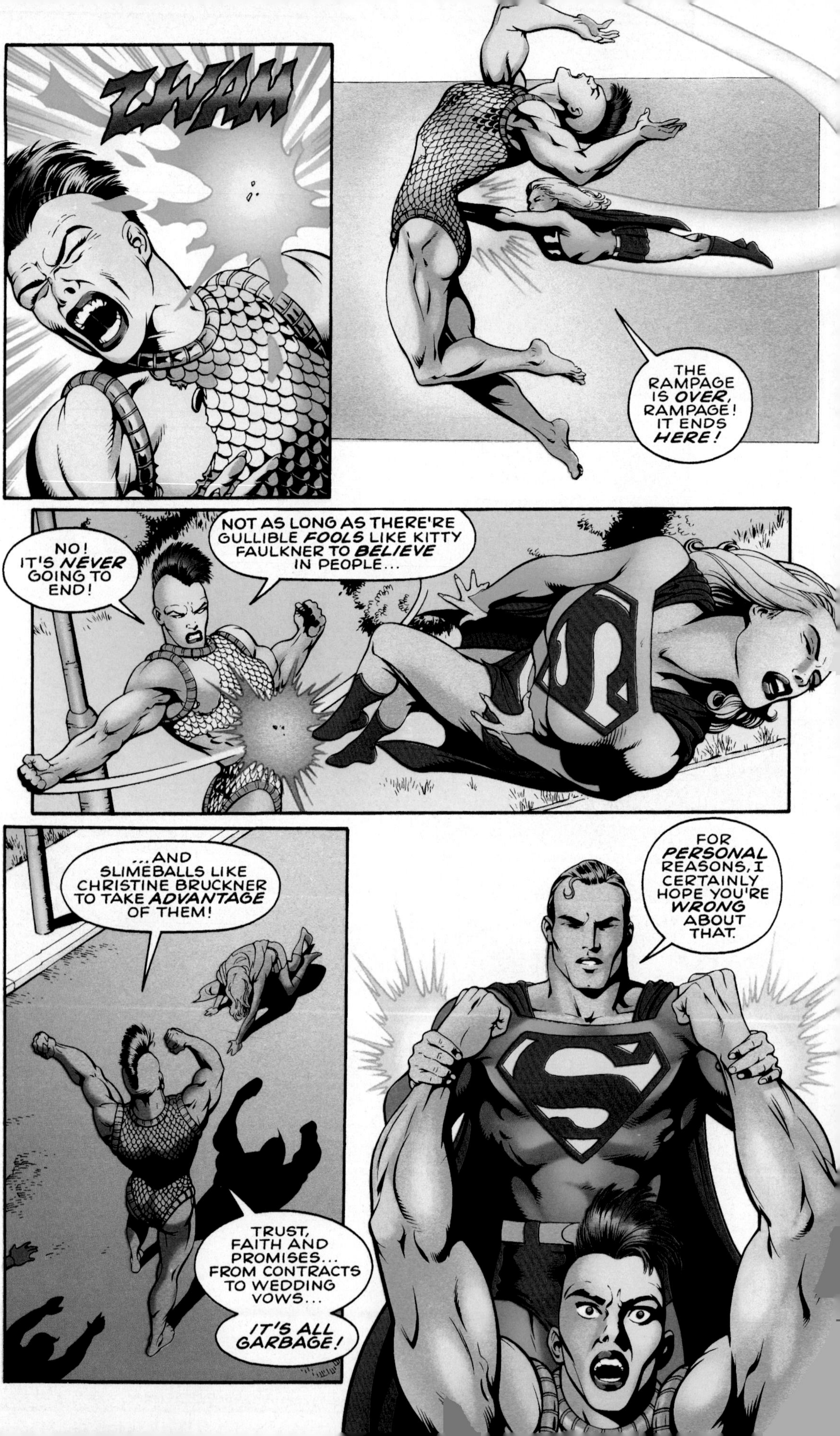
ZWAM
THE RAMPAGE IS OVER, RAMPAGE! IT ENDS HERE!
NO! IT'S NEVER GOING TO END!
NOT AS LONG AS THERE'RE GULLIBLE FOOLS LIKE KITTY FAULKNER TO BELIEVE IN PEOPLE...
...AND SLIMEBALLS LIKE CHRISTINE BRUCKNER TO TAKE ADVANTAGE OF THEM!
TRUST, FAITH AND PROMISES... FROM CONTRACTS TO WEDDING VOWS...
IT'S ALL GARBAGE!
FOR PERSONAL REASONS, I CERTAINLY HOPE YOU'RE WRONG ABOUT THAT.

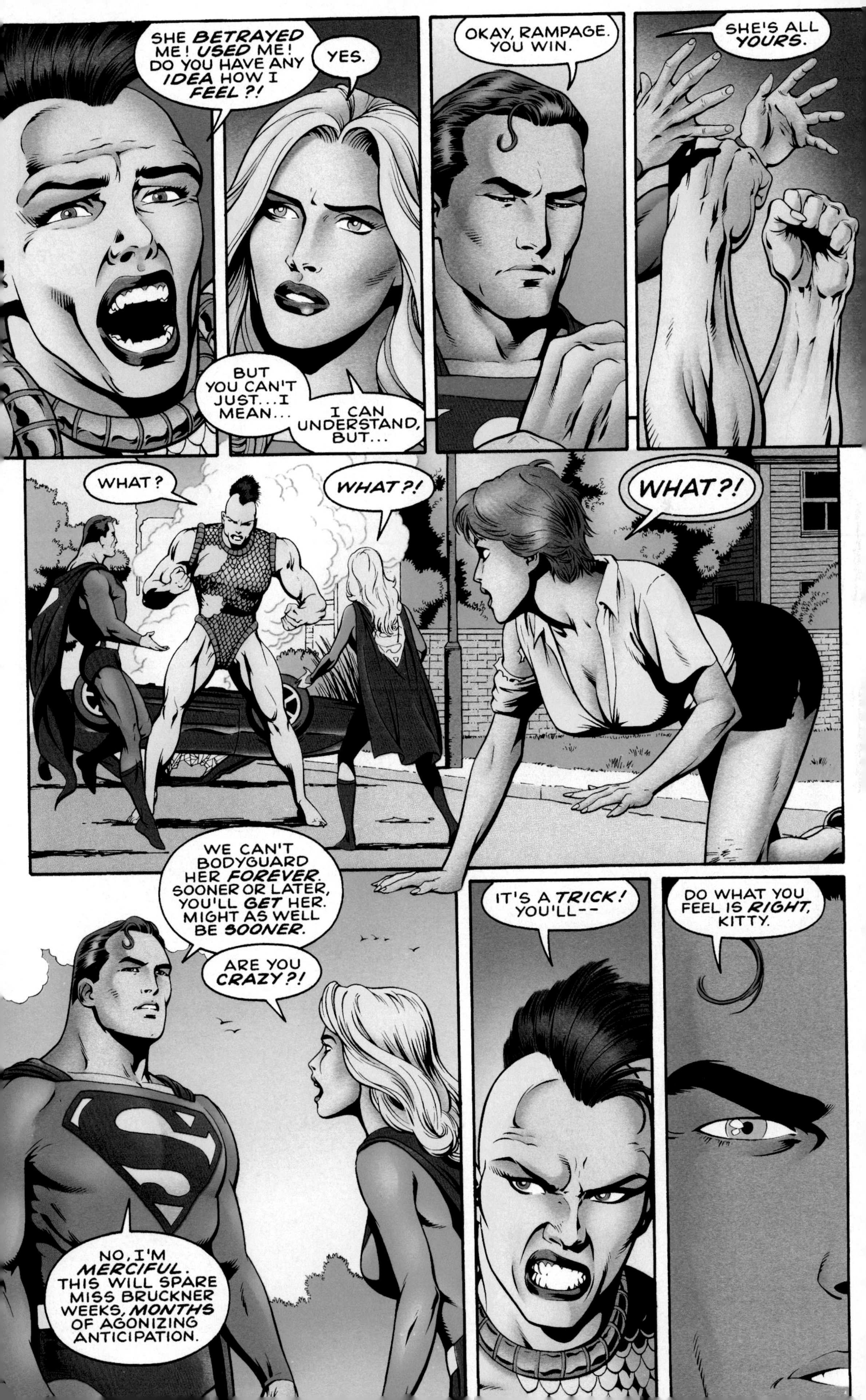
SHE BETRAYED ME! USED ME! DO YOU HAVE ANY IDEA HOW I FEEL?!
YES.
BUT YOU CAN'T JUST...I MEAN...
I CAN UNDERSTAND, BUT...
OKAY, RAMPAGE. YOU WIN.
SHE'S ALL YOURS.
WHAT?
WHAT?!
WHAT?!
WE CAN'T BODYGUARD HER FOREVER. SOONER OR LATER, YOU'LL GET HER. MIGHT AS WELL BE SOONER.
ARE YOU CRAZY?!
NO, I'M MERCIFUL. THIS WILL SPARE MISS BRUCKNER WEEKS, MONTHS OF AGONIZING ANTICIPATION.
IT'S A TRICK! YOU'LL--
DO WHAT YOU FEEL IS RIGHT, KITTY.

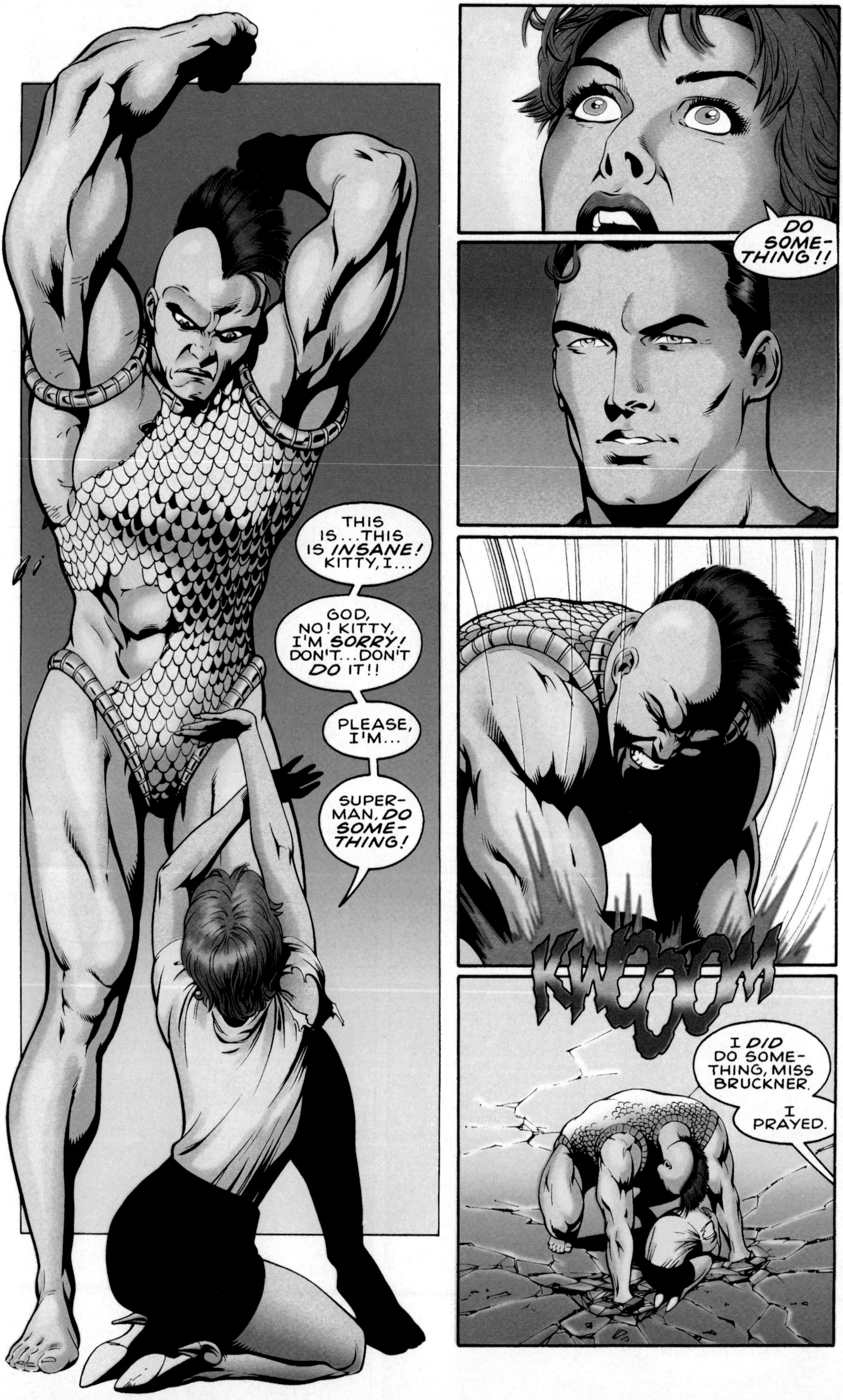
THIS IS...THIS IS INSANE! KITTY, I...
GOD, NO! KITTY, I'M SORRY! DON'T...DON'T DO IT!!
PLEASE, I'M...
SUPER-MAN, DO SOME-THING!
DO SOME-THING!!
KWOOOM
I DID DO SOME-THING, MISS BRUCKNER.
I PRAYED.

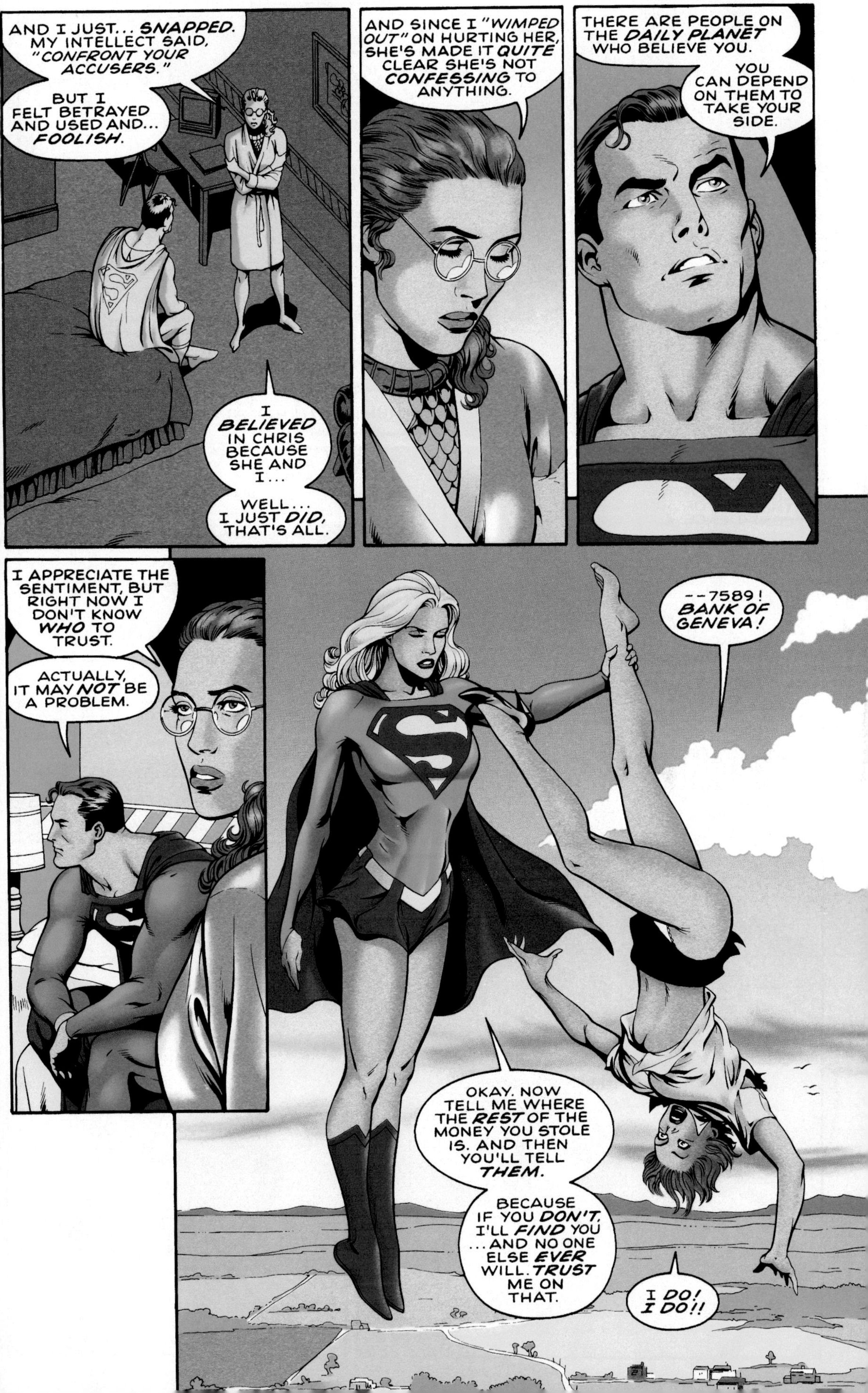
AND I JUST... SNAPPED. MY INTELLECT SAID, "CONFRONT YOUR ACCUSERS."
BUT I FELT BETRAYED AND USED AND... FOOLISH.
I BELIEVED IN CHRIS BECAUSE SHE AND I...
WELL... I JUST DID, THAT'S ALL.
AND SINCE I "WIMPED OUT" ON HURTING HER, SHE'S MADE IT QUITE CLEAR SHE'S NOT CONFESSING TO ANYTHING.
THERE ARE PEOPLE ON THE DAILY PLANET WHO BELIEVE YOU.
YOU CAN DEPEND ON THEM TO TAKE YOUR SIDE.
I APPRECIATE THE SENTIMENT, BUT RIGHT NOW I DON'T KNOW WHO TO TRUST.
ACTUALLY, IT MAY NOT BE A PROBLEM.
--7589! BANK OF GENEVA!
OKAY. NOW TELL ME WHERE THE REST OF THE MONEY YOU STOLE IS. AND THEN YOU'LL TELL THEM.
BECAUSE IF YOU DON'T, I'LL FIND YOU ...AND NO ONE ELSE EVER WILL. TRUST ME ON THAT.
I DO! I DO!!

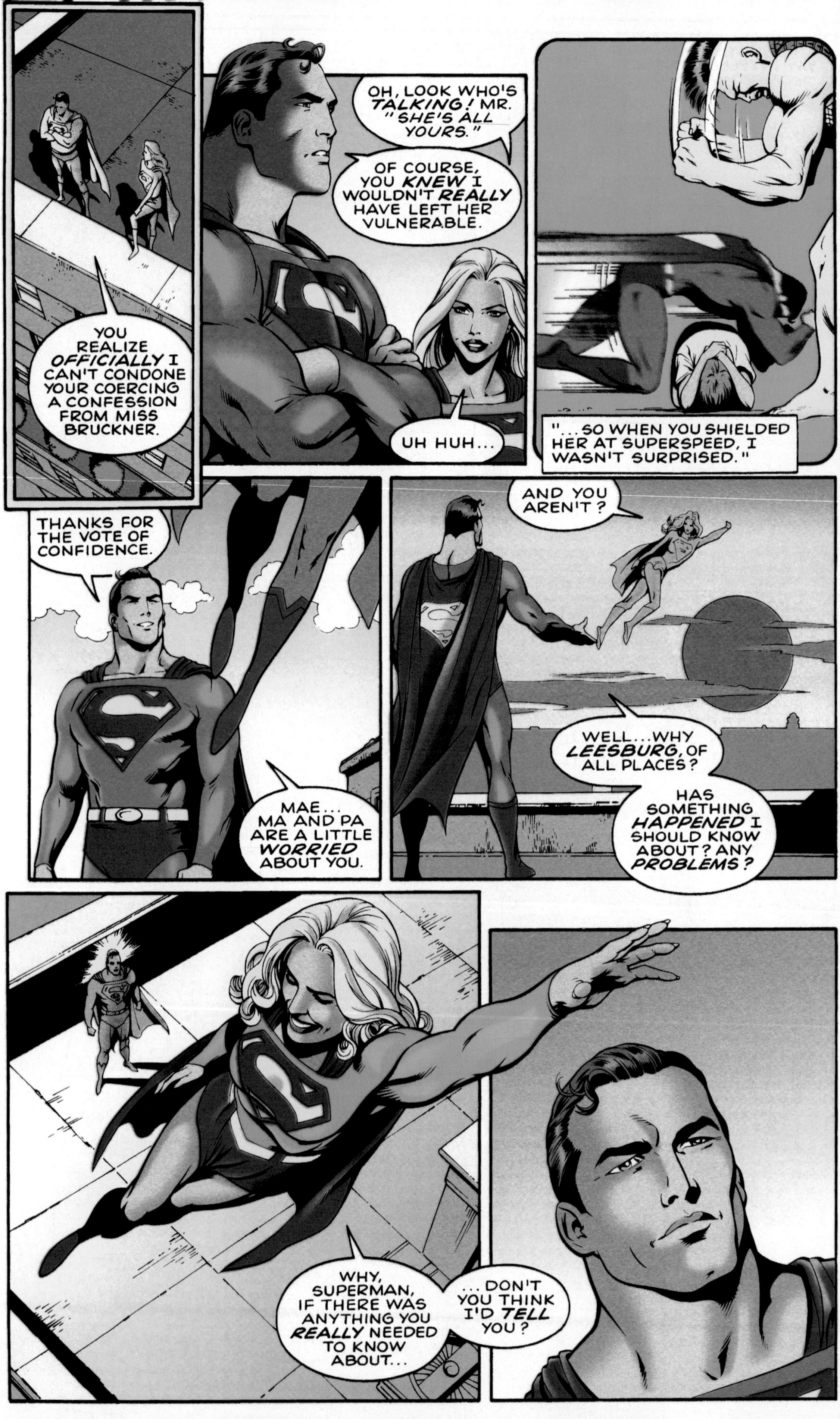
YOU REALIZE OFFICIALLY I CAN'T CONDONE YOUR COERCING A CONFESSION FROM MISS BRUCKNER.
OH, LOOK WHO'S TALKING! MR. "SHE'S ALL YOURS."
OF COURSE, YOU KNEW I WOULDN'T REALLY HAVE LEFT HER VULNERABLE.
UH HUH...
"...SO WHEN YOU SHIELDED HER AT SUPERSPEED, I WASN'T SURPRISED."
THANKS FOR THE VOTE OF CONFIDENCE.
MAE... MA AND PA ARE A LITTLE WORRIED ABOUT YOU.
AND YOU AREN'T?
WELL...WHY LEESBURG, OF ALL PLACES?
HAS SOMETHING HAPPENED I SHOULD KNOW ABOUT? ANY PROBLEMS?
WHY, SUPERMAN, IF THERE WAS ANYTHING YOU REALLY NEEDED TO KNOW ABOUT...
...DON'T YOU THINK I'D TELL YOU?

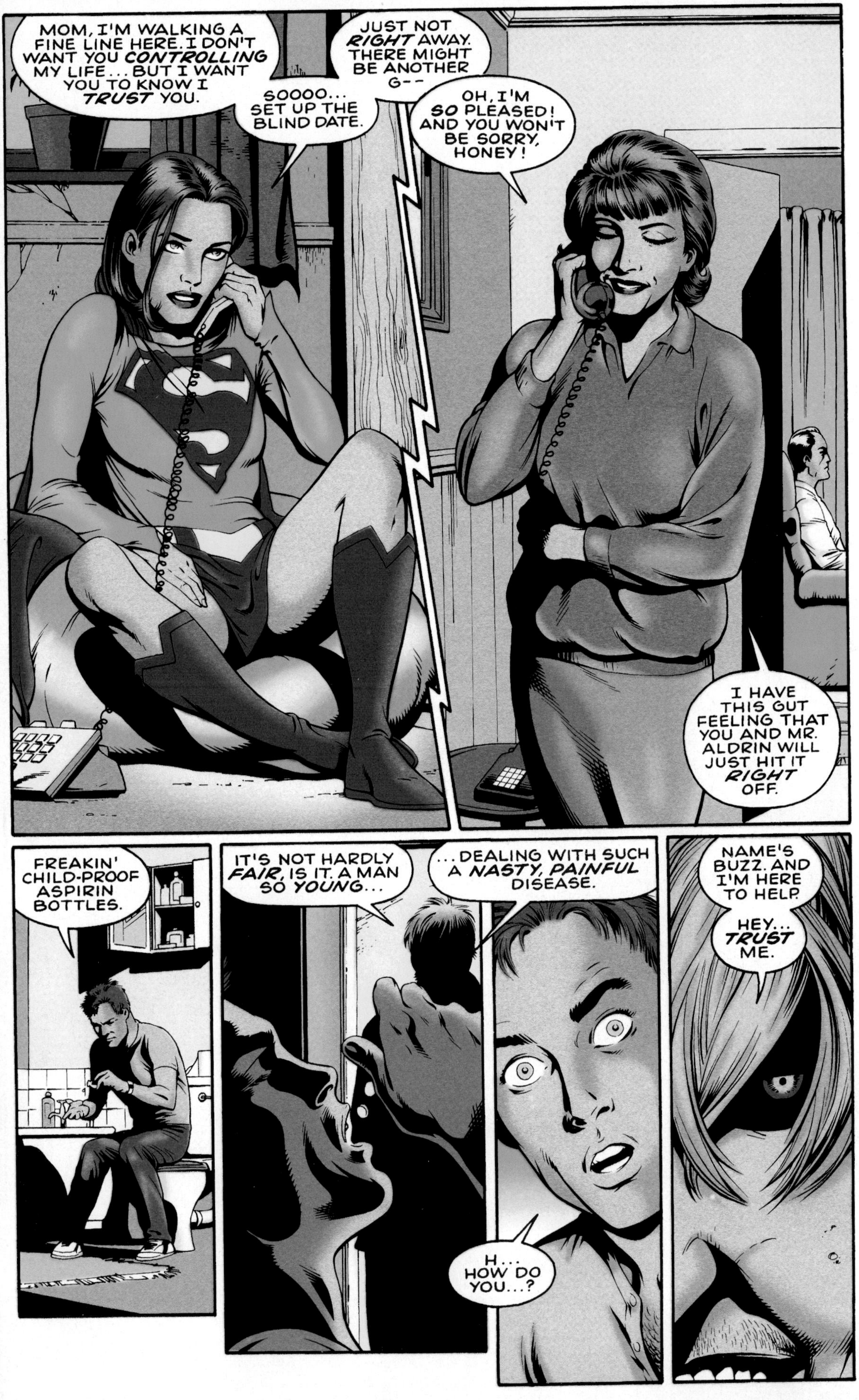
MOM, I'M WALKING A FINE LINE HERE. I DON'T WANT YOU CONTROLLING MY LIFE... BUT I WANT YOU TO KNOW I TRUST YOU.
SOOOO... SET UP THE BLIND DATE.
JUST NOT RIGHT AWAY. THERE MIGHT BE ANOTHER G--
OH, I'M SO PLEASED! AND YOU WON'T BE SORRY, HONEY!
I HAVE THIS GUT FEELING THAT YOU AND MR. ALDRIN WILL JUST HIT IT RIGHT OFF.
FREAKIN' CHILD-PROOF ASPIRIN BOTTLES.
IT'S NOT HARDLY FAIR, IS IT. A MAN SO YOUNG...
...DEALING WITH SUCH A NASTY, PAINFUL DISEASE.
H... HOW DO YOU...?
NAME'S BUZZ. AND I'M HERE TO HELP.
HEY... TRUST ME.

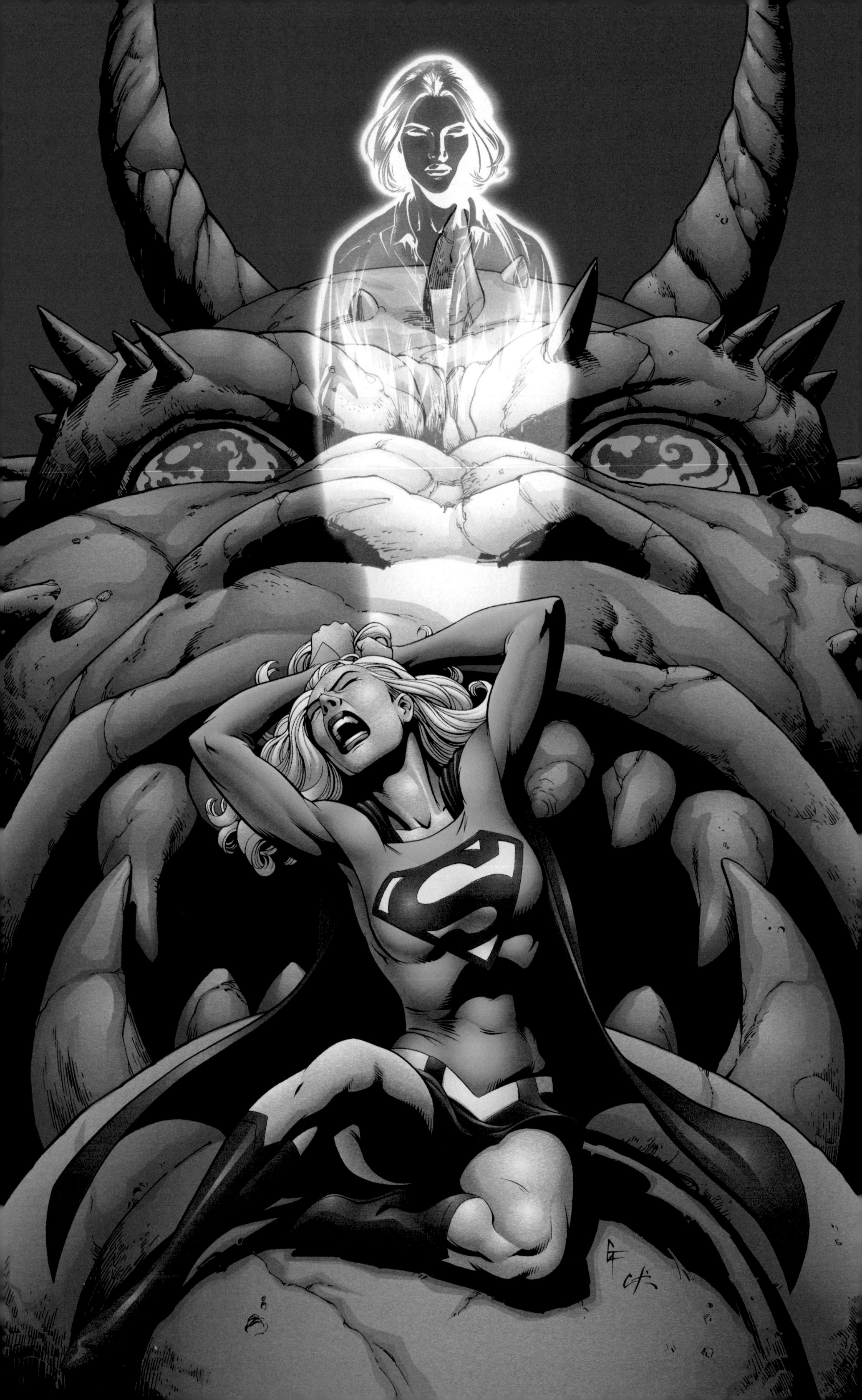

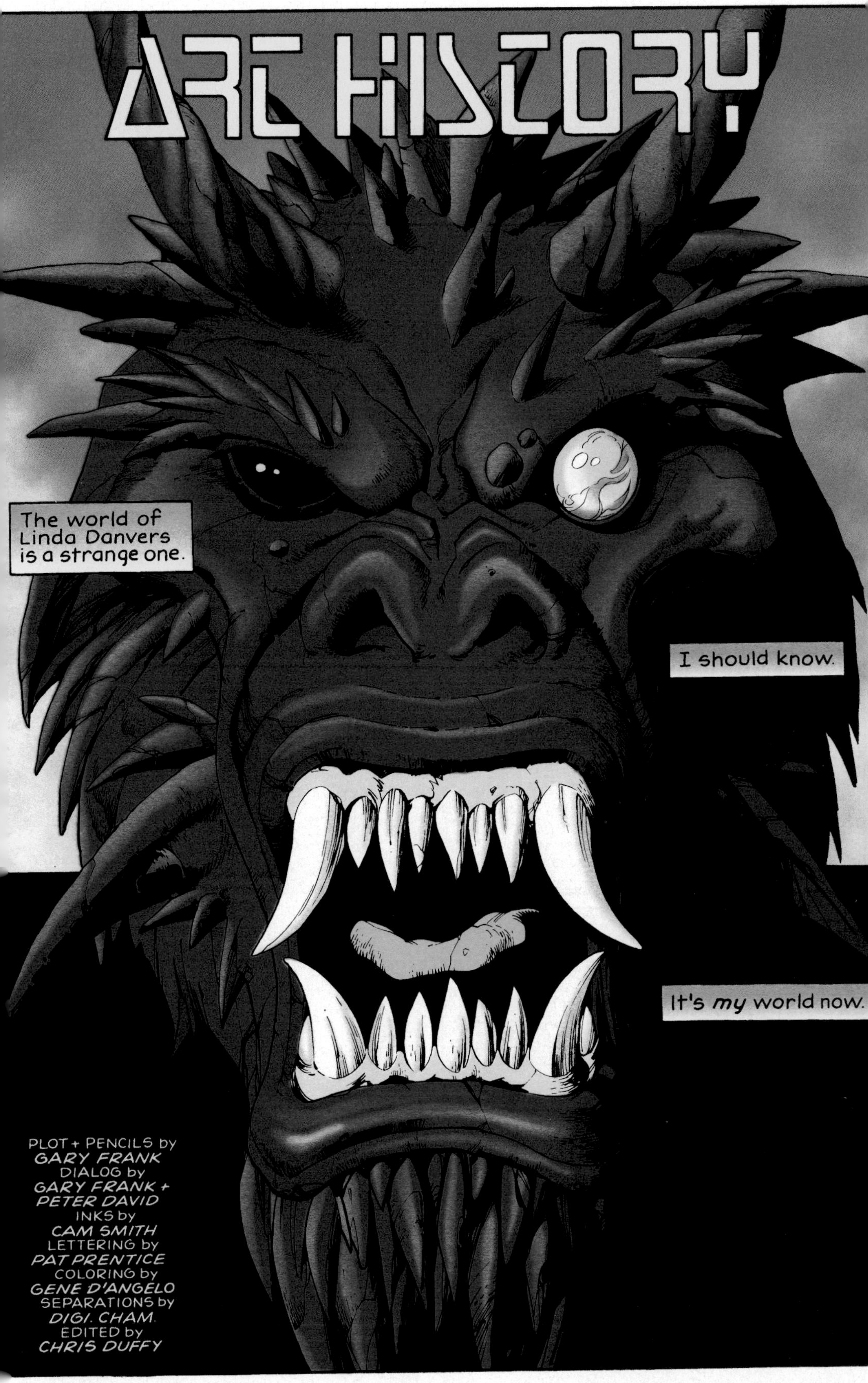
ART HISTORY
The world of Linda Danvers is a strange one.
I should know.
It's *my* world now.
PLOT + PENCILS by GARY FRANK
DIALOG by GARY FRANK + PETER DAVID
INKS by CAM SMITH
LETTERING by PAT PRENTICE
COLORING by GENE D'ANGELO
SEPARATIONS by DIGI. CHAM.
EDITED by CHRIS DUFFY

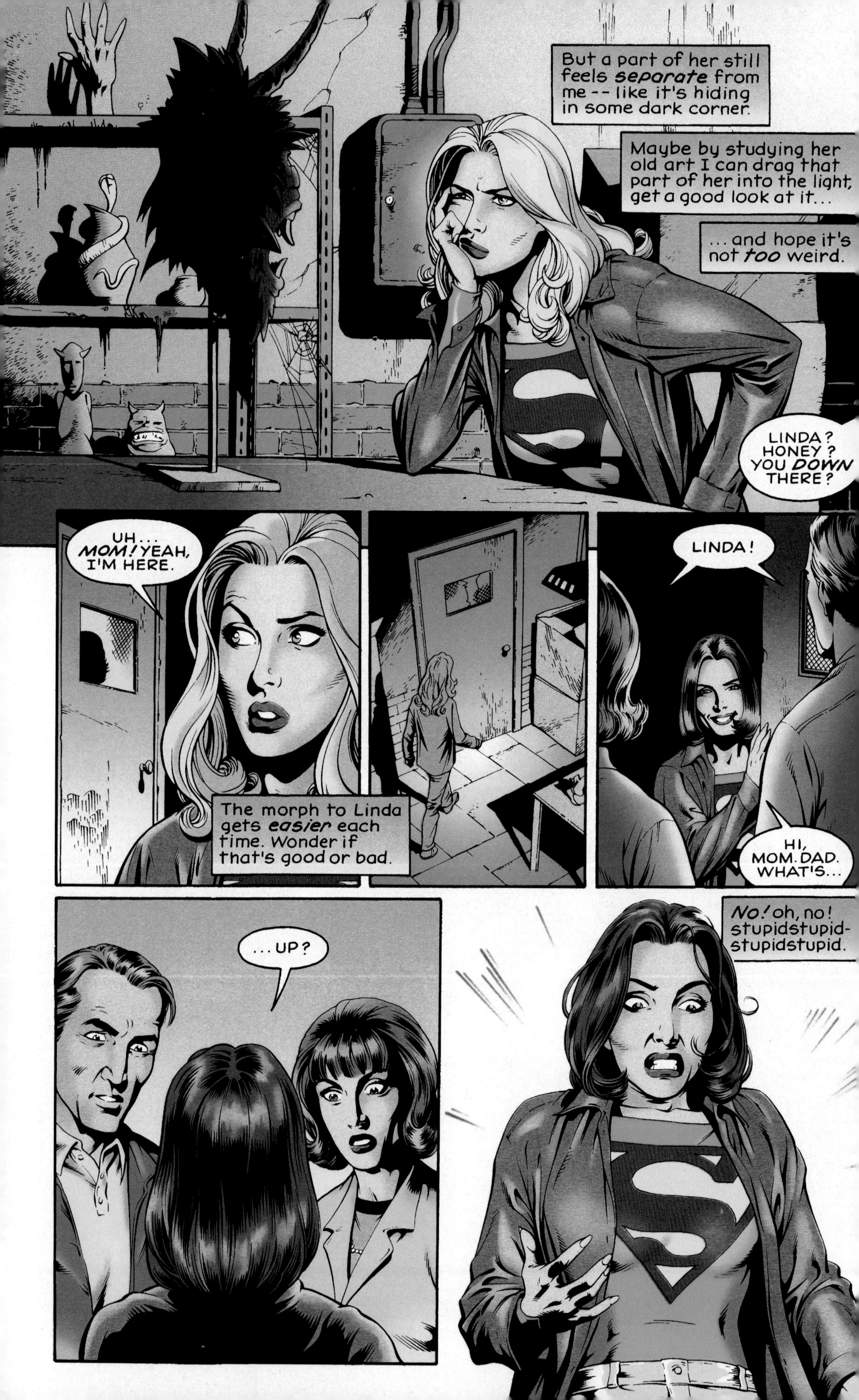
But a part of her still feels *separate* from me -- like it's hiding in some dark corner.
Maybe by studying her old art I can drag that part of her into the light, get a good look at it...
...and hope it's not *too* weird.
LINDA? HONEY? YOU *DOWN* THERE?
UH... *MOM!* YEAH, I'M HERE.
The morph to Linda gets *easier* each time. Wonder if that's good or bad.
LINDA!
HI, MOM. DAD. WHAT'S...
...UP?
No! oh, no! stupidstupid-stupidstupid.

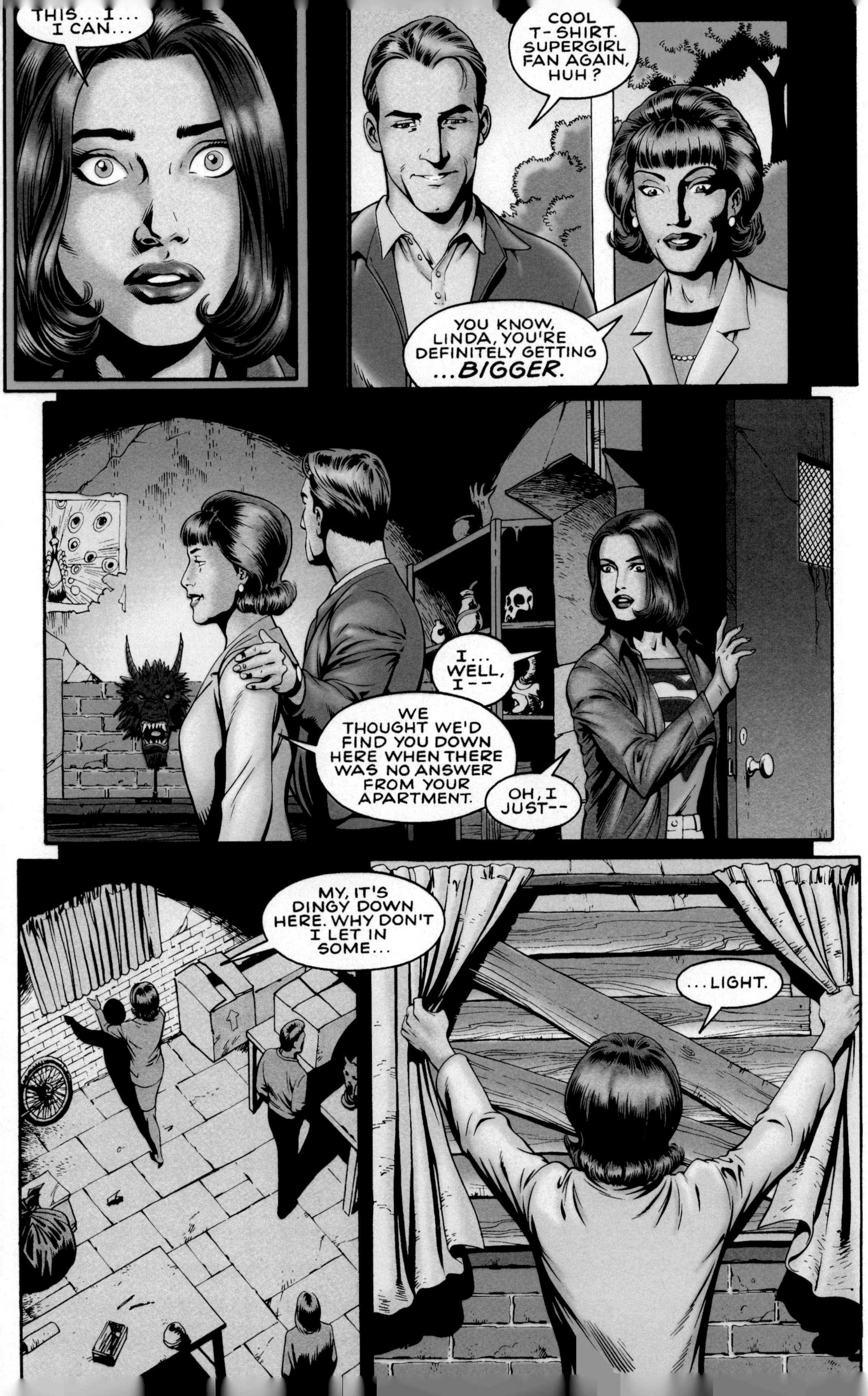
THIS... I... I CAN...
COOL T-SHIRT. SUPERGIRL FAN AGAIN, HUH?
YOU KNOW, LINDA, YOU'RE DEFINITELY GETTING ...BIGGER.
I... WELL, I--
WE THOUGHT WE'D FIND YOU DOWN HERE WHEN THERE WAS NO ANSWER FROM YOUR APARTMENT.
OH, I JUST--
MY, IT'S DINGY DOWN HERE. WHY DON'T I LET IN SOME...
...LIGHT.

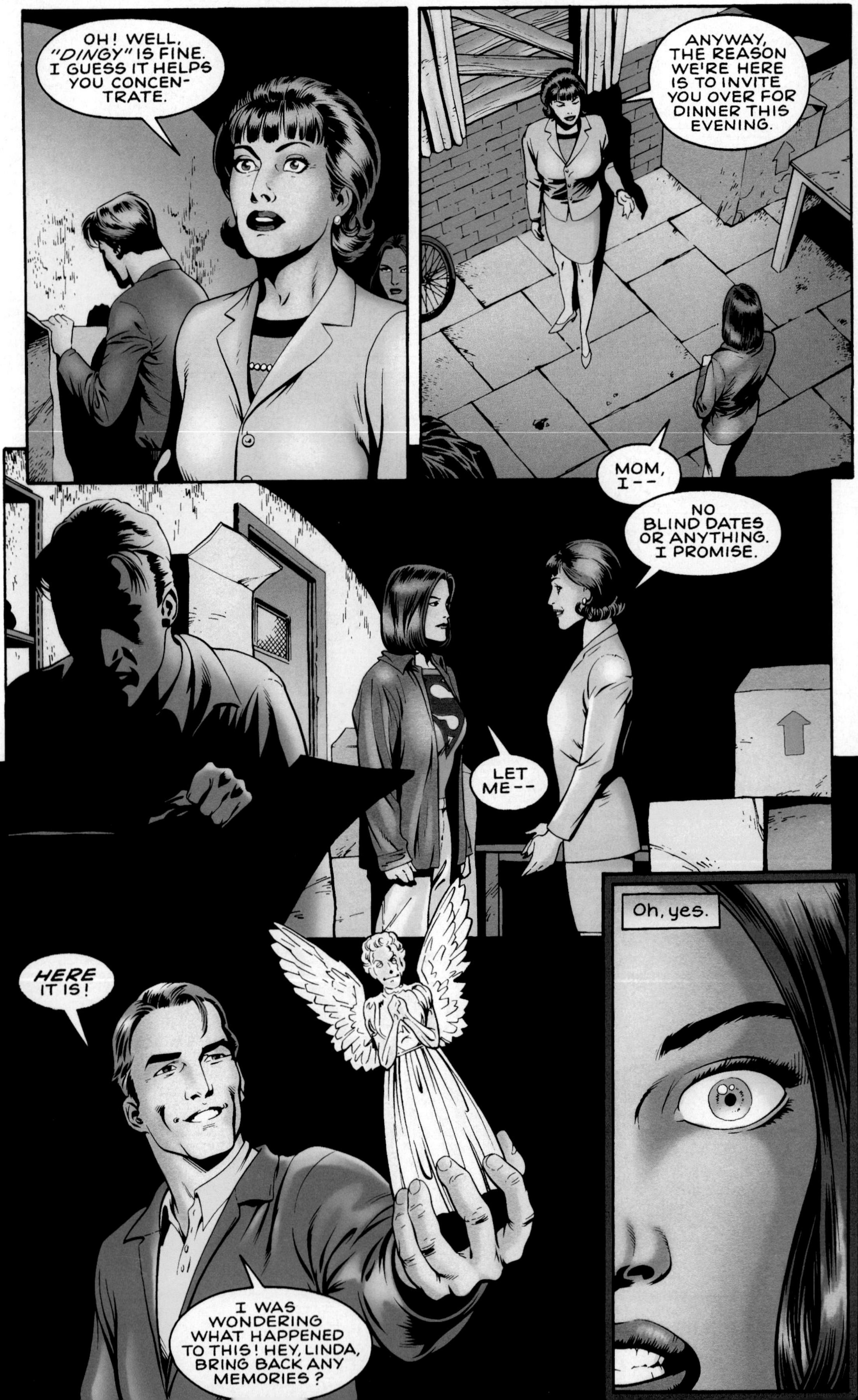
OH! WELL, "DINGY" IS FINE. I GUESS IT HELPS YOU CONCEN-TRATE.
ANYWAY, THE REASON WE'RE HERE IS TO INVITE YOU OVER FOR DINNER THIS EVENING.
MOM, I--
NO BLIND DATES OR ANYTHING. I PROMISE.
LET ME--
HERE IT IS!
I WAS WONDERING WHAT HAPPENED TO THIS! HEY, LINDA, BRING BACK ANY MEMORIES?
Oh, yes.

Memories of Reverend Meeke leading the congregation in applause...

...and of Mrs. Meeke, his wife.

My... *Linda's* friend.

1st

OH, LINDA, IT REALLY IS A BEAUTIFUL PIECE. IF YOU CAN BEAR TO PART WITH HER, I'M SURE SHE'D BE *VERY* HAPPY ON MY MANTLEPIECE.

I feel Linda's happiness the next day. I feel her anticipation, her...

YOU DIRTY COW!

I'VE HAD IT WITH YOUR *LIES!*

DO YOU HEAR ME?

NO...

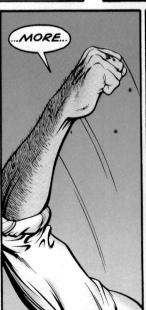

...MORE...

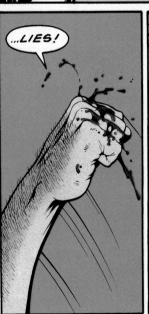

...LIES!

...her fear.

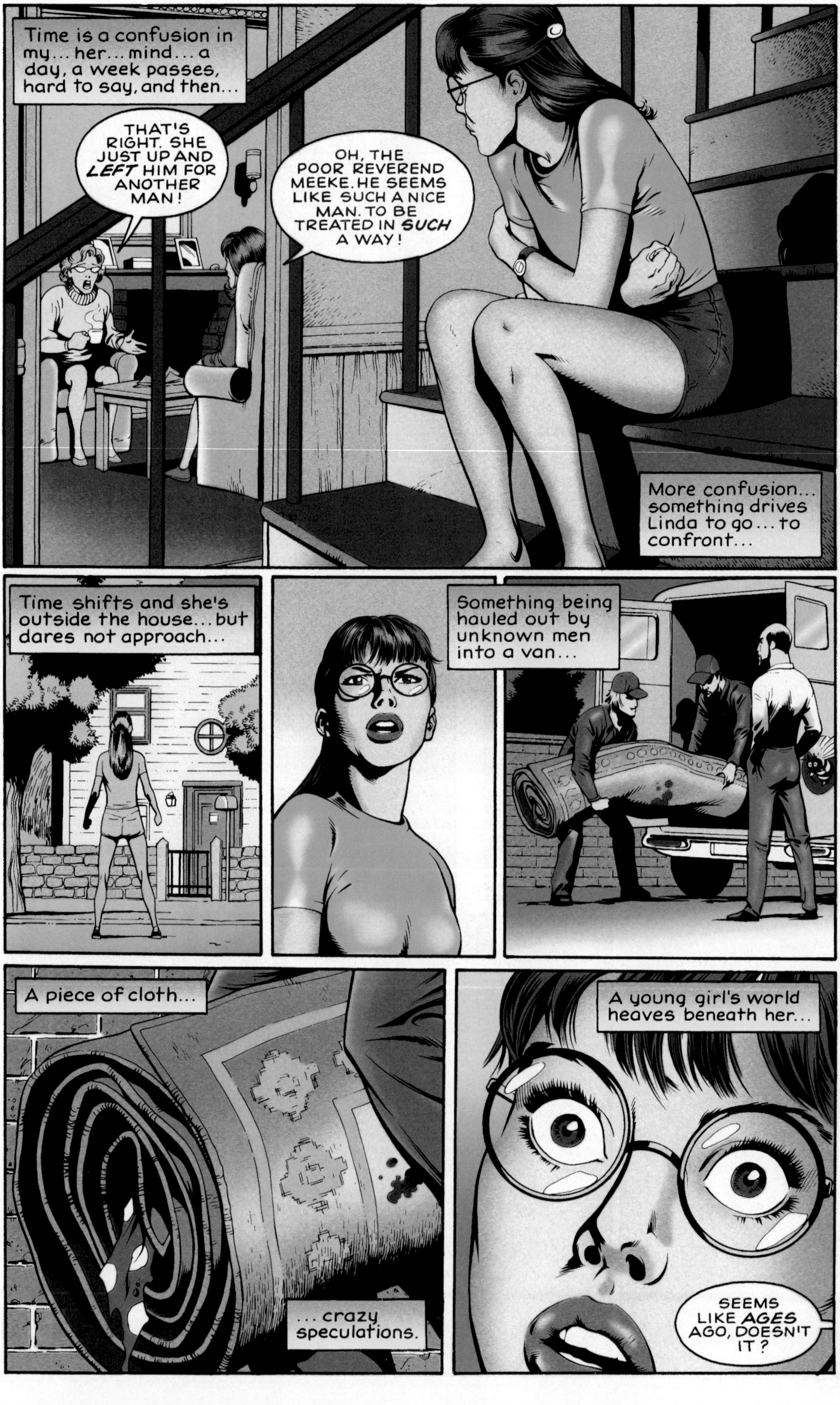

Time is a confusion in my... her... mind... a day, a week passes, hard to say, and then...
THAT'S RIGHT. SHE JUST UP AND LEFT HIM FOR ANOTHER MAN!
OH, THE POOR REVEREND MEEKE. HE SEEMS LIKE SUCH A NICE MAN. TO BE TREATED IN SUCH A WAY!
More confusion... something drives Linda to go... to confront...
Time shifts and she's outside the house... but dares not approach...
Something being hauled out by unknown men into a van...
A piece of cloth...
...crazy speculations.
A young girl's world heaves beneath her...
SEEMS LIKE AGES AGO, DOESN'T IT?

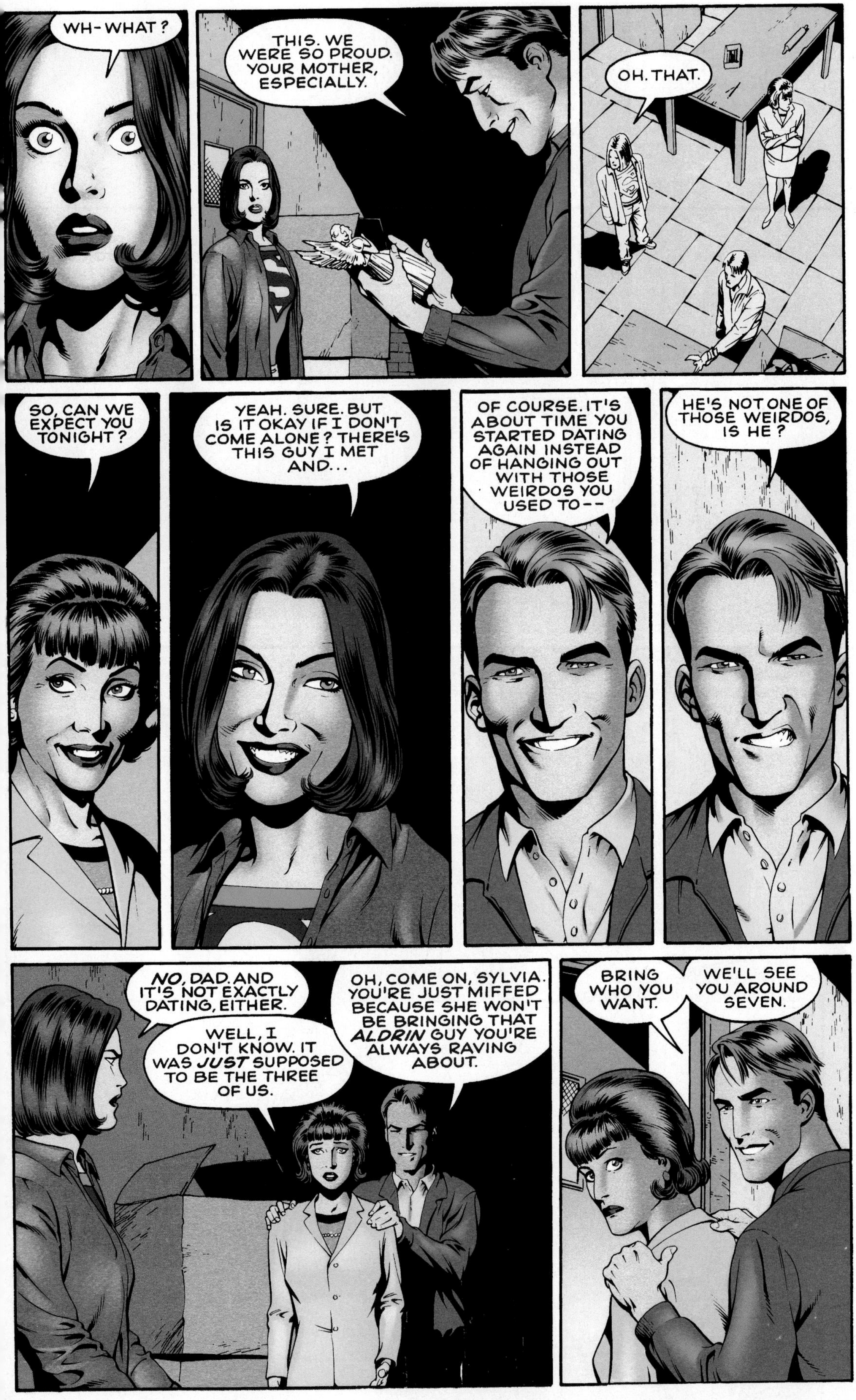
WH-WHAT?
THIS. WE WERE SO PROUD. YOUR MOTHER, ESPECIALLY.
OH. THAT.
SO, CAN WE EXPECT YOU TONIGHT?
YEAH. SURE. BUT IS IT OKAY IF I DON'T COME ALONE? THERE'S THIS GUY I MET AND...
OF COURSE. IT'S ABOUT TIME YOU STARTED DATING AGAIN INSTEAD OF HANGING OUT WITH THOSE WEIRDOS YOU USED TO--
HE'S NOT ONE OF THOSE WEIRDOS, IS HE?
NO, DAD. AND IT'S NOT EXACTLY DATING, EITHER.
WELL, I DON'T KNOW. IT WAS *JUST* SUPPOSED TO BE THE THREE OF US.
OH, COME ON, SYLVIA. YOU'RE JUST MIFFED BECAUSE SHE WON'T BE BRINGING THAT *ALDRIN* GUY YOU'RE ALWAYS RAVING ABOUT.
BRING WHO YOU WANT.
WE'LL SEE YOU AROUND SEVEN.

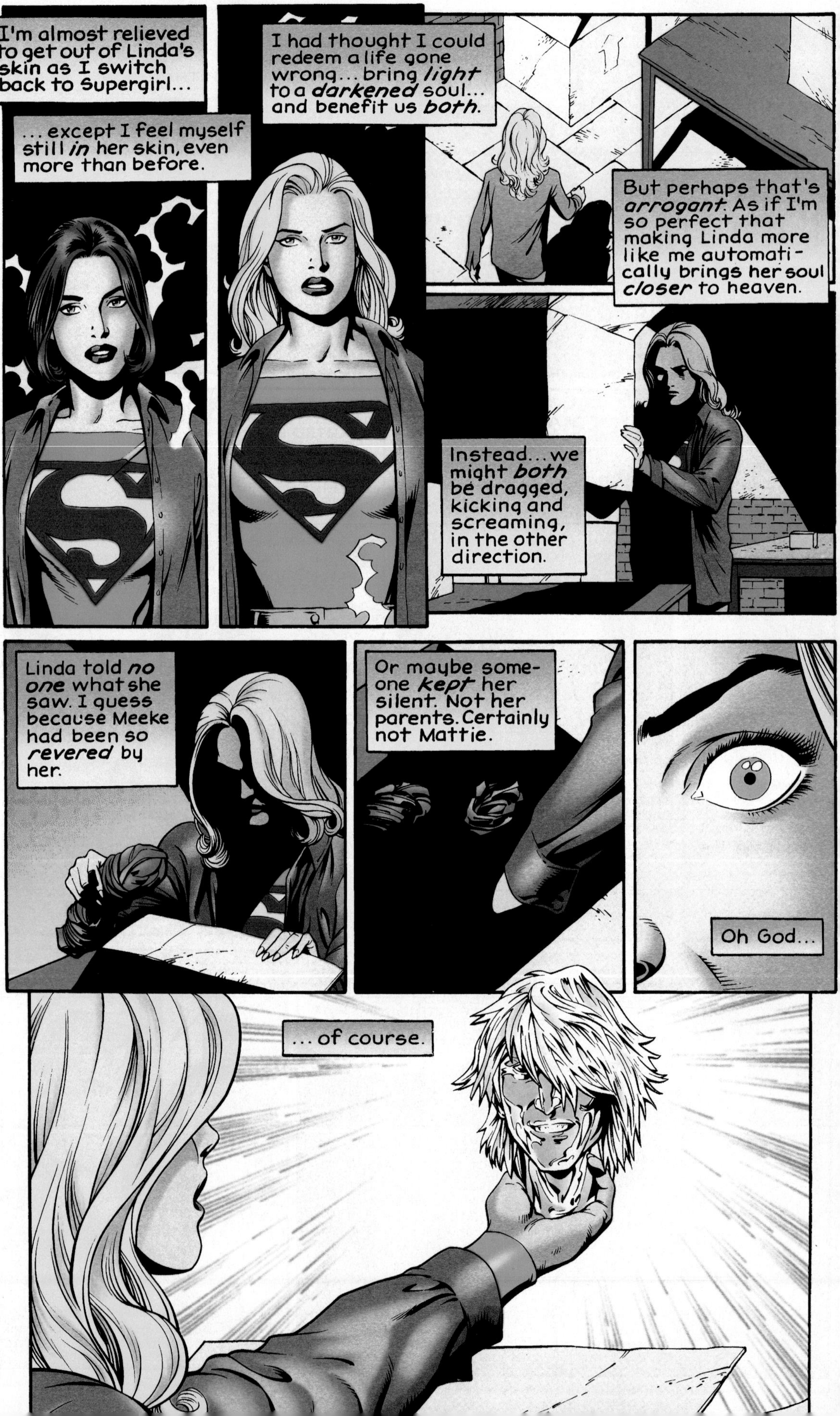

I'm almost relieved to get out of Linda's skin as I switch back to Supergirl...
... except I feel myself still *in* her skin, even more than before.
I had thought I could redeem a life gone wrong... bring *light* to a *darkened* soul... and benefit us *both*.
But perhaps that's *arrogant*. As if I'm so perfect that making Linda more like me automatically brings her soul *closer* to heaven.
Instead... we might *both* be dragged, kicking and screaming, in the other direction.
Linda told *no one* what she saw. I guess because Meeke had been so *revered* by her.
Or maybe someone *kept* her silent. Not her parents. Certainly not Mattie.
Oh God...
... of course.

AW, COME ON, LINDA. YOU CAN'T SIT OVER HERE ON YOUR OWN.

JESUS SAVES

I'M OKAY. REALLY! I CAN HEAR THE REVEREND FINE.

A LITTLE TOO WELL, ACTUALLY.

JUST LISTEN TO THAT PILE OF DRIVEL.

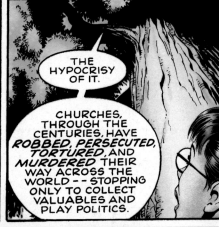

THE HYPOCRISY OF IT.

CHURCHES, THROUGH THE CENTURIES, HAVE *ROBBED, PERSECUTED, TORTURED,* AND *MURDERED* THEIR WAY ACROSS THE WORLD -- STOPPING ONLY TO COLLECT VALUABLES AND PLAY POLITICS.

AND THEY STAND UP AND TELL US TO DO WHAT THEY SAY OR WE'RE *EVIL*, AND GOD'S GONNA 'AVE OUR GUTS FOR GARTERS.

WHO ARE--

THEN WHEN SOMEONE LIKE YOU OR I DISCOVERS THE TRUTH-- SOME DIRTY LITTLE SECRET-- WHAT CAN WE DO?

EH?

NOTHING!

IF ENOUGH PEOPLE *KNEW,* THEN--

I MEAN, WHO'D BELIEVE US?

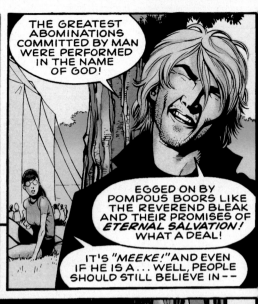
THE GREATEST ABOMINATIONS COMMITTED BY MAN WERE PERFORMED IN THE NAME OF GOD!

EGGED ON BY POMPOUS BOORS LIKE THE REVEREND BLEAK AND THEIR PROMISES OF *ETERNAL SALVATION!* WHAT A DEAL!

IT'S *"MEEKE!"* AND EVEN IF HE IS A... WELL, PEOPLE SHOULD STILL BELIEVE IN--

BELIEF? HE'S GOT NOTHING *BUT* THAT. NO FACTS! HE THUMPS THE BIBLE AS IF IT WERE THE WORD OF GOD INSTEAD OF *MEN!* MEN LIKE *HIM!*

BUT... MY *MOM* SAYS IT--

DON'T BREAK THIS TO MUMSY, BUT THAT THING WAS KNOCKED TOGETHER IN ROME BY POLITICIANS. *"OPIUM OF THE MASSES"* AND ALL THAT.

HOW CAN YOU SAY THAT?

THE BIBLE IS--

A TOOL! *"BE MEEK BE POOR. YOU'LL BE REWARDED WHEN YOU'RE DEAD!"* WAKE UP!

MY FRIEND AL USED TO SAY *"DO WHAT THOU WILT SHALL BE THE WHOLE LAW."*

REMEMBER THAT.

DO WHAT THOU WILT.

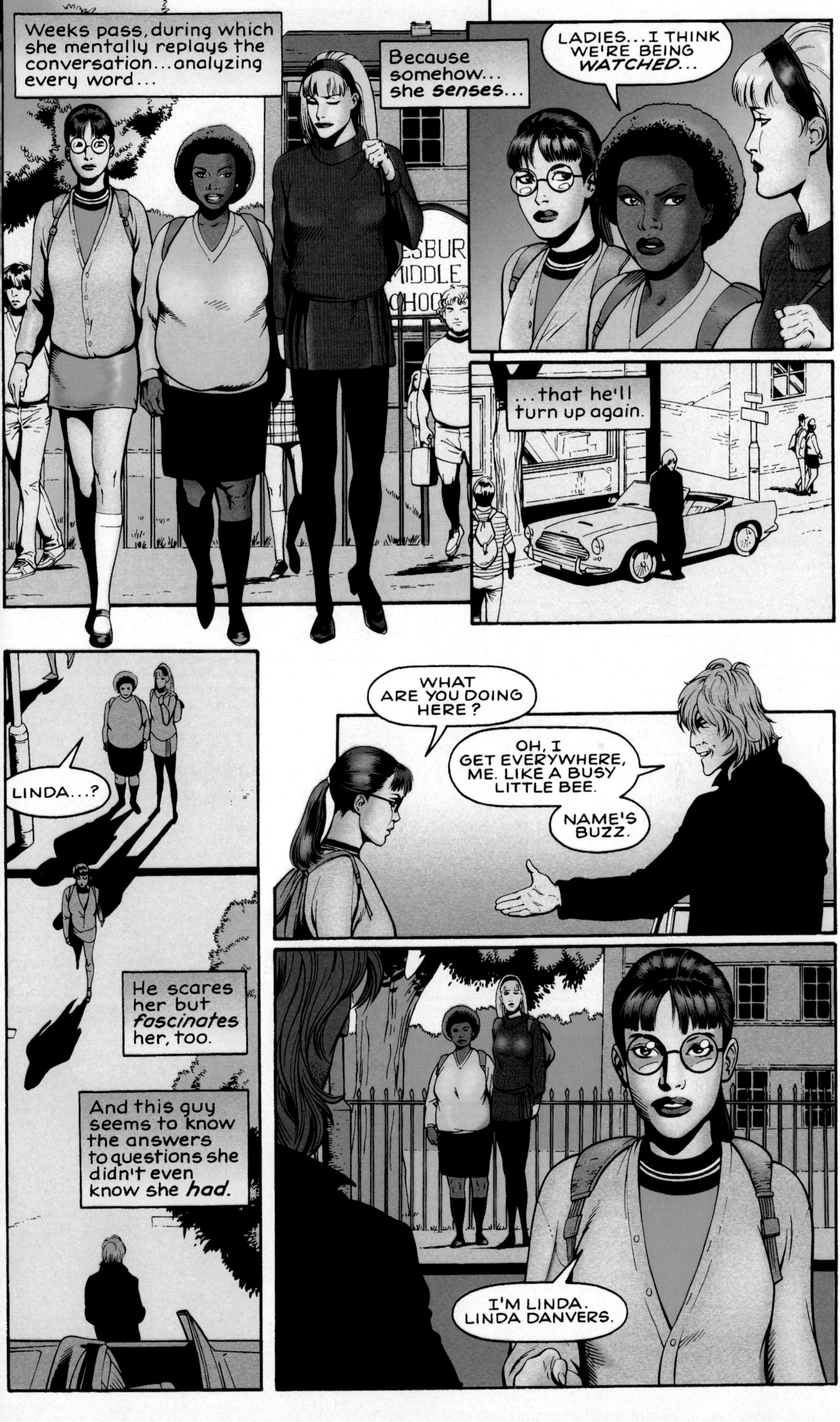
Weeks pass, during which she mentally replays the conversation...analyzing every word...
Because somehow... she *senses*...
...ESBUR... MIDDLE ...CHOO...
LADIES...I THINK WE'RE BEING *WATCHED*...
...that he'll turn up again.
LINDA...?
He scares her but *fascinates* her, too.
And this guy seems to know the answers to questions she didn't even know she *had*.
WHAT ARE YOU DOING HERE?
OH, I GET EVERYWHERE, ME. LIKE A BUSY LITTLE BEE.
NAME'S BUZZ.
I'M LINDA. LINDA DANVERS.

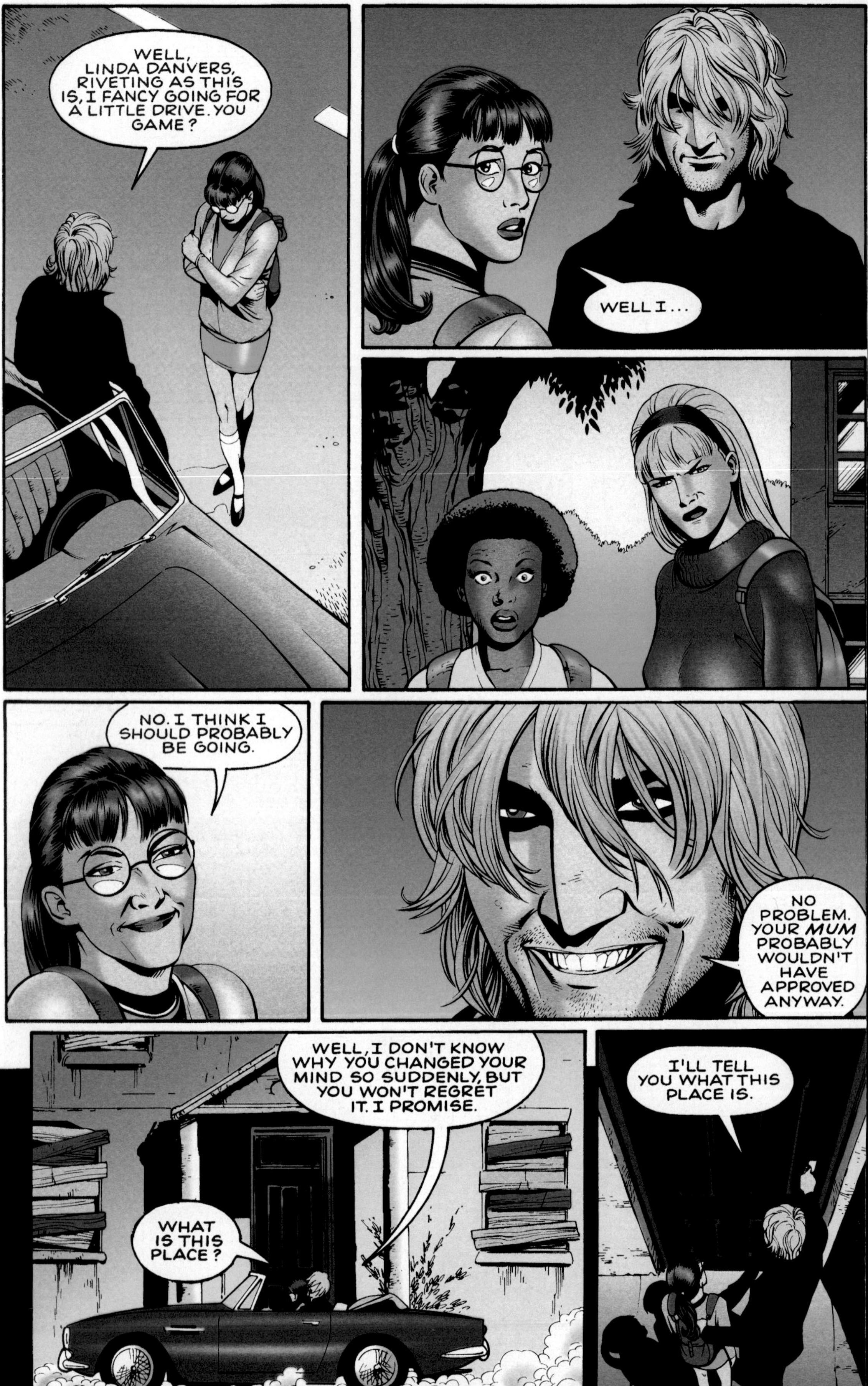
WELL, LINDA DANVERS, RIVETING AS THIS IS, I FANCY GOING FOR A LITTLE DRIVE. YOU GAME?
WELL I...
NO. I THINK I SHOULD PROBABLY BE GOING.
NO PROBLEM. YOUR MUM PROBABLY WOULDN'T HAVE APPROVED ANYWAY.
WELL, I DON'T KNOW WHY YOU CHANGED YOUR MIND SO SUDDENLY, BUT YOU WON'T REGRET IT. I PROMISE.
WHAT IS THIS PLACE?
I'LL TELL YOU WHAT THIS PLACE IS.

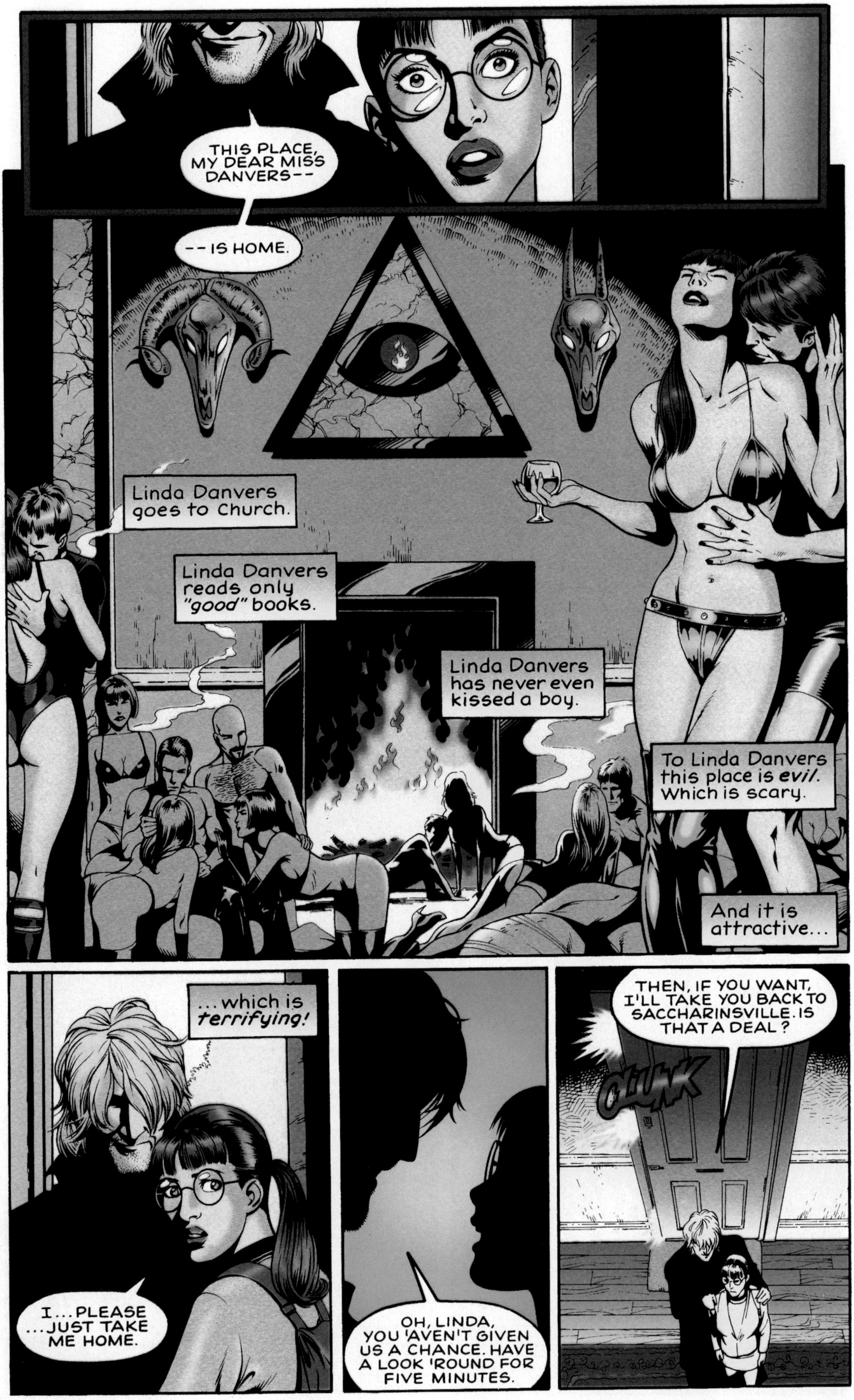
THIS PLACE, MY DEAR MISS DANVERS--
--IS HOME.
Linda Danvers goes to Church.
Linda Danvers reads only "good" books.
Linda Danvers has never even kissed a boy.
To Linda Danvers this place is evil. Which is scary.
And it is attractive...
...which is terrifying!
I... PLEASE ...JUST TAKE ME HOME.
OH, LINDA, YOU 'AVEN'T GIVEN US A CHANCE. HAVE A LOOK 'ROUND FOR FIVE MINUTES.
THEN, IF YOU WANT, I'LL TAKE YOU BACK TO SACCHARINSVILLE. IS THAT A DEAL?
CLUNK

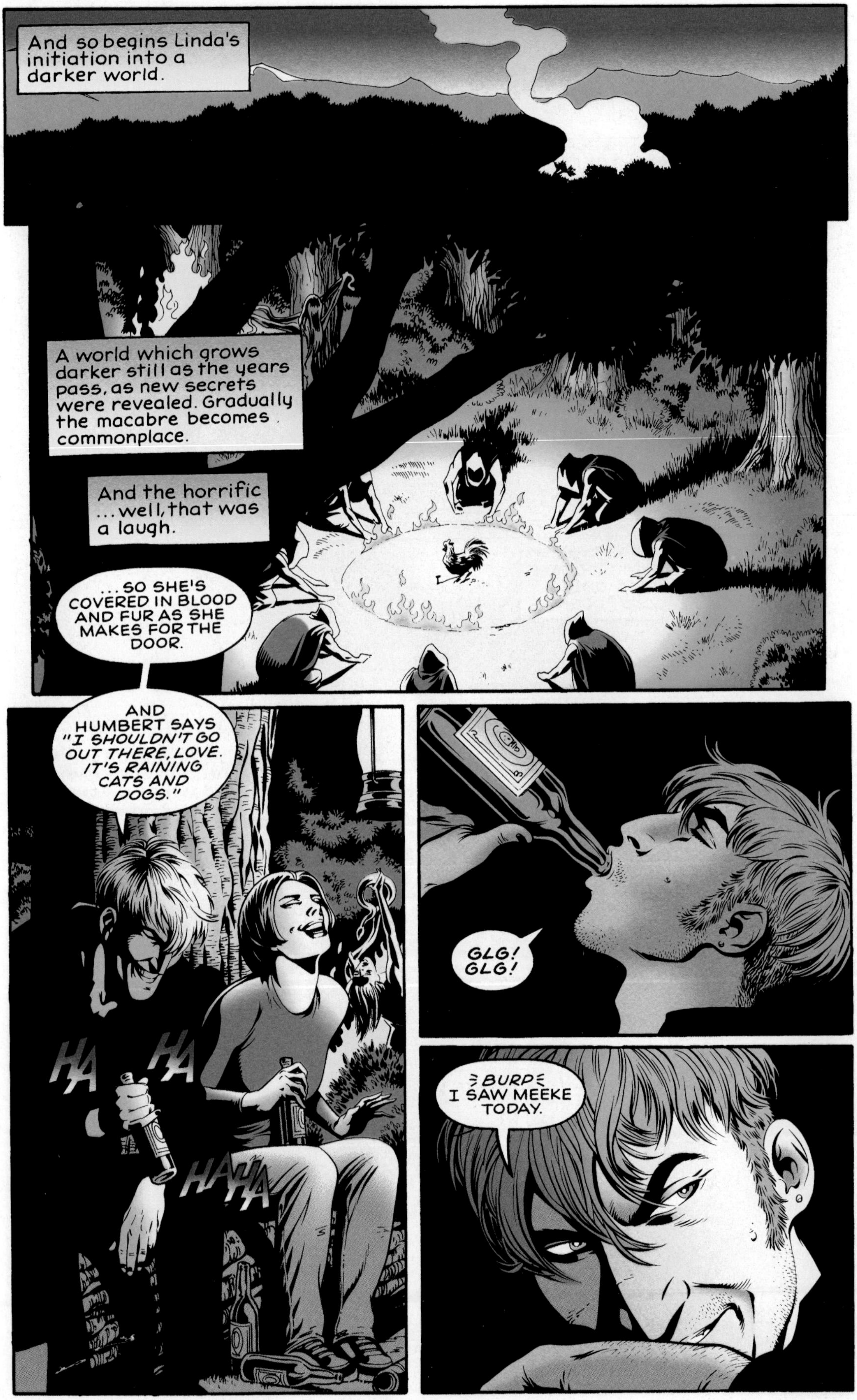

And so begins Linda's initiation into a darker world.
A world which grows darker still as the years pass, as new secrets were revealed. Gradually the macabre becomes commonplace.
And the horrific ...well, that was a laugh.
...SO SHE'S COVERED IN BLOOD AND FUR AS SHE MAKES FOR THE DOOR.
AND HUMBERT SAYS "I SHOULDN'T GO OUT THERE, LOVE. IT'S RAINING CATS AND DOGS."
HA HA
HAHAHA
GLG! GLG!
BURP
I SAW MEEKE TODAY.

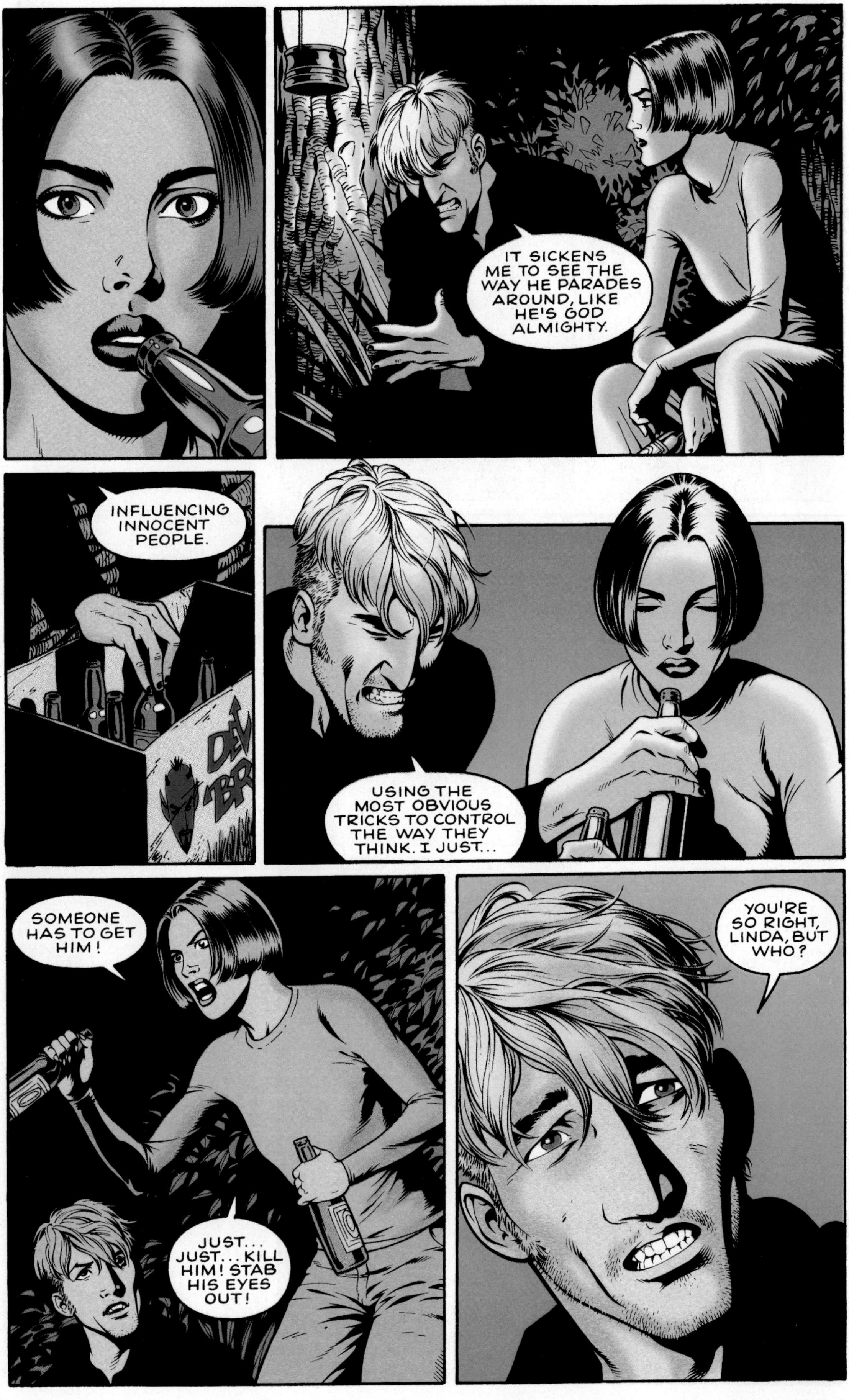
IT SICKENS ME TO SEE THE WAY HE PARADES AROUND, LIKE HE'S GOD ALMIGHTY.
INFLUENCING INNOCENT PEOPLE.
USING THE MOST OBVIOUS TRICKS TO CONTROL THE WAY THEY THINK. I JUST...
SOMEONE HAS TO GET HIM!
JUST... JUST... KILL HIM! STAB HIS EYES OUT!
YOU'RE SO RIGHT, LINDA, BUT WHO?

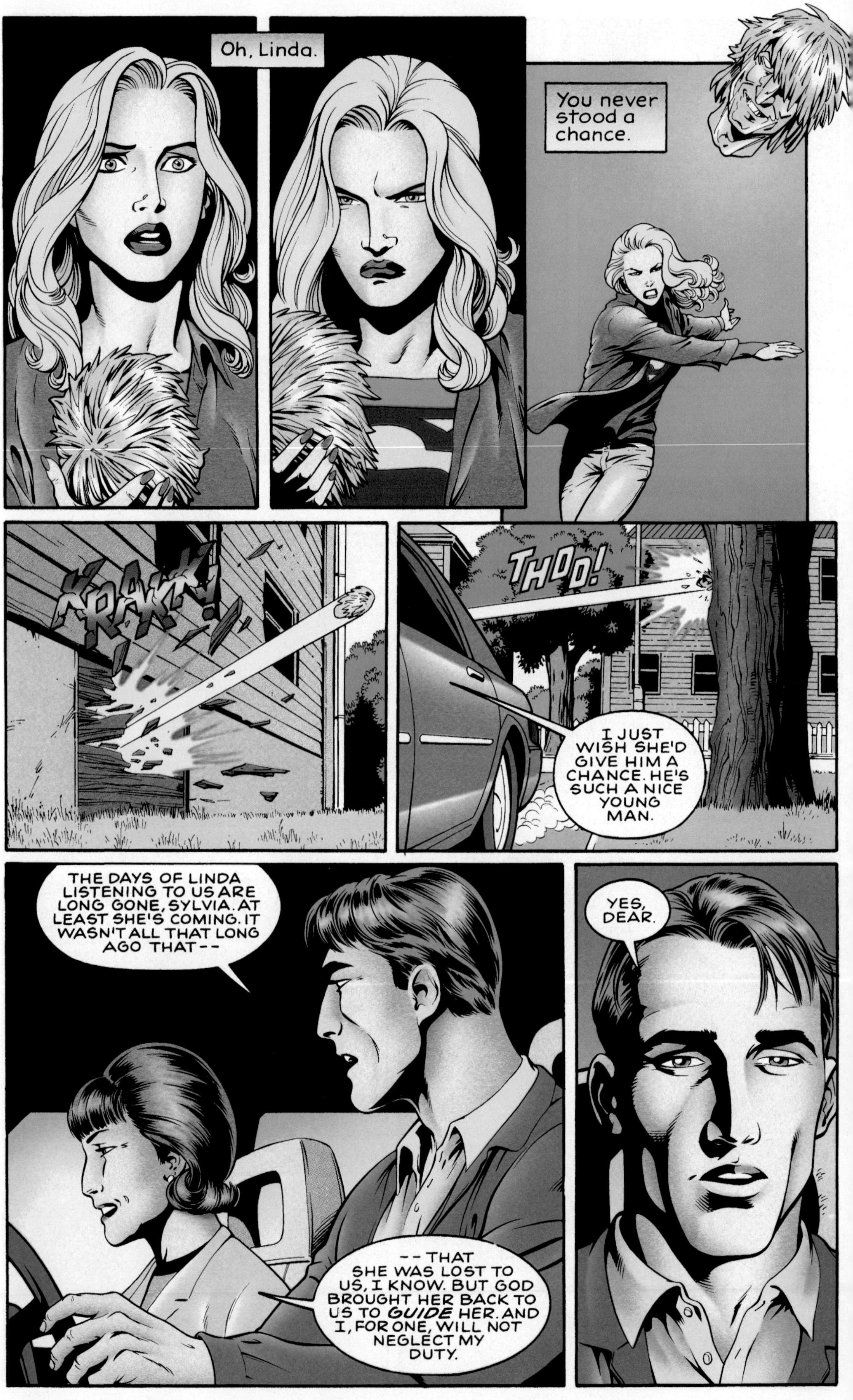
Oh, Linda.
You never stood a chance.
KRAKK!
THOD!
I JUST WISH SHE'D GIVE HIM A CHANCE. HE'S SUCH A NICE YOUNG MAN.
THE DAYS OF LINDA LISTENING TO US ARE LONG GONE, SYLVIA. AT LEAST SHE'S COMING. IT WASN'T ALL THAT LONG AGO THAT--
--THAT SHE WAS LOST TO US, I KNOW. BUT GOD BROUGHT HER BACK TO US TO GUIDE HER. AND I, FOR ONE, WILL NOT NEGLECT MY DUTY.
YES, DEAR.

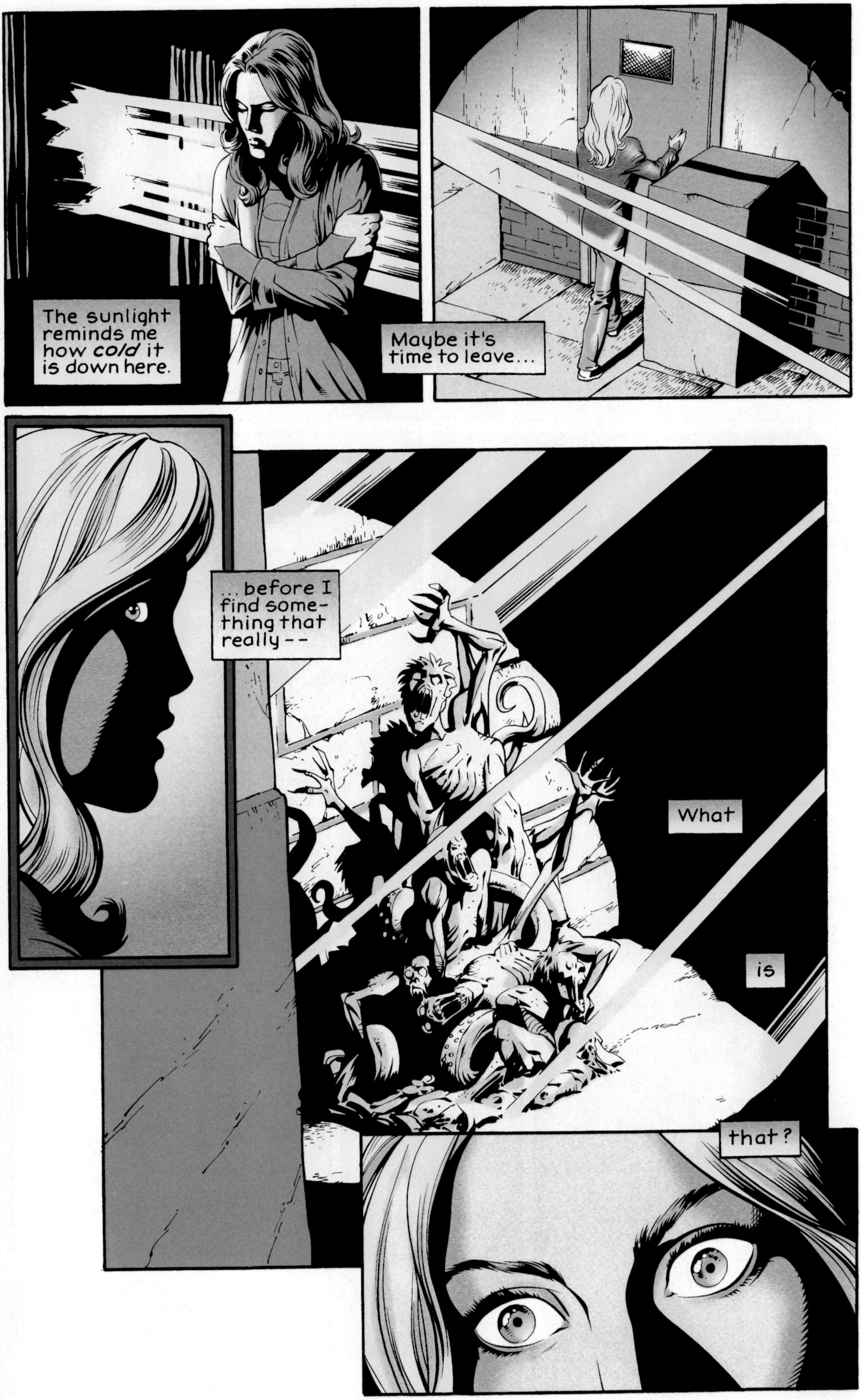
The sunlight reminds me how *cold* it is down here.
Maybe it's time to leave...
...before I find something that really --
What
is
that?

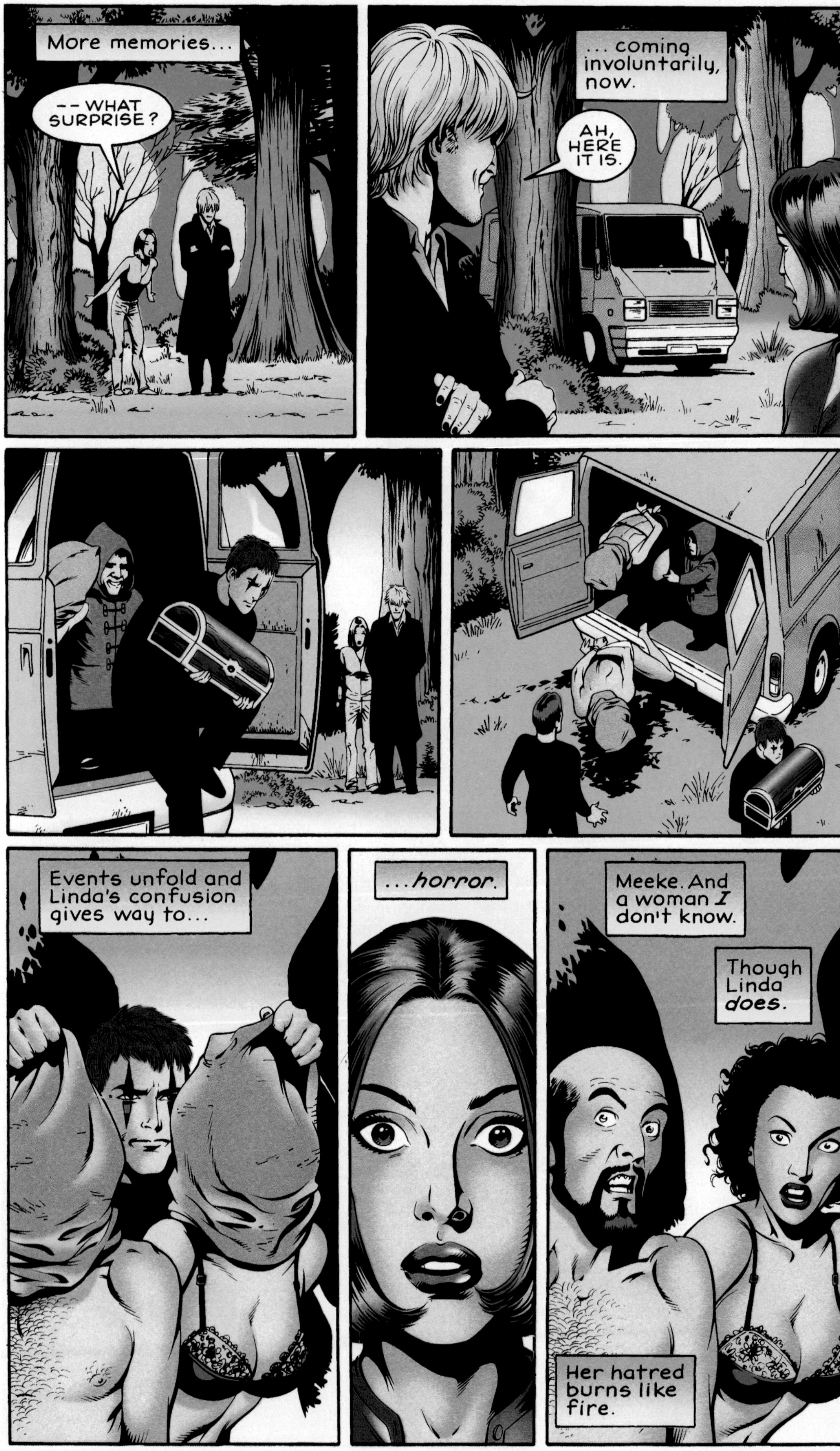
More memories...
-- WHAT SURPRISE?
... coming involuntarily, now.
AH, HERE IT IS.
Events unfold and Linda's confusion gives way to...
...horror.
Meeke. And a woman I don't know.
Though Linda does.
Her hatred burns like fire.

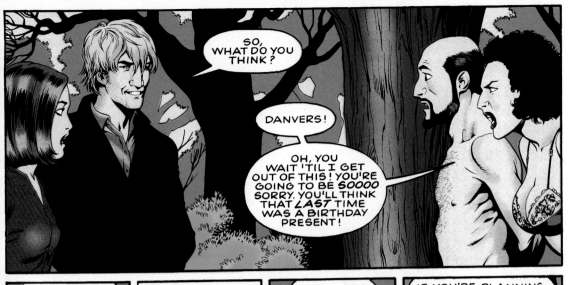

SO, WHAT DO YOU THINK?

DANVERS!

OH, YOU WAIT 'TIL I GET OUT OF THIS! YOU'RE GOING TO BE *SOOOO* SORRY. YOU'LL THINK THAT *LAST* TIME WAS A BIRTHDAY PRESENT!

OH, NO, LINDA! SHE'S REALLY *MAD!* GEE I DIDN'T--

HANG ABOUT. DID YOU SAY *"WHEN I GET OUT OF THIS"*?

OH, WHAT A RELIEF.

IF YOU'RE PLANNING ON SOILING THOSE LOVELY KNICKERS...

CREEAK

...NOW MIGHT BE THE APPROPRIATE TIME.

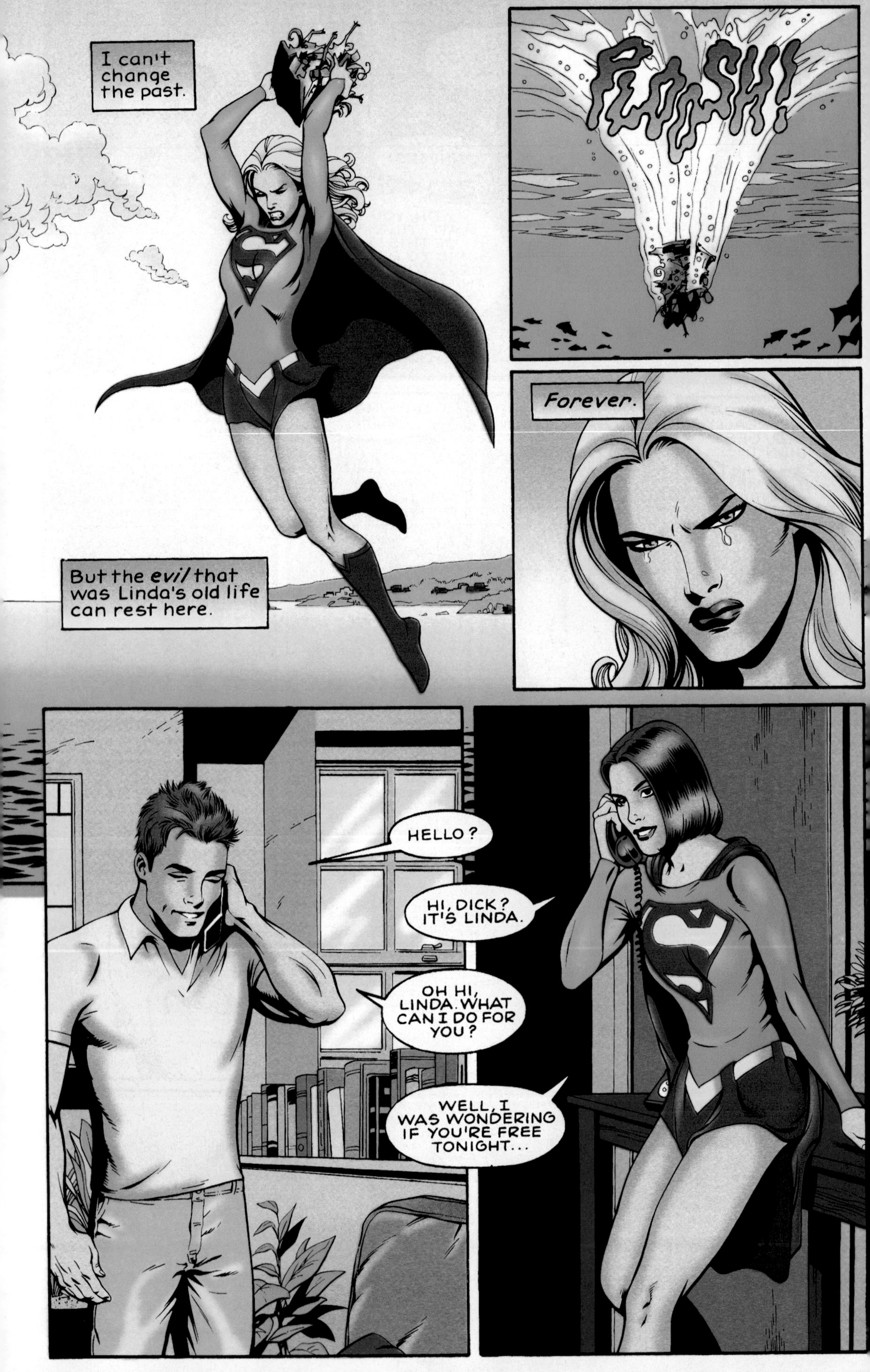
I can't change the past.
FLOOSH!
Forever.
But the evil that was Linda's old life can rest here.
HELLO?
HI, DICK? IT'S LINDA.
OH HI, LINDA. WHAT CAN I DO FOR YOU?
WELL, I WAS WONDERING IF YOU'RE FREE TONIGHT...

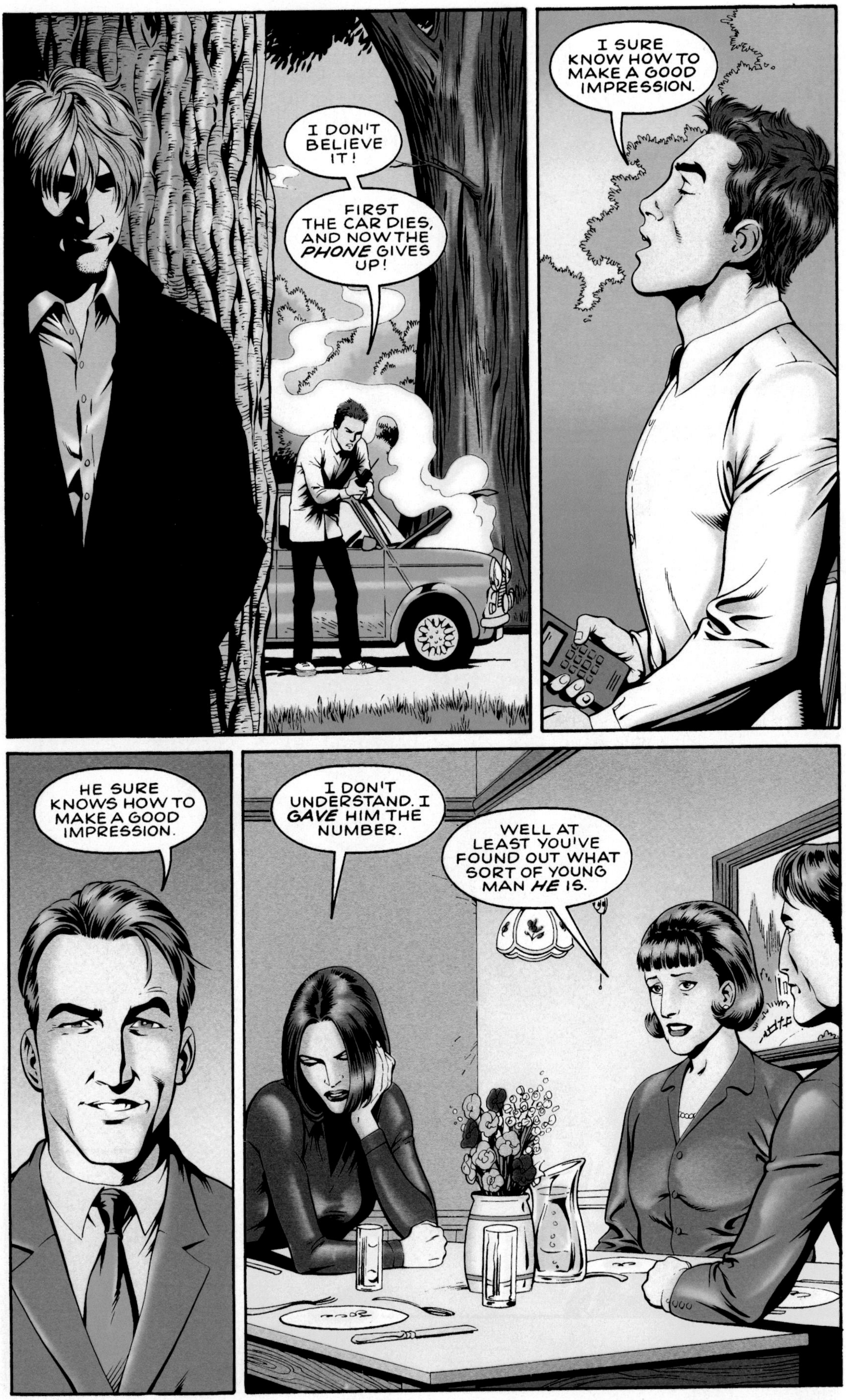
I DON'T BELIEVE IT!
FIRST THE CAR DIES, AND NOW THE *PHONE* GIVES UP!
I SURE KNOW HOW TO MAKE A GOOD IMPRESSION.
HE SURE KNOWS HOW TO MAKE A GOOD IMPRESSION.
I DON'T UNDERSTAND. I *GAVE* HIM THE NUMBER.
WELL AT LEAST YOU'VE FOUND OUT WHAT SORT OF YOUNG MAN *HE* IS.

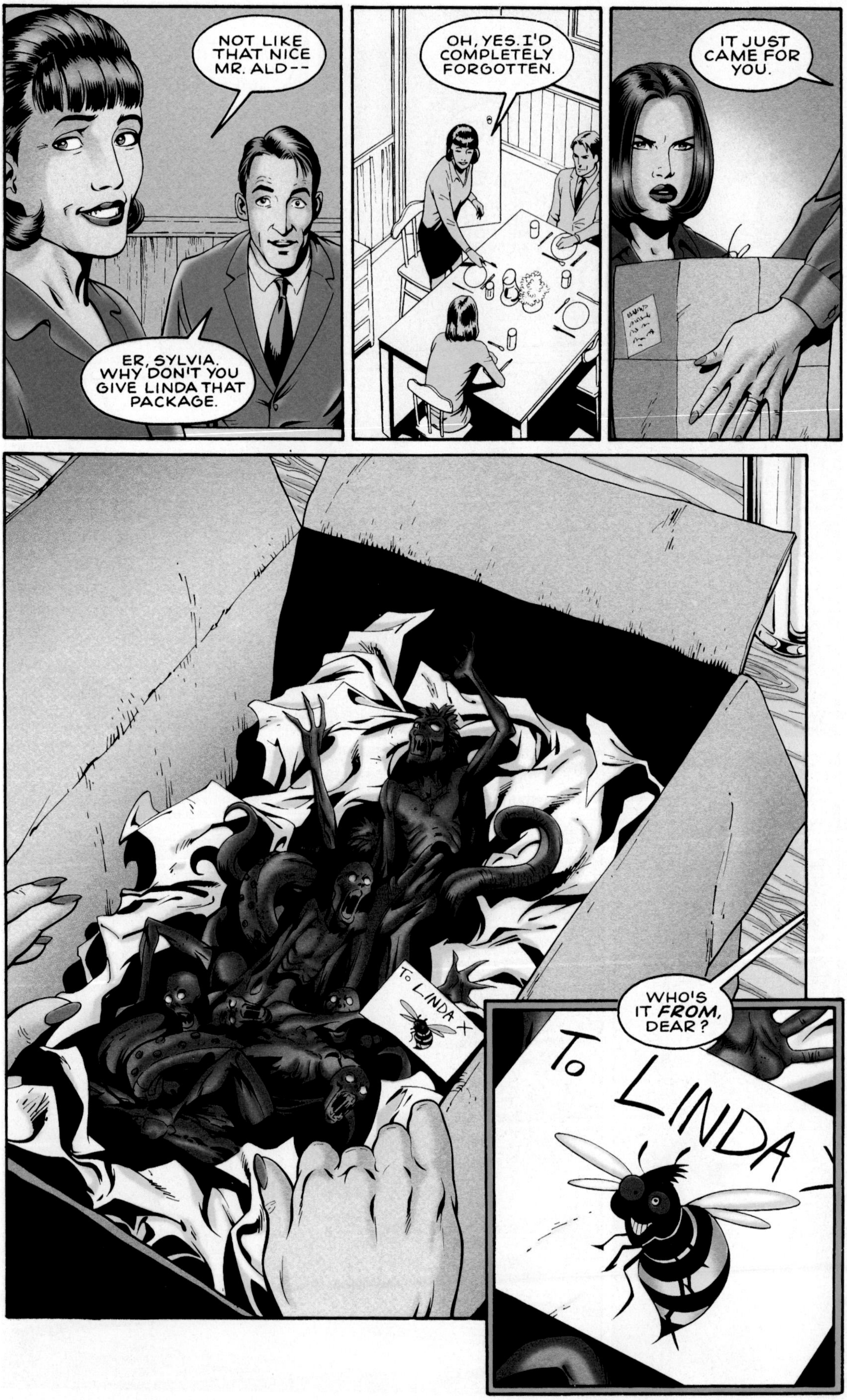
NOT LIKE THAT NICE MR. ALD--
ER, SYLVIA. WHY DON'T YOU GIVE LINDA THAT PACKAGE.
OH, YES. I'D COMPLETELY FORGOTTEN.
IT JUST CAME FOR YOU.
TO LINDA X
WHO'S IT FROM, DEAR?
TO LINDA

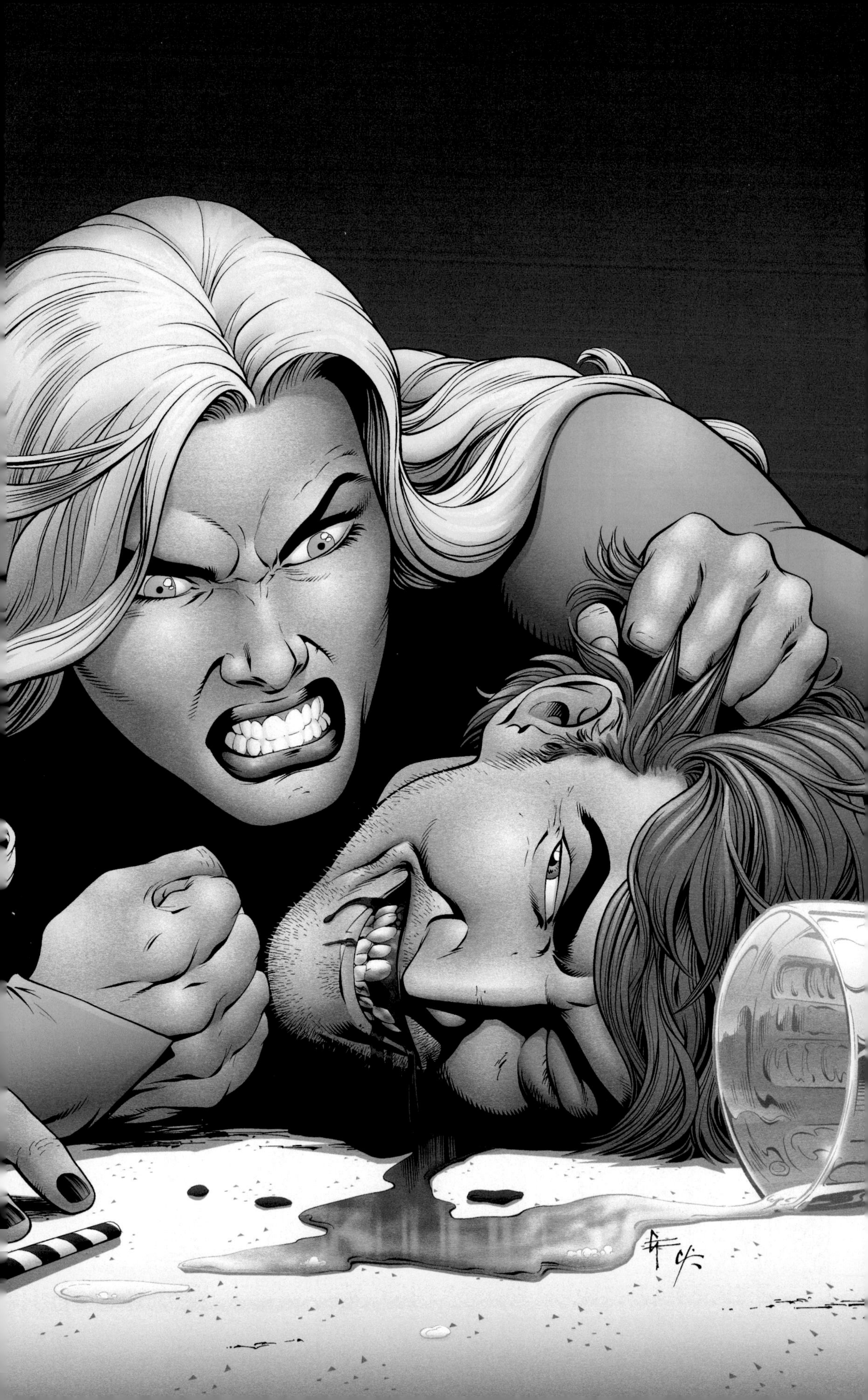

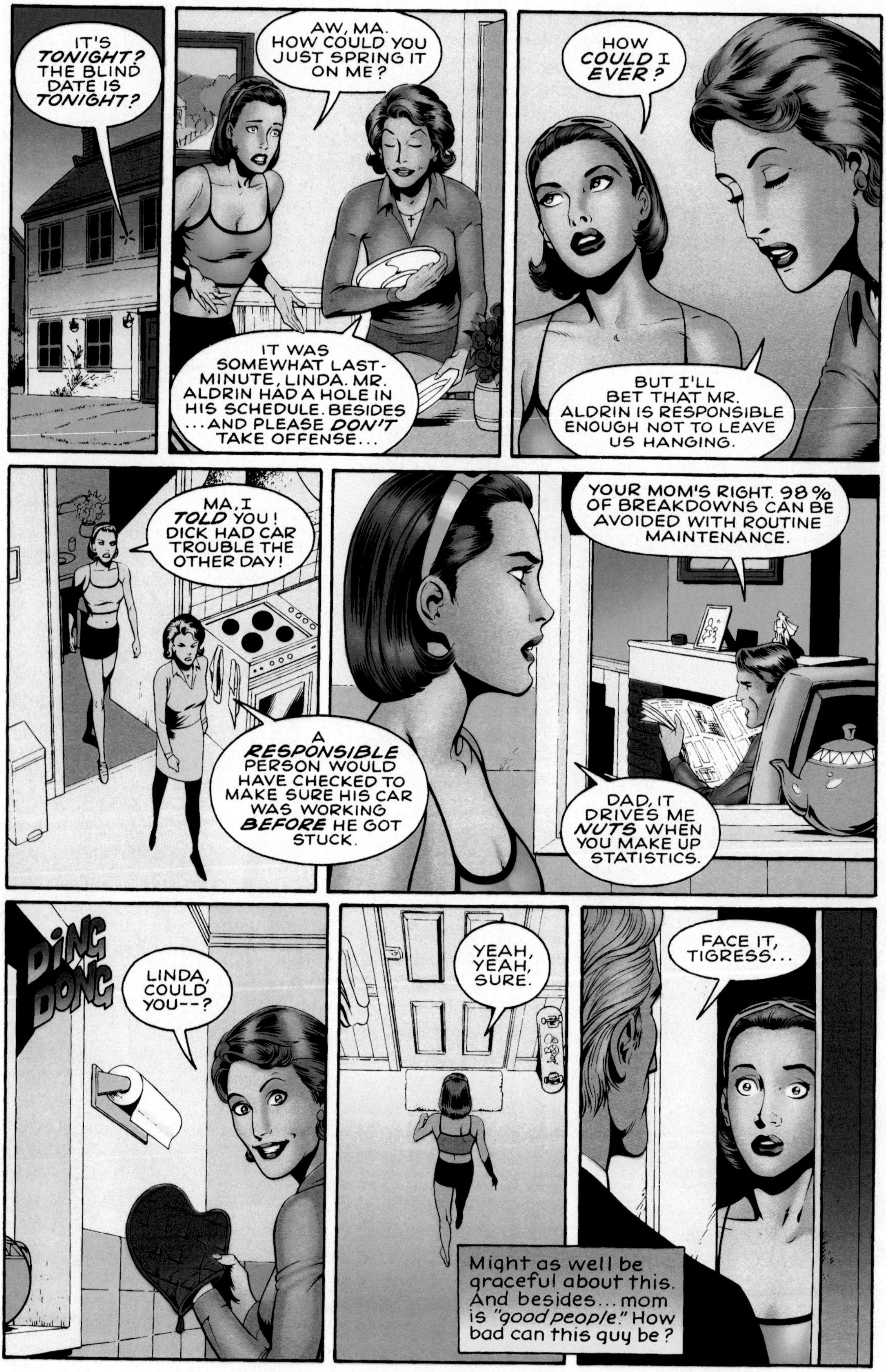
IT'S TONIGHT? THE BLIND DATE IS TONIGHT?
AW, MA. HOW COULD YOU JUST SPRING IT ON ME?
IT WAS SOMEWHAT LAST-MINUTE, LINDA. MR. ALDRIN HAD A HOLE IN HIS SCHEDULE. BESIDES ...AND PLEASE DON'T TAKE OFFENSE...
HOW COULD I EVER?
BUT I'LL BET THAT MR. ALDRIN IS RESPONSIBLE ENOUGH NOT TO LEAVE US HANGING.
MA, I TOLD YOU! DICK HAD CAR TROUBLE THE OTHER DAY!
A RESPONSIBLE PERSON WOULD HAVE CHECKED TO MAKE SURE HIS CAR WAS WORKING BEFORE HE GOT STUCK.
YOUR MOM'S RIGHT. 98% OF BREAKDOWNS CAN BE AVOIDED WITH ROUTINE MAINTENANCE.
DAD, IT DRIVES ME NUTS WHEN YOU MAKE UP STATISTICS.
DING DONG
LINDA, COULD YOU--?
YEAH, YEAH, SURE.
Might as well be graceful about this. And besides... mom is "good people." How bad can this guy be?
FACE IT, TIGRESS...

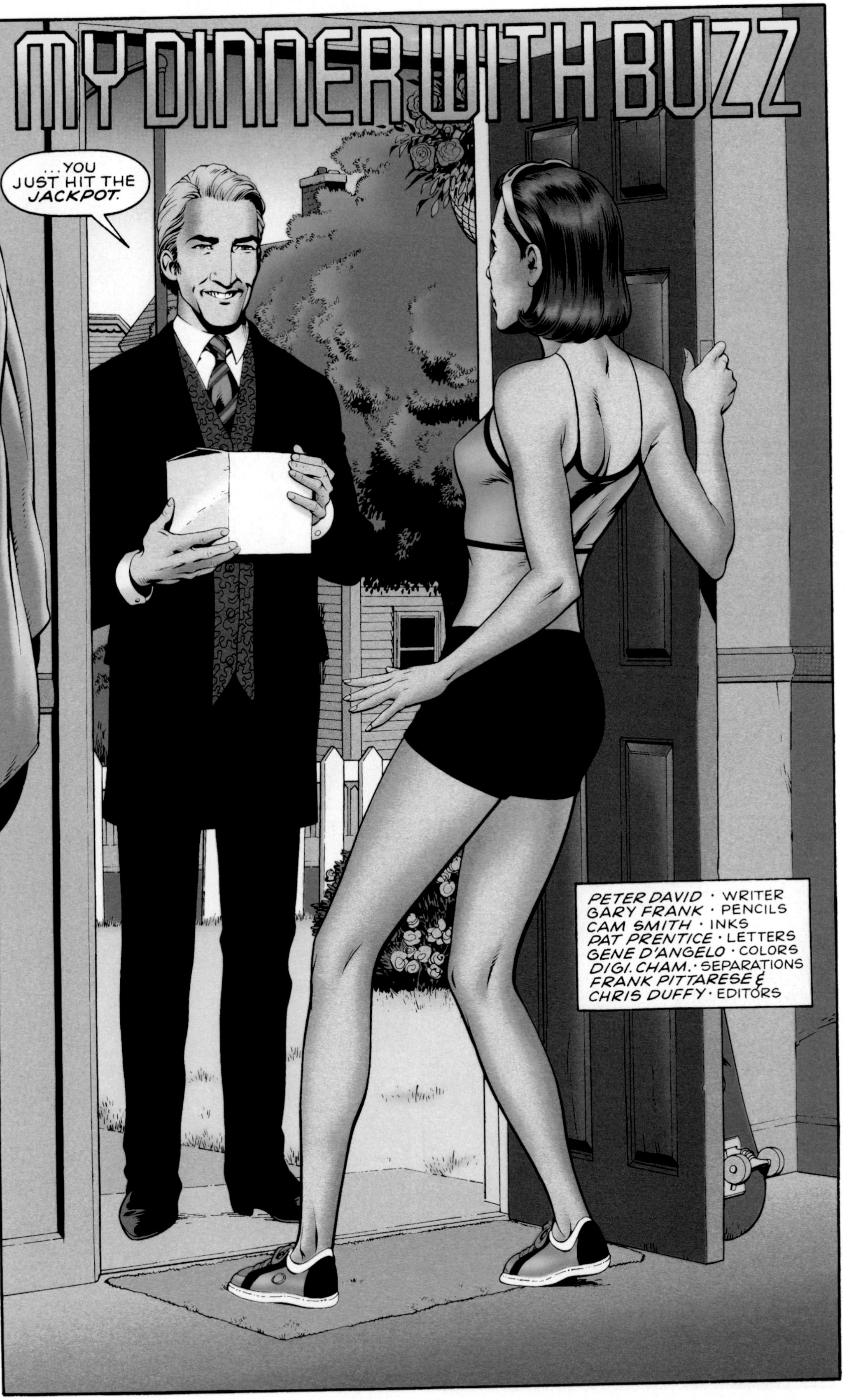
MY DINNER WITH BUZZ
...YOU JUST HIT THE JACKPOT.
PETER DAVID · WRITER
GARY FRANK · PENCILS
CAM SMITH · INKS
PAT PRENTICE · LETTERS
GENE D'ANGELO · COLORS
DIGI. CHAM. · SEPARATIONS
FRANK PITTARESE & CHRIS DUFFY · EDITORS

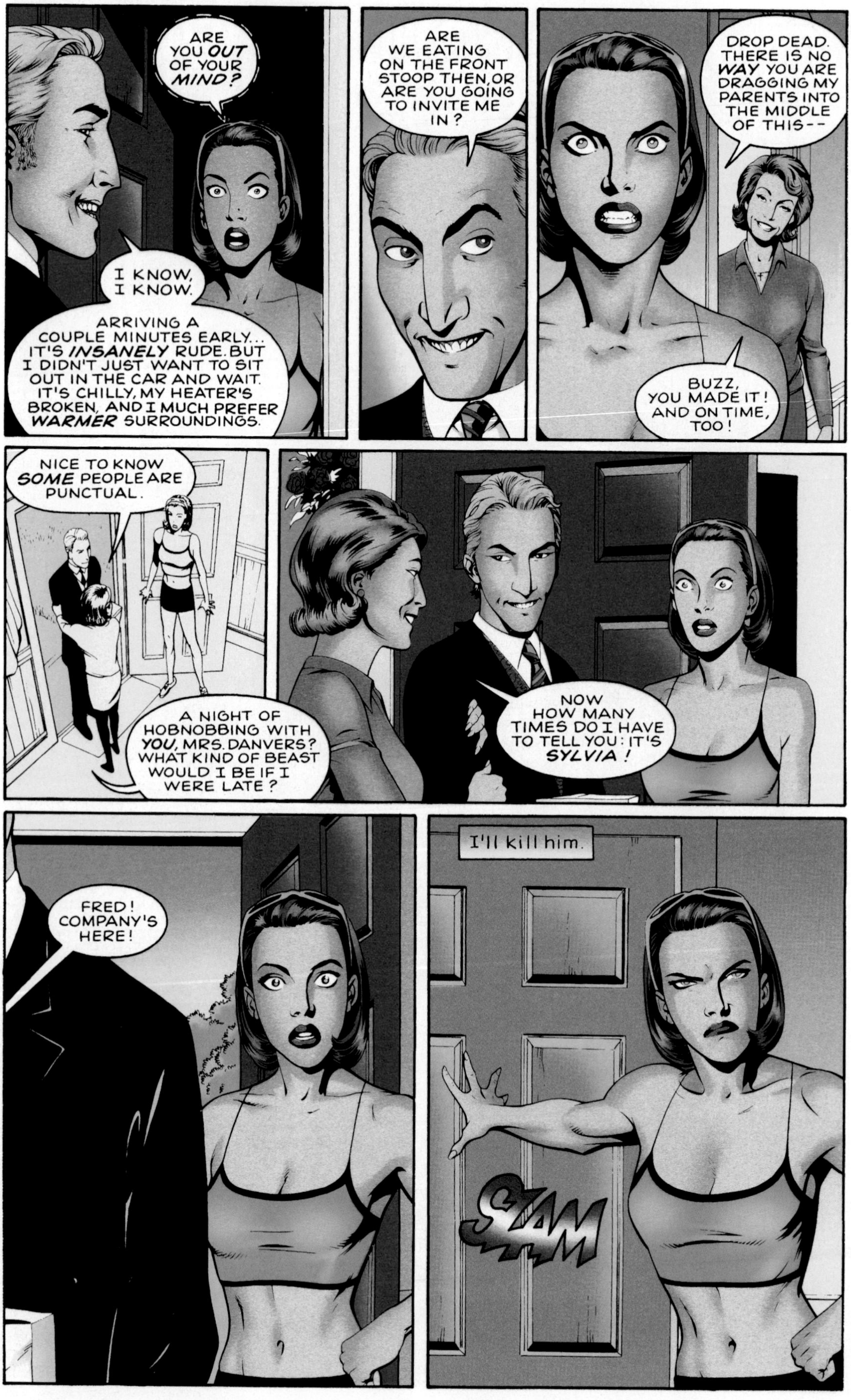
ARE YOU OUT OF YOUR MIND?
I KNOW, I KNOW.
ARRIVING A COUPLE MINUTES EARLY... IT'S INSANELY RUDE. BUT I DIDN'T JUST WANT TO SIT OUT IN THE CAR AND WAIT. IT'S CHILLY, MY HEATER'S BROKEN, AND I MUCH PREFER WARMER SURROUNDINGS.
ARE WE EATING ON THE FRONT STOOP THEN, OR ARE YOU GOING TO INVITE ME IN?
DROP DEAD. THERE IS NO WAY YOU ARE DRAGGING MY PARENTS INTO THE MIDDLE OF THIS--
BUZZ, YOU MADE IT! AND ON TIME, TOO!
NICE TO KNOW SOME PEOPLE ARE PUNCTUAL.
A NIGHT OF HOBNOBBING WITH YOU, MRS. DANVERS? WHAT KIND OF BEAST WOULD I BE IF I WERE LATE?
NOW HOW MANY TIMES DO I HAVE TO TELL YOU: IT'S SYLVIA!
FRED! COMPANY'S HERE!
I'll kill him.
SLAM

LINDA...?

SORRY. WIND.

FRED DANVERS. PARDON ME FOR NOT LEAPING TO MY FEET.

NOT A PROBLEM, FRED. BUZZ ALDRIN.

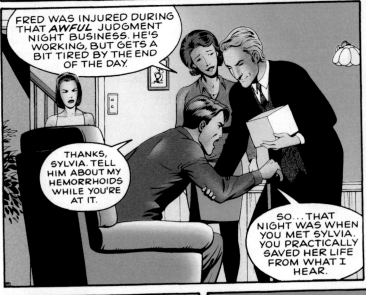

FRED WAS INJURED DURING THAT *AWFUL* JUDGMENT NIGHT BUSINESS. HE'S WORKING, BUT GETS A BIT TIRED BY THE END OF THE DAY.

THANKS, SYLVIA. TELL HIM ABOUT MY HEMORRHOIDS WHILE YOU'RE AT IT.

SO... THAT NIGHT WAS WHEN YOU MET SYLVIA. YOU PRACTICALLY SAVED HER LIFE FROM WHAT I HEAR.

OH, NOTHING OF THE *SORT.* JUST FOUND THE POOR THING LYING IN THE SNOW AND MADE SURE SHE GOT HOME SAFELY.

REGARDLESS, I APPRECIATE IT. THESE DAYS IT'S RARE TO FIND SOMEONE CONCERNED WITH OTHER PEOPLE'S WELFARE.

SO TRUE, FRED. SO TRUE.

YOUR FATHER SEEMS RATHER *TAKEN* WITH HIM. WHAT DO *YOU* THINK, LINDA?

LINDA?

HE'S REALLY... SOMETHING.

I'd pick him up and smash him through a wall. But I think my folks just *might* tumble to my secret if I did that.

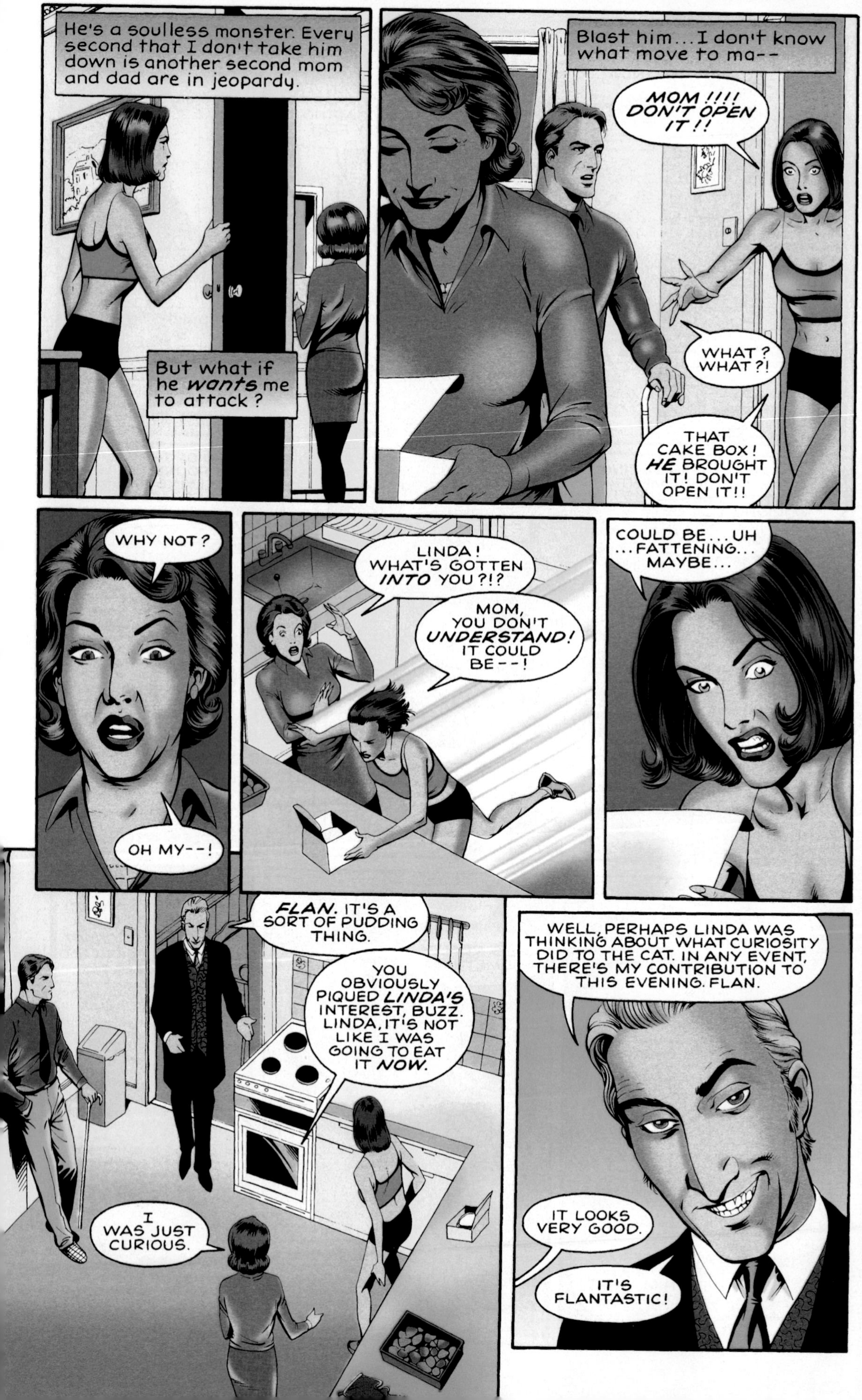
He's a soulless monster. Every second that I don't take him down is another second mom and dad are in jeopardy.
But what if he *wants* me to attack?
Blast him... I don't know what move to ma--
MOM!!!! DON'T OPEN IT!!
WHAT? WHAT?!
THAT CAKE BOX! *HE* BROUGHT IT! DON'T OPEN IT!!
WHY NOT?
OH MY--!
LINDA! WHAT'S GOTTEN *INTO* YOU?!?
MOM, YOU DON'T *UNDERSTAND!* IT COULD BE--!
COULD BE...UH ...FATTENING... MAYBE...
FLAN. IT'S A SORT OF PUDDING THING.
YOU OBVIOUSLY PIQUED *LINDA'S* INTEREST, BUZZ. LINDA, IT'S NOT LIKE I WAS GOING TO EAT IT *NOW.*
I WAS JUST CURIOUS.
WELL, PERHAPS LINDA WAS THINKING ABOUT WHAT CURIOSITY DID TO THE CAT. IN ANY EVENT, THERE'S MY CONTRIBUTION TO THIS EVENING. FLAN.
IT LOOKS VERY GOOD.
IT'S FLANTASTIC!

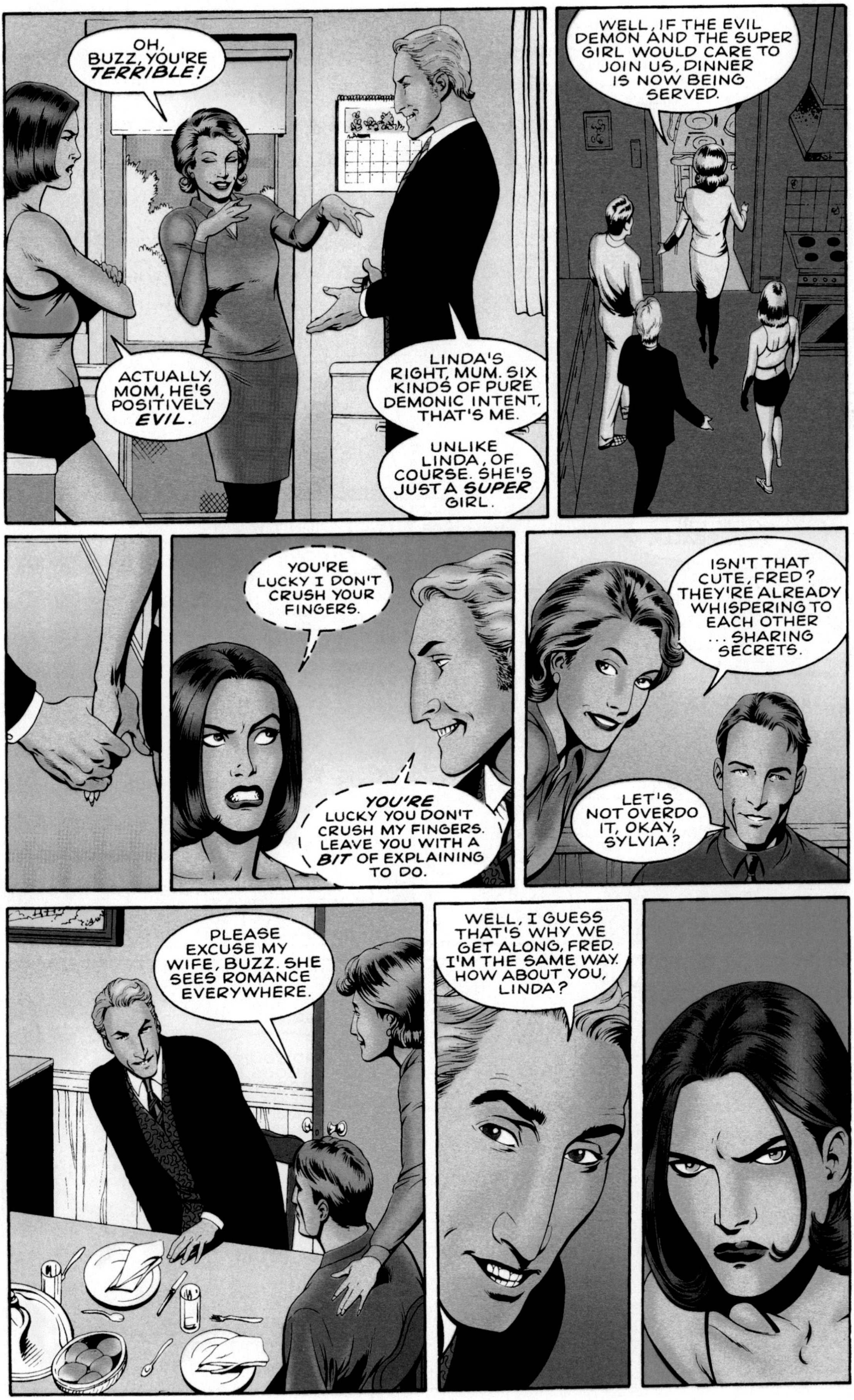
OH, BUZZ, YOU'RE TERRIBLE!
ACTUALLY, MOM, HE'S POSITIVELY EVIL.
LINDA'S RIGHT, MUM. SIX KINDS OF PURE DEMONIC INTENT, THAT'S ME.
UNLIKE LINDA, OF COURSE. SHE'S JUST A SUPER GIRL.
WELL, IF THE EVIL DEMON AND THE SUPER GIRL WOULD CARE TO JOIN US, DINNER IS NOW BEING SERVED.
YOU'RE LUCKY I DON'T CRUSH YOUR FINGERS.
YOU'RE LUCKY YOU DON'T CRUSH MY FINGERS. LEAVE YOU WITH A BIT OF EXPLAINING TO DO.
ISN'T THAT CUTE, FRED? THEY'RE ALREADY WHISPERING TO EACH OTHER ... SHARING SECRETS.
LET'S NOT OVERDO IT, OKAY, SYLVIA?
PLEASE EXCUSE MY WIFE, BUZZ. SHE SEES ROMANCE EVERYWHERE.
WELL, I GUESS THAT'S WHY WE GET ALONG, FRED. I'M THE SAME WAY. HOW ABOUT YOU, LINDA?

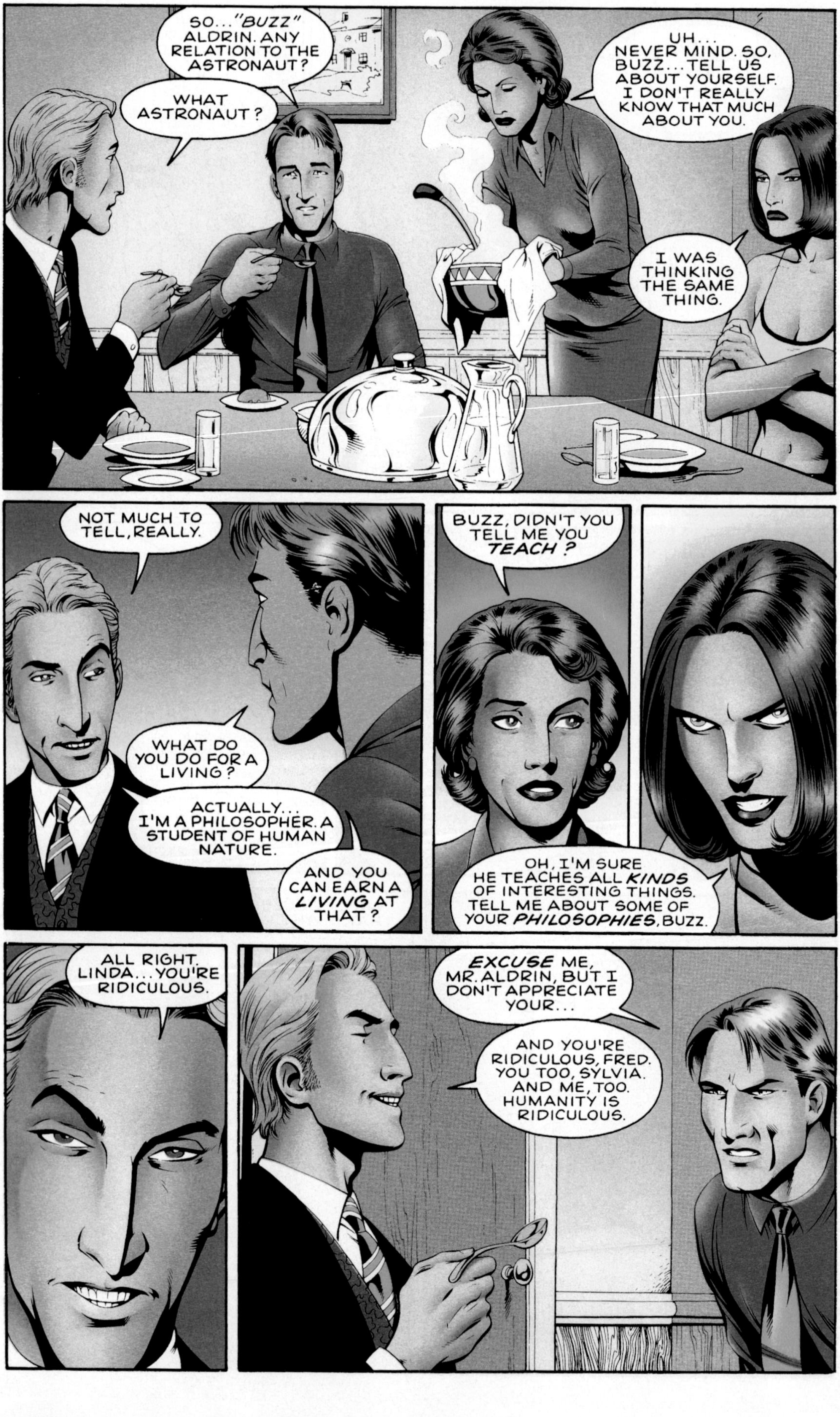
SO..."BUZZ" ALDRIN. ANY RELATION TO THE ASTRONAUT?
WHAT ASTRONAUT?
UH... NEVER MIND. SO, BUZZ... TELL US ABOUT YOURSELF. I DON'T REALLY KNOW THAT MUCH ABOUT YOU.
I WAS THINKING THE SAME THING.
NOT MUCH TO TELL, REALLY.
WHAT DO YOU DO FOR A LIVING?
ACTUALLY... I'M A PHILOSOPHER. A STUDENT OF HUMAN NATURE.
AND YOU CAN EARN A LIVING AT THAT?
BUZZ, DIDN'T YOU TELL ME YOU TEACH?
OH, I'M SURE HE TEACHES ALL KINDS OF INTERESTING THINGS. TELL ME ABOUT SOME OF YOUR PHILOSOPHIES, BUZZ.
ALL RIGHT. LINDA... YOU'RE RIDICULOUS.
EXCUSE ME, MR. ALDRIN, BUT I DON'T APPRECIATE YOUR...
AND YOU'RE RIDICULOUS, FRED. YOU TOO, SYLVIA. AND ME, TOO. HUMANITY IS RIDICULOUS.

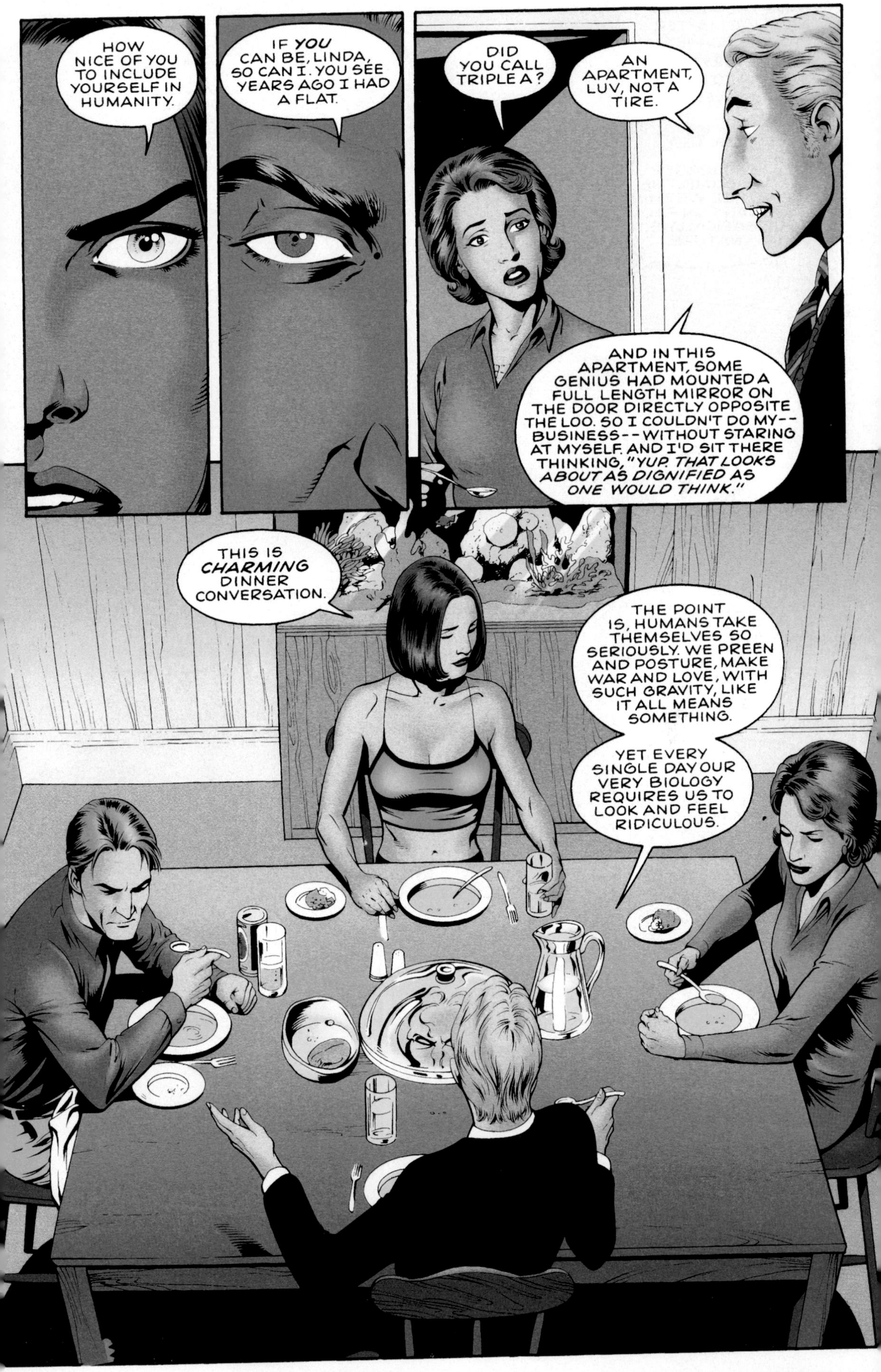
HOW NICE OF YOU TO INCLUDE YOURSELF IN HUMANITY.
IF *YOU* CAN BE, LINDA, SO CAN I. YOU SEE YEARS AGO I HAD A FLAT.
DID YOU CALL TRIPLE A?
AN APARTMENT, LUV, NOT A TIRE.
AND IN THIS APARTMENT, SOME GENIUS HAD MOUNTED A FULL LENGTH MIRROR ON THE DOOR DIRECTLY OPPOSITE THE LOO. SO I COULDN'T DO MY-- BUSINESS--WITHOUT STARING AT MYSELF. AND I'D SIT THERE THINKING, *"YUP. THAT LOOKS ABOUT AS DIGNIFIED AS ONE WOULD THINK."*
THIS IS *CHARMING* DINNER CONVERSATION.
THE POINT IS, HUMANS TAKE THEMSELVES SO SERIOUSLY. WE PREEN AND POSTURE, MAKE WAR AND LOVE, WITH SUCH GRAVITY, LIKE IT ALL MEANS SOMETHING.
YET EVERY SINGLE DAY OUR VERY BIOLOGY REQUIRES US TO LOOK AND FEEL RIDICULOUS.

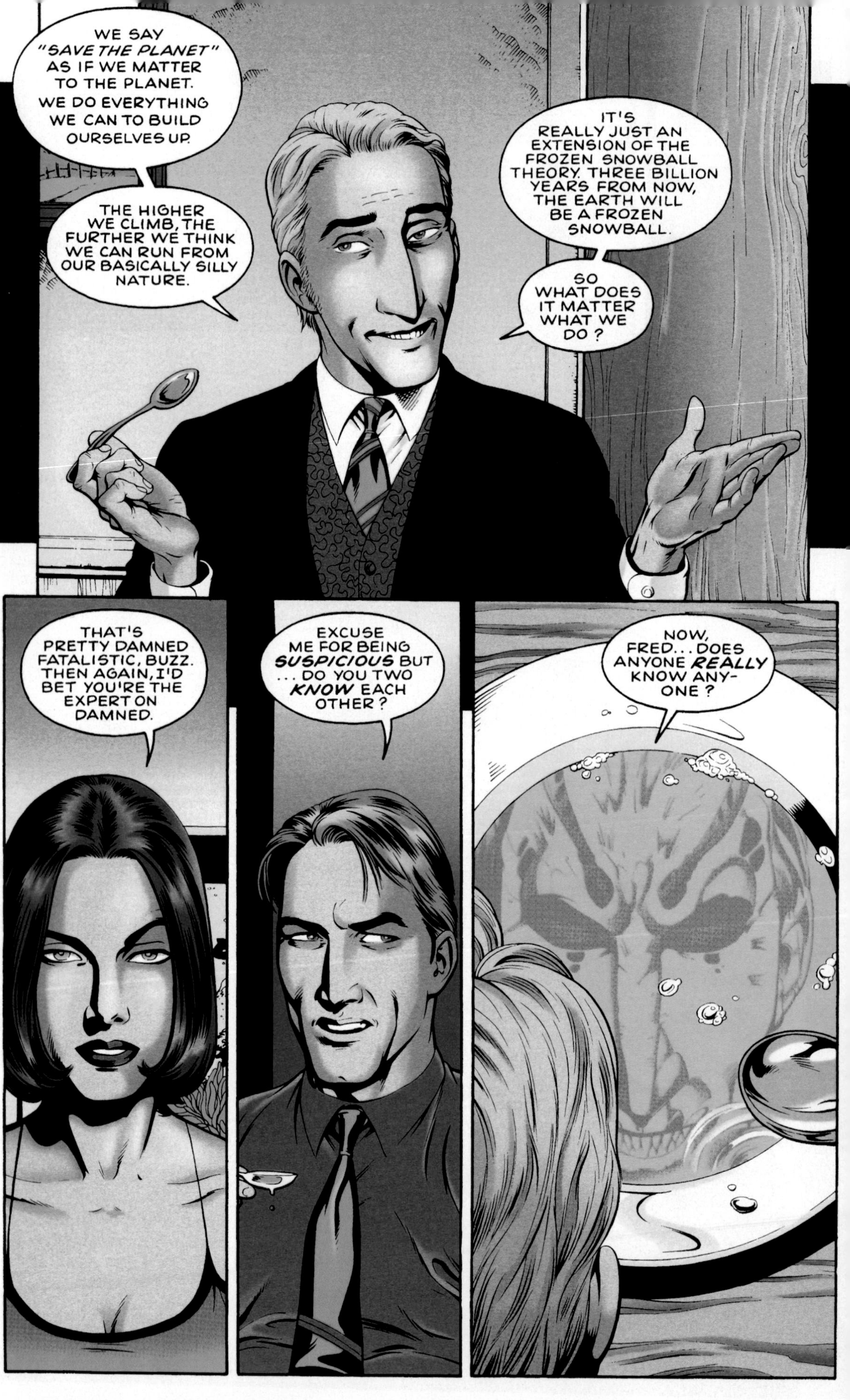
WE SAY "SAVE THE PLANET" AS IF WE MATTER TO THE PLANET.
WE DO EVERYTHING WE CAN TO BUILD OURSELVES UP.
THE HIGHER WE CLIMB, THE FURTHER WE THINK WE CAN RUN FROM OUR BASICALLY SILLY NATURE.
IT'S REALLY JUST AN EXTENSION OF THE FROZEN SNOWBALL THEORY. THREE BILLION YEARS FROM NOW, THE EARTH WILL BE A FROZEN SNOWBALL.
SO WHAT DOES IT MATTER WHAT WE DO?
THAT'S PRETTY DAMNED FATALISTIC, BUZZ. THEN AGAIN, I'D BET YOU'RE THE EXPERT ON DAMNED.
EXCUSE ME FOR BEING SUSPICIOUS BUT ... DO YOU TWO KNOW EACH OTHER?
NOW, FRED... DOES ANYONE REALLY KNOW ANY-ONE?

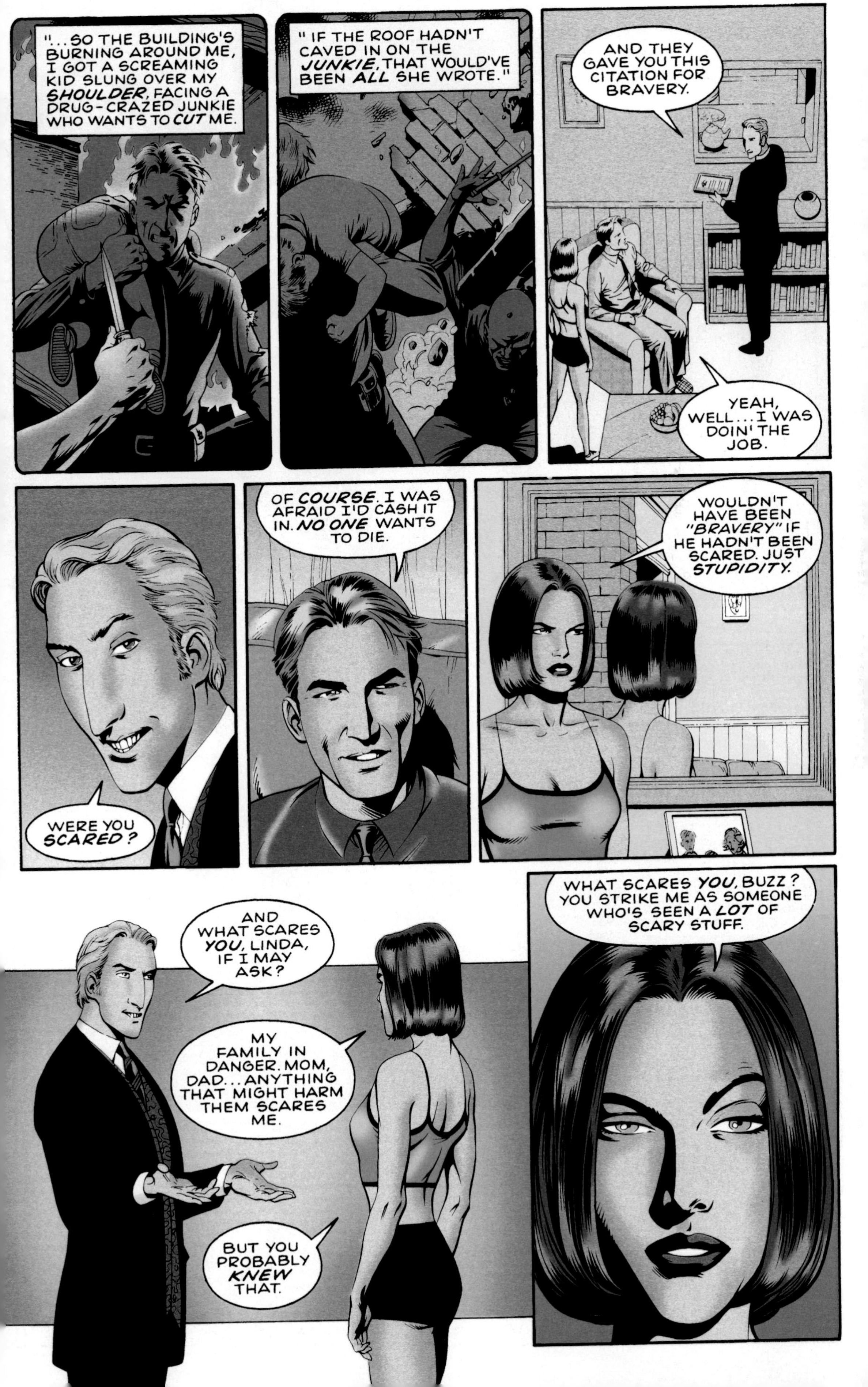
"...SO THE BUILDING'S BURNING AROUND ME, I GOT A SCREAMING KID SLUNG OVER MY SHOULDER, FACING A DRUG-CRAZED JUNKIE WHO WANTS TO CUT ME.
"IF THE ROOF HADN'T CAVED IN ON THE JUNKIE, THAT WOULD'VE BEEN ALL SHE WROTE."
AND THEY GAVE YOU THIS CITATION FOR BRAVERY.
YEAH, WELL... I WAS DOIN' THE JOB.
WERE YOU SCARED?
OF COURSE. I WAS AFRAID I'D CASH IT IN. NO ONE WANTS TO DIE.
WOULDN'T HAVE BEEN "BRAVERY" IF HE HADN'T BEEN SCARED. JUST STUPIDITY.
AND WHAT SCARES YOU, LINDA, IF I MAY ASK?
MY FAMILY IN DANGER. MOM, DAD... ANYTHING THAT MIGHT HARM THEM SCARES ME.
BUT YOU PROBABLY KNEW THAT.
WHAT SCARES YOU, BUZZ? YOU STRIKE ME AS SOMEONE WHO'S SEEN A LOT OF SCARY STUFF.

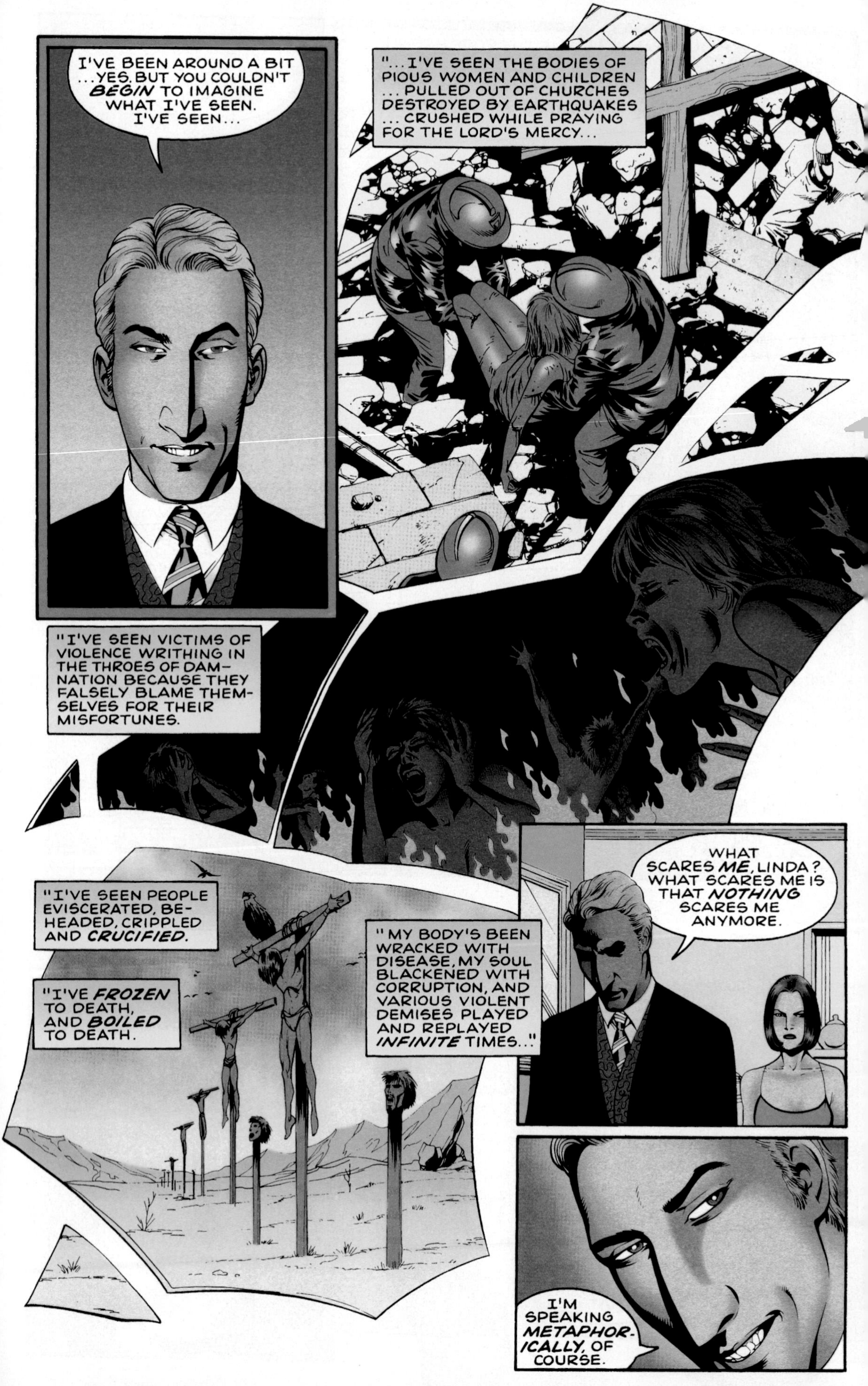
I'VE BEEN AROUND A BIT ...YES. BUT YOU COULDN'T *BEGIN* TO IMAGINE WHAT I'VE SEEN. I'VE SEEN...
"...I'VE SEEN THE BODIES OF PIOUS WOMEN AND CHILDREN ... PULLED OUT OF CHURCHES DESTROYED BY EARTHQUAKES ... CRUSHED WHILE PRAYING FOR THE LORD'S MERCY...
"I'VE SEEN VICTIMS OF VIOLENCE WRITHING IN THE THROES OF DAMNATION BECAUSE THEY FALSELY BLAME THEMSELVES FOR THEIR MISFORTUNES.
"I'VE SEEN PEOPLE EVISCERATED, BEHEADED, CRIPPLED AND *CRUCIFIED*.
"I'VE *FROZEN* TO DEATH, AND *BOILED* TO DEATH.
"MY BODY'S BEEN WRACKED WITH DISEASE, MY SOUL BLACKENED WITH CORRUPTION, AND VARIOUS VIOLENT DEMISES PLAYED AND REPLAYED *INFINITE* TIMES..."
WHAT SCARES *ME*, LINDA? WHAT SCARES ME IS THAT *NOTHING* SCARES ME ANYMORE.
I'M SPEAKING *METAPHORICALLY*, OF COURSE.

WHERE DID YOU *FIND* THIS GUY?! HE'S *CREEPY!*

FRED, DON'T YOU *GET* IT? HE'S A STUDENT OF HUMAN BEHAVIOR.

HE SAYS OUTRAGEOUS THINGS TO SEE PEOPLE'S REACTIONS.

"LINDA WILL WARM TO HIM. *YOU'LL* SEE."

GET OUT. *NOW!*

BEFORE WE'VE EVEN GOTTEN TO THE FLAN? WHAT AN ABSURD...

CUT THE CRAP!

ENOUGH! YOU HEAR? *ENOUGH!* YOU'RE A MURDERER, A MONSTER! I SHOULD PULP YOU HERE AND NOW.

WHAM

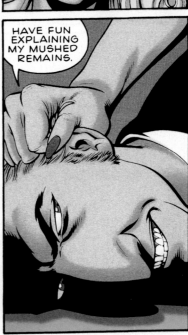

HAVE FUN EXPLAINING MY MUSHED REMAINS.

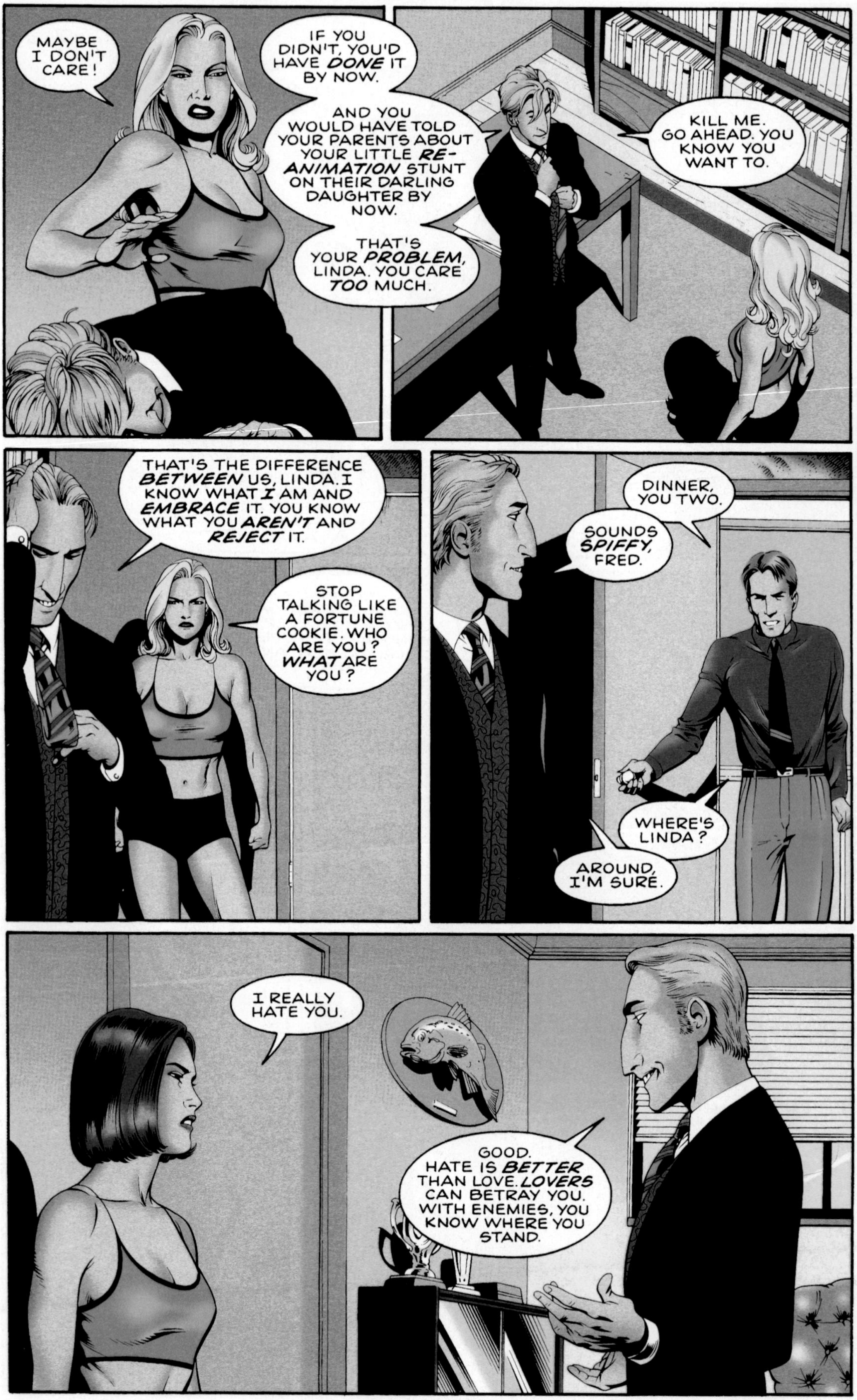
MAYBE I DON'T CARE!
IF YOU DIDN'T, YOU'D HAVE DONE IT BY NOW.
AND YOU WOULD HAVE TOLD YOUR PARENTS ABOUT YOUR LITTLE RE-ANIMATION STUNT ON THEIR DARLING DAUGHTER BY NOW.
THAT'S YOUR PROBLEM, LINDA. YOU CARE TOO MUCH.
KILL ME. GO AHEAD. YOU KNOW YOU WANT TO.
THAT'S THE DIFFERENCE BETWEEN US, LINDA. I KNOW WHAT I AM AND EMBRACE IT. YOU KNOW WHAT YOU AREN'T AND REJECT IT.
STOP TALKING LIKE A FORTUNE COOKIE. WHO ARE YOU? WHAT ARE YOU?
DINNER, YOU TWO.
SOUNDS SPIFFY, FRED.
WHERE'S LINDA?
AROUND, I'M SURE.
I REALLY HATE YOU.
GOOD. HATE IS BETTER THAN LOVE. LOVERS CAN BETRAY YOU. WITH ENEMIES, YOU KNOW WHERE YOU STAND.

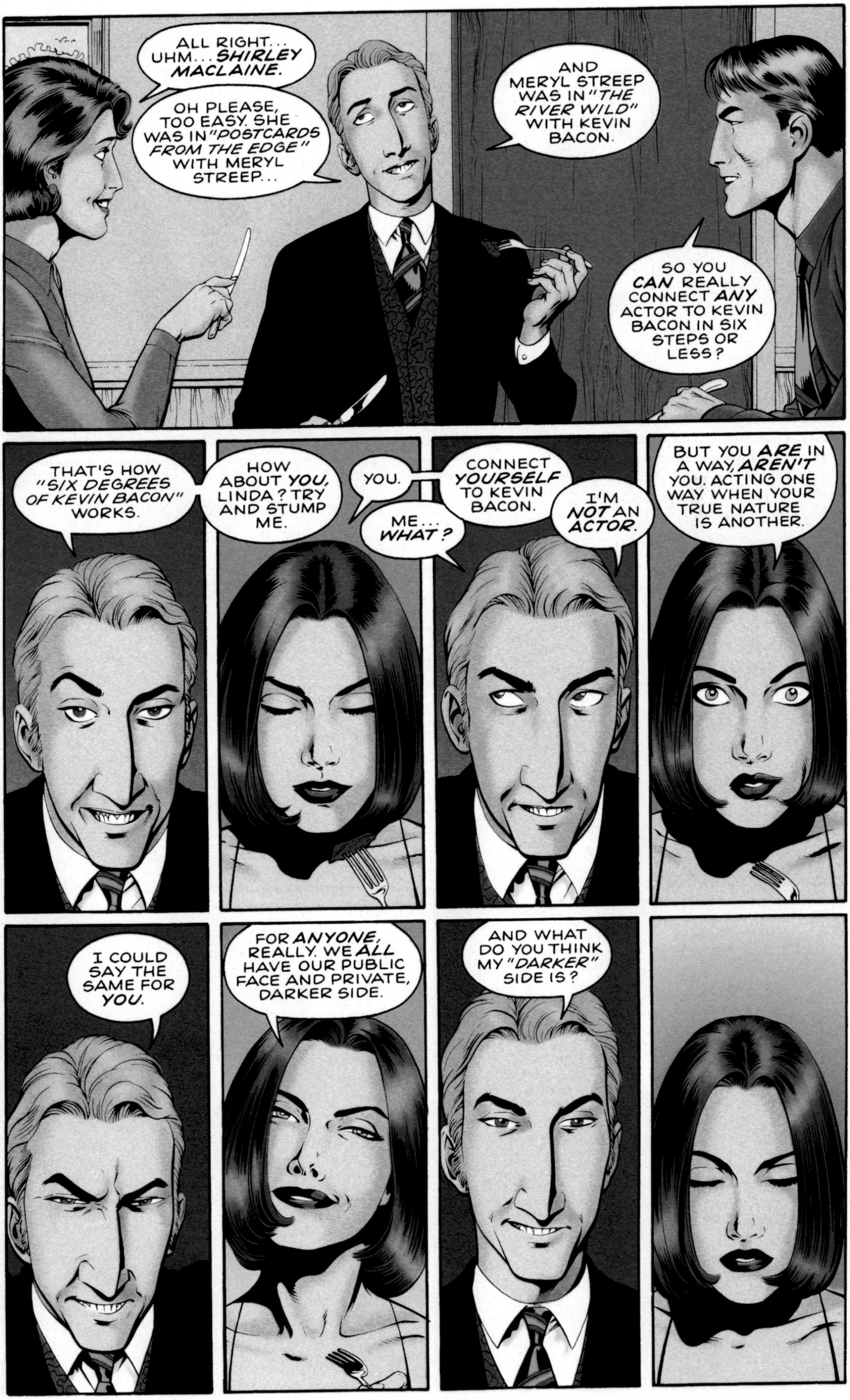
ALL RIGHT... UHM... SHIRLEY MACLAINE.
OH PLEASE, TOO EASY. SHE WAS IN "POSTCARDS FROM THE EDGE" WITH MERYL STREEP...
AND MERYL STREEP WAS IN "THE RIVER WILD" WITH KEVIN BACON.
SO YOU CAN REALLY CONNECT ANY ACTOR TO KEVIN BACON IN SIX STEPS OR LESS?
THAT'S HOW "SIX DEGREES OF KEVIN BACON" WORKS.
HOW ABOUT YOU, LINDA? TRY AND STUMP ME.
YOU.
ME... WHAT?
CONNECT YOURSELF TO KEVIN BACON.
I'M NOT AN ACTOR.
BUT YOU ARE IN A WAY, AREN'T YOU. ACTING ONE WAY WHEN YOUR TRUE NATURE IS ANOTHER.
I COULD SAY THE SAME FOR YOU.
FOR ANYONE, REALLY. WE ALL HAVE OUR PUBLIC FACE AND PRIVATE, DARKER SIDE.
AND WHAT DO YOU THINK MY "DARKER" SIDE IS?

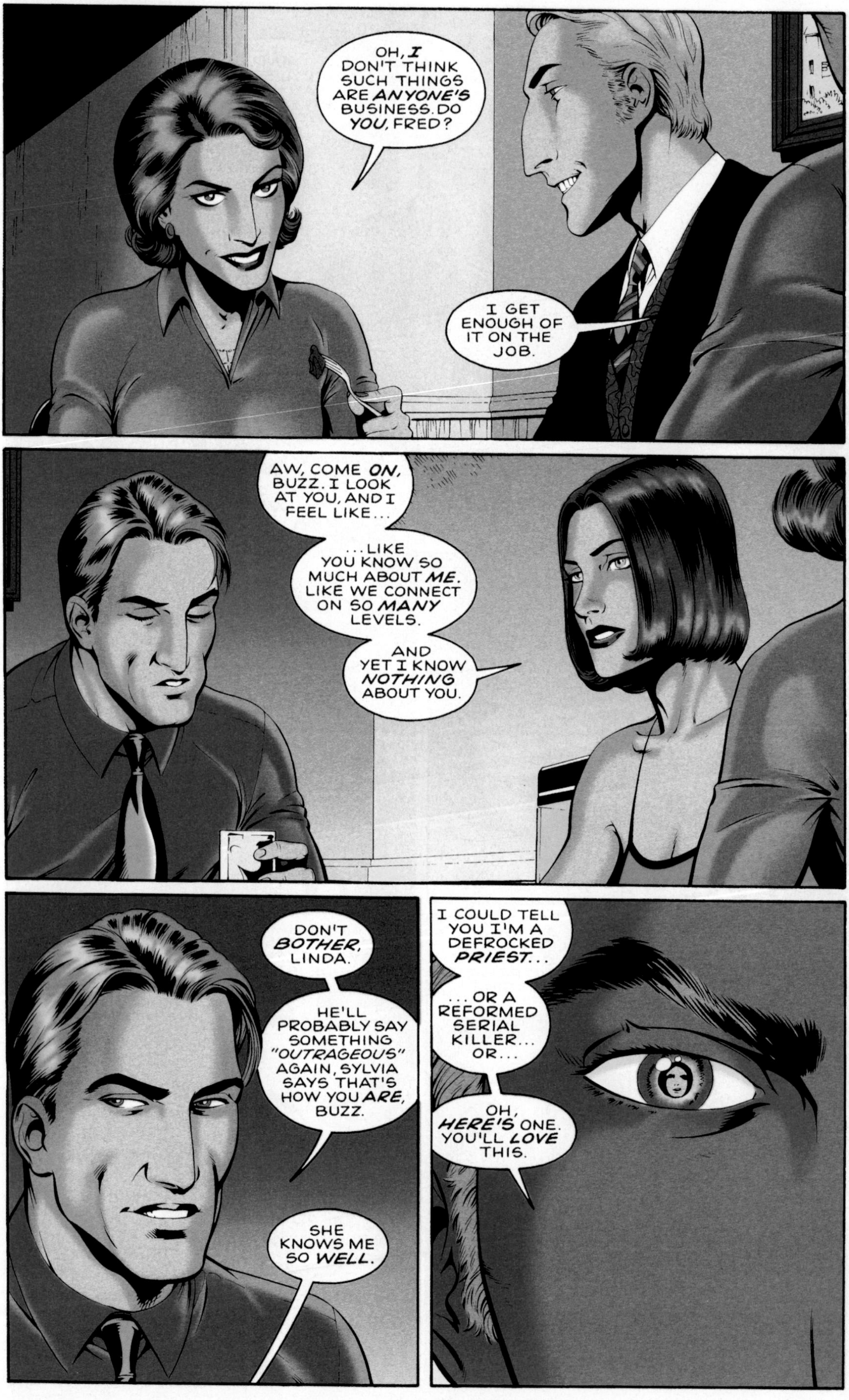
OH, I DON'T THINK SUCH THINGS ARE ANYONE'S BUSINESS. DO YOU, FRED?
I GET ENOUGH OF IT ON THE JOB.
AW, COME ON, BUZZ. I LOOK AT YOU, AND I FEEL LIKE...
...LIKE YOU KNOW SO MUCH ABOUT ME. LIKE WE CONNECT ON SO MANY LEVELS.
AND YET I KNOW NOTHING ABOUT YOU.
DON'T BOTHER, LINDA.
HE'LL PROBABLY SAY SOMETHING "OUTRAGEOUS" AGAIN, SYLVIA SAYS THAT'S HOW YOU ARE, BUZZ.
SHE KNOWS ME SO WELL.
I COULD TELL YOU I'M A DEFROCKED PRIEST...
...OR A REFORMED SERIAL KILLER... OR...
OH, HERE'S ONE. YOU'LL LOVE THIS.

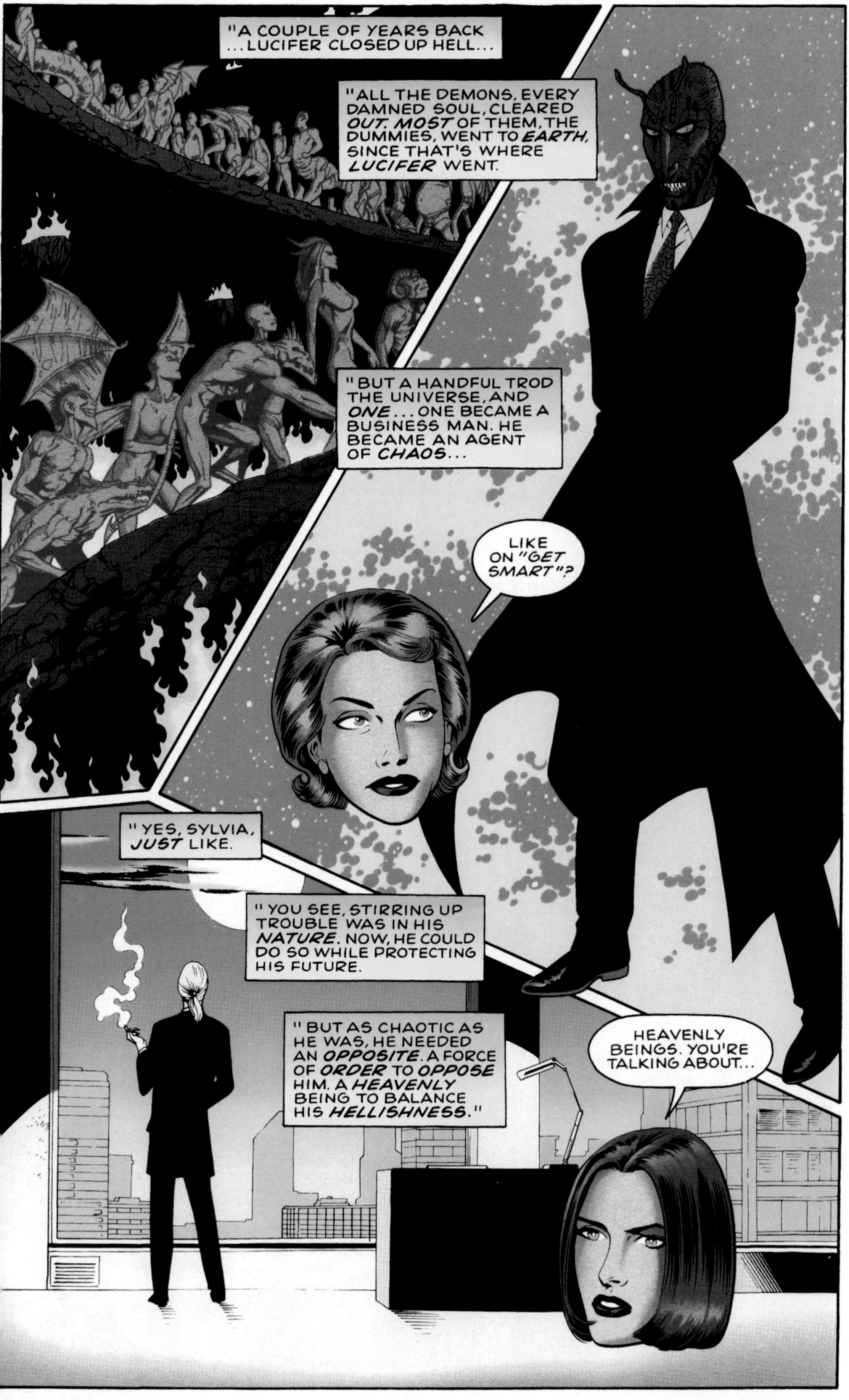
"A COUPLE OF YEARS BACK ...LUCIFER CLOSED UP HELL...
"ALL THE DEMONS, EVERY DAMNED SOUL, CLEARED OUT. MOST OF THEM, THE DUMMIES, WENT TO EARTH, SINCE THAT'S WHERE LUCIFER WENT.
"BUT A HANDFUL TROD THE UNIVERSE, AND ONE... ONE BECAME A BUSINESS MAN. HE BECAME AN AGENT OF CHAOS...
LIKE ON "GET SMART"?
"YES, SYLVIA, JUST LIKE.
"YOU SEE, STIRRING UP TROUBLE WAS IN HIS NATURE. NOW, HE COULD DO SO WHILE PROTECTING HIS FUTURE.
"BUT AS CHAOTIC AS HE WAS, HE NEEDED AN OPPOSITE. A FORCE OF ORDER TO OPPOSE HIM. A HEAVENLY BEING TO BALANCE HIS HELLISHNESS."
HEAVENLY BEINGS. YOU'RE TALKING ABOUT...

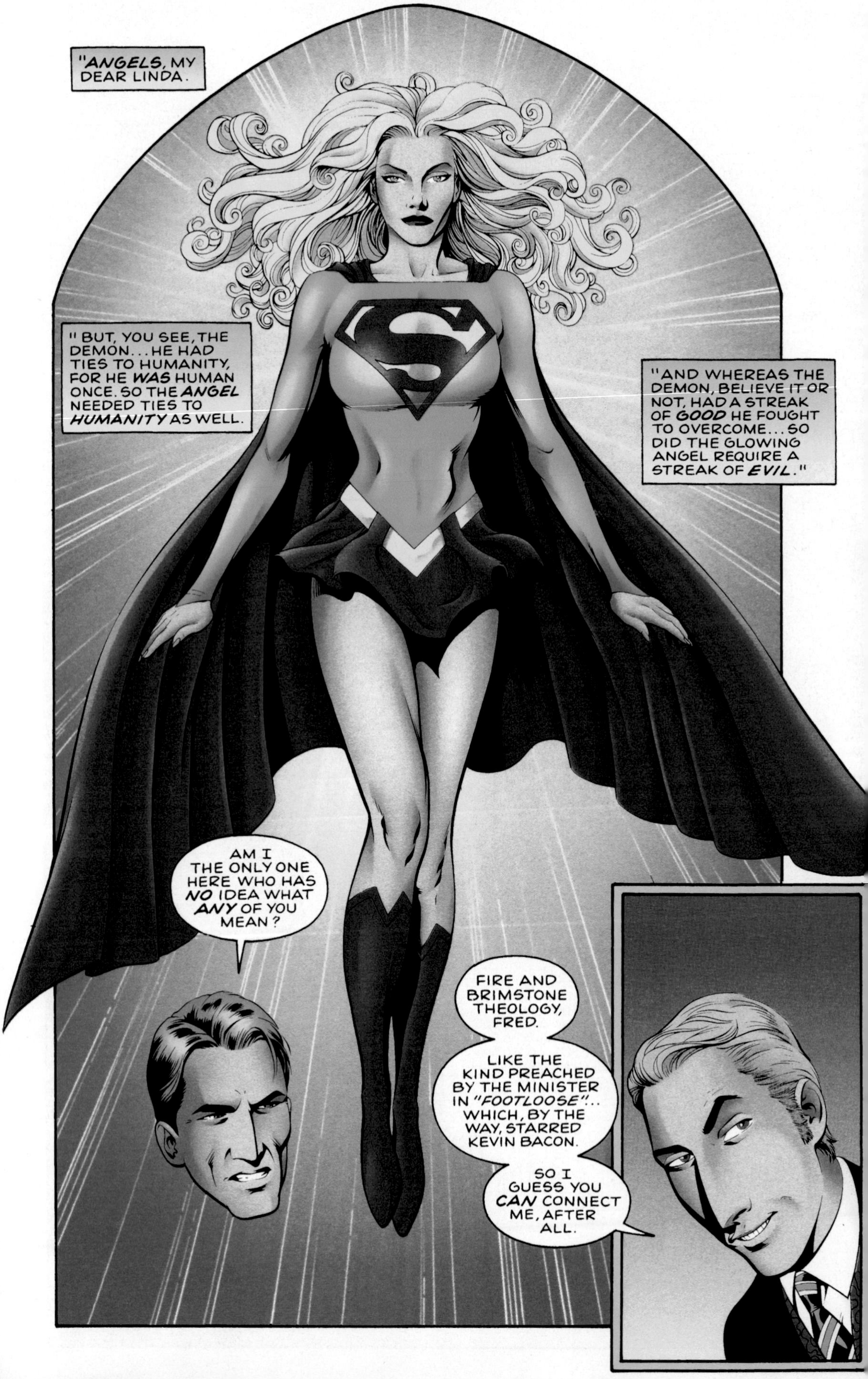
"ANGELS, MY DEAR LINDA.
" BUT, YOU SEE, THE DEMON... HE HAD TIES TO HUMANITY, FOR HE WAS HUMAN ONCE. SO THE ANGEL NEEDED TIES TO HUMANITY AS WELL.
"AND WHEREAS THE DEMON, BELIEVE IT OR NOT, HAD A STREAK OF GOOD HE FOUGHT TO OVERCOME... SO DID THE GLOWING ANGEL REQUIRE A STREAK OF EVIL."
AM I THE ONLY ONE HERE WHO HAS NO IDEA WHAT ANY OF YOU MEAN?
FIRE AND BRIMSTONE THEOLOGY, FRED.
LIKE THE KIND PREACHED BY THE MINISTER IN "FOOTLOOSE"... WHICH, BY THE WAY, STARRED KEVIN BACON.
SO I GUESS YOU CAN CONNECT ME, AFTER ALL.

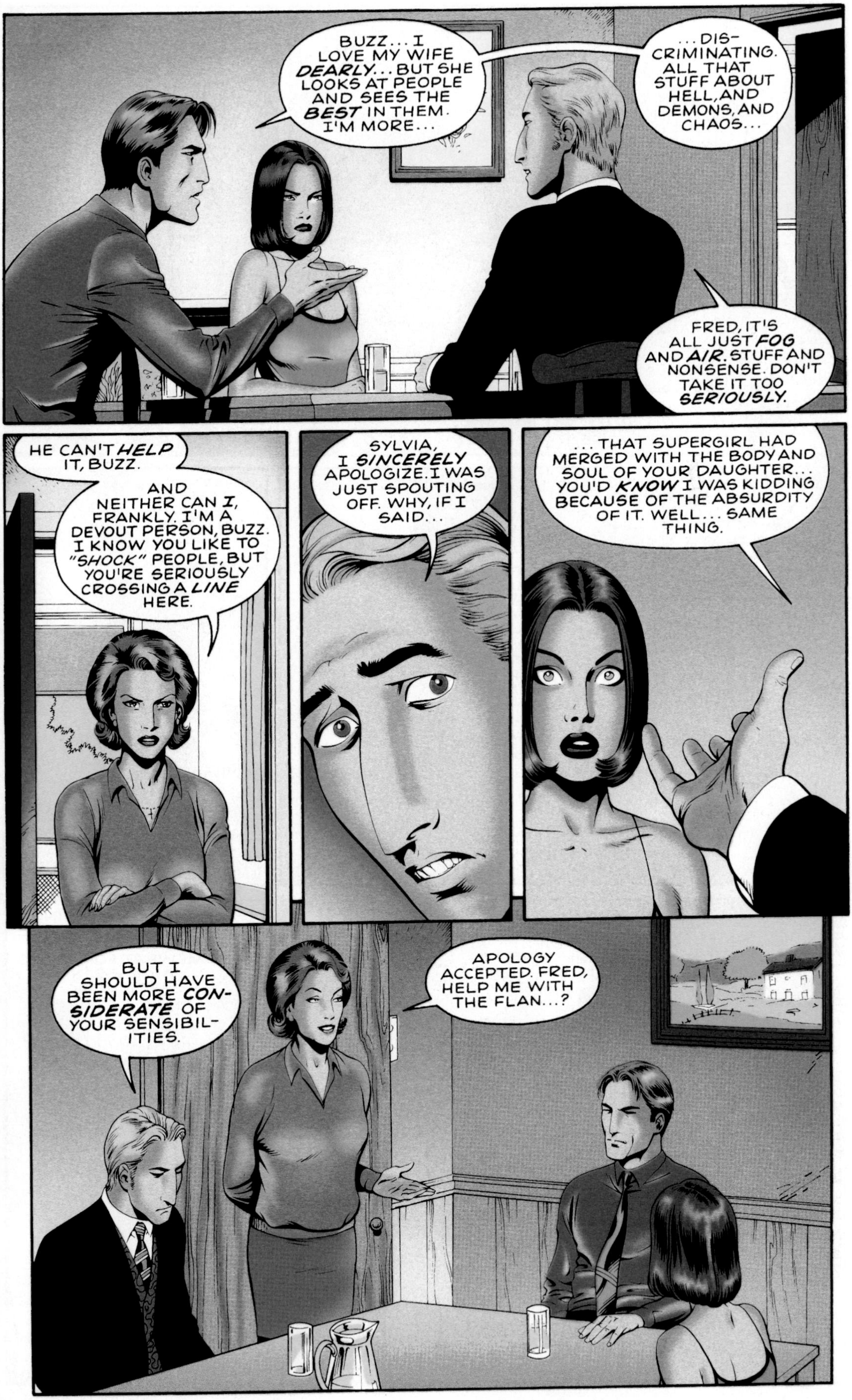
BUZZ... I LOVE MY WIFE DEARLY... BUT SHE LOOKS AT PEOPLE AND SEES THE BEST IN THEM. I'M MORE...
...DIS-CRIMINATING. ALL THAT STUFF ABOUT HELL, AND DEMONS, AND CHAOS...
FRED, IT'S ALL JUST FOG AND AIR. STUFF AND NONSENSE. DON'T TAKE IT TOO SERIOUSLY.
HE CAN'T HELP IT, BUZZ.
AND NEITHER CAN I, FRANKLY. I'M A DEVOUT PERSON, BUZZ. I KNOW YOU LIKE TO "SHOCK" PEOPLE, BUT YOU'RE SERIOUSLY CROSSING A LINE HERE.
SYLVIA, I SINCERELY APOLOGIZE. I WAS JUST SPOUTING OFF. WHY, IF I SAID...
...THAT SUPERGIRL HAD MERGED WITH THE BODY AND SOUL OF YOUR DAUGHTER... YOU'D KNOW I WAS KIDDING BECAUSE OF THE ABSURDITY OF IT. WELL... SAME THING.
BUT I SHOULD HAVE BEEN MORE CON-SIDERATE OF YOUR SENSIBIL-ITIES.
APOLOGY ACCEPTED. FRED, HELP ME WITH THE FLAN...?

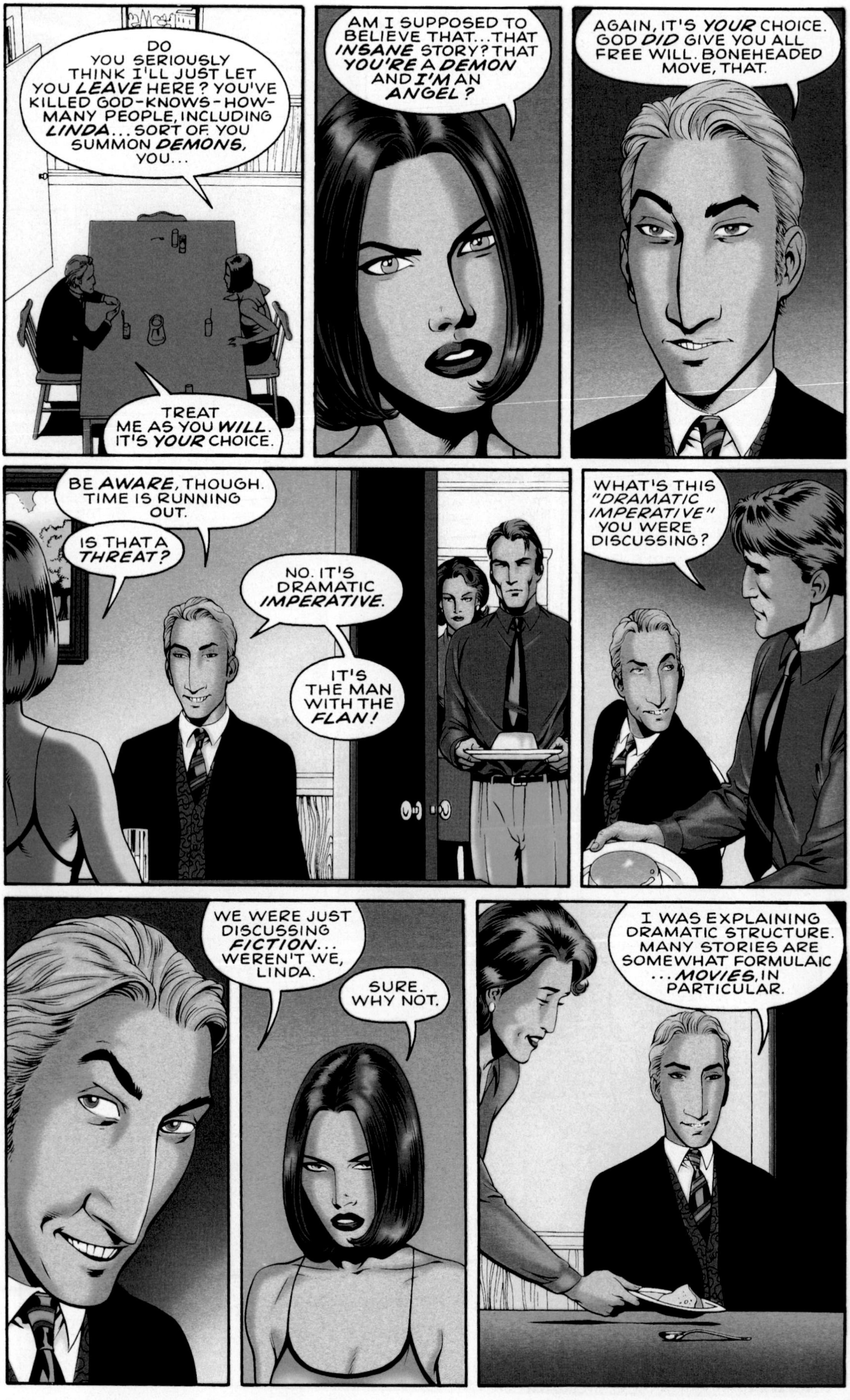
DO YOU SERIOUSLY THINK I'LL JUST LET YOU LEAVE HERE? YOU'VE KILLED GOD-KNOWS-HOW-MANY PEOPLE, INCLUDING LINDA... SORT OF. YOU SUMMON DEMONS, YOU...
TREAT ME AS YOU WILL. IT'S YOUR CHOICE.
AM I SUPPOSED TO BELIEVE THAT...THAT INSANE STORY? THAT YOU'RE A DEMON AND I'M AN ANGEL?
AGAIN, IT'S YOUR CHOICE. GOD DID GIVE YOU ALL FREE WILL. BONEHEADED MOVE, THAT.
BE AWARE, THOUGH. TIME IS RUNNING OUT.
IS THAT A THREAT?
NO. IT'S DRAMATIC IMPERATIVE.
IT'S THE MAN WITH THE FLAN!
WHAT'S THIS "DRAMATIC IMPERATIVE" YOU WERE DISCUSSING?
WE WERE JUST DISCUSSING FICTION... WEREN'T WE, LINDA.
SURE. WHY NOT.
I WAS EXPLAINING DRAMATIC STRUCTURE. MANY STORIES ARE SOMEWHAT FORMULAIC ...MOVIES, IN PARTICULAR.

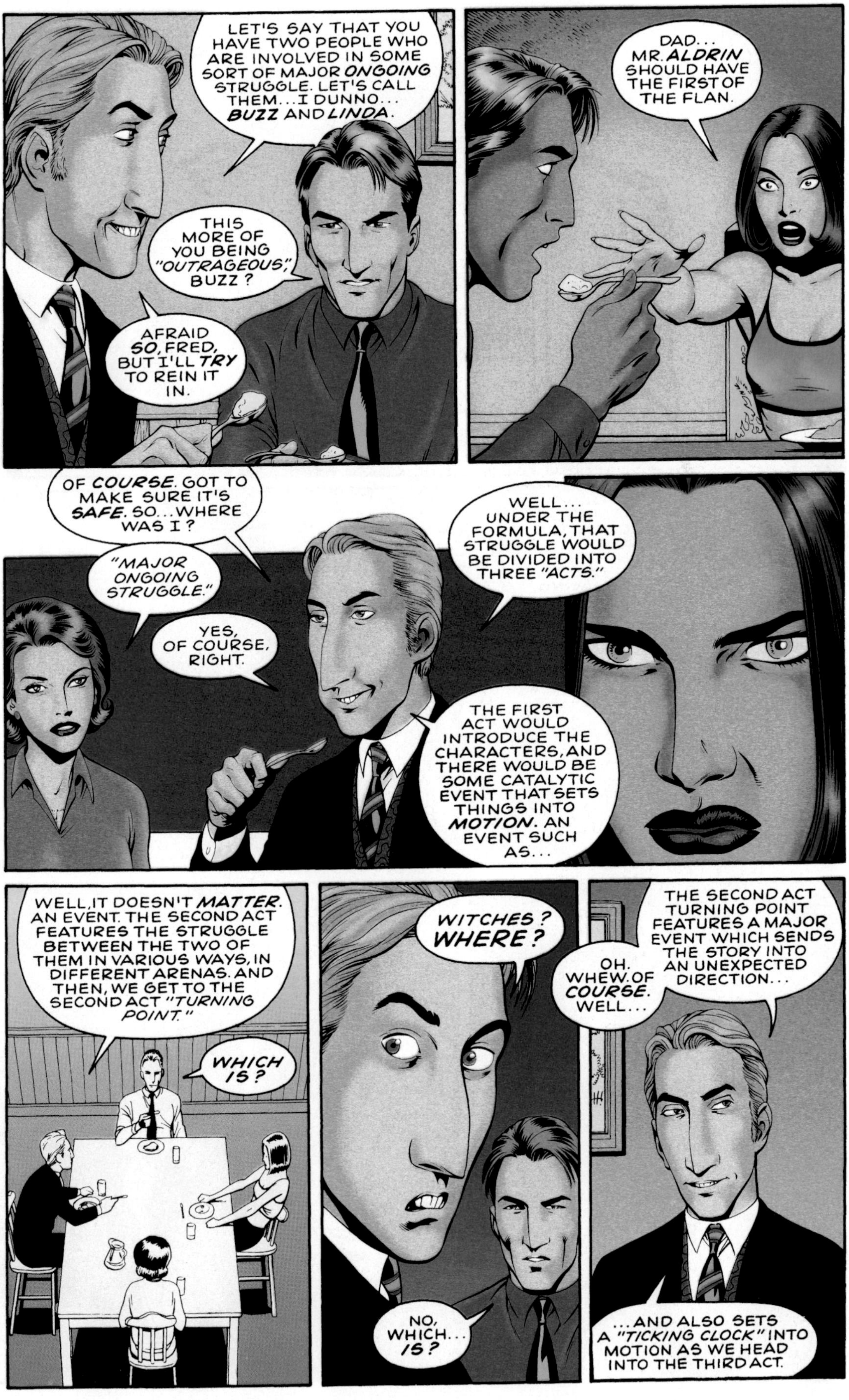
LET'S SAY THAT YOU HAVE TWO PEOPLE WHO ARE INVOLVED IN SOME SORT OF MAJOR *ONGOING* STRUGGLE. LET'S CALL THEM... I DUNNO... *BUZZ* AND *LINDA*.
THIS MORE OF YOU BEING *"OUTRAGEOUS,"* BUZZ?
AFRAID *SO,* FRED, BUT I'LL *TRY* TO REIN IT IN.
DAD... MR. *ALDRIN* SHOULD HAVE THE FIRST OF THE FLAN.
OF *COURSE*. GOT TO MAKE SURE IT'S *SAFE*. SO... WHERE WAS I?
"MAJOR ONGOING STRUGGLE."
YES, OF COURSE, RIGHT.
WELL... UNDER THE FORMULA, THAT STRUGGLE WOULD BE DIVIDED INTO THREE *"ACTS."*
THE FIRST ACT WOULD INTRODUCE THE CHARACTERS, AND THERE WOULD BE SOME CATALYTIC EVENT THAT SETS THINGS INTO *MOTION*. AN EVENT SUCH AS...
WELL, IT DOESN'T *MATTER*. AN EVENT. THE SECOND ACT FEATURES THE STRUGGLE BETWEEN THE TWO OF THEM IN VARIOUS WAYS, IN DIFFERENT ARENAS. AND THEN, WE GET TO THE SECOND ACT *"TURNING POINT."*
WHICH IS?
WITCHES? WHERE?
NO, WHICH... *IS?*
OH. WHEW. OF *COURSE*. WELL...
THE SECOND ACT TURNING POINT FEATURES A MAJOR EVENT WHICH SENDS THE STORY INTO AN UNEXPECTED DIRECTION...
...AND ALSO SETS A *"TICKING CLOCK"* INTO MOTION AS WE HEAD INTO THE THIRD ACT.

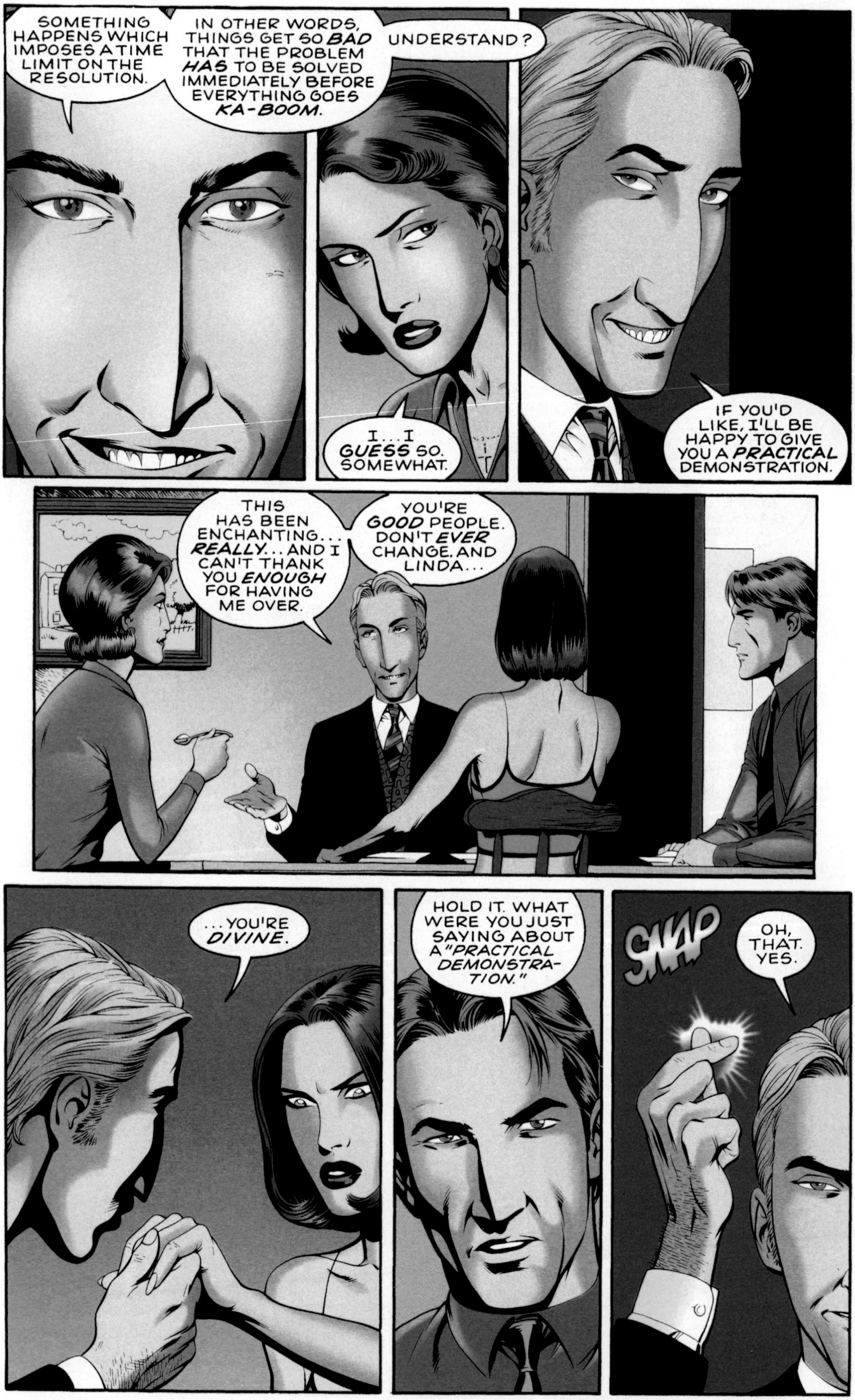
SOMETHING HAPPENS WHICH IMPOSES A TIME LIMIT ON THE RESOLUTION.
IN OTHER WORDS, THINGS GET SO BAD THAT THE PROBLEM HAS TO BE SOLVED IMMEDIATELY BEFORE EVERYTHING GOES KA-BOOM.
UNDERSTAND?
I...I GUESS SO. SOMEWHAT.
IF YOU'D LIKE, I'LL BE HAPPY TO GIVE YOU A PRACTICAL DEMONSTRATION.
THIS HAS BEEN ENCHANTING... REALLY... AND I CAN'T THANK YOU ENOUGH FOR HAVING ME OVER.
YOU'RE GOOD PEOPLE. DON'T EVER CHANGE. AND LINDA...
...YOU'RE DIVINE.
HOLD IT. WHAT WERE YOU JUST SAYING ABOUT A "PRACTICAL DEMONSTRATION."
SNAP
OH, THAT. YES.

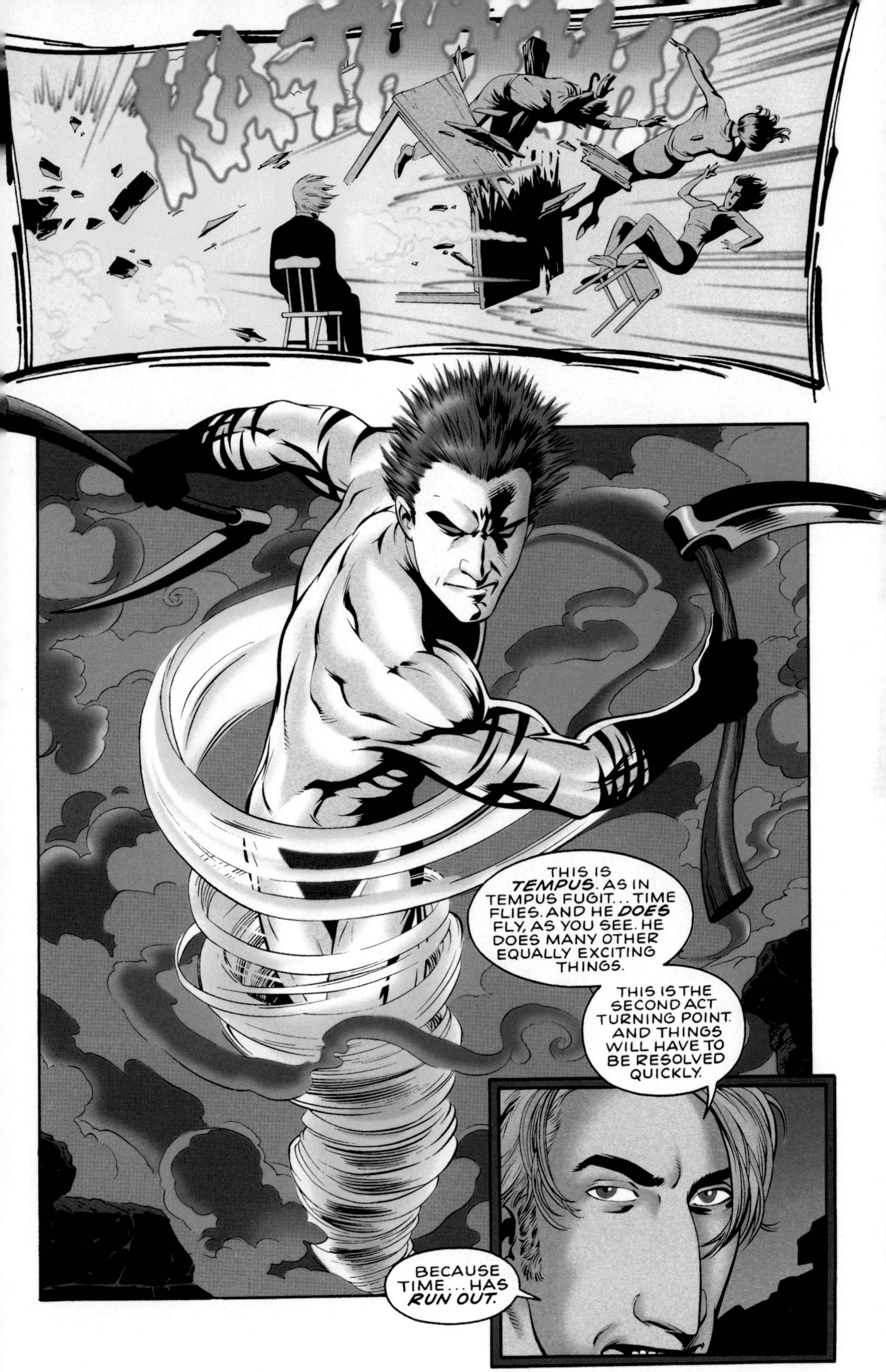
THIS IS *TEMPUS*. AS IN TEMPUS FUGIT... TIME FLIES. AND HE *DOES* FLY, AS YOU SEE. HE DOES MANY OTHER EQUALLY EXCITING THINGS.
THIS IS THE SECOND ACT TURNING POINT. AND THINGS WILL HAVE TO BE RESOLVED QUICKLY.
BECAUSE TIME... HAS *RUN OUT*.

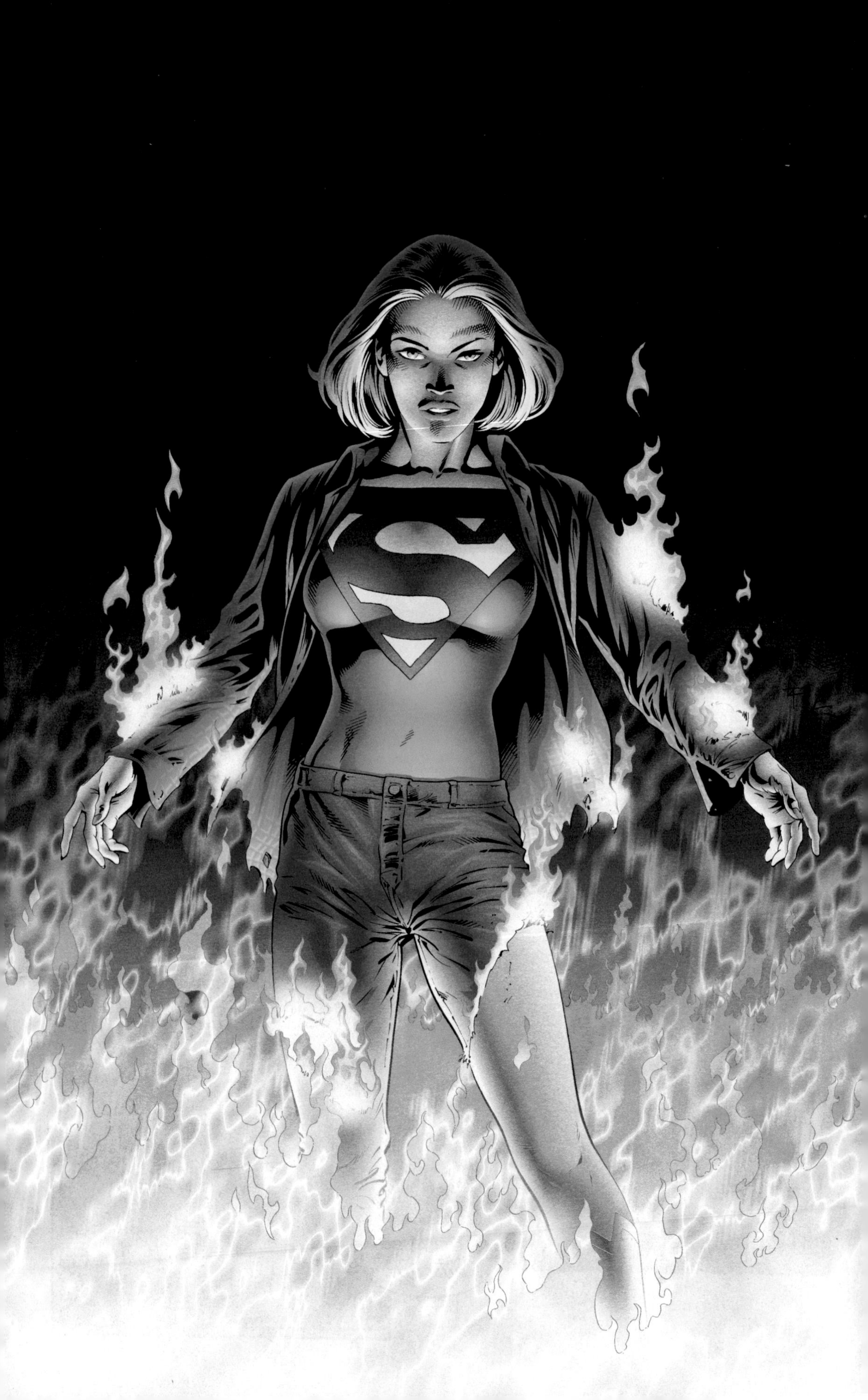

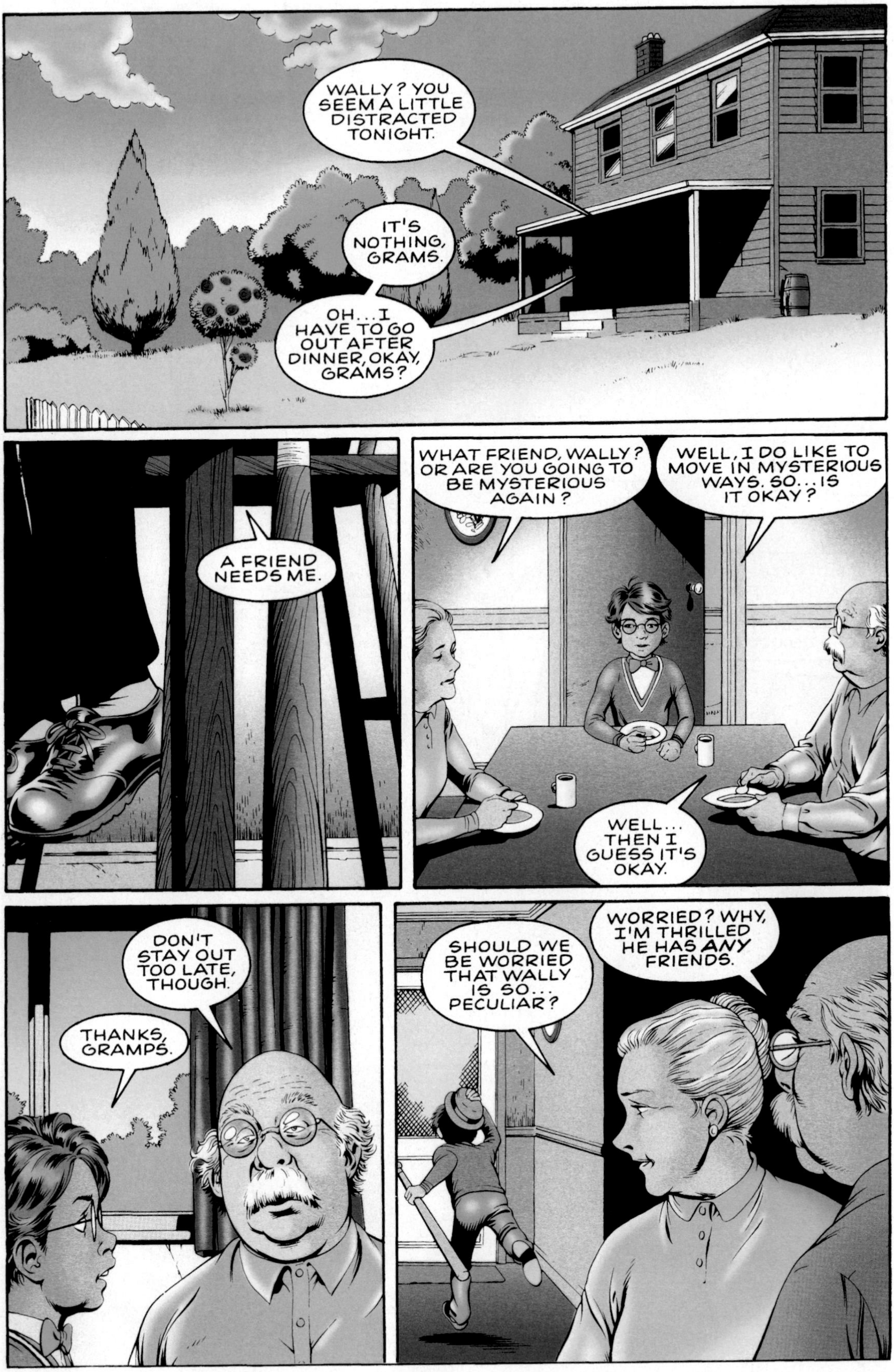
WALLY? YOU SEEM A LITTLE DISTRACTED TONIGHT.
IT'S NOTHING, GRAMS.
OH...I HAVE TO GO OUT AFTER DINNER, OKAY, GRAMS?
A FRIEND NEEDS ME.
WHAT FRIEND, WALLY? OR ARE YOU GOING TO BE MYSTERIOUS AGAIN?
WELL, I DO LIKE TO MOVE IN MYSTERIOUS WAYS. SO...IS IT OKAY?
WELL... THEN I GUESS IT'S OKAY.
DON'T STAY OUT TOO LATE, THOUGH.
THANKS, GRAMPS.
SHOULD WE BE WORRIED THAT WALLY IS SO... PECULIAR?
WORRIED? WHY, I'M THRILLED HE HAS ANY FRIENDS.

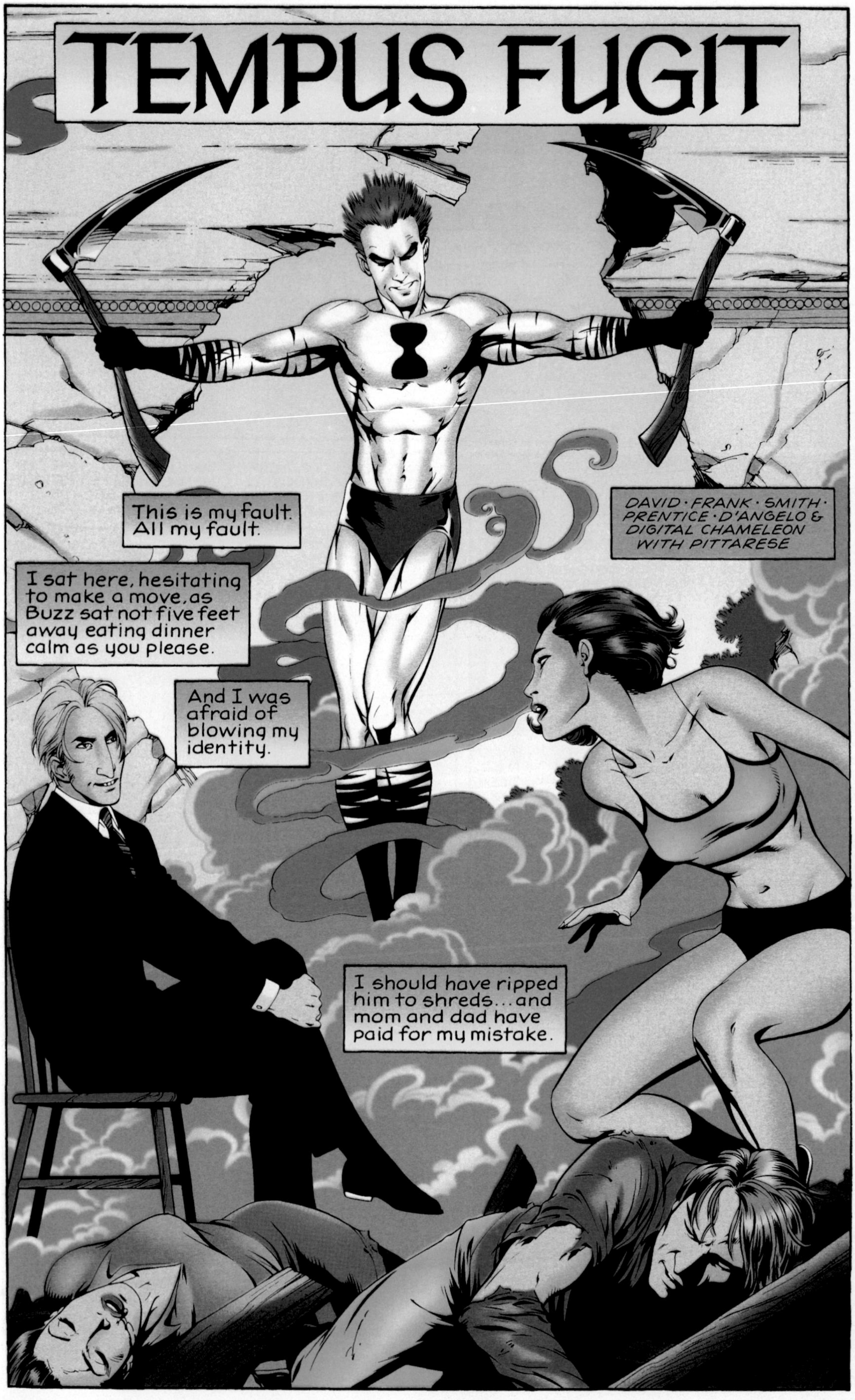
TEMPUS FUGIT
This is my fault. All my fault.
DAVID · FRANK · SMITH · PRENTICE · D'ANGELO & DIGITAL CHAMELEON WITH PITTARESE
I sat here, hesitating to make a move, as Buzz sat not five feet away eating dinner calm as you please.
And I was afraid of blowing my identity.
I should have ripped him to shreds... and mom and dad have paid for my mistake.

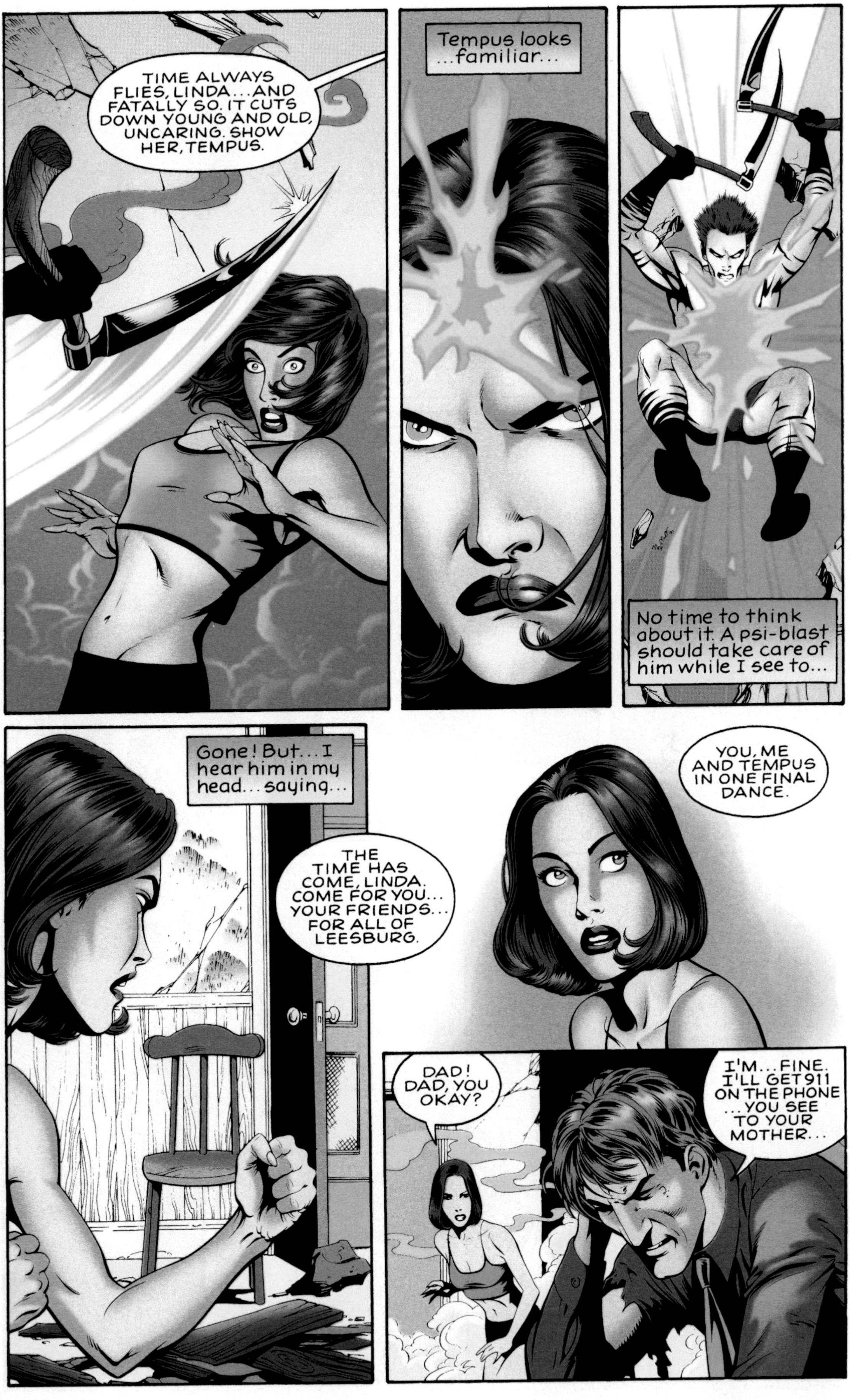
TIME ALWAYS FLIES, LINDA... AND FATALLY SO. IT CUTS DOWN YOUNG AND OLD, UNCARING. SHOW HER, TEMPUS.
Tempus looks ...familiar...
No time to think about it. A psi-blast should take care of him while I see to...
Gone! But... I hear him in my head... saying...
THE TIME HAS COME, LINDA. COME FOR YOU... YOUR FRIENDS... FOR ALL OF LEESBURG.
YOU, ME AND TEMPUS IN ONE FINAL DANCE.
DAD! DAD, YOU OKAY?
I'M... FINE. I'LL GET 911 ON THE PHONE ...YOU SEE TO YOUR MOTHER...

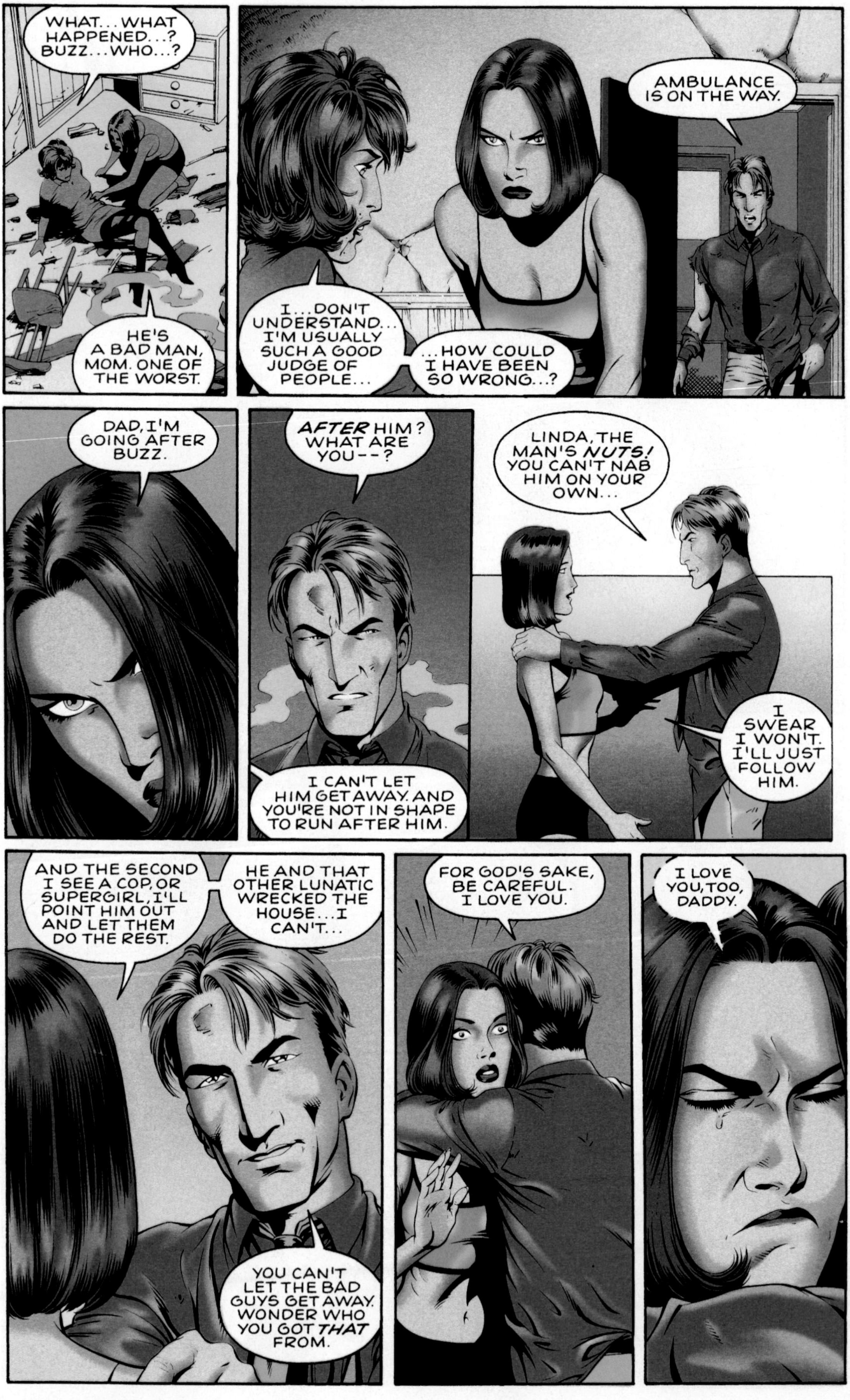
WHAT... WHAT HAPPENED...? BUZZ... WHO...?
HE'S A BAD MAN, MOM. ONE OF THE WORST.
I... DON'T UNDERSTAND... I'M USUALLY SUCH A GOOD JUDGE OF PEOPLE...
...HOW COULD I HAVE BEEN SO WRONG...?
AMBULANCE IS ON THE WAY.
DAD, I'M GOING AFTER BUZZ.
AFTER HIM? WHAT ARE YOU--?
I CAN'T LET HIM GET AWAY. AND YOU'RE NOT IN SHAPE TO RUN AFTER HIM.
LINDA, THE MAN'S NUTS! YOU CAN'T NAB HIM ON YOUR OWN...
I SWEAR I WON'T. I'LL JUST FOLLOW HIM.
AND THE SECOND I SEE A COP, OR SUPERGIRL, I'LL POINT HIM OUT AND LET THEM DO THE REST.
HE AND THAT OTHER LUNATIC WRECKED THE HOUSE... I CAN'T...
YOU CAN'T LET THE BAD GUYS GET AWAY. WONDER WHO YOU GOT THAT FROM.
FOR GOD'S SAKE, BE CAREFUL. I LOVE YOU.
I LOVE YOU, TOO, DADDY.

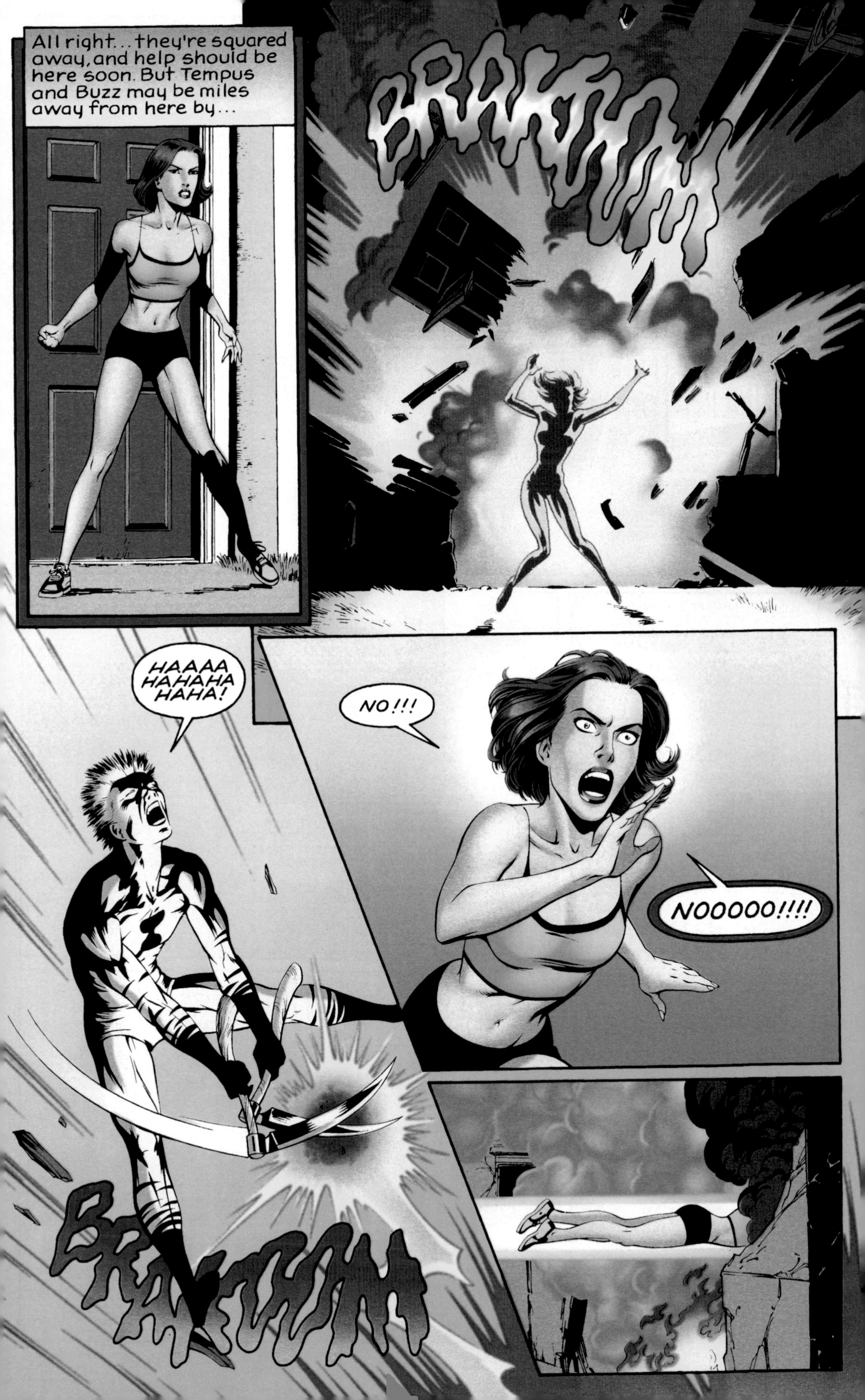
All right... they're squared away, and help should be here soon. But Tempus and Buzz may be miles away from here by...
BRAKOOM
HAAAA HAHAHA HAHA!
NO!!!
NOOOOO!!!!
BRAKOOM

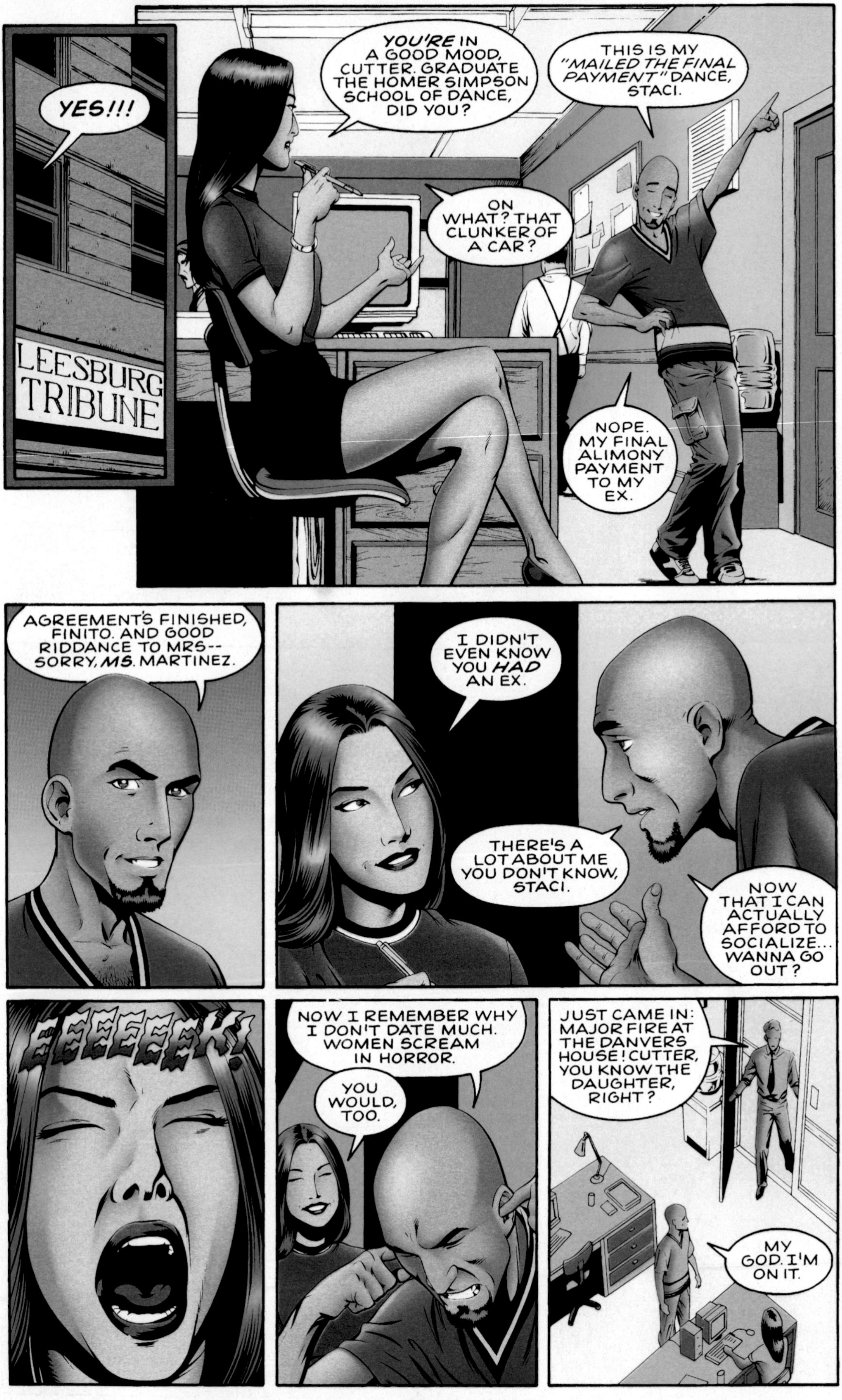
YES!!!
LEESBURG TRIBUNE
YOU'RE IN A GOOD MOOD, CUTTER. GRADUATE THE HOMER SIMPSON SCHOOL OF DANCE, DID YOU?
THIS IS MY "MAILED THE FINAL PAYMENT" DANCE, STACI.
ON WHAT? THAT CLUNKER OF A CAR?
NOPE. MY FINAL ALIMONY PAYMENT TO MY EX.
AGREEMENT'S FINISHED, FINITO. AND GOOD RIDDANCE TO MRS-- SORRY, MS. MARTINEZ.
I DIDN'T EVEN KNOW YOU HAD AN EX.
THERE'S A LOT ABOUT ME YOU DON'T KNOW, STACI.
NOW THAT I CAN ACTUALLY AFFORD TO SOCIALIZE... WANNA GO OUT?
EEEEEEK!
NOW I REMEMBER WHY I DON'T DATE MUCH. WOMEN SCREAM IN HORROR.
YOU WOULD, TOO.
JUST CAME IN: MAJOR FIRE AT THE DANVERS HOUSE! CUTTER, YOU KNOW THE DAUGHTER, RIGHT?
MY GOD. I'M ON IT.

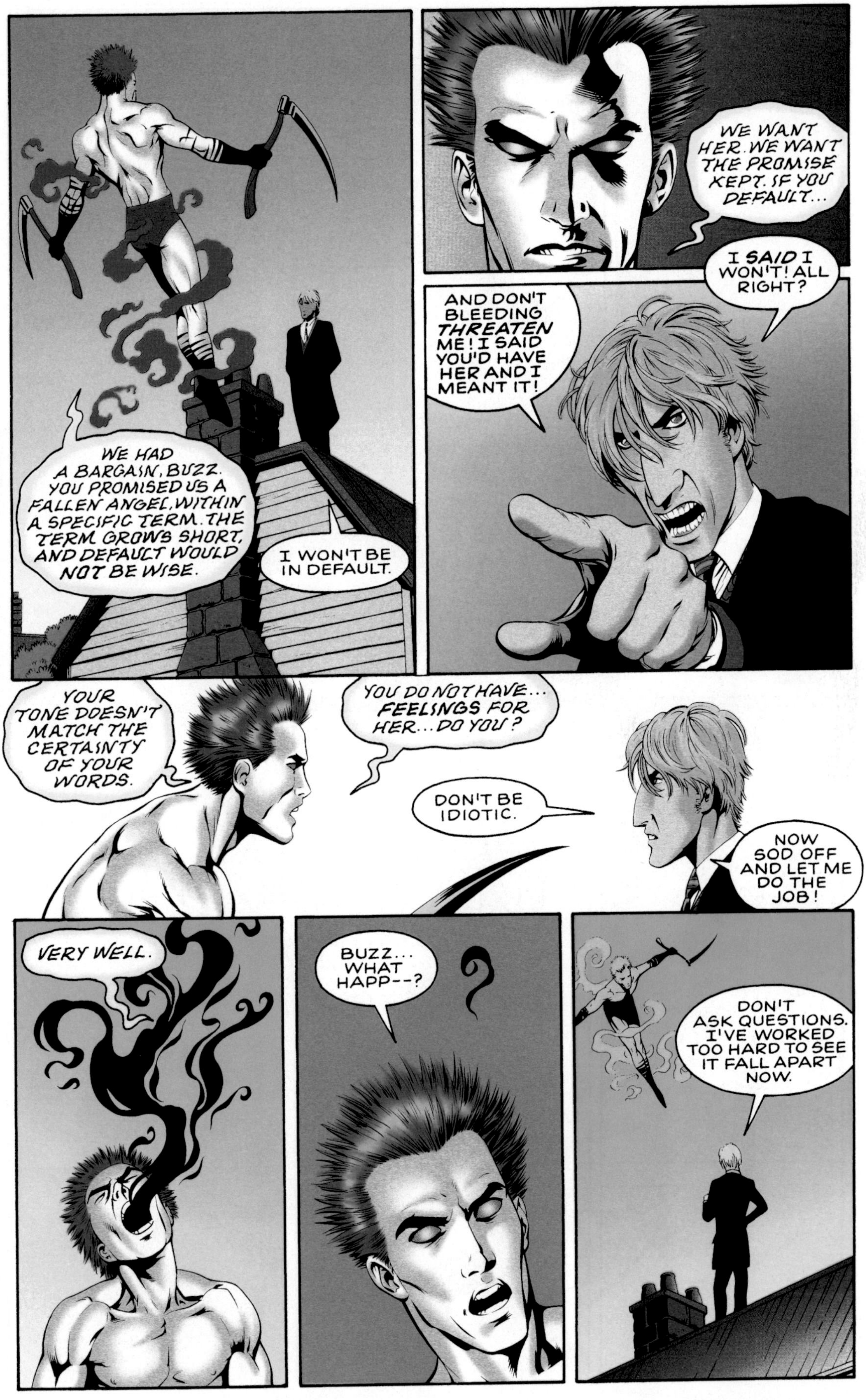
WE HAD A BARGAIN, BUZZ. YOU PROMISED US A FALLEN ANGEL, WITHIN A SPECIFIC TERM. THE TERM GROWS SHORT, AND DEFAULT WOULD NOT BE WISE.
I WON'T BE IN DEFAULT.
WE WANT HER. WE WANT THE PROMISE KEPT. IF YOU DEFAULT...
I SAID I WON'T! ALL RIGHT?
AND DON'T BLEEDING THREATEN ME! I SAID YOU'D HAVE HER AND I MEANT IT!
YOUR TONE DOESN'T MATCH THE CERTAINTY OF YOUR WORDS.
YOU DO NOT HAVE... FEELINGS FOR HER... DO YOU?
DON'T BE IDIOTIC.
NOW SOD OFF AND LET ME DO THE JOB!
VERY WELL.
BUZZ... WHAT HAPP--?
DON'T ASK QUESTIONS. I'VE WORKED TOO HARD TO SEE IT FALL APART NOW.

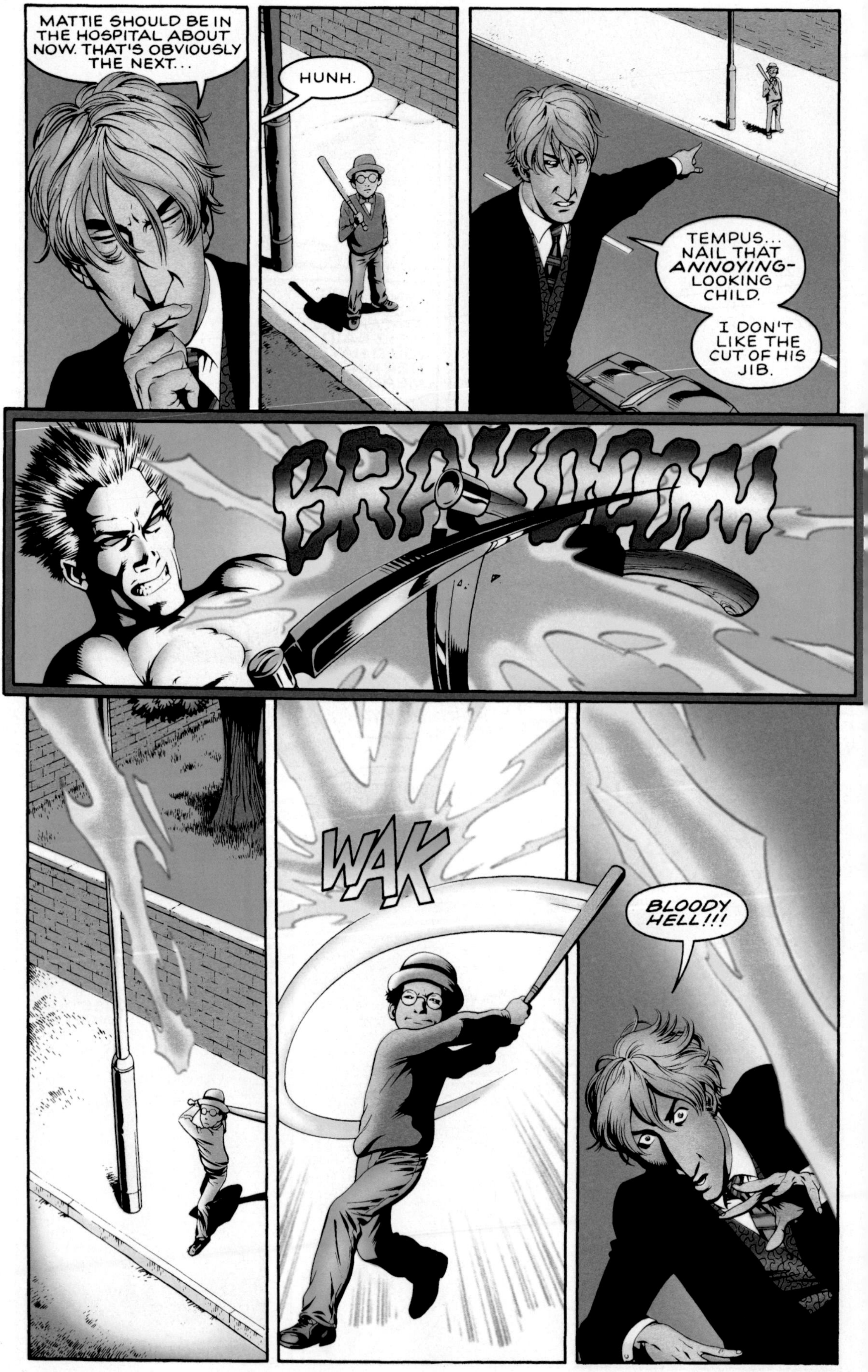
MATTIE SHOULD BE IN THE HOSPITAL ABOUT NOW. THAT'S OBVIOUSLY THE NEXT...
HUNH.
TEMPUS... NAIL THAT ANNOYING-LOOKING CHILD.
I DON'T LIKE THE CUT OF HIS JIB.
BRAKOOOM
WAK
BLOODY HELL!!!

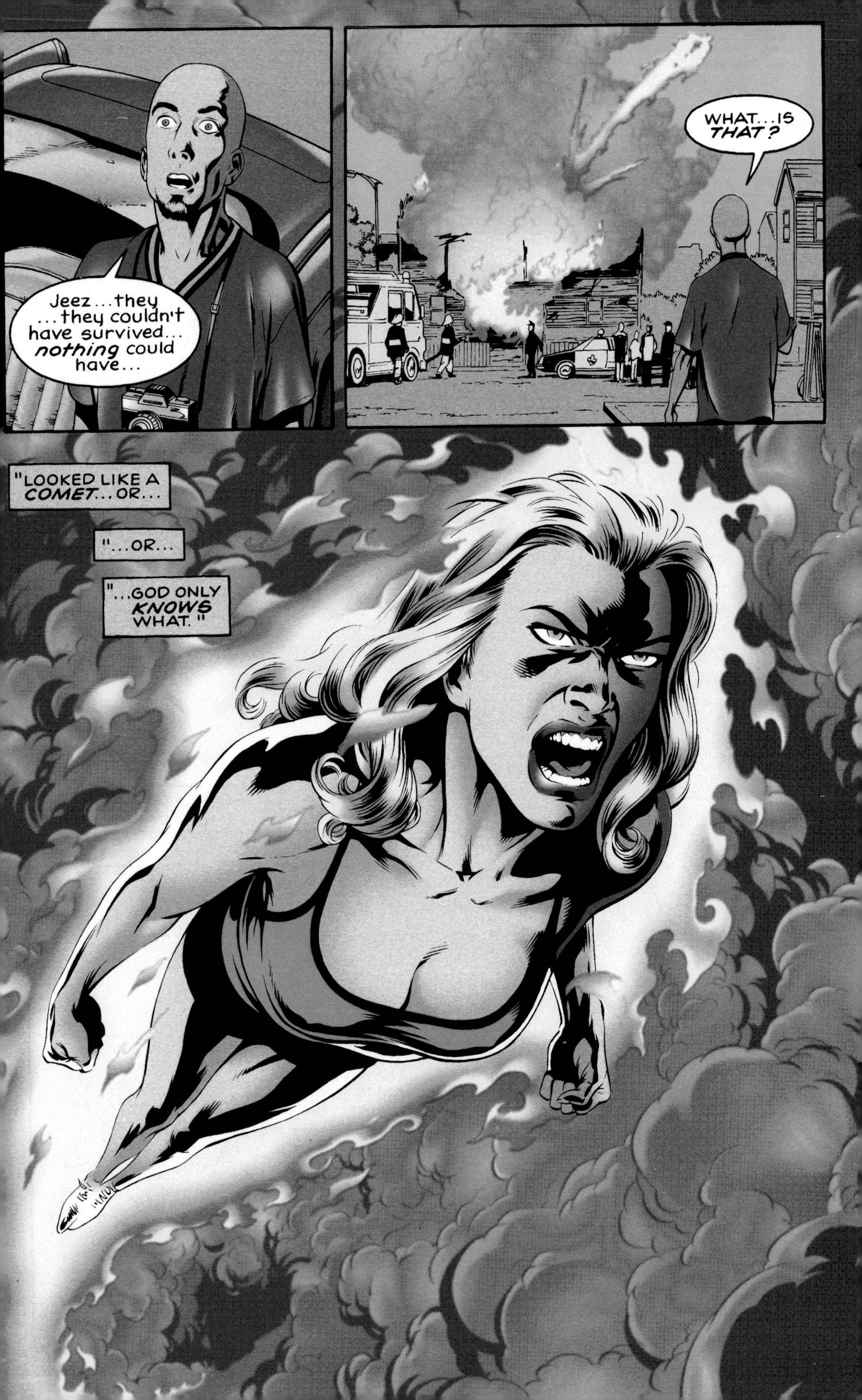
Jeez...they ...they couldn't have survived... *nothing* could have...
WHAT...IS *THAT*?
"LOOKED LIKE A *COMET*...OR...
"...OR...
"...GOD ONLY *KNOWS* WHAT."

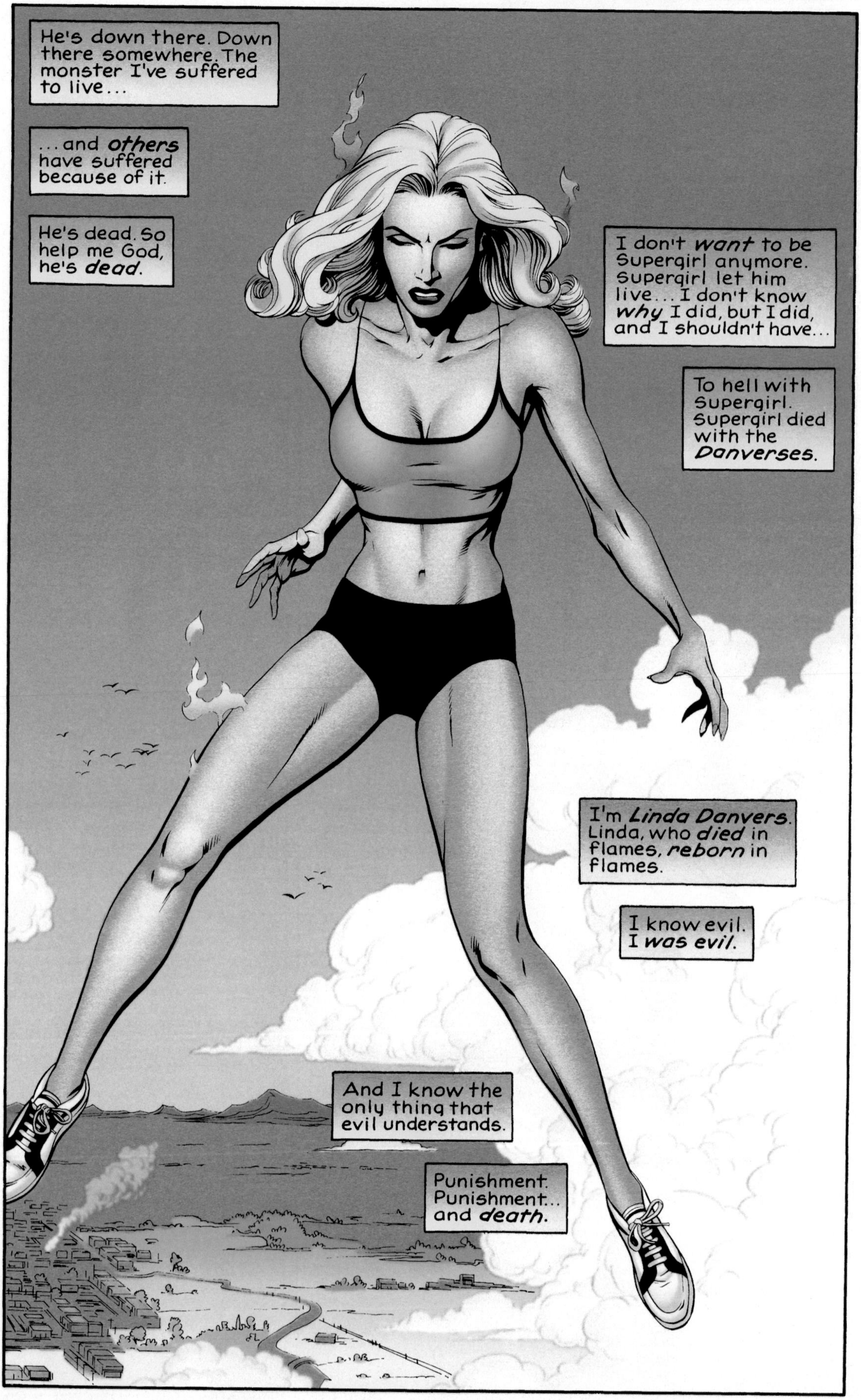
He's down there. Down there somewhere. The monster I've suffered to live...
...and *others* have suffered because of it.
He's dead. So help me God, he's *dead*.
I don't *want* to be Supergirl anymore. Supergirl let him live... I don't know *why* I did, but I did, and I shouldn't have...
To hell with Supergirl. Supergirl died with the *Danverses*.
I'm *Linda Danvers*. Linda, who *died* in flames, *reborn* in flames.
I know evil. I *was evil*.
And I know the only thing that evil understands.
Punishment. Punishment... and *death*.

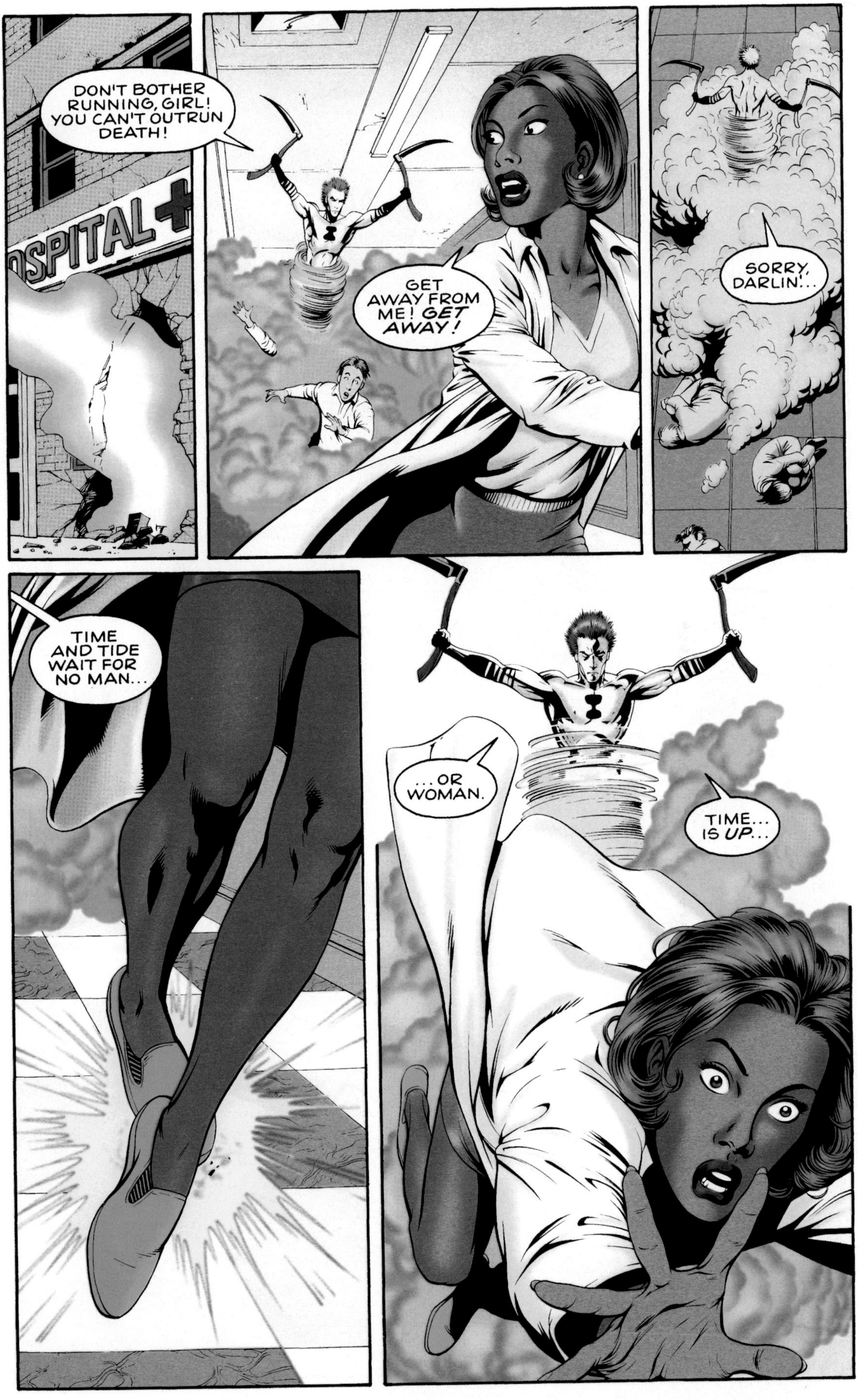

OSPITAL
DON'T BOTHER RUNNING, GIRL! YOU CAN'T OUTRUN DEATH!
GET AWAY FROM ME! GET AWAY!
SORRY, DARLIN'...
TIME AND TIDE WAIT FOR NO MAN...
...OR WOMAN.
TIME... IS UP...

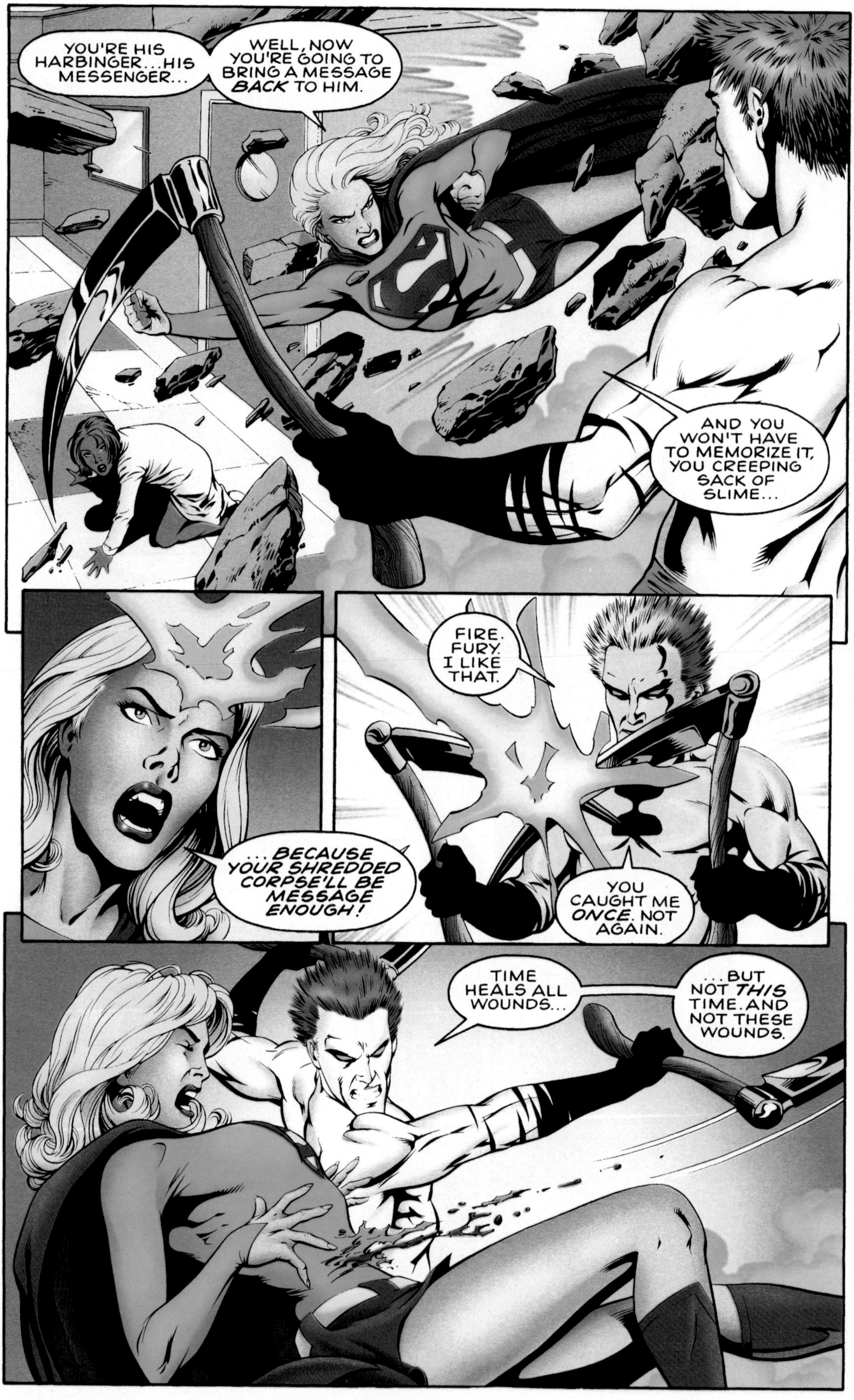
YOU'RE HIS HARBINGER...HIS MESSENGER...
WELL, NOW YOU'RE GOING TO BRING A MESSAGE BACK TO HIM.
AND YOU WON'T HAVE TO MEMORIZE IT, YOU CREEPING SACK OF SLIME...
...BECAUSE YOUR SHREDDED CORPSE'LL BE MESSAGE ENOUGH!
FIRE. FURY. I LIKE THAT.
YOU CAUGHT ME ONCE. NOT AGAIN.
TIME HEALS ALL WOUNDS...
...BUT NOT THIS TIME. AND NOT THESE WOUNDS.

He cut me ...cut me twice...

He shouldn't have been able to do that.

He slices through my psi-defenses as if they're not even there.

Was it...against my will? Or did I...*allow* it...as if I need the final pain to drive me forward...to do what my soul screams to do...

Screams...

Screams with the pain of loss... the fury of vengeance, denied but demanded...

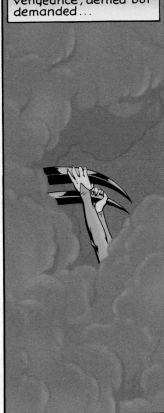

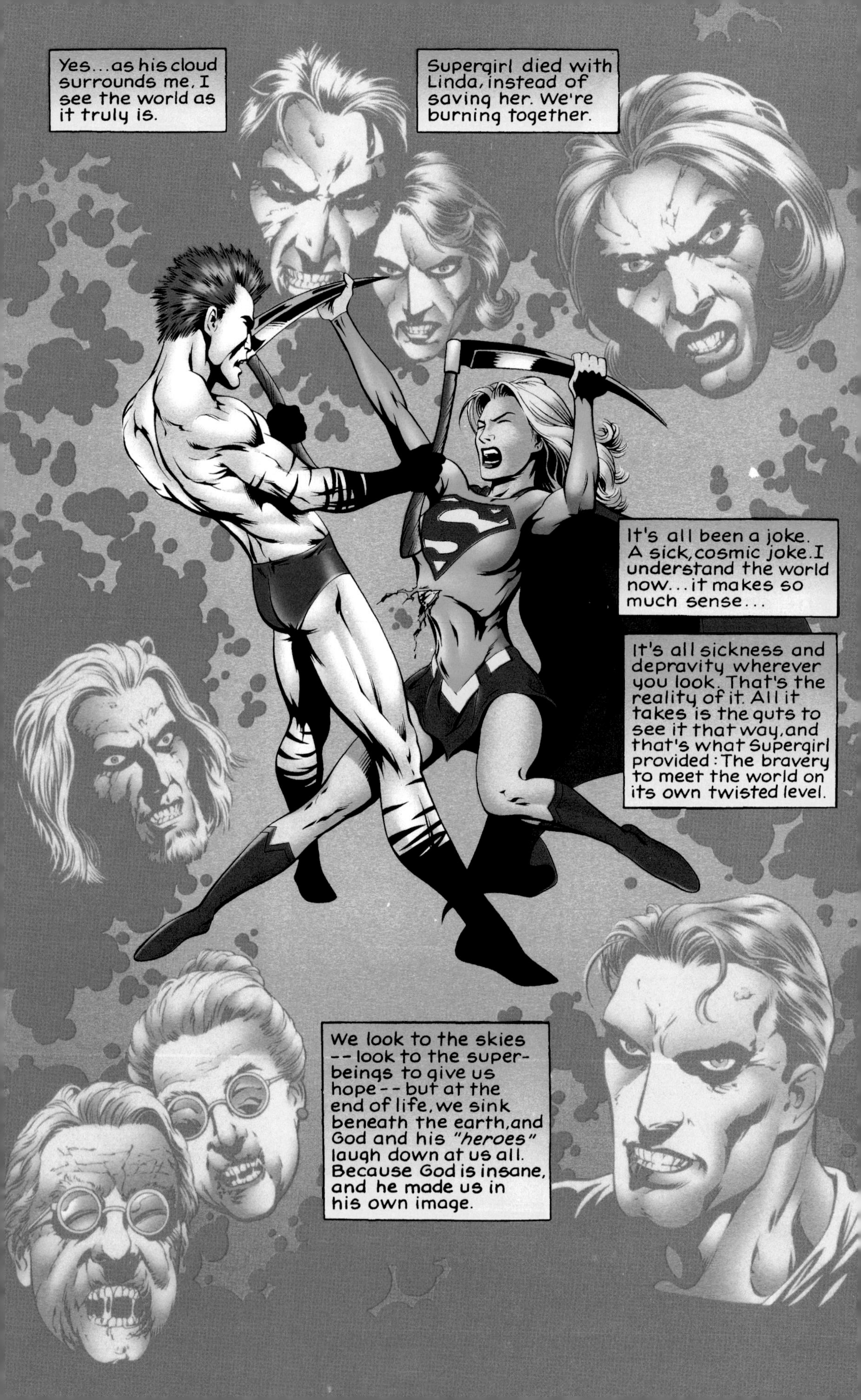
Yes...as his cloud surrounds me, I see the world as it truly is.
Supergirl died with Linda, instead of saving her. We're burning together.
It's all been a joke. A sick, cosmic joke. I understand the world now...it makes so much sense...
It's all sickness and depravity wherever you look. That's the reality of it. All it takes is the guts to see it that way, and that's what Supergirl provided: The bravery to meet the world on its own twisted level.
We look to the skies -- look to the super-beings to give us hope -- but at the end of life, we sink beneath the earth, and God and his "heroes" laugh down at us all. Because God is insane, and he made us in his own image.

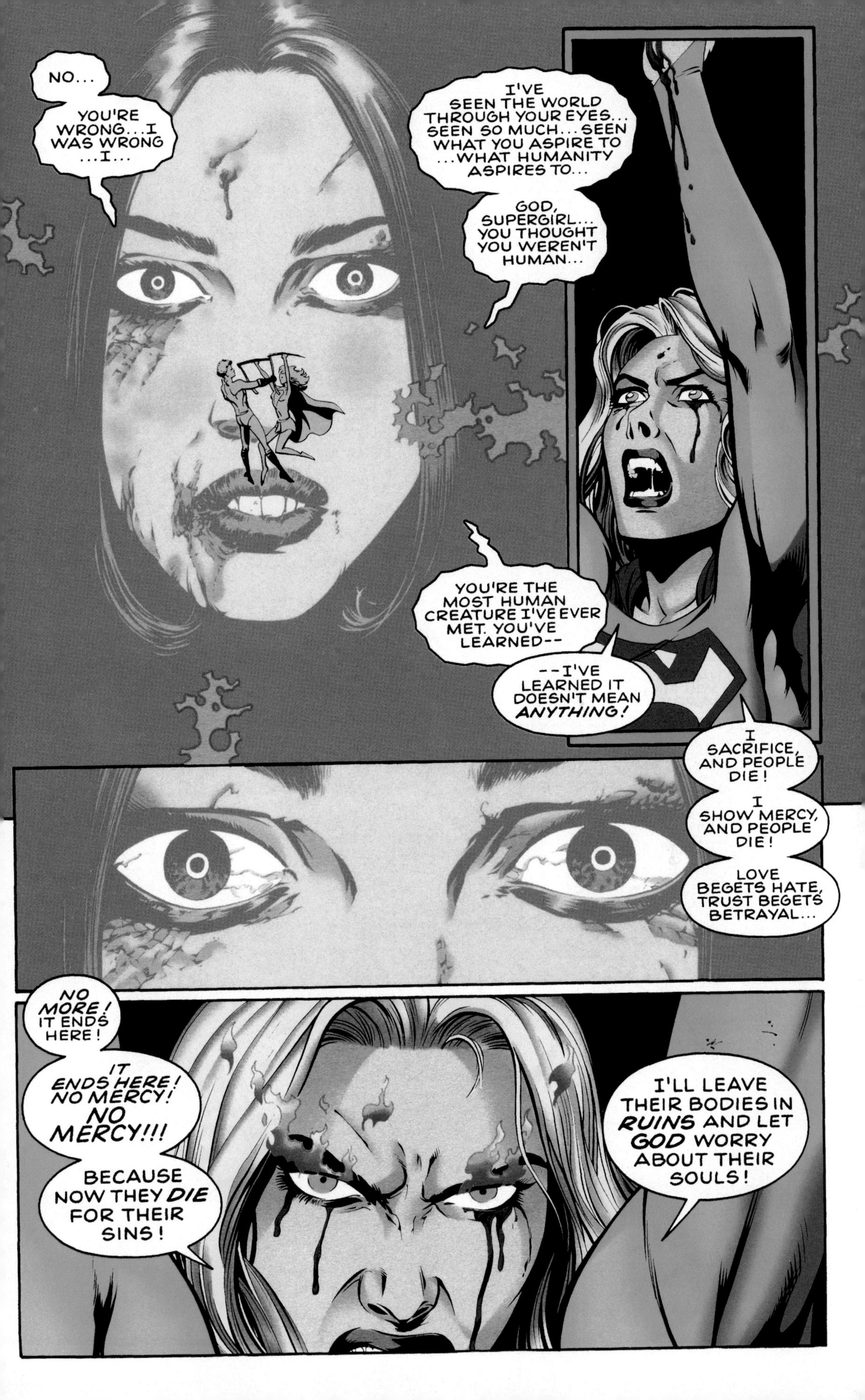
NO...
YOU'RE WRONG...I WAS WRONG ...I...
I'VE SEEN THE WORLD THROUGH YOUR EYES... SEEN SO MUCH...SEEN WHAT YOU ASPIRE TO ...WHAT HUMANITY ASPIRES TO...
GOD, SUPERGIRL... YOU THOUGHT YOU WEREN'T HUMAN...
YOU'RE THE MOST HUMAN CREATURE I'VE EVER MET. YOU'VE LEARNED--
--I'VE LEARNED IT DOESN'T MEAN ANYTHING!
I SACRIFICE, AND PEOPLE DIE!
I SHOW MERCY, AND PEOPLE DIE!
LOVE BEGETS HATE, TRUST BEGETS BETRAYAL...
NO MORE! IT ENDS HERE!
IT ENDS HERE! NO MERCY! NO MERCY!!!
BECAUSE NOW THEY DIE FOR THEIR SINS!
I'LL LEAVE THEIR BODIES IN RUINS AND LET GOD WORRY ABOUT THEIR SOULS!

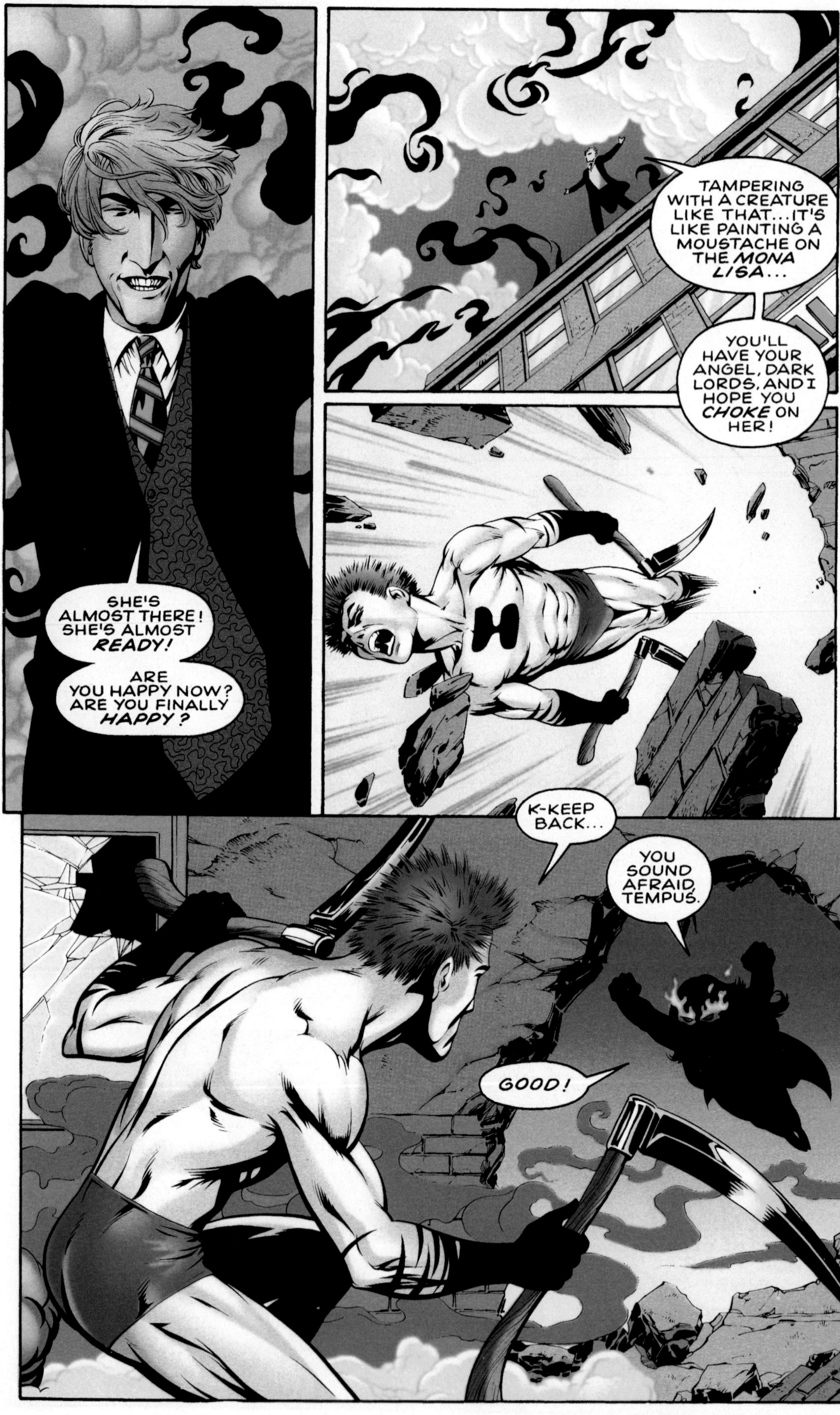
SHE'S ALMOST THERE! SHE'S ALMOST READY!
ARE YOU HAPPY NOW? ARE YOU FINALLY HAPPY?
TAMPERING WITH A CREATURE LIKE THAT...IT'S LIKE PAINTING A MOUSTACHE ON THE MONA LISA...
YOU'LL HAVE YOUR ANGEL, DARK LORDS, AND I HOPE YOU CHOKE ON HER!
K-KEEP BACK...
YOU SOUND AFRAID, TEMPUS.
GOOD!

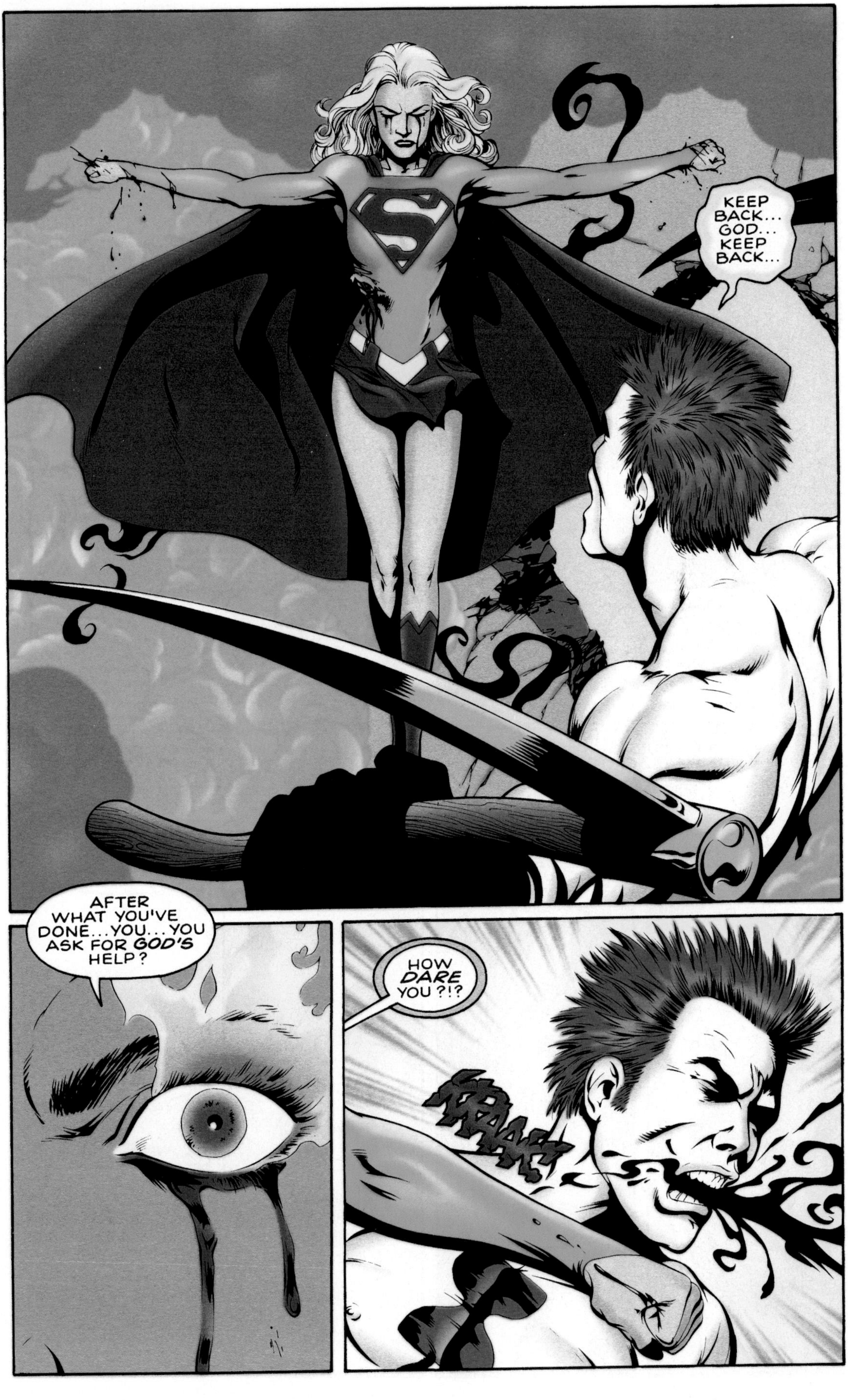
KEEP BACK... GOD... KEEP BACK...
AFTER WHAT YOU'VE DONE...YOU...YOU ASK FOR *GOD'S* HELP?
HOW *DARE* YOU?!?

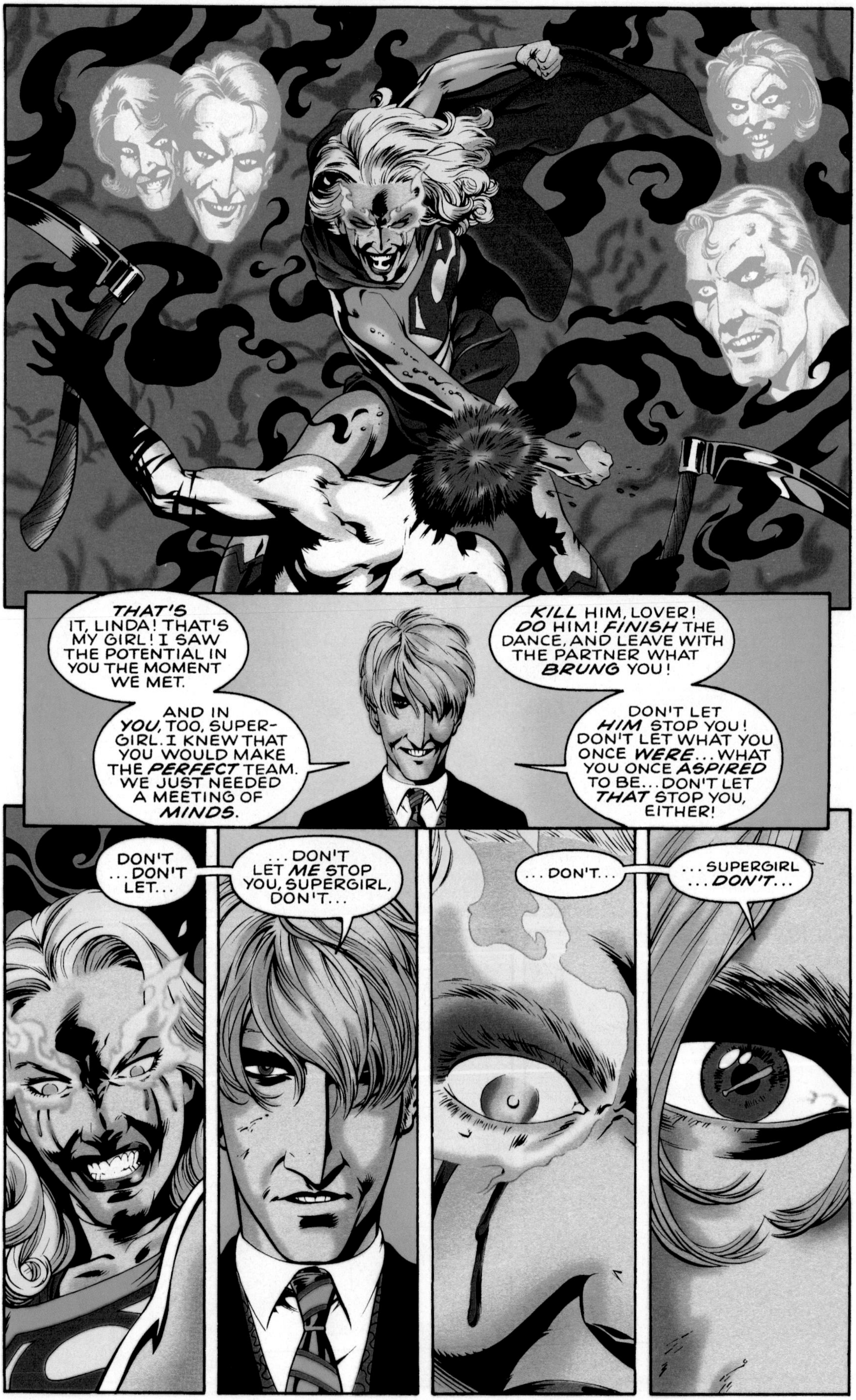
THAT'S IT, LINDA! THAT'S MY GIRL! I SAW THE POTENTIAL IN YOU THE MOMENT WE MET.
AND IN YOU, TOO, SUPER-GIRL. I KNEW THAT YOU WOULD MAKE THE PERFECT TEAM. WE JUST NEEDED A MEETING OF MINDS.
KILL HIM, LOVER! DO HIM! FINISH THE DANCE, AND LEAVE WITH THE PARTNER WHAT BRUNG YOU!
DON'T LET HIM STOP YOU! DON'T LET WHAT YOU ONCE WERE... WHAT YOU ONCE ASPIRED TO BE... DON'T LET THAT STOP YOU, EITHER!
DON'T ...DON'T LET...
...DON'T LET ME STOP YOU, SUPERGIRL, DON'T...
...DON'T...
...SUPERGIRL ...DON'T...

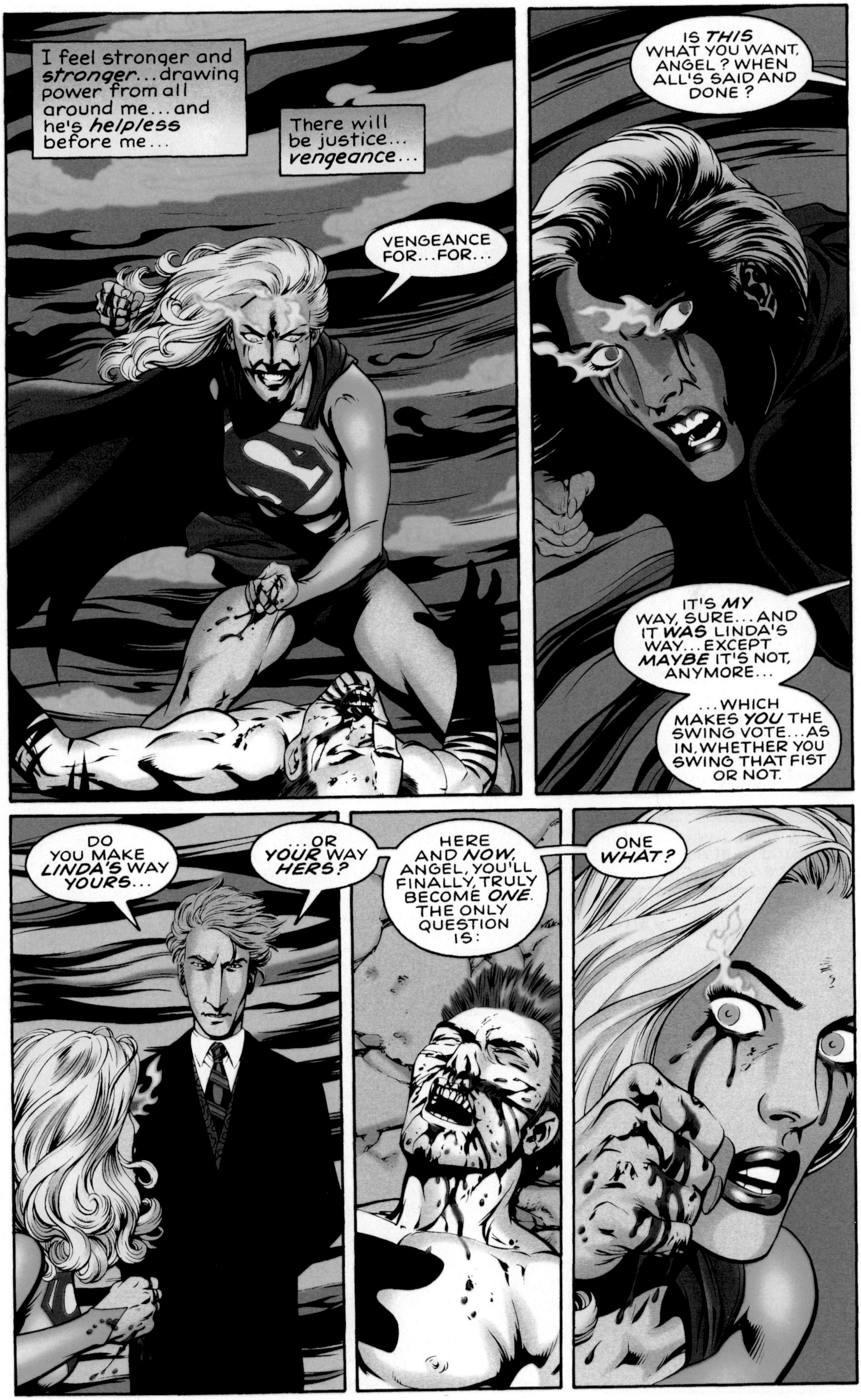
I feel stronger and stronger... drawing power from all around me... and he's helpless before me...
There will be justice... vengeance...
VENGEANCE FOR... FOR...
IS THIS WHAT YOU WANT, ANGEL? WHEN ALL'S SAID AND DONE?
IT'S MY WAY, SURE... AND IT WAS LINDA'S WAY... EXCEPT MAYBE IT'S NOT, ANYMORE...
...WHICH MAKES YOU THE SWING VOTE... AS IN, WHETHER YOU SWING THAT FIST OR NOT.
DO YOU MAKE LINDA'S WAY YOURS...
...OR YOUR WAY HERS?
HERE AND NOW, ANGEL, YOU'LL FINALLY, TRULY BECOME ONE. THE ONLY QUESTION IS:
ONE WHAT?

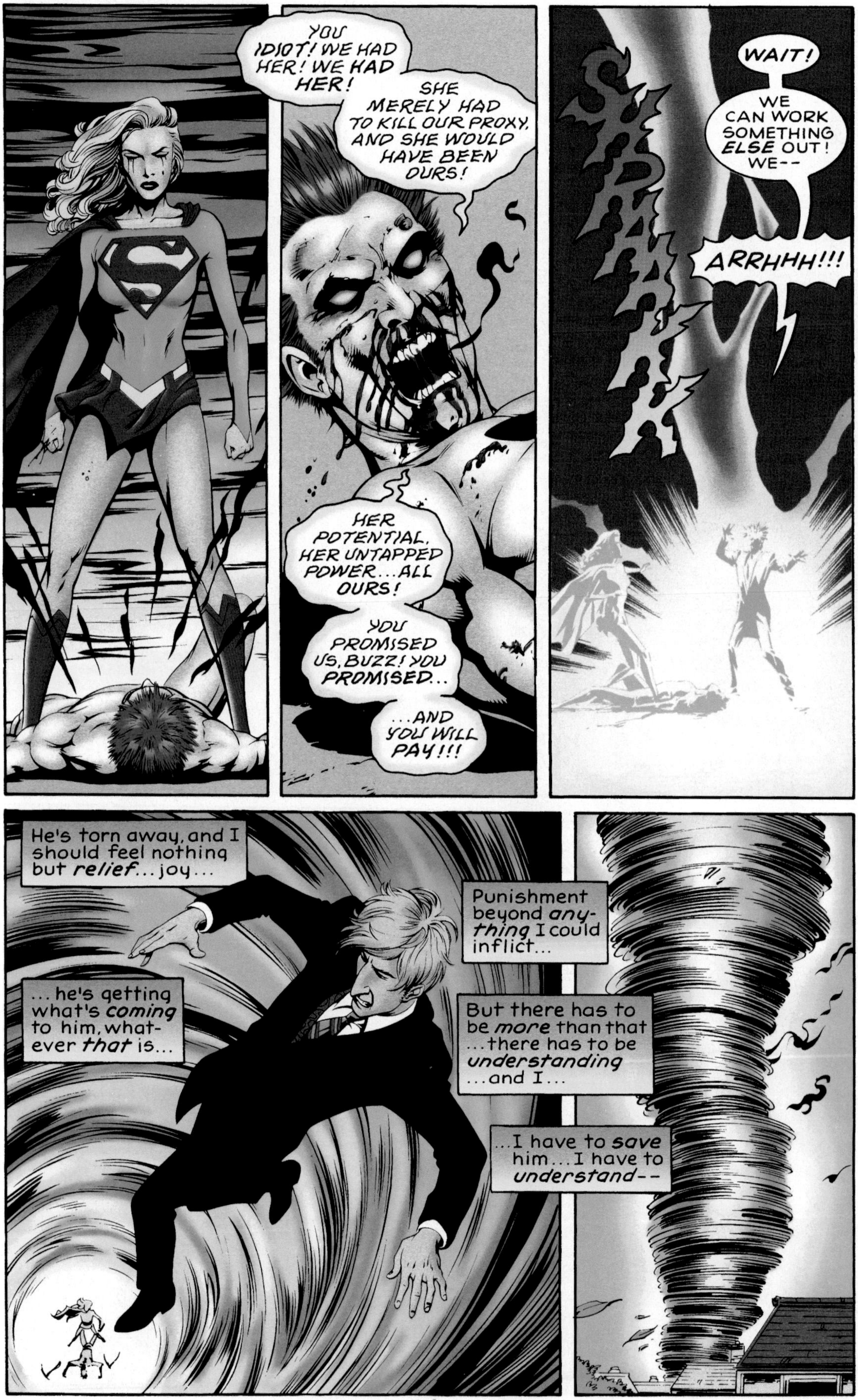
YOU IDIOT! WE HAD HER! WE HAD HER!
SHE MERELY HAD TO KILL OUR PROXY, AND SHE WOULD HAVE BEEN OURS!
HER POTENTIAL, HER UNTAPPED POWER... ALL OURS!
YOU PROMISED US, BUZZ! YOU PROMISED...
...AND YOU WILL PAY!!!
SPRAKK
WAIT!
WE CAN WORK SOMETHING ELSE OUT! WE--
ARRHHH!!!
He's torn away, and I should feel nothing but relief... joy...
... he's getting what's coming to him, whatever that is...
Punishment beyond anything I could inflict...
But there has to be more than that ...there has to be understanding ...and I...
...I have to save him... I have to understand--

-- WHY?! WHY!?

I'M CLEAN OUT OF *ANSWERS*, ANGEL, LUV! SOMETIMES YOU HAVE TO TAKE THINGS...

...ON *FAITH*.

BRAKOOM

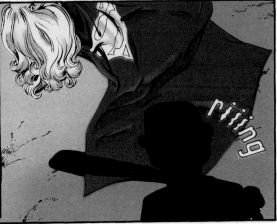

riiing

riiing

OH!

D...*Dick Malverne*?! Of ...course! He was Tempus ...in thrall to Buzz...

But how'd we get in my *apartment*? How did...

...*riinng*

ALL RIGHT, I'M COMING! JEEZ--!

riing

HELLO?

D...DAD? *DAD?*

LINDA? YOU'RE STILL THERE? I THOUGHT WE WERE HAVING DINNER TONIGHT.

ARE... ARE YOU AND MOM... *OKAY?*

OF *COURSE* WE'RE OKAY.

YES, THE HOUSE, TOO. WHAT KIND OF QUESTION IS...?

YEAH, I GUESS WE CAN MAKE IT ANOTHER NIGHT. FINE. SURE.

I TELL YOU, SYLVIA, LINDA IS THE *FLIGHTIEST* GIRL I'VE EVER KNOWN. *COMPLETELY* IRRESPONSIBLE.

I KNOW, FRED, BUT SHE'S ALL OURS, AND WE HAVE TO TRUST AND LOVE HER.

YOU MAKE A CHILD, DO THE BEST YOU CAN...

"...AND THEN JUST HAVE FAITH IT WILL ALL WORK OUT IN *THE END*."

DAI
GARY F
THANKS R
FOR SUPPO

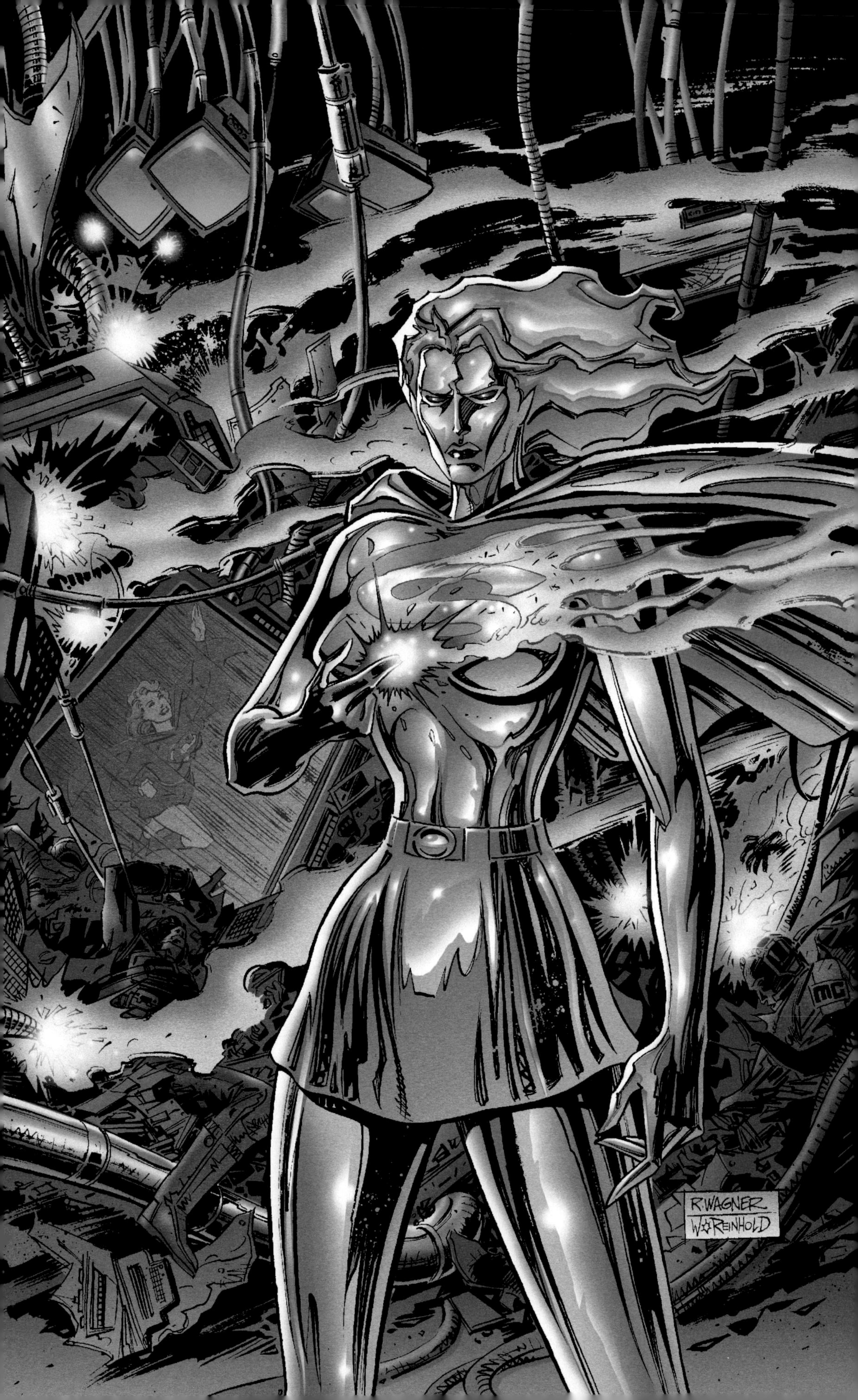
R.WAGNER
W☆REINHOLD

EARTH IS DEAD.

THOSE WHO ONCE MIGHT
HAVE CALLED IT HOME
ARE LONG SCATTERED
TO THE ENDLESS STARS.

BUT IN THAT SCATTERING,
ON A THOUSAND
DIFFERENT WORLDS,
BY A THOUSAND
DIFFERENT WAYS . . .
EARTH'S GREATEST
LEGENDS LIVE ON.

LEGENDS OF THE DEAD EARTH

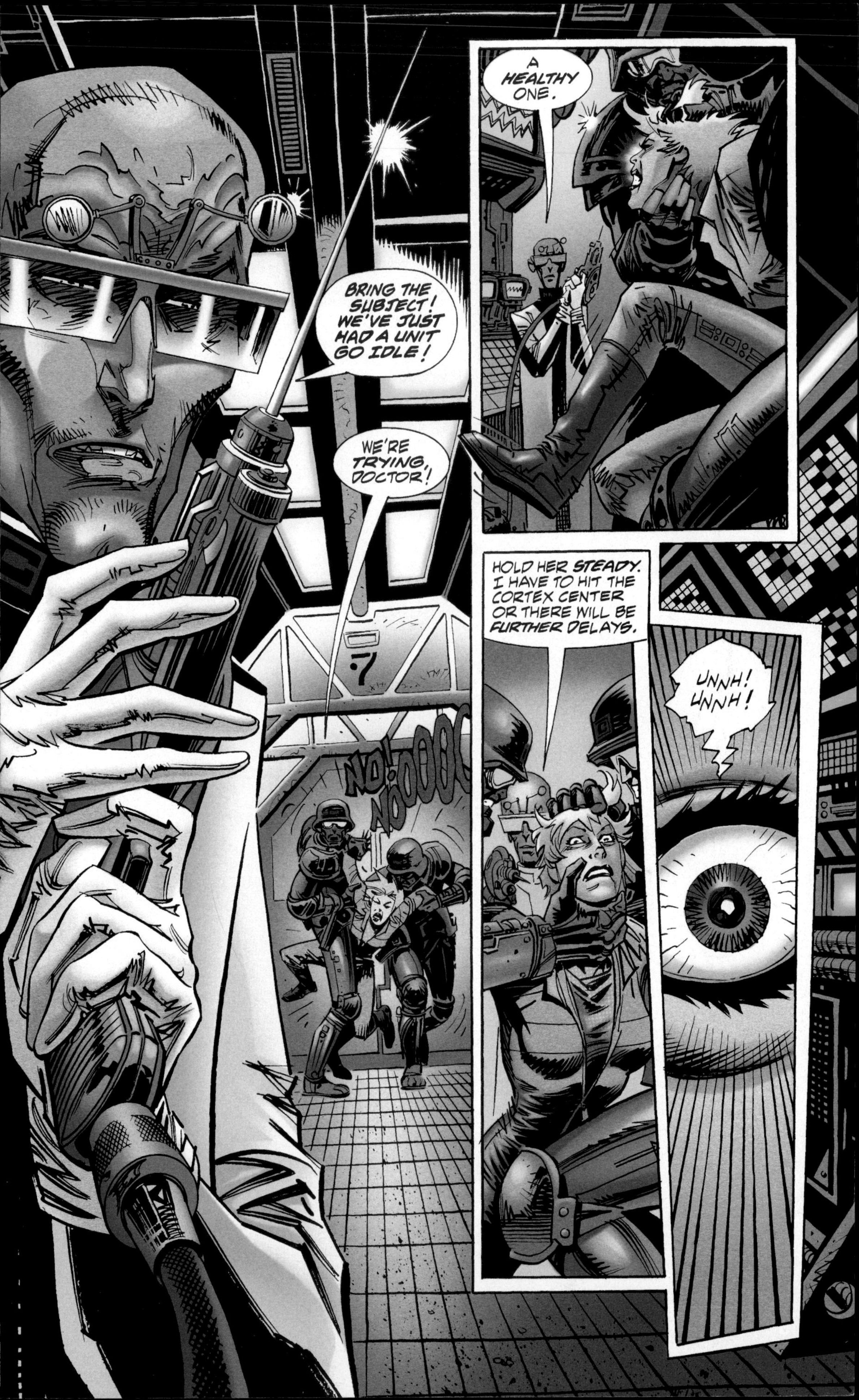
BRING THE SUBJECT! WE'VE JUST HAD A UNIT GO IDLE!
WE'RE TRYING, DOCTOR!
NO! NOOOOO
A HEALTHY ONE.
HOLD HER STEADY. I HAVE TO HIT THE CORTEX CENTER OR THERE WILL BE FURTHER DELAYS.
UNNH! UNNH!

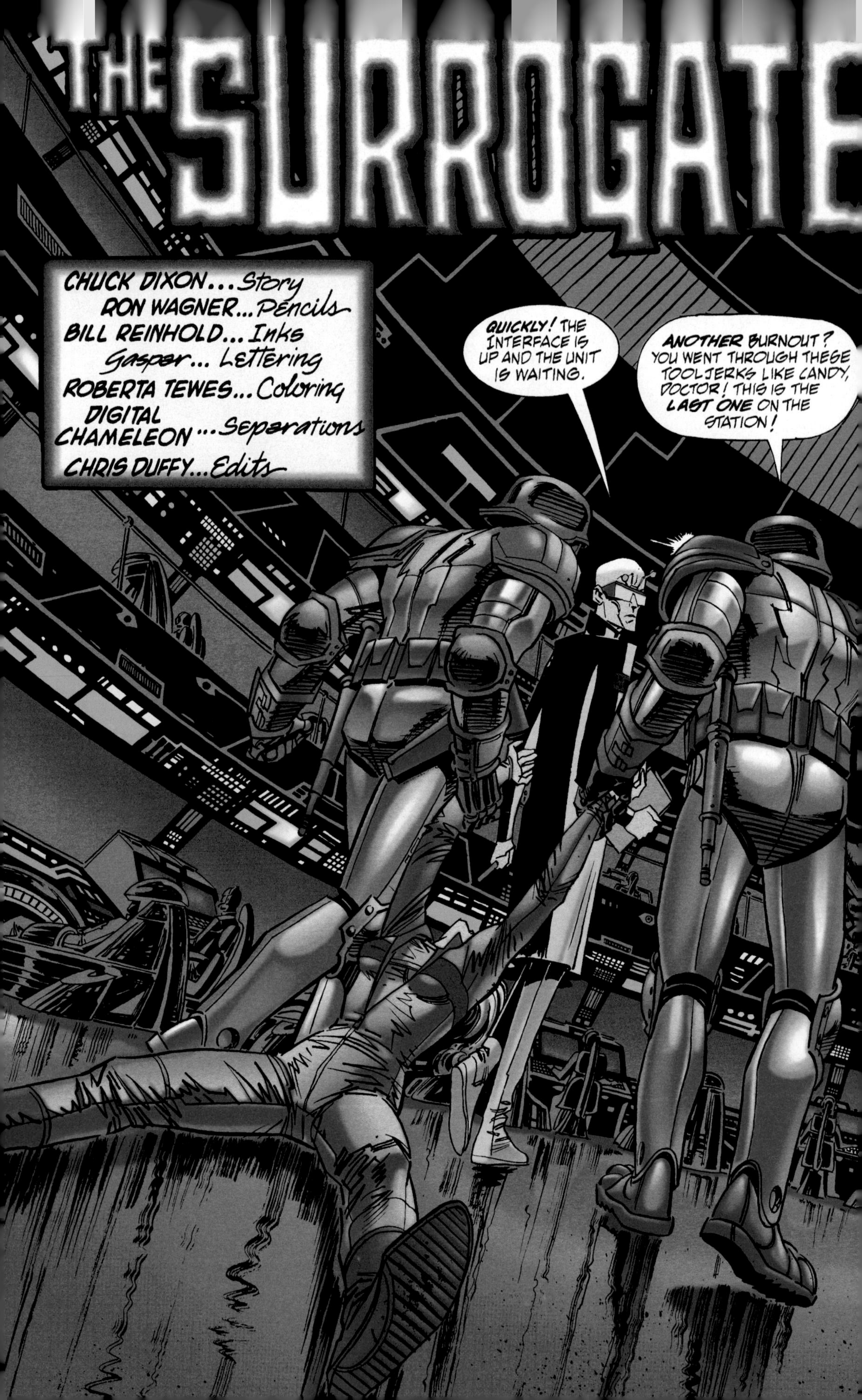
THE SURROGATE
CHUCK DIXON...Story
RON WAGNER...Pencils
BILL REINHOLD...Inks
Gasper...Lettering
ROBERTA TEWES...Coloring
DIGITAL CHAMELEON...Separations
CHRIS DUFFY...Edits
QUICKLY! THE INTERFACE IS UP AND THE UNIT IS WAITING.
ANOTHER BURNOUT? YOU WENT THROUGH THESE TOOLJERKS LIKE CANDY, DOCTOR! THIS IS THE LAST ONE ON THE STATION!

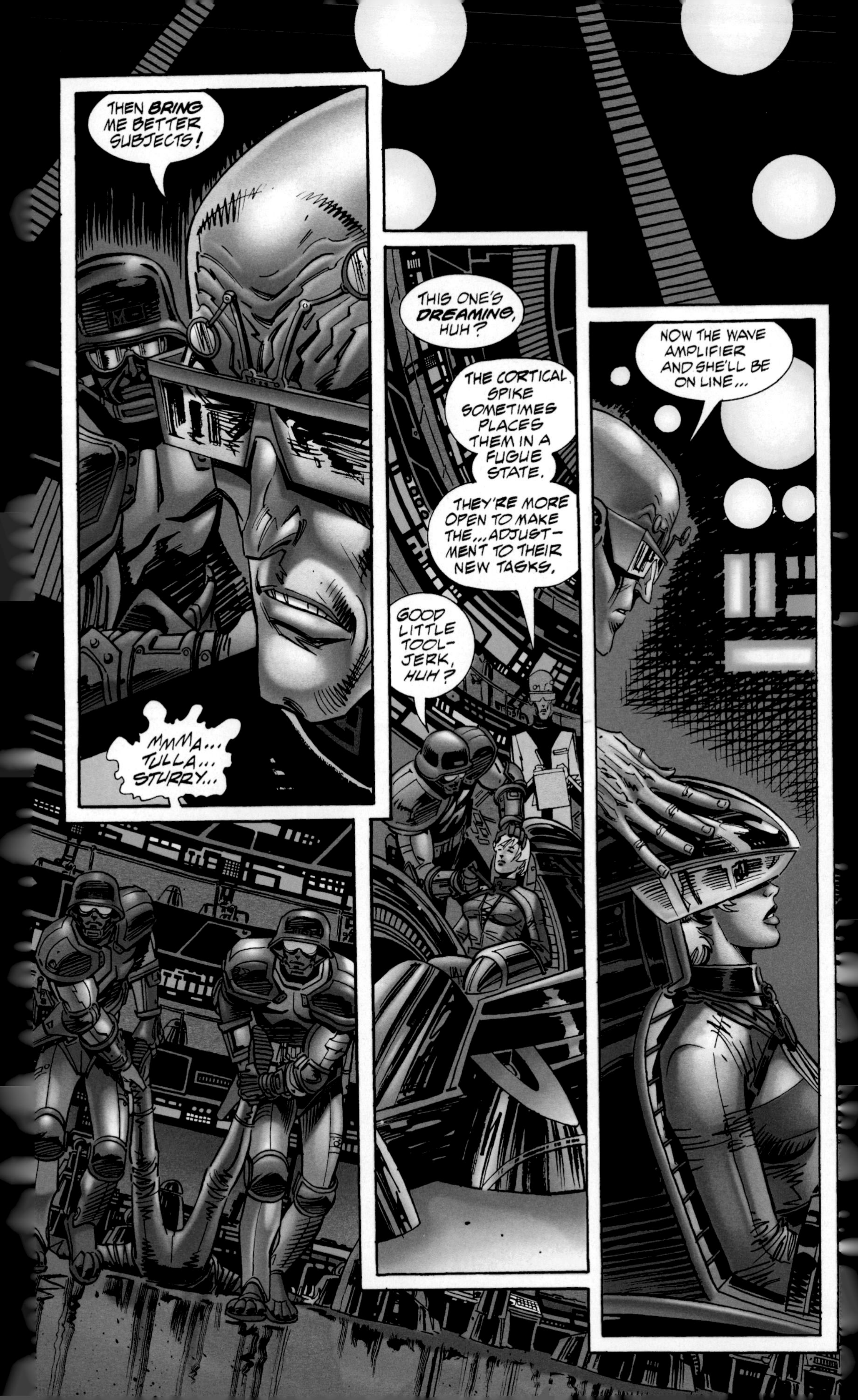
THEN BRING ME BETTER SUBJECTS!
MMMA... TULLA... STURRY...
THIS ONE'S DREAMING, HUH?
THE CORTICAL SPIKE SOMETIMES PLACES THEM IN A FUGUE STATE.
THEY'RE MORE OPEN TO MAKE THE... ADJUSTMENT TO THEIR NEW TASKS.
GOOD LITTLE TOOL-JERK, HUH?
NOW THE WAVE AMPLIFIER AND SHE'LL BE ON LINE...

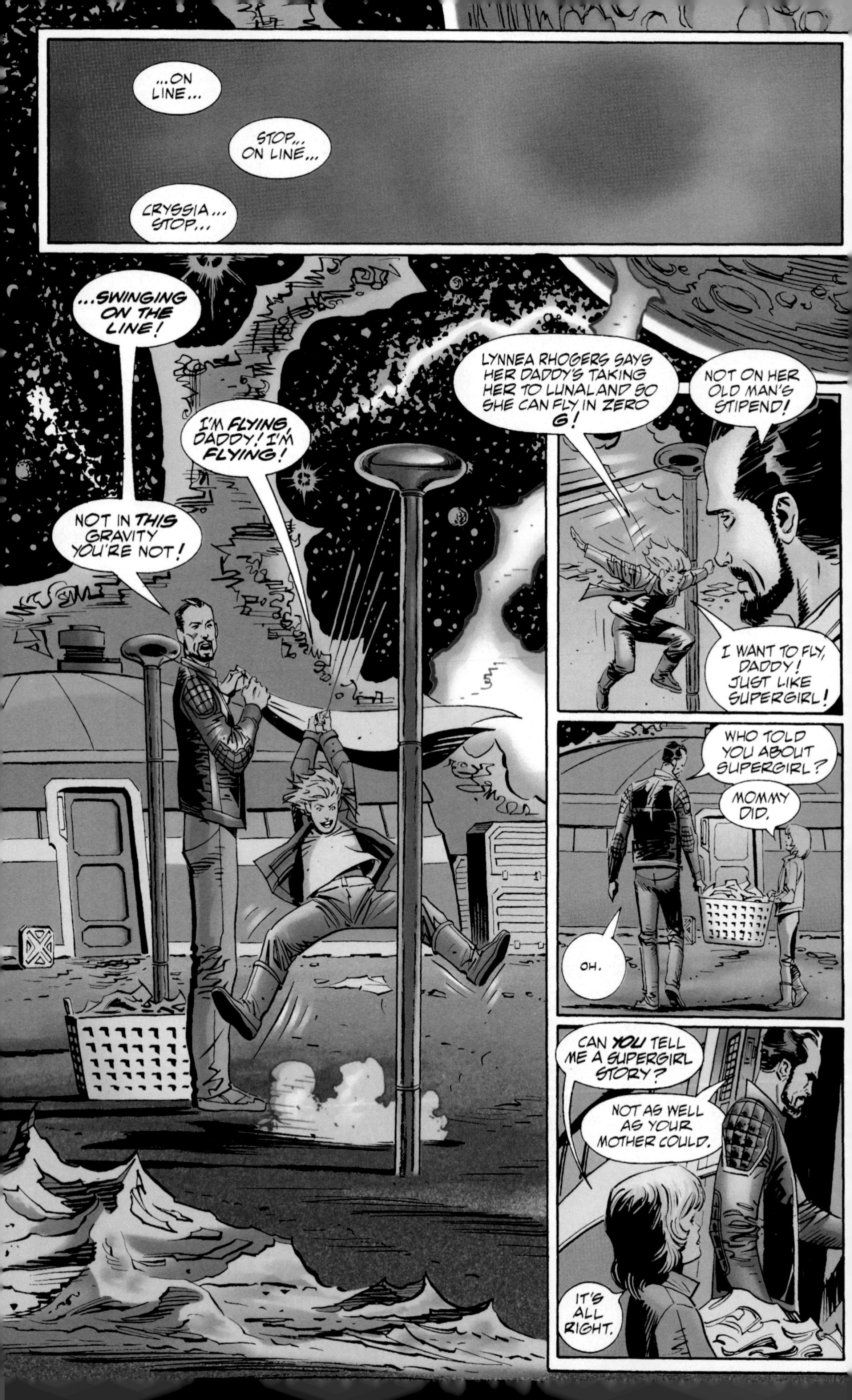
...ON LINE...
STOP... ON LINE...
CRYSSIA... STOP...
...SWINGING ON THE LINE!
I'M FLYING, DADDY! I'M FLYING!
NOT IN THIS GRAVITY YOU'RE NOT!
LYNNEA RHOGERS SAYS HER DADDY'S TAKING HER TO LUNALAND SO SHE CAN FLY IN ZERO G!
NOT ON HER OLD MAN'S STIPEND!
I WANT TO FLY, DADDY! JUST LIKE SUPERGIRL!
WHO TOLD YOU ABOUT SUPERGIRL?
MOMMY DID.
OH.
CAN YOU TELL ME A SUPERGIRL STORY?
NOT AS WELL AS YOUR MOTHER COULD.
IT'S ALL RIGHT.

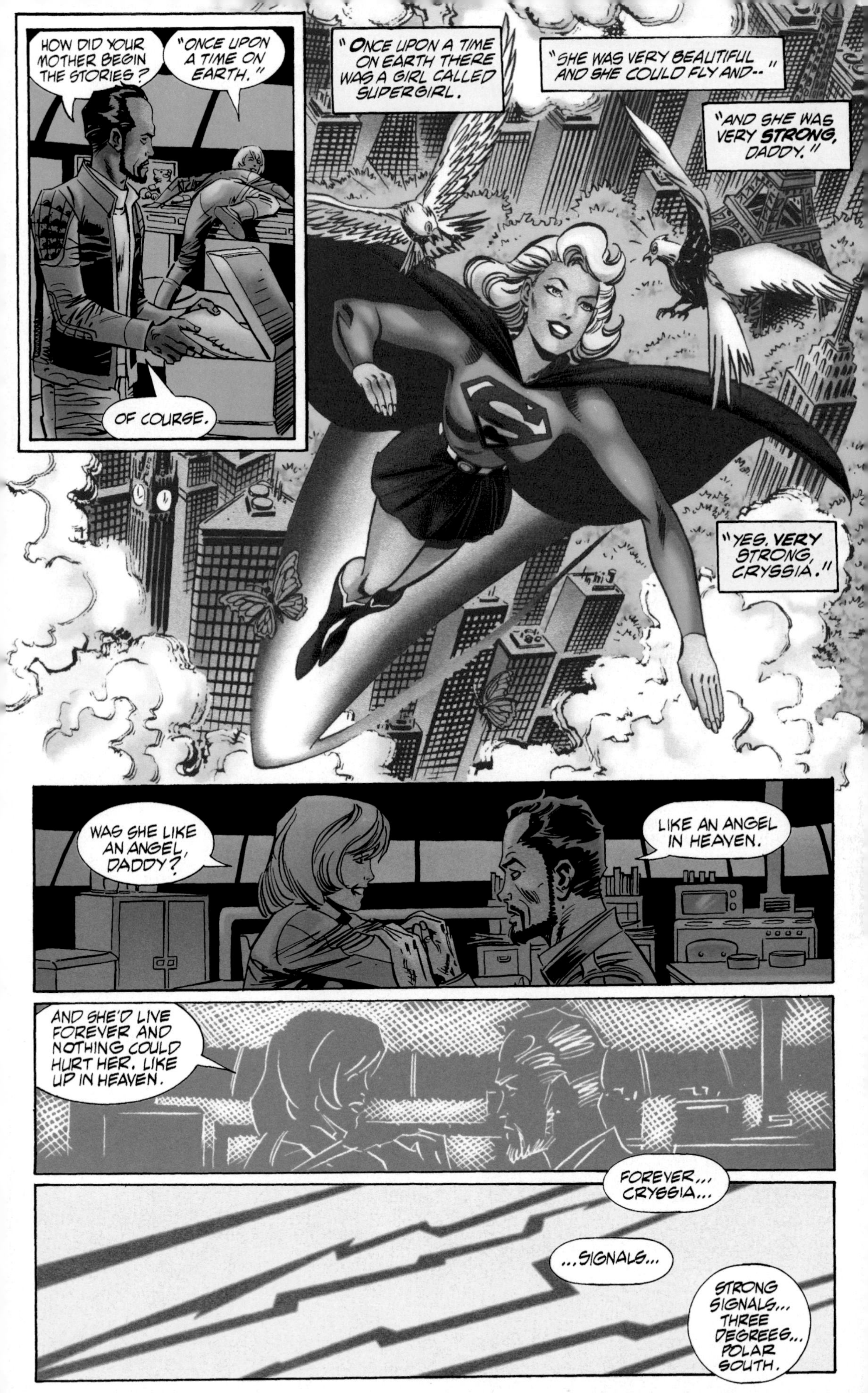
HOW DID YOUR MOTHER BEGIN THE STORIES?
"ONCE UPON A TIME ON EARTH."
OF COURSE.
"ONCE UPON A TIME ON EARTH THERE WAS A GIRL CALLED SUPERGIRL.
"SHE WAS VERY BEAUTIFUL AND SHE COULD FLY AND--"
"AND SHE WAS VERY STRONG, DADDY."
"YES. VERY STRONG, CRYSSIA."
WAS SHE LIKE AN ANGEL, DADDY?
LIKE AN ANGEL IN HEAVEN.
AND SHE'D LIVE FOREVER AND NOTHING COULD HURT HER. LIKE UP IN HEAVEN.
FOREVER... CRYSSIA...
...SIGNALS...
STRONG SIGNALS... THREE DEGREES... POLAR SOUTH.

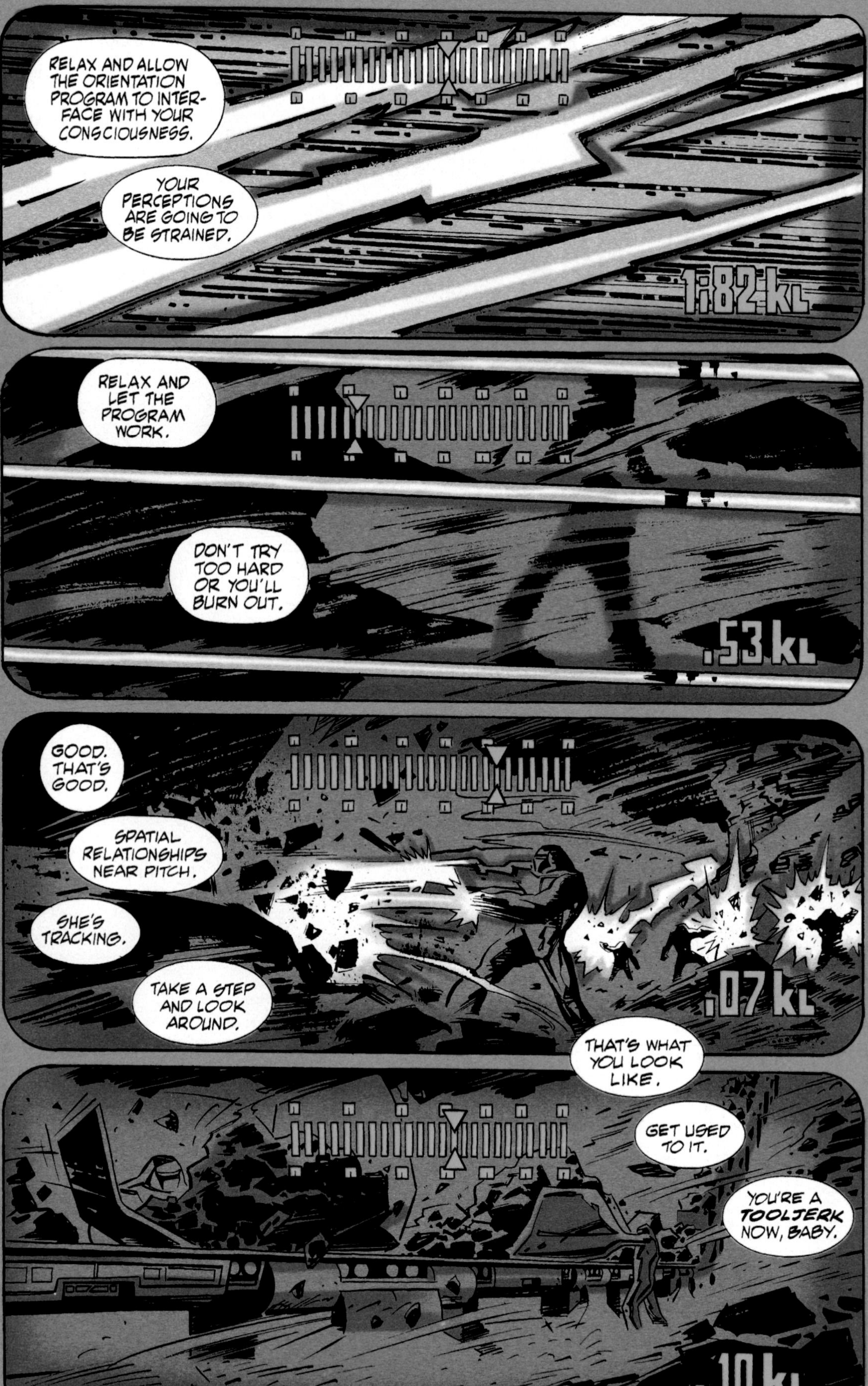

RELAX AND ALLOW THE ORIENTATION PROGRAM TO INTER-FACE WITH YOUR CONSCIOUSNESS.
YOUR PERCEPTIONS ARE GOING TO BE STRAINED.
1.82 KL
RELAX AND LET THE PROGRAM WORK.
DON'T TRY TOO HARD OR YOU'LL BURN OUT.
.53 KL
GOOD. THAT'S GOOD.
SPATIAL RELATIONSHIPS NEAR PITCH.
SHE'S TRACKING.
TAKE A STEP AND LOOK AROUND.
.07 KL
THAT'S WHAT YOU LOOK LIKE.
GET USED TO IT.
YOU'RE A *TOOLJERK* NOW, BABY.
.10 KL

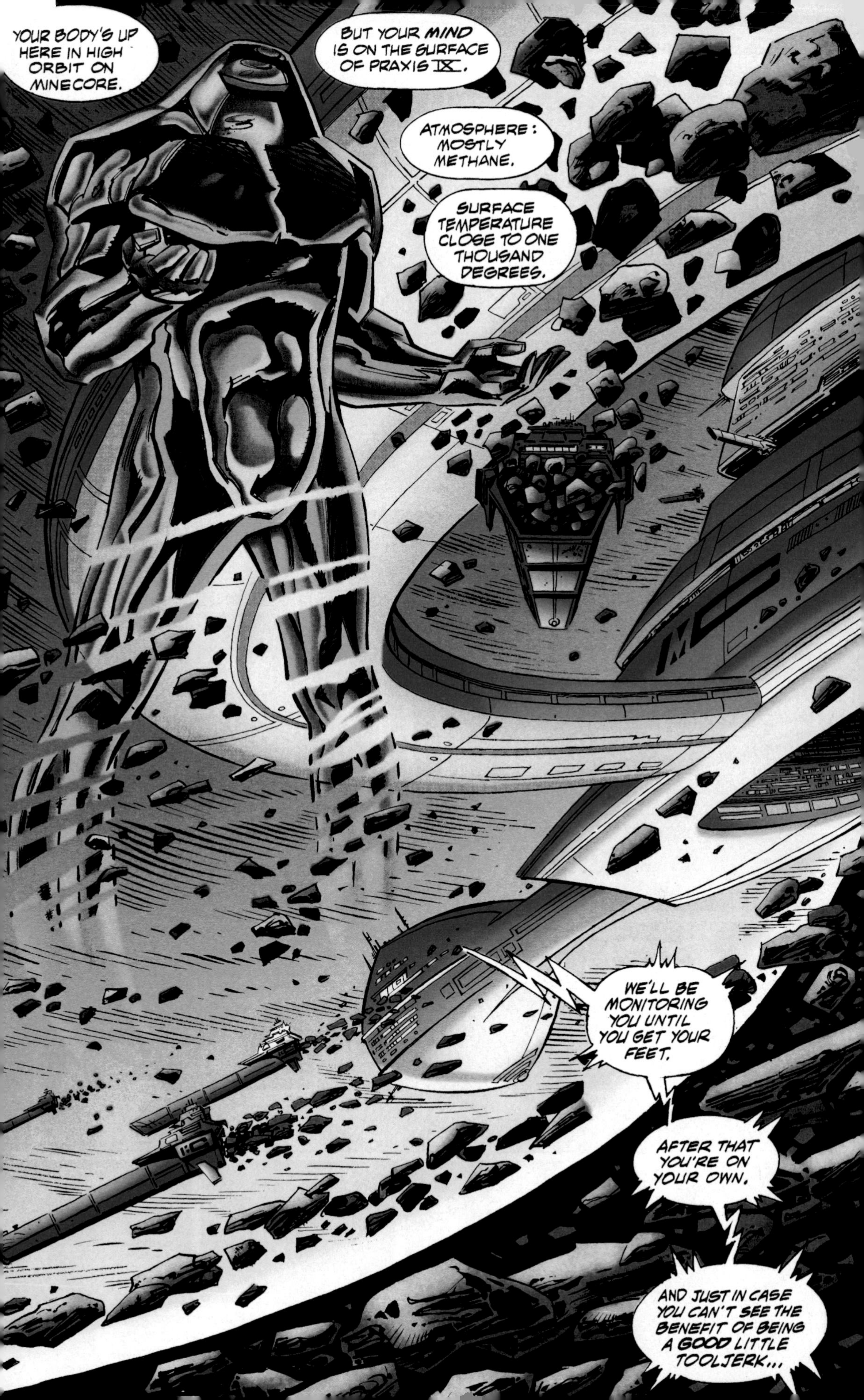
YOUR BODY'S UP HERE IN HIGH ORBIT ON MINECORE.
BUT YOUR MIND IS ON THE SURFACE OF PRAXIS IX.
ATMOSPHERE: MOSTLY METHANE.
SURFACE TEMPERATURE CLOSE TO ONE THOUSAND DEGREES.
WE'LL BE MONITORING YOU UNTIL YOU GET YOUR FEET.
AFTER THAT YOU'RE ON YOUR OWN.
AND JUST IN CASE YOU CAN'T SEE THE BENEFIT OF BEING A GOOD LITTLE TOOLJERK...

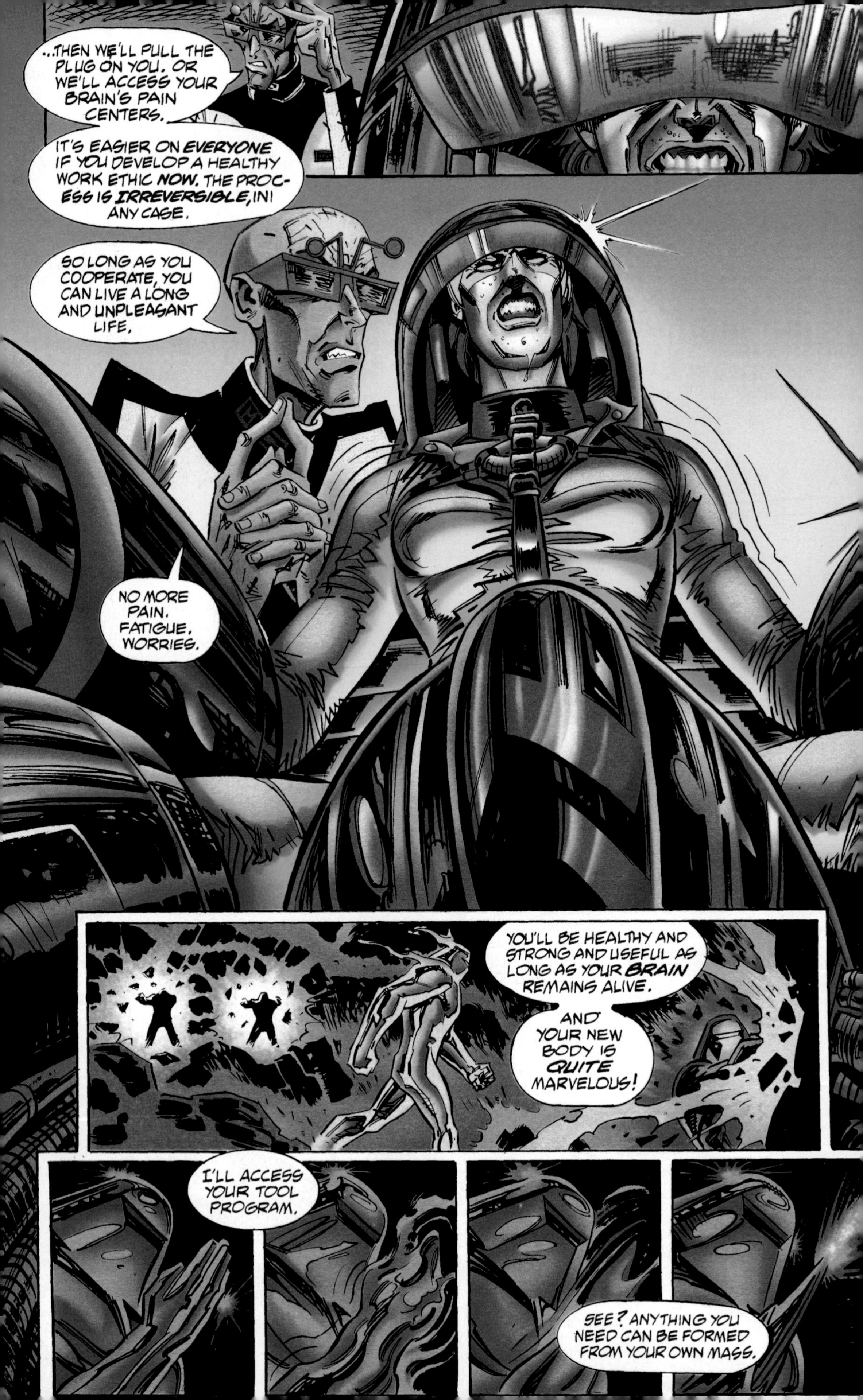
...THEN WE'LL PULL THE PLUG ON YOU. OR WE'LL ACCESS YOUR BRAIN'S PAIN CENTERS.
IT'S EASIER ON EVERYONE IF YOU DEVELOP A HEALTHY WORK ETHIC NOW. THE PROCESS IS IRREVERSIBLE, IN ANY CASE.
SO LONG AS YOU COOPERATE, YOU CAN LIVE A LONG AND UNPLEASANT LIFE.
NO MORE PAIN. FATIGUE. WORRIES.
YOU'LL BE HEALTHY AND STRONG AND USEFUL AS LONG AS YOUR BRAIN REMAINS ALIVE.
AND YOUR NEW BODY IS QUITE MARVELOUS!
I'LL ACCESS YOUR TOOL PROGRAM.
SEE? ANYTHING YOU NEED CAN BE FORMED FROM YOUR OWN MASS.

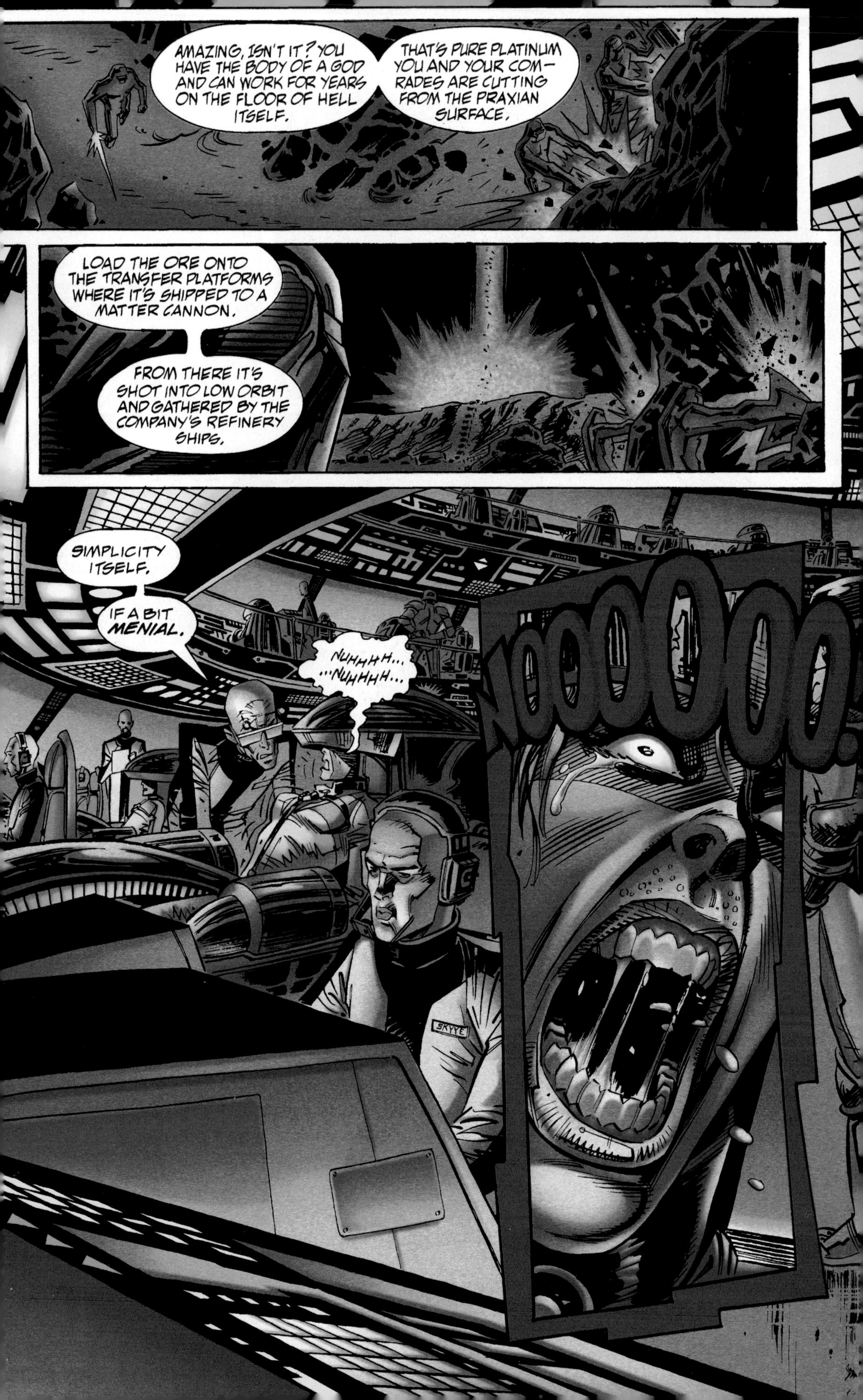
AMAZING, ISN'T IT? YOU HAVE THE BODY OF A GOD AND CAN WORK FOR YEARS ON THE FLOOR OF HELL ITSELF.
THAT'S PURE PLATINUM YOU AND YOUR COM-RADES ARE CUTTING FROM THE PRAXIAN SURFACE.
LOAD THE ORE ONTO THE TRANSFER PLATFORMS WHERE IT'S SHIPPED TO A MATTER CANNON.
FROM THERE IT'S SHOT INTO LOW ORBIT AND GATHERED BY THE COMPANY'S REFINERY SHIPS.
SIMPLICITY ITSELF.
IF A BIT *MENIAL*.
NUHHHH... ...NUHHHH...
NOOOOOO..
SKYYE

SKYYE! LOCK THIS DOWN!

I'M SORRY, DOCTOR. SHE'S GOING!

I CAN'T AFFORD ANOTHER SETUP AND DELAY!

I'M STILL GETTING SURFACE READINGS FROM THAT UNIT.

THEY'RE GETTING STRONGER. IT'S STILL ACTIVE.

BUT THE TOOLJERK GOES IDLE WHEN THE FLESH SUBJECT DIES!

I'M TELLING YOU SHE'S STILL OPERATING DOWN ON THE SURFACE.

I'VE THEORIZED ABOUT THIS...

IT'S THE NEXT STEP! LOG ALL DATA FOR ANALYSIS!

IF WE CAN RECREATE THIS PHENOMENON WE CAN CUT COSTS BY BILLIONS!

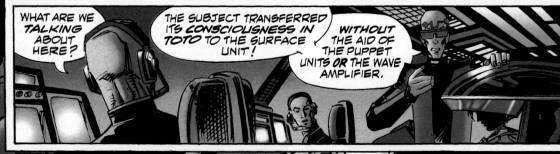

WHAT ARE WE TALKING ABOUT HERE?

THE SUBJECT TRANSFERRED ITS CONSCIOUSNESS IN TOTO TO THE SURFACE UNIT!

WITHOUT THE AID OF THE PUPPET UNITS OR THE WAVE AMPLIFIER.

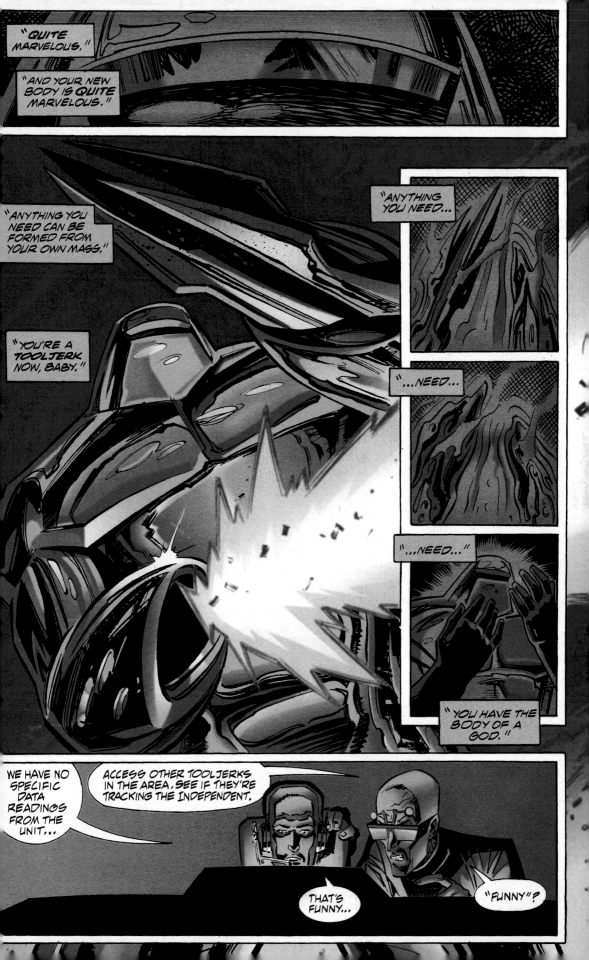

"QUITE MARVELOUS."

"AND YOUR NEW BODY IS QUITE MARVELOUS."

"ANYTHING YOU NEED CAN BE FORMED FROM YOUR OWN MASS."

"YOU'RE A TOOLJERK NOW, BABY."

"ANYTHING YOU NEED..."

"...NEED..."

"...NEED..."

"YOU HAVE THE BODY OF A GOD."

WE HAVE NO SPECIFIC DATA READINGS FROM THE UNIT...

ACCESS OTHER TOOLJERKS IN THE AREA. SEE IF THEY'RE TRACKING THE INDEPENDENT.

THAT'S FUNNY...

"FUNNY"?

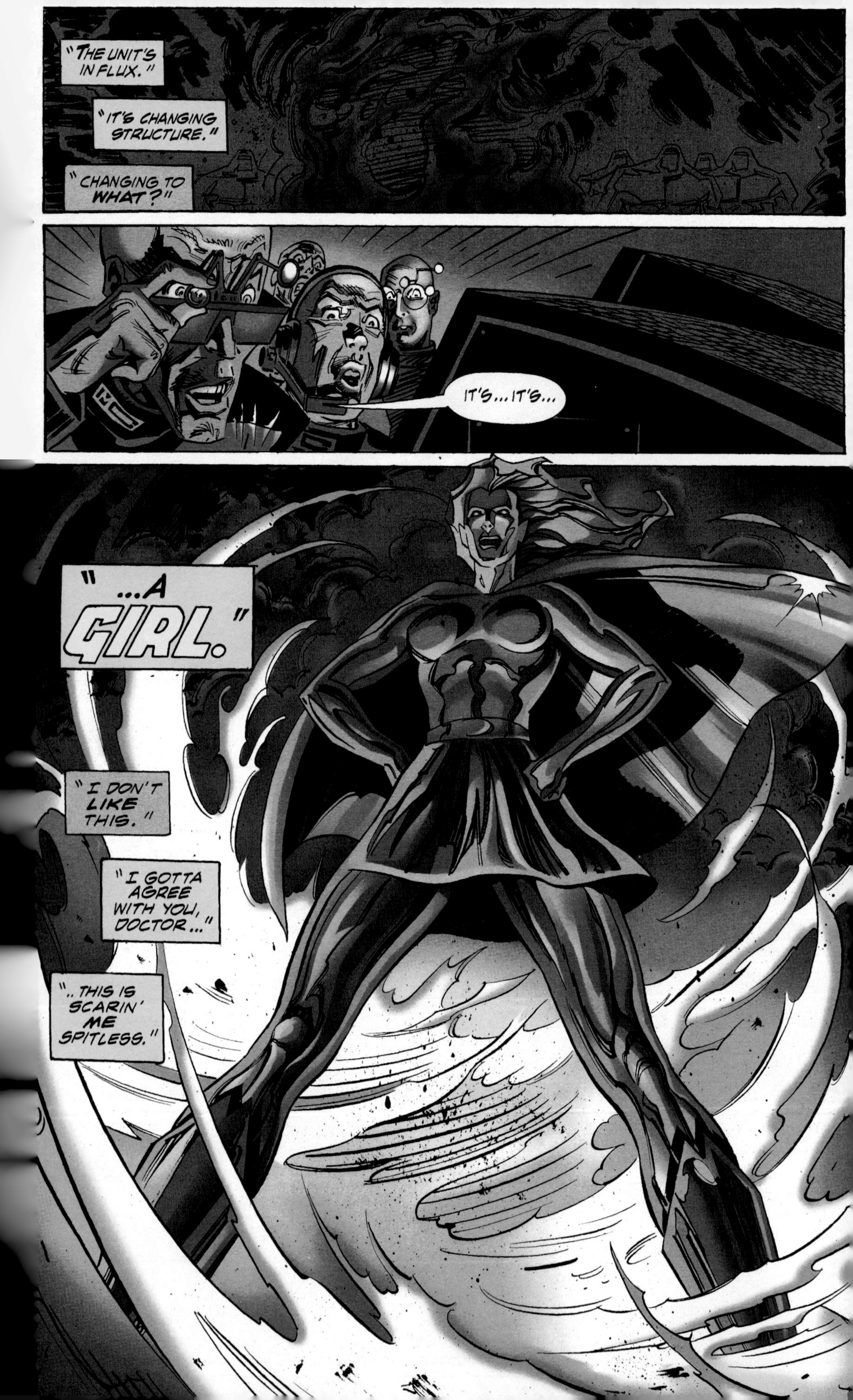

"THE UNIT'S IN FLUX."
"IT'S CHANGING STRUCTURE."
"CHANGING TO WHAT?"
IT'S... IT'S...
"...A GIRL."
"I DON'T LIKE THIS."
"I GOTTA AGREE WITH YOU, DOCTOR..."
"..THIS IS SCARIN' ME SPITLESS."

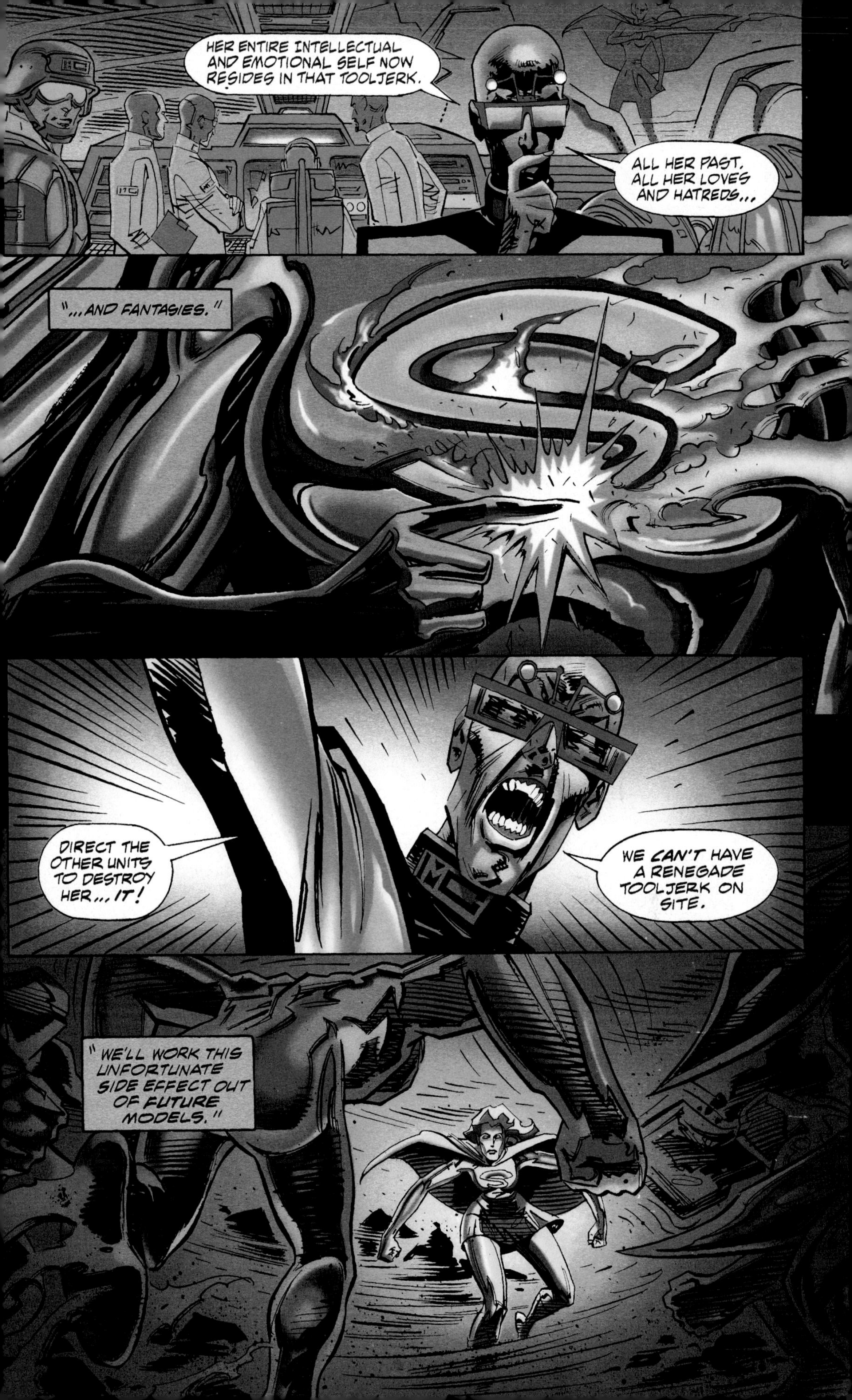
HER ENTIRE INTELLECTUAL AND EMOTIONAL SELF NOW RESIDES IN THAT TOOLJERK.
ALL HER PAST, ALL HER LOVES AND HATREDS...
"...AND FANTASIES."
DIRECT THE OTHER UNITS TO DESTROY HER... IT!
WE CAN'T HAVE A RENEGADE TOOLJERK ON SITE.
"WE'LL WORK THIS UNFORTUNATE SIDE EFFECT OUT OF FUTURE MODELS."

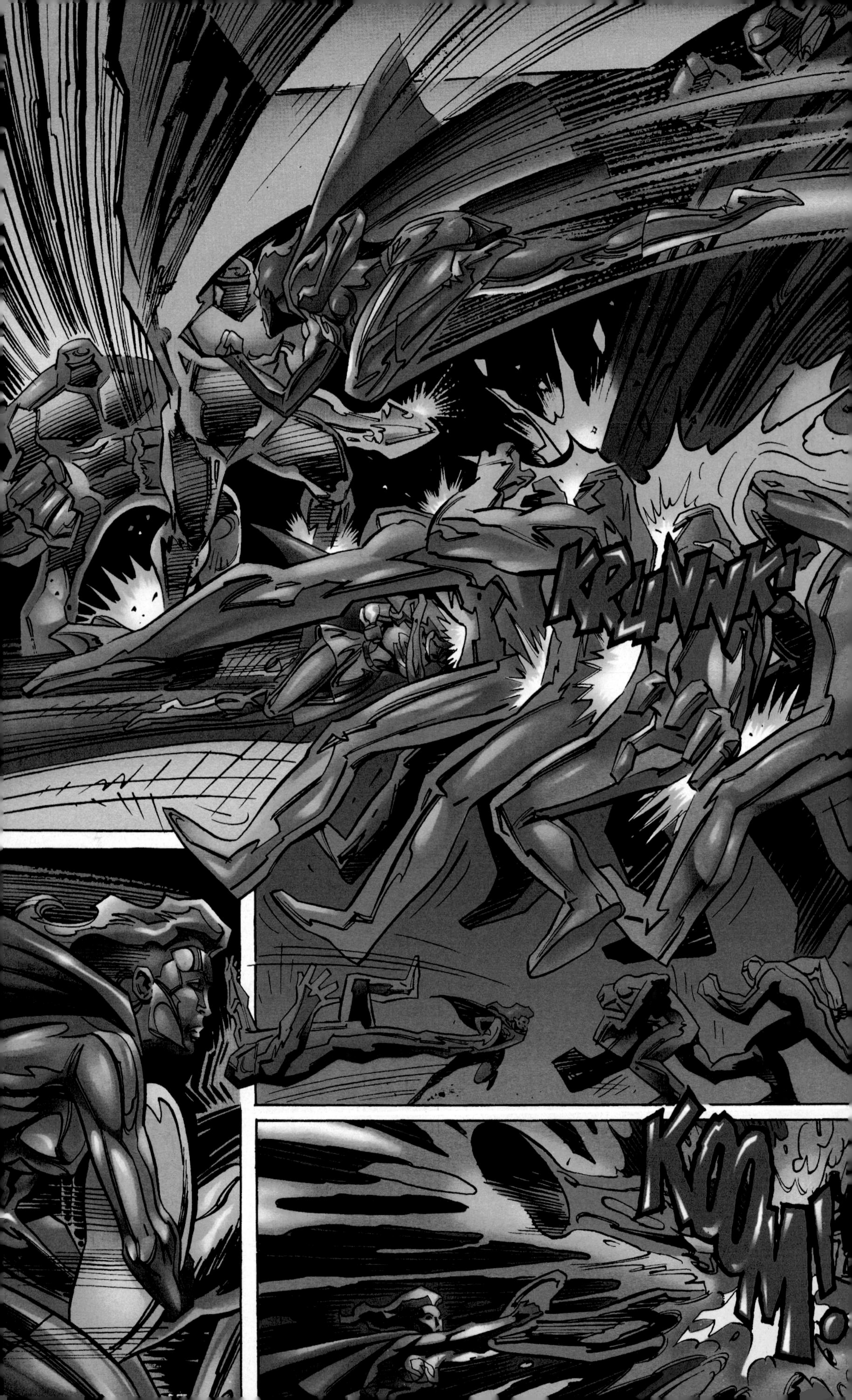
KRUNNK!
KOOM!

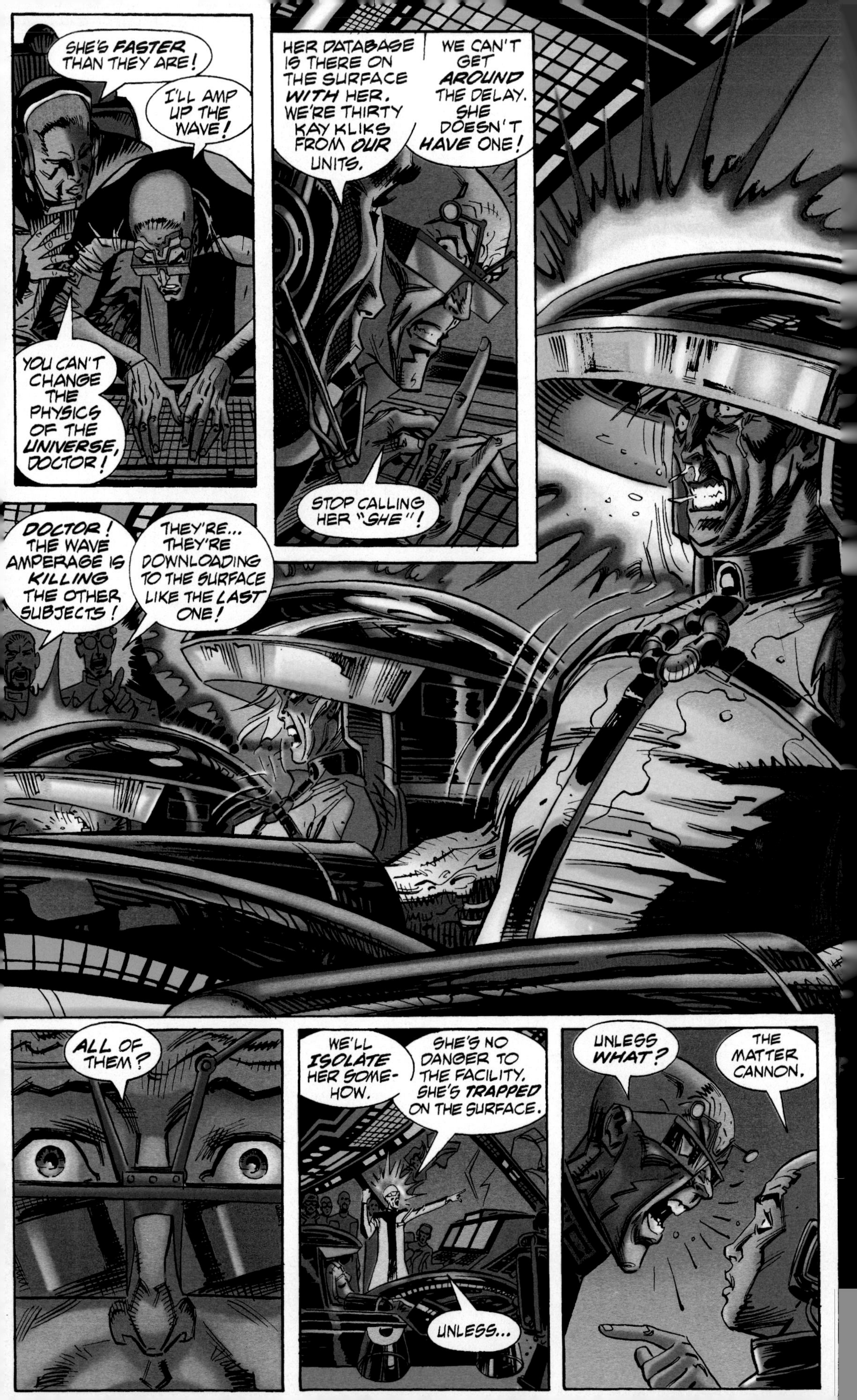
SHE'S FASTER THAN THEY ARE!
I'LL AMP UP THE WAVE!
YOU CAN'T CHANGE THE PHYSICS OF THE UNIVERSE, DOCTOR!
HER DATABASE IS THERE ON THE SURFACE WITH HER. WE'RE THIRTY KAY KLIKS FROM OUR UNITS.
WE CAN'T GET AROUND THE DELAY. SHE DOESN'T HAVE ONE!
STOP CALLING HER "SHE"!
DOCTOR! THE WAVE AMPERAGE IS KILLING THE OTHER SUBJECTS!
THEY'RE... THEY'RE DOWNLOADING TO THE SURFACE LIKE THE LAST ONE!
ALL OF THEM?
WE'LL ISOLATE HER SOMEHOW.
SHE'S NO DANGER TO THE FACILITY. SHE'S TRAPPED ON THE SURFACE.
UNLESS...
UNLESS WHAT?
THE MATTER CANNON.

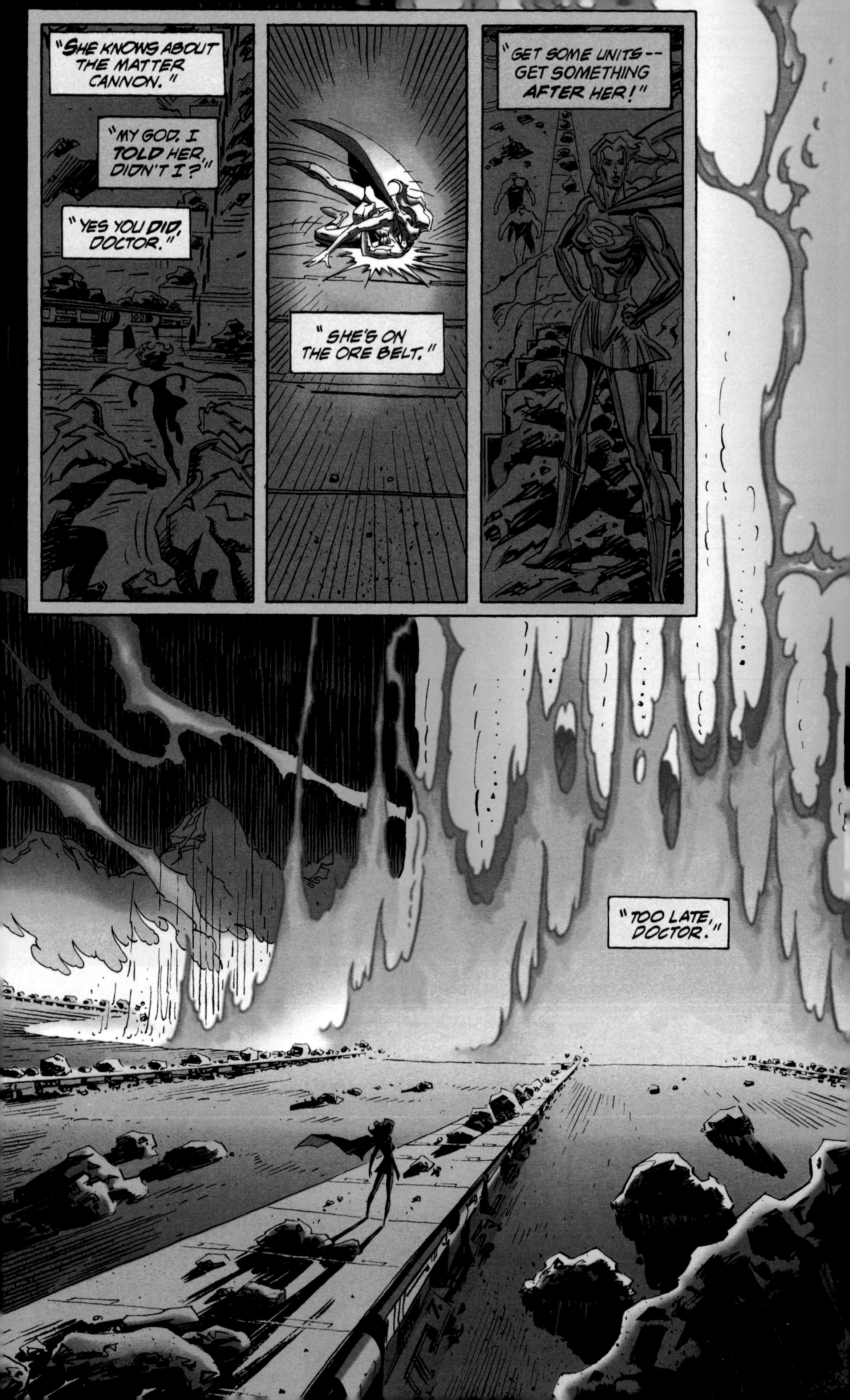
"SHE KNOWS ABOUT THE MATTER CANNON."
"MY GOD. I TOLD HER, DIDN'T I?"
"YES YOU DID, DOCTOR."
"SHE'S ON THE ORE BELT."
"GET SOME UNITS -- GET SOMETHING AFTER HER!"
"TOO LATE, DOCTOR."

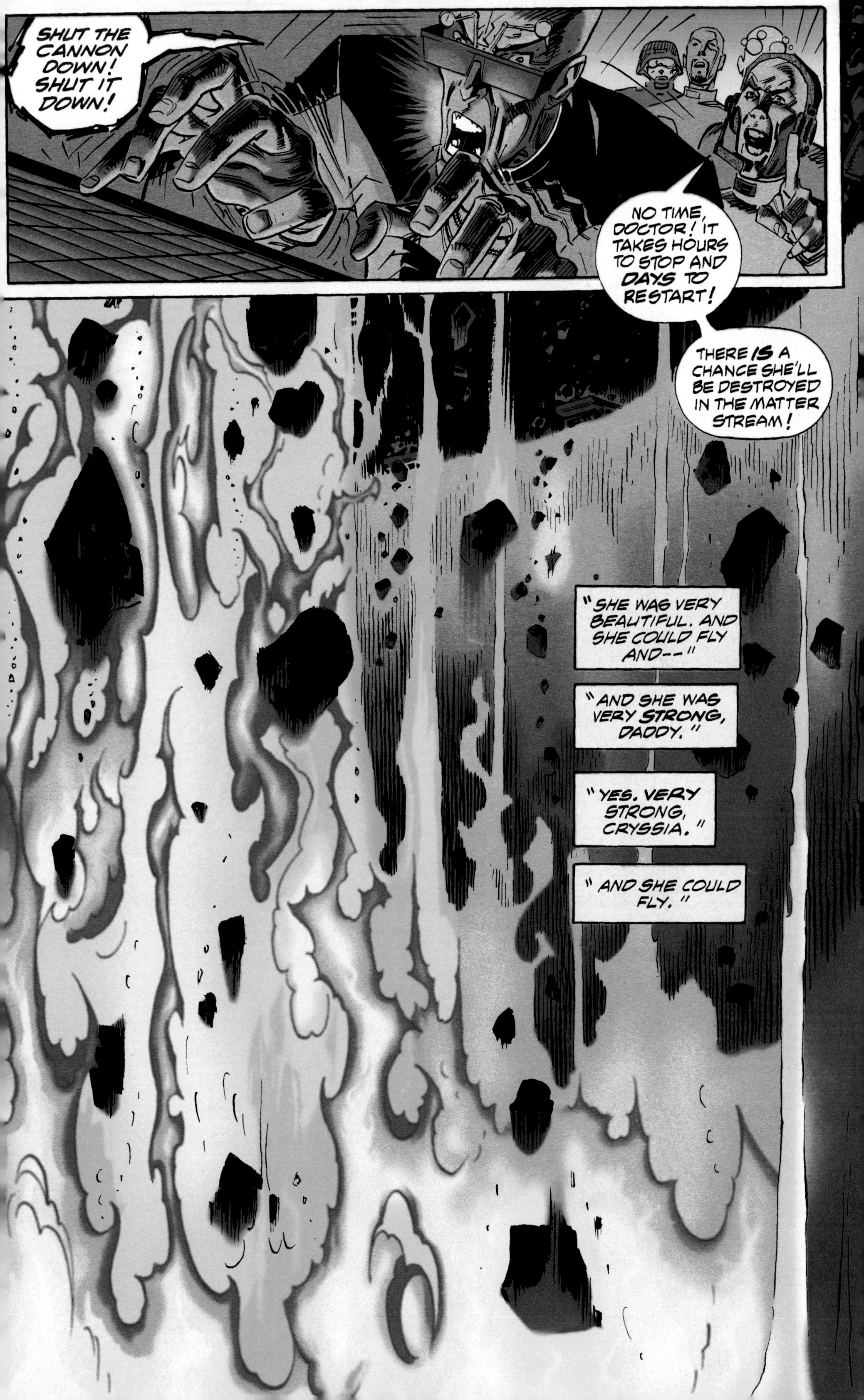
SHUT THE CANNON DOWN! SHUT IT DOWN!
NO TIME, DOCTOR! IT TAKES HOURS TO STOP AND DAYS TO RESTART!
THERE IS A CHANCE SHE'LL BE DESTROYED IN THE MATTER STREAM!
"SHE WAS VERY BEAUTIFUL. AND SHE COULD FLY AND--"
"AND SHE WAS VERY STRONG, DADDY."
"YES. VERY STRONG, CRYSSIA."
"AND SHE COULD FLY."

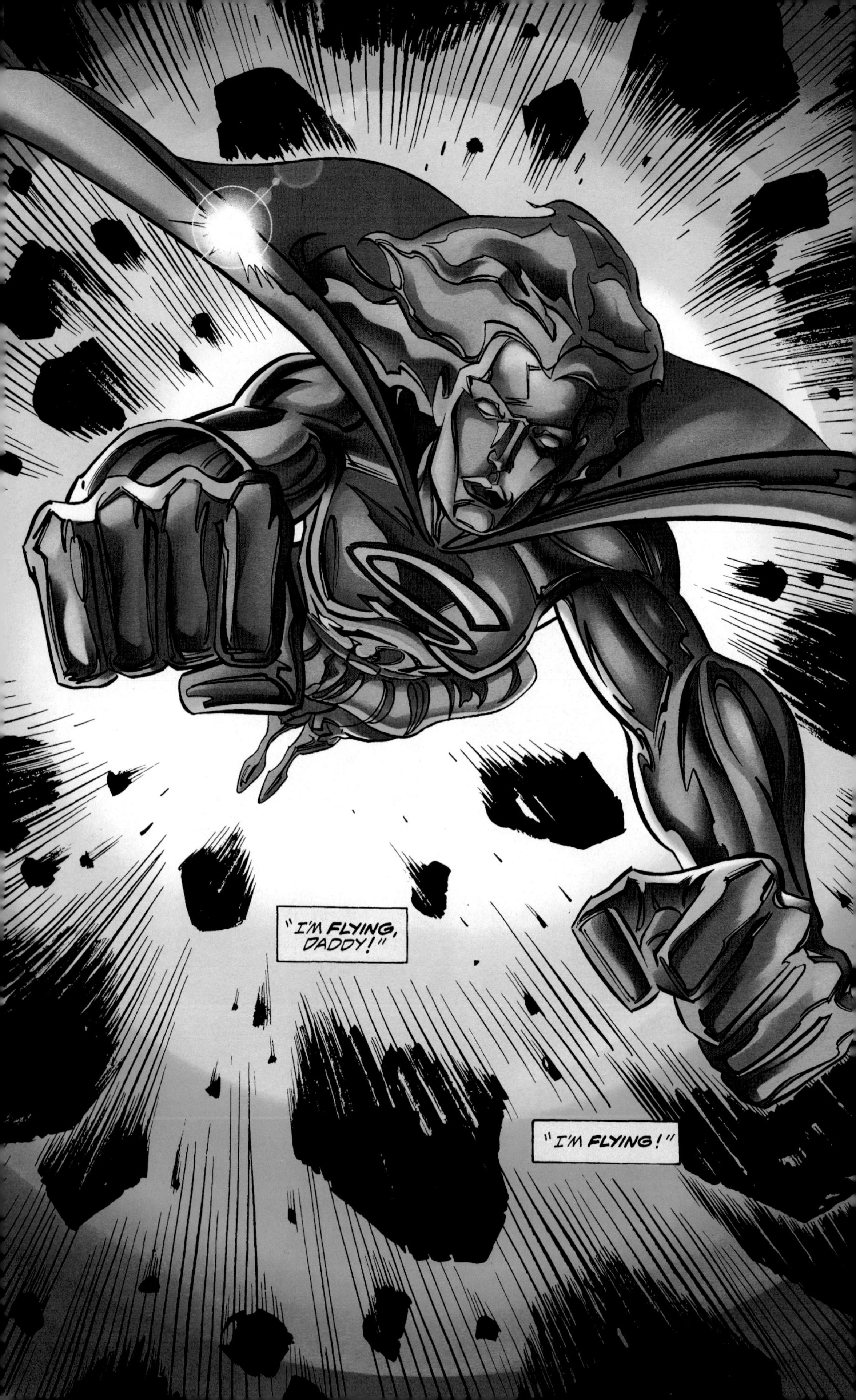
"I'M FLYING, DADDY!"
"I'M FLYING!"

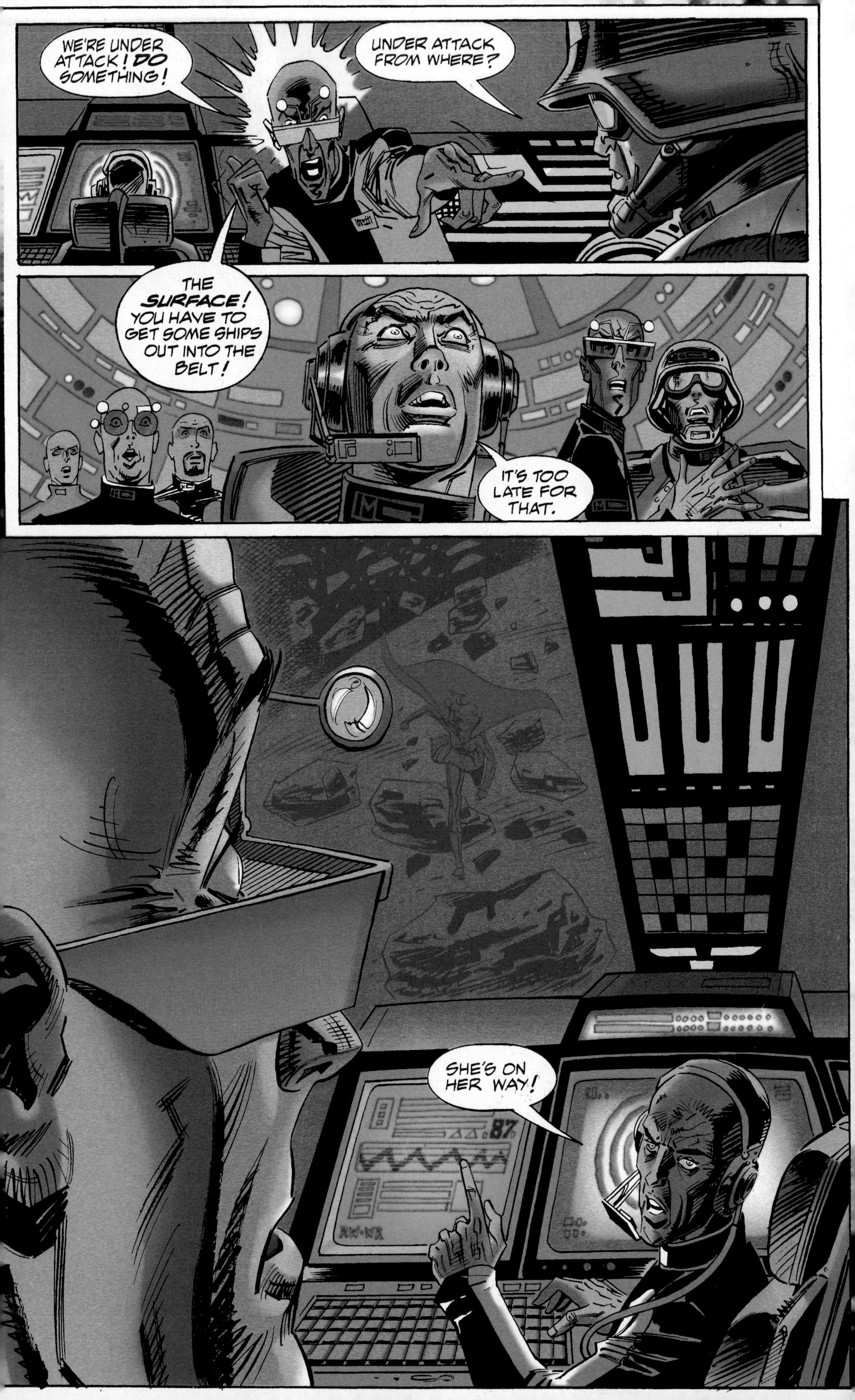
WE'RE UNDER ATTACK! DO SOMETHING!
UNDER ATTACK FROM WHERE?
THE SURFACE! YOU HAVE TO GET SOME SHIPS OUT INTO THE BELT!
IT'S TOO LATE FOR THAT.
SHE'S ON HER WAY!

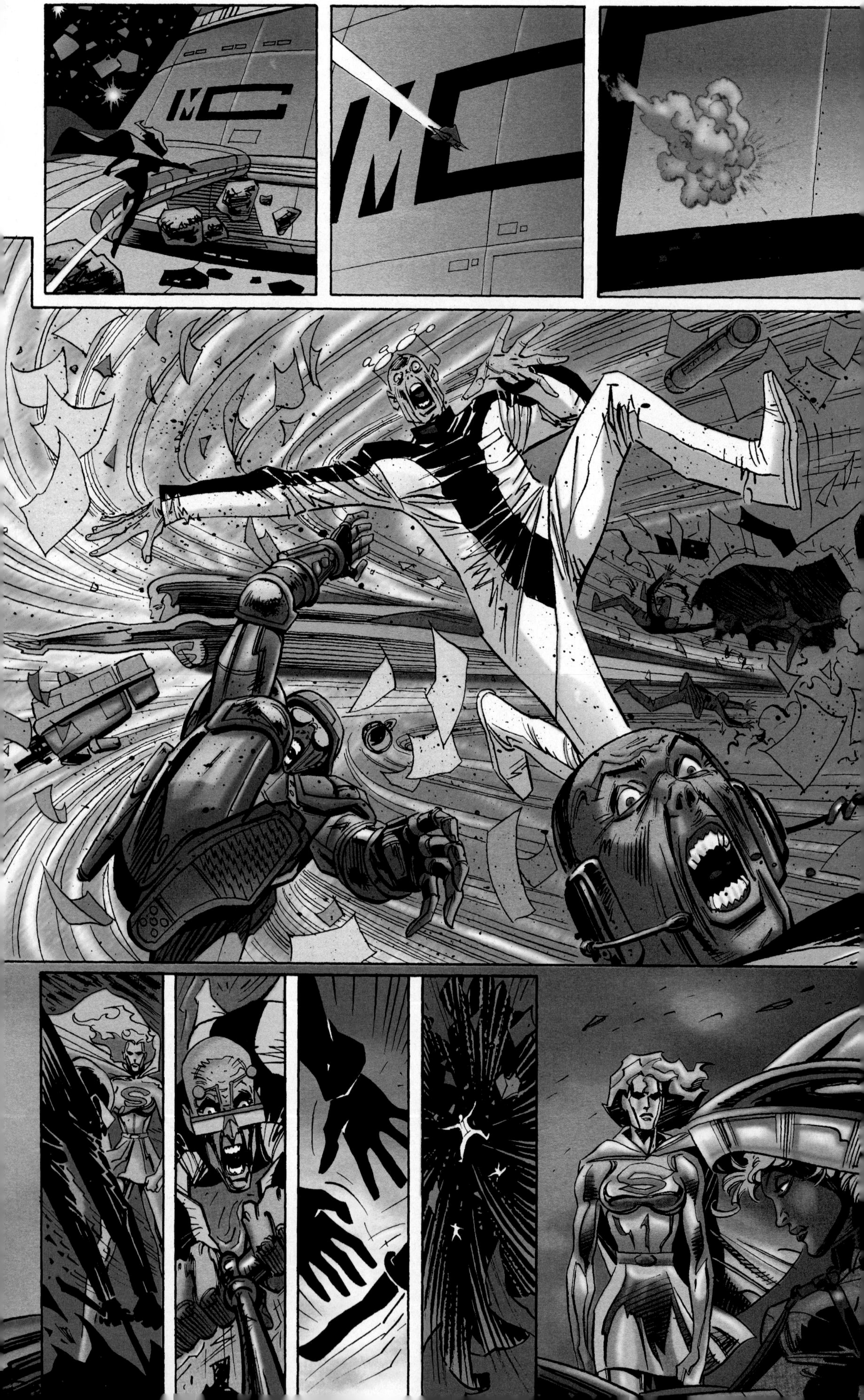

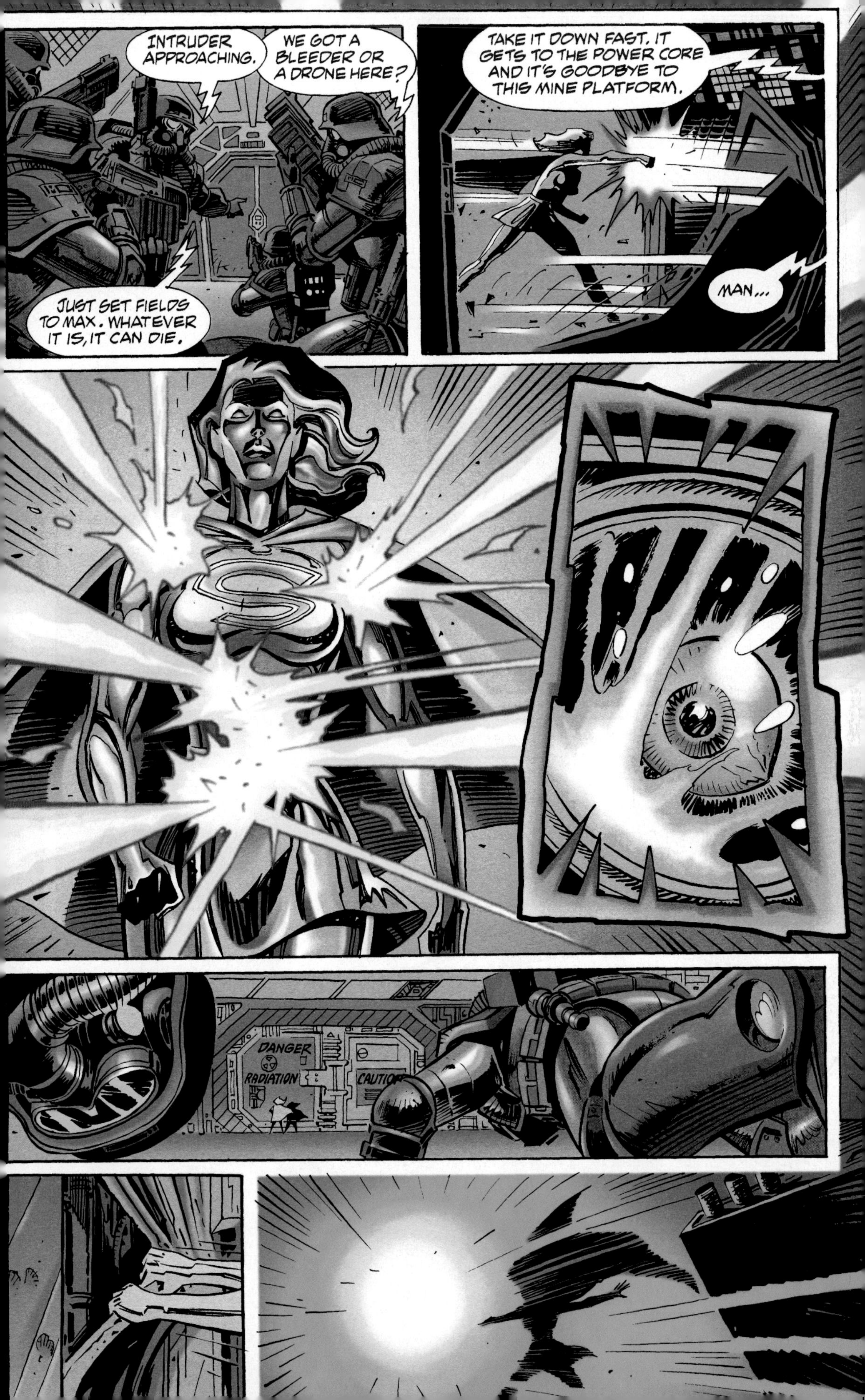
INTRUDER APPROACHING.
WE GOT A BLEEDER OR A DRONE HERE?
JUST SET FIELDS TO MAX. WHATEVER IT IS, IT CAN DIE.
TAKE IT DOWN FAST. IT GETS TO THE POWER CORE AND IT'S GOODBYE TO THIS MINE PLATFORM.
MAN...
DANGER
RADIATION
CAUTION

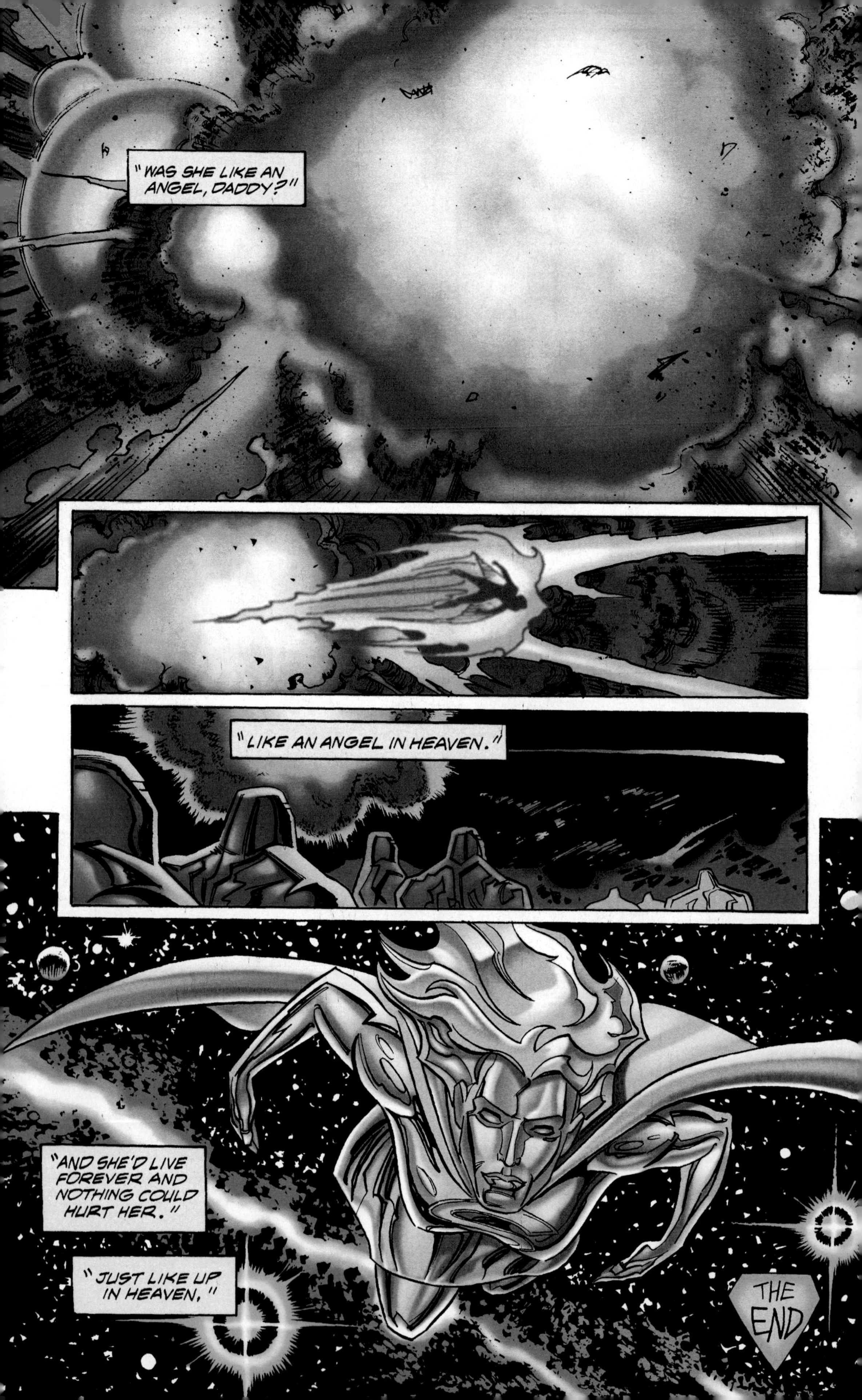
"WAS SHE LIKE AN ANGEL, DADDY?"
"LIKE AN ANGEL IN HEAVEN."
"AND SHE'D LIVE FOREVER AND NOTHING COULD HURT HER."
"JUST LIKE UP IN HEAVEN."
THE END

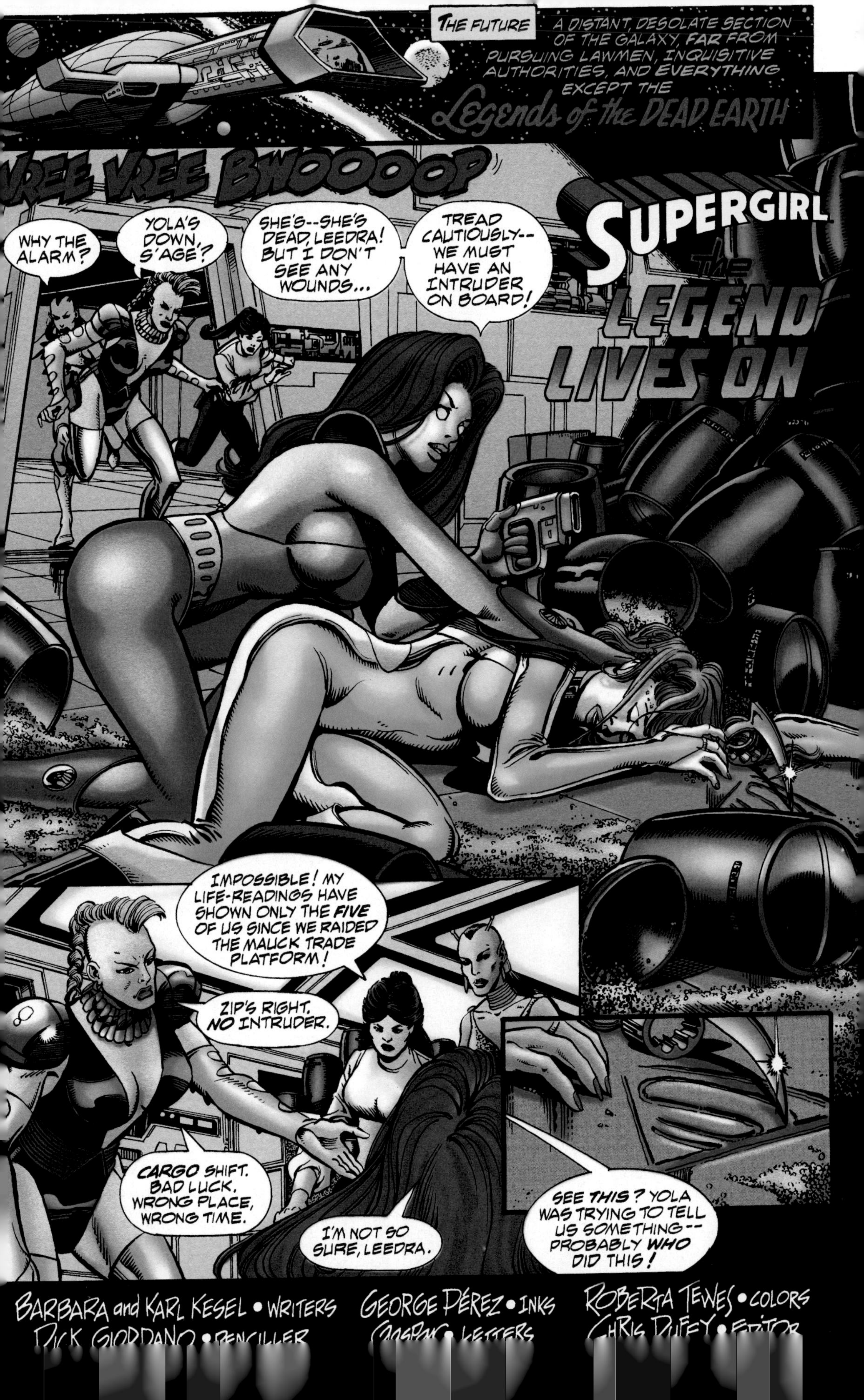
THE FUTURE
A DISTANT, DESOLATE SECTION OF THE GALAXY, FAR FROM PURSUING LAWMEN, INQUISITIVE AUTHORITIES, AND EVERYTHING EXCEPT THE
Legends of the DEAD EARTH
VREE VREE BWOOOOOP
SUPERGIRL
THE LEGEND LIVES ON
WHY THE ALARM?
YOLA'S DOWN, S'AGE?
SHE'S--SHE'S DEAD, LEEDRA! BUT I DON'T SEE ANY WOUNDS...
TREAD CAUTIOUSLY--WE MUST HAVE AN INTRUDER ON BOARD!
IMPOSSIBLE! MY LIFE-READINGS HAVE SHOWN ONLY THE FIVE OF US SINCE WE RAIDED THE MAUCK TRADE PLATFORM!
ZIP'S RIGHT. NO INTRUDER.
CARGO SHIFT. BAD LUCK. WRONG PLACE, WRONG TIME.
I'M NOT SO SURE, LEEDRA.
SEE THIS? YOLA WAS TRYING TO TELL US SOMETHING--PROBABLY WHO DID THIS!
BARBARA and KARL KESEL • WRITERS
GEORGE PÉREZ • INKS
ROBERTA TEWES • COLORS

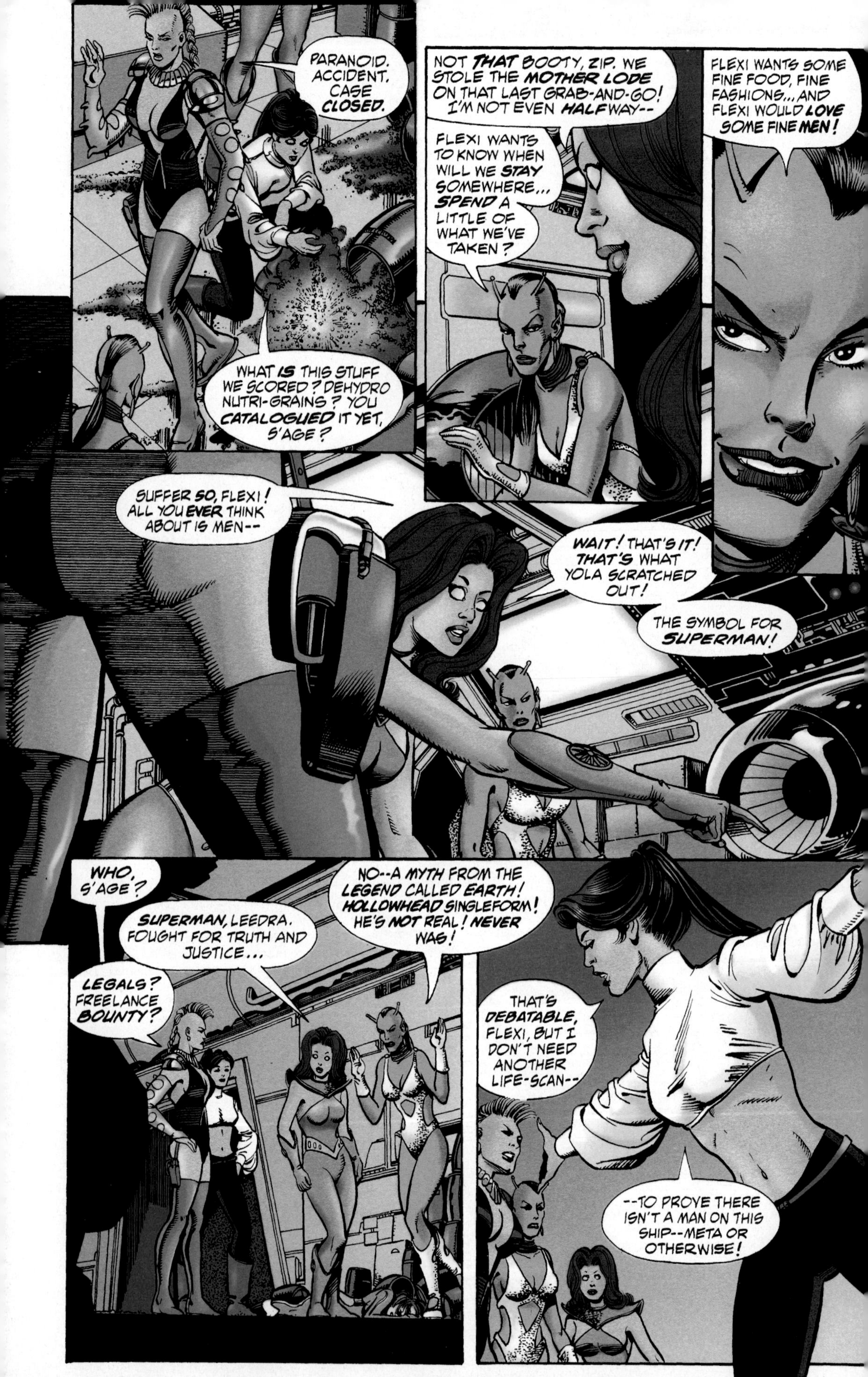
PARANOID. ACCIDENT. CASE CLOSED.
WHAT IS THIS STUFF WE SCORED? DEHYDRO NUTRI-GRAINS? YOU CATALOGUED IT YET, S'AGE?
NOT THAT BOOTY, ZIP. WE STOLE THE MOTHER LODE ON THAT LAST GRAB-AND-GO! I'M NOT EVEN HALFWAY--
FLEXI WANTS TO KNOW WHEN WILL WE STAY SOMEWHERE... SPEND A LITTLE OF WHAT WE'VE TAKEN?
FLEXI WANTS SOME FINE FOOD, FINE FASHIONS... AND FLEXI WOULD LOVE SOME FINE MEN!
SUFFER SO, FLEXI! ALL YOU EVER THINK ABOUT IS MEN--
WAIT! THAT'S IT! THAT'S WHAT YOLA SCRATCHED OUT!
THE SYMBOL FOR SUPERMAN!
WHO, S'AGE?
SUPERMAN, LEEDRA. FOUGHT FOR TRUTH AND JUSTICE...
LEGALS? FREELANCE BOUNTY?
NO--A MYTH FROM THE LEGEND CALLED EARTH! HOLLOWHEAD SINGLEFORM! HE'S NOT REAL! NEVER WAS!
THAT'S DEBATABLE, FLEXI, BUT I DON'T NEED ANOTHER LIFE-SCAN--
--TO PROVE THERE ISN'T A MAN ON THIS SHIP--META OR OTHERWISE!

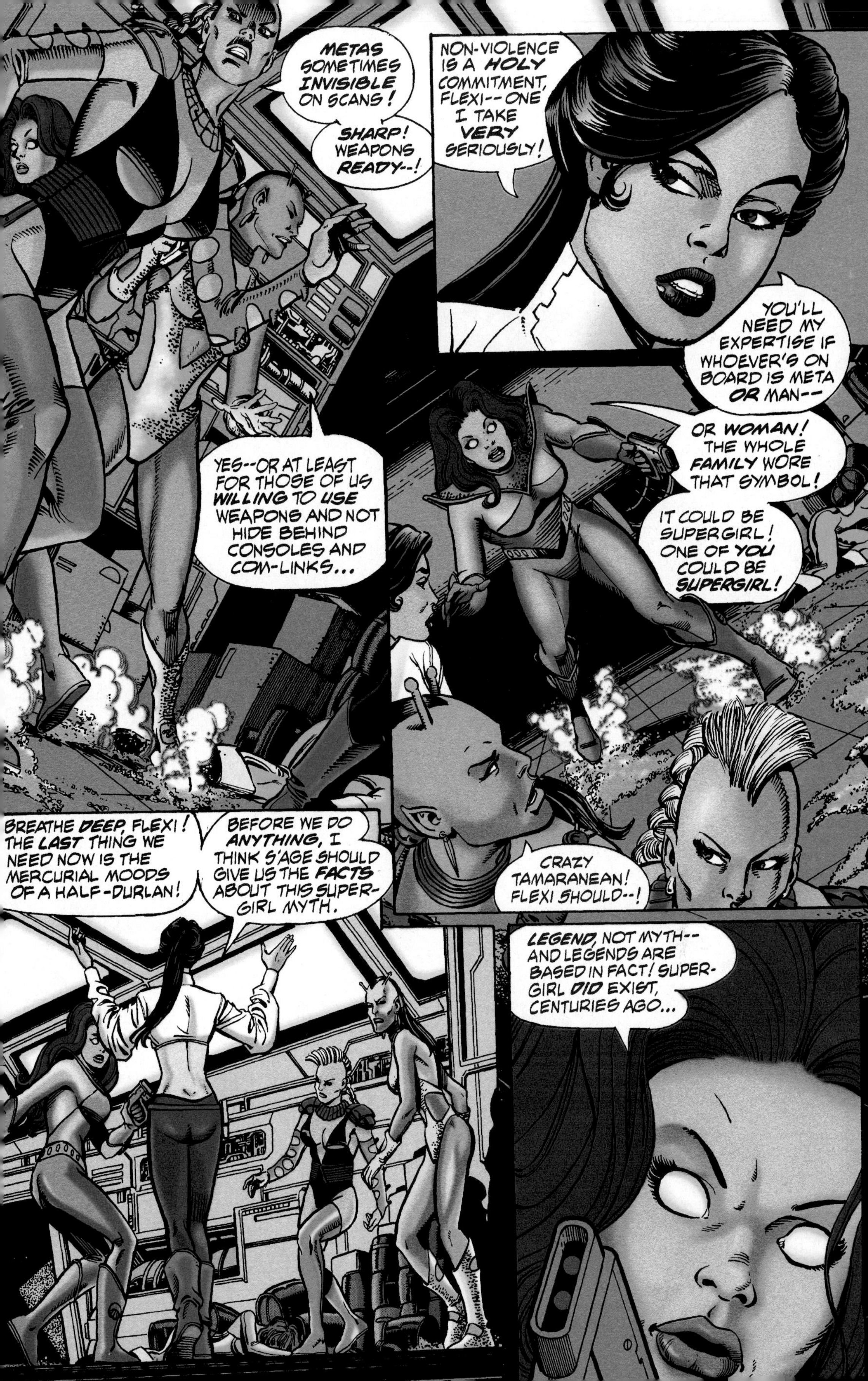

METAS SOMETIMES INVISIBLE ON SCANS!
SHARP! WEAPONS READY--!
NON-VIOLENCE IS A HOLY COMMITMENT, FLEXI--ONE I TAKE VERY SERIOUSLY!
YES--OR AT LEAST FOR THOSE OF US WILLING TO USE WEAPONS AND NOT HIDE BEHIND CONSOLES AND COM-LINKS...
YOU'LL NEED MY EXPERTISE IF WHOEVER'S ON BOARD IS META OR MAN--
OR WOMAN! THE WHOLE FAMILY WORE THAT SYMBOL!
IT COULD BE SUPERGIRL! ONE OF YOU COULD BE SUPERGIRL!
CRAZY TAMARANEAN! FLEXI SHOULD--!
BREATHE DEEP, FLEXI! THE LAST THING WE NEED NOW IS THE MERCURIAL MOODS OF A HALF-DURLAN!
BEFORE WE DO ANYTHING, I THINK S'AGE SHOULD GIVE US THE FACTS ABOUT THIS SUPER-GIRL MYTH.
LEGEND, NOT MYTH--AND LEGENDS ARE BASED IN FACT! SUPER-GIRL DID EXIST, CENTURIES AGO...

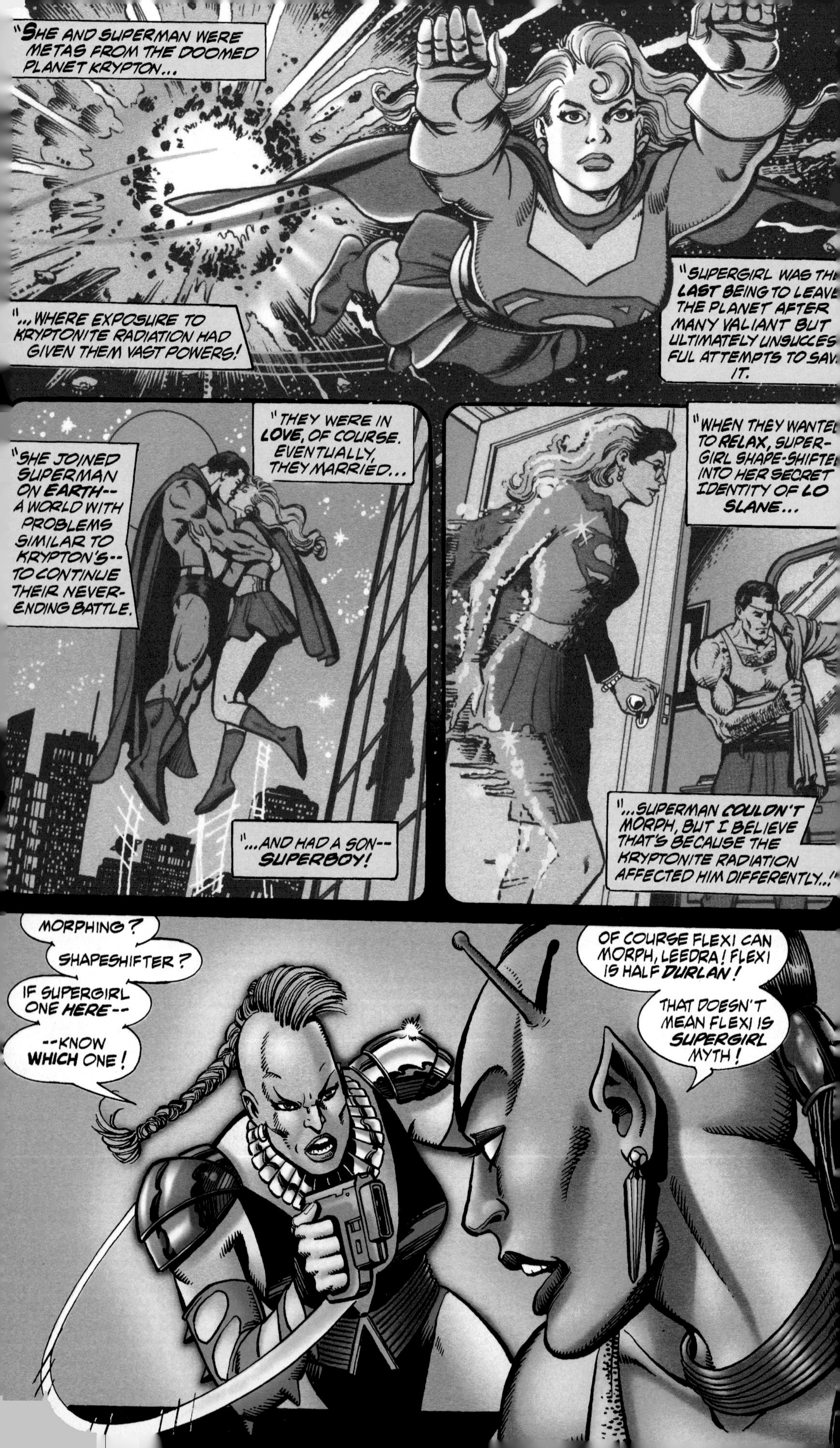
"SHE AND SUPERMAN WERE METAS FROM THE DOOMED PLANET KRYPTON...
"...WHERE EXPOSURE TO KRYPTONITE RADIATION HAD GIVEN THEM VAST POWERS!
"SUPERGIRL WAS THE LAST BEING TO LEAVE THE PLANET AFTER MANY VALIANT BUT ULTIMATELY UNSUCCESSFUL ATTEMPTS TO SAVE IT.
"SHE JOINED SUPERMAN ON EARTH-- A WORLD WITH PROBLEMS SIMILAR TO KRYPTON'S-- TO CONTINUE THEIR NEVER-ENDING BATTLE.
"THEY WERE IN LOVE, OF COURSE. EVENTUALLY, THEY MARRIED...
"...AND HAD A SON-- SUPERBOY!
"WHEN THEY WANTED TO RELAX, SUPER-GIRL SHAPE-SHIFTED INTO HER SECRET IDENTITY OF LO SLANE...
"...SUPERMAN COULDN'T MORPH, BUT I BELIEVE THAT'S BECAUSE THE KRYPTONITE RADIATION AFFECTED HIM DIFFERENTLY..!
MORPHING?
SHAPESHIFTER?
IF SUPERGIRL ONE HERE--
--KNOW WHICH ONE!
OF COURSE FLEXI CAN MORPH, LEEDRA! FLEXI IS HALF DURLAN!
THAT DOESN'T MEAN FLEXI IS SUPERGIRL MYTH!

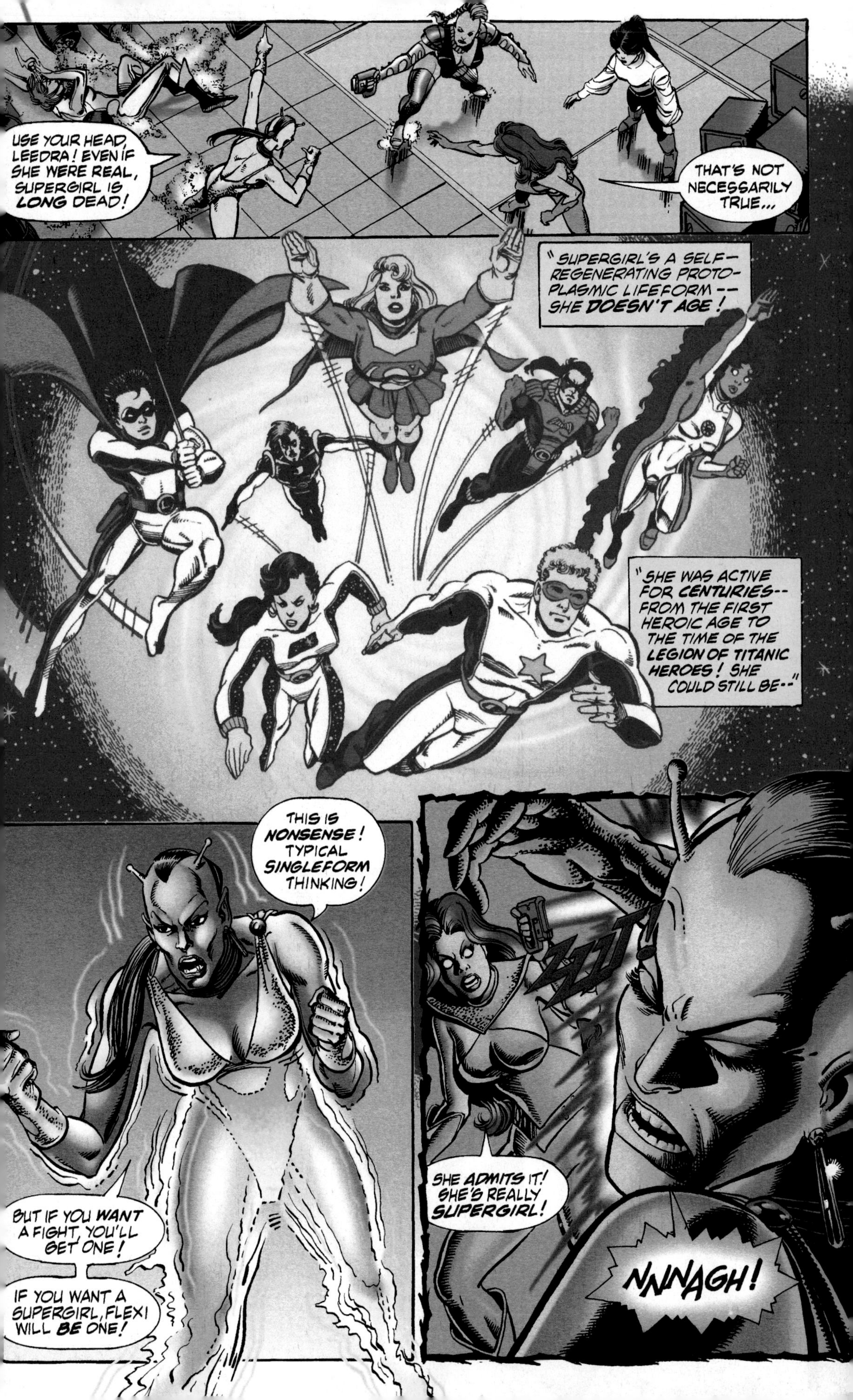
USE YOUR HEAD, LEEDRA! EVEN IF SHE WERE REAL, SUPERGIRL IS LONG DEAD!
THAT'S NOT NECESSARILY TRUE...
"SUPERGIRL'S A SELF-REGENERATING PROTO-PLASMIC LIFEFORM -- SHE DOESN'T AGE!
"SHE WAS ACTIVE FOR CENTURIES-- FROM THE FIRST HEROIC AGE TO THE TIME OF THE LEGION OF TITANIC HEROES! SHE COULD STILL BE--"
THIS IS NONSENSE! TYPICAL SINGLEFORM THINKING!
BUT IF YOU WANT A FIGHT, YOU'LL GET ONE!
IF YOU WANT A SUPERGIRL, FLEXI WILL BE ONE!
SHE ADMITS IT! SHE'S REALLY SUPERGIRL!
NNNAGH!

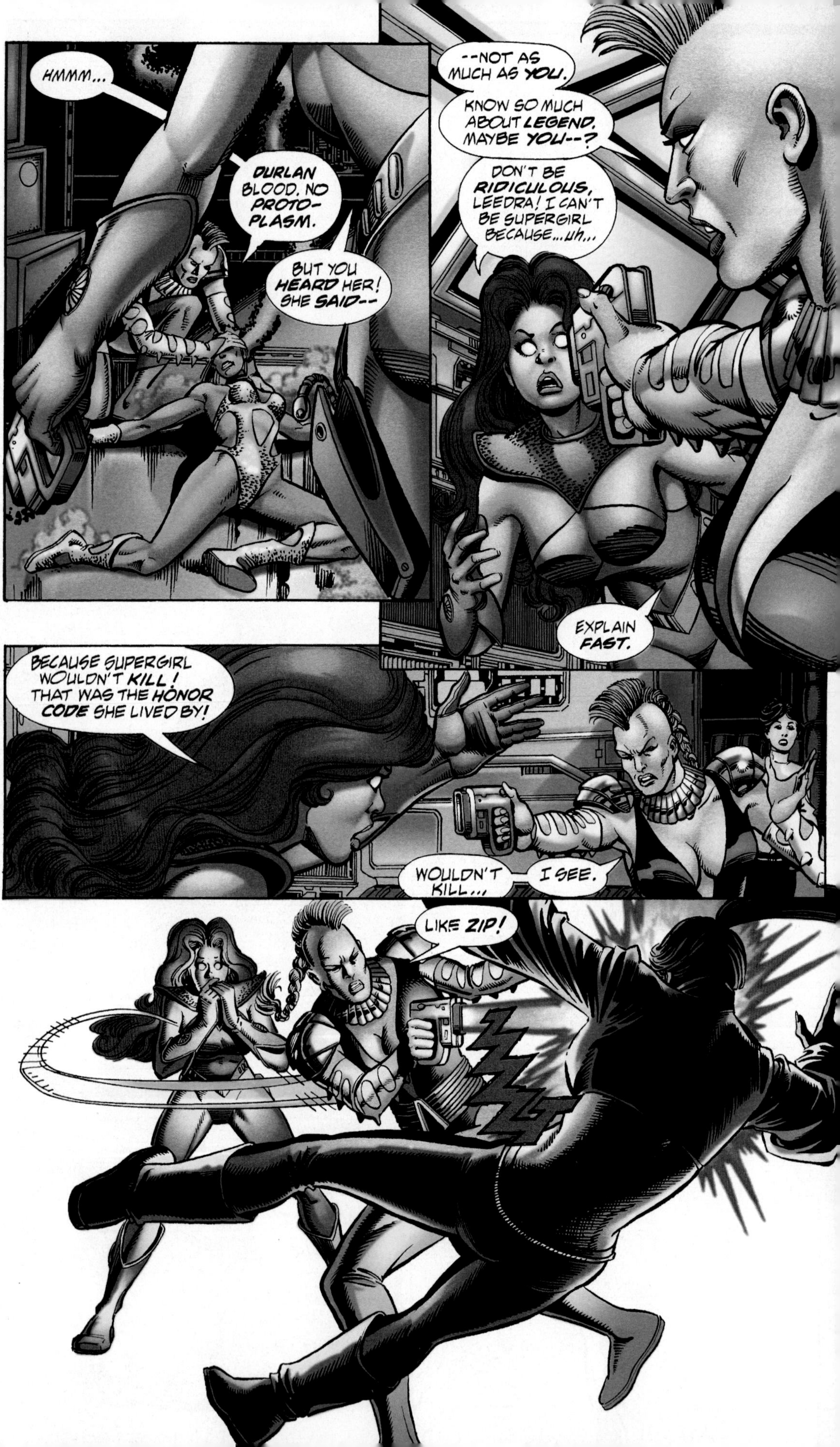
HMMM...
DURLAN BLOOD. NO PROTO-PLASM.
BUT YOU HEARD HER! SHE SAID--
--NOT AS MUCH AS YOU.
KNOW SO MUCH ABOUT LEGEND. MAYBE YOU--?
DON'T BE RIDICULOUS, LEEDRA! I CAN'T BE SUPERGIRL BECAUSE...uh...
EXPLAIN FAST.
BECAUSE SUPERGIRL WOULDN'T KILL! THAT WAS THE HONOR CODE SHE LIVED BY!
WOULDN'T KILL...
I SEE.
LIKE ZIP!

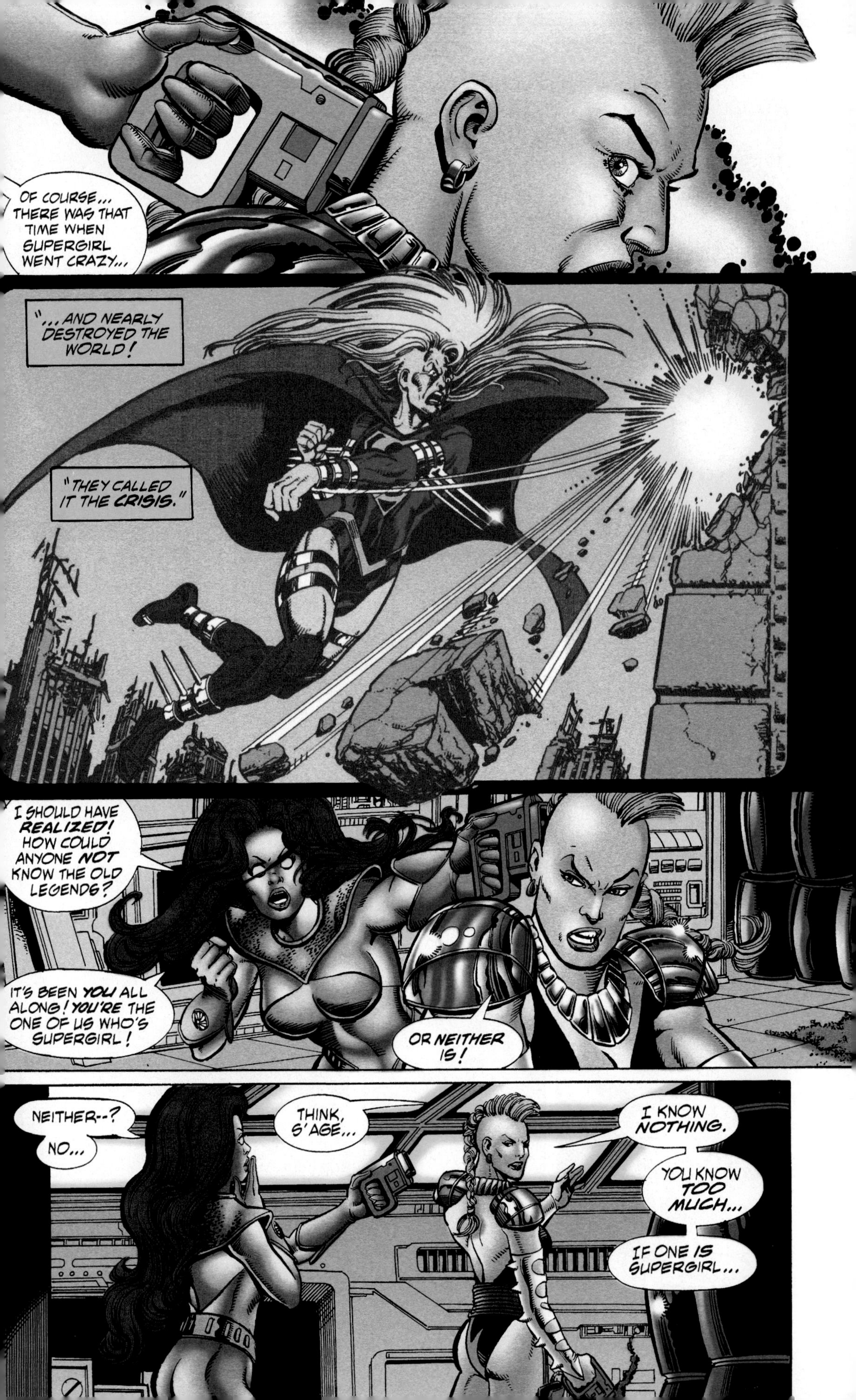

OF COURSE... THERE WAS THAT TIME WHEN SUPERGIRL WENT CRAZY...
"...AND NEARLY DESTROYED THE WORLD!
"THEY CALLED IT THE CRISIS."
I SHOULD HAVE REALIZED! HOW COULD ANYONE NOT KNOW THE OLD LEGENDS?
IT'S BEEN YOU ALL ALONG! YOU'RE THE ONE OF US WHO'S SUPERGIRL!
OR NEITHER IS!
NEITHER--?
NO...
THINK, S'AGE...
I KNOW NOTHING.
YOU KNOW TOO MUCH...
IF ONE IS SUPERGIRL...

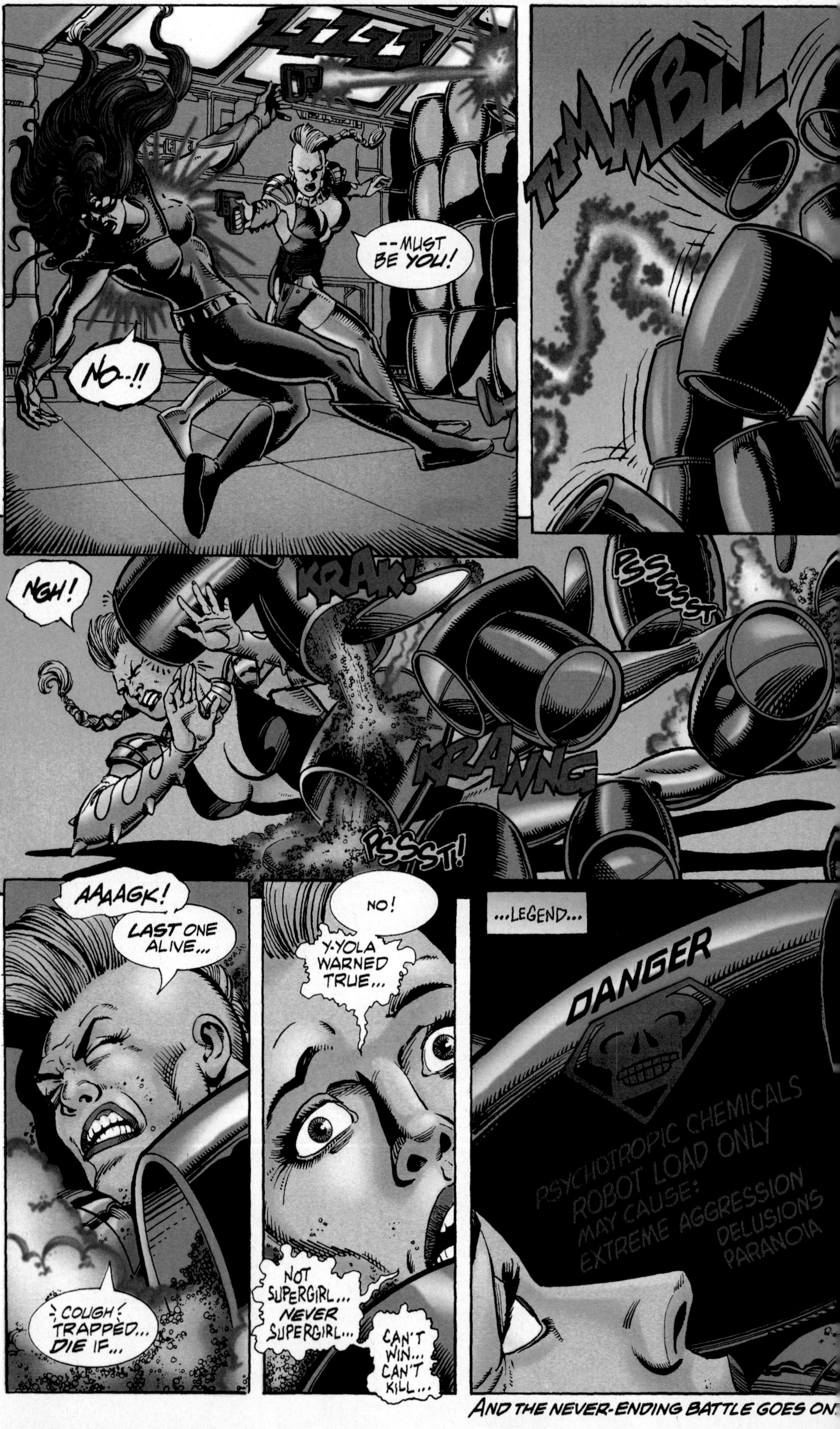
ZZZZT
--MUST BE YOU!
NO--!!
TUMMBLL
NGH!
KRAK!
PSSSSST
KRANNG
PSSST!
AAAAGK!
LAST ONE ALIVE...
COUGH TRAPPED... DIE IF...
NO!
Y-YOLA WARNED TRUE...
NOT SUPERGIRL... NEVER SUPERGIRL...
CAN'T WIN... CAN'T KILL...
...LEGEND...
DANGER
PSYCHOTROPIC CHEMICALS
ROBOT LOAD ONLY
MAY CAUSE:
EXTREME AGGRESSION
DELUSIONS
PARANOIA
AND THE NEVER-ENDING BATTLE GOES ON

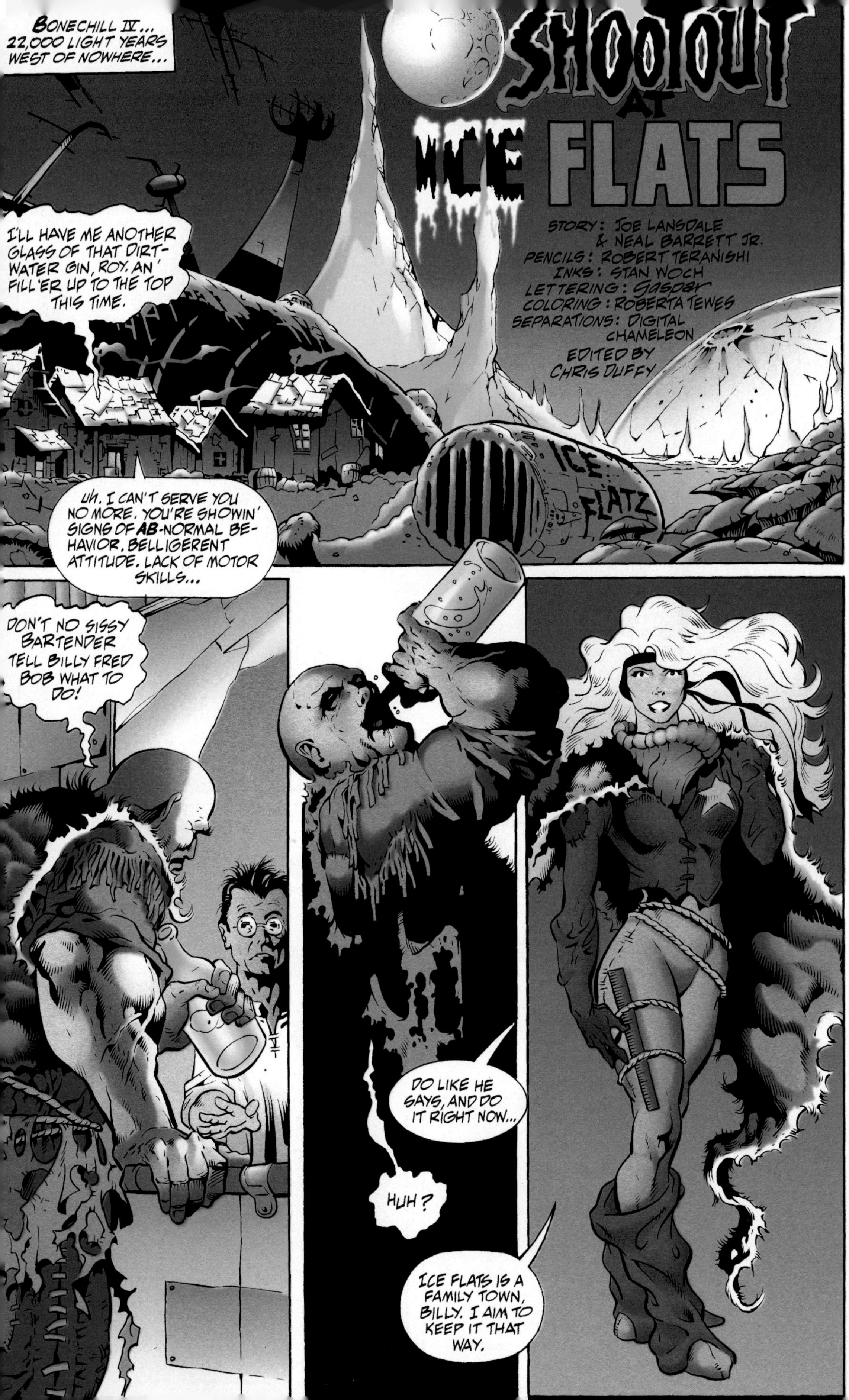
BONECHILL IV... 22,000 LIGHT YEARS WEST OF NOWHERE...
SHOOTOUT AT ICE FLATS
STORY: JOE LANSDALE & NEAL BARRETT JR.
PENCILS: ROBERT TERANISHI
INKS: STAN WOCH
LETTERING: Gaspar
COLORING: ROBERTA TEWES
SEPARATIONS: DIGITAL CHAMELEON
EDITED BY CHRIS DUFFY
I'LL HAVE ME ANOTHER GLASS OF THAT DIRT-WATER GIN, ROY. AN' FILL 'ER UP TO THE TOP THIS TIME.
ICE FLATZ
UH. I CAN'T SERVE YOU NO MORE. YOU'RE SHOWIN' SIGNS OF AB-NORMAL BEHAVIOR. BELLIGERENT ATTITUDE. LACK OF MOTOR SKILLS...
DON'T NO SISSY BARTENDER TELL BILLY FRED BOB WHAT TO DO!
DO LIKE HE SAYS, AND DO IT RIGHT NOW...
HUH?
ICE FLATS IS A FAMILY TOWN, BILLY. I AIM TO KEEP IT THAT WAY.

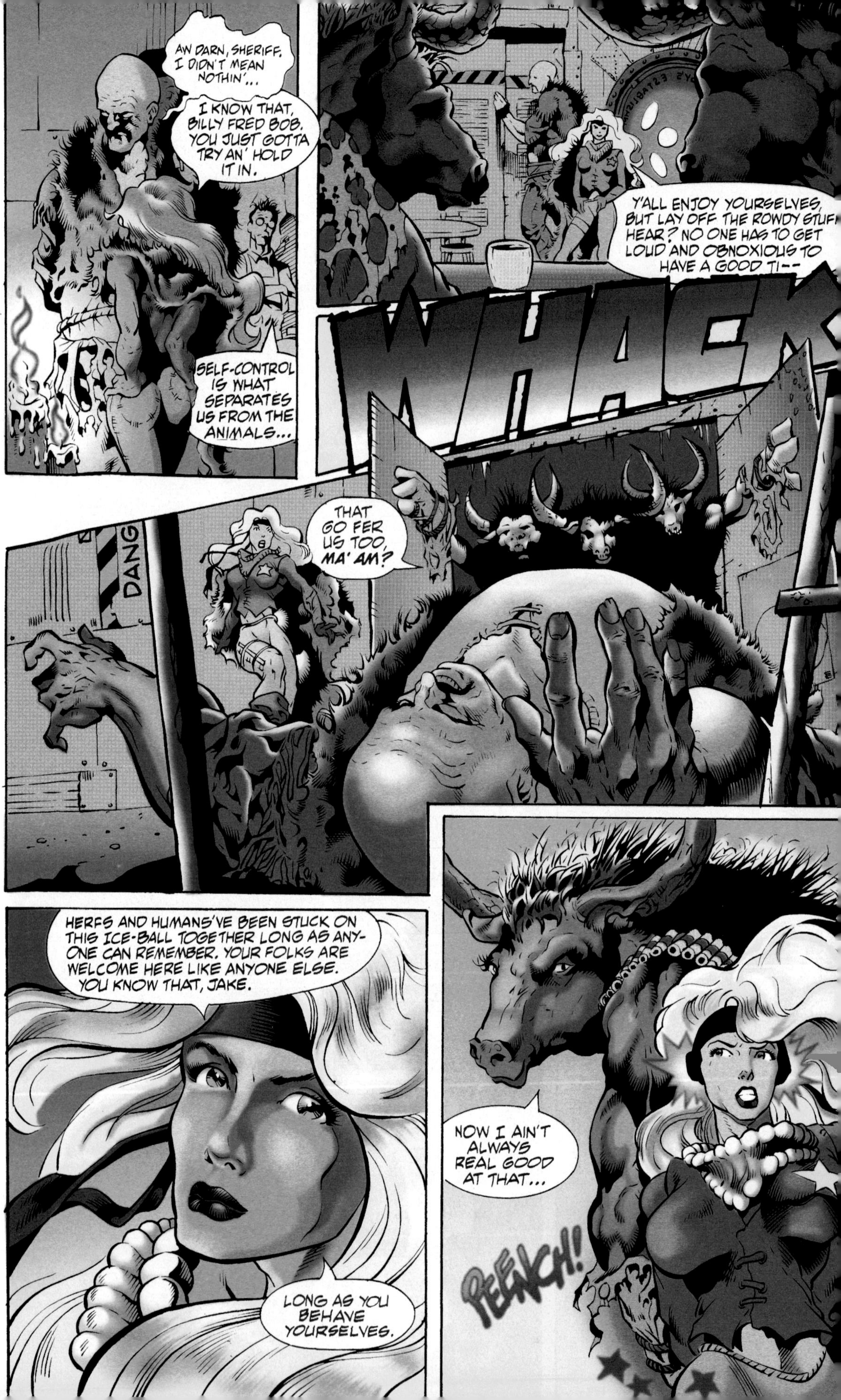
AW DARN, SHERIFF. I DIDN'T MEAN NOTHIN'...
I KNOW THAT, BILLY FRED BOB. YOU JUST GOTTA TRY AN' HOLD IT IN.
SELF-CONTROL IS WHAT SEPARATES US FROM THE ANIMALS...
Y'ALL ENJOY YOURSELVES, BUT LAY OFF THE ROWDY STUFF, HEAR? NO ONE HAS TO GET LOUD AND OBNOXIOUS TO HAVE A GOOD TI--
WHACK
THAT GO FER US TOO, MA' AM?
DANG
HERFS AND HUMANS'VE BEEN STUCK ON THIS ICE-BALL TOGETHER LONG AS ANYONE CAN REMEMBER. YOUR FOLKS ARE WELCOME HERE LIKE ANYONE ELSE. YOU KNOW THAT, JAKE.
LONG AS YOU BEHAVE YOURSELVES.
NOW I AIN'T ALWAYS REAL GOOD AT THAT...
PEENCH!

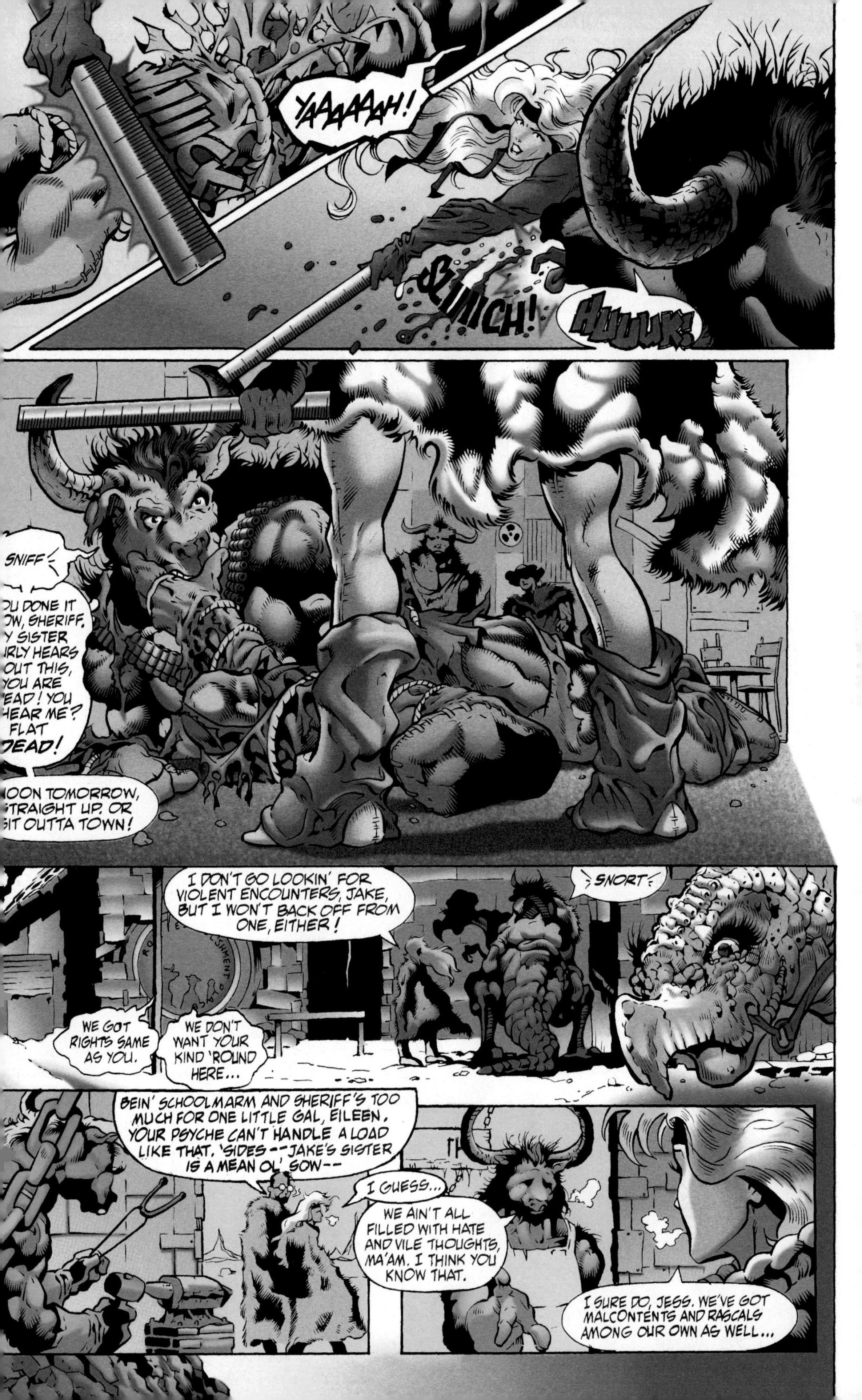
YAAAAAAH!
HUUUK!
SNIFF
OU DONE IT OW, SHERIFF. Y SISTER URLY HEARS OUT THIS, YOU ARE EAD! YOU HEAR ME? FLAT DEAD!
OON TOMORROW, TRAIGHT UP. OR IT OUTTA TOWN!
I DON'T GO LOOKIN' FOR VIOLENT ENCOUNTERS, JAKE, BUT I WON'T BACK OFF FROM ONE, EITHER!
SNORT
WE GOT RIGHTS SAME AS YOU.
WE DON'T WANT YOUR KIND 'ROUND HERE...
BEIN' SCHOOLMARM AND SHERIFF'S TOO MUCH FOR ONE LITTLE GAL, EILEEN. YOUR PSYCHE CAN'T HANDLE A LOAD LIKE THAT. 'SIDES-- JAKE'S SISTER IS A MEAN OL' SOW--
I GUESS...
WE AIN'T ALL FILLED WITH HATE AND VILE THOUGHTS, MA'AM. I THINK YOU KNOW THAT.
I SURE DO, JESS. WE'VE GOT MALCONTENTS AND RASCALS AMONG OUR OWN AS WELL...

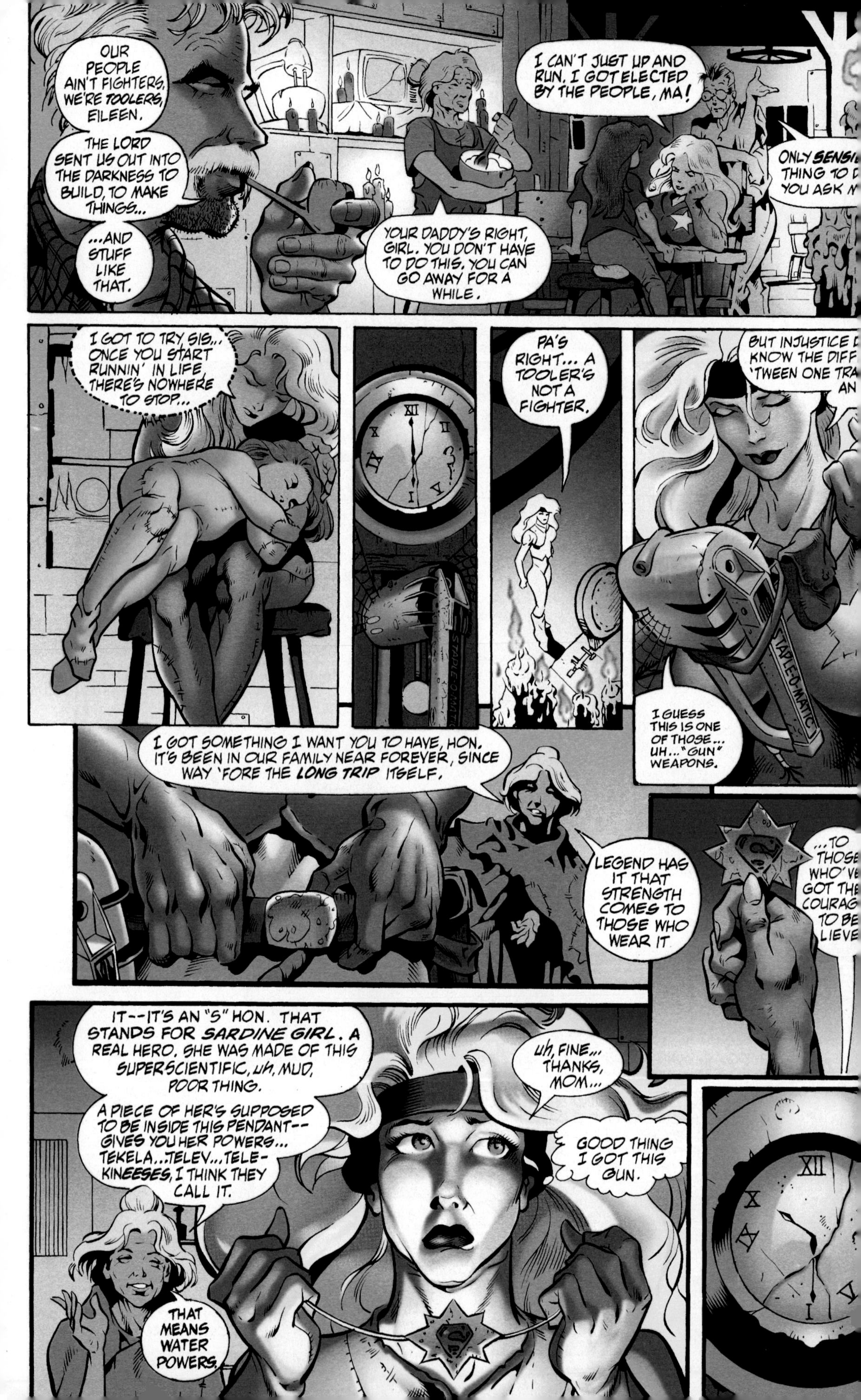
OUR PEOPLE AIN'T FIGHTERS. WE'RE TOOLERS, EILEEN.
THE LORD SENT US OUT INTO THE DARKNESS TO BUILD, TO MAKE THINGS...
...AND STUFF LIKE THAT.
YOUR DADDY'S RIGHT, GIRL. YOU DON'T HAVE TO DO THIS. YOU CAN GO AWAY FOR A WHILE.
I CAN'T JUST UP AND RUN. I GOT ELECTED BY THE PEOPLE, MA!
I GOT TO TRY, SIS... ONCE YOU START RUNNIN' IN LIFE, THERE'S NOWHERE TO STOP...
PA'S RIGHT... A TOOLER'S NOT A FIGHTER.
I GUESS THIS IS ONE OF THOSE... UH..."GUN" WEAPONS.
STAPLE-O-MATIC
I GOT SOMETHING I WANT YOU TO HAVE, HON. IT'S BEEN IN OUR FAMILY NEAR FOREVER, SINCE WAY 'FORE THE LONG TRIP ITSELF.
LEGEND HAS IT THAT STRENGTH COMES TO THOSE WHO WEAR IT
IT--IT'S AN "S" HON. THAT STANDS FOR SARDINE GIRL. A REAL HERO. SHE WAS MADE OF THIS SUPERSCIENTIFIC, UH, MUD, POOR THING.
A PIECE OF HER'S SUPPOSED TO BE INSIDE THIS PENDANT-- GIVES YOU HER POWERS... TEKELA...TELEV...TELEKINEESES, I THINK THEY CALL IT.
THAT MEANS WATER POWERS.
UH, FINE... THANKS, MOM...
GOOD THING I GOT THIS GUN.

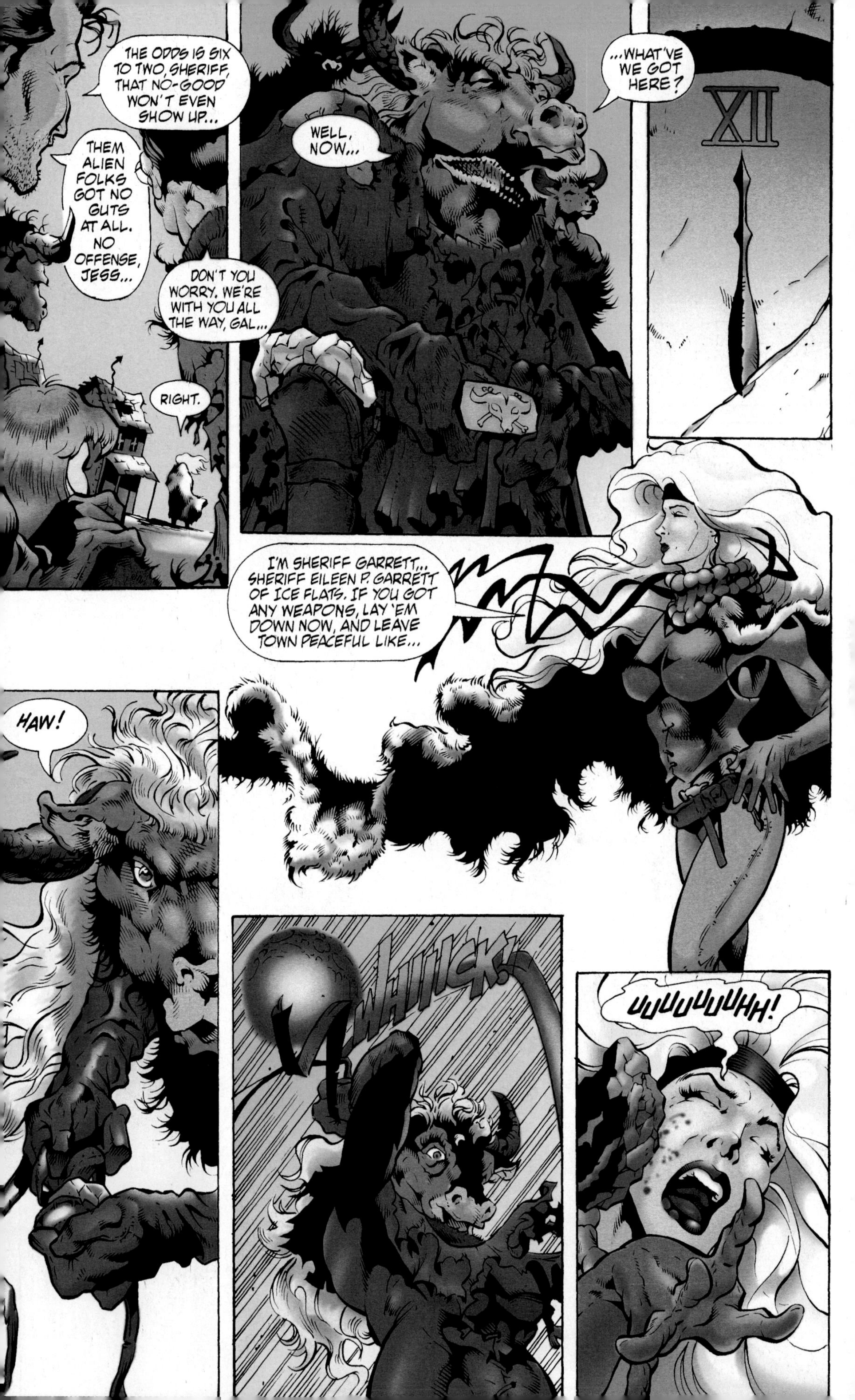
THE ODDS IS SIX TO TWO, SHERIFF, THAT NO-GOOD WON'T EVEN SHOW UP...
THEM ALIEN FOLKS GOT NO GUTS AT ALL. NO OFFENSE, JESS...
DON'T YOU WORRY. WE'RE WITH YOU ALL THE WAY, GAL...
RIGHT.
WELL, NOW...
...WHAT'VE WE GOT HERE?
XII
I'M SHERIFF GARRETT... SHERIFF EILEEN P. GARRETT OF ICE FLATS. IF YOU GOT ANY WEAPONS, LAY 'EM DOWN NOW, AND LEAVE TOWN PEACEFUL LIKE...
HAW!
WHIIICK!
UUUUUUUHH!

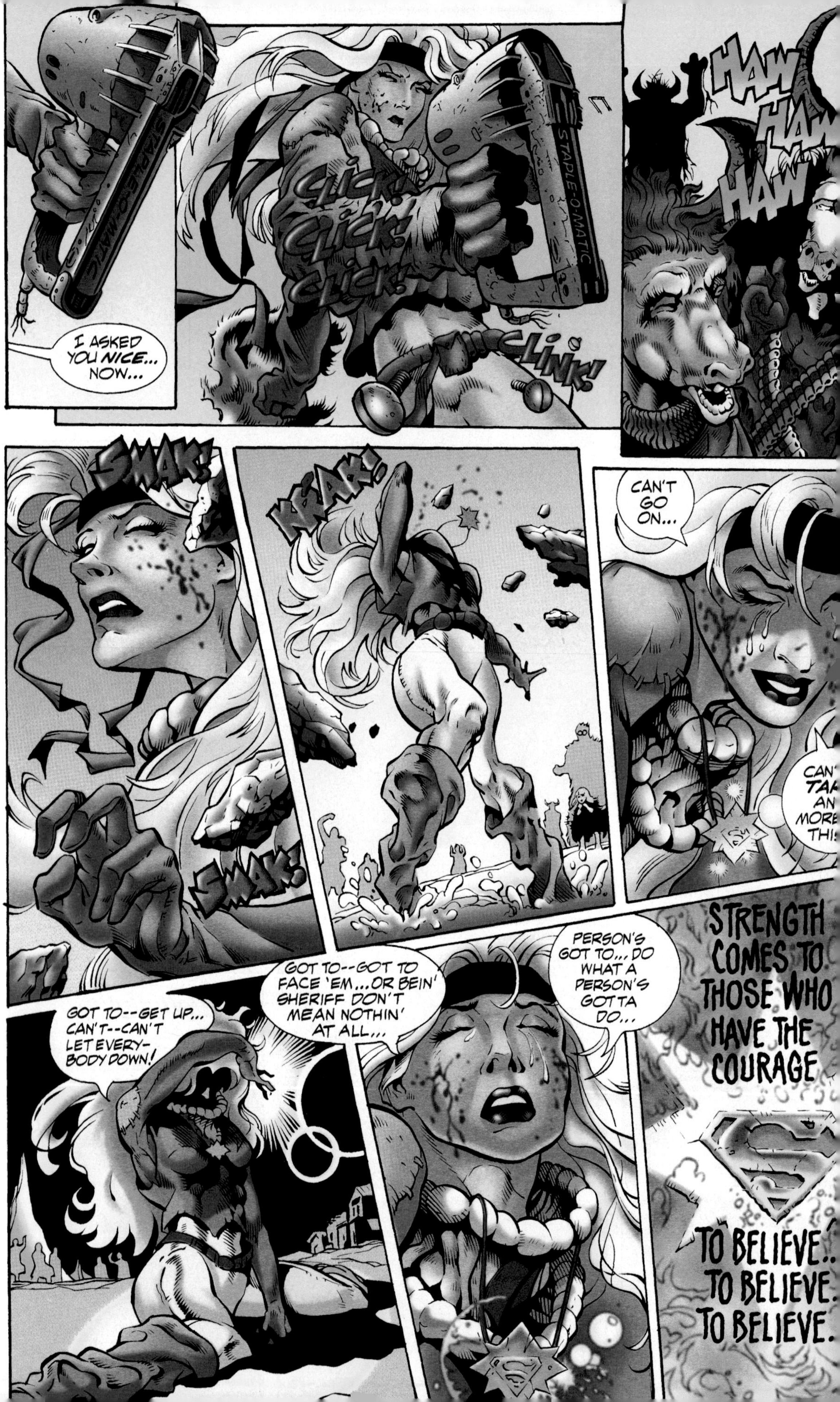
STAPLE-O-MATIC
STAPLE-O-MATIC
CLICK! CLICK! CLICK!
CLINK!
I ASKED YOU NICE... NOW...
HAW HAW HAW HAW
SMAK!
SMAK!
KRAK!
CAN'T GO ON...
GOT TO--GET UP... CAN'T--CAN'T LET EVERY-BODY DOWN!
GOT TO--GOT TO FACE 'EM... OR BEIN' SHERIFF DON'T MEAN NOTHIN' AT ALL...
PERSON'S GOT TO... DO WHAT A PERSON'S GOTTA DO...
STRENGTH COMES TO THOSE WHO HAVE THE COURAGE
TO BELIEVE... TO BELIEVE. TO BELIEVE.

DC COMICS™

"Combines the real world elements that have made the Christopher Nolan movies so successful with stylized visuals that only the comic medium can provide."
—COMPLEX MAGAZINE

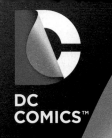

MUST-READ TALES OF THE DARK KNIGHT!

BATMAN EARTH ONE: VOL. 1

GEOFF JOHNS & GARY FRANK

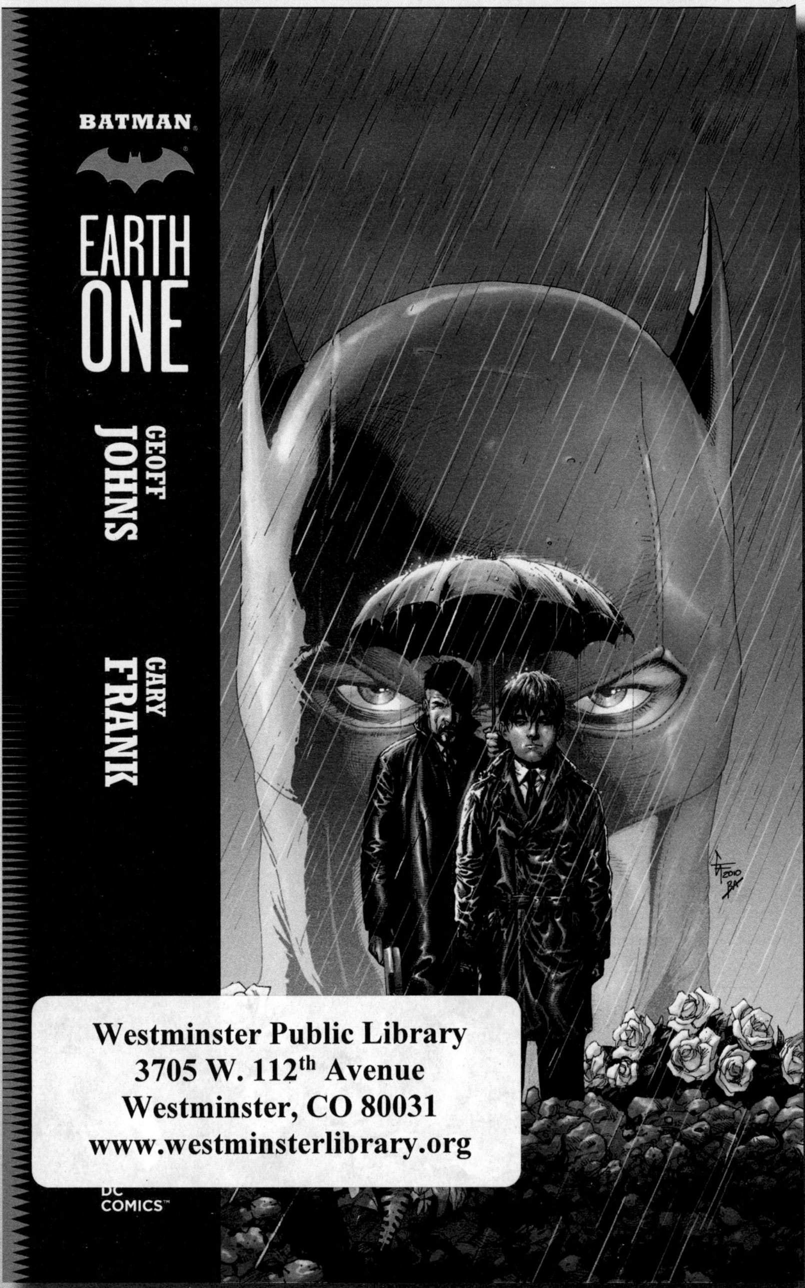
BATMAN
EARTH ONE
GEOFF JOHNS
GARY FRANK
DC COMICS™

BATMAN VOL. 3: DEATH OF THE FAMILY

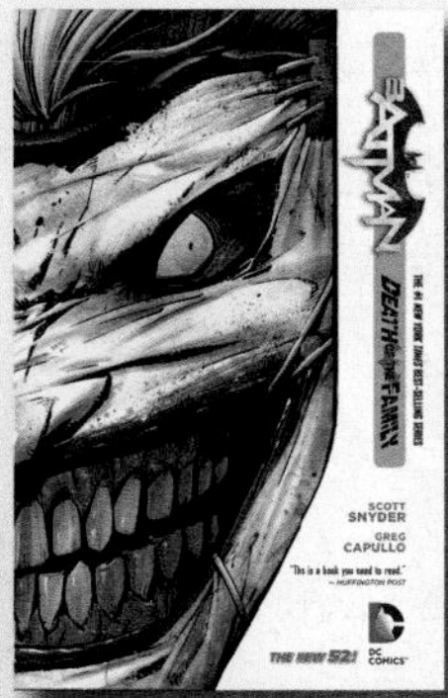
SCOTT SNYDER
GREG CAPULLO
THE NEW 52!

by SCOTT SNYDER & GREG CAPULLO

BATMAN: KNIGHTFALL VOLS. 1-3

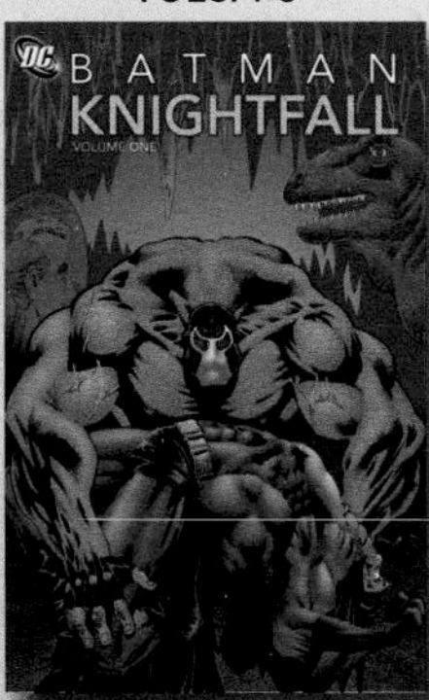
BATMAN
KNIGHTFALL
VOLUME ONE

BATMAN: NO MAN'S LAND VOLS. 1-4

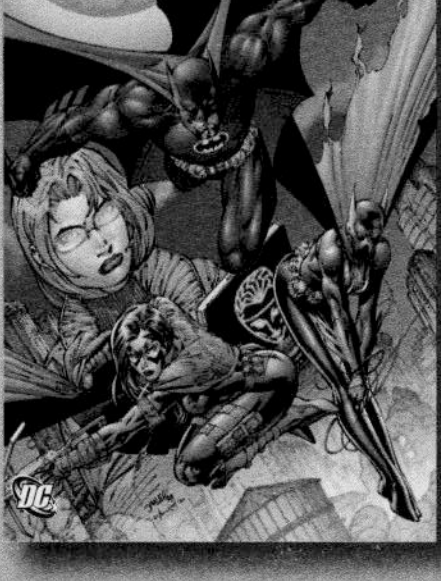
BATMAN
NO MAN'S LAND
1

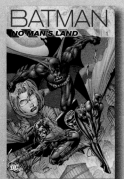

"It's fresh air. I like this all-too-human Superman, and I think a lot of you will, too."
—SCRIPPS HOWARD NEWS SERVICE

START AT THE BEGINNING!

SUPERMAN: ACTION COMICS VOLUME 1: SUPERMAN AND THE MEN OF STEEL

SUPERMAN
VOLUME 1: WHAT
PRICE TOMORROW?

GEORGE PEREZ JESUS MERINO NICOLA SCOTT

SUPERGIRL VOLUME 1:
THE LAST DAUGHTER
OF KRYPTON

MICHAEL GREEN MIKE JOHNSON MAHMUD ASRAR

SUPERBOY VOLUME 1:
INCUBATION

SCOTT LOBDELL R.B. SILVA ROB LEAN

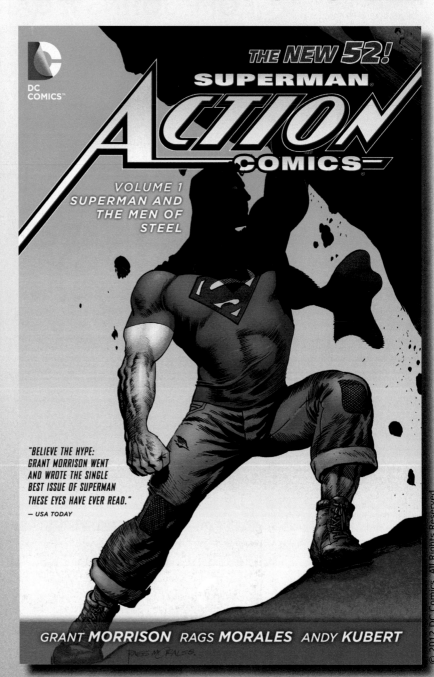

THE NEW 52!

SUPERMAN

ACTION COMICS

VOLUME 1
SUPERMAN AND
THE MEN OF
STEEL

*"BELIEVE THE HYPE:
GRANT MORRISON WENT
AND WROTE THE SINGLE
BEST ISSUE OF SUPERMAN
THESE EYES HAVE EVER READ."*
— USA TODAY

GRANT **MORRISON** RAGS **MORALES** ANDY **KUBERT**

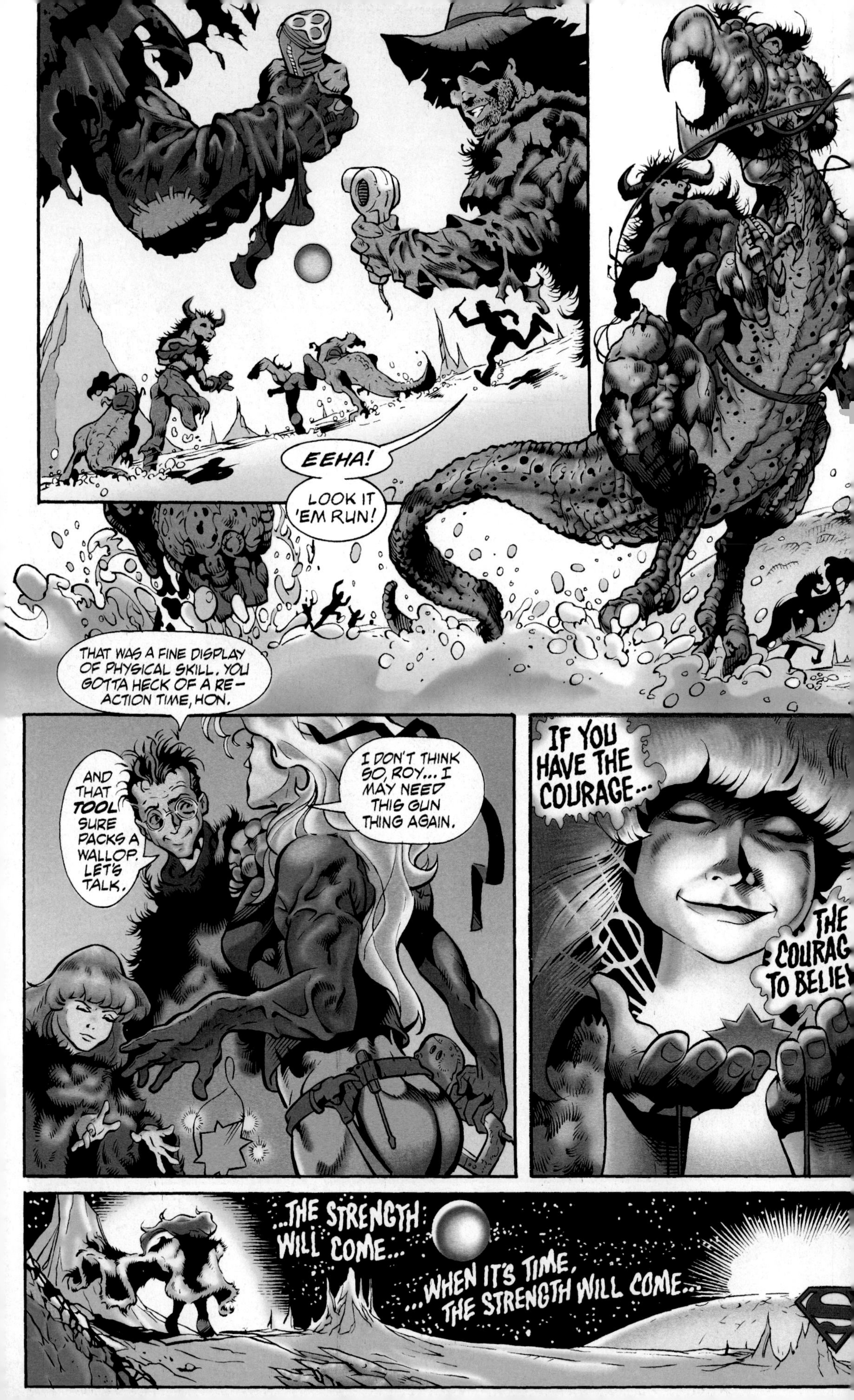

EEHA!
LOOK IT 'EM RUN!
THAT WAS A FINE DISPLAY OF PHYSICAL SKILL. YOU GOTTA HECK OF A RE-ACTION TIME, HON.
AND THAT TOOL SURE PACKS A WALLOP. LET'S TALK.
I DON'T THINK SO, ROY... I MAY NEED THIS GUN THING AGAIN.
IF YOU HAVE THE COURAGE...
...THE STRENGTH WILL COME...
...WHEN IT'S TIME, THE STRENGTH WILL COME...

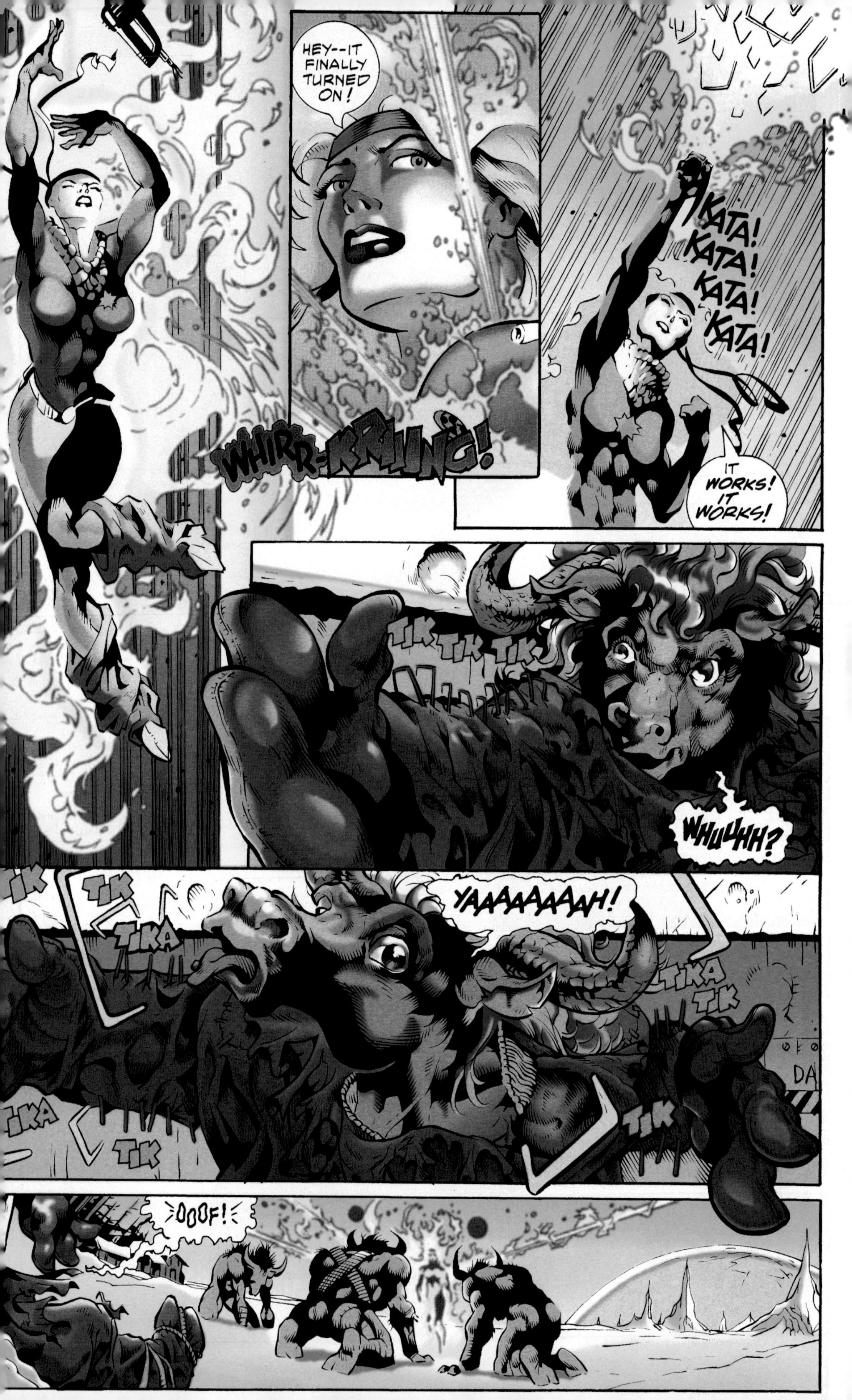
HEY--IT FINALLY TURNED ON!
WHIRR-KRIIING!
KATA! KATA! KATA! KATA!
IT WORKS! IT WORKS!
TIK TIK TIK
WHUHHH?
TIK
TIKA
YAAAAAAAAH!
TIKA
TIK
TIKA
TIK
TIK
OOOF!